Preface

Primatology, the study of primate behavior, ecology, and biology, is a large and ever-growing discipline. No one book can hope to cover more than a modest portion of all the topics and species of nonhuman primates investigated by people in many fields. We invited a broad range of expert researchers to write essays specifically for this book that would provide an introduction to the nonhuman primates: their past, present, and future. By bringing together this array of experts in one volume, we hope to offer a cutting edge overview of our closest relatives: the prosimians, monkeys, and apes.

We have much in common with these mammals because of our shared evolutionary history. We also share this planet and, as a result, to an alarming extent we control their future. If we learn to appreciate the nature, value, and richness of their lives, perhaps we will take care to ensure their continued survival. Some of them, those closest to us, can be of great usefulness in helping us reconstruct aspects of our past adaptations and behavior. They can also offer us an important set of comparisons as we investigate our present patterns of life.

ORGANIZATION

The book is divided into two parts. Part 1, "The Nonhuman Primates," describes who they are, where they live, and how well or precariously they are surviving in their present habitats. The first section of Part 1 discusses primate diversity, taxonomy, and phylogeny. Our approach throughout the book is an evolutionary one, and to illustrate this point of view we present a model system for the study of adaptation at the molecular level. The next sections introduce and describe representative nonhuman primates, starting with apes, then Old World monkeys, New World monkeys, and finally, prosimians. Because a particular species is omitted does not indicate that it has not been studied or that it is in any way less important than another species that has been included. In an introductory text one is forced to make choices due to space limitations. In some instances we have selected primates because the studies on them are very recent or the work is ongoing and steadily adding new information to what we know of primates. The final section of Part 1, "Primate Conservation," addresses vitally important issues of survival for the living nonhuman primates. These essays cover the primate status in Asia, a case study of the impact humans have on a species of macaque monkey, and the use of translocation and rehabilitation as conservation tools.

Part 2, "The Realm of Primate Behavior," introduces the reader to the study of different aspects of primate behavior from the evolution of social organization to reconstructing the behavior of our ape ancestors. In addition, special topics of social behavior such as aggression, reproduction, kinship, social dominance, communication, and aging are investigated in some detail. These are the essays that will provide a view of what life is really like for a prosimian, a monkey, or an ape. The distinctive biology of each kind of primate is used as the basis for understanding the dimensions of its social experience. The section concludes with a review of part of the history of primate studies to show the reader how much influence the investigators' training and interests have on their work. The last essay illustrates some of the important roles primates have played in many aspects of human culture.

FEATURES

Several key features distinguish this introduction to primates:

- *A flexible organization.* The sequencing of the essays can be rearranged easily to suit the structure of the course, whether it be by topic or by taxa. Essays address issues and examples that will hold the interest of beginning students, and primate taxa are introduced in a complete section. Some may find it convenient to start with the individual primate species and then move to their evolution and questions of conservation. Other sequences could work equally well because no section requires another as background. A topical table of contents suggests various ways in which each essay may be used to illustrate topics ranging from behavioral ecology to conservation and evolution.

- *Currency and breadth of coverage.* Because the contents of this book are derived from recent or ongoing studies, the essays will be of interest to readers with diverse backgrounds in primatology or animal behavior, as well as to the reader who is being introduced to the field. By mixing paradigms, styles, and levels of analysis, this collection reflects the growth and diversification of the field of primate studies.

- *Abundant pedagogical support.* To help students better comprehend what they read, this collection includes illustrations; worldwide distribution maps of the primates; an index; an extensive bibliography; part and article introductions; and a 16-page, full-color portfolio of primates. The glossary provides definitions of terms that appear in individual essays and offers additional information. Readers wanting to know more about specific kinds of nonhuman primates not discussed in this book are encouraged to follow Suggested Readings offered at the end of the book. This list of supplementary readings is included to assist in locating related information about species and topics introduced in each essay.

The Nonhuman Primates

Phyllis Dolhinow
University of California, Berkeley

Agustín Fuentes
Central Washington University

Mayfield Publishing Company
Mountain View, California
London · Toronto

To all those we study, may they prosper
and survive long into the future.

Copyright © 1999 by Mayfield Publishing Company

Library of Congress Cataloging-in-Publication Data

The nonhuman primates / [edited by] Phyllis Dolhinow, Agustín
    Fuentes.
        p.   cm.
    Includes bibliographical references (p. 284) and index.
    ISBN 1-55934-974-3
    1. Primates.   2. Primates—Behavior.   I. Dolhinow, Phyllis.
II. Fuentes, Agustín.
QL737.P9N597   1999
599.8—dc21   98-45272
                                                        CIP

Manufactured in the United States of America

10   9   8   7   6   5   4   3   2   1

Mayfield Publishing Company
1280 Villa Street
Mountain View, California 94041

Sponsoring editor, Jan Beatty; production editor, Linda Ward; manuscript editor, Kay Mikel; design manager, Jeanne Schreiber; text and cover designer, Linda M. Robertson; art editor, Robin Mouat; illustrators, Judy Waller and Cartographics; photo researcher, Brian Pecko; manufacturing manager, Randy Hurst. The text was set in 10/12 Berkeley Book by TBH Typecast, Inc., and printed on 45# Chromatone Matte by Banta Book Group.

Cover photos (from left to right): mandrill, © Noel Rowe; mountain gorilla silverback, © Tim Laman; three ringtailed lemurs, © Benjamin Freed; two Philippine tarsiers, © Noel Rowe; capuchin monkey, © Phyllis Dolhinow; chimpanzees digging for termites, © Jane Goodall/National Geographic Society Image Collection.

The published results of modern primate studies are scattered widely in the literature—often in very specialized and highly technical journals and books. This text presents current views and information in a manner reflective of the variety of perspectives and approaches that characterize modern primate studies. Our purpose in putting together this selection of leading research is to provide all who are interested in and fascinated by primate behavior with a well-rounded sample of information that is new and exciting.

ACKNOWLEDGMENTS

We wish to express our thanks and appreciation to all those at Mayfield who helped make this book possible. Jan Beatty, our sponsoring editor, translated our early conversations and perceived needs into a real project, allowing, encouraging, and guiding us the entire way. Her understanding of anthropology and its relatedness to the behavior of all primates made our volume a reality. Linda Ward, our production editor, guided us step by step through the maze that ended in the book and did so with patience, good humor, and diplomacy. Kay Mikel, our copy editor, translated our verbiage into Standard English with helpful nudges and consistent effort. And, to the many other people that make up the Mayfield team, we give our sincere thanks.

We thank our colleagues Mark Taff, Robert Sussman, and many others for their generous sharing of ideas. Many disciplines and backgrounds are represented as well as differing points of view. We're especially grateful to the following reviewers of the manuscript: James M. Calcagno, Loyola University Chicago; Laurie Godfrey, University of Massachusetts; Deborah J. Overdorff, University of Texas, Austin; R. W. Sussman, Washington University; and Linda D. Wolfe, East Carolina University.

This set of essays would not have taken its present shape without the tremendously important stimulus of our students over the years. Their interests and questions about the nonhuman primates have helped structure the design of this book. Students at both University of California, Berkeley, and Central Washington University played an important role in its production. Katie MacKinnon, Erin Gemienhart, and Professor Fuentes's Spring 1998 primate behavior class are among them. Elsworth Ray, Allisa Carter, and Melissa Panger, contributors to the book, also helped in other ways. Penelope Anderson of Central Washington University provided excellent secretarial assistance.

Phyllis Dolhinow is grateful for the encouragement and support of Jack and Becky and appreciates the diversion provided by a miscellaneous group of non-primates. Agustín Fuentes thanks his parents, Elizabeth and Victor, his family in Espana and the United States, his partner Devi Snively, and Audrey the wonder-dog for support and inspiration. Agustín Fuentes especially thanks Phyllis Dolhinow for being a friend and mentor.

Contents

Preface   vii
Topical Table of Contents   xv
Contributors   xvii
Introduction   1

PART 1
The Nonhuman Primates: Who Are They,
Where Are They, and How Are They Doing?   5

Taxonomy and Phylogeny of the Primates   6
1. WALTER CARL HARTWIG, Primate Evolution   10
2. JUAN CARLOS MORALES, TODD R. DISOTELL, AND DON J. MELNICK,
   Molecular Phylogenetic Studies of Nonhuman Primates   18
3. CARO-BETH STEWART, The Colobine Old World Monkeys
   as a Model System for the Study of Adaptive Evolution
   at the Molecular Level   29

The Nonhuman Primates   39

The Apes   41
4. THAD BARTLETT, The Gibbons   44
5. CHERYL KNOTT, Orangutan Behavior and Ecology   50
6. MICHELE GOLDSMITH, Gorilla Socioecology   58
7. BARBARA FRUTH, GOTTFRIED HOHMANN,
   AND WILLIAM C. McGREW, The *Pan* Species   64

The Old World Monkeys   73
8. FRED B. BERCOVITCH AND MICHAEL A. HUFFMAN, The Macaques   77
9. JANICE CHISM, Decoding Patas Social Organization   86
10. R. CRAIG KIRKPATRICK, Colobine Diet and Social Organization   93

The New World Monkeys   106
11. KAREN B. STRIER, The Atelines   109
12. MELISSA PANGER, Capuchin Object Manipulation   115

The Prosimians   121
13. BENJAMIN Z. FREED, An Introduction to the Ecology
    of Daylight-Active Lemurs   123
14. LISA GOULD, How Female Dominance and Reproductive Seasonality
    Affect the Social Lives of Adult Male Ringtailed Lemurs   133
15. SHARON GURSKY, The Tarsiidae: Taxonomy, Behavior,
    and Conservation Status   140

Primate Conservation   146
16. ARDITH A. EUDEY, Asian Primate Conservation—My Perspective   151
17. BRUCE P. WHEATLEY, REBECCA STEPHENSON, AND HIRO KURASHINA,
    The Effects of Hunting on the Longtailed Macaques
    of Ngeaur Island, Palau   159

18. CAREY P. YEAGER AND SCOTT C. SILVER, Translocation
     and Rehabilitation as Primate Conservation Tools:
     Are They Worth the Cost? 164
19. LOIS K. LIPPOLD, Doing Fieldwork Among the Doucs in Vietnam 170

PART 2
The Realm of Primate Behavior 175
20. IRWIN S. BERNSTEIN, The Study of Behavior 176

How Things Came to Be 181
21. AGUSTÍN FUENTES, Variable Social Organization:
     What Can Looking at Primate Groups Tell Us
     About the Evolution of Plasticity in Primate Societies? 183
22. PHYLLIS DOLHINOW, Understanding Behavior:
     A Langur Monkey Case Study 189
23. CRAIG B. STANFORD, Great Apes and Early Hominids:
     Reconstructing Ancestral Behavior 196

The Primate Group 201
24. IRWIN S. BERNSTEIN, Kinship and the Behavior
     of Nonhuman Primates 202
25. ELSWORTH RAY, Social Dominance in Nonhuman Primates 206
26. ELSWORTH RAY, Hierarchy in Primate Social Organization 211

Behavioral and Biological Dimensions of the Life Span 218
27. M. S. M. PAVELKA, Primate Gerontology 220
28. MICHAEL L. POWER, Aspects of Energy Expenditure
     of Callitrichid Primates: Physiology and Behavior 225
29. PHYLLIS DOLHINOW, Play: A Critical Process
     in the Developmental System 231
30. FRED B. BERCOVITCH, The Physiology
     of Male Reproductive Strategies 237

The Mind 245
31. SUE TAYLOR PARKER, The Comparative Method
     in Studies of Cognitive Evolution 246
32. ROGER S. FOUTS AND DEBORAH H. FOUTS,
     Chimpanzee Sign Language Research 252

Primates in the Broader Context 257
33. LINDA MARIE FEDIGAN AND SHIRLEY C. STRUM, A Brief History
     of Primate Studies: National Traditions, Disciplinary Origins,
     and Stages in North American Field Research 258
34. ALLISA CARTER AND CHRIS CARTER, Cultural Representations
     of Nonhuman Primates 270

Suggested Readings 277
Glossary 279
References 284
Index 331

Topical Table of Contents

Topic	Essay	Authors
Behavioral Ecology	4–15	Bartlett; Knott; Goldsmith; Fruth, Hohmann, and McGrew; Bercovich and Huffman; Chism; Kirkpatrick; Strier; Panger; Freed; Gould; Gursky
	28	Power
	30	Bercovitch
Cross-Species Comparisons	4	Bartlett
	6	Goldsmith
	7	Fruth, Hohmann, and McGrew
	8	Bercovitch and Huffman
	10	Kirkpatrick
	11	Strier
	13	Freed
	15	Gursky
	21	Fuentes
	28	Power
Conservation	15	Gursky
	16	Eudey
	17	Wheatley, Stephenson, and Kurashina
	18	Yeager and Silver
	19	Lippold
Current Topics in Primatology	12	Panger
	18	Yeager and Silver
	21	Fuentes
	23	Stanford
	24	Bernstein
	25	Ray
	26	Ray
	27	Pavelka
	32	Fouts and Fouts
	33	Fedigan and Strum

Topic	Essay	Authors
Evolution	1	Hartwig
	2	Morales, Disotell, and Melnick
	3	Stewart
	20	Bernstein
	21	Fuentes
	22	Dolhinow
	23	Stanford
	31	Parker
Field Methods	14	Gould
	17	Wheatley, Stephenson, and Kurashina
	19	Lippold
Genetics	2	Morales, Disotell, and Melnick
	3	Stewart
Reproduction/Sexual Behavior	4	Bartlett
	7	Fruth, Hohmann, and McGrew
	8	Bercovitch and Huffman
	11	Strier
	28	Power
	30	Bercovitch
Social Behavior	4–15	Bartlett; Knott; Goldsmith; Fruth, Hohmann, and McGrew; Bercovitch and Huffman; Chism; Kirkpatrick; Strier; Panger; Freed; Gould; Gursky
	20	Bernstein
	22	Dolhinow
	24	Bernstein
	25	Ray
	27	Pavelka
	29	Dolhinow
Socioecology	5	Knott
	6	Goldsmith
	7	Fruth, Hohmann, and McGrew
	10	Kirkpatrick
	11	Strier
	28	Power

Contributors

THAD BARTLETT
Department of Anthropology
Dickinson College

FRED B. BERCOVITCH
Caribbean Primate Research Center

IRWIN S. BERNSTEIN
Department of Psychology
University of Georgia

ALLISA CARTER
Department of Anthropology
University of California, Berkeley

CHRIS CARTER
Department of Anthropology
University of California, Berkeley

JANICE CHISM
Department of Biology
Winthrop University

TODD DISOTELL
Department of Anthropology
New York University

PHYLLIS DOLHINOW
Department of Anthropology
University of California, Berkeley

ARDITH EUDEY
Editor, *Asian Primates*

LINDA M. FEDIGAN
Department of Anthropology
University of Alberta

DEBORAH H. FOUTS
Chimpanzee and Human Communication
   Institute
Central Washington University

ROGER S. FOUTS
Chimpanzee and Human Communication
   Institute
Central Washington University

BENJAMIN Z. FREED
Department of Anthropology
Washington University

BARBARA FRUTH
Max Plank Institut fur Verhaltenphysiologie

AGUSTÍN FUENTES
Department of Anthropology
Central Washington University

MICHELE GOLDSMITH
Center for Animals and Public Policy
Department of Environmental and Population
   Health
Tufts University School of Veterinary Medicine

LISA GOULD
Department of Anthropology
Okanagan University College

SHARON GURSKY
Department of Anthropology
CUNY–Queens College

WALTER C. HARTWIG
Department of Basic Sciences
San Francisco College of Osteopathic
   Medicine

GOTTFRIED HOHMANN
Max Plank Institut fur Verhaltenphysiologie

MICHAEL A. HUFFMAN
Primate Research Institute
Kyoto University

R. CRAIG KIRKPATRICK
Research Fellow, Center for Reproduction
of Endangered Species

CHERYL KNOTT
Department of Anthropology
Harvard University

HIRO KURASHINA
Department of Anthropology
University of Guam

LOIS K. LIPPOLD
Director, Douc Langur Project,
Department of Anthropology
San Diego State University

WILLIAM C. MCGREW
Departments of Anthropology and Zoology
Miami University

DON MELNICK
Center for Environmental Research and
Conservation
Columbia University

JUAN CARLOS MORALES
Center for Environmental Research and
Conservation
Columbia University

MELISSA PANGER
Department of Anthropology
University of California, Berkeley

SUE T. PARKER
Department of Anthropology
Sonoma State University

M. S. M. PAVELKA
Department of Anthropology
University of Calgary

MICHAEL L. POWER
National Zoological Park, Washington, D.C.
(Nutrition Lab)

ELSWORTH RAY
Department of Anthropology
University of California, Berkeley

SCOTT C. SILVER
Wildlife Conservation Society

CRAIG B. STANFORD
Department of Anthropology
University of Southern California

REBECCA STEPHENSON
Department of Anthropology
University of Guam

CARO-BETH STEWART
Department of Biological Sciences
State University of New York at Albany

KAREN B. STRIER
Department of Anthropology
University of Wisconsin

SHIRLEY STRUM
Department of Anthropology
University of California, San Diego

BRUCE WHEATLEY
Department of Anthropology
University of Alabama

CAREY P. YEAGER
World Wildlife Fund—Indonesia Programme,
Jakarta

Introduction

The field of primate studies has escalated in size and scope at an exponential rate since its inception in the early part of the twentieth century. The initial focus on a few field observations in Africa, Asia, and Central America and ethological investigations with captive apes has grown to encompass field and captive research of more than one hundred species at locations across the globe (see Fedigan and Strum for a historical review, Essay 33). The breadth of modern primate studies encompasses specializations that include ecology, genetics, physiology, neuroanatomy, biomechanics, and behavioral ecology/socioecology. This rapid growth has made it impossible for texts and overviews of the field to keep pace without an annual edition, and even then several volumes would be required.

Having acknowledged the impossibility of doing justice to all that is happening in modern primatology, we have elected to rely on the power of sampling to produce a small survey of what we know and think about the nonhuman primates at the end of the twentieth century. We have been delighted with the generosity of good advice and enthusiasm from our colleagues and contributors—each of whom is an expert in his or her own area. However, we offer the usual caveat and take full responsibility for omissions and commissions in this volume. Far more has been left out than has been included; dozens of volumes are possible.

The prodigious growth in information on many primate species in numerous locations has simultaneously aided and complicated our efforts to understand those that share our order. In our search for generalizations the untidy nature of the facts often defies organization into easy, manageable categories. It was a far simpler task when we knew far less. As we study more primates for longer periods of time, and in different locations, our conception of normal or usual is stretched further and further to include substantial variability even within a single species. We have tapped an enormous diversity of behavioral and ecological patterns. Although we persist in our attempts to analyze and generalize, we are faced with an ever increasing challenge to identify the genesis of diversity, to place it within ecological and evolutionary contexts.

In these essays the contributors present a view through a small window into the fascinating world of nonhuman primates—incomplete, to be certain, but representative. There is considerable variation in emphasis and theoretical position among the contributors, and as a result, you can expect an occasional contradiction in conclusions. All, however, seek to understand primate behavior using the tools at their command. A diversity of academic backgrounds (for example, anthropology, biology, psychology, zoology, animal and human medicine, mathematics, and linguistics) and diverse theoretical orientations both contribute to the strength of the field of primatology. The contributors to this volume include a fair sampling of academic training and technology, of biases and beliefs.

The book has been organized in parts to incorporate the wide variety of viewpoints and the differing fields of emphasis within the study of nonhuman primates. The essays are succinct and readable and avoid discipline-specific jargon. The essays sample a wide array of primate field studies—some complete, some in progress, others just beginning. By introducing our subjects we hope to fire the imagination that will drive future studies. We are at a complex intersection in our study and understanding of primate behavior. New techniques of investigation and insights into the causes and effects of behavior are increasing our comprehension of what we see and measure.

We begin with a brief overview of the primates—who they are and when they came into being. This sample of primate evolutionary history sets the stage for a discussion of the modern primates. What we see today does not exist merely in the present but is part of a long and well-documented history. Relationships between the living primates present us with a family picture of the primate order, a cluster of taxonomically and phylogenetically related groups.

With a background in primate evolution as a means of introduction to the order, we turn to the major divisions of living primates. There are many more prosimians and monkeys than are presented here, but these essays represent a range of ecological adaptations, behaviors, and lifeways. It is a sample—not random but deliberately chosen—that illustrates major geographical areas and well-studied species. Familiarity with the general ecology and behavior of these taxa will assist your understanding of the specific behaviors and physiological systems presented in the final part of the book.

After introducing the living nonhuman primates, we focus attention on the ever increasing serious threat to their very existence on this planet. The human primate is responsible for the loss or degradation of a multitude of habitats in which nonhuman primates cling to life. No scientist or even the casual observer or tourist can ignore the fact that the world's major primate habitats are shrinking at an alarming rate. If we are to continue to coexist, enjoy, and study prosimians, monkeys, and apes, we must move to conserve them. To do less will be to lose them forever.

Part 2, the realm of primate behavior, begins with an essay on general attributes of behavior and is followed by five groups of related essays. The different primates introduced and described in Part 1 provide a background for the special topics of behavior selected for discussion in each of the five sections. Evolution is a key concept for the first group of essays as we look closely at the broad arena of variable social organizations and then at specific patterns of behavior. Being our closest living relatives, the nonhuman primates serve as models for the reconstruction of the history of our own behavior.

The next section, on group living, concerns two central aspects of social life—kinship and social hierarchies—that are critical to our entire conception of social life, for us as well as for them. Development, the life cycle, physiology, and anatomy provide the structure of the next group of essays. It is easy to overlook the fact that much of behavior results from and is facilitated by the physical structure of our bodies. To identify primate abilities and limitations, we must look closely at their capabilities and the environments in which they exist. These essays deal with specific cases and reflect the complex and engaging realities of the primate body.

From development and the body we move to the primate mind. The latter is no less critical to existence than is the body; indeed, they are inseparable. Primates are considered a relatively intelligent set of animals, and studies of cognition and language lend support to this evaluation. Finally, the last two essays provide us with an overview of the history of primatology and the place of our subjects in literature, art, and history. It is extremely important to appreciate how much the training and biases of the people who study a subject affect the results of their study. Just as evolution itself is a product as much of chance as any other factor, so too are the disciplines that produced the information on which this and all primate essays are based. It is fascinating to examine the focus and motivation of primate researchers. As to the pervasive and widespread place of primates in culture, this might surprise some of you. Our cousins have provided us with a panoply of gratifications, food for thought, and insights on the nature of life.

What would we like you to get from this book? Our goal is to provide an introduction to the nonhuman primates and to illustrate elements of their fascinating and complex social lives. You will learn who the primates are, where they live, and how they behave. You should come away with a feeling of what living in a group entails as well as an understanding of the evolutionary pressures and pathways that have shaped modern primate behavior. Finally, through general overviews and specific discussions alike, you will have the opportunity to discover the ordinary activities of their day-to-day existence. This is truly an exciting time to be studying the nonhuman primates. The field itself is a work in progress.

PART 1

The Nonhuman Primates:
Who Are They, Where Are They,
and How Are They Doing?

Part 1 of this book is divided into three sections: **taxonomy** and **phylogeny**, the living primates, and case studies of primate conservation. This effectively represents the past, the present, and the future of our **order.** We can see where we began and trace our route to where we are at present. Finally, we must become aware of the many challenges that exist today if we are to assure that all living primate species will continue into the future.

Essay 1 provides a historical or evolutionary background for the consideration of individual species in Essays 4–15. Sixty million years of change has produced the array of forms we study today. An understanding of the phylogenetic relatedness of primates provides guidelines for interpreting their current adaptations. Our understanding of the distribution, behavior, and ecology of living primates is enriched by knowing their place of origin and their evolutionary history. Essays 1, 2, and 3 outline the evolutionary history and genetic relationships of the primates as a basis for our overview of select living primate groups.

The next set of essays presents the results of field studies of a sizable (yet far from complete) sampling of the more than two hundred species of living nonhuman primates. These essays are divided into four sections with each section presenting examples from one of the four major divisions of the order Primates: apes, Old World monkeys, New World monkeys, and prosimians. Each section is preceded by a brief overview outlining the major subdivisions and groupings in the lineage and including general behaviors and ecological information. Many additional kinds of primates have been well studied in the field and in captivity, and it is only because of limited space that so few are presented here.

The final set of essays in Part 1 presents accounts of the conservation status of many primates and the often grim reality of the struggle for survival of some nonhuman primates. Many more could have been added to this short overview, but even this brief survey clearly illustrates the major issues confronting both human and nonhuman primates in a competition for living space and survival. Humans have changed the face of the planet, and adaptations that ensured survival in past times no longer guarantee life today. Knowledge is power. We can serve our close relatives well and ensure their continued presence and health if we attend to what we know to be their needs in concert with our own.

Taxonomy and Phylogeny of the Primates

In the 1700s the anatomist Carl von Linné (better known by his Latin name Carolus Linnaeus) developed a method for classifying the diversity of life on Earth. His system arranged organisms into groups, or taxa, based on shared similarities in their morphological structures. This basic system of classification—combining and segregating organisms according to similarity in **morphology**—creates a nested hierarchy of seven basic levels: kingdoms, phyla, classes, orders, families, genera, and species. The Linnean method is still the most common classificatory system in use today.

Linnaeus also developed the system we use to name **taxa.** This system is referred to as **binomial nomenclature,** a two-name naming system. Those organisms that are alike in general form a **genus** (genera is the plural), and this is the first of the two names. Those organisms sharing more specific features are called **species,** the second of the two names in the Linnean system. Using the taxonomic methods established by Linnaeus, scientists are able to produce a classification of all living forms on Earth.

This traditional taxonomy shows the relation between primates and the rest of the animals. However, a traditional taxonomy provides no information about evolutionary relationships. The dimension of time, the ancestor-descendent relation, is absent. Taxonomies are useful for classification but only coarsely reveal evolutionary relations. To describe the latter we use phylogenies.

By no means does everyone agree about the details of how primates should be classified. There are many disputes over taxonomy reflecting basic disagreements about how it ought to be done. This is particularly the case at the species and subspecies level for a number of tropical forest living taxa. For example, recent revisions of the genus *Aotus,* the South American night monkey, have increased the number of species from three to eleven to thirteen. The South-Southeast Asia genus *Presbytis* is currently undergoing a split into three genera. There is constant heated debate as to the appropriate subspecific classifications within nearly every large genus of primates.

There are at least three main reasons for this taxonomic turmoil. First, two major tendencies or styles are employed by those who classify: lumping and splitting. **Lumpers** tend to consolidate subspecies and species, thereby reducing the number of taxa, whereas **splitters** do the reverse and divide what was formerly a single unit. There is a longstanding debate between the two camps, an argument based on differing concepts of the natural world and a real disagreement over how different is different.

A second cause of taxonomic turmoil, and one to surface only recently, results from advances in our knowledge and our ability to analyze and compare molecular information. These skills have altered the playing field of taxonomy and are changing the amount and quality of the information available for use in arranging the taxa of organisms. A classification of primates based on coat (or pelage) can produce a classification at variance with one based on skeletal structures. Researchers using molecular data have produced still different classifications. But these molecular-based rearrangements of the order Primates, created with modern high-tech methods, do not automatically become the best classification systems. The degree of DNA identity between humans and chimpanzees, for example, must be evaluated according to obvious differences in development between members of these two genera. Clearly, humans are not just 2 percent different from chimpanzees.

The third element in this taxonomic uproar has to do with politics, economics, and a host of other cultural and national realities. Due to the structure and procedures of the global and national bodies regulating and instituting conservation programs, and to economic realities of the countries in which nonhuman primates live, endangered or critically threatened species are in urgent need of being granted top priority for help. It is critically important to identify these endangered groups and to conserve them. But limited funds and incomplete natural history data on many primates can lead to a taxonomic status assignment based on factors other than scientific criteria.

Using multiple lines of evidence, including structural and molecular data, we can provide an overview of the evolutionary relations of living primates. To accomplish this with structural traits we examine modern forms and their ancestors. Classifying organisms based on their evolutionary histories is one way scientists deal with these issues. Evolution is the unifying principle of biology. To accomplish an evolutionary classification it is necessary to use multiple lines of evidence, including both morphological structure and molecular data. Within an evolutionary classification the structures of living and fossil forms are compared to establish the evolutionary pathways of different species. Traits, or characters, shared by all or most species are considered "primitive." These features are seen in all species because they were inherited from a common ancestral species. Characters that are unique to a species, or taxa, are termed **derived traits** as they evolved after the species being compared last shared an ancestor. Those features common to some species but not to others, traits that evolved after the common ancestor to all the taxa being compared but prior to more recent speciation events, are **shared derived traits.** Establishing whether characters are primitive, derived, or shared derived traits allows scientists to confirm the evolutionary history, and consequently the evolutionary relationships, among a group of species.

Examining molecular data is a complementary technique scientists use to establish evolutionary relationships and to designate the validity of a species or subspecies. Instead of morphological features, the scientists compare the sequences of DNA bases and the mutations, or changes, in the sequence of a portion of DNA to establish primitive, derived, and shared derived molecular states. The patterns of DNA sequences provide an independent method from morphology for testing hypotheses regarding the taxonomic status and evolutionary histories of different species.

If we wish to examine behavior in a similar fashion, we are limited to living forms for direct comparisons. Behavior can change far more rapidly than morphology and may exist for many generations and not be the result of **natural selection.** However, all is not lost because we can tell a great deal about an animal's life patterns from its morphology. We study the living primates and realize that certain structures are associated with a specific array of behavior patterns. For example, leg and arm bones tell us whether the animal leaped from one limb to another, swung by the arms, or walked on all four limbs. Size of eye orbits offers a clue as to whether day or night activity was the norm.

One of our most important goals is to understand the living primates and the relations among them. To accomplish this goal requires information on an organism's evolutionary history. Ultimate, or evolutionary, causes lie buried in the past, to be teased out with comparison and reconstruction, assisted by as much phylogenetic and taxonomic information as is available. The ecological context of life, the habitat and all that it contains, is then added to this mix to produce the most complete picture of the living primates (Figure 1).

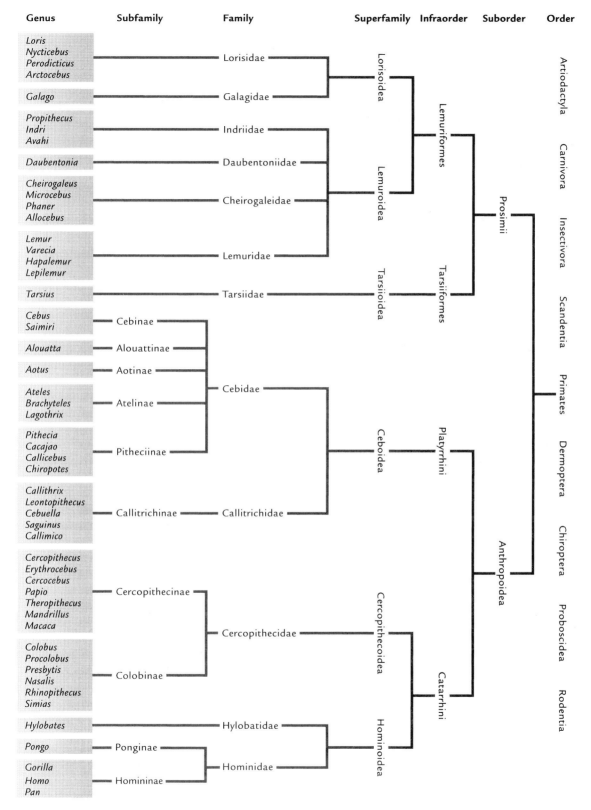

Genus	Subfamily	Family	Superfamily	Infraorder	Suborder	Order

Loris
Nycticebus
Perodicticus
Arctocebus
Lorisidae
Lorisoidea
Lemuriformes
Prosimii

Galago
Galagidae

Propithecus
Indri
Avahi
Indriidae
Lemuroidea

Daubentonia
Daubentoniidae

Cheirogaleus
Microbus
Phaner
Allocebus
Cheirogaleidae

Lemur
Varecia
Hapalemur
Lepilemur
Lemuridae

Tarsius
Tarsiidae
Tarsioidea
Tarsiiformes

Cebus
Saimiri
Cebinae

Alouatta
Alouattinae

Aotus
Aotinae
Cebidae
Ceboidea
Platyrrhini
Anthropoidea

Ateles
Brachyteles
Lagothrix
Atelinae

Pithecia
Cacajao
Callicebus
Chiropotes
Pitheciinae

Callithrix
Leontopithecus
Cebuella
Saguinus
Callimico
Callitrichinae
Callitrichidae

Cercopithecus
Erythrocebus
Cercocebus
Papio
Theropithecus
Mandrillus
Macaca
Cercopithecinae
Cercopithecidae
Cercopithecoidea

Colobus
Procolobus
Presbytis
Nasalis
Rhinopithecus
Simias
Colobinae
Catarrhini

Hylobates
Hylobatidae
Hominoidea

Pongo
Ponginae
Hominidae

Gorilla
Homo
Pan
Homininae

Order column: Artiodactyla, Carnivora, Insectivora, Scandentia, Primates, Dermoptera, Chiroptera, Proboscidea, Rodentia

FIGURE 1   Primate taxonomy

1

Primate Evolution

Walter Carl Hartwig

*Fossil prosimians, monkeys, and apes are the only direct records of primate ancestry, and these **fossils** are often fragmentary and difficult to interpret. The recovery of fossils is a relatively straightforward objective of field research and a cumulatively positive contribution to our understanding of primate evolution. The process of discovery naturally leads to contemplation, and our appetite for more discovery is never satisfied. The transition from discovery to understanding, however, is neither direct nor automatic. As scientists who must reconstruct the past by examining fossil evidence of individuals, we are influenced by the history of fossil discovery and by the quality of the fossils themselves. As you will see, some localities have produced numerous fossils, and these sites exert a tremendous influence over our interpretation of primate evolution. However, no single locality can represent all of the diversity of a species living at any one time. Therefore, primate evolution is a subject in a constant state of revision as more evidence is discovered.*

*The story of primate evolution as told in this essay is both helped and limited by the fortunes of recovering primate fossils. You cannot design an expedition to test a hypothesis or to find a particular type of fossil. Not all fossils are well preserved, and erosion and other factors can confuse the fossil record. Answers to some very interesting questions in primate evolution—How did primates originate? or How did the earliest New World monkeys get to South America?—will always be beyond the reach of an **inductive inquiry** such as deciphering the **fossil record**. Fossils do, however, present the direct links, once vital, often spectacular, and always intriguing, between living primates and their ultimate common ancestors.*

PRIMATE ORIGINS

Primates are characterized by a unique combination of anatomical traits, including a bar of bone that encircles (or fully encloses) the eye socket, nails instead of claws on most of the digits, opposability of the thumb, and growth of the bone that encloses the inner ear (auditory bulla) from the petrosal bone. The fossil record of primate evolution dates from the present back to approximately fifty million years ago (Table 1). The fossil record has little to say about where and when primates originated, but theories abound on the nature of this profound event. Historically, these theories have emphasized the physical characteristics that make primates different from other mammals—grasping thumbs and toes and stereoscopic vision. They have also assumed that only one aspect of early primate life, such as an arboreal habitat or foraging for insects by grabbing at them, could be the root of primate origins.

As the century turns, however, an idea that puts the earliest primate in a more generalized light is gaining support. Because many primate species are multivorous,[1] primate origins may be predicated

---

[1]"Multivorous" is used here to describe a diet that includes many different things, such as fruits, leaves, nectar, insects, and small vertebrates. This term is used explicitly to distinguish "multivory" from "omnivory," a more formal term that really means the consumption of all things. Although primates frequently are described as omnivorous, only humans actually approach the true meaning of omnivory. This distinction is important because even subtle shifts in the dietary preferences of a population can lead to evolutionary divergence.

10

TABLE 1 A Geological Timeline of Major Trends in Primate Evolution

Geologic Epoch (millions of years)	North America	Europe	Asia	Africa	South America
Pleistocene (2–present)		Old World monkeys diminish, hominoids go extinct.	Old World monkeys persist and ultimately colonize insular Southeast Asia; giant hominoids found in southern China and Vietnam.	Old World monkeys proliferate on the continent; giant prosimians found on Madagascar; hominoids limited to tropical belt.	Unusual fossil monkeys found on Caribbean islands; large fossils resembling spider and howler monkeys found in Brazil.
Pliocene (5–2)		Great diversity of Old World monkeys and a few surviving hominoids that resemble living apes and early hominids.	Presumed loss of hominoid diversity in temperate areas (very few fossil deposits of this age are known).	Old World monkeys greatly diversify; no fossil evidence of hominoids except for earliest known hominids.	
Miocene (23–5)		Hominoids flourish in the middle and late Miocene, including the earliest known definite brachiator.	Hominoids flourish in the middle and late Miocene, including a probable direct ancestor of living orangutans; no known Old World monkeys.	Emergence and diverse radiation of hominoids in sub-Saharan Africa; first evidence of distinct Old World monkeys.	Diverse radiation in southern South America in early Miocene; very diverse radiation of more modern-looking forms in northern South America in middle and late Miocene.
Oligocene (35–23)	Primates go extinct.	Remaining adapid and omomyid primates go extinct.	Fragmentary anthropoid fossils in Myanmar.	Proliferation of early anthropoids and possibly the earliest distinct catarrhine.	Earliest known fossil New World monkeys.
Eocene (53–35)	Two different types of prosimian-like primates, adapids and omomyids, flourish.	Two different types of prosimian-like primates, adapids and omomyids, flourish.	Several fragmentary jaws of potential early anthropoids in China and Southeast Asia.	Appearance of earliest definite anthropoids in Fayum deposits.	
Paleocene (65–53)	Possible origin of primates, but fossil record offers no definitive evidence.		A logical tropical area for primate origins, but no evidence yet in the fossil record.	A logical tropical area for primate origins, but no evidence yet in the fossil record.	

on a dietary approach more generalized than just insect predation. By analogy to the opossum—a nonprimate that has adapted certain primate-like characteristics such as a relatively large brain, a bony postorbital process, and a short snout—the earliest primates may have been as frugivorous as they were insectivorous, and a large part of their divergence from other mammals may have been due to foraging on fruits where no other mammal could go. Thus, the best explanation for primate origins may be one in which both habit (visual predation) *and* habitat (the slight outer branches of the forest canopy and undergrowth) drove the evolution of characteristic primate features.

Much of our understanding of primate origins reflects our sense of how they spread out afterward. Primates have diversified into a greater variety of habits and habitats than most other orders of mammals. Such a broad radiation is due to the potential of their persistent generality, both anatomically and behaviorally, compared to other mammal species that are linked more closely to the predator-prey pyramid. We can thus be certain that novelty without loss of versatility was a central theme in primate origins, even if we cannot pin the sequence of **adaptations** to a particular point in the distant fossil record.

EARLY RADIATIONS

How would you know an early primate if you found one in the fossil record? Identifying a fossil as a primate is straightforward if the fossil has key features such as a postorbital bar of bone, but many times fossils consist only of teeth or parts of jaws. In these cases identification is not as certain but is based on the relative generality of the chewing surface of the teeth compared to other mammal groups living at the same time (Figure 1). Although there is no obvious earliest primate in the fossil record, two radiations of early primates are apparent in the **Eocene** fossil records of North America and Europe.

Geological exposures of Eocene age in the northern latitudes contain fossils of small mammals that are indisputably primate because they present

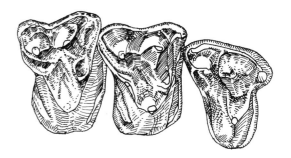

FIGURE 1   *Purgatorius.* These fifty-million-year-old fossilized teeth are often identified as the oldest primate, mostly because the pattern of crests on the chewing surfaces is more generalized than that of other mammals at this time. Whether or not *Purgatorius* is part of primate ancestry is less important than the general concept behind its symbolic status as the earliest primate: primate evolution is the record of how a relatively unspecialized line of mammals radiated. Scale ⇒ 1mm.

the postorbital bar of bone and auditory bulla that minimally define all living primates (Figure 2). The fossil record of their radiation has grown enormously over the last one hundred years, but additional discoveries have only confirmed very early interpretations of how they relate to one another. One group, found in both North America and Europe, bears a striking resemblance to living lemurs and is classified in the family Adapidae. Another group, also found in both North America and Europe, is slightly smaller on average and bears a striking resemblance to the living nocturnal prosimians. These are the Omomyidae.

Despite their geographic restriction to the northern latitudes, one or the other of these early prosimian-like primate radiations repeatedly has been linked to the origins of the **Anthropoidea.** This tendency drew from the historical significance that these fossils have played in building an old record of primate evolution, but recent discoveries of equally old anthropoids have altered our sense of how closely related the adapids and omomyids are to later anthropoids. They clearly demonstrate an extensive range of diversity and adaptation of primates at a prosimian grade of biological organization early in the primate evolutionary radiation.

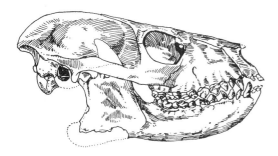

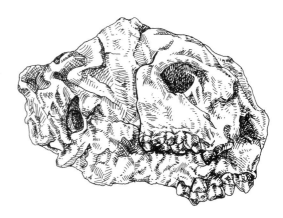

FIGURE 2   *Notharctus*. A nearly complete skeleton of this early primate was found in the western United States and described in 1920. As the most apparent evidence of early primate evolution, *Notharctus* became the genus from which both living prosimians and living anthropoids must have descended. For more than half a century, anthropoid origin was considered a phenomenon of the northern hemisphere and a product of a particular notharctid lineage of Eocene (35–50 mya) prosimians. Neither of these ideas is supported now. *Notharctus* illustrates how debate over the origin of different types of primates is influenced by the history of fossil discovery and the completeness of fossil remains.

FIGURE 3   *Catopithecus* (35–40 mya). This broken specimen from the productive El Fayum locality preserves enough anatomy to challenge long-held beliefs about the rise of anthropoid primates. The skull shows a complete wall of bone behind the eyeball (an anthropoid feature) and has only two premolar teeth (a defining feature of catarrhine anthropoids: Old World monkeys, apes, and humans). However, all anthropoids have fused mandibles, but *Catopithecus* does not. Thus, depending on how you classify *Catopithecus*, one of these three characteristics (unfused mandible, postorbital closure, two premolars) must be justified. If one of these major trait complexes evolved in parallel in anthropoids, as is clearly demonstrated by *Catopithecus,* so could the other two. *Catopithecus* is an example of how our predictions of what we will find in the fossil record can be completely logical and at the same time completely wrong.

ANTHROPOID ORIGINS AND EVOLUTION

Early Anthropoids

The most exciting growth area in primate evolution in the last ten years has been the discovery of several very early anthropoids in neotropical latitudes of the Old World. Several of these fossils have been found at the single large locality of the Fayum in Egypt, but intriguing fragments have also been found throughout North Africa, China, and South Asia. Anthropoids differ from prosimians in having a relatively larger braincase, fewer teeth, and complete bony closure behind the eyes. The fossil record of the near tropics in the forty-million-year time range has been offering glimpses of these traits in controversial fossils that are raising as many questions as answers.

The Egyptian locality of El Fayum has dominated our understanding of early anthropoid evolution because of the numerous genera found there

under exacting stratigraphic control. Historically, the fossils could be grouped into a primitive branch (the Parapithecidae, with three premolars) and an advanced branch (the Propliopithecidae, with two premolars) that reflect the roots of living New World monkeys and living catarrhines, respectively. Recently, however, fossils such as *Catopithecus* from lower in the stratigraphy have demonstrated a combination of primitive and advanced features that upset this logical scheme (Figure 3).

At the same time, less complete specimens from deposits dated more than forty million years ago in South Asia and China may indicate a widespread radiation of early anthropoids (as well as the possibility that Africa was not the source of anthropoid evolution). The fossils lack preservation of the critical parts of the skull necessary to confirm whether or not they are truly anthropoid, but their discovery has indicated a more general revision in our sense of how old, and how global, was the emergence of anthropoids.

The Evolution of New World Monkeys

The division of living anthropoids into New World monkeys, Old World monkeys, apes, and humans is a convenient framework for interpreting the fossil record of definite anthropoids. For example, it is easier to interpret a fossil *within* the lineage of New World monkeys than to identify a possible *ancestor* of the radiation. In this sense, the fossil record of South American primates is one of the more straightforward stories in primate evolution.

The earliest South American monkeys known so far date to approximately twenty-six million years ago and do not resemble any living forms. For the next ten million years the fossil record has been productive only in southern South America, where numerous small and fragmentary remains show a wider radiation of forms still unlike the living New World monkeys. The final pulse of fossil recoveries in South America, dating from sixteen to twelve million years ago, is found on the opposite end of the continent in a very productive region of Colombia known as La Venta. More than a dozen different kinds of New World monkeys have been found here, almost all of which clearly resemble living monkeys (Figure 4).

The primate fossil record in South America continues to grow, but the abundance of recent discoveries has been limited to the very productive **Miocene** locality of La Venta in Colombia. As with the Fayum, then, our sense of how diverse New World monkeys were fifteen million years ago is largely the function of discovery within a single, geographically peripheral region. Undeniably, the pattern of New World monkey evolution is conservative, but we must remember that vast areas of their current distribution do not contain fossils and vast time gaps (the last ten million years, for example) in their known fossil record persist.

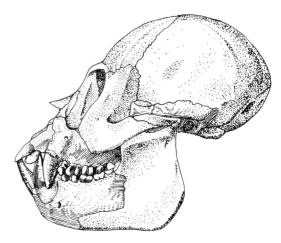

FIGURE 4   *Cebupithecia* (12–16 mya). Extinct primates in South America bear a striking resemblance to their living descendants. This pattern was established with the discovery of *Cebupithecia,* which closely resembles the living saki monkey and other fossils found in Colombia in the 1950s. By the time of the middle Miocene epoch (10–15 mya), however, examples of each major type (subfamily) of living New World monkey can be found in the fossil record.

The Evolution of Old World Monkeys

The evolution of Old World monkeys has received the least attention of all the major radiations, despite the fact that living Old World monkeys are relatively successful compared to other primate groups. The fossil record as we know it is limited to a few early specimens from the Miocene of Africa and many specimens from the recent past (**Pleistocene**) in Africa, Europe, and Asia. Although the presence of many Miocene hominoid fossils in Africa is enough to signal the separate radiation of the Old World monkeys, the absence of early Old World monkey fossils has kept us from understanding the nature of the separation.

One of the most recent discoveries in primate evolution may now satisfy that gap in understanding. Ongoing excavations on Maboko Island in Kenya have yielded the first complete cranium of the earliest-known Old World monkey (Figure 5), and it shows that the Old World monkey lineage

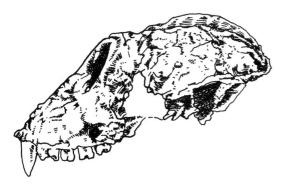

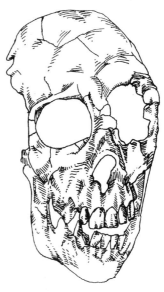

FIGURE 5   *Victoriapithecus* (17–19 mya). The evolution of Old World monkeys can be traced to this genus, one of the only known specimens of its kind from the Miocene of Africa. Until recent fieldwork on Maboko Island, in Kenya, only teeth and fragmentary cranial bones of early Old World monkeys were known. This specimen, found in 1996, finally reveals the characteristic face of primitive Old World monkeys, which retains the profile and other features of *Aegyptopithecus* and is quite different from the facial profile of early hominoids.

FIGURE 6   *Proconsul* (17–21 mya). This specimen was found on Rusinga Island in Kenya by Mary Leakey in 1948 and remains one of the most evocative images of primate evolution. The distorted cranium is instantly recognizable as a hominoid, even though the features that it shares with living apes are considered primitive for catarrhines (monkeys, apes, and humans) in general. Anatomically, *Proconsul* reflects the essential nature of hominoid evolution—a generalized diet (as inferred from tooth morphology) and a notable increase in relative brain size as compared to other primates. Recently discovered postcranial material of *Proconsul* and other Miocene hominoids indicates that early hominoid locomotion emphasized quadrupedalism, not suspension and brachiation.

may be more similar to early catarrhine precursors of the Fayum than previously believed. Both Old World monkeys and the **Hominoidea** have diverged from a common early catarrhine ancestry, but this discovery indicates that anatomically neither can be positioned as a conservative extension of the primitive structural form.

The fossil record of Old World monkeys also tracks a general trend in primate evolution for hominoid diversity to dwindle over the last ten million years while Old World monkey diversity expanded. In **Pliocene** and Pleistocene deposits throughout the range of living Old World monkeys, fossil forms can be found that support the interpretation of global expansion perhaps as a result of more temperate climates replacing more tropical ones over large areas of the Old World.

The Evolution of Hominoid Primates

With the exception of the human fossil record, no other storyline in primate evolution is more captivating to students than the evolutionary history of apes. Unfortunately, the story is one of great promise early but great fragility in modern times. The fossil record of hominoid primates definitively reaches back to a landmark fossil from the early Miocene of the African Rift Valley, *Proconsul* (Figure 6). From the early through the middle Miocene a wide variety of hominoid primates appeared in the tropical latitudes of eastern Africa. The radiation spread to neotropical latitudes of Europe, Asia, and Southeast Asia over the next ten million years (Figure 7). After a zenith in the middle Miocene, however, hominoid diversity dwindled steadily until

FIGURE 7 *Sivapithecus* (8–12 mya). One of the best examples of great ape evolution in progress is the radiation of *Sivapithecus,* which is found from Turkey to Pakistan in the late Miocene. The facial features it shares with the living orangutan are striking. The logical interpretation of *Sivapithecus* as a direct ancestor of the living orangutan, however, is not without its critics, who feel that some specific differences outweigh the general similarities. Understanding the fossil record ultimately requires an informed but subjective assessment of which anatomical characters are most informative.

the fossil record virtually disappears at the end of the Miocene. The living apes and some Pleistocene fossils are the only evidence of the once predominant radiation.

Two questions pervade interpretation of the hominoid fossil record: How ape-like were the extinct apes? and Which of them is the most likely ancestor to humans? Recent fossil discoveries have demonstrated that ape-like brachiation may date back to the earliest descendants of *Proconsul,* particularly in the form of a very long-armed skeleton of *Dryopithecus* from Europe. On the highly charged matter of the second question, the lack of fossil material from the cornerstone region of eastern Africa keeps the debate regarding the **Hominidae** speculative. Late Miocene candidates from southern Europe, such as *Ouranopithecus* (Figure 8), may not be given the credit they are due because we are compelled to match a late African hominoid to an early African hominid in our search for the proverbial "missing link."

PATTERN AND PROCESS IN PRIMATE EVOLUTION

In general primates are a radiation of mammals in which growth of structures related to the brain has taken precedence over growth of structures related to the body. This trend can be observed by comparing the oldest fossils within each lineage (prosimians, monkeys, apes, and humans) to living species. Within each lineage, primate evolution is also the story of a wide variety of limb sizes and shapes, tooth sizes and shapes, and social systems that have changed over time as a result of traditional selective pressures.

The number of primate species living at any time in the past almost certainly exceeded the number of species living today. This is due to larger areas of tropical climate in the past and the absence of humans. We must remember, therefore, that the anatomy of living primates underestimates the range of possible anatomies we will find in the fossil record (Figure 9). A major challenge in the study of primate evolution is to balance the rules that seem to govern the biology of living species against the unruly nature of past biodiversity. We must allow for the possibility that many distinctive traits of living species have appeared and disappeared several times in primate evolutionary history, even though this defeats the expectations of a deductive scientific approach to the fossil record. Indeed, the two major questions of primate evolution—How do we explain the fossil record? and What is the ancestry of living primates?—have often been addressed independently. Future fossil discoveries will focus the picture of how primates have evolved, the resolution of which is limited only by our own imagination.

ACKNOWLEDGMENTS
I thank Lou Phan (Figures 1–9a) and Humberto do Espirito Santo (Figure 9b) for the illustrations.

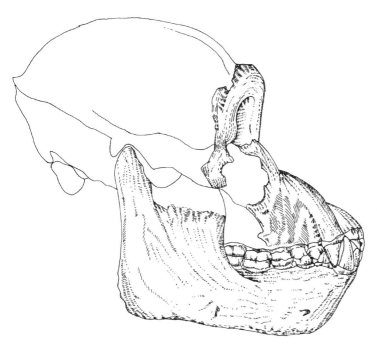

FIGURE 8 *Ouranopithecus* (7–9 mya). Hominoid evolution may have begun in Africa, but it had reached the entire Old World by the end of the Miocene. *Ouranopithecus*, from Greece, is one of the best examples of a late Miocene hominoid that may have given rise to the hominid line, based on the features it shares with *Australopithecus*. Circumstantial evidence favors Africa as the place where hominids originated, but at the moment the most compelling fossil evidence for their hominoid ancestry may be the European *Ouranopithecus*.

(a)   (b)

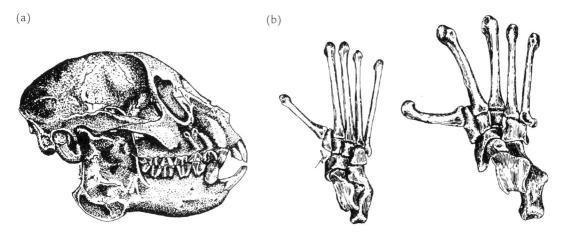

FIGURE 9 Dramatic size increase is a feature of all primate radiations during the late Pleistocene epoch (100,000–10,000 B.P.). The causes of this trend across mammals are both environmental and phylogenetic, but the abrupt extinction of megafauna probably was a function of human contact on top of changing environments. (a) A giant extinct lemur (*Archeolemur*) is just one of several examples of this phenomenon on the island of Madagascar. (b) The foot bones of a giant South American monkey (*Protopithecus*, right) compared to a living spider monkey (*Ateles*, left).

2

Molecular Phylogenetic Studies of Nonhuman Primates

Juan Carlos Morales, Todd R. Disotell, and Don J. Melnick

Beginning with George Nuttall's 1904 book, *Blood Immunity and Blood Relationship,* which opened with a discussion of the classification of the order Primates, molecular data have played a role in deciphering the evolutionary history of the primates. However, it was not until the 1960s and 1970s that genetic research into primate relationships blossomed, leading to what Pilbeam (1996) called the "Goodman-Wilson-Sarich genetic revolution" in primate evolutionary studies.

Over the past twenty-five years considerable progress has been made, not only in the quality and quantity of data that can now be collected in the laboratory but in the theoretical methods and analytical procedures used to interpret these data. The first molecular classification studies collected similarity (or distance) data and used a **cluster technique** as well as other distance-based techniques that group species based on overall genetic similarity. First developed in the 1960s, these

techniques were used extensively throughout the 1970s. In recent years improved data collection techniques, such as **restriction site mapping, nucleotide sequencing,** and microsatellite typing, have changed the way we analyze and interpret molecular data. These newer techniques produce discrete character data (e.g., nucleotide sequences), which are used to infer relationships either in a cladistic framework or by using complex maximum likelihood models. **Cladistics** is a method that groups species using shared derived characteristics. Under this method, a hypothesis about evolutionary relationships is generated by estimating a tree that requires the least number of steps (that is, the least amount of evolutionary change) between taxa. This is usually referred to as the most parsimonious tree. Under the maximum likelihood approach, one actually starts with a specific hypothesis on taxa relationships and then calculates the probability that such an evolutionary scenario

---

Editors' Note: Technological and analytical advances in the last thirty years have changed the ways we seek knowledge about our past. In primate studies the practice of using DNA, enzymes, and other molecules to illustrate evolutionary relationships has become a form of high-tech, biochemical detective work. Current studies of primate evolution rely as much on specialized computer analyses, mathematical modeling, and biochemistry as on the more traditional approaches of comparing shapes and sizes of fossils and living primates.

Essays 2 and 3 introduce the amazing diversity of techniques, types of molecules, and computer analyses currently used to create and understand primate phylogenies and molecular evolution. The molecules and methods can become a confusing cluster of terminology, but it is important to remember what these studies are all about: primate evolutionary relationships. Focus on the results—the phylogenies provided—to gain a sense of how these researchers are uncovering primate histories through current technology and molecular biology.

would give rise to the observed data. An evolutionary model that has a higher probability of producing the data at hand is preferred over one with less probability (see Swofford et al. 1996).

Additionally, along with this increasing sophistication of analytical models and methods, a greater understanding of their relative strengths and weaknesses is being gained. For instance, the recognition of the potential differences between a "gene tree" and a "species tree" has led many researchers to utilize several independent genetic systems to corroborate phylogenetic hypotheses based on molecular data (see Ruvolo 1997 for an example). A gene tree is the actual evolutionary history of a specific fragment of the genome. If such a region was variable in an ancestral species, then the descendent species may inherit different variants, purely by chance, which could lead researchers to erroneously reconstruct the species' evolutionary history. Another way that the gene tree may differ from the species tree is if divergent variants of a genetic region are lost, again purely by chance, in one or more of the descendent species. Thus, the only way to be confident that the two types of tree represent the evolutionary history of the animals themselves is when a number of genetic systems all lead to the same tree shape, which, given the random nature of the effects we have mentioned, would be unlikely unless they share a common evolutionary history.

Another difficulty in interpreting molecular data is due to the difficulty in analyzing lineages that exhibit different rates of evolution and the "long-branch attraction" phenomenon. Under both of these circumstances, very distantly related species' genes may superficially come to resemble each other due to parallel or convergent evolution. All of these phenomena require using greater caution in inferring evolutionary history from molecular data and are leading to the reassessment of certain primate relationships (e.g., see the discussion of tarsier relationships in this essay).

The primates have always been subdivided into two major groups, nevertheless, there is still some discussion over how these two groups should be partitioned. Simpson's (1945) division of the primates into the Prosimii (lemurs, lorisids, and tar-

siers) and Anthropoidea (monkeys and apes), which is still supported by many primate researchers (Martin 1990), has long stood in opposition to Pocock's (1918) division of the order into Strepsirrhini (lemurs and lorisids) and Haplorhini (tarsiers and anthropoids), which seems currently to be more widely accepted (Szalay and Delson 1979). Genetic and other molecular data have generally been claimed to provide support for the strepsirrhine-haplorhine division (Goodman et al. 1994). Now let's take a closer look at each of the major groups of primates.

THE TARSIERS

The earliest immunological work that included tarsiers concluded they were more closely related to anthropoids, supporting the haplorhine concept (Dene, Goodman, and Prychodko 1976). Later, more refined immunological studies could not resolve a trichotomy (a co-equal three-way relationship) composed of one branch that included lemurs and lorises, one branch of tarsiers, and one branch for all of the anthropoids (Sarich and Cronin 1976). Analysis of tandem alignments of protein sequences supports the haplorhine concept, but tarsiers were not sequenced for most of the proteins involved (Goodman et al. 1982). Chromosomal analyses have been unable to place tarsiers because of their extremely unusual chromosomal complement (the highest number among primates) and the inability of various researchers to align chromosomal banding patterns in tarsiers with anything homologous in the other primates (see Martin 1990 for an extensive discussion of tarsier chromosomal evolution). DNA-DNA hybridization studies (Bonner, Heinemann, and Todaro 1980) cluster tarsiers with anthropoids, though with a very short common ancestral branch. This study also revealed widely different rates of evolution among the Malagasy lemurs, anthropoids, tarsiers, and galagos.

More recently, five nuclear genes have been sequenced in tarsiers and other primates. Three globin loci (gamma, pseudo eta, and epsilon) provide conflicting results (Bailey et al. 1991; Goodman et al. 1994). Analyses of these sequences do yield most parsimonious trees that support a haplorhine **clade,** but the next most parsimonious trees support a prosimian grouping and only require one, two, and three more evolutionary changes, respectively (Disotell, unpublished analysis). The most parsimonious tree, derived from interphotoreceptor retinoid binding protein (IRBP) nucleotide sequences, links tarsiers most closely with lemurs (Stanhope et al. 1992), but again, only one more evolutionary change yields a tree that links them to anthropoids. The aA-Crystallin locus does not link tarsiers with anthropoids but rather with either other lemurs and lorisids or other nonprimate mammals, depending on the method and model of phylogenetic analysis (Jaworski 1995).

Analysis of a tandem alignment of three regions of the mitochondrial genome for which 2739 nucleotide bases have been sequenced for tarsier, lemur, a New World monkey, several apes, and a cow as an outgroup (data from Hayasaka, Gojobori, and Horai 1988; Adkins and Honeycutt 1994; Yoder, Ruvolo, and Vigalys 1996; Andrews, Jermiin, and Easteal 1998) was carried out by one of the authors (Disotell, unpublished analysis). The most parsimonious tree shows tarsiers as the **sister-taxon** to the rest of the primates. A tree one step longer supports a prosimian grouping, whereas a tree supporting the haplorhine grouping requires an additional six steps. Although different analytical schemes and choices of outgroups (for reference) are possible (and even desirable), analysis of mitochondrial data collected to date do not unambiguously support *Tarsius* as either a haplorhine or a prosimian.

The mitochondrial results, coupled with the protein and nuclear DNA data and analyses discussed here, reveal that the evidence for the Haplorhini is underwhelming at best. Clearly, more data and more realistic models of nucleotide sequence evolution will be needed to unambiguously resolve the relationship of tarsiers to the other primates using genetic data. This is not unexpected given the very long branch lengths (and the problems they create for phylogenetic analyses) that connect the tarsier lineage to either the prosimian group or the anthropoid group. Disparate rates of evolution among the lemur group, tarsiers, and an-

thropoids (discussed in Martin 1990) may also be confounding such analyses.

LEMURS AND LORISES

Molecular phylogenetic analyses of strepsirrhines have resolved several major issues while leaving many of the minor ones open to debate. Yoder (1997) presents a particularly useful summary of the state of strepsirrhine systematics that incorporates both morphological and molecular data. The two most debated issues in strepsirrhine systematics have been the relationships of the cheirogalids (dwarf and mouse lemurs) found in Madagascar with respect to the other Malagasy lemurs and the African and Asian lorisids, and the position of the aye-aye (also from Madagascar).

The first question revolves around whether or not the Malagasy species form a single lineage. If not, at least two migrations across the Mozambique channel need to be invoked to explain a potential close relationship between cheirogalids and lorisids. Various morphologically oriented studies have proposed a close relationship between lorisids and cheirogalids based on several shared derived traits of the postcrania and cranial base (see discussion in Martin 1990). Despite this evidence, every molecular study to date supports the view that the Malagasy primates are a single group. Genetic evidence in support of this conclusion includes immunodiffusion (Dene, Goodman, and Prychodko 1980), chromosome banding (Dutrillaux 1988), DNA-DNA hybridization (Bonner, Heinemann, and Todaro 1980), and nucleotide sequences of the g-globin (Koop et al. 1989), e-globin (Porter et al. 1995), COII (Adkins and Honeycutt 1994), cytochrome b (Yoder, Ruvolo, and Vigalys 1996), and IRBP (Yoder 1996) genes.

The aye-aye (*Daubentonia*), with its suite of uniquely derived characteristics, has proven particularly difficult for morphologists to place among the other lemurs. However, as with the issue of the Malagasy group, molecular and chromosomal analyses are remarkably congruent regarding the aye-aye's relationships. The aye-aye consistently falls as the most basal member of the Malagasy lemur lineage when DNA sequences of two independent nuclear loci—e-globin (Porter et al. 1995) and IRBP (Yoder 1996)—and a combination of two mitochondrial loci are analyzed cladistically after removing replacement sites (those causing an amino acid replacement) that may be subject to selection (Adkins and Honeycutt 1994; Yoder, Ruvolo, and Vigalys 1996; Yoder 1997). Chromosomal banding analysis also supports this view (Dutrillaux 1988), as does a distance analysis using immunodiffusion data (Dene, Goodman, and Prychodko 1980).

Unfortunately, in-depth sampling of the majority of the Malagasy lineages for multiple genes has not yet been carried out. As a result, only the composition of the five major lineages of Malagasy primates is relatively noncontroversial, though the relationships among them are still questioned. The aye-aye is best considered the basal member of the entire group, whereas the cheirogalids, lemurids (*Lemur, Hapalemur, Eulemur,* and *Varecia*), indrids (*Indri, Propithecus,* and *Avahi*), and the many species of *Lepilemur* can currently be described as members of an undifferentiated four-way split. Different genetic systems suggest different relationships among these four clades resulting in this unresolved bush (see Yoder 1997 for a review). More work needs to be done to resolve several issues of strepsirrhine phylogeny, but the broad outlines are now clearly laid out (Figure 1).

NEW WORLD MONKEYS

According to Horovitz and Meyer (1997), the New World monkeys invaded South America about 25 mya and underwent an **adaptive radiation** that resulted in about sixteen different recognized genera, and up to sixty-four different species. Most taxonomists agree with the division of these primates into three groups: the callitrichids, represented by the marmosets (*Callithrix*) and tamarins (*Saguinus, Leontopithecus*); the pithecins, represented by the sakis (*Pithecia, Chiropotes*) and uakaris (*Cacajao*); and the atelins, represented by the howler (*Alouatta*), the spider (*Ateles*), the woolly (*Lagothrix*), and the woolly spider (*Brachyteles*) monkeys. In ad-

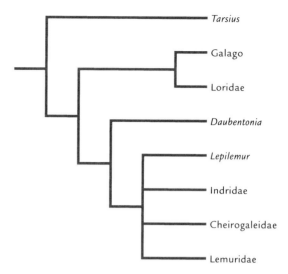

FIGURE 1 Phylogenetic hypothesis of the "Prosimians," based on our interpretation of the molecular data.

dition to these groups, four other genera have been very difficult to classify: the capuchins (*Cebus*), the squirrel (*Saimiri*), the owl (*Aotus*), and the titi (*Callicebus*) monkeys. To a somewhat lesser extent, the position of the Goeldi's monkey (*Callimico*) among the callitrichids has also been controversial.

Morphological studies have done little to elucidate the relationships among the different New World monkeys. Most authors recognize the callitrichids (including *Callimico*) as members of a single family (Callitrichidae) separate from the rest of the New World monkeys, or what is generally referred to as the family Cebidae, but fail to agree on the phylogenetic relationships of its constituents. However, even this minimal level of agreement is not universal. Rosenberger (1992) suggests a markedly different phylogenetic split in which the Cebidae include the callitrichids, *Cebus,* and *Saimiri,* whereas all the other genera are placed in the family *Atelidae*.

Molecular phylogenetic studies of New World monkeys began with the work of Cronin and Sarich in 1975 using microcomplement fixation distances. These studies were followed by the immunodiffusion work of Baba, Darga, and Goodman (1979) and the chromosomal work of Chiarelli (1980). More recently, DNA phylogenies have been developed using sequence data from nuclear genes such as the e-globin (Schneider et al. 1993; Harada et al. 1995), the IRBP (Harada et al. 1995; Schneider et al. 1996); and the G6PD (von Dornum 1997) loci; and also from the mitochodrial 16S (Horovitz and Meyer 1995), 12S (Horovitz, Zardoya, and Meyer 1998), the COII (von Dornum 1997), and the ND3/ND4 (Pastorini et al. 1998) loci.

The emerging consensus of molecular data (Figure 2) is as follows: *Lagothrix* and *Brachyteles* form a **sister-group,** and are closely related to *Ateles*. These, in turn, are a sister-group to *Alouatta*, and together they constitute the subfamily *Atelinae*. The so-called seed predator monkeys—*Chiropotes, Cacajao,* and *Pithecia*—also form a well-supported monophyletic assemblage, and together with the titi monkey (*Callicebus*) form the subfamily Pithecinae. Molecular data also suggest that the Atelinae and the Pithecinae should be regarded as sister-taxa and included in one family, the Atelidae.

DNA sequence data also support the callitrichids as a monophyletic group, and clearly place *Callimico* as a sister-taxon to the marmosets. *Callimico* resembles marmosets and tamarins in having claws on all digits except the **hallux,** but it resembles all other New World monkeys in having third molars and producing one infant at a time. Because of this, *Callimico* is usually placed as a basal member of the callitrichids; however, most molecular sequence data clearly support its placement as a sister-taxon to the marmosets *Callithrix* and *Cebuella,* to the exclusion of the tamarins. There is also rather weak support for the **monophyly** of the tamarins, *Saguinus* and *Leontopithecus*.

Finally, there appears to be an emerging consensus among molecular studies that *Cebus* and *Saimiri* are sister-taxa and that these genera, together with the callitrichids and *Aotus*, constitute a monophyletic assemblage (family Cebidae) separate from the Atelinae-Pithecinae clade. Even further, Bauer and Schreiber (1997) suggest that, based on immunogenetics studies of sixty-nine serum proteins, these two groups of New World monkeys may have invaded South America on two different occasions; therefore, the New World monkeys may not constitute a monophyletic group.

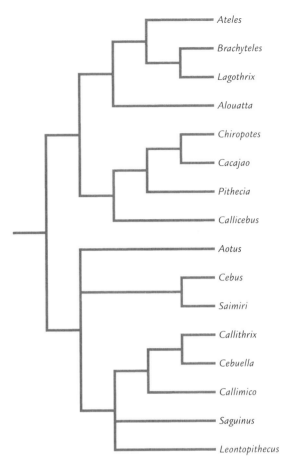

FIGURE 2   Phylogenetic hypothesis of the New World monkeys, based on our interpretation of the molecular data.

OLD WORLD MONKEYS

The living Old World monkeys (family Cercopithecidae) have long been divided into two subfamilies, the leaf-eating Colobinae and the cheek-pouched Cercopithecinae. Two recent works provide overviews of Old World monkey molecular systematics in general (Disotell 1996) and the Cercopithecinae in particular (Disotell 1998). Molecular studies of the Colobinae, in contrast, are only in their infancy.

Within the cercopithecines, there are two groups: the cercopithecins (guenons, vervets, patas and swamp monkeys, and talapoins) and the papionins (macaques, mandrills, mangabeys, and baboons). For the cercopithecins, several excellent chromosomal studies (Ledbetter 1981; Dutrillaux et al. 1982; Stanyon et al. 1988) and a comprehensive electrophoretic study of fourteen proteins in eighteen species (Ruvolo 1988) have been carried out, but little DNA-level research has been done to date. Unfortunately, the results of these earlier studies are not congruent. For instance, chromosomal data from multiple independent analyses (Ledbetter 1981; Dutrillaux et al. 1982; Stanyon et al. 1988) find a group composed of the guenon species *Cercopithecus aethiops, C. sabaeus,* and *C. lhoesti* and the patas monkey *Erythrocebus patas* that is separate from the other species of guenons in the genus *Cercopithecus.* The protein-based study conversely places *Erythrocebus* as a very basal cercopithecin not at all closely related to *C. aethiops* or *C. lhoesti.* In her study *C. aethiops* is, however, not grouped exclusively with other members of the genus *Cercopithecus* but rather in a three-way split with the talapoin (*Miopithecus*) and the other guenons.

The single published DNA-based study of cercopithecins (van der Kuyl et al. 1995) based on a portion of the mitochondrial 12S rRNA locus does not group *C. aethiops* and *Erythrocebus* (*C. sabaeus* and *C. lhoesti* were, unfortunately, not sampled). Research in progress (Disotell, Steiper, and Di Iorio, unpublished), analyzing three unlinked nuclear genes in cercopithecins, supports a close relationship between *C. aethiops* and *Erythrocebus patas,* mirroring part of the chromosomal-based picture. Much more work on the molecular systematics of the guenons needs to be carried out before a robust molecular-based phylogeny can be proposed. A consensus based on work to date (Figure 3) suggests that the genus *Cercopithecus* is paraphyletic; *C. aethiops* is perhaps best referred to the genus *Chlorocebus* (Groves 1989), which groups with *Erythrocebus patas; Miopithecus* is most likely a member of the guenon lineage (including *Erythrocebus, Chlorocebus,* and *Cercopithecus* spp.); and *Allenopithecus* (the swamp monkey) is probably best temporarily considered to be the most basal member of the cercopithecins, or perhaps even a basal

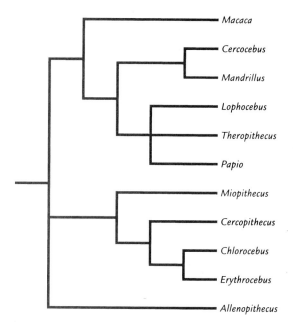

FIGURE 3   Phylogenetic hypothesis of the Cercopithecins, based on our interpretation of the molecular data.

member of the entire subfamily Cercopithecinae (see Disotell 1996).

Fortunately, the phylogeny of the papionins is much clearer. A recent study (Harris and Disotell 1998) has strongly corroborated the phylogenetic hypothesis for these primates proposed by Disotell (1994), which is based partly on mitochondrial DNA sequences (see Figure 3). The five unlinked nuclear genes studied corroborate the original assertion of Cronin and Sarich (1976) that mangabeys are polyphyletic (that is, they belong to two unrelated lineages). The mangabey species in the genus *Cercocebus* are most closely related to *Mandrillus* (drills and mandrills), and the mangabey species in the genus *Lophocebus* are in a clade with *Papio* (baboons) and *Theropithecus* (geladas). As a consequence, *Papio* and *Mandrillus* are not closely related as has been proposed by most morphologists (Strasser and Delson 1987) and even assumed by early molecular workers (Goodman and Moore 1971). Unlike the case for the African apes (including humans), no conflicting chromosomal or molecular phylogenies (out of a dozen or so constructed) have been proposed that refute the major elements of papionin relationships, including mangabey **polyphyly** and the distant relationship of mandrills and baboons. The only issue remaining to be resolved is the precise relationships among *Lophocebus, Theropithecus,* and *Papio* (Harris and Disotell 1998).

MACAQUES

The macaques (genus *Macaca*) represent a group of papionin primates that deserve special consideration. This genus has the widest distribution of any nonhuman primate, occurring in much of southern and eastern Asia and in parts of North Africa. It has undergone a very extensive adaptive radiation (with up to nineteen different species recognized) and is the most heterogeneous for habitat and ecology within the cercopithecins. The most accepted classification subdivides the macaques into four distinct species groups based largely on penis morphology; the *silenus-sylvanus* group, the *fascicularis* group, the *sinica* group, and the *arctoides* group (Fooden 1976). However, Delson (1980) suggests that *silenus-sylvanus* should be divided into two different groups (since *sylvanus* is the only species found in Africa and all other macaques are found in Asia), and *M. arctoides* (the only species in the group) should be included within the *sinica* group (based on morphological similarities and geographic distribution). Although the phylogenetic relationships among these species groups are not very clear, most morphologists agree that these groupings represent monophyletic assemblages. Nevertheless, genetic studies on the macaques tend to disagree with this contention. Most notably, allozyme and mitochondrial DNA studies fail to clearly unite the members of the *fascicularis* group, or to clarify the position of *arctoides* (see Fooden and Lanyon 1989; Morales and Melnick 1998). Molecular data so far have helped to confirm that: the Barbary ape (*M. sylvanus*), the sole living African representative of the genus, is clearly a sister-taxon separate from the rest of the Asian macaques; the *fascicularis* group apparently

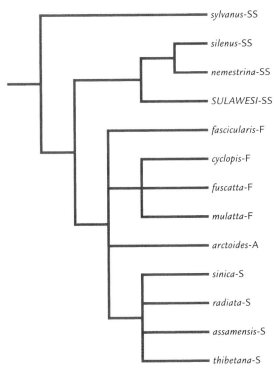

FIGURE 4   Phylogenetic hypothesis among the macaque species, based on our interpretation of the molecular data. The letters after the species name refer to the species groups according to Fooden (1976). SS—*silenus-sylvanus* group; F—*fascicularis* group; A—*arctoides* group; S—*sinica* group.

is a paraphyletic assemblage from which both the *sinica* group and *arctoides* originated, and in most cases *arctoides* is not strongly associated with the *sinica* group (Figure 4). Nonetheless, some preliminary nuclear DNA sequences produced in our lab (Tosi, Morales, and Melnick, unpublished) do suggest a sister relationship between *arctoides* and the *sinica* group.

Another interesting aspect of the macaque radiation can be seen on the island of Sulawesi, Indonesia. There are up to seven well-recognized macaque species on the island, which some authors believe are the products of different dispersal events of the closely related species *Macaca nemestrina* from Borneo. Mitochondrial DNA data confirm that at least two major dispersal events occurred into Sulawesi, one in the northern portion of the island and the other in the south (Evans, Morales, and Melnick, in press). Each one of these colonizations, in turn, led to a radiation of three or four species.

COLOBINES

The colobines are a group of cercopithecid monkeys distributed in Africa and Asia; they are characterized by their ecology and stomach morphology. They all possess a multichambered stomach with a forestomach that supports a bacterial microflora with cellulose-digesting capabilities. This enables the colobines to digest plant fibers and, thus, include large quantities of foliage in their diets (Oates and Daves 1994).

The African colobines appear to be a monophyletic assemblage based on some morphological characteristics (Oates, Davies, and Delson 1994) and are clearly divided into two genera, *Colobus* and *Procolobus*. The black-and-white *Colobus* include four or five recognized species. The genus *Procolobus* includes two major groups: red (subgenus *Piliocolobus*) and olive (subgenus *Procolobus*) colobus monkeys. Among the red colobus, up to fourteen different taxa are recognized, which some authors consider either different species or a single species with different local forms (subspecies). Clearly, molecular studies are necessary among the African colobines to establish species limits and phylogenetic relationships.

The Asian colobines are considered by most authors as a single monophyletic group separate from the African colobines, although their collective taxonomic rank remains somewhat controversial. They are variably referred to as the subtribe Semnopithecina (Szalay and Delson 1979), subtribe Presbytina (Delson 1994), or tribe Presbytini (McKeena and Bell 1997).

Almost nothing is known about the phylogenetic relationships of the Asian colobines. To begin with, there is little agreement on how many genera should be recognized. The basic assemblages include the leaf monkeys (*Presbytis*), the langurs (*Trachypithecus*), the hanuman langur (*Semnopithecus*), the douc langur (*Pygathrix*), the snub-nosed monkeys (*Rhinopithecus*), the proboscis monkey (*Nasalis*), and the pigtailed langur (*Simias*). Some authors suggest that the leaf monkeys, the langurs, and the hanuman langur should be included in one genus (*Presbytis*), the douc langur and the snub-nosed monkeys in another (*Pygathrix*), and the proboscis monkey and the pigtailed langur in another (*Nasalis*). However, the basic groups are easy to identify and will be treated here as different assemblages, irrespective of their taxonomic allocation.

Using morphological data, Delson (1994) proposes an unresolved trichotomy between *Pygathrix* (including *Rhinopithecus*), *Nasalis* (including *Simias*), and a clade containing *Semnopithecus* (including *Trachypithecus*) and *Presbytis*. Groves (1989) suggests that one of the Asian colobines, the proboscis monkey (genus *Nasalis*), is in fact not closely related to the Asian colobines but should be placed at the base of the entire colobine radiation. Chromosomal studies support this idea because *Nasalis* has a diploid chromosome number (2n) of 48, whereas all other colobines have 2n = 44 (Giusto and Margulis 1981). Nevertheless, studies of microcomplement fixation (Sarich 1970), DNA sequences of the lysozyme gene (Messier and Stewart 1997), and the mtDNA genes COII (Disotell 1996), cyt b (Collura and Stewart 1996), and ND3 and ND4 (our data, unpublished) clearly support the idea that *Nasalis* is an Asian colobine.

Besides this single consensus, the available molecular data are still very inconclusive about the relationships among Asian colobines. Wang et al. (1997), working on Chinese colobines, showed that *Pygathrix* and *Rhinopithecus* are sister-taxa but that they should be regarded as different genera because the genetic distance between these groups is much larger than the genetic differences between the species of *Rhinopithecus*. Collura and Stewart (1996) found four main branches among the Asian colobines: the *Nasalis* branch, an "Indian subcontinent" branch (including *Semnopithecus* from India and *Trachypithecus vetulus* from Sri Lanka), a langur line (with three species of *Trachypithecus*), and the snub-nosed line (with *Pygathrix* and *Rhinopithecus* as distantly related sister-taxa). Nevertheless, the relationships among these branches are not fully resolved. Zhang and Ryder (1998), based on a portion of the cytochrome b gene, found also a close association among the Indian subcontinent species, and that *Pygathrix* and *Rhinopithecus* are not sister-taxa. Our own preliminary data on the ND3 and ND4 mtDNA genes support the recognition of *Semnopithecus* and *Trachypithecus* as different genera, a sister relationship of *Trachypithecus* and *Presbytis,* and a possible sister relationship of *Nasalis* and the snub-nosed monkeys (*Pygathrix* and *Rhinopithecus*).

A summary of what is known about colobine relationships based on molecular data is presented in Figure 5. Clearly much more needs to be done to clarify the phylogenetic relationships among the colobine radiation. Although it is clear that the African and Asian colobines represent two different radiations, we need more data to resolve the deep branches and the relationships within such diverse genera as *Procolobus, Trachypithecus* and *Presbytis*. It has been proposed by Groves (1989) that within *Trachypithecus* and *Presbytis* the older species are found toward the periphery and the more derived species toward the center of the distribution of the genera, in what he refers to as a pattern of centrifugal speciation. Molecular data should be able to test this hypothesis.

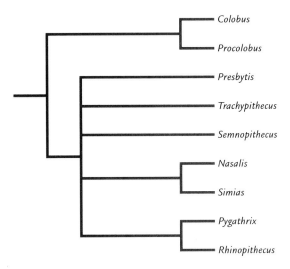

FIGURE 5   Phylogenetic hypothesis of the colobines, based on interpretation of the limited amount of molecular data available.

HOMINOIDS

Gibbons

Over the last hundred years or more, morphologists have proposed just about every possible arrangement of ape relationships, with all ape species at one time or another put forth as the closest relative of humans. However, most recognize the gibbons as the first of the living species to diverge. Cronin, Sarich, and Ryder (1984) suggest that the gibbon lineage separated from the main hominoid lineage 13 to 15 mya (based largely on immunological, DNA-DNA hybridization, and allozyme data). However, their molecular data also indicate a long period of common ancestry for the living gibbons, radiating into the modern forms no sooner than 4 to 5 mya.

The gibbons are an endemic family that occur only in the Indochinese and the Sundaic subregions (Corbet and Hill 1992). They are represented by eleven or twelve different species, which are divided into four subgenera based on distinctive chromosomal diploid number (2n). These are: *Hylobates* with 2n = 44, *Bunopithecus* with 2n = 38, *Nomascus* with 2n = 52, and *Symphalangus* with 2n = 50. Nevertheless, the relationships among these four major **karyotype** forms is somewhat controversial. Shafer, Meyers, and Saltzman (1984) suggest that based on chromosomal data *Symphalangus* and *Nomascus* split first from the gibbon radiation and that *Bunopithecus* falls within the *Hylobates* radiation. Some believe that *Symphalangus* was the first to split from the main gibbon stem (Bruce and Ayala 1979; Creel and Preuschoft 1984; Garza and Woodruff 1992), whereas others suggest that *Nomascus* was the first to split (Groves 1972; Haimoff et al. 1984). More recently, molecular studies based on the cytochrome oxidase subunit II gene (Zehr et al. 1996) suggest that *Bunopithecus* is the first subgenus to split. Clearly much more work is needed to determine how all these subgenera are related to each other.

Identification of species and subspecies based largely on coat color has proven problematic (especially with zoo animals that have been extensively artificially hybridized), and other characters such as vocalizations, which tend to be more reliable in identifying different groups in the gibbons, are not easily available to the nonspecialist. Nevertheless, species of gibbons are known to produce species specific and sex specific patterns of vocalizations (Marshall, Sugardito, and Markaya 1984; Geissmann 1995).

Species limits and phylogenetic relationships within some of the putative gibbon genera or subgenera are also controversial. In the subgenus *Hylobates,* the so-called *lar* species-group includes five different species (based on call patterns and pelage characters), nevertheless it is considered by Creel and Preuschoft (1984) to be a single species based on craniometric analysis. The subgenus *Nomascus* includes three widely accepted species, but the relationships among these, and the level of subdivision (e.g., subspecies) within them is still controversial. Clearly, a much more comprehensive molecular analysis is needed that includes not only several molecular markers but a more thorough geographic sampling of the gibbons as well.

Great Apes

A consensus eventually developed among morphologists who classified the so-called great apes—orangutans, gorillas, and chimpanzees—into a single group variously referred to as the Pongidae, Ponginae, or pongids. However, the molecular work of Goodman, Wilson, Sarich, and colleagues (Goodman 1963; Wilson and Sarich 1969; Sarich and Cronin 1976) in the 1960s and 1970s overturned this consensus (Pilbeam 1996), leading most researchers to recognize that orangutans were more distantly related to gorillas, chimpanzees, and humans than any of the latter were to each other.

Resolution of the so-called African hominoid trichotomy (three-way split) has proven rather difficult and contentious (e.g., Marks 1991; Bailey et al. 1992; Rogers 1994). Ruvolo (1997) provides a very thorough review of hominoid systematics to date. She examined fourteen independent genetic data sets and found eleven in favor of a chimp-human clade, two in support of a chimp-gorilla clade, and

one in support of a gorilla-human clade. Using Wu's (1991) multiple locus test, she concluded that the chimp-human clade could be accepted at a p = 0.002 confidence level. To our knowledge, only a few studies have been carried out since Ruvolo's review that are relevant to questions about hominoid systematics, and they are not necessarily incongruent with her results. For instance, analysis of a portion of the dystrophin muscular promoter gene yields either a trichotomy or a chimpanzee-gorilla grouping with very weak support depending on the model and method of phylogenetic analysis used (Fracasso and Patarnello 1998). However, unless over a dozen new molecular data sets supporting a chimpanzee-gorilla clade are found (with no

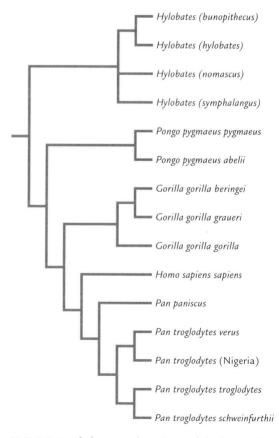

FIGURE 6 Phylogenetic hypothesis of the hominoids, based on our interpretation of the molecular data.

additional evidence for the human-chimpanzee clade), Ruvolo's conclusion that "the problem of hominoid phylogeny can be confidently considered solved" (1997: 248) may indeed be warranted.

Recently, several studies of chimpanzee subspecific genetic differentiation have been carried out. Chimpanzees (Morin et al. 1994; Wise et al. 1997), like gorillas (Ruvolo et al. 1994), show large genetic differences between eastern and central populations and those of West Africa (Figure 6). Indeed, like gorillas in which the eastern lowland and mountain gorilla subspecies cannot be differentiated (Ruvolo et al. 1994), the eastern and central species of chimpanzees, *Pan troglodytes troglodytes* and *P. t. schweinfurthii,* cannot be clearly distinguished, at least at the mtDNA level (Goldberg and Ruvolo 1997; Gonder et al. 1997). Chimpanzees from Nigeria that have only recently been sampled cluster with those from the West African subspecies *P. t. verus,* though with a very long period of separation, leading to a proposal to resurrect the subspecific nomen *vellerosus* (Gonder et al. 1997). Another species, the pygmy chimpanzee or bonobo (*P. paniscus*), has been shown to be quite distinct from the common chimpanzee based on mitochondrial DNA sequences (Morin et al. 1994; Gonder et al. 1997).

CONCLUSION

Within the next twenty years it is likely that most of the major issues of primate interrelationships will be resolved (at least at the genus and, perhaps also, at the species level). Such resolution of primate phylogeny will not portend the end of molecular anthropological studies, however. With completion of the Human Genome Project and studies linking human and nonhuman primate chromosomal regions at both the gross level (Weinberg et al. 1992) and to a finer degree (Perelygin et al. 1996), more detailed studies of the processes of evolution, speciation, and diversification will be possible. Linking specific genes to developmental, morphological, and behavior systems in primates will open up numerous new avenues of research into all aspects of primate evolution.

3

The Colobine Old World Monkeys as a Model System for the Study of Adaptive Evolution at the Molecular Level

Caro-Beth Stewart

The long-term goal of the research described in this essay is to understand the molecular basis for adaptive evolution of complex, multicellular organisms, such as the mammals. For reasons that will be explained, the colobine Old World monkeys are being used as a model system for these studies on adaptive evolution at the molecular level. Some possible genetic mechanisms used in adaptive evolution include changes in protein structure and function, changes in gene regulation and tissue expression patterns, and gene duplication involving the selected locus. Following the duplication, the duplicated genes can diverge regarding their sequences and regulation, thus allowing diversification and specialization. To identify the actual genetic mechanisms used by mammals during **evolution,** *it is necessary to use a phylogeny-based comparative approach, preferably coupled with experimental testing.*

THE COMPARATIVE METHOD

A powerful way to detect adaptive evolution is to compare organisms that have made similar adaptive shifts through apparently similar mechanisms (Wilson 1985). Such solving of the "same" problem in the "same" way—a phenomenon referred to as **convergent evolution** (Box 1)—has long been considered to be evidence of adaptive evolution (Futuyma 1986). For example, the artiodactyl ru-

minants (e.g., cows, goats, and deer) and the leaf-eating colobine monkeys (e.g., langur, proboscis, and colobus monkeys) convergently evolved complex foreguts in which bacteria ferment leafy plants and unripe fruits that mammalian enzymes are not able to digest efficiently, if at all (Bauchop and Martucci 1968; Bauchop 1971; Bauchop 1977; Bauchop 1978; Stevens 1988).

A potential pitfall of the **comparative method** is that adaptive mutations can become masked by **neutral mutations** that accumulate over time. To identify adaptive events, comparisons thus should be made between closely related organisms. The colobine monkeys "invented" foregut fermentation more recently (probably within the last 15 million years) than did the artiodactyls; thus, the primates offer an opportunity to more easily identify the initial genetic events involved in evolution of foregut fermentation.

Researchers in my laboratory are examining the molecular basis for the evolution of foregut fermentation in the colobine Old World monkeys and comparing our findings to those from the ruminant artiodactyls. Both of these mammalian groups appear to have recruited certain proteins that are normally involved in host defense, including lysozyme (Jollès 1996) and ribonuclease (Barnard 1969; Beintema 1990), to act as digestive enzymes on the foregut bacteria. The research in my laboratory focuses on the adaptive evolution of lysozyme and

Box 1 Understanding Convergence in Biology and Biochemistry

In the biological sciences the independent evolution of similar traits is formally termed **homoplasy** (Sanderson and Hufford 1996); homoplasy can occur by chance or through selection. When the same or similar traits evolve in different taxa under the same or similar selection pressures, such homoplasy is commonly known as convergence. Convergence is considered strong indication of adaptive evolution or positive selection for the new trait (Futuyma 1986). When speaking of DNA or protein sequences, the concept of convergence can be applied either to evolutionarily related (i.e., **homologous**) or evolutionarily unrelated (i.e., **analogous**) molecules. Convergence of unrelated molecules to have the same general function (such as an enzymatic mechanism) is not uncommon; however, there are no documented cases of unrelated molecules gaining statistically significant levels of sequence identity (Doolittle 1994). Convergence between homologous proteins by the same amino acid replacements has been documented (see, e.g., Stewart et al. 1987; Stewart and Wilson 1987; Yokoyama and Yokoyama 1990) but appears to be rare (Kreitman and Akashi 1995). Indeed, molecular evolution is usually divergent; that is, over evolutionary time two related sequences will become progressively more different from each other and different from their common ancestor. Some biochemists wish to reserve the term "convergent evolution" to refer to evolutionarily unrelated molecules that have solved "structural problems by generating long strings of amino acids with similar sequences" (Doolittle 1994). However, such a limited definition would undermine the traditional biological (and widely used) meaning of the term and, thus, would appear to serve no useful purpose, especially as this form of convergence has never been documented. Here the term "convergence" is used in the biological sense—which implies adaptive evolution—and refers to homologous molecules.

---

ribonuclease in the primates, with emphasis on the colobine monkeys. As a framework for these studies, we are also determining the molecular phylogeny of the colobines (Collura, Auerbach, and Stewart 1996; Collura and Stewart 1996; Stewart and Disotell 1998).

MOLECULAR PHYLOGENY OF THE COLOBINE MONKEYS

For reference, a simplified phylogeny of the anthropoid primates is shown in Figure 1. The anthropoid primates are ideal for comparative molecular studies because they are generally one of the best known groups of mammals regarding their evolutionary relationships. However, the branching order of the colobine monkeys has had relatively little study until recently.

There are approximately 31 living species of colobines currently recognized (Oates, Davies, and Delson 1994), including the colobus monkeys of Africa (about 7 species), the langur and leaf monkeys of southern Asia (about 23 species), and the proboscis monkeys of Borneo (1 species, *Nasalis larvatus*). Based on morphological studies, the branching order of even these three major lineages has remained controversial, with some authors arguing that the proboscis monkeys form a sister group to the African and Asian clades (Groves 1989) and other authors arguing that the proboscis monkeys branch with the Asian colobines (for discussion see Oates et al. 1994). Therefore, as a foundation for our studies on lysozyme and ribonuclease evolution, we have been determining the molecular phylogeny of the colobines.

Resolving the branching order of closely related species requires sequencing molecules that are evolving rapidly, such as mitochondrial DNA (**mtDNA**) and nuclear pseudogenes. The mitochondrial cytochrome b gene is evolving at an appropriate rate for resolving the branching order of many mammalian species (Kocher et al. 1989), so it was chosen for our mtDNA studies. We initially ampli-

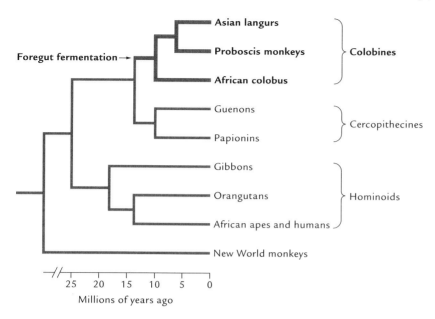

FIGURE 1   Simplified phylogenetic tree of the anthropoid primates. Along the anthropoid lineage, the New World monkeys (platyrrhines) probably diverged from the lineage leading to the Old World monkeys and apes (catarrhines) around 35–45 million years ago, and the Old World monkey lineage diverged from the lineage leading to apes and humans (hominoids) around 25 million years ago. The Old World monkey family is divided into two subfamilies, the cercopithecines and the colobines, which diverged from one another around 14–15 million years ago (Delson 1994; Stewart and Disotell 1998). The African and Asian colobines probably diverged about 10 million years ago (Stewart and Disotell 1998). The colobines are unique among the primates in having evolved a complex forestomach (indicated by the arrow) in which bacteria digest leafy plant food. The colobines, in turn, digest the foregut bacteria. A similar digestive strategy evolved independently in the ruminant artiodactyls (Bauchop 1977; Chivers and Hladik 1980; Stevens 1988). This is the comparative framework for the studies on adaptive molecular evolution described in this essay.

fied the cytochrome b gene from various species of primates by means of the **polymerase chain reaction (PCR)** and then sequenced the PCR products directly, as is commonly done in molecular phylogenetic studies. However, during these studies, we have found that the "universal" mtDNA primers (Kocher et al. 1989) amplify nuclear pseudogenes as well as, or better than, the intended mtDNA target sequence in many species of primates (Collura and Stewart 1995; Collura et al. 1996; Collura and Stewart 1996). These nuclear transfer problems have interfered with the rapid determination of the mtDNA phylogeny of the colobines by my laboratory and others (van der Kuyl et al. 1995a; van der Kuyl et al. 1995b; Zhang and Ryder 1998).

Such nuclear pseudogenes are a fairly recently recognized, yet serious, problem for phylogenetic and population genetic studies that use mtDNA (reviewed in Perna and Kocher 1996; Zhang and Hewitt 1996), as well as for biomedical studies concerning mitochondrial diseases (Wallace et al. 1997). In many cases it has proven difficult, if not impossible, to tell the pseudogenes from the real mitochondrial versions based on the DNA sequences alone. Fortunately, we have shown that identification of the expressed (thus presumably mitochondrial) version of the gene is a fairly simple matter, if one uses reverse transcriptase-coupled PCR (RT-PCR) to amplify mitochondrial mRNAs (Collura et al. 1996) rather than using routine cellular DNA-based PCR methods. With the use of this RT-PCR method when needed, we have sequenced and analyzed the entire cytochrome b gene from many species of colobines (Collura et al. 1996; Collura and Stewart 1996; Collura, Karanth, and Stewart, in preparation).

We have found that the purple-faced langur (currently named *Trachypithecus vetulus*) forms a genetic clade with the hanuman langur (currently named *Semnopithecus entellus*). Because these two species appear to have a recent common ancestor, we propose that they be classified in the same genus, probably *Semnopithecus* (as we did in Messier and Stewart 1997). In addition, we find that the dusky, silvered, and Francois's langurs form a genetic clade separate from the hanuman and purple-faced langurs, so a separate genus name, such as *Trachypithecus,* is warranted for these species. We find four or five deep lineages of Asian colobines among the species so far sampled; these include the *Semnopithecus* and *Trachypithecus* clades already mentioned, and the genera *Rhinopithecus, Pygathrix,* and *Nasalis.* The branching order of these five lineages is not resolved with statistical certainty by the cytochrome b gene (Collura and Stewart 1996; Zhang and Ryder 1998; Collura, Karanth, and Stewart, in preparation). We are now sequencing additional nuclear **genes** and longer segments of the mitochondrial genomes from selected species to attempt to determine the phylogeny of the colobines.

Importantly, based on both nuclear and mitochondrial DNA sequences (Collura et al. 1996; Messier and Stewart 1997; Zhang and Ryder 1998; Collura, Messier, and Stewart, submitted), we have found that the proboscis monkey branches with the Asian colobines (see Figure 1) rather than being a sister group to the African and Asian colobines, as has been proposed by Groves (1989). This phylogeny provides a foundation for our studies on the molecular mechanisms underlying the evolution of foregut fermentation.

CONVERGENT EVOLUTION OF FOREGUT FERMENTATION

The colobines have complex, multichambered stomachs in which bacteria ferment and detoxify plant food (Bauchop and Martucci 1968). Remarkably, this foregut-fermenting mode of digestion evolved convergently in some distant mammalian relatives of the colobines, including the ruminant artiodactyls (Stevens 1988). Comparison of convergent molecular events associated with the acquisition of foregut fermentation in these distantly related groups can reveal what is necessary for this dietary adaptation (Prager 1996). Thus, the other groups of foregut fermenters serve as natural "positive control groups" for our studies on the colobines. Conversely, the cercopithecines, which do not exhibit this characteristic, serve as a natural "negative control group" for these studies.

Most mammals with simple stomachs—including the cercopithecine monkeys—have low to moderate levels (.03–.2 mg/gm tissue) of the bacteriolytic enzyme lysozyme in the *posterior* (antral and pyloric) regions of the stomach (Dobson, Prager, and Wilson 1984; Stewart 1986). In human guts, lysozyme is normally made in glands of the pyloric antrum, in the Brunner's glands of the proximal duodenum, and in Paneth cells of the small intestine (Erlandsen, Parsons, and Taylor 1974; Klockars and Reitamo 1975). In contrast, in both the artiodactyl ruminants and the hanuman langur, lysozyme is found at high levels (about 1–2 mg/gm tissue) in the *anterior* regions of the true stomach (Pahud et al. 1983; Dobson et al. 1984; Stewart 1986; Stewart and Wilson 1987). One goal of our research is to understand the genetic basis of this change in the pattern of lysozyme **gene expression** in the primates. Some of our progress in this area is described next.

The presumed role of lysozyme in the digestive process for foregut-fermenting animals is to break open, or **lyse,** bacterial cell walls so that the cell contents are made available to other digestive enzymes (Figure 2). Given the fact that many bacterial species are resistant to the action of lysozyme, it is likely that other molecules act synergistically with lysozyme to lyse bacteria in the guts of animals. Indeed, humans are known to produce the antibacterial peptides known as "defensins" in the Paneth cells of the small intestine (Mallow et al. 1996; Ouellette and Selsted 1996); this same cell type also makes lysozyme. In preliminary studies, we have found high levels of antibacterial peptide activity in stomach and intestinal tissues of the hanuman langur (Messier and Stewart, unpublished). Whatever the mechanism, it is known that foregut bacteria are lysed in the stomach and intestine of ruminants and that the bacterial contents are digested by pancreatic enzymes. Similar to the lysozyme case, the ruminants make extremely high levels (500–1200 µg/gram tissue), and the colobines make moderately high levels (about 280 µg/gram), of secretory ribonuclease in pancreatic acinar cells (Barnard 1969; Beintema and Lenstra 1982; Beintema 1990). In contrast, primates with simple stomachs, including humans and cercopithecines, would appear to have little (1–2 µg/gram of tissue) secretory ribonuclease in the pancreas. The hypothesized role of pancreatic ribonu-clease in foregut-fermenting animals is to digest the bacterial RNAs to retrieve nitrogen and phosphorous (Barnard 1969).

Stomach lysozymes from the ruminants and the langur monkey display similar characteristics that are consistent with them functioning in stomach fluid (reviewed in Irwin 1996; Prager 1996). For example, these stomach lysozymes are more active under moderately acidic conditions than are conventional lysozymes (Dobson et al. 1984; Stewart and Wilson 1987). Rumen contents are buffered by the saliva to pH values around 5 to 7 (Kay and Davies 1994), so lysozyme secreted into the anterior region of the true stomach should have ample opportunity to begin digesting the bacterial cell walls before the pH of the stomach contents drops too low. In addition, the ruminant and langur stomach lysozymes are more resistant to degradation by pepsin, a protease found in the stomach, than are conventional lysozymes (Dobson 1981; Dobson et al. 1984; Jollès et al. 1984).

As will be explained, after the invention of foregut fermentation along the colobine lineage, the

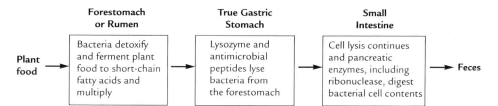

FIGURE 2   Hypothesized roles of the host defense molecules (lysozyme, antimicrobial peptides, and ribonuclease) in the digestion of bacteria in the gastrointestinal tracts of foregut-fermenting mammals. The foregut contains up to about 10^{12} bacteria per milliliter of contents. These bacteria ferment the plants that are eaten by the mammals to short-chain volatile fatty acids, which are then used as carbon sources (Rogers 1958). The ruminants and colobines make moderate to high levels of the bacteriolytic enzyme lysozyme in the anterior regions of their stomachs, whereas most other mammals make low amounts of this enzyme in the pyloric region of the stomach. Foregut bacteria are known to be dissolved when they pass into the true stomach (Kay, Hoppe, and Maloiy 1976); lysozyme and antimicrobial peptides, both of which are made at high levels in the gut, may be involved in this bacterial cell lysis. The bacterial cell contents, including proteins and nucleic acids, are then digested to retrieve nitrogen and phosphorous (Rogers 1958; Bauchop and Martucci 1968; Bauchop 1978). Much of this digestion is done by pancreatic enzymes, including ribonuclease (Barnard 1969; Beintema et al. 1973; Beintema and Lenstra 1982). *Source:* Modified from Stewart and Wilson, 1987.

ancestral colobine lysozyme evolved rapidly and converged in amino acid sequence with cow stomach lysozyme (Stewart, Schilling, and Wilson 1987; Stewart and Wilson 1987; Swanson, Irwin, and Wilson 1991; Prager 1996; Messier and Stewart 1997). Thus, it appears that colobine and ruminant stomach lysozymes adapted both at the functional and protein sequence levels, presumably for their new roles as digestive enzymes.

ADAPTIVE MOLECULAR EVOLUTION

Although the Darwinian concept of adaptation has been central to biological thought for about a century, it has generally been difficult to demonstrate at the molecular level (Kreitman 1991; Kreitman and Akashi 1995). Indeed, much evolution at the molecular level appears to fit the neutral theory of evolution (Kimura 1983), which states that most DNA and protein sequence differences observed between different species result from fixation of harmless mutations through random genetic drift. The selectionist theory, in contrast, asserts that genetic differences accumulate exclusively through the action of positive Darwinian selection; that is, for a mutation to become fixed in a species it must have a selective advantage. Both theories accept that negative selection, imposed by functional constraints on the molecule, is common. The point at issue is whether those mutational changes that spread through a species do so by Darwinian selection acting on advantageous mutations or by genetic drift acting on neutral or nearly neutral mutations (Kimura 1983). As both processes appear to occur during molecular evolution, our task is to uncover the cases of positive selection because they are key to understanding adaptive evolution.

Few studies have directly addressed the adaptive genetic mechanisms used by multicellular organisms in natural environments. Analysis of the limited data available by the mid-1970s led to formulation of the regulatory theory of adaptive evolution. This theory states that the primary mechanisms of adaptive evolution involve changes in gene regulation rather than changes in protein

structure and function (Wilson 1975; Wilson, Carlson, and White 1977). More recently, numerous literature reports regarding mechanisms of resistance to toxic agents by a wide range of species (from bacteria to mammals) have been compiled, and lessons regarding the primary adaptive mechanisms have been learned (Taylor and Feyereisen 1996). Importantly, amino acid replacements in target loci (such as cell surface receptors and enzymes that degrade the toxic agent) were the predominant form of resistance found, both in laboratory experiments and in the wild. Moreover, gene amplification (or gene duplication) was the most common mechanism of up-regulation of toxin metabolizing enzymes, although other mutations that altered gene regulation were also found (Taylor and Feyereisen 1996). These observations suggest that changes in protein sequence and function may play a more important role in adaptive evolution of complex organisms than originally theorized by the regulatory hypothesis. Several methods for detecting positive selection in protein-coding genes from divergent species have been proposed.

POSITIVE SELECTION IN PROTEIN-CODING REGIONS

There are currently two major classes of tests for positive Darwinian selection in protein-coding regions of genes from different species, *sequence convergence* (Box 1) and *neutral rate violation* (Kreitman and Akashi 1995). To demonstrate sequence convergence, the amino acid replacements in question must be inferred to have happened independently on the lineages in question, either by convergent or parallel amino acid replacements (Sneath and Sokal 1973; Stewart et al. 1987; Stewart and Wilson 1987). Ideally, these amino acid replacements should either have a known functional consequence or exceed the number of such independent events expected by chance alone. The neutral rate violation test depends on demonstrating that the rate of amino acid replacement in a given protein from different species exceeds the rate that can be explained by neutral evolutionary processes alone

(Nei 1987; Li and Graur 1991; Kreitman and Akashi 1995). Both of these types of tests are rather stringent, and thus are likely to miss many cases of adaptive sequence evolution, if they involve a limited number of amino acid replacements. The primate lysozyme case, however, meets both tests (Messier and Stewart 1997; Sharp 1997).

ADAPTIVE SEQUENCE EVOLUTION OF PRIMATE LYSOZYMES

Our earliest comparative studies were performed at the lysozyme protein sequence level (Dobson 1981; Jollès et al. 1984; Stewart 1986; Stewart et al. 1987; Stewart and Wilson 1987; Jollès et al. 1989; Jollès et al. 1990) because it was then easier to sequence the lysozyme protein than its gene. When the sequence of lysozyme purified from the stomach of the hanuman langur was compared to the other lysozyme sequences available, several unusual observations about its evolution were made (Stewart 1986; Stewart et al. 1987; Stewart and Wilson 1987). First, it was found that the langur stomach lysozyme lineage evolved more than twice as fast as the baboon and human lysozyme lineages. Even more striking, approximately half of the amino acid replacements reconstructed to have occurred along the langur lysozyme lineage after it diverged from the baboon lysozyme lineage were homoplastic (see Box 1) with ones that occurred on the lineage leading to cow stomach lysozyme. Both convergent and parallel amino acid replacements were found on the langur and cow lysozyme lineages, and were significantly more numerous between these two lineages than between other pairs of lysozymes. Furthermore, these convergent and parallel amino acid replacements caused the langur lysozyme to gain in overall amino acid sequence similarity to cow stomach lysozyme during the period of adaptation (Stewart 1986; Stewart et al. 1987; Stewart and Wilson 1987). Thus, by any reasonable biological definition of the term "convergence" (see Box 1), it is safe to say that the langur and cow stomach lysozymes *converged* in amino acid sequence, even though only a few positions in the molecules were involved (Prager 1996).

More recently, we have shown that the DNA sequences of the lysozyme genes from the colobine monkeys also meet the neutral rate violation definition of positive selection (Messier and Stewart 1997). We used ancestral sequence reconstruction to pinpoint adaptive episodes to specific lineages of the primate phylogeny. By doing this, we discovered that both the ancestral colobine lysozyme lineage and the ancestral hominoid lysozyme experienced episodes of positive Darwinian selection, followed by episodes of negative selection. The adaptive episode on the ancestral colobine lineage was predicted from the previous research showing accelerated and convergent protein sequence evolution on the langur lysozyme lineage (Stewart et al. 1987; Stewart and Wilson 1987; Swanson et al. 1991). This more detailed DNA-based study confirmed our previous conclusions regarding the "convergence" of the amino acid sequences of colobine and ruminant stomach lysozymes: about half of the amino acid replacements reconstructed on the ancestral colobine lineage happened in parallel or convergently along the lineage leading to ruminant stomach lysozymes (Messier and Stewart 1997).

The colobine lysozymes thus meet both the sequence convergence and neutral rate violation tests for positive Darwinian selection. Furthermore, there is a plausible selection pressure—new digestive function in the stomach—to explain this adaptation.

EVOLUTION OF LYSOZYME GENE EXPRESSION IN THE COLOBINES

In contrast to the ruminants, the primates appear to have only one gene for lysozyme, which is made both in the gut and in leukocytes (Stewart 1986; Swanson et al. 1991). One of the first questions we needed to answer about the regulatory evolution of the lysozyme gene was when in evolutionary time it was first turned on in the anterior stomach of the colobines. Answering this question has involved looking for lysozyme in the stomachs of primate species that were selected based on their phylogenetic relationships (see Figure 1). Specifically, we obtained and examined tissues from species representing each major lineage of anthropoid primates, including colobines representing the most distantly related lineages of colobine monkeys (African colobus and Asian langurs). Tissues from these species have been examined for protein electrophoretic type (Figure 3) and level of lysozyme in various glandular regions of the tubular stomach (Figure 4) that differ by macroscopic examination (presumably equivalent to the cardiac, fundic, and pyloric regions of monogastric stomachs) and in macrophage-containing tissues (e.g., liver, lung, spleen). All of the New World monkeys, hominoids, and cercopithecines that have been examined have a single form of lysozyme in various tissues, and in the stomach it is found only in the pyloric region (Stewart 1986). In contrast, we have found lysozyme at moderate levels (estimated at about .1–.2 mg lysozyme per gram of tissue, using purified langur lysozyme as standard) throughout the entire tubular stomachs of the dusky langur and guereza colobus monkey. This result is similar to what was found in protein extracts from stomachs of two olive colobus monkeys brought to me from Africa by John Oates in the mid-1980s (Stewart 1986). This level is similar to that found in the pyloric region of all hanuman langurs examined. In contrast, the anterior regions of the tubular stomachs of some, but not all, individual hanuman langurs make about 10 to 20 times higher levels of lysozyme. These results are summarized in phylogenetic context in Figure 4.

As illustrated in Figure 3, in some individual hanuman langurs, two different electrophoretic forms of lysozyme were found in milk and macrophage-containing tissues, M (for macrophage/milk) and S (for anterior stomach). Some individual langurs had only one form (S) in all tissues. Importantly, even in those individuals with two forms of lysozyme in most tissues, only the S form was found at high levels in the anterior stomach, whereas M and S were found in equal amounts in the pyloric region of the stomach of the same individuals.

Thus, it appears that we have found either an **allele,** or a very recent duplicate, of the lysozyme

FIGURE 3 Nondenaturing protein electrophoresis showing two alleles of lysozyme in hanuman langurs. When tissue extracts and milks (shown here) from hanuman langurs are electrophoresed at pH 4.3 in nondenaturing polyacrylamide gels, some individuals display two forms of lysozyme, M (for *milk/*macrophage) and S (for stomach). Anterior stomach extracts from all individuals examined display only the S form at high levels (Stewart 1986).

gene that has a dramatically different expression level in the anterior stomach of hanuman langurs. Indeed, we seem to have caught this species "in the act" of recruiting lysozyme to be made at high levels in the anterior stomach. The two models that are consistent with the data are illustrated in Figure 5. Under the allelic model (Figure 5a), one must propose that there are three alleles at the hanuman langur lysozyme locus, S (which has the ancestral colobine expression pattern and the same amino acid sequence as is found in many other langur species; see Messier and Stewart 1997), ↑S (which is expressed at high levels in the anterior stomach, and has the same amino acid sequence as the S allele), and M (which has the ancestral colobine expression pattern and differs from the S allele by at least one amino acid that is charged at pH 4). Under the gene duplication model (Figure 5b), one must propose that one of the duplicates (of the S electrophoretic form) is made at high levels in the anterior stomach, whereas the other gene is made in the posterior region of the stomach and in nonstomach tissues (and can be of either the M or S form).

Discovery of this regulatory mutation in the hanuman langur allows us to make better sense of the evolution of lysozyme gene expression in colobine stomachs. Figure 4 presents our best working hypothesis regarding the evolution of lysozyme gene expression in the stomachs of primates. Parsimonious reasoning in this evolutionary

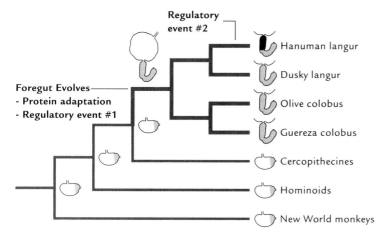

Regulatory event #2

Foregut Evolves
- Protein adaptation
- Regulatory event #1

Hanuman langur
Dusky langur
Olive colobus
Guereza colobus
Cercopithecines
Hominoids
New World monkeys

FIGURE 4   Evolution of lysozyme gene in the anterior stomachs of colobine monkeys. Shown alongside the species names of primates examined for lysozyme are simplified drawings of their stomachs. The lightly shaded portions of the stomachs indicate moderate levels of lysozyme, whereas the black portion indicates high levels of this enzyme. The levels and locations of lysozyme were examined for the extant species (on right) and inferred for the ancestral species (on left). *Source:* Stewart 1986, and recent unpublished studies.

framework leads to the inference that the ancestor of all living colobines made moderate levels of lysozyme throughout the tubular stomach; this would mean that some type of regulatory mutation (event #1) caused this gene to be expressed in a cell

(a) Regulatory and protein allelic polymorphism

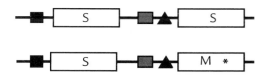

S

↑ S

M *

(b) Gene duplication and protein allelic polymorphism

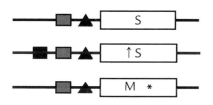

S   S

S   M *

FIGURE 5   Two models to explain hanuman langur lysozyme electrophoretic and stomach enzyme level data. Triangles indicate a hypothetical macrophage/mammary gland control region. Grey boxes indicate gene control regions that specify moderate levels found in the anterior stomach. Black boxes indicate an enhancer for high levels found in the anterior stomach.

type found in the anterior regions of the colobine stomach. Later, a second regulatory mutation (event #2) greatly increased the level of lysozyme in the anterior region of the stomach in the hanuman langur. In addition, we have evidence that this second event involves a regulatory allele of lysozyme or recent gene duplication (↑S) that has not reached fixation in this species. At present, we do not know what cell types are making lysozyme in the stomachs of colobine monkeys, although a likely candidate for high level expression in the anterior stomach is Chief cells, which are known to secrete large amounts of pepsin in many animal species.

Mapping these regulatory events and the amino acid replacements in the lysozyme protein (Messier and Stewart 1997) on the primate phylogeny allows us to infer that most of the adaptive changes in the colobine lysozyme protein sequences happened on the lineage of the primate phylogeny that represents the common ancestor of the African and Asian colobines (see Figure 4). Thus, the first regulatory event is inferred to have happened during the same period as the episode of positive selection on the lysozyme protein; we estimate this period to be about 4 million years ago, based on DNA sequences and the fossil record (Stewart and Disotell 1998). It should be noted that the colobine foregut itself most likely evolved to its complex state during this relatively short period of evolutionary time. The second regulatory mutation of lysozyme (event #2) maps to the hanuman langur lineage. Thus, the lysozyme protein adaptation occurred before the second regulatory mutation that greatly increased the level of lysozyme in the anterior stomach of the hanuman langur. Studies are currently in progress to identify the mutations responsible for these dramatic changes in lysozyme gene expression patterns.

CONCLUSIONS AND FUTURE PROSPECTS

The lysozyme gene locus in the colobine monkeys appears to have been under strong selection pressure to evolve a new function, presumably as a digestive enzyme in the true stomach. The genetic events associated with this adaptive recruitment include a dramatic change in expression pattern of the gene and positive Darwinian selection of the protein sequence. Similar genetic events have been documented for ruminant stomach lysozymes (Irwin 1996; Prager 1996), bolstering their adaptive significance in both groups. Lysozyme sequences from the colobine monkeys have served as a model system for the study of adaptive sequence evolution (Stewart et al. 1987; Stewart and Wilson 1987; Swanson et al. 1991; Messier and Stewart 1997)

and are driving the development of new theoretical methods and computer programs in the field of molecular evolution (Yang, Kumar, and Nei 1995; Zhang and Kumar 1997; Zhang, Kumar, and Nei 1997; Yang 1998). We hope that our forthcoming studies on the regulatory evolution of the primate lysozyme and ribonuclease genes may similarly serve as models in the field.

ACKNOWLEDGMENTS

The ruminant and colobine lysozyme projects were begun in the laboratory of the late Allan C. Wilson in the Department of Biochemistry at the University of California, Berkeley. This research was built on the efforts of Deborah Dobson, Tyler White, Ellen Prager, James Schilling, Janet Kornegay, Kara Swanson, and especially David Irwin, who is continuing the ruminant lysozyme studies at the University of Toronto. The recent research on colobine molecular evolution described in this essay was funded by grants from the NSF (Presidential Faculty Fellow Award, DEB-9453469) and the NIH (R01-GM47474) to the author and was performed by her students and collaborators at the State University of New York at Albany. These include Walter Messier, Randall Collura, Deidre Gilday, Robert Holt, Shou-hsien Li, Hung Lee, Marcy Auerbach, Glenn Maston, Deborah Anselma, Alia Khan, and Dianne Schwarz. I thank the many friends and collaborators who provided primate specimens for these studies, including John Oates, George Amato, Oliver Ryder, Barbara Lester, Cathi Lehn, and—most especially—Phyllis Dolhinow.

The Nonhuman Primates

The next twelve essays represent a very small portion of the living nonhuman primates (see Appendix B), but they are selected to illustrate major groupings, behavior patterns, and ecological adaptations. The essays discuss behavior and ecology at the level of the genus, species, group, and in some instances, the individual. The information on each primate is up to date and reflects recent or ongoing research.

The twelve essays are presented in four groups representing the major divisions in the order *Primates:* apes, Old World monkeys, neotropical monkeys, and prosimians. Each segment is introduced with a brief overview. Our main tool for learning about the nonhuman primates is observational study, primarily in the field but also in captive settings. These observations, along with experimental studies usually carried out in captivity, lay the groundwork for all theorizing and discussion. Our generalizations are only as good as our data make them. A brief overview of key elements in primate studies will help you to interpret and understand the essays in this section.

One such element in the study of primates is location. Although many species of primates have been observed in only one location, others have been studied for years in many different habitats. Some species live only in one kind of habitat, whereas other species are successful in a variety of locations (see Dolhinow on langurs, Berkovitch and Huffman on macaques, this volume). Keep in mind that the distribution and condition of life for many living primates has been affected tremendously by human life patterns. Because a specific primate does not live in another habitat does not mean it cannot or that in the past it has not. Where species exist today may be a far from accurate reflection of the past. However, there are habitats today, such as villages and cities, that did not exist in even the fairly recent past.

Some aspects of primate life that are seriously affected by where primates live include group size and structure, development, health, reproduction, and life expectancy. It matters greatly where primates live. The quantity, quality, and distribution of food, the amount and seriousness of harassment by humans, population density, competitors for space and food, and predation are all elements affecting primates physiologically, socially, and psychologically. To comprehend the factors affecting primate life we need to focus on the individual. Access to life's necessities and perks is regulated by interindividual relations, which are in turn affected by a host of environmental factors. Individual parameters of variability, such as sex, age, health, reproductive condition, experience, social status, and biological thresholds, along with environmental elements shape and direct the patterns that we, as observers, record. By collating all we see with the context in which it occurs, we construct pictures of primate life that then can be compared to arrive at larger scale generalizations about primate existence.

Because comparisons enable us to gain broad understandings, the majority of essays in this section are comparative in nature. Therein lies an interesting problem. Although comparative studies are essential, they are difficult because of the differences among primates and their habitats. Variability, so valuable to understand, compromises easy comparison.

Observers often ask different questions, and these questions plus the objects of study vary with academic discipline, experience, and theoretical predisposition. Ultimately, the observer who plans the research makes all decisions as to where to study and which units of behavior to record and how. Once these decisions are made, they serve to structure the data produced by the study. Methods of data collection have become very systematic, as have our methods of data analysis via computer programs and statistical packages. Despite the potential problems inherent in comparative studies, we feel that the best way to introduce the range of primate behavior and ecology is through general comparative essays. What follows is a range from very focused essays, such as those on the patas monkey and cebus object manipulation, to more general essays, such as those on the atelines and colobines.

The Apes

The apes are the nonhuman primates classified with humans in the superfamily Hominoidea. They are distinguished from the monkeys by lacking a tail, having a generally larger brain compared to body size, and having a suite of upper body characteristics that are adaptive for suspensory locomotion.

The lesser apes are the gibbons and siamangs of Southeast Asia. The nine to eleven species in the genus *Hylobates* can be grouped into four subgenera based on coloration and chromosome number. They are the only true brachiators among the primates, using their hook-like hands, long arms, and flexible shoulders to move rapidly through the forest by swinging underneath branches. Gibbons and siamangs are small-bodied apes (5–15 kg), not much bigger than many monkey species, and they show no **sexual dimorphism.** They live primarily in one-male, one-female pair-bonded social groups, in which the male and female duet in a vocal chorus to defend their territory. As offspring mature, the adult of the same sex typically drives the offspring out of the territory, although the parents may assist the youngster in carving out his or her own territory. Fruit is the primary component of the diet of the gibbons, whereas the siamang is larger in body size and consumes a significant amount of leaves.

The great apes are the orangutans, chimpanzees, and gorillas. They are larger and heavier than any of the other nonhuman primates and have relatively larger brains than other nonhuman primates. Like the lesser apes, the great apes inherited the upper body adaptations that permit **brachiation;** however, they do not use this as a primary form of locomotion. The great apes build nests in the trees to rest and sleep in, which is unique among the nonhuman primates.

Orangutans (*Pongo pygmaeus*) are found in the Southeast Asian islands of Borneo and Sumatra. They are large in size and have long red hair. The males are twice the size of the females (females average 40 kg, males average 80 kg) and have fatty cheek pads, which make their faces look dish-like. They are the most arboreal of the great apes and use their grasping hands and feet to suspend themselves in the forest canopy. The adults disperse their weight between different branches to minimize the chance of breaking a branch and falling to the ground.

The orangs have a very interesting social system. Male and female orangutans rarely encounter each other. When they do, it is usually only to mate. Adult male and female orangutans forage independently of each other, with the male having a large territory that overlaps the ranges of several females. The male defends his territory from incursion by other males. Such a lack of social interaction is fairly unique among **diurnal** primates. This odd social system is usually explained as a compromise resulting from such a large fruit-eating primate living almost completely arboreally. The minimal group size may be necessary for the large males and females to each obtain enough food.

Sexual maturity is reached between seven and ten years of age, and gestation lasts 260 days. Orangutans have been known to modify and use sticks as tools to extract honey and insects from holes in trees.

The gorilla (*Gorilla gorilla*) is the largest living primate: females weigh 70+ kg and males average 175+ kg. This primate is found in three discontinuous and extremely limited ranges in equatorial Africa; each of these gorilla populations is classified as a separate subspecies. Gorillas move about by quadrupedal "knuckle-walking," in which much of the weight is borne by the knuckles and middle digits of the fingers. The mountain gorilla's diet is composed almost entirely of leaves, whereas the diet of both eastern and western lowland gorillas includes significantly more fruit.

Mature males are recognized by the whitish hue of the coat on their backs; these males are called "silverbacks." The silverback is the dominant male in the one-male, multifemale social groups. Group sizes can range from three to twenty-one individuals.

There are two species of chimpanzee (genus *Pan*). They are partly **arboreal** and partly **terrestrial**, making nests in the trees at night and feeding in trees, but knuckle-walking terrestrially. The chimpanzee (*Pan troglodytes*) is found in the tropical rain forest and surrounding woodland across western, central, and eastern Africa and in Tanzania in a series of discontinuous populations. The bonobo (*Pan paniscus*) is limited to tropical rain forest in Zaire.

Both species of chimpanzee have highly complex fission-fusion, or community, social organizations. The community is a large, multimale, multifemale social grouping that does not forage as a unit. Instead, individual chimpanzees forage in smaller temporary groups that are subsets of the larger community. There are several types of subgroups: all-male, nursery groups (females with young offspring); groups of males with an estrous female, and so forth. Both bonobos and chimps share this social organization, yet the interactions and demography of both the community and the smaller subgroups are distinctive for each species. *Pan paniscus* forms more cohesive groups and subgroups, and bonobo females tend to be in proximity with each other more often. *Pan troglodytes* males form more stable subgroups, and the community as a whole is more likely to be dispersed even in times of food abundance.

Fruit is the major component in the chimpanzee diet, augmented by leaves and a variety of animal prey such as termites, ants, and reptiles. *Pan troglodytes* are known to hunt and eat mammalian prey, including other primates, bushbucks, and rodents. Chimpanzees use a variety of self-made tools to increase their access to food resources. They will modify sticks and grasses to gather ants and termites from insect nests, use modified leaves as sponges to soak up water, and use a "hammer and anvil" technique to crack open nuts with wood and stones.

Chimpanzees (both species) weigh 30–60 kg, with some sexual dimorphism. Female chimpanzees reach sexual maturity between nine and twelve years of age. Similar to the baboons, female chimpanzees have prominent sexual swellings around their perineum. Gestation lasts approximately eight months, and young are dependent on the mother for an extended period.

4

The Gibbons

Thad Bartlett

WHAT IS A GIBBON?

Gibbons (family Hylobatidae) are small bodied, arboreal apes that live in monogamous social groups. They are often mistakenly identified as monkeys, partly because they match so closely the popular conception of what monkeys are. In particular, gibbons are extremely vocal and highly acrobatic. The primary mode of locomotion exhibited by gibbons is brachiation, which means they swing from their arms below the branches of a tree rather than walking on all fours above them. But gibbons also jump, leap, and run bipedally over the tops of branches as they travel from one tree to another. As a result, they can move very rapidly through their range without coming to the ground. Like all apes, gibbons display several traits that distinguish them from monkeys, including very long arms, an upright body posture, and the absence of a tail.

Gibbons are much smaller than the more familiar "great apes" (i.e., gorillas, chimpanzees, and orangutans). Because of their small stature, gibbon species are often referred to collectively as the "lesser apes." In addition to overall body size, gibbons differ from the great apes in a number of ways. First, they are almost completely arboreal, spending most of their lives in the trees. Although all apes feed in trees, at least some members of all other ape species habitually come to the ground to travel. Second, gibbons have **ischial callosities,** hairless sitting pads on their buttocks, a trait they share with Old World monkeys (Napier and Napier 1985). Finally, unlike the great apes, gibbons do

not make sleeping nests. When gibbons are ready to retire for the night, they simply find a comfortable crook in a branch.

TAXONOMY AND DISTRIBUTION

Gibbons are distributed throughout Southeast Asia including the islands of Java, Sumatra, and Borneo, as well as further north into Thailand, Vietnam, Laos, China, Burma, Bangladesh, and the northeast extreme of India. Most researchers recognize nine species belonging to a single genus, *Hylobates* (Groves 1972; Marshall and Sugardjito 1986). The genus can be broken into four subgenera based on the number of chromosomes each species has (Prouty et al. 1983a, 1983b; van Tuinen and Ledbetter 1983; Table 1). The least well studied of all gibbon species is *H. concolor,* and the taxonomy of this species is particularly disputed. Eames and Robson (1993) recognize two distinct species *H. concolor* (the black-crested gibbon) and *H. leucogenys* (the white-cheeked gibbon, which incorporates two previously recognized subspecies). Geismann (1995a), however, argues that the *concolor* group may consist of as many as four separate species.

Aside from the siamang (*H. syndactylus*), all gibbon species have **allopatric** distributions with the exception of small areas of overlap between *H. lar* and *H. pileatus* in central Thailand, between *H. lar* and *H. agilis* on the Malay Peninsula, and between *H. agilis* and *H. muelleri* in central Borneo (Brockel-

44

TABLE 1 Species of the Genus *Hylobates*

Subgenus	Species	Common Name(s)
Nomascus (diploid number, 52)	*Hylobates concolor**	Black- or white-cheeked gibbon
Symphalangus (diploid number, 50)	*Hylobates syndactylus*	Siamang
Hylobates (diploid number, 44)	*Hylobates agilis*	Agile gibbon
	Hylobates klossii	Kloss's gibbon
	Hylobates lar	White-handed gibbon
	Hylobates moloch	Silvery gibbon
	Hylobates muelleri	Mueller's or Bornean gibbon
	Hylobates pileatus	Pileated or capped gibbon
Bunopithecus (diploid number, 38)	*Hylobates hoolock*	Hoolock or white-browed gibbon

*Taxonomy disputed. See text.

man and Gittins 1984). The siamang overlaps members of the subgenus *Hylobates* in parts of the Malay Peninsula and Sumatra.

Adults of most gibbon species weigh between 5 and 6 kilograms. *H. hoolock* weighs slightly more (6–8 kg), and the siamang is twice the size of the smaller species (10–12 kg). Though they may appear much larger, the average weight of the smaller gibbon species is equivalent to that of a large domestic cat. Much of the gibbons' apparent bulk comes from a thick fur coat. Unlike the great apes, gibbons exhibit **sexual monomorphism**. Males and females are the same size, both in terms of body weight and the length of their canine teeth. The size difference between the siamang and the other species likely accounts for the ecological and behavioral differences siamangs display relative to other gibbons. These include a greater proportion of leaves in their diet, shorter day ranges, smaller home ranges, less intense **territorial** behavior, and a more cohesive social structure. Dietary differences between siamang and smaller gibbons may also allow for the large areas of **sympatry** between these species (Chivers 1977; MacKinnon 1977; Raemaekers 1979).

The behavior and ecology of the lesser apes have been the subject of numerous field studies, including one of the earliest field studies of wild primates (Carpenter 1940). With the exception of the sia-

mang as noted, all members of the family share a number of basic characteristics of their behavior and ecology—they are highly territorial, live in monogamous social groups, and feed selectively on ripe fruit, especially figs. These characteristics will be considered in greater detail in the sections that follow.

FEEDING BEHAVIOR

Ripe fruit is a major component of the diet of all gibbons, making up well over 50% of feeding time in all but the siamang. The majority of the remaining feeding time is generally spent on young leaves and shoots, though *H. klossii* spends 25% of feeding time foraging for insects (Whitten 1984). Figs (*Ficus* spp.) are a major food item for most species, probably because they are high in energy, have a low level of secondary compounds, and are available throughout the year (Vellayan 1981; see also, Chivers 1977; Raemaekers 1980; Gittins 1982; Islam and Feeroz 1992). As is the case with many other primate species, gibbons appear to be especially dependent on figs when other fruit species are less abundant (Leighton and Leighton 1983).

Gibbons are highly selective with regard to food species. Comparison of trees used by *H. lar* and siamang to the frequency of those trees in sampled botanical plots shows that most of the plant species used occur at a density equal to or less than one tree per hectare (Gittins and Raemaekers 1980). MacKinnon and MacKinnon (1980b) found that, with all fig species combined, the percentage of feeding time accounted for by the five most used food species was greater in *H. lar* (46%) and siamang (51%) than for any of the three other primates—two species of leaf monkey and one species of macaque—occupying the same forest.

Another perceived aspect of gibbon feeding is their selection of small inconspicuous food sources (Gittins 1982). Quantitative estimates of crown volume for gibbon feeding trees are rarely reported, though Robbins, Chapman, and Wrangham (1991) indicate that the average size of trees used by *H. muelleri* was 40.7 cm in diameter at breast height, which is comparable to patch sizes used by small foraging groups of spider monkeys. Significantly, the fact that fig trees tend to be large, superabundant food sources stands in contrast to the suggestion that gibbons actively seek out small food patches.

RANGE USE AND TERRITORIALITY

According to Chivers (1984), the average range size for *Hylobates* is 34.2 hectares, but range sizes may reach as much as 50 hectares (e.g., *H. lar*, Malay Peninsula). Day ranges are long relative to home range size. The longest average day ranges (1300–1700 m) have been found among smaller species, particularly in the Malay Peninsula, whereas day ranges of siamang and *H. muelleri* are considerably shorter (approximately 850 m). A number of authors have observed that long relative day ranges allow gibbons to cover all portions of their range at short intervals, which may facilitate territorial maintenance (MacKinnon 1977; Mitani and Rodman 1979).

Roughly 75% of the gibbon home range is defended against incursion by **conspecifics.** Territorial activity takes the form of loud morning calls (referred to as "songs") often given from well within the territory and, less often, branch-shaking displays and active chasing, usually by adult males,

at territorial borders (Ellefson 1974; Gittins 1980, 1984). Calling in most species is characterized by predawn solos sung by adult, subadult, and juvenile males. In addition, male and female **pairmates** perform complex duets. These songs are species specific, but the duets of most species follow the same general sequence (Marshall and Marshall 1976; Haimoff 1984). From a distance these highly coordinated calls appear to come from a single animal but are in fact made up of distinct male and female parts. The female's contribution to the duet is known as a great call. It can be heard from distances of over a kilometer, and groups will frequently respond to the songs of neighbors and begin to sing themselves. The male, who is silent during the female's great call, responds to the female with a coda, which resembles the male's solo call (Raemaekers, Raemaekers, and Haimoff 1984; Raemaekers and Raemaekers 1985a, 1985b).

Singing is most frequent during the morning hours. Duetting can occur as frequently as once a day, though in some species (e.g., *H. klossii*) rates can be as low as once every four days (Whitten 1984). Duets often follow territorial disputes between neighboring groups and may function to advertise territory ownership (see Brockelman and Srikosomatara 1984). Alternatively, it has been suggested that duets act as a form of mate guarding, identifying the participants as paired and therefore unavailable to unmated animals in neighboring territories (Cowlishaw 1992).

Intergroup conflicts generally occur much less frequently than singing bouts. When they do occur, disputes may last for only a few minutes or for as long as several hours. On rare occasions disputes may occupy much of a day and involve multiple neighboring groups. Territorial disputes mostly involve males. Less frequently, females without dependent offspring will join their pairmates in border chases. Older juveniles, especially males, periodically join territorial encounters, but they rarely participate in chases. As they enter subadulthood, these males gradually take a more active role.

Much of the time during a dispute is occupied by alternating periods of quiet vigilance and solo calls sung as the males sit on exposed branches within plain view of one another (Ellefson 1968;

Gittins 1980). These standoffs are punctuated with sudden vigorous chases. Typically, one male will chase another 40 or 50 meters into his territory, after which the pursuer becomes pursuee as the retreating male changes direction and chases the intruder back in the direction from which he came. It is difficult to objectively identify a "winner" in the majority of these encounters. In fact, at the end of most territorial disputes, both social groups will move away from the border area. The majority of such encounters amount to posturing, but on rare occasions more vigorous encounters may have lethal consequences. Palombit (1993) observed a violent attack by one *H. lar* male (Group A) on another (Group G). Palombit reports that during the attack "one of these males produced a scream of unprecedented duration and amplitude" (p. 312). Following the encounter, the G male was clearly injured, and his health gradually deteriorated until he disappeared twenty-four days later. Brockelman et al. (1998) also report the disappearance of an adult male *H. lar* after being bitten during a border dispute.

It is widely held that both small group size and territoriality in gibbons is a response to their dependence on small scattered fruit trees, which are unable to support larger social groups (Gittins and Raemaekers 1980; Leighton 1987). Gittins (1982) reports that "a conspicuous aspect of [agile] gibbons' ranging behavior is that the group splits up and the individuals feed independently" (p. 67), which allows exploitation of many small feeding sites. Division of the social group during feeding has also been described for *H. lar* (Ellefson 1974; Raemaekers 1979). Siamang, *H. klossii,* and *H. hoolock* groups are more cohesive (Chivers 1974; Tenaza 1975; Raemaekers 1979; Whitten 1982a; Mukherjee 1986).

Although patterns of range use by gibbons are assumed to be related to the location of food sources, only limited quantitative data are available to substantiate this claim. Based on analysis of several years of data on range use by siamang at Kuala Lompat, Chivers (1977) found that range use was closely related to the distribution of major feeding trees. One study group spent 80% of its time in 45% of their home range, where 75% of the food

trees were located. Whitten (1982a) reports that feeding time in *H. klossii* correlated positively with the amount of potential food sources in sampled quadrants. However, according to Whitten, overall time spent in various portions of the range did not correlate with food availability, suggesting that food availability was not the only important determinant of range use for the species. The way in which gibbons distribute their time over their home range may also be related to, for example, patrolling territorial borders (MacKinnon 1977) or the distribution of sleeping trees (Tenaza 1975, 1985).

Seasonal variation in range use by gibbons is not reported to be extensive. Whitten (1982b) observed that although seasonal changes do occur "these are changes in emphasis rather than presence or absence of visits to certain areas" (p. 182). Gibbons of most species often halt activity during heavy downpours (Chivers 1974; Ellefson 1974; Raemaekers 1980; Gittins 1982; Mukherjee 1986). This may account for observed seasonal differences in day range length. Raemaekers (1980), however, found that reduced travel distances for *H. lar* and siamang corresponded to months when the abundance of preferred food was low. But during these periods they continued to feed on highly favored food items, including figs and other ripe fruit.

The majority of field studies on hylobatids have been conducted in complex equatorial rain forests; this geographical focus may have biased conclusions about the degree of seasonal differences in range use. Data available from study areas characterized by more seasonal forest structure indicate that seasonal variation in range use may be more pronounced in those areas. Mukherjee (1986), in particular, reports that groups of *H. hoolock* in Tripura, India, "may remain in one area of the home range for several days before moving depending on resources" (p. 117). In addition, preliminary studies have documented the occurrence of *H. concolor* populations in areas where it is known to snow, and where fruit is unavailable for several months each year (Haimoff et al. 1987; Lan, He, and Shu 1990). The impact these factors have on gibbon foraging behavior is not understood, but clearly this calls into question statements such as that by Gittins and Raemaekers (1980) that gibbons are limited to "relatively aseasonal forests throughout their geographical range" (p. 97).

MATING AND SOCIAL ORGANIZATION

Some of the most exciting revelations about gibbons to come to light in recent years concern their mating behavior and social organization. Most notable are the observations of extra-pair copulations. All of the well-studied species of gibbon—those that have been studied in the wild for one year or more—have been shown to form long-term monogamous bonds. As Palombit notes (1994b: 721), "fidelity to one's mate has long been considered an implicit corollary of" gibbon social organization. Recent observations of copulations involving pairmates from different social groups requires that this assumption be reevaluated.

Observations of extra-pair copulations in gibbons have come from two long-term study sites: the Ketambe Research Station in the Gunung Leuser National Park, Sumatra, Indonesia (Grether, Palombit, and Rodman 1992; Palombit 1993, 1994a, 1994b, 1995, 1996; Unger 1996) and the Mo Singto study area, Khao Yai National Park, Thailand (Raemaekers and Raemaekers 1984, 1985a, 1985b; Raemaekers et al. 1984; Whitington and Treesucon 1991; Whitington 1992; Reichard and Sommer 1994, 1997; Reichard 1995; Brockelman et al. 1998).

The first observation of extra-pair copulations in gibbons was that of Palombit (1994b). He observed five instances of extra-pair copulation involving a paired female siamang (Group C) and three males from a neighboring group (Group P). Three of the five episodes involved a single juvenile male over an eight-month period; the remaining two instances involved successive pairmates of the neighboring P female. In each case copulations occurred during border disputes when the C male was separated from his mate.

Matings between members of different social groups have also been observed among *lar* gibbons. Reichard (1995) witnessed eight extra-pair copulations involving a single paired adult female

(Group A) and the adult males of two neighboring groups. As in the above cases, these too occurred during border disputes. In one case the sexual encounter was cut short when the A female's mate detected the foreign male. Reichard reports that "[the A male] charged towards the couple and vigorously pursued the escaping [neighbor male] for more than 30 m" (p. 106). According to Reichard, extra-pair copulations accounted for 12% of all copulations observed during his study.

The implications of such findings could be quite profound, although the genetic consequences of extra-pair matings have not yet been documented. Palombit notes that extra-pair copulations observed at Ketambe did not result in the birth of an infant. But in the case of the *lar* gibbons, Reichard concludes that some of the extra-pair copulations took place over the period during which the A female is believed to have conceived. Without genetic testing, however, it is impossible to determine which male sired the offspring.

In the cases I have described so far, extra-pair copulations involved members of otherwise stable pair-bonds. In other cases potential breeding opportunities may have led to the dissolution of established pair-bonds. Palombit (1994a) reports that of eleven total pair-bonds that existed at some point during his study, three ended when one of the pairmates left to take another mate. In fact, gibbon pair-bonds may dissolve under a variety of conditions, for example, desertion (as described here), death of a mate (Palombit 1994a), or **displacement** (Treesucon and Raemaekers 1984; Bartlett and Brockelman 1996). If the preexisting pair had offspring, the addition of a new adult will result in a new, non-nuclear family group.

In fact, long-term observations at both Ketambe and Khao Yai suggest that many, if not most, gibbon social groups represent non-nuclear family groups during at least some portion of their group history. Taken together this evidence argues forcefully that gibbon social structure, cloaked for so long under the single term "monogamy," is much more complex than has previously been recognized (Palombit 1996). And there are important implications for the broader population. Local gibbon communities may have a social superstructure composed of both genetic and **affiliative** (residence-based) **relationships.** It is likely that neighboring family groups frequently consist, in part, of both closely related animals and unrelated individuals who have lived in the same social group during some portion of their lives. This is a much different characterization of gibbon social organization than that implied by the idea of largely isolated **nuclear family** groups.

The importance of recent findings about gibbon social organization are significant; however, the fact remains that the social organization exhibited by gibbons is unlike that exhibited by the overwhelming majority of primates (or even mammals). Although it is clearly an overgeneralization to suggest that hylobatids "mate for life," some pair-bonds are very persistent: one pair of *H. lar* monitored by Palombit remained intact over the six and a half years of observation; a single pair of siamang initially studied by Chivers remained together for eight years; and the longest studied pair of *H. lar* in Khao Yai National Park have remained together for over fourteen years (Brockelman et al. 1998).

THE FUTURE OF GIBBON RESEARCH

H. lar and siamang continue to be the best studied gibbon species, but long-term studies have only been conducted at a few sites. As a result, the degree of intraspecific variation has perhaps been underestimated. This is particularly significant in the case of *H. lar,* which has the broadest geographical distribution of any gibbon species. In contrast, long-term studies of Javan gibbons (*Hylobates moloch*) and members of the *concolor* group have yet to be made; however, the conservation of these critically endangered primates must be a first priority (Eames and Robson 1993; Geissmann 1995b).

Little information is available about the social behavior of wild gibbons. Most studies have concluded that gibbons engage in very little social activity (e.g., grooming and play; see Leighton 1987). But it is a mistake to assume that this characterizes all species or all populations of a given species. In Khao Yai National Park, rates of social interaction appear to be higher than those reported in other published gibbon studies. Play bouts involving infants and juveniles (and less often adults of both sexes) may last up to thirty minutes or more and, at times, occupy as much as one hour of the activity period (Brockelman et al. 1998). Furthermore, juveniles occasionally engage in play bouts with individuals from neighboring groups during neutral group encounters (Reichard and Sommer 1997; pers. observ.).

Finally, Palombit (1996) argues compellingly that blanket terms such as "monogamous" and "territorial" used to characterize the hylobatids (e.g., Leighton 1987) conceal more subtle distinctions in the social interactions of these species. According to Palombit, careful observations of the social interactions between *H. lar* and siamang pairmates revealed subtle distinctions between the pair-bonds of these closely related species. In particular, male siamang, which are known to provide more infant care, also maintain higher rates of physical proximity and contact with their mates. This research provides an important caveat for students of gibbon ecology. Similarly, in-depth observations may reveal overgeneralizations about the feeding behavior of hylobatids who, until now, have been characterized as ripe fruit specialists adapted to small feeding resources.

5

Orangutan Behavior and Ecology

Cheryl Knott

The striking orangutan, the red ape of Asia, has intrigued scientists from the days of nineteenth-century explorers like Alfred Russell Wallace. However, as recently as 1965, George Schaller wrote that "there have been no field studies of the orangutan." This situation has changed dramatically over the intervening years. Many long- and short-term studies on orangutan behavior and ecology have now been conducted in the wild. Through these investigations we have found that orangutans are extreme or unusual among primates in a number of fascinating ways. They are the most solitary, have the longest interbirth intervals, display an unusually high degree of forced copulation, and adult males may possibly come in two different morphological types. However, orangutans still remain difficult to study due to their predominantly solitary nature and the often difficult to access habitats where they are found. Much still remains unknown or unexplained. In this essay I will briefly review the literature regarding orangutan ecology and behavior, highlighting some of the newest findings from my own research in Gunung Palung National Park in Western Borneo, as well as recent studies in Suaq Balimbing Forest and Ketambe Forest in Gunung Leuser National Park, Sumatra.

Orangutans may best be understood by placing them within their ecological context, that is, by studying how the environment in which they are found has shaped their evolution and continues to influence their behavior and physiology. This approach helps us to move beyond description and begin to understand *why* certain behaviors are observed. To answer these questions in orangutans, as well as other primates, we now have some new tools: hormonal measurements, nutritional biochemistry, urinalysis, and genetic studies. These techniques provide noninvasive ways to test hypotheses about behavior and physiology that have not been possible before in the wild. Working within an ecological framework, these new techniques allow us to study the "ecophysiology" of wild primates and to investigate what determines survival and reproduction—the key elements of evolution.

TAXONOMY AND DISTRIBUTION

Orangutan literally means "person of the forest" in the Malaysian and Indonesian languages spoken in the countries where orangutans are found. Currently, orangutans are restricted to the islands of Borneo and Sumatra, although during the Pleistocene they were more widespread across Southeast Asia (MacKinnon 1971). Orangutans from the two islands are normally divided into two separate subspecies: *Pongo pygmaeus pygmaeus*, from Borneo, and *Pongo pygmaeus abelii*, from Sumatra. Bornean and Sumatran orangutans are quite behaviorally and morphologically similar, but there is a higher degree of genetic difference between them than is found within other great ape species (Caccone and Powell 1989; Ruvolo et al. 1995; Lu et al. 1996; Uchida 1996). This genetic difference has led some to suggest that the two subspecies should be separated into two species (Ryder and Chemnick 1993).

However, there is a lack of general agreement about the degree of genetic difference that justifies a species level distinction (Jolly, Oates, and Disotell 1995), and in captivity Bornean and Sumatran orangutans can easily interbreed and produce fertile offspring (Muir, Galdikas, and Beckenbach 1995).

ENVIRONMENT

Orangutans live in rain forest habitats ranging from sea-level swamp forests to mountain slopes rarely exceeding 1200 m (Djojosudharmo and van Schaik 1992). These forests are true wet, rain forests with average rainfall ranging from slightly over 2000 mm per year (Galdikas 1988) to 4500 mm per year (Lawrence and Leighton 1996), depending on the site and year sampled. One of the principal orangutan habitats is forest dominated by the large trees of the *Dipterocarpaceae* family. This type of forest is characterized by "mast fruitings," a phenomenon that occurs approximately every two to ten years (Ashton, Givinish, and Appanah 1998) in which up to 88% of rain forest tree species may fruit at the same time (Medway 1972; Appanah 1986; van Schaik 1986). This fruiting pattern is unique to the rain forests of Southeast Asia (Janzen 1974). Some orangutan habitats, such as peat swamp forests, do not exhibit mast fruiting, but fruit production is still highly variable (Galdikas 1988). Although African and South American rain forests also have fluctuations in fruit availability, Asian forests in general are characterized by more temporal and spatial variability in fruit production (Fleming, Breitwisch, and Whitesides 1987). This causes dramatic fluctuations in the type and quantity of fruit available to orangutans (Knott 1998a). This resource unpredictability may help us explain many of the unique aspects of orangutan physiology and biology.

GENERAL DESCRIPTION

Orangutans are the largest of all canopy animals with wild adult males weighing 86.3 kg on average and females 38.5 kg (Markham and Groves 1990). Such large animals move through the canopy by **quadrumanual clambering** (using all four hands and feet to grasp and pull themselves along) and occasional brachiation (particularly by smaller individuals). They also effectively use their body weight to bend and sway small trees, using the stored momentum in the tree as a spring to propel themselves across a gap until they can grasp an adjacent branch.

Compared to humans and other great apes, the orangutan's arms, hands, and feet are extremely long (Fleagle 1988). Their shallow hip joint permits them to extend their legs by more than 90 degrees (MacLatchy 1996), allowing them to hang suspended by any hand-foot combination. These features help them contort their bodies into unusual positions to reach hard to access fruit and to negotiate their way through the rain forest canopy where they spend almost their entire lives. Orangutans rarely descend to the ground, although adult males do so more often than females (Rodman and Mitani 1987). This sex difference in ground locomotion may be due to constraints posed by canopy travel on adult males (Rodman and Mitani 1987), or, alternatively, females with offspring may be more vulnerable to the occasional ground predator (Rodman and Mitani 1987; Setiawan, Knott, and Budhi 1996).

Female orangutans are less than half the size (approximately 45%) of developed adult males (Markham and Groves 1990). This is one of the highest degrees of sexual dimorphism seen in primates. The ultimate causes of this sexual dimorphism have been attributed to male-male competition (Rodman and Mitani 1987), female choice (Fox 1998), and sexual coercion (Smuts and Smuts 1993). All may have been important in the evolution of large male body size in orangutans. Female orangutans are considered to be the "ecological" sex, that is, to exhibit a body size that is primarily constrained by nutritional factors rather than competition (Demment 1983; Rodman and Mitani 1987).

Fully adult males are also striking for their secondary sexual characteristics, such as the production of the long call and their projecting cheek "pads." Experiments indicate that the loud, bellowing long calls seem to function primarily to mediate spacing between males (Mitani 1985a). The production of and response to long calls varies depending on dominance (Mitani 1985a; Utami and Setia 1995). Further studies of receptive females are needed to adequately test whether females also respond to male long calls (Mitani 1985a). The jutting cheek pads of adult males are composed of fibrous fatty tissue (Winkler 1989) and are one of the most unusual features of the orangutan's appearance. It has been speculated that they seem to help locate (Galdikas 1983) or concentrate the sound of a long call (Rodman and Mitani 1987). However, an alternative explanation may be that these cheek pads have evolved because they help increase the male's apparent size. There has been strong selection for large body size in adult male orangutans (Rodman and Mitani 1987), but males may not have been able to evolve any bigger and still maintain their primarily arboreal lifestyle. Selection may instead have operated to increase the width of the face and, thus, the apparent overall size of the animal.

Intriguingly, it has been proposed that there may be two types of fully "adult" males (Kingsley 1982, 1988; Schürmann and van Hooff 1986; te Boekhorst, Schürmann, and Sugardjito 1990; Graham and Nadler 1990; Maggioncalda 1995b) with one type, which I will call "developed" males, exhibiting the large male body size and secondary sexual characteristics I have described, and the other, "undeveloped" males, retaining a smaller, "subadult" size morphology. Some of these small males may just be in transition before full maturation. Other males seem to remain longer in an undeveloped stage. Males have been reported to still be "subadults" at an estimated age of twenty years in the wild (Schürmann and van Hooff 1986) and up to eighteen years in captivity (Kingsley 1988). Studies of orangutan skulls have shown that there are males whose cranial sutures have closed, although they remain small (Uchida 1996). Thus, it appears that the timing of development of secondary sexual characteristics may occur within a broad age range in orangutan males, anywhere between ten and twenty years of age, and that males may remain undeveloped for ten years or longer (Kingsley 1988; Schürmann and van Hooff 1986). Review of the literature indicates that all males, however, do eventually develop secondary sexual characteristics; there are no known individuals from zoos or in captivity that have remained undeveloped beyond twenty years.

Males who remain undeveloped for an extended period have significantly lower levels of testosterone (Kingsley 1982; Maggioncalda 1995a) and growth hormones (Maggioncalda 1995a) than do males who are in the process of developing. However, these undeveloped males appear to have adequate production of testosterone and are fully capable of fathering offspring (Kingsley 1982, 1988). Interestingly, testosterone levels were significantly higher in developing males than in fully developed males in captivity (Maggioncalda 1995a) as well as in the wild (Knott 1997b). Kingsley (1982) did not find this difference in captivity, but her sample was limited to two developing males.

What triggers the timing of full development in males? It has been proposed that the presence of a developed adult male may "suppress" maturation in undeveloped males (Kingsley 1982; Schürmann and van Hooff 1986; Maggioncalda 1995b). This is based on inferences from captivity in which some undeveloped males mature soon after they are separated from their developed cagemates. These correlations, however, do not rule out the possibility that such males would have matured at that time regardless of the presence of a developed male. Males are also seen to develop cheek pads while still in the presence of an already developed male (Kingsley 1982). It is also difficult to imagine how an inhibitory mechanism could operate in the wild where orangutan males are rarely within visual or olfactory contact. Maggioncalda (1995b) suggests that undeveloped males may use long calls to monitor the density of developed males as a cue for when to initiate full maturation. However, not all developed males regularly produce long calls (Utami and Setia 1995; Knott, pers. obser.). Thus, long calls are not an accurate indicator of density. Alternatively, differing ages of maturation in adult males may result from changes in energetic status brought about by fluctuating nutrition, or males may simply vary genetically in their developmental timetables.

ACTIVITY PATTERNS

The time orangutans spend in different activities varies depending on the availability of food, social conditions, and reproductive status. Averaging across three studies (MacKinnon 1974; Rodman 1979a; Mitani 1989), orangutans spend approximately 44% of their time resting, 41% feeding, 13% traveling, 2% nest building, and less than 1% engaging in other activities, such as fighting, mating, and socializing. These percentages may, however, vary tremendously. Because orangutans are primarily solitary, their activity patterns may be very individualistic. Each animal may react in a different way to the same environmental conditions. For example, during periods of low fruit availability, I have found that some individuals will travel between habitats, expending more energy than during periods of high fruit availability to search out the few species that are fruiting, whereas other individuals may severely limit their foraging time and maintain their body reserves (Knott 1998c). An individual's condition, reproductive status, and territory quality may influence these decisions.

FEEDING ECOLOGY

The orangutan diet varies dramatically depending on what foods are available. Fruit, both pulp and seeds, is the preferred food of orangutans (e.g., Sugardjito, te Boekhorst, and van Hooff 1987; Galdikas 1988; Leighton 1993). Orangutans prefer to feed in trees with large patches of fruit when it is available (Leighton 1993). Sugardjito (1986) found that adult males have longer feeding bouts than do adult females, and Rodman (1979a) noted that males tend to feed in fewer food patches per day than do females. When fruit is abundant, such as during a mast fruiting, the orangutan diet may consist of 100% fruit (Knott 1998a). However, during fruit poor times, orangutans must rely on more abundant, but relatively lower quality, food such as the inner cambium layer of bark, leaves, pithy plants, and insects. During a several month period of particularly poor fruit availability following a mast fruiting, I found that orangutans at Gunung Palung ate 37% bark, 25% leaves, 21% fruit, 10% pith, and 7% insects (Knott 1998a).

These changes in dietary composition also result in dramatic differences in nutritional intake. During a period of high fruit availability, orangutans at Gunung Palung were able to obtain an average of 8422 Kcal/day for males and 7404 Kcal/day for females, whereas during periods of low fruit availability, their caloric intake decreased dramatically to 3824 Kcal/day for males and 1793 Kcal/day for females (Knott 1998a). These differences were primarily due to the increased nutritional and caloric content of foods available during these two periods. During the mast period of high fruit availability, fruits most commonly eaten by orangutans were significantly higher in caloric content as well as in lipids and carbohydrates than were foods eaten during the low fruit period (Knott 1999).

Orangutans have been seen to eat meat only on rare occasions. In Sumatra, three adult females have been observed on seven occasions to hunt and eat slow lorises (*Nycticebus coucang*) (Utami 1997), and one female was observed to eat a gibbon (Sugardjito and Nurhada 1981). At Gunung Palung in Borneo I've witnessed a juvenile female orangutan catch and eat a rat (Knott 1998b). Thus, the ability to capture other mammalian prey may be a relatively ancient ability in hominoids as it is also observed in chimpanzees (e.g., Teleki 1973; Goodall 1986; Boesch and Boesch 1989; Stanford et al. 1994), and bonobos (Ihobe 1992a).

ENERGY BALANCE

Orangutans seem to have a pronounced ability to store excess food resources as fat (Wheatley 1982, 1987; Leighton 1993; Knott 1998a). In captivity, in fact, they have a greater tendency toward obesity than do other great apes (MacKinnon 1971). These dramatic fluctuations in caloric and nutritional intake may have serious consequences for orangutan physiology and energy balance. During periods of low fruit availability, I have found that orangutans burn up their own fat deposits to utilize as energy (Knott 1998a). When caloric intake is particularly low, they may start producing "ketone bodies," which are products of fat metabolism and can be detected in urine using single dipstick tests (Knott 1997a, 1998a). These fluctuations in fruit availability provide orangutans with the *opportunity* to store excess energy as fat, which they can then utilize during fruit poor times.

SOCIAL SYSTEM AND RANGING PATTERNS

The orangutan social system has been difficult to characterize because these animals often range over extensive areas and their residence in a given study area may vary widely across time. Mounting evidence suggests that females tend to stay in their natal area, whereas males disperse (Rodman 1973; Rijksen 1978; Galdikas 1988; Knott, pers. obser.). Horr (1975) and Rodman (1973) saw little overlap in female ranges, but longer term studies (Galdikas 1988; van Schaik and van Hooff 1996; Utami 1997; Knott 1998c) have found that female ranges can overlap considerably.

Developed adult males can have overlapping ranges, with the number of developed males using a given area at the same time ranging from one (Rodman 1973) to as many as six (Knott 1998c, 1999). Some males may stay resident in an area, whereas others appear to be transient. However, this may be a false distinction (van Schaik and van Hooff 1996) as the researcher's perception of residence patterns may depend on the length of time sampled and the inability to know where individuals are when they are not in the core study area. At Gunung Palung, these differences in male ranging patterns seem to be tied to fluctuations in fruit availability, with more males using the study area during periods of high fruit availability (Knott 1998c).

Thus, developed males appear to have large and widely overlapping ranges within which they search for receptive females. This evidence suggests that the orangutan social system can best be characterized as "roving male promiscuity" in which "males cannot defend access to female ranges and females do not congregate at particular areas" (van Schaik and van Hooff 1996). Small, undeveloped

males, however, are often seen to travel in groups and to corral females for mating. Thus, undeveloped males practice a form of roving male promiscuity wherein they sometimes form associations, whereas developed males never do. Genetic data will help us resolve some of the long-standing questions regarding relatedness between individuals within an orangutan population as well as the relative paternity success of developed versus undeveloped males.

SOCIAL BEHAVIOR

Why do orangutans differ so much from the gregarious nature of most other primates? Why don't adult males bond together to defend female home ranges from other males? The answer may lie in the comparison between the ecology of orangutans living in Asian rain forests and the ecology of the more convivial African apes. It has been suggested that orangutan fruit trees are more widely dispersed compared to African fruit trees (Fleming et al. 1987). However, no systematic studies have been done comparing ecological differences between these different rain forests as they might relate to great apes. It appears, though, that fruit trees preferred by orangutans in Asian rain forests are significantly smaller in diameter compared to those used by chimpanzees and bonobos (Knott 1999). Thus, the scarcity of large patches of fruit may limit the ability of orangutans to forage together as a group.

Examining the occasions when orangutans *are* social can help us understand why they are usually solitary. Aggregations of orangutans have been found in large fig trees (MacKinnon 1974; Rijksen 1978; Sugardjito et al. 1987), in large dipterocarp trees that only fruit during mast fruitings (Knott 1998c), and other times when closely packed trees, such as *Palaquium* are fruiting (Knott 1998c). These aggregations are primarily composed of mothers with offspring, undeveloped males, and an occasional lone developed male. During periods of increased sociability, orangutans may modify their time spent feeding (MacKinnon 1974; Rodman 1977; Galdikas 1988; Mitani 1989), traveling (Galdikas 1988; Mitani 1989; Knott 1998c), and resting (Mitani 1989). Costs of grouping may constrain group travel of orangutans except during exceptional periods when the nature and distribution of fruit resources permits it. Increased sociability (Knott 1998c) and density (te Boekhorst et al. 1990) have been strongly correlated with periods of high fruit availability. Furthermore, some orangutan populations may not be as solitary as was once thought. In Suaq Balimbing forest in Ketambe, van Schaik and Fox (pers. comm.) have found that orangutans are much more social than has previously been described at other sites.

Another cause of grouping, the risk of predation, appears to be not very important for orangutans given their large body size (Sugardjito 1983; Setiawan et al. 1996). Because individuals rarely form groups, threats by groups of orangutans directed at lone individuals have not been observed except in the case of forced matings. Lethal aggression does occur in orangutans, particularly between developed adult males, but this threat does not lead to the formation of bonds between developed males. Undeveloped males, however, may form bonds as a response to threats from developed males and as a way to gain group access to cycling females.

REPRODUCTION AND LIFE HISTORY VARIABLES

Like humans, orangutans have no estrus swellings and no visual indicators of ovulation (Schultz 1938; Graham-Jones and Hill 1962), and the orangutan menstrual cycle has a mean length of 28 days (Nadler 1988; Markham 1990). Females reach sexual maturity at approximately eleven to fifteen years in the wild (Galdikas 1981), although maturation can occur as early as seven to nine years in captivity (Asano 1967; Masters and Markham 1991). The ability of females to conceive is also reduced during adolescence (Schürmann and van Hooff 1986; Galdikas 1995). Sexual maturation in males ranges broadly. Males have been known to father offspring as early as 6.5 years in captivity (Kingsley 1982). The transition from an adolescent to an undeveloped adult male stage occurs at ap-

proximately seven to ten years of age (Graham and Nadler 1990). After that, as explained previously, full development may proceed directly or may be delayed for ten years or more (te Boekhorst et al. 1990). Average completed orangutan life span in the wild is not known, but captive individuals have lived into their late fifties (Bond, National Oranguatan Studbook Keeper, pers. comm.).

Orangutans have been reported to have an average completed interbirth interval of eight years—the longest of any primate and indeed one of the longest in any mammal (Galdikas and Wood 1990; Tilson et al. 1993). This interbirth interval ranges between 5.9 years and 10.4 years at Tanjung Puting in Central Borneo where orangutans have been studied the longest (Galdikas and Wood 1990). Infants and juveniles nurse for approximately six years (Galdikas 1980), during which time female hormonal levels appear to be suppressed (Knott 1999). The length of gestation is approximately eight months (Markham 1990).

What causes this long interbirth interval in orangutans? In my study, I have shown that hormonal levels respond to changes in energetic status brought about by fluctuations in fruit availability. During periods of high fruit availability, orangutans have significantly higher levels of urinary estrogens than during periods of low fruit availability (Knott 1997a, 1999). Thus, when times are poor, orangutans may find it more difficult to conceive, lengthening the interbirth interval. Given that a period of fruit abundance may come along only once every few years in the Southeast Asian rain forest, it may be difficult for orangutans to reproduce more quickly. This is supported by examining captive orangutans, wherein dramatically reduced energy expenditure and increased caloric intake compared to the wild are associated with much faster reproductive parameters. Captive orangutans reach sexual maturity earlier (Masters and Markham 1991), conceive sooner after giving birth (Lasley, Presley, and Czekala 1980), and have shorter interbirth intervals (Markham 1990) than wild orangutans. Low body weight in captivity has also been associated with amenorrhea, and weight gain has been shown to increase urinary hormonal levels (Masters and Markham 1991).

SOCIOSEXUAL BEHAVIOR

A surprisingly large percentage of orangutan matings have been characterized as forced copulations (MacKinnon 1974; Rijksen 1978; Galdikas 1981, 1985a; Mitani 1985b). In the wild, undeveloped males appear to engage in more forced copulations (Schürmann 1982; Rodman and Mitani 1987) and, usually, more copulations in general than do fully developed males (MacKinnon 1974; Rodman and Mitani 1987). However, both developed and undeveloped males can and do force females to copulate (Mitani 1985b). Orangutan females, due to their mostly solitary ranging patterns, may be particularly vulnerable to this type of sexual coercion compared to other primates (Smuts and Smuts 1993). Whether females *choose* to mate with developed males or whether they cooperate due to threat of injury from these large males is not well understood. Fox (1998) found that females showed active mate choice. Nadler (1977) looked at the relationship between the female hormonal cycle and mating in captive orangutans and found that when male access to the female was not limited copulations occurred on a nearly daily basis. However, during the midcycle period, female resistance to males was lower, and multiple copulations occurred more frequently. In later experiments, when females were allowed to *choose* when to enter a male's cage, mating was limited to midcycle (Nadler 1988). Current studies are examining the relationship between the menstrual cycle and reproductive activity in the wild (Fox 1998; Knott 1999). In my study, I have found that matings are much more common during periods of high fruit availability when urinary estrogen levels are higher in females (Knott 1997b).

ORANGUTAN COGNITIVE ABILITIES AND TOOL USE

Orangutans in captivity have been found to be highly intelligent, habitually making and using tools (Lethmate 1982). Orangutans raised in people's homes and later brought to rehabilitation cen-ters have been taught sign language (Shapiro and Galdikas 1995) and regularly emulate human activities (Russon and Galdikas 1995). It has thus been surprising that almost no reports have been made of habitual tool-using behavior in wild orangutans. However, new evidence of tool use in the wild is now emerging. Van Schaik and Fox (1996) report from the recently established site at Suaq Balimbing in Sumatra that orangutans regularly use tools to extract seeds from *Neesia* fruits as well as to access insects from tree holes. Stick tools of specified lengths are made for each of these tasks. This behavior is not explained by simple availability of foods, as orangutans at Gunung Palung also eat *Neesia* but do not use tools to extract them (van Schaik and Knott 1998). The greater density of orangutans at Suaq Balimbing, perhaps due to increased fruit availability, may have allowed for more social encounters than at Gunung Palung and more opportunities for transmission of cultural information.

Other tool-using behaviors are also observed in the wild. Orangutans regularly make leaf umbrellas to cover themselves during heavy downpours and use branches in agonistic displays (MacKinnon 1974; Rijksen 1978; Galdikas 1982; Knott, pers. obser.). Occasional observations have been made of orangutans using leaves for self-cleaning (MacKinnon 1974; Rijksen 1978) and as protection in food acquisition (Rijksen 1978), dead wood for opening up durian fruits (Rijksen 1978), and sticks for scratching (Galdikas 1982). At Gunung Palung we have recently witnessed orangutans using leaves as drinking tools. Although these behaviors may remain rarer in orangutans than in chimpanzees, they demonstrate that orangutans *do* have the capacity for tool use in the wild and, like chimpanzees (McGrew 1992), there may be population or "cultural" differences in tool usage.

CONSERVATION STATUS

Orangutans are internationally recognized as endangered species. Their rain forest habitat has declined by more than 80% over the past twenty years due to timber extraction and conversion of rain forest for plantations and agriculture (Tilson et al. 1993). This, augmented by hunting orangutans for meat and killing adult females to obtain infants for the illegal pet trade, has resulted in an estimated decline in the orangutan population of 30 to 50% over the past ten years. Uncontrolled forest fires have also destroyed significant portions of orangutan habitat in both Sumatra and Borneo. The continued survival of the orangutan is in significant peril. Only through concerted efforts to preserve orangutan habitat and prevent continued hunting of individuals can we hope to sustain populations of wild orangutans into the twenty-first century.

ACKNOWLEDGMENTS

Primary support for this research came from the National Geographic Society, the National Science Foundation, the Wenner-Gren Foundation, Harvard University's Frederick Sheldon Traveling Fellowship, the Leakey Foundation, the Mellon Foundation, and the Department of Anthropology at Harvard University. I thank the Directorate of Nature Conservation (PHPA) for permission to conduct research in Gunung Palung National Park and the Indonesian Institute of Sciences (LIPI), the Center for Research and Development in Biology, and PHPA for their sponsorship. Tim Laman provided support in the field, and I thank him and Richard Wrangham for useful comments on an earlier version of the manuscript. I thank Drs. Fuentes and Dolhinow for inviting me to contribute to this publication.

6

Gorilla Socioecology

Michele Goldsmith

The gorilla (*Gorilla gorilla*) is one of three great ape species, including chimpanzees (*Pan troglodytes*) and bonobos (*Pan paniscus*), living in Africa. These African great apes are our closest living relatives, having shared their most recent common ancestor with humans. Gorillas, being the largest of all primates, have attracted the attention of researchers and the general public for decades. Early field anecdotes from "great white hunters" filled our heads with the notion that gorillas were ferocious man-eaters. These descriptions found their way into our culture via King Kong and museum displays of large silverback males mounted on their hind legs with angry teeth bared. Our attitude about and fascination with gorillas changed when George Schaller and Dian Fossey provided the first ecological and behavioral information on these gentle vegetarians (Schaller 1963; Fossey 1983).

Traditionally, three subspecies are recognized (Groves 1970). The best known population is the mountain gorillas (*Gorilla gorilla beringei*) in the Virunga Volcano region along the borders of Democratic Republic of the Congo (Zaire), Rwanda, and Uganda. Approximately 320 individuals (Sholley 1991) live at altitudes up to 3650 m in this now war-torn region. Thirty-five kilometers to the south, another isolated population of about 290 mountain gorillas (McNeilage and Plumptre, pers. comm.) live in Bwindi-Impenetrable National Park, Uganda, at altitudes between 1400 and 2300 m. Although their status as mountain gorillas has been challenged based on preliminary information regarding their morphology, ecology, and behavior

(Sarmiento, Butynski, and Kalina 1996), genetic distance data suggest that the Virunga and Bwindi populations are indistinguishable from each other (Garner and Ryder 1996). The second subspecies, eastern lowland gorillas or Grauer's gorilla (*Gorilla gorilla graueri*), are the largest in size with males averaging 360 pounds. These 17,000 individuals (Hall et al. 1998) inhabit lowland and certain highland forests between 600 and 2400 m in northeastern Zaire.

Mountain and eastern lowland gorillas are separated geographically from western lowland gorillas (*Gorilla gorilla gorilla*), which are smallest in body size and are found at altitudes up to 1500 m in Equatorial Guinea, Gabon, Cameroon, Central African Republic, Congo, and Nigeria. There may be as many as 110,000 individuals throughout these regions (Oates, 1996), but the bushmeat trade in Cameroon, Central African Republic, and Congo steadily decreases this number. The western lowland gorilla comprises almost all gorillas in captivity and most of those displayed in museums. Genetic distance data of western and eastern subspecies suggest that these two populations are as distinct from each other as are bonobos and chimpanzees and that genetic differences within western lowland gorillas are great (Garner and Ryder, 1996). These findings suggest that western lowland gorillas should be considered a separate species from the two eastern populations and that western lowland gorillas may represent more than one subspecies.

As demonstrated by other essays in this volume, primates display an array of social systems. Among the apes, for example, we see as many social systems as there are genera. In Asia, gibbons and siamangs are pair-bonded, sometimes mating for life, whereas the larger orangutans are solitary, with male ranges overlapping those of a number of solitary females. In contrast, chimpanzees and bonobos are more gregarious, displaying a **fission-fusion society** in which temporary foraging parties fluctuate in size but are all part of a larger community. Gorillas are generally described as living in stable, harem social groups with a single male and multiple females, although this is not always the case. An explanation for the differences among ape social systems is ecology, especially the availability and distribution of food sources. The study of how aspects of an animal's ecology influences its behavior and social organization is called **socioecology.**

SOCIOECOLOGY

Primatologists have long sought explanations for the diversity of social systems found among and within primate species. For example, Crook and Gartlan (1966) showed how certain social systems were highly correlated with different ecologically based grades. They found that large-bodied, terrestrial primates tended to live in large, one-male groups. Furthermore, Eisenberg, Muckenhein, and Rudran (1972) demonstrated the strong influence of ecology on behavior by showing how howler monkeys living in areas with different food supplies displayed different social organizations.

To examine socioecological issues, investigators often focus on group size because this variable is intricately related to the type of social system a species displays (Terborgh and Janson 1986). As with other adaptations, group size can be viewed as the result of a balance of costs and benefits, with groups generally increasing in size for added protection from predators and decreasing in size as a result of increased competition within the group for food. The degree of competition within groups varies with diet category, and diet categories differ in their nutritional quality, temporal availability, and spatial pattern. Leaves or herbaceous vegetation, for example, are often difficult to digest and

low in energy, but they are also high in protein, available year-round, and abundantly and evenly distributed in the environment. As a result, **folivores** (leaf eaters) do not need to travel far each day, and they can live in relatively large groups without experiencing high levels of competition among members. In contrast, fruits are easily digested and high in energy, but they are low in protein, usually only seasonally available, and not evenly distributed in the environment. Thus, **frugivores** (fruit eaters) often have to travel great distances each day in search of food, and members in large groups often experience high levels of feeding competition.

For fruit-eating primates, the distance a group needs to travel each day is intrinsically related to the size of the social group (e.g., groups with high ranging costs live in small social groups; Janson and Goldsmith 1995). These groups experience high levels of within-group feeding competition, which may explain why frugivorous apes either live in small social groups (e.g., monogamous gibbons and solitary orangutans) or display grouping patterns that allow group size to fluctuate (e.g., fission-fusion system of chimpanzees and bonobos). These systems may have evolved to reduce the energetic costs that large-bodied animals face when feeding on these types of resources. Interestingly, there is no predictable relationship between ranging costs and group size for folivorous primates, suggesting that group size may be a major selective force on group size and social structure in frugivorous but not folivorous primates.

This distinction between frugivore and folivore becomes critical in light of the commonplace description of gorillas as folivorous primates. This feeding preference is unlike all other apes, which are typically classified as frugivores. This prevalent view of gorilla behavioral ecology, however, is based on information from mountain gorillas living at their highest altitudes in the Virunga Volcanoes. Although long-term studies of this population are useful, the behavioral ecology and social organization of Virunga gorillas may not be representative of all gorillas.

Studies on the more numerous lowland subspecies have been limited because of difficulties with habituation and low visibility in dense forest settings, but much has been learned about their basic ecology that suggests they are quite different from Virunga mountain gorillas. This essay reviews the influence of ecology on gorilla dietary, ranging, and grouping behavior. The approach is new in that it considers altitude as the independent variable influencing ecology and, ultimately, behavior.

GORILLA ECOLOGY

Mountain Gorillas

In the high elevations of the Virunga Volcanoes, a number of different vegetation zones exist. These include mostly herbaceous vegetation, nettles, vines, and shrubs, with very few flowering and fruiting plants (Fossey and Harcourt 1977). Accordingly, Virunga mountain gorillas are described as "relatively specialized folivores," with a high nutrient quality diet consisting of perennially available and abundant foliage such as leaves, pith, stems, and bark. Bamboo is the only food source that is seasonally available (Waterman et al. 1983; Watts 1984).

In general, mountain gorillas spend only 6% to 7% of the day moving, with day ranges varying from 0.1 to 2.5 km, with a mean of 0.48 km (Watts 1991). When food availability does not fluctuate seasonally, **ranging patterns** do not differ throughout the year (Watts 1991). When groups feed on seasonally available foods such as bamboo, however, they increase their rate of travel and cover a larger foraging area (Vedder 1984). In general, studies on mountain gorilla ranging behavior show that the quality and diversity of food sources, as well as food biomass, density, and habitat patch size influence ranging behavior. Because most of their foods are herbs, Virunga gorillas spend most of their foraging and resting time on the ground.

Mountain gorillas live in relatively stable groups of 2 to 34 members, with an average of 9.2 individuals. Although they are generally described as living in single-male, polygynous social groups, 28% of the groups have two breeding silverback males.

There is much variation, but females generally transfer from their **natal group** and engage in secondary transfer, whereas males either remain solitary or form all-male groups. As seen in other mammals that live in single-male groups, takeovers may result in infanticide, wherein the new resident male kills offspring he has not sired.

The extent to which mountain gorillas experience within-group feeding competition is low due to abundant and evenly distributed food sources. Daily path length increases with group size, but only weakly, and competition for food between group members is low. Based on these findings, Watts (1985, 1991) suggests that the cost to individual gorillas of adding another member to the social group appears to be slight. Adding new members to a group may initially increase its spread, thereby increasing travel distances. However, there are disadvantages to being too far from the group center, such as greater exposure to infanticide, that constrain group size and force the group to travel farther per day (Watts 1989).

New research on the Bwindi mountain gorillas at lower elevations (Achoka 1994; Lyons 1995; Goldsmith et al. 1998) shows that this population lives in fruit rich areas and are sympatric with chimpanzees (*Pan troglodytes shweinfurthii*), a situation quite different from that of the Virungas. As predicted from their environment, Bwindi gorillas incorporate more fruit in their diet than do Virunga gorillas. Daily distances traveled by Bwindi gorilla groups average 900 m, almost twice that of the Virunga population. Preliminary data suggest that more frugivorous groups travel farther each day than more folivorous groups. The Bwindi gorillas are also much more arboreal than the Virunga population, with all age and sex classes feeding and resting up in trees.

Little is known about the grouping behavior of Bwindi gorillas. Mean group size estimates between 7.2 and 11.7 individuals (see Butynski 1984) suggest that they are similar in size to the Virunga population. Groups within the region often have more than one male, and one group had six mature males before it disbanded. A preliminary study on their nesting behavior demonstrates that groups with more folivorous diets nest in a more cohesive fashion than those feeding on more sparsely distributed foods (Hanke and Goldsmith 1998).

Western Lowland Gorillas

Long-term ecological studies on western lowland gorillas make it clear that their feeding habits are significantly different from those of Virunga mountain gorillas. Gorillas in Lopé Reserve, Gabon, use primary-type forests often, and rely heavily on fruit, suggesting that western lowland gorillas are not accurately classified as folivores (Williamson et al. 1990). Recent studies from the Nouabalé-Ndoki National Park in northeastern Congo and the Bai Hoköu research site in the Dzanga-Ndoki National Park in southwestern Central African Republic further demonstrate the frugivorous nature of this subspecies (Nishihara 1995; Remis 1997a). Although large amounts of fruit are consumed, the importance of herbaceous and woody vegetation such as pith, stems, bark, and leaves in the gorillas' diet should not be underestimated. During certain times of the year, more than 90% of fecal samples contain fiber and leaf fragments (Tutin and Fernandez 1985), and in some cases, herbaceous pith is eaten in equal amounts throughout the year (Goldsmith 1996).

The average daily path length of western lowland gorillas has been recorded as low as 1.1 km/day in Lopé (Tutin 1996) and as great as 2.6 km/day in Bai Hoköu (Goldsmith 1998). Distances at Bai Hoköu were five times greater than those recorded for Virunga mountain gorillas. When fruits are readily available in the environment, groups travel farther than when fruits are scarce. Western lowland gorillas are highly arboreal with all age and sex classes feeding, resting, and sleeping in trees (Remis 1995).

Wrangham (1979) suggests that because of their frugivorous diet, western lowland gorillas should live in smaller groups than mountain gorillas. Using estimates from the literature, Harcourt and others (1981) conducted a comparison between group sizes of western lowland and Virunga mountain subspecies that tended to support this idea. The data for this study, however, were taken from Equatorial Guinea, where it's been argued that group

sizes may have been artificially small due to intense habitat disturbance (Tutin et al. 1992). The latest evidence from Lopé, Gabon (Tutin et al. 1992), the Ndoki Forest, Congo (Olejniczak 1996), and Bai Hoköu, Central African Republic (Goldsmith 1996), suggests a mean group size of about 9.5 individuals for western lowland gorillas, similar to that of Virunga mountain gorillas, but western lowland gorilla groups rarely exceed 16 to 18 individuals. Although most of the information on the ecology and behavior of western lowland gorillas comes from limited observations and indirect data (due to lack of habituation), there have been no documented or suspected cases of infanticide.

Data on the relationship between group size and day range in Lopé suggests that groups differing in size travel similar daily distances (Tutin et al. 1992). The groups' continued reliance on herbaceous vegetation reduces feeding competition within groups. Therefore, western lowland gorillas do not need to modify their group size and display a social system similar to that of mountain gorillas. In contrast, at Bai Hoköu gorilla groups adapt different strategies depending on the availability of fruit. When fruits are readily available, large groups travel significantly farther than small groups, suggesting high levels of within-group feeding competition. When fruits are not as available, larger groups become travel minimizers, reducing travel distance and eating foods of lesser quality, whereas small groups increase travel distance (over 4 km/day) and visit more fruit sources (Goldsmith 1996).

Although western lowland gorilla groups are frugivorous and experience within-group feeding competition, they do not live in smaller groups as predicted. How, then, do they reduce competition that results from feeding on sparsely distributed fruits? Western lowland gorillas increase their group spread and form smaller temporary foraging subgroups. More than five years of study at Bai Hoköu has documented that gorillas form temporary subgroups that feed separately and, on occasion, sleep separately from each other (Goldsmith 1996; Remis 1997b). Although temporary subgroups form throughout the year, they occur significantly more often during the rainy season months when feeding on fruits. This behavior is newly described for gorillas and is similar to what we see in other frugivorous African apes. For example, like lowland gorillas, bonobo diets are a combination of fruits and herbaceous vegetation. It is suggested that the incorporation of herbaceous foods by bonobos relaxes feeding competition and allows larger, stable, mixed-sexed groups.

For western lowland gorillas, the mechanism that probably allows for less cohesive groups is the number of silverback males in each group. The number of males in a group is related to group size, and having multiple males is a prerequisite to flexibility, making group spread and subgroup formation possible. Therefore, the number of silverbacks in a group may constrain both overall group size and the lowland gorillas' flexible grouping behavior (Goldsmith 1996).

Western lowland gorillas are sympatric with chimpanzees (Pan troglodytes troglodytes) in all regions where they have been studied. Long-term studies in Lopé, Gabon, show that most gorilla plant foods are harvested arboreally (69%), that dietary overlap between gorillas and chimpanzees is high (60–80%), and that the diet of Lopé gorillas is much closer to that of chimpanzees than it is to that of Virunga gorillas (Rogers et al. 1990; Tutin and Fernandez 1993). Gorillas were more likely to feed on terrestrial herbaceous vegetation than chimpanzees and to concentrate on this resource when fruit was scarce. Chimpanzee and gorilla diets diverge most at times when fruit is not abundant, although it is mainly gorillas that shift foraging strategies. Chimpanzees generally continue to forage for sparsely available ripe fruits. Direct interspecific competition between the two species has not been observed. Similar findings on sympatric populations come from Bai Hokōu, Central African Republic, and Ndoki Forest, Congo (Remis 1994; Goldsmith 1996; Kuroda et al. 1996).

Eastern Lowland Gorillas

Eastern lowland gorillas have been studied in and around the Kahuzi-Biega region in Zaire. Research shows that groups in the more mountainous regions, such as the Fizi, Utu, Mt. Tschiaberimu, and Kahuzi, are more like mountain gorillas in their diet and behavior (Casimir and Butenandt 1973), whereas groups at lower altitudes, such as the Itebero and Masisi regions, are more similar to western lowland gorillas (Yamagiwa et al. 1992). Eastern lowland gorillas in the highlands feed primarily on stems, pith, and shoots (and cultivated banana plants) in secondary forest and in stands of bamboo. In some regions, such as Utu, they eat figs and fruits when they are available. In these areas, gorillas traveled about 0.6 to 1.1 km/day or perhaps longer, about 0.1 to 3.4 km/day (Goodall, 1977). Average group size was relatively large in the Kahuzi region, averaging 10.8 (Yamagiwa et al. 1993) and 15.6 individuals (Murnyak 1981).

At lower elevations, such as Masisi and Itebero, there is a high density of tropical forests, and this may be the only true lowland area where these gorillas have been studied. The proportion of fruit in the gorilla diet here is significantly greater than that of eastern lowland gorillas at higher altitudes and that of the Virunga mountain gorillas (Yamagiwa et al. 1992). Daily travel distances measured for a group in the Itebero region suggest a mean daily path length (2.2 km/day) greater than those recorded for any eastern lowland or mountain gorilla group (but sample size is small). Little information is available on the social organization of these groups, but researchers at lower elevation sites suggest that ranging distances are influenced by the availability of fruit and that groups are generally less cohesive than those of either mountain gorillas or eastern lowland gorillas living at higher altitudes (Yamagiwa, Maruhashi, and Yumoto 1996).

Eastern lowland gorillas are also sympatric with chimpanzees (Pan troglodytes shweinfurthii). At lower elevations dietary overlap between gorillas and chimpanzees is high, and gorillas and chimpanzees occur at equal population densities. In contrast, at higher elevations where fewer fruits are available, chimpanzees consumed fibrous plant parts and lived at much lower densities than gorillas (Yamagiwa et al. 1996). The gorillas ate a more diverse diet and traveled shorter daily distances (mean = 0.8 km/day) than chimpanzees (mean = 1.4 km/day). Both species ate fruit over the entire annual cycle, although not necessarily the same plant species at the same time.

SUMMARY

Gorilla populations differ from one another in aspects of their ecology and behavior. At the lowest altitudes forests are fruit-rich, and chimpanzee densities are high. In these regions gorillas are highly frugivorous, more arboreal, travel far daily distances, and, in some cases, may live in less cohesive social groups. This is similar to what we see in other African apes, especially bonobos. At the other end of the scale—at high altitudes where there are few fruit sources and no chimpanzees—gorillas are folivorous, terrestrial, travel short daily distances, and live in cohesive, stable groups. The mountain gorillas in the Virungas appear to be the only strictly folivorous ape population. Some gorilla populations, such as the Kahuzi-Biega eastern lowland gorillas and the Bwindi mountain gorillas, live in forests where fruit and chimpanzee densities vary with altitude. These situations allow for direct tests of how these two factors affect gorilla ranging and grouping patterns.

It is important that we reevaluate the usefulness of the Virunga population as a model of all gorilla behavior because studies show that their behavioral ecology should not be generalized to other populations. This may have important implications for conservation. Methods to manage the Virunga population may not be viable for other populations. In addition, all gorillas in captivity are lowland gorillas. Therefore, it is essential that we apply what we know about the behavioral ecology of wild western lowland gorillas to captive situations to encourage species specific behaviors.

7

The *Pan* Species

Barbara Fruth, Gottfried Hohmann, and William C. McGrew

Chimpanzees (*Pan troglodytes*) have been known to science for 350 years, but only at the beginning of this century did more detailed scientific investigation lift the fog around this mysterious species. After Nissen's early study in French Guinea in the 1930s (Nissen 1931), many decades passed before chimpanzees were observed regularly in their natural habitats. Field research started in the 1960s with Jane Goodall and Junichero Itani in Tanzania, Vernon Reynolds in Uganda, and Adriaan Kortlandt in Belgian Congo. By now, studies at forty-one sites in seventeen countries (Goodall 1996) have compiled about two hundred years of combined field research, but only a few well-known long-term studies provide most of what we know. Today, chimpanzee populations spread along a west-east equatorial belt from the dry savannas of far west Africa, over the evergreen rain forests of central Africa, to the montane forests and dry woodland-savanna mosaics of the east African rift valley (Goodall 1986; Figure 1, A–C). Chimpanzees show impressive flexibility in their adaptation to so many different environments. Recent genetic findings suggest a split into different species (Morin et al. 1994a), as well as a "new" subspecies (Gonder et al. 1997). This variation makes clear why caution is needed in drawing a picture of "The Chimpanzee."

But chimpanzees also have a closely related cousin, known only since 1929. In the Tervuren Museum in Belgium (Musée Royal de l'Afrique Centrale), Harold Coolidge (1933) serendipitously discovered that skulls previously thought to be young chimpanzees were instead adult bonobos, *Pan paniscus*. Bonobos live mostly in the cuvette centrale of the Democratic Republic of Congo (formerly Zaire) in homogenous habitat south of the Congo River (see Figure 1, D). This massive river, reaching a width of 20 km in the north and west and lined by constantly inundated swamp in the east, is the geographical barrier that separates bonobos from chimpanzees. Field research started only in 1974, when Takayoshi Kano and Alison and Noël Badrian independently founded two study sites, Wamba and Lomako. Another four study sites were later established in the Congo basin, but only Lomako and Wamba persist today. Most bonobos live in evergreen lowland rain forest, although recently their presence was confirmed in the mosaic habitat of Lukuru at the southern fringe of distribution. There, savanna regularly interleafs with rain forest fragments, and bonobos make use of both habitats (Thompson, pers. comm.). Collectively, fifty years of accumulated research on this great ape species make clear why *Pan paniscus* is considered more mysterious today than *Pan troglodytes*. The bonobo is often labeled the "unknown," "last," or "forgotten" ape.

CHARACTERISTICS IN COMMON

Both *Pan* species show many common characteristics. Their anatomy is fundamentally similar; that is, there is sexual dimorphism, with males being heavier and having larger canine teeth than females (Jungers and Susman 1984; Parish, under review).

Both species live in groups or communities of 20 to 120 members (Nishida 1968; Kuroda 1979;

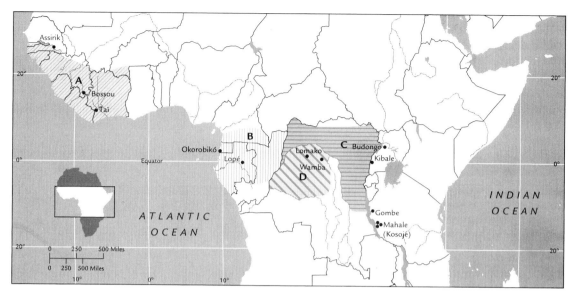

FIGURE 1 Distribution of chimpanzees and bonobos across Africa. Chimpanzees: A = *Pan troglodytes verus*, B = *Pan troglodytes troglodytes*, C = *Pan troglodytes schweinfurthii*. Bonobos: D = *Pan paniscus*. Black dots indicate long-term study sites (> 1 year of research).

Goodall 1986). Both are diurnal, wide-ranging, and regularly form subgroups of differing number and composition, so-called parties, that range independently in a common home range. This fluid pattern is called fission-fusion social organization. Home range size varies and depends strongly on both habitat quality and community size, ranging from 6 to more than 300 km² (Kano 1971; Baldwin, McGrew, and Tutin 1982; Sugiyama 1984). Communities consist of both sexes, but females usually outnumber males. (Male-to-female ratio may be as much as 1:4.) Males remain in their natal community, but females generally migrate to neighboring communities, usually at sexual maturity. As a result, males know one another from childhood until death and many are closely related, whereas females are less familiar and more distantly related (Morin et al. 1994b).

Depending on habitat, food patch size, and food distribution, both species daily travel distances ranging from several 100 m up to 10 km, with an average of about 3 km/day, to meet their nutritional needs (Wrangham 1977; Fruth 1995). They are omnivorous, eating ripe fruit, leaves, piths, flowers,

and a small but important proportion of animal prey, such as insects or mammals. Between 60 and 328 species of plant food have been recorded for different chimpanzee populations, which on average equals that known for bonobos. For example, 147 species were recorded for the Wamba population (Nishida and Uehara 1983; McGrew, Baldwin, and Tutin 1988; Kano 1992; Tutin and Fernandez 1993). Food is eaten both in the trees and on the ground. The degree of arboreality, however, reflects habitat structure more than species' preferences (Figure 2), with both species spending at least half of their daily activity on the ground (Doran 1996; Fruth 1996).

At night, both *Pan* species are arboreal. Each weaned individual makes a platform of leafy branches and twigs on which to sleep. Construction takes only a few minutes and results in a springy interwoven bed or nest. Usually, new nests are built each night, and both nest material and nest sites are chosen selectively (Fruth and Hohmann 1994).

Pan fears predators such as leopards and lions, and the apes may be threatened by diseases such as

FIGURE 2   Arboreal nursery group of mothers and offspring. (Photo by C. E. G. Tutin)

pneumonia or ebola (Goodall 1986; Boesch 1991; Morell 1995), but the main threat is *Homo sapiens*. Despite protection through international legislation, these species are still hunted for meat, sold in pet markets, and used in biomedical research. The biggest danger, however, is the systematic destruction of their habitats through deforestation and increasing human population density.

DIFFERENCES ACROSS *PAN* SPECIES

Party Composition

The most striking differences between the two *Pan* species occur in social organization and structure. An eye-catching difference concerns party composition (Figure 3). Chimpanzee females spend most of their time only with dependent offspring. They

join males seasonally or when in estrus, whereas males range in parties year-round. Community boundaries are frequented by males, and encounters with neighboring communities are either avoided or hostile (Goodall 1986). Bonobo females, in contrast, are typically found in mixed-sex parties, independent of season and reproductive status. All-female parties are frequent, whereas all-male parties are almost absent (Kuroda 1979). Community boundaries exist, but attractive resources in zones of overlap lead to occasional encounters between neighboring communities. These encounters begin with agonistic displays but end up with members of both communities eating together and interacting peacefully (Kano 1992).

Cooperation

This apparent difference of social organization is even more striking at the level of individual social ties. According to evolutionary theory, the high degree of relatedness of males in a community should result in cooperation and male bonding (Wrangham 1986; cf. van Schaik 1996). Equally, female dispersal should lead to a low degree of relatedness among females, with correspondingly low levels of mutual affiliation and cooperation. Patterns of residence are similar in both species, but social relations are not. Unlike chimpanzees, bonobo females cooperate and bond, whereas males do not (Parish and de Waal, under review).

Sharing Food

Both *Pan* species regularly share food, most commonly from mother to offspring. Plant food is most often shared and may promote independent feeding and foraging by infants being weaned earlier (McGrew 1975). Although such sharing can best be explained as parental investment (Trivers 1972), sharing among unrelated individuals needs different explanations. Chimpanzees strikingly differ from bonobos in terms of what food is shared and who shares with whom. Sharing by mature *Pan troglodytes* mostly involves meat (Teleki 1973; McGrew 1979; Nishida et al. 1992). In *Pan paniscus*, large monopolizable fruits such as *Treculia africana*

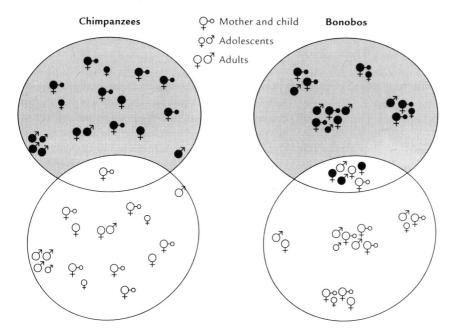

FIGURE 3   Schematic depiction of chimpanzee (left) and bonobo (right) social organization. Each circle indicates the home range of one community, with the intermediate section showing zones of overlap. Chimpanzee parties are composed of females ranging with dependent offspring, males who form all-male bands to engage in border patrols, or potentially reproductive male-female units. Bonobo parties are mostly mixed sex, containing members of all age and sex classes.

or *Anonidium mannii* are most commonly shared (Kuroda 1984; Hohmann and Fruth 1996).

In chimpanzees, males usually control the carcass and distribute meat to allied males and to certain adult females (Figure 4), especially those in estrus (Boesch and Boesch 1989; McGrew 1996). This likely reflects that chimpanzees mostly hunt together, and future cooperation must be encouraged by dividing the precious resource among fellow hunters and allied individuals.

In bonobos, females take the role of owner and food distributor, sharing mostly with other females and only rarely with males. Males almost never share with one another (Hohmann and Fruth 1996). If female community members are unrelated, such sharing cannot bring benefits from inclusive fitness. However, benefits may result from reciprocity and the status of controlling access and distribution of key resources.

Dominance

In chimpanzees all males dominate all females, but some bonobo females are able to dominate some males (Nishida 1979; Parish 1994; Furuichi 1997). This is true although both *Pan* species exhibit a pronounced sexual dimorphism, with females weighing less than 85% of males (Parish, under review). Whether or not female dominance in bonobos is based on female-female cooperation or persists in a one-to-one situation against a male remains to be seen. Our data from Lomako suggest that sexes are codominant.

Material Culture

Chimpanzees are famous for their cognitive abilities (for a review see Byrne 1995). In the wild, their use of tools gives insight into this ability (Figure 5). They prepare probes to fish for termites or sticks to dip for ants (McGrew 1979), create leaf sponges to drink water (van Lawick-Goodall 1968), or use hammer and anvil to crack open nuts (Boesch and Boesch 1984). The variety of tools chosen or fabricated across populations gives proof of the plastic-

FIGURE 4   Young adult female watches adult male. (Photo by C. E. G. Tutin)

FIGURE 5   Two adult females and one adult male (center) fish for termites. Female on left opens fishing hole with left index finger; male in center withdraws grass tool held in precision grip in left hand; female on right "mops" termites from back of left hand. (Photo by L. F. Marchant)

ity of this behavior and the breadth of chimpanzee material culture (McGrew 1992).

Bonobos, in contrast, show little evidence of tool use in the wild, although in captivity they are equal to chimpanzees in every way (Jordan 1982). At Lomako individuals occasionally cover their bodies with leafy twigs for insulation during very cold nights. At Wamba, bonobos use twigs to shelter their sleeping places (Kano 1982). Bonobos use saplings to perform a ritualized display. This branch dragging sparks attention from party members, and when these branches are left behind, they may serve late arriving individuals as indicators of direction (Ingmanson 1996). Whether or not this is intentional remains to be shown. In short, bonobos in the wild show little material culture in comparison with that of chimpanzees.

Mating

Chimpanzees mate only during a period of estrus signaled by the pink swelling of the female's genital area. This period of tumescence covers about a third of the female's menstrual cycle (Wallis 1992; Takahata, Ihobe, and Idani 1996). There are seasonal changes in cyclicity, and females who travel together may synchronize the time and length of tumescence. Males respond (Figure 6) according to the females' attractivity (Wallis 1992). Once in estrus, females may travel with several males and mate promiscuously or be monopolized by the alpha male or be cloistered and mated by one male in consort. Which of the three mating strategies is practiced depends on the ranks and the ages of the mating partners (Hasegawa and Hiraiwa-Hasegawa 1983). Although opportunistic matings are more frequent, the rate of conception is higher during consortship (Tutin 1979).

In bonobos sexuality is an everyday event, and sexual interactions occur between all age and sex classes (Figures 7 and 8). Females also exhibit conspicuous swellings. Their period of tumescence may be longer than that of chimpanzees, but this varies both across and within populations (Stanford 1998). Long-lasting swellings may give the impression of continuous receptivity or, alternatively, of attractivity. Both homo- and heterosexual interactions take place throughout the menstrual cycle,

FIGURE 6 Adolescent male about to intromit with young adult female who presents for copulation. (Photo by C. E. G. Tutin)

FIGURE 7 Adolescent male copulates with adult female. (Photo by C. E. G. Tutin)

although mating frequency and female proceptivity are positively correlated with the degree of tumescence (Furuichi 1987).

What are the consequences of these different estrus patterns for the social organization of the two *Pan* species?

Group Relations and Mate Guarding

Chimpanzee social organization has been thought to be a prime example of resource defense polygyny, a male strategy to promote reproductive success. In chimpanzees, females range primarily on their own within the overall community home range, guarded indirectly by the community males through regular boundary patrols. During encounters between communities, males may fiercely defend their territory and thus, potentially, their mates (Manson and Wrangham 1991). Chimpanzee females who escape control by community males during estrus—for example, by ranging on the periphery to neighboring communities where they may be impregnated by neighboring males—may risk losing their offspring to infanticidal males of their own community (Goodall 1983; Nishida and Kawanaka 1985). Here, male investment in a particular female is short and coincides with female receptivity.

Bonobo males seem to have a different strategy. When communities meet, males rarely prevent females from mating with neighbors, and no infanti-

cide has been seen. Males and females roam together in mixed-sex parties year-round. Data from Lomako suggest that a male's investment in a particular female is long term and exceeds her period of tumescence.

For chimpanzees the strategy pays. At Gombe close genetic relations among males is confirmed (Morin et al. 1994b), but data from the Taï Forest in Ivory Coast provided a shocking contrast. More than half of the infants born into the community were not sired by resident males (Gagneux, Woodruff, and Boesch 1997).

Although we have no evidence for polygynous resource defense in bonobos, Lomako males' strategy is fairly successful. More than 80% of the Eyengo community infants are fathered by resident males.

Social Sex

Besides the differences in heterosexual behavior, there is a striking contrast in homosexual behavior of the *Pan* species. Genito-genital rubbing, absent in chimpanzee females, is the most often cited pattern of homosexual behavior in female bonobos. It has been termed homoerotic (Wrangham 1993)

FIGURE 8 Infant male copulates bipedally with adult female (lying on her side) as she is groomed by the infant's mother. (Photo by C. E. G. Tutin)

and, together with heterosexual activities, is said to reduce tension, dampen arousal, or allow reconciliation (Kano 1980; Kuroda 1980; de Waal and Lanting 1997).

SOCIALITY IN *PAN* SPECIES

What causes such dramatic differences in the sociality of *Pan* species? Why do male bonobos not bond? What promotes alliances among unrelated females in bonobos? What allowed bonobo females to evolve dominance based on female alliances?

Attempts to explain these differences across *Pan* species in sociality focus on either ecological or social factors as prime movers. Two contradicting hypotheses illustrate the different approaches.

Ecological Scenario

Richard Wrangham (1980) proposed that availability and distribution of food is the driving force in the evolution of social organization. His observations from the wild show that chimpanzee habitats provide small food patches and that competition among group members is keen. Because of this, chimpanzee females forage alone in their small subranges and only occasionally join larger parties during estrus or when food is more abundant.

According to Wrangham, bonobo habitat provides larger food patches, seasonality lacks sharp contrasts, and fallback foods such as terrestrial herbaceous vegetation (THV) are continuously available. Thus, females do not compete over food and so can afford to socialize. Wrangham therefore interprets female-female proximity as mutual tolerance instead of true affiliation. Grooming and sociosexual contacts may help to reduce tension among these unrelated group members. Grouped bonobo females draw the attention of males, which helps to reduce potential harassment. The more females gather, the more males they attract.

Social Scenario

Amy Parish (1994) contrasts this hypothesis by conclusions drawn from data on both *Pan* species collected in captivity. According to Parish, bonobo females develop affiliative and persisting social bonds, as expressed by affiliative behavior such as grooming and social sex. The friendly relationships among bonobo females allow them to monopolize key resources against males, whereas the lack of such relationships among chimpanzee females does not. Parish suggested that in contrast to chimpanzees, bonobo females dominate males.

Support for Both Hypotheses

Data from bonobos in the wild tie increased sociality to food abundance and to a low level of food competition enabled by THV being available year-round (White and Wrangham 1988; Malenky and Wrangham 1994). Independently, fusion of parties overnight, when food competition is absent, is a regular pattern and may demonstrate a tendency toward increased gregariousness (Fruth and Hohmann 1994).

Problems with Both Hypotheses

Recent data from Lomako show that bonobo habitat is no paradise. There is marked seasonality in food abundance, and competition over food occurs regularly. During lean seasons, community members split into smaller parties, but regardless of party size, composition and socionomic sex ratio persist. Data from Lomako indicate that sociosex among females is negatively correlated with grooming, so that such sex may be an acknowledgment of status rather than an expression of mutual attraction. Female dominance over males seems to depend on cooperation rather than on female superiority, as it does not occur in one-to-one situations but only when females outnumber males. Forced copulation or infanticide has not been seen in wild bonobos.

Both hypotheses assume that adult females in a community of the genus *Pan* are genetically unrelated. Long-term studies of wild chimpanzees show that most females emigrate, but not all. At Taï 88% of females dispersed, and at Mahale 100%, but at Gombe only 13% of the females transferred, leaving the potential for female cooperation among those that remain (Goodall 1983; Nishida, Takasaki, and Takahata 1990; Boesch 1997). For bonobos neither exact figures of female migration nor genetic data are available, so it cannot yet be said

whether or not this contrasting pattern of cooperation—male-male cooperation in chimpanzees and female-female cooperation in bonobos—is truly independent of genetic relatedness.

KINSHIP

During the first six years of our research at Lomako, we never saw males immigrate, but three adolescent females temporarily joined the Eyengo community and both males and females of different age classes disappeared. From 1992 onward we collected feces of identified individuals, and DNA was extracted and typed in the laboratory of Diethard Tautz at Munich University (Gerloff et al. 1995). For most subadult and adult males, we found matching maternal **genotypes** in the group, giving evidence for male **philopatry**. In contrast, except for one mother-daughter pair, female community members never were closely related. However, in spite of this result, the calculation of average genetic relatedness among males and among females did not provide evidence for one sex being more closely related than the other. This could result from occasional male migration, which has been seen in chimpanzees (Goodall 1986), although it is not the only way to obtain similar relatedness among the sexes. Even if individuals stay in their community from birth or date of immigration onward, this may not guarantee fidelity to the community throughout the life span (Gagneux et al. 1997).

In sum, differences between chimpanzees and bonobos need not mirror differences of genetic relatedness.

DISCUSSION AND SYNTHESIS

The key to a better understanding of the differences in the two species of *Pan* may be in correcting overemphasized contrasts (Stanford 1998). Given recent data on forest-dwelling chimpanzees, some behavioral traits of bonobos fit well into the range of the behavioral diversity of chimpanzees (Boesch 1996; Fruth and Hohmann 1996). Just as "the chimpanzee" for decades was represented by Goodall's apes at Gombe, "the bonobo" described here is composed of fragments from only two places, Wamba and Lomako. Whether or not more research will reveal a higher behavioral diversity among bonobos remains to be seen.

Male-male bonds may be the fundamental basis of chimpanzee society, but female-female bonds in bonobos are not equivalent. Bonobos instead appear to be a male-female society supported by two major columns: long-lasting relationships among females and their adult sons (Ihobe 1992b; Kano 1992) and close associations among males and unrelated females.

Increased knowledge about bonobos crossing the boundary between forest and savanna and about chimpanzees living in the equatorial rain forest of the Congo basin may help to bridge the gap between the "fierce" chimpanzee and the "gentle" bonobo. Eventually, different populations of *Pan* will be seen as links in a long chain of rich diversity.

The Old World Monkeys

All of the Old World monkeys belong to one family: the Cercopithecidae. This taxonomic group is found only in Africa, Asia, and Europe. All members of the Cercopithecidae have **bilophodont molars** specialized for grinding, which each have four cusps that are connected by two ridges. They also have callused pads on their buttocks called ischial callosities. In contrast to the New World monkeys, Old World monkeys (and apes as well), have narrow, downward-facing nostrils that are close together. They are generally larger in body size than the New World monkeys and spend more time on the ground. The Cercopithecidae are further subdivided into two subfamilies: the Cercopithecinae and the Colobinae. The Cercopithecinae is composed of nine genera. As a group, they share the dietary adaptation of cheek pouches, which allow them to store food for short periods of time.

The most extensive genus of the group is *Macaca*. The nineteen species of macaques together form the most widely distributed nonhuman primate genus. They are found on the island of Gibraltar, across North Africa, throughout the Near East and India, Japan, and throughout Southeast Asia. Macaques are extremely adaptable and thrive in many different environments, ranging from tropical rain forest to montane forest and bustling cities. Adults range in size from 3 to 18 kg, with some species showing more sexual dimorphism than others. Their diet is varied, including flowers, seeds, bird eggs, leaves, bark, and invertebrates. Age at sexual maturity averages between 3 and 4 years. Most are found in multimale, multifemale social groups, with females forming matrilineal hierarchies.

Baboons are in the genus *Papio* and are widely distributed throughout Africa. Five species are included within this genus. Baboons are fairly large, stocky **quadrupeds;** they show a considerable amount of sexual dimorphism in both size and weight. In addition, the males have impressively large canine teeth, which they use in displays. The upper canine teeth are kept sharp by the first lower premolar, which is modified to hone the upper canine each time the mouth is closed. Baboon social groups are generally large, some containing up to 200 individuals, and except for the Hamadryas baboon of Ethiopia are multimale, multifemale in composition. The Hamadryas baboons live in one-male, multifemale groups, several of which gather together at night in large sleeping groups. Baboon females have conspicuous pink sexual swellings across their rumps, clearly indicating when they are in estrus or fertile. Gestation lasts

6–7 months, and sexual maturity is reached from 3.5 to 6 years of age, later for males than for females.

The sexually dimorphic gelada baboon was formerly included in the genus *Papio* but is now classified as the sole extant species in the genus *Theropithecus.* Based on the many fossils which have been found, this genus flourished in the past but currently has dwindled to only the species *gelada,* which is found in Ethiopia. They live in one-male, multifemale breeding groups that join together into bands, which in turn may gather into large herds of up to 600 individuals. Their diet consists primarily of grasses, and they live in a montane grassland habitat. This genus is unique in having an hourglass-shaped patch of pink skin on the neck and chest, which swells during female estrus.

A genus closely related to the baboon is *Mandrillus,* which includes the mandrill and the drill. They are forest dwellers found in Africa, Cameroon, Gabon, southeast Nigeria, and the Congo. The males weigh in at 25 kg and are twice as big as the females. The males also have large nasal ridges and long canine teeth. Male mandrills have brilliantly colored blue and red faces, whereas the drill's face is black. Both species have brilliantly colored **perineums.**

The mangabeys mostly live in multimale, multifemale groups across equatorial Africa. All six species eat fruit primarily. They are divided into two genera, *Cercocebus* and *Lophocebus.*

The most distinctively marked group of monkeys found throughout sub-Saharan Africa are the guenons, which all belong to the genus *Cercopithecus.* Each population shows marked differences in coat colors and patterns, which perhaps help them identify each other in the forest habitat where they live. Even though each guenon group looks different, many of them can interbreed, which causes some difficulty in classifying them. There are generally considered to be twenty to twenty-two species, which can be organized into more closely related species groups. All but two species are found in one-male, multifemale groups, ranging in size from five to thirty-five individuals. Most are primarily fruit eaters, but they include some leaves and animal prey in their diet as well. None weigh over 9 kg, and they show little to moderate sexual dimorphism.

The semiterrestrial vervet monkey was formerly classified as *Cercopithecus* but is now classified in it's own genus, *Chlorocebus.* Vervets live in large multimale, multifemale social groups in savanna habitat. An interesting characteristic shared by the vervet monkey and the patas monkey (*Erythrocebus patas*) is that the males in both genera have bright blue scrotums.

The smallest monkey is the talapoin (*Miopithecus talapoin*), which weighs in at .75–1.28 kg. They are found in Angola and Zaire in multimale, multifemale groups of up to fifty individuals. Despite their smaller size, these tiny monkeys don't reach **sexual maturity** until they are 4 years old.

The colobine monkeys do not have cheek pouches but share the adaptation of having a large **sacculated** (many-chambered) **stomach,** which houses bacteria that enables digestion of mature leaves, an important part of their diet. Their teeth are also adapted to a leaf-eating diet by having sharp crests that shear the leaves into small pieces. Infants are easily recognizable in this subfamily because in most species they are born a different color from the adults. Their coat color changes to the adult shade sometime between 3 and 6 months of age. These infants are often baby-sat or **allomothered** for periods of time by troop members other than the mother, often a juvenile female. This gives the young female some infant-handling experience and frees up the mother to forage or spend more time interacting with other group members.

There are currently eight recognized genera in the subfamily Colobinae, two found in equatorial Africa and the other six found in India and Southeast Asia. The African colobines include the black and white colobus monkeys from the genus *Colobus* and the red colobus (genus *Procolobus*). They live in multifemale, multimale groups, or in one-male, multifemale groups. They range in size from 6 to 12 kg, except for the olive colobus, which weighs in at 4.5 kg and is the smallest of the colobines. They eat leaves and seeds primarily, supplemented with fruit. As you might guess, the five species of red colobus monkeys all have varying amounts of red fur. The five species of black and white colobus monkeys are quite distinctive looking, with long flowing capes of white hair and long fluffy tails accenting their black bodies. The infants are born all white with pink faces.

The leaf monkeys of the genus *Presbytis* are found in Asia and are quite variable in appearance. There are eight recognized species found in the Southeast Asian islands of Borneo, Sumatra, and the Mentawai Islands, as well as in Java and on the Malay Peninsula. Most species have white fronts, with basic coat colors of gray, black, orange, or a mix. They range in size from 4 to 9 kg, with little or slight sexual dimorphism. These arboreal monkeys are mostly found in one-male, multifemale groups, except for the Mentawai Island leaf monkey, which is found in one-male, one-female pairs.

The hanuman langur is currently classified as the only species in the genus *Semnopithecus*. They are very widespread monkeys, found in India, Pakistan, Bangladesh, Sri Lanka, and Burma. They thrive in a wide variety of habitats, ranging from tropical rain forest to urban areas, and live at altitudes ranging from sea level to 14,000 feet, the widest range of elevations recorded for any non-human primate. The hanuman langurs are the most terrestrial of the colobines.

The remaining ten species of langurs and leaf monkeys are classified in the genus *Trachypithecus* and are found in India and Bangladesh, Sri Lanka, Burma, China, Malaysia, and the Sunda Islands. Most are gray and black or black and white in color, with bright orange infants. The golden langur and the capped leaf monkey are the exceptions, having cream and orange colored adult coats. The spectacled leaf monkey has rings of white skin around each eye and around the mouth, which stand out on their otherwise dark faces. Many *Trachypithecus* species have tufted crests of hair on top of their heads and prominent tufts of hair that resemble sideburns along their cheeks. Their one-male, multifemale social groups range from 6 to 30 individuals. The smallest species weighs 5 kg, and the largest 11 kg. There is very little sexual dimorphism.

In Vietnam, Laos, and Cambodia, we find one of the most exotic looking genera of primates, *Pygathrix*. Both species of douc langurs are brilliantly marked, with patches of different colors and shades of blue or orange on their faces. These 8–10 kg monkeys live in multimale, multifemale groups and eat a diet of leaves, fruit, seeds, and flowers. Group sizes can reach up to forty individuals.

The snub-nosed monkeys (*Rhinopithecus*) are also quite distinctive with bright patches of color on their heads and across their lips and faces. They have limited distribution in Vietnam and China. Their one-male, multifemale groups and all-male bands are known to join together into large groups numbering in the hundreds of individuals. They feed on leaves, fruit, buds, and grasses. The females weigh 8–9 kg, and the males weigh 14–20 kg. All are endangered.

Another remarkable looking monkey is the proboscis monkey from the genus *Nasalis*. This monkey is named for the extremely large and pendulous noses found on the males, who use them to make a honking vocalization. They are located on the Southeast Asian island of Borneo. They live in one-male, multifemale groups, and males form all-male bachelor bands. Having partially webbed feet makes them excellent swimmers, and they can swim underwater for up to 20 meters.

The colobine monkey with the shortest tail is the pigtailed langur, *Simias concolor*. They are found on the Mentawai Islands of Indonesia. They have a variable social structure which includes one-male, one-female pairs, as well as one-male, multifemale and multimale, multifemale social groups.

8

The Macaques

Fred B. Bercovitch and Michael A. Huffman

MACAQUES AND PRIMATOLOGY

The macaques are the most widespread nonhuman primate genus on the planet today. Investigations on the behavior of free-ranging rhesus and Japanese macaques have resulted in the longest continuous observations of any nonhuman primate species, extending through multiple generations of monkeys and observers.

Pioneer primatologist Clarence R. Carpenter, a student of Robert Yerkes (the namesake of the Yerkes Regional Primate Research Center, Georgia), was one of the first scientists to study primates in their natural habitat with his observations of howler monkeys in Panama (Carpenter 1934). He also observed gibbons in Southeast Asia and was responsible for establishing the population of free-ranging rhesus monkeys on the island of Cayo Santiago, off the coast of Puerto Rico in 1938 (Rawlins and Kessler 1986). Carpenter's landmark paper on the sexual behavior of rhesus macaques (Carpenter 1942) was quite prescient in many of its observations. World War II, and an array of political problems, resulted in a hiatus in research, but in the mid-1950s a new generation of scientists began to work on the island. Stuart Altmann, a graduate student of E. O. Wilson, the "father" of sociobiology, followed in Carpenter's tracks by initially observing howler monkeys in Panama and then shifting to a lengthy study of the rhesus monkeys on Cayo Santiago (Altmann 1962). His insights into monkey social structure and communication as a network of individual interactions resulted in a more solid framework for understanding primate societies. In addition to Altmann, Carl Koford, John Kaufmann, and Donald Sade were instrumental in contributing to early observations on the Cayo Santiago rhesus macaques (Rawlins and Kessler 1986).

Halfway around the world, in 1948, the Primate Research Group was established in Japan by Denzaburo Miyagi and Kinji Imanishi at Kyoto University. A survey of Japanese macaque, *M. fuscata,* habitats, from the southernmost boundary on Yakushima Island to the northernmost edge at the tip of Honshu Island, was initiated in 1951 by Imanishi and his students, Junichiro Itani, Shunzo Kawamura, Masao Kawai, Kisaburo Tokuda, and others. Provisioning with sweet potatoes and grain enabled the researchers to collect detailed information about individual differences in behavior and social relationships, and, as at Cayo Santiago, the early work has continued on many of the same social groups. In these formative years, emphasis was placed on the description of social relationships and the impact of individual life histories on group organization in Japanese macaques (Huffman 1991a). *Primates,* the first journal specifically devoted to the study of primates, was launched by the Kyoto University group of primatologists.

Genealogical records from the long-term studies at both Cayo Santiago and Japan have had a tremendous impact on primatology by revealing that the foundation of cercopithecine society is based on matrilineal social relationships (Itani 1954; Sade 1965) coupled with rank transmission from mother to offspring (Kawamura 1958; Koford 1963). Along with this social structure is a pattern of male troop transfer suggestive of inbreeding avoidance (Itani

1954; Nishida 1966; Sade 1968). Studies of Japanese macaques demonstrated the social transmission of cultural behavior (Itani 1958; Huffman 1996), and research on Cayo Santiago provided the first evidence from the field connecting population structure, social groups, and genetic relationships (Buettner-Janusch et al. 1974a, 1974b).

EVOLUTION AND DISTRIBUTION

Macaques evolved about 5–6 million years ago, concurrent with the advent of the hominid lineage (Fa 1989). Emerging in North Africa, they radiated throughout Europe, southern Russia, and Asia. Possessed of a generalized morphology, macaques are renowned for their diversity and adaptability. They dwell in a greater variety of habitats and climates than any other nonhuman primate genus (Lindburg 1991).

Macaques have been classified into nineteen species (Table 1; Fa 1989; Hoelzer and Melnick 1996). Macaque evolution was largely influenced by glacial events that yielded geographically isolated island populations (Hoelzer and Melnick 1996). The Sulawesi macaques present a peculiar evolutionary history. Sulawesi Island is approximately 750 miles northwest of Darwin, Australia, and is home to seven of the nineteen macaque species (Fooden 1976; Takanaka et al. 1987). The route of island occupancy is unclear and could have involved either land bridges that later became submerged or transit by rafting (Fa 1989). Why and how the Sulawesi macaques evolved into such a variety of species in such a small area, whereas other macaque species such as the rhesus failed to speciate even though they colonized a greater variety of habitats, remains a mystery.

ECOLOGY AND DIET

Macaques are frugivores, with fruits constituting 60 to 90% of dietary items (Clutton-Brock and Harvey 1977a). Ripe fruits generally occur in discrete, dispersed food patches, and macaques have fairly large home ranges compared to folivorous species

TABLE 1 The Macaques

Species	Common Name
Macaca assamensis	Assamese macaque
M. sylvanus	Barbary macaque
M. radiata	Bonnet macaque
M. fuscata	Japanese macaque
M. silenus	Liontailed macaque
M. fascicularis	Longtailed macaque
M. nemestrina	Pigtailed macaque
M. mulatta	Rhesus macaque
M. arctoides	Stumptailed macaque
M. cyclopsis	Taiwan macaque
M. thibetana	Tibetan macaque
M. sinica	Toque macaque
Sulawesi Macaques	
M. nigriscens	Gorontalo macaque
M. hecki	Heck's macaque
M. maura	Moor macaque
M. brunnescens	Muna-Buntung macaque
M. ochreata	Ochre macaque
M. nigra	Sulawesi crested macaque
M. tonkean	Tonkean macaque

(Clutton-Brock and Harvey 1977b). Although subsisting primarily on fruits, macaques ingest a variety of foods. For example, seasonal differences in the diet of Japanese macaques are quite distinct, and food availability is highly variable from month to month (Agetsuma 1995a). Sufficient calorie and protein intake is difficult in winter, especially in the northern regions, when the menu may consist largely of bark, winter buds, and twigs (Nakagawa et al. 1996).

Most macaques are generalists in terms of their overall food intake (Lindburg 1991). Ingestion of over 100 plant species during the year by a single population is common. A wide selection of leaves, bark, buds, flowers, seeds, and insects are consumed. Japanese macaques on the island of Koshima also eat limpets on the rocky shoreline as well as an occasional fish or octopus stranded in the shallows (Watanabe 1989).

Macaques spend a large portion of the day in search of small, widely dispersed sources of nutrition. They concentrate on feeding in the trees at the end of branches, and are called "terminal branch feeders" (Grand 1972). Again, however, a lot of diversity occurs in the amount of time that different species actually spend moving in the trees or walking on the ground looking for food. Male moor macaques spend 80% or more of their time on the ground (Matsumura, pers. comm.). In contrast, bonnet and liontailed macaques spend 90% or more of their time in the trees (Fooden 1986; Kurup and Kumar 1993).

Foraging habits are intimately associated with anatomy (Rodman 1979b). Longtailed, liontailed, and bonnet macaques are well adapted for arboreal travel, whereas pigtailed macaques forage mostly on the ground. Food sources of pigtailed macaques tend to be more widely dispersed, and they move longer distances between food patches than sympatric longtailed macaques. As a consequence, pigtailed macaques have larger home ranges and longer day ranges than longtailed macaques. Longtailed macaques tend to be gracile and possess long tails (hence, their name) for assistance when leaping across branches, whereas pigtailed macaques tend to be stocky and have stubby tails (hence, their name). Troops of both species fragment into smaller subgroups while foraging (Fittinghoff and Lindburg 1980; Caldecott, Feistner, and Gadsby 1996).

Foraging efficiency varies as a function of food availability and group size. Life in a social group yields competition for preferred food items, depending on the size of the group, the amount of food available, and its defendability. Among wild female longtailed macaques, relative rates of aggression are significantly higher over access to fruit than to leaves, especially in trees where at least half of the available fruit is ripe (Sterck and Steenbeek 1997). In wild Japanese macaques in the cold temperate forest on Kinkazan Island, female dominance and feeding success were significantly correlated when food was clumped and defensible during lean winter months of the year (Saito 1996). In the warm temperate forests of Yakushima Island, where food is abundant and widely distributed throughout the year, competition for food is less intense. Subordinate individuals can avoid competition by maintaining a tolerable distance from dominant nonkin (Furuichi 1983). Synchrony of troop members' feeding activity is significantly lower when they feed on more highly clumped fruit and seeds than when they feed on leaves (Agetsuma 1995b).

Female-female competition over access to specific food resources mediates both troop fission and troop fusion. Competition between troops of toque macaques results in disputes usually linked to access to fruit trees (Dittus 1987). Fissioning results from reduced social cohesion among females within a group (Dittus 1988). Among toque macaques, troop fusioning occurs less often than fissioning, with the process resembling a hostile takeover more than a cooperative merger (Dittus 1987). Among the Japanese macaques on Yakushima Island, intergroup competition for access to food has led to group extinction. Troop fusion occurs when the home range is small, resources are limited, and females are unable to defend special resources (Takahata et al. 1994). Evidence indicates that a minimum troop size is probably necessary among macaques to meet the demands posed by intertroop competition for restricted food resources.

SOCIAL STRUCTURE

Macaque societies range in size from about a dozen individuals to over one hundred monkeys under natural conditions, but most groups are in the vicinity of twenty to fifty animals (Lindburg 1991). The record is probably held by the Takasakiyami A troop of Japanese macaques, who maintained a single cohesive group of more than 1000 individuals under provisioned conditions (Ohsawa and Sugiyama 1996). Group size reflects food availability, predator pressure, and disease susceptibility. All macaque social systems are composed of female-bonded, multimale, multifemale configurations.

Female-bonded cercopithecine troops are characterized by intense kinship ties among females. Social interactions, such as **grooming** and alliance formation, often map onto matrilineal relatedness. However, kinship appears to have less influence on feeding competition and patterns of social interactions in moor, Tonkean, and bonnet macaques than in other macaques (Simonds 1965; Thierry, Gauthier, and Peignot 1990; Matsumura and Okamoto 1997). Moor macaques often feed in the same tree in close physical contact with nonkin. Male bonnet macaques groom other males more often than females groom each other (Simonds 1965), with only a weak association connecting grooming preferences to alliance partnerships (Silk 1992).

The core of macaque society is clusters of matrilineal subgroups. Female macaques usually maintain strict linear **dominance hierarchies,** with members of a dominant **matriline** consistently higher ranking than members of a subordinate matriline, regardless of age (Koyama 1967; Berman 1986). Daughters occupy rank positions immediately below that of their mothers. Two-year-old high-ranking females have little problem supplanting 10-year-old low-ranking females three times their size from desirable food commodities. Females are philopatric and generally maintain the same rank position throughout life, although dominance transitions occur (e.g., Ball 1996). Males alter troop membership, as well as dominance status, during their lifetimes.

Male troop tenure is quite variable, but males tend to reside in a single group for about two to four years (Huffman 1991b; Manson 1995). Male dispersal appears to be driven by a combination of inbreeding avoidance and female preference for novelty (Huffman 1991b; Bercovitch 1997; Kuester and Paul 1998). Troop tenure is associated with group size and the number of available mating partners (Huffman 1991b). Male influxes can occur for short durations during the mating season (Sprague 1991a, 1991b) and mating with nontroop males is common (Sprague 1991a; Berard et al. 1994).

All macaques reside in troops with many adult males and females. Although birth sex ratios are equal, adult females in a troop outnumber adult males due to patterns of natal male migration, reduced survivorship of migrating males, and the earlier reproductive maturation of females compared to males (Norikoshi and Koyama 1975; Dittus 1980; Lindburg 1991).

Macaque societies can be divided on the basis of symmetry of social interactions, which reflect their dominance styles (de Waal and Luttrell 1989; Thierry 1990; Matsumura 1997). In some species, such as rhesus, Japanese, and pigtailed macaques,

dominance relationships are striking and often enforced, with interactions tending to be strongly nepotistic. In other species, such as bonnet, Barbary, stumptailed, and Sulawesi macaques, dominance interactions are more relaxed and egalitarian or tolerant, with nepotism exhibiting a reduced role in patterning social relationships. In the less rigid species, infants tend to interact with nonmatriline members at younger ages, and rank transmission rules are less stringent. In macaque societies, the structure of social relationships is mediated by patterns of both peaceful and aggressive interventions in dyadic conflicts, as well as by reconciliation after such conflicts (Ehardt and Bernstein 1992; de Waal 1993; Petit and Thierry 1994; Silk 1997).

REPRODUCTIVE BIOLOGY AND BEHAVIOR

Female macaques have a sexual skin in the perineal region that intensifies in color during the follicular phase of the cycle, as well as increasing in size in some species (Fooden 1976; Dixson 1983; Thierry et al. 1996). The ovarian cycle of macaques ranges from 28 to 40 days, with a mode of about 31 days (Robinson and Goy 1986; Lindburg 1991). Species with protuberant sex skin swellings (e.g., liontailed, moor, pigtailed, Sulawesi crested, Tonkean) tend to have cycles in the vicinity of 30 to 40 days, whereas macaque species lacking pronounced sex skin swelling tend to have shorter ovarian cycles of 25 to 35 days. Complex penile morphology among macaques coincides with minimal female sex skin development, whereas simple penile morphology corresponds with pronounced sex skin swellings (Dixson 1983). The penis of male macaques varies from blunt and broad to narrow and elongate (Fooden 1976). Some male macaques have a sex skin in the facial region that becomes bright red during the mating season.

Mating activity is restricted to a two- to three-month period in about one-third to one-half of macaque species (Lindburg 1991). Copulation rates reach their zenith within four days of the estradiol peak (Wilson, Gordon, and Collins 1982), but adolescent females mate with males for a longer period of time than do adult females (Bercovitch and Goy 1990). Mating associations between females and males range from a few minutes to several days (Lindburg 1991). Barbary macaque females may wander from male to male, with about two minutes elapsing from associating with a male until copulating with him, and about a half hour separating consecutive ejaculations (Taub 1980; Kuester and Paul 1992).

Mating with multiple males combined with the absence of obvious signals denoting ovulation camouflages paternity but does not necessarily result in complete confusion about sire identity (see Bercovitch 1995). Recent investigations using DNA fingerprint technology have found that dominant males tend to out-reproduce subordinate males (longtailed macaques: de Ruiter et al. 1992; Barbary macaques: Paul and Kuester 1996; Japanese macaques: Soltis et al. 1997a, 1997b; rhesus macaques: Smith 1994), but the connection is inconsistent and probably offset by male adoption of alternative mating tactics, as well as female preference for nondominant males (Huffman 1992; Berard et al. 1994; Soltis et al. 1997a, 1997b). Female dominance rank also has an impact on reproductive success, but results vary widely across species and localities (Silk 1987).

Female macaques produce first offspring prior to full body growth (Bercovitch and Goy 1990) but surpass a minimum body weight prior to first conception (Bercovitch et al. 1998). Male macaques require about one year longer to reach sexual maturity than females (Bercovitch 1998). The timing of first birth is affected by dominance rank, population density, and food availability (Sugiyama and Ohsawa 1982; Bercovitch and Goy 1990; Bercovitch and Berard 1993), but an accelerated age at first birth does not correspond to a greater lifetime reproductive success (Fedigan et al. 1986; Bercovitch and Berard 1993; Paul and Kuester 1996). Breeding life span is the best predictor of female lifetime reproductive success.

Females usually give birth every year or two and nurse infants until 6 to 12 months of age. Reproductive senescence and irregular ovarian cycles occur at about 20 to 25 years of age (Takahata 1980;

Paul, Kuester, and Podzuweit 1993; Nozaki, Mitsunaga, and Shimizu 1995; Walker 1995). Older female siblings and matrilineal relatives support the mother in infant caretaking responsibilities, with the male parental role ranging from intense (e.g., Barbary macaques) to indifferent (e.g., pigtailed macaques).

SPECIAL TOPICS

Male-Infant Bonds in Macaques

Male-infant affiliations are not only quite common but extremely intense in some macaques. The adaptive significance of these bonds is shrouded in controversy and has been studied most extensively in Barbary macaques. Originally, male-infant bonds in Barbary macaques were regarded as a form of **agonistic buffering**, a social skill adopted by subordinate animals to mitigate aggression by dominant animals (Deag and Crook 1971). Taub (1980, 1984) subsequently reasoned that male care of infants functioned as a form of paternal investment involving male offspring or kin. A third suggestion is that males bond with infants as a form of mating effort that promotes the prospects for sex with the infants' mothers (Smuts and Gubernick 1992).

Paul, Kuester, and Arnemann (1996) subjected these three ideas to systematic analysis using data obtained from DNA fingerprints. Their results confirmed earlier reports that males do not preferentially associate with their own offspring. They also questioned the suggestion that male care derives from paternal confusion resulting from female sexual behavior aimed at preventing infanticide. Many infants were ignored by all males, despite their mothers' promiscuity, and each male had extremely strong bonds with specific infants, despite their mating activities with multiple females. Paul et al. (1996) dismissed the mating effort hypothesis because they found that caretaking by males did not enhance prospects for mating with the infants' mothers. Male caretakers were not more likely to sire the infants' next sibling. They concluded that male care of infants does not occur in response to aggression, so it is not "agonistic buffering." But male use of infants does mediate social relationships between males. Paul et al. (1996) propose that alliance formation between males could enhance fitness and might develop partly as a consequence of triadic interactions involving two males and an infant.

Triadic relationships involving two males and an infant take the form of "bridging" behavior in stumptailed (Estrada 1984) and Tibetan (Ogawa 1995a, 1995b) macaques. In these situations, two males simultaneously interact with an infant, who creates a "bridge" between the males. Among Tibetan macaques, low-ranking males often establish a bridge with high-ranking males by using a preferred infant companion of the more dominant individual prior to initiating grooming (Ogawa 1995b). This pattern is similar to "agonistic buffering" (Ogawa 1995b) but seems to be a prelude to positive social interactions rather than a device to inhibit negative social interactions. Some evidence indicates that male Assamese (Kawamoto as cited in Ogawa 1995b) and longtailed (de Waal, van Hooff, and Netto 1976) macaques also establish bridges with specific infants and other males. In both rhesus (Hill 1986) and Japanese (Itani 1959) macaques, males protect particular infants against conspecific attacks. Although male macaques do not have a reputation for extensive bonding with infants, males in many species of macaques establish preferential associations with specific infants in their social group. The functional and adaptive significance of these affiliative relationships remains unclear.

Female Matriarchies in Japanese Macaques (*M. fuscata*)

Macaque society is founded on matrilineal relationships, and the following is a true life drama of the lives of some members of the Arashiyama troop of Japanese macaques. At Arashiyama records go back to 1948, with the first reported encounter by a local school teacher, Eiji Ohta. Detailed observations were subsequently begun by Kyoto University researcher Nanosuke Hazama (1899–1981) on 15 October 1954, and since then the troop has been closely monitored (see Huffman 1991a).

Mino was born on 25 May 1957. At birth, she had a 2-year-old brother, Ala, and an infant sister, Kojiwa-56 (numbers after matriline name denote the year of birth followed by mother's year of birth, grandmother's year of birth, and so forth in the case of multiple two-digit markers). Two years earlier, shortly before Ala was born, Kojiwa had moved with her troop of forty-seven to Iwatayama. Life was good, their diet of acorns, berries, seeds, leaves, and insects was supplemented daily with potatoes and apples provided by their benevolent new landlords.

The leaders of the troop were Zao, the alpha male, and Tokiwa, the alpha female. Zao had only recently become the new alpha after his predecessor, Mars, left. As a member of a middle-ranking family, young Mino viewed Tokiwa and her four offspring as unapproachable. She could only watch from a distance as they had first choice of all the best apples and potatoes. Tokiwa's oldest son, Chikusha was a dashing young male on the threshold of adolescence—4 years old, already flirting in the fall mating season. His status in life had always assured him the most and best of everything. But he was restless and in August 1959, shortly before the beginning of the mating season, Chikusha gave up his birth given status and headed east toward Mt. Hiezan. At the time, it was believed that primate groups were closed societies, yet on 15 January 1960, Chikusha was found by Hazama as a **peripheral male** of the Hiezan troop, about 17 km NE of Iwatayama, thus shattering the myths of mindless meandering males and impenetrable societies.

Back at Iwatayama, Zao had begun to lose his grip on the group, and he left that same mating season. Tokiwa, the matriarch, became the most dominant individual in the group until Lincoln, an adult male, took over the role. Tokiwa remained the alpha female until her death on 15 November 1962. At that time, her first born and only daughter, Matsu (born in 1952), already a mother of six, inherited her mother's alpha status.

By March 1966 the troop had reached 163 members, the neighborhood became overcrowded, and tension was building among the adult leader male class. In June 1966, the once sleepy little community divided the neighborhood down the middle between the two mid-ranking female matriline groups of Betta and Kojiwa. Daughters followed mothers, but maturing males moved into the social group of opposite rank position rather than follow kin. Males of the high-ranking matrilines moved into B troop with females of lower ranking matrilines and vice versa, producing a grand scheme in social disintegration that helped avoid inbreeding.

By this time Mino was 9 years old and had produced one daughter, Mino-63, and one son, Mino-65. As a consequence of the troop fission, Mino was now a female of high status. In fact, her matriline was now the highest in the newly formed B troop. Mino's mother, Kojiwa, was aging, and she became the victim of a series of attacks by her daughter. Mino emerged as the alpha female in the group shortly after the fission, and her mother died a year later.

Mino and other low-ranking females had begun courting the alpha male Zola prior to the troop fission and had established nonsexual friendships. With Zola as the alpha male, and Mino as the alpha female, B troop became the dominant group at Iwatayama. In 1972, A troop started a new life among the cactus and mesquite in southwestern Texas and became known as Arashiyama West (Fedigan 1991).

In 1970 with the departure of Zola, Matsu-59 became alpha male. He was the son of the alpha female who reigned in A troop, but he had followed Zola into B troop and taken position as beta male. He retained his alpha rank for a record 11 years. Mino remained alpha female from 1966 to 1975, and three of her descendents have maintained the alpha slot for the next two decades. The most dramatic of these changeovers was the attack on Mino-63 by her daughter, Mino-6369, and granddaughter, Mino-636974. Mino-63 died as an indirect cause of those injuries on 27 January 1979.

Mino herself went on to lead a long life, as famous old queen mothers often do. She gave birth to her last infant, Mino-82, a daughter, at the age of 25 (Figure 1). She was not seen to mate the last 5 years of her life, and she died on 23 January 1991 at the age of 33. To this day she maintains the distinction of being the longest lived wild born, free-ranging Japanese macaque in recorded history.

Caller ID in Pigtailed Macaques (*M. nemestrina*)

Pigtailed macaques emit at least four acoustically distinct screams that provide information about the dominance rank of the opponent and the severity of aggressive attack (Gouzoules and Gouzoules 1989a). Vocalizations produced by victims of attack that function to elicit support from allies are called recruitment screams. Juvenile females are more efficient than juvenile males in the use of recruitment screams (Gouzoules and Gouzoules 1989b). Sex differences in proficiency probably result from sex differences in life history patterns. Female pigtailed macaques remain in their natal group throughout life and depend on recruiting allies to maintain dominance position, whereas males migrate to other groups and rarely scream to attract defenders.

Although acoustically distinct screams could mirror differences in motivational state rather than reflect references to external events, the discrete structure of the calls provides strong evidence for **symbolic communication** (Snowdon 1990b). Recruitment screams are extremely loud and exhibit features enhancing prospects for locating the sender. Information about caller identity is also encoded into recruitment screams using vocal signatures, or distinctive attributes, characteristic of matriline membership (Gouzoules and Gouzoules 1990). Pigtailed macaque recruitment screams are analogous to a telephone caller ID system because the signal conveys information that enables the recipients to either ignore or respond to the call based on the identity of the caller. The auditory communication system of pigtailed macaques, as well as other nonhuman primates, provides evidence that primate societies are structured on the basis of recognition of social relationships among animals (Seyfarth and Cheney 1994).

Sexual Dalliances in Stumptailed Macaques (*M. arctoides*)

Stumptailed macaques posess bizarre male and female genitalia. The baculum, or *os penis,* is longer (53 mm) in stumptailed macaques than in any

FIGURE 1 Mino (1957–1991) being groomed by her daughter Mino-82 at Arashiyama a few weeks before her death. (Photo by M. A. Huffman.)

other extant primate species (Dixson 1987), and the penis is twice as long as in rhesus or Japanese macaques. Females have an elaborate, lengthy, cervical vestibular colliculus (i.e., a long, bumpy, cavity leads into the cervix), which is specialized to receive the javelin-shaped elongated penis (Fooden 1967). The coevolution of specialized male and female genitalia is associated with unusual copulatory behavior.

Male stumptailed macques ejaculate with females about five to ten times per day under a variety of conditions (Nieuwenhuijsen, de Neef, and Slob 1986), and maintain intromission for about two minutes after ejaculation (Chevalier-Skolnikoff 1974). Following ejaculation, the duo adopts a "postejaculatory pair sit" (Goldfoot et al. 1975), where the male sits down while his penis remains inserted and his mating partner sits in his lap. Formation of a genital "lock" by stumptailed macaques is probably related to their specialized genitalia (Dixson 1983).

Male stumptailed macaques masturbate using a unique style. Their "directed masturbation" involves grasping the hair of a female and looking at her while masturbating, or positioning oneself near a copulating couple and, while watching the female, stroking one's penis (Nieuwenhuijsen et al. 1986). Masturbation is not restricted to males, but females increase the amount of genital stimulation they obtain by mounting other females (Chevalier-Skolnikoff 1974, 1976; Goldfoot et al. 1980). When females mount other females, the pelvic thrusting of the mounter stimulates the genitalia and results in a pseudo-ejaculatory response that includes body rigidity, vocal exhalation, display of a "round mouth ejaculation face," uterine contractions, and increased heart rate, all of which suggest that females achieve orgasm by mounting other females (Chevalier-Skolnikoff 1974, 1976; Goldfoot et al. 1980). Such homosexual activity by females is of-ten stimulated by heterosexual behavior in the group (Chevalier-Skolnikoff 1976), a pattern common to the directed masturbation of males.

The specialized genital morphology, copulatory tie, and high rates of sexual activity indicate that stumptailed macaques would be an excellent species for examining issues related to sexual selection and sperm competition.

ACKNOWLEDGMENTS

We thank Agustín Fuentes, Phyllis Dolhinow, and Bernard Thierry for their input and suggestions. MAH would also like to thank many colleagues in Japan, especially Junichiro Itani, Jiro Ikeda, Masao Kawai, Shunzo Kawamura, Yukimuru Sugiyama, Naoki Koyama, Koshi Norikoshi, Yukio Takahata, and the Asaba family for their faithful support of my research and their endearing friendship spanning the last twenty years. FBB would like to thank Matt Kessler for his unwavering support over the last decade. The Caribbean Primate Research Center is supported by NIH Grant RR03640.

9

Decoding Patas Social Organization

Janice Chism

Patas monkeys (Erythrocebus patas) *are slender, long-legged monkeys of the African Guinea and Sahel savanna regions. They are distributed from Senegal in West Africa to Kenya in the east. Their scientific name describes their color: Erythrocebus means red monkey, and the species name* patas *is derived from the word for "red" in the language of the Wolof people of western Sudan. Adult males are a deep mahogany color on their backs with white limbs and bellies. Females and juveniles are more discreetly colored, light red on the back and cream below. Adults are dimorphic in size; males weigh 12–14 kg and females 7–8 kg (Hall 1965). Like many monkeys, patas infants have a distinct natal coat. They are born with black fur that gradually turns red by about 3 months of age.*

Primatologists conducted several brief field studies of patas monkeys in the 1960s and 1970s (e.g., Hall 1965, Struhsaker and Gartlan 1970, Gartlan 1975). They described patas groups as small (approx. 15–30 animals) with a few adult females and their young and with a classic one-male or **harem,** *social structure. In a one-male group, an adult male establishes himself as the sole resident male and mates exclusively with the group's reproductive females. A resident male was presumed to maintain exclusive access to the group's females by driving out maturing males and aggressively deterring outside males from entering the group (Hall 1965). Mating systems like this are typical of herd-living ungulates such as antelope, and Hall (1965) specifically suggested that patas monkeys had converged on a typical African ungulate social system in adapting to a savanna* **herbivore** *way of life.*

When I went to the Laikipia District of Kenya to conduct a two-year field study of patas monkeys in *1979, I didn't expect any surprises about patas social organization or basic ecology. Previous field studies and five years of observations of a captive patas group at the University of California, Berkeley, appeared to have securely established patas as having a one-male group structure. Observations of the Laikipia patas population over the next several years, however, revealed the behavioral ecology to be more complicated and variable than previously suspected. As many primatologists in the 1970s and 1980s were discovering, social organization and ecology are not as fixed and universal as had been supposed.*

THE MUTARA PATAS

My field site, a mosaic of open grassland and woodland areas dominated by umbrella-shaped acacia trees on ADC Mutara Ranch, was located on a high plateau just above Africa's great Eastern Rift Valley. Along the permanent river courses, tall fever trees (*Acacia xanthophloea*) and a dense tangle of bushes and vines formed narrow bands of gallery forest. The patas shared this habitat with many species of ungulates, including giraffe, zebra, and several different gazelles, and with a full range of predators such as lions, leopards, cheetahs, hyenas, wild dogs and jackals, and with at least two other primates, vervet monkeys and galagos. Baboons also lived in the district, although they had been eliminated from Mutara by the ranch manager who considered them pests (Chism and Rowell 1988).

The Mutara patas study focused on two groups, a small one of about fifteen to twenty monkeys, including about ten adult females, and a larger group which averaged about fifty monkeys, including about twenty adult females. Each group also had a varying number of infants and juveniles. At the beginning of the study, both groups had the one-male structure I had expected to find. Although no previous observer had actually witnessed a change in adult male membership in a wild patas group, the theoretical expectation was that this would be a relatively rare but dramatic event in which a usurper male would appear, fight with the resident male, and then the winner of the contest would remain while the loser slunk off to lick his wounds in solitude. To my surprise, however, there were three changes of male membership in the two study groups over the first ten months of observation. In early 1980, during a rare bout of out-of-season mating by two females, two adult males appeared to be in the group simultaneously for a few days. This was such an unexpected event that I and another colleague observing the groups simply didn't believe our own eyes. We each saw and carefully described two different males but kept telling ourselves that we must have been mistaken—patas monkeys live in one-male groups!

The popular image of scientists is that they make observations and then come to objective conclusions about the meaning of these observations, free from any preconceptions. In fact, scientists more often work with a preexisting idea of what a system (in this case a social system of a species) is like. They then test this idea using a very formal process in which, paradoxically, they try to falsify hypotheses, or predictions, based on this idea. If the paradigm the scientist is working from is wrong or only partially correct, however, sometimes it takes a while to recognize and accept the "new" view emerging from the data. This was exactly what kept me from immediately grasping the implications of the two different males I had seen in the patas group in early 1980.

Observations of the two study groups during their regular conception period later that year, however, left no doubt about what was happening. From June to August both study groups contained several males for varying periods (Chism and Rowell 1986). Three different males mated with females

in the small group, and eight males (up to seven at one time) mated in the large group. This was a stunning development, and it took several more years of observations of this study population to understand more fully what factors caused this variability in patas group structure (Harding and Olson 1986; Chism and Rogers 1997).

PATAS SOCIAL STRUCTURE

The picture of patas social organization based on several years of study at Mutara is now a more complex but, I think, a more interesting one. It involves very different patterns of social life for males and females. Patas females grow up to become adult members of the group into which they were born (Figure 1). They interact throughout their lives with a set of familiar females, many of them close maternal relatives, including mothers, sisters, daughters, aunts, nieces, even grandmothers and grandchildren. Perhaps these small, kin-based groups allow patas female relationships to be fairly relaxed, lacking the rigidly organized matrilineal dominance

FIGURE 1   A patas mother forages with her infant at the Mutara field study site in Kenya. (Photo by D. K. Olson and J. Chism)

hierarchies found among many baboons and macaques (Gouzoules and Gouzoules 1987). The most
disruptive interactions occur when young patas females enter puberty and briefly, but energetically,
strive to establish their place among the adult females (Rowell and Chism 1986).

In contrast to the stable, kin-centered social environment of the females, the lives of patas males
(Figure 2) are characterized by frequent change of
group and the consequent need to interact with
new social companions. Males leave their natal
groups as 2- to 3-year-olds, either alone or with
other adolescent males; brothers, especially, may
leave groups together. Thus, most young males
have kin or familiar companions around when they
are first on their own in a hostile world filled with
predators, other patas groups that do not want to
share their range or resources with nonmembers,
and adult males, both inside and outside groups,
who view them as potential competitors for mates.

For several years after leaving their natal groups,
young males form brief associations with a series
of other males before finally becoming large (and
aggressively competent) enough to contest with
residents for more permanent membership in
female-based groups (Chism and Rowell 1986;
Chism and Rogers 1997). During this period,
males may briefly enter and mate in the females'
groups during breeding periods. Even as adults,
however, male residence in groups is brief, averaging only about three months at Mutara, with the
longest tenures being less than a full year (Chism
and Rowell 1986). Thus, over their lives, males
must repeatedly attempt to establish relationships
with males, females, and immatures with whom
they have had little or no previous experience. This
suggests that reproductive success for males includes both the ability to compete aggressively with
other males for access to females and an effective
set of social skills that allow them to enter and get
along in many social groups.

Patas female reproductive strategy can be described as "breed early and often." Females can
conceive at 2½, have their first babies at 3 years
of age, then give birth annually. This means that
patas infants must develop very quickly to be able
to feed themselves and keep up with their group

FIGURE 2   An adult male patas sits in the crown of an
acacia tree at the Mutara field site in Kenya. (Photo by
J. Chism and D. K. Olson)

on their own at least by the time they are 1 year
old. At Mutara, infants orphaned as young as 7
months managed to survive without being adopted
(Chism, Rowell, and Olson 1984). This is one of
the fastest rates of maturation and reproduction
of any Old World monkey (Rowell 1977). Only
the closely related vervet monkey (*Cercopithecus
aethiops*) achieves anything like this rate of maturation and reproduction on a regular basis. Patas reproduction is also highly synchronized. At Mutara,
females became receptive and mated in about a 10-
week period from June to mid-August. Births occurred in a brief period from mid-December to
February (Chism et al. 1984).

The mating and birth seasons were exciting but
exhausting times for the human observer as they
also appeared to be for the monkeys. During mating seasons, several males were present, and it often seemed as if the social order had completely
broken down (Chism and Rogers 1997). New
males entered the groups, fought with the resident
male, and followed females doggedly for hours at a
time attempting to copulate with them. Infants got
separated from their mothers and cooed piteously
while trying to reconnect with them. The group

occasionally seemed to be directionless, just milling around rather than purposely moving from one feeding site to another as it usually did. Keeping track of the identity of new males and of who was mating or fighting with whom was a strenuous and confusing business for the observer (perhaps it was for the monkeys too).

During the birth season the presence of many new infants also resulted in a change in the tenor of life. Like most primates, patas females are very interested in new babies and are anxious to sniff, touch, and hold them. Although patas mothers are reluctant to let other monkeys take their infants for the first day or two after birth, very soon, usually within the first week, infants are taken, held, carried, and even nursed by other females (Chism 1986). Juvenile females, and to a lesser extent males, are also interested in babies and are eager to get possession of them, but adult females mostly monopolize access to the infants until they are 2 to 3 months old.

Interestingly, patas mothers do not initially take advantage of these willing baby-sitters to go off and forage. Rather, mothers usually remain nearby, resting or socializing with other females. Only when infants are about 3 months old do mothers leave them with caretakers while they forage and feed. At this age several patas infants may be left together in a sort of play group, or creche, under the care of a single adult or juvenile female while all the other mothers forage 100 meters or more away (Chism 1995).

The willingness of the group's females to share the care of dependent infants may be crucial to the patas' ability to maintain their rapid and highly synchronized reproduction (Chism, in press). A high level of foraging and feeding efficiency is necessary if a patas female is to conceive again when her previous infant, just 6 months old, is still nursing and being carried for at least part of the long day's trek for food and water. Sharing the task of infant care during this critical period may help females to return to good nutritional condition quickly and maintain their very short birth intervals. In addition, when immature females look after infants, they gain maternal experience that will help them rear their own first infants. In many

species, first-time, inexperienced females are more likely to lose their infants than are more experienced mothers (e.g., Drickamer 1974). Patas, however, are as successful with their first infants as with later ones (Chism et al. 1984).

Male patas reach full maturity much later than females, at about 5 to 6 years of age (Rowell 1977). In our captive patas group in Berkeley, young males began to be harassed by the resident adult male (often their fathers) when they were about 2 years old. This harassment continued relentlessly until we removed the young males from the group. We were not especially surprised by this pattern of behavior; indeed, we expected it because maturing males would have to be excluded from their natal groups to maintain a one-male group structure. What was surprising was that in the wild patas groups at Mutara no such harassment of young males occurred. Although young males could not be kept in the captive group past the age of about 2 years, in the wild some males stayed in groups until they were nearly 3½. When they did leave, it appeared to be entirely of their own volition (Chism and Rowell 1986).

Here, it might seem that the confined conditions of captivity promoted an unnatural behavior, the harassment of young males. Observation of males in the captive group aided our understanding of male emigration from wild groups, however. Wild males start to become almost invisible socially in their third year, staying out of sight of the adult male and very close to their mothers most of the time. Since patas mothers and indeed all females will vigorously defend immatures against any hint of aggression from adult males, this is a very effective strategy in the wild. Why didn't it work in captivity? The inability of young males to remain out of sight for long in the enclosure was probably responsible for their constant harassment. We were able to keep one young male in the group much longer than usual, although it was hard to observe him, because he found a hiding place under the observation booth. We hypothesized that young males in wild groups, too, would eventually become the objects of adult male aggression. They forestall this, however, by leaving just as they are beginning to show distinctive adult male secondary sex characters, such as the blue scrotum, which would provoke attack (Chism and Rowell 1986).

PATAS ECOLOGY

In addition to altering our view of patas social organization, the Mutara study provided a somewhat different picture of patas ecology. Surrounded all their lives by a sea of grass, patas rarely eat it and treat open expanses of grassland with great caution (Chism and Rowell, 1988; Chism and Wood 1994). This requires some explanation. If a primate species is going to leave the comparative abundance, predictability, and safety of the forest to move into the savanna with its strongly seasonal food supply and rich collection of predators, why wouldn't it make more use of the most common feature of that habitat?

Some primates, notably baboons, utilize grassland resources more thoroughly than do patas. Although cercopithecines lack specialized stomachs to cope with the cellulose grass contains, grass seeds and roots have nutrients they can readily use. But grass seeds are only available for a very brief period of the year in many areas and are laborious to collect in large quantities. Digging up the underground roots of grasses requires strong fingers, which baboons have but patas and other *Cercopithecus* monkeys do not.

Social organization and ecological requirements together help determine what habitat and resources a species can exploit. Savanna baboon males are much larger than patas males, and there are nearly always several males in each baboon group. Therefore, baboon males are able to defend their groups very effectively against many of the predators found on the savanna. Patas males do not do this. Instead, patas have adopted a three-pronged antipredator strategy that relies heavily on crypticity, a high level of vigilance, and speed. It is amazing how a bright red monkey can become invisible against a background of tawny grass. Unlike forest monkeys, who constantly chirp to each other while moving through the trees, patas rarely call while moving and foraging. They frequently interrupt their foraging or progressions to stand bipedally

and scan the environment for any sign of danger (Figure 3). The higher the vantage point, the better the view, so patas scan from fenceposts, the tops of trees, and even from telephone lines.

Different kinds of predators elicit different responses. Big cats such as leopards cause patas to climb high in the trees and to call loudly while looking toward the predator, whereas cape hunting

FIGURE 3   Patas monkeys bipedal scan on the ground at the Mutara study site (top). Patas monkeys bipedal scan from a fence at Mutara (bottom). (Photos by J. Chism and D. K. Olson)

dogs or domestic dogs with or without their humans cause patas to flee rapidly but silently on the ground (Chism and Rowell 1988). Patas can run very fast on their long legs to escape predators, possibly as fast as 55 km per hour (Hall 1965). Even so, they are no match for cheetahs, which can run 110 km per hour in a final sprint. In general the patas' strategy seems to be to attract as little attention to themselves as possible, to see predators long before the predators see them, and when possible to get rapidly out of the way.

Patas males, females, and immatures are all active in looking for and giving alarm calls to predators (Chism and Rowell 1988). This equal opportunity predator detection system contrasts with that proposed by Hall based on his observations of patas in Uganda (Hall 1965). Although Hall suggested that patas males might lead predators away from their groups by running off conspicuously while females and young hid in the grass, this wasn't what the patas actually did. Instead, when a predator approached the group, it was every patas for itself, with even infants as young as 6 months mostly responsible for getting themselves to safety.

Although patas are often characterized as being a grassland species, the Mutara patas groups relied heavily on trees for food, sleeping sites, and protection from predators (Figure 4). Analysis of their patterns of habitat use showed a preference for woodland edges that provided access to fruits, seeds, flowers, gum, and new leaves of woodland trees and shrubs. Using edges also allowed simultaneous exploitation of the more seasonally variable resources of the grassland, such as insects and the herbs that come up after the rains (Chism and Rowell 1988). Although abundant, most trees in this habitat are relatively short (approx. 4–5 m), and the crowns often do not form a continuous canopy. Woodland of this type does not provide many trees suitable for a whole group to sleep in together at night, so patas have adopted the rather unusual pattern of sleeping separately and spread over a wide area, each monkey (or mother-infant pair) in its own tree (Chism and Rowell 1988).

Patas differ in their diet, social organization, and antipredator strategies both from savanna baboons and from the more closely related vervets with

FIGURE 4   A patas monkey sits in a tree in acacia woodlands at the Mutara field study site. (Photo by J. Chism)

which they share the savanna habitat. At Mutara, vervets had small home ranges based in the more heavily wooded areas along river courses. They sometimes ventured out to feed in more open areas but always retreated at night into the taller trees near the river in which the entire vervet group could sleep together (Chism and Rowell 1988). Vervets also differ from patas in having a permanent multimale group structure and a more highly developed system of female dominance relations based on matrilines such as those common among baboons and macaques (Fedigan and Fedigan 1988). Thus, these three species occupy distinctly different niches, or ways of life, in the savanna habitats they share.

Patas social organization, like that of most well-studied *Cercopithecus* species, is much more variable than earlier researchers suspected (e.g., Cords 1987, Rowell 1988). This variable social structure is part of the species' response to a highly seasonal environment and to food and water resources that show both annual seasonality and dramatic fluctuations from year to year (Chism et al. 1984). Patas social organization and reproductive strategy appear to facilitate the most rapid reproduction possible for an anthropoid primate in this often harsh and unpredictable environment. Rapid reproduction allows a patas group to increase its numbers to recover quickly from high mortality in poor years.

The ability to shift from a one-male to a multimale mating system allows patas flexibility in the face of the rapid and dramatic changes in numbers of breeding females due to differences in survivorship (Chism and Rogers 1997). When female survivorship and numbers of reproductive females in patas groups are high, many males enter groups and mate. Females facilitate male influxes by soliciting copulation with males in all-male groups, in other female-based groups, or with solitary males.

Why do females do this? As the number of females in a group increases, the opportunities for females to mate near the middle of the conception period are reduced (Chism and Rogers 1997). Observations at Mutara in the drought year of 1980 suggested that females who give birth at either end of the birth period experience higher infant mortality and may themselves be more likely to die (Chism et al. 1984). Having several males to mate with may help females conceive as close to the middle of the breeding season as possible. When numbers of females are relatively small, multimale influxes are less likely because females in the group may have sufficient opportunity to mate with the sole resident male (Chism and Rogers 1997).

CONCLUSION

Since modern studies of nonhuman primates began, there have been many shifts in the paradigms used to explain their behavior. The research questions of primatologists, like those of all scientists, have been influenced by the prevailing social climate as well as by the current dominant paradigm in biology. Thus, emphasis shifted from the descriptions of species-specific social organization of the 1960s to the fitness of individuals in the 1970s and 1980s, influenced by sociobiologists such as W. D. Hamilton, Robert Trivers, and E. O. Wilson

(Gilmore 1981). Haraway (1978) suggested that the presence of many women in primatology and the rise of feminist theory also influenced questions researchers addressed and their views of primate social organization.

Both social organization and individual fitness would seem best examined in wild primates, but studies of captive animals also make important contributions to our understanding of group and individual social dynamics. Captive settings allow study of the subtle mechanisms involved in maintenance of social structure. Examples include Rowell's work on the role of monitoring and adjustment in patas social interactions (Rowell and Olson 1983) and Loy's long-term studies of patas dominance relations (Loy et al. 1993). Research on captive rhesus macaques (Stern and Smith 1984), with the precision it allowed in visibility and knowledge of genetic relationships, provided early definitive evidence that the males observed to copulate with particular females often were not the genetic fathers of the offspring of these females. This observation substantially altered the way field researchers approached discussions of male reproductive success. Whereas previously researchers had assumed a positive relationship existed between how many times a male was seen mating and the number of offspring he fathered, now field-workers use new, noninvasive, and very sensitive molecular genetic techniques to determine actual paternity of offspring in wild primate groups (e.g., Ohsawa, Inoue, and Takenaka 1993).

A combination of short- and long-term field studies and observations of captive groups has so far helped decode patas social organization. Ongoing studies of patas populations in East and West Africa will no doubt demonstrate additional regional as well as within-population differences in the social and ecological adaptations of patas monkeys. New studies will also continue to reflect the influence of new paradigms that may help future researchers understand aspects of patas behavior that puzzle the current generation of primatologists.

10

Colobine Diet and Social Organization

R. Craig Kirkpatrick

Thesis, antithesis, synthesis: this is the way science progresses.

—E. H. Haeckel, 1834–1919

Colobines seem designed to eat leaves. Sharp molars shear leaves, enlarged salivary glands produce chemicals that help degrade them, and the foreguts of colobine stomachs contain symbiotic microbes that break down leaf fibers (Bauchop and Martucci 1968; Kay and Davies 1994). The nutrients in leaves then are absorbed in the main stomach and in the caecum and large intestine. The morphological features that aid leaf eating are adaptations that unify and help to define the subfamily Colobinae. Colobine morphology also leads to a behavioral adaptation: as a whole, colobines eat more leaves than the other Cercopithecoidae subfamily, the cercopithecines, which includes macaques and baboons.

Diets that emphasize leaves can lead to certain types of social organization. Leaves are more abundant than flowers and fruits, so there is less direct competition for leaves. This low level of direct competition means that most colobines have weak dominance hierarchies, if such hierarchies exist at all. Further, a small area can contain enough food for several animals. Animals that eat lots of leaves often have smaller home ranges and smaller group sizes than animals that eat less foliage (Clutton-Brock and Harvey 1977a). Two common forms of primate social organization are the one-male unit (OMU) and the multimale group. OMUs consist of one male, several females, and associated immatures, usually the females' offspring. OMUs typically are smaller than multimale groups,

which commonly have two or more males, many females, and many immatures. Leaf eating may be one reason that the typical breeding group for colobines is the smaller of the two, the OMU.

Notwithstanding their well-deserved reputation as leaf eaters, colobines have diverse diets. Some colobines eat over 75% leaves. Other colobines, however, eat substantially less foliage, and the major part of their diet comes from seeds and fruits. The diet of the red leaf monkey, Presbytis rubicunda, *for example, is made up of only 37% leaves, with seeds and fruits at 49%. In the black colobus,* Colobus satanas, *seeds and fruits provide over half the diet. Further, leaves of different plant species or leaves at different stages of growth often differ in nutritional quality, and young leaves usually are easier to digest than mature leaves (Waterman and Kool 1994).*

Over the past four decades, long-term field studies (defined here as studies covering at least six months) have been conducted on twenty-four of the twenty-eight species of colobines. Table 1 on pages 99–105 chronicles the results of these studies. As knowledge of colobine ecology has grown, early ideas about colobine feeding and its influence on social behavior have changed. Inference from morphology and the results of early studies led to a monolithic view of colobines as "leaf eaters." Subsequent studies have broadened our understanding of colobine feeding adaptations, of the diversity of colobine social systems, and of the complex role food plays in the development of those social systems.

This essay reviews colobine ecology in historical perspective. The way in which ideas have changed about colobine food choice and its influence on social behavior is a good example of the way science works. Initial studies provided a framework for discussion. The incorporation of subsequent studies required modification of that framework. The first section of this essay reviews studies published in the seventeen years between 1960 and 1977. The year 1977 was marked by the publication of the seminal volume Primate Ecology *(Clutton-Brock 1977) and by Clutton-Brock and Harvey's (1977a) extensive review of correlates to primate socioecology. At that time, all quantification of colobine feeding was on populations that had leaves as the major part of their diet. The second section covers the subsequent seventeen years, 1978 to 1994. During this period, the diversity of colobine food choice was documented; the landmark book* Colobine Monkeys *(Davies and Oates 1994) reviewed much of this new information. The remaining sections of this essay look at continuing challenges to colobine research, particularly the ongoing attempt to integrate feeding ecology and social organization.*

THESIS: COLOBINES AS LEAF EATERS (1960–1977)

The first long-term studies of colobines in the wild were on the hanuman langur, *Presbytis entellus,* the guereza, *Colobus guereza* (also known as the black and white colobus) and the red colobus, *Colobus badius.* Starting with Dolhinow's (1972b) study in 1959 and 1960, the hanuman langur came to be the best-documented colobine. Dolhinow found that hanuman langurs at Orcha had weak dominance hierarchies and were organized in multimale units. Although their home ranges partially overlapped, fighting between groups was never observed. Sugiyama (1964) found a very different situation at Dharwar. There, one-male units were common, with about two-thirds of the males that were in bisexual groups being in OMUs and one-third in multimale groups. Males at Dharwar were quite aggressive with one another. Subsequent studies added to the complexity: some locations mainly had multimale groups, and other locations mainly had OMUs (see Table 1). However, the causes of these differences were unclear.

Most early studies of hanuman langurs focused on social organization and behavior. Few of these studies quantified diet. An important exception was in a two-year study by a team of scientists in Sri Lanka (Eisenberg et al. 1972; Hladik 1977). These researchers compared the social organization and diet of two species at Polonnaruwa: the hanuman langur and the purple-faced langur, *Presbytis senex.* The diets of both species were strongly seasonal, with shifts between reproductive parts (fruits and flowers) and vegetative parts (leaves). Rare food items, such as young leaves and fruits, were preferred, and mature leaves were eaten only when other foods were not available. Hanuman langurs fed on fewer leaves (48% of diet) and lived in large multimale units. Purple-faced langurs had a diet with more leaves (60%), had smaller home ranges, and lived in OMUs.

Strong data sets were developed during this period for guereza and red colobus as well. Guereza at Kibale were highly folivorous and had a monotonous diet (Struhsaker and Oates 1975; Oates 1977a). Three tree species provided about 70% of the diet, which was quite similar to the low diet diversity of purple-faced langurs (Hladik 1977). Guereza lived primarily in OMUs, and group size appeared to be based on food availability. The number of food trees in a group's home range predicted the number of animals in that group (Dunbar and Dunbar 1974).

In contrast to guereza, red colobus typically lived in multimale groups. Groups of red colobus at Kibale had an average of forty-four members, and the home ranges of these groups overlapped extensively (Struhsaker 1975). Although red colobus were highly folivorous (82% of diet), they ate fewer mature leaves than guereza and had greater diet diversity (Struhsaker and Oates 1975). Groups of red colobus living in marginal habitat also were often smaller than groups living in rain forest habitat; these smaller groups often were OMUs. This led Struhsaker (1975) to suggest that smaller groups came about due to lower food availability in poor quality habitat.

Other studies during this period also set initial ideas about colobines. Bernstein (1968) found tremendous OMUs averaging thirty-two individuals in the silvered leaf monkey, *Presbytis cristata*. Poirier (1967, 1970) found that about half the males in the Nilgiri langur, *Presbytis johnii*, lived in OMUs, whereas the other half lived in multimale units. Diet appeared folivorous, and the size of groups appeared to be related to the density of food trees within a group's range, although Poirier did not actually quantify diet. Curtin (1976), working at Kuala Lompat, found the dusky leaf monkey, *Presbytis obscura*, was more folivorous than the banded leaf monkey, *Presbytis melalophos*. Curtin also found that dusky leaf monkeys were in OMUs, whereas banded leaf monkeys lived in multimale groups.

These studies gave a first good look at colobines. Colobines generally were folivorous, and OMUs seemed the main type of social organization. The multimale units of some populations of hanuman langur, red colobus, and banded leaf monkey were seen as anomalous. Comparative information for purple-faced langurs with hanuman langurs and for guereza with red colobus gave particularly strong support to the hypothesis that leaf eating led to smaller groups. Purple-faced langurs ate more leaves than hanuman langurs and had a less diverse diet, smaller ranges, and smaller groups. The same was true for guereza and red colobus: guereza ate more mature leaves and had a less diverse diet, smaller ranges, and smaller groups. The abundance and distribution of foods appeared to be strong determinants of colobine social organization (Clutton-Brock and Harvey 1977b).

ANTITHESIS: COLOBINES ARE SEED EATERS (1978–1994)

Initial studies provided a framework for the continued investigation of colobine ecology. By 1977, however, there was little information from East and Southeast Asia, where most colobines lived. Many early studies—particularly those on hanuman langurs—were on populations that interacted with humans, and wild populations might differ in behavior. Primatologists also had become aware of sampling biases and the need to standardize data collection. There was a concerted effort to better understand colobine food choice by quantifying the nutrition and availability of foods.

In this period the variability of colobine food choice became clearer (see Table 1). Seeds and fruits were found to be the major food of the banded leaf monkey, the red leaf monkey, the black colobus, and the Angolan colobus, *Colobus angolensis*. Still, leaves were found to contribute over 50% of the diet in numerous other colobines, such as the Nilgiri langur, the capped langur, *Presbytis pileata*, the olive colobus, *Colobus verus*, and the ursine colobus, *Colobus polykomos*.

More striking than the amount of seeds or leaves in particular diets was the finding that, almost universally, colobine diets were extremely seasonal. In both the red leaf monkey and the banded leaf monkey, for example, seeds and fruits provided almost 90% of the diet in some months whereas in other months they provided less than 30% (Davies, Bennett, and Waterman 1988). Capped langurs at Madhupur shifted seasonally between mature leaves, young leaves, and seeds and fruits, as did ursine colobus at Tiwai (Stanford 1991a; Dasilva 1994). Young leaves and unripe seeds were preferred to mature leaves, but young leaves and seeds were only available in certain seasons.

A major achievement of this period was in the search for correlates to colobine food choice. Limited nutritional analysis of foods in early studies suggested that high levels of protein might be one reason certain foods were preferred, and that high levels of tannins (which inhibit the digestion of protein) might be one reason certain foods were avoided (Struhsaker 1975; Oates, Swain, and Zantovska 1977). Subsequent studies looked at a wider range of nutritional components and at a wider variety of plants in the habitat. Researchers found that young leaves had more protein and less indigestible fiber than mature leaves and other food items. The ratio of protein to fiber was a significant factor in food choice (Davies et al. 1988; Mitchell 1994). High levels of tannins and other plant poisons made food items undesirable (McKey et al. 1981; Maisels, Gautier-Hion, and Gautier 1994), although the influence of tannins and other poisons was less consistent than the influence of protein-fiber ratios. In addition, colobines were very selective in their food choices: often, the most abundant tree species did not provide foods, whereas rare species provided a major portion of the diet (Oates, Waterman, and Choo 1980; Davies et al. 1988).

This new information led to revision of the idea that colobines were best categorized as leaf eaters with an abundant food supply. Rather, colobines were now seen as highly selective feeders in an inhospitable environment (Waterman and Kool 1994). For several species, there was strong evidence that seeds were preferred foods. Further, colobines typically ate young leaves before mature leaves, and young leaves were available only in certain seasons. The digestive morphology that earlier had been seen as aiding the digestion of leaves was subsequently seen, instead, to aid the digestion of seeds and unripe fruits (Chivers and Hladik 1980; Chivers 1994). Leaves, it was argued, were only a "fall-back" for those seasons in which seeds were unavailable (Davies 1991; Stanford 1991b).

Between 1978 and 1994, the variability of colobine social organization also became clearer. Angolan colobus, for example, lived in multimale groups that at times came together in aggregations (Moreno-Black and Bent 1982). OMUs formed the basic unit of association for many species, but in some of these species OMUs had complete range overlap and at times traveled together (capped langurs: Stanford 1991b; proboscis monkey, *Nasalis larvatus:* Bennett and Sebastian 1988). This reached an extreme in the Guizhou snub-nosed monkey, *Rhinopithecus brelichi,* in which OMUs were found in bands with hundreds of individuals (Bleish et al. 1993).

As variability in colobine feeding and social organization became clear, the way in which feeding ecology related to social organization became cloudy. Diets were extremely seasonal, and low diet diversity in certain seasons correlated with smaller ranges (e.g., black colobus: McKey and Waterman 1982). This was similar to the way in which low diet diversity correlated with smaller ranges in guereza (when compared with red colobus) and purple-faced langurs (when compared with hanuman langurs). The relationship was complex, how-

ever. In red leaf monkeys, for example, a smaller range was used when low diet diversity was the result of a diet high in young leaves, but a larger range was used when low diversity was the result of a diet high in seeds (Davies 1984). There also was some indication that seasonal diets resulted in seasonal changes in social structure. When red leaf monkeys fed on small patches of young leaves, OMUs fragmented into sub-groups—smaller food patches led to smaller social groups.

Generally, however, social organization in colobines did not change seasonally, even though the availability and distribution of food changed seasonally. Further, differences in biomass of the same species between sites, generally assumed to indicate differences in total food availability (Denham 1971), did not affect social organization. A trio of studies on proboscis monkeys, for example, found biomass differed by an order of magnitude among sites, yet social organization remained constant (Bennett and Sebastian 1988; Yeager 1989, 1991; Boonratana 1994). In a counterexample, red colobus at Kibale and Tana River had similar biomass, yet different social systems (Marsh 1979).

SYNTHESIS: DIVERSE DIETS AND DIVERSE SOCIAL SYSTEMS

Studies since 1994 continue to show the complexity of colobine diets and social systems. Although nutrition influences colobine food choice, other factors, such as food availability, can be equally important (Kirkpatrick 1996; Mowry, Decker, and Shure 1996). Species with similar diets also can have quite different social systems, as found for guereza and Angolan colobus at Basakwe (Bocian 1997).

What continues to emerge is a picture of colobines, as a whole, having diverse diets that change substantially between seasons. Early studies were on populations that tended to feed on more leaves than did populations later studied (a mean of 59% for studies of 1977 and before [n = 10], a mean of 52% for studies of 1978 and after [n = 37], see Table 1). Seeds and fruits are more important to colobines than originally thought, and colobine social organization is more variable than originally thought.

But the pendulum may have swung too far. Just as the monolithic idea of colobines as "leaf eaters" was incomplete, so too is the revisionist idea that colobines are "seed eaters." Considering the subfamily as a whole, the mean level of leaves in the diet is 52%, even if two-thirds of this leaf diet is from young leaves (Table 1, Figure 1). It also is unclear whether seeds or fruits are more important to colobine diets: both contribute about 15%. All told, the colobine feeding adaptation is unlikely to have evolved for a specific plant part. It allows colobines access to nonstructural carbohydrates in both leaves and seeds, and in other food types as well (e.g., lichens and nonlignified bark; reviewed in Kirkpatrick, in press). To argue for the primacy of one food type misses a fundamental point: the colobine feeding adaptation allows these species to have tremendously diverse diets, both within and between species.

As for social organization, the original idea that OMUs typified the subfamily disregarded variability in the search for a modal category. Clearly, OMUs are fundamental to colobine social organization. There is much variation on this basic theme, however. Some OMUs are stable in membership over many years (e.g., hanuman langurs at Kanha: Newton 1994), whereas other OMUs have substantial change within one year (e.g., proboscis monkeys at Samunsam: Rajanathan and Bennett 1990). Further, in some species OMUs come together in large aggregations, whereas in other species they do not.

Colobine feeding ecology explains some of the variation in colobine social systems. Early findings remain robust on higher folivory and smaller groups in hanuman langurs and purple-faced leaf monkeys at Polonnaruwa and guereza and red colobus at Kibale. The food resources of red colobus are spatially and temporally clumped compared to those of guereza, and this may lead to larger groups (Oates 1994). Further, hanuman langurs in the temperate Himalayas (where food resources are poor) form larger, less-stable groups than lowland hanuman langurs (Bishop 1979). This is similar to the large groups and fission-fusion

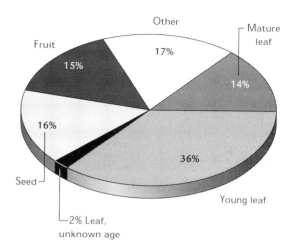

FIGURE 1   The Colobine Diet. Leaf products, as a whole, contribute 52% of the colobine diet, and so the title "leaf eaters" is appropriate to this group. (This figure uses the mean of twenty-four species of colobines, with each species given equal weight in the calculation of summation numbers.)

found in temperate-living snub-nosed monkeys (Kirkpatrick, in press). Adjustment of group size to food patch size also is seen in seasonal changes in range use by red leaf monkeys (Davies 1984).

Feeding ecology has limits in explaining social organization, however. Proboscis monkeys do not appear to change social organization in response to food availability, for example, and guereza and Angolan colobus at Basakwe have different social organizations but similar diets. Factors in addition to feeding ecology influence grouping patterns and social systems. In some cases, changes in social organization may be tied more closely to reproductive cycles than to food cycles (e.g., Himalayan hanuman langur: Bishop 1975; Boggess 1976). Predation on red colobus, which takes 20–40% annually of some populations, may cause red colobus to take refuge in larger groups (Busse 1977; Wrangham and van Zinnicq Bergmann Riss 1990). Phylogeny (i.e., a species' evolutionary history) also can play a role in a species' social system (Rendall and DiFiore 1995).

CONCLUSION

The history of knowledge about colobine ecology is a good example of how science works. Initial studies provided ideas about colobines. The cross-species comparisons of hanuman langurs with purple-faced langurs and of red colobus with guereza, in particular, stimulated hypotheses of how social organization was dependent on feeding ecology. As new data were collected, hypotheses had to be revised. For many colobines, we have only one long-term study on which to base conclusions about that species' behavior. Studies of hanuman langurs and of red colobus—two of the most-studied colobines—show that behavior varies widely among populations of the same species. As more data have accumulated, ideas about colobines have had to change.

Field studies of colobine ecology have provided strong data to test predictions developed from general ecological theory. Studies of colobine food nutrition, for example, provided strong support for Milton's (1979) hypothesis that protein-fiber ratios determined food choice in all small mammals. Models of optimal foraging predicted that a less diverse diet should decrease range size (see Pyke, Pullinam, and Charnov 1977); this prediction held for numerous colobines. Optimal foraging also predicted that larger groups should increase daily travel distances, but larger groups of colobines do not travel farther than smaller groups, allowing investigation of why this prediction was not upheld and revision of the model (e.g., Isbell 1991). Studies of colobine ecology have shown where theory must be modified to more closely resemble the real world.

Colobines are, primarily, leaf eating primates. They show a strong preference for young leaves and seeds, however, and their digestive morphology allows them to weather strong seasonal variation in diet. Variability in diet also helps to explain variability in colobine social systems. Contrary to early hypotheses, however, social organization does not show strict correspondence to ecological variables; direct causal links between the environment and social organization remain unclear. Teasing apart the influences of feeding ecology and other factors on social organization remains an exciting challenge for the next generation of field biologists who study the leaf eating monkeys.

TABLE 1 Colobine Diet and Social Organization

Long-term studies (≥ 6 months) of colobine feeding and social organization. Colobines are leaf eaters and the one-male unit (OMU) is their primary form of social organization. There is much variation on these basic themes, however. In this table, "young leaves" includes leaf buds and "primary social org." is the type of group in which the majority of reproductively-active males live. Studies published from 1960 to 1977 are listed in bold type. Summation numbers are calculated as means (mode for social organization) of (1) studies published from 1960 to 1977, (2) studies after 1977, and (3) the colobine subfamily as a whole. The summation for colobines as a whole is weighted by species (that is, species means are used to calculate these numbers). Not all studies distinguish between mature and young leaves and between seeds and fruits. The ratio of mature to young leaves and of seeds to fruits is calculated for those studies making the distinction, and this ratio is used, as necessary, to apportion subfamily numbers for leaves and seeds/fruits. The phylogeny in this table follows Fleagle (1988), modified by the addition of *Rhinopithecus bieti*.

Species and Site	Diet (percentages)						Primary Social Org.	Mean No. Animals per Group	Reference
	All Leaves	Mature Leaves	Young Leaves	All Seeds/ Fruits	Seeds	Fruits			
African colobines									
Colobus angolensis (Angolan colobus)									
Diani Beach (Kenya)	**27**	**(6)**	**(21)**	**67**	**(50)**	**(17)**	**MM**	**8**	Moreno-Black and Maples 1977
Botsima (Salonga, Zaire)	51	(>2)	(>26)	27	(22)	(5)	(n. r.)	~5	Maisels et al. 1994
Basakwe (Ituri Forest, Zaire)							MM	14	Bocian 1997
(species mean)	39	(4)	(24)	47	(36)	(11)	MM	9	
Colobus [Piliocolobus] badius (red colobus)									
Gombe (Tanzania)	**79**	**(44)**	**(35)**	**11**			**MM**	**82**	Clutton-Brock 1975
Kanyawara (Kibale Forest, Uganda)	**82**	**(23)**	**(59)**	**6**			**MM**	**44**	Struhsaker 1975
Abuko (Gambia)							**MM?**	**33**	Gunderson 1977
Fathala (Senegal)	47	(5)	(42)	36	(18)		MM	25	Gatinot 1978
Mchelelo (Tana River, Kenya)	65	(12)	(52)	25	(1)	(24)		18	Marsh 1979, 1981
Tai (Cote d'Ivoire)	83			10			MM		Galat and Galat-Luong 1985
Abuko (Gambia)	47	(12)	(35)	42	(3)	(39)	MM	26	Starin 1991
Jozani (Zanzibar)	65	(5)	(55)	29			MM		Mturi 1993
Botsima (Salonga, Zaire)	61	(6)	(54)	38	(31)	(7)	MM	> 60	Maisels et al. 1994
(species mean)	66	(15)	(47)	25	(13)	(23)	MM	41	

(continued)

TABLE 1 Colobine Diet and Social Organization continued

Species and Site	All Leaves	Mature Leaves	Young Leaves	All Seeds/Fruits	Seeds	Fruits	Primary Social Org.	Mean No. Animals per Group	Reference
Colobus guereza (guereza, or black and white colobus)									
Budongo Forest (Uganda)	47			53			**OMU**	**8**	Marler 1969
Bole Valley (Ethiopia)	77	(12)	(58)	14	(0)	(14)	**OMU**	**7**	Dunbar and Dunbar 1974
Kanyawara (Kibale, Uganda)							**OMU**	**10**	Oates 1977a, 1977b
Budongo Forest (Uganda)							OMU	7	Suzuki 1979
Basakwe (Ituri Forest, Zaire)	58	(>4)	(>30)	25	(22)	(3)	OMU/MM	8	Bocian 1997
(species mean)	61	(8)	(44)	31	(11)	(9)	OMU	8	
Colobus polykomos (ursine colobus)									
Tai (Cote d'Ivoire)	53			32					Galat and Galat-Luong 1985
Bai (Ghana)							MM	~15	
Tiwai (Sierra Leone)	56	(26)	(30)	35	(32)	(3)	MM	~10	Dasilva 1994
(species mean)	55	(26)	(44)	34	(32)	(3)	MM	13	
Colobus satanas (black colobus)									
Lombe (Douala-Edea, Cameroon)	43	(20)	(21)	53			MM	15	McKey et al. 1981
de Brazza Hills (Lope, Gabon)	26	(3)	(23)	60					Harrison 1986
(species mean)	35	(12)	(22)	57			MM	15	
Colobus [*Procolobus*] *verus* (olive colobus)									
Tai (Cote d'Ivoire)	94			6					Galat and Galat-Luong 1985
Tiwai (Sierra Leone)	74	(11)	(59)	19	(14)	(2)	MM	~8	Oates 1988
(species mean)	84	(11)	(59)	13	(14)	(2)	MM	8	

Diet (percentages)

Species and Site	All Leaves	Mature Leaves	Young Leaves	All Seeds/ Fruits	Seeds	Fruits	Primary Social Org.	Mean No. Animals per Group	Reference
Asian colobines									
Nasalis larvatus (proboscis monkey)									
Samunsam (Sarawak, Malaysia)	41	(3)	(38)	58	(15)	(35)	OMU	9	Bennett and Sebastian 1988
Tanjung Puting (Kalimantan, Indonesia)	52	(3)	(41)	40	(21)	(1)	OMU	13	Yeager 1989
Kinabatangan (Sabah, Malaysia)	61	(0)	(61)	21	(7)	(14)	OMU	17	Boonratana 1994
(species mean)	51	(2)	(47)	40	(14)	(17)	OMU	13	
Presbytis aygula (Java leaf monkey, ~*comata*)									
Kamojang (Java, Indonesia)	65	(6)	(59)	14	(1)	(13)	OMU	8	Ruhiyat 1983
Presbytis hosei (white-fronted leaf monkey, ~*frontata*)									
Kutai (Kalimantan, Indonesia)	65		(44)	27			OMU	8	Rodman 1978
Lipad (Sabah, Malaysia)	69	(4)	(44)	30	(19)	(11)	OMU	8	Mitchell 1994
(species mean)	67	(4)	(44)	29	(19)	(11)	OMU	8	
Presbytis melalophus (banded leaf monkey, ~*femoralis*)									
Kuala Selangor (peninsular Malaysia)	**35**	**(11)**	**(24)**	**56**	**(8)**	**(48)**	**OMU**	**15**	Bernstein 1967, 1968
Kuala Lompat (peninsular Malaysia)							**MM**	**17**	Curtin 1976, 1980
Kuala Lompat (peninsular Malaysia)	38			50			(n. r.)	15	MacKinnon and MacKinnon 1978
Kuala Lompat (peninsular Malaysia)	36	(8)	(28)	49	(25)	(10)	OMU	15	Bennett 1983; Davies et al. 1988
(species mean)	36	(10)	(26)	52	(17)	(29)	OMU	16	

(continued)

TABLE 1 Colobine Diet and Social Organization *continued*

Species and Site	Diet (percentages)						Primary Social Org.	Mean No. Animals per Group	Reference
	All Leaves	Mature Leaves	Young Leaves	All Seeds/ Fruits	Seeds	Fruits			
Presbytis potenziani (Mentawai leaf monkey)									
Sirimuri (Siberut Islands, Indonesia)							OMU[3]	4	Tilson and Tenaza 1976
Betumonga (Pagai Islands, Indonesia)	55			32			OMU[3]	3	Fuentes 1994
(species mean)	55			32			OMU	4	
Presbytis rubicunda (red leaf monkey)									Davies et al. 1988; Davies 1991 Supriatna, Manullang, and Soekara 1986
Sepilok (Sabah, Malaysia)	37	(1)	(36)	49	(30)	(19)	OMU	6	
Tanjung Puting (Kalimantan, Indonesia)	36			52			OMU	6	
(species mean)	37	(1)	(36)	51	(11)	(9)	OMU	6	
Presbytis thomasi (Thomas's leaf monkey)									Gurmaya 1986 Assink and van Dijk 1990 Unger 1992[1] [2]
Bohorok (Sumatra, Indonesia)	36			53			OMU	8	
Ketambe (Sumatra, Indonesia)							OMU	9	
Ketambe (Sumatra, Indonesia)	51	(17)	(34)	26			OMU	8	
Ketambe (Sumatra, Indonesia)	44	(13)	(31)	36			OMU	8	
(species mean)	44	(15)	(33)	38			OMU	8	
Presbytis [Trachypithecus] cristata (silvered leaf monkey)									Bernstein 1968
Kuala Selangor (peninsular Malaysia)							OMU	32	
Pangandaran (Java, Indonesia)	46	(1)	(45)	27	(7)		OMU	14	Kool 1993[4]
(species mean)	46	(1)	(45)	27	(7)	(9)	OMU	23	
Presbytis [Trachypithecus] francoisi (Francois's leaf monkey) —no long-term studies									

Diet (percentages)

Species and Site	All Leaves	Mature Leaves	Young Leaves	All Seeds/ Fruits	Seeds	Fruits	Primary Social Org.	Mean No. Animals per Group	Reference
Presbytis [Trachypithecus] geei (golden leaf monkey) —no long-term studies									
Presbytis [Trachypithecus] obscura (dusky leaf monkey)									
Kuala Selangor (peninsular Malaysia)							OMU	13	Bernstein 1967, 1968
Kuala Lompat (peninsular Malaysia)	58	(22)	(36)	35	(3)	(32)	MM	17	Curtin 1976, 1980
(species mean)	58	(8)	(44)	35	(11)	(9)	OMU/MM	11	
Presbytis [Trachypithecus] phayrei (Phayre's leaf monkey) —no long-term studies									
Presbytis [Trachypithecus] pileata (capped leaf monkey)									
Madhupur (Bangladesh)	61	(42)	(11)	30	(9)	(24)	OMU/MM	6	Islam and Husain 1982
Madhupur (Bangladesh)	67	(42)	(11)	34	(9)	(24)	OMU	8	Stanford 1991a, 1991b
(species mean)	64	(42)	(11)	32	(9)	(24)	OMU	7	
Presbytis [Semnopithecus] entellus (hanuman langur)									
Orcha (Madhya Pradesh, India)							MM	18	Dolhinow 1972b
Dharwar (Mysore, India)	>53			>6			OMU	15	Sugiyama 1964; Yoshiba 1967 (tab. 5)
Polonnaruwa and Bundala (Sri Lanka)							MM	26	Ripley 1965
Polonnaruwa and Wilpattu (Sri Lanka)							MM	24	Muckenhirn 1972
Melemchi (Himalayan Nepal)							MM	32	Bishop 1975
Junbesi (Solu, Himalayan Nepal)	>45	(>31)	(>14)	>1			OMU/MM	~10	Curtin 1975; Boggess 1976

(continued)

TABLE 1 Colobine Diet and Social Organization *continued*

Species and Site	Diet (percentages)						Primary Social Org.	Mean No. Animals per Group	Reference
	All Leaves	Mature Leaves	Young Leaves	All Seeds/ Fruits	Seeds	Fruits			
Presbytis [Semnopithecus] entellus (hanuman langur)									
Polonnaruwa (Sri Lanka)	48	(21)	(27)	45			**OMU**	**21**	Hladik 1977
Abu (Rajasthan, India)							**MM**	46	Hrdy 1977b
Rajaji (Uttar Pradesh)							**OMU**	~38	Laws and Vonder Haar Laws 1984
Jodhpur (Rajashtan, India)	52	(35)	(14)			(24)	**OMU**	20	Sommer and Rajpurohit 1989
Kanha (Madhya Pradesh, India)				24		(24)	MM	23	Newton 1992
(species mean)	50	(29)	(18)	19					
Presbytis [Semnopithecus] johnii (Nilgiri leaf monkey)									
Ootacamund (Madras, India)							**OMU/MM**	**9**	Poirier 1967, 1970
Nilgiri Hills (Mysore, India)							**OMU**	**9**	Poirier 1967
Kakachi (Tamal Nadu, India)	58	(27)	(25)	25			OMU	8	Oates et al. 1980
Mundanthurai							OMU	9	Hohmann 1989
(species mean)	58	(27)	(25)	25					
Presbytis [Semnopithecus] senex (purple-faced leaf monkey, = *vetulus*)									
Polonnaruwa (Sri Lanka)	58	(31)	(27)	27			**OMU**		Rudran in Muckenhirm 1972; Rudran 1973
Polonnaruwa (Sri Lanka)	60	(40)	(20)	28					Hladik 1977
(species mean)	59	(36)	(24)	28					
Pygathrix nemaeus (douc langur) —no long-term studies									
Rhinopithecus avunculus (Tonkin snub-nosed monkey)									
Ta Ke (Tuyen Qiang, Vietnam)	38	(0)	(38)	62			OMU		Boonratana and Le 1994
Rhinopithecus bieti (Yunnan snub-nosed monkey)									
Wuyapiya (Yunnan, China)	>6		0	0			OMU		Kirkpatrick 1996

Diet (percentages)

Species and Site	All Leaves	Mature Leaves	Young Leaves	All Seeds/ Fruits	Seeds	Fruits	Primary Social Org.	Mean No. Animals per Group	Reference
Rhinopithecus brelichi (Guizhou snub-nosed monkey) Fanjingshan (Guizhou, China)	71			15			OMU	6	Bleish et al. 1993; Bleish and Xie, in press (tab. 2)
Rhinopithecus roxellana (Sichuan snub-nosed monkey) Shennongjia (Hubei, China)							OMU		Ren et al., in press
Simias concolor (simakobu) **Siberut (Mentawai Archipelago, Indonesia)**							**OMU**[3]	**~4**	Tilson 1977
Pagai (Mentawai Archipelago, Indonesia)							OMU[3]	4	Tenaza and Fuentes 1995
(species mean)							OMU	4	
Mean, studies 1960 to 1977 (unweighted)	59	(26)	(33)	23	(3)	(20)			
Mean, studies 1978 to 1997 (unweighted)	52	(10)	(37)	35	(19)	(16)			
Colobines (weighted)	52	(14)	(36)	31	(16)	(15)	OMU	12	

[1] Mean of scan and focal estimates
[2] Data for females only
[3] These OMUs with only one female (i.e., monogamous)
[4] Data taken from group studied eight months, not from group studied five months

The New World Monkeys

The neotropical or New World monkeys are found in southern Mexico and Central and South America. They are characterized as a group by having a third premolar and round, outward-facing nostrils that are placed farther apart than their Old World counterparts. The New World monkeys weigh between .1 kg and 10 kg. They are divided into two families, the smaller Callitrichidae and the Cebidae.

The Callitrichidae includes marmosets, tamarins, and Goeldi's monkey. They are highly derived and specialized monkeys. All weigh under 1 kg and have claws on all but their big toe. The marmosets and tamarins have only two molars, one less than all other anthropoid nonhuman primates. They typically give birth to twin offspring, and care of those offspring is shared by the entire group. These are all rare traits in anthropoids.

The eleven species of marmosets (*Callithrix* and *Cebuella*) are found primarily in Brazil and are the smallest of the callitrichids. They vary in color, and many are distinguished by tufts of hair around their ears. They are distinguished from tamarins by having enlarged incisors, which they use for making holes in trees to feed on gums and saps. The marmosets form social groups that may include multiple adult males and females but usually only one breeding pair. These tiny monkeys reach sexual maturity between 12 and 24 months of age. The average gestation is between 4 and 5 months, and females often give birth every 6 months. Group size typically varies from two to fifteen individuals. The marmoset diet consists of fruit, insects and small fauna, gums, and saps.

The twelve species of tamarins (genus *Saguinus*) can be found from the tip of Costa Rica through northern South America. They lack the enlarged incisors seen among the marmosets but are also very small, colorful monkeys, accented by tufts of hair on the head or face. Tamarins form smaller groups (average five individuals) that may be multimale, one-female (unusual for primates) or multimale, multifemale. The females reach sexual maturity between 15 and 24 months, giving birth every 8 months or so. The diet is the same as that of the marmosets but generally includes fewer gums and saps.

There are four species in the genus *Leontopithecus,* the critically endangered Lion tamarins, and they are all found in Brazil. They are larger than the other callitrichids. They form one-male, one-female groups or multimale, multifemale groups of three to eight individuals.

The phylogenetic placement of the one species of Goeldi's monkey (*Callimico goeldi*) is difficult. It has some features that align it with callitrichids, and others that resemble cebids. It is small, has claw-like nails, and lives in either one-male, one-female or multimale, multifemale groups with only one breeding pair, all of which are callitrichid traits. However, *Callimico* has the third molar and does not bear twins, which are cebid traits. Most researchers classify Goeldi's monkey as the callitrichid most closely related to the cebids, and molecular studies of platyrrhine phylogeny support this position. The nonbreeding adults are thought to be grown offspring or siblings of the breeding pair.

The Cebidae are larger in body size and have three molars. Unlike the marmosets and tamarins, they do not have claws or regularly give birth to twins. This group is divided into eleven genera, which can be further divided into six subfamilies collectively containing thirty-one species.

The subfamily Aotinae contains only the genus *Aotus,* commonly called the night or owl monkeys. There are two visually distinct species, one of which is found in Brazil, Peru, Bolivia, and Paraguay; the other is limited only to Brazil. This genus has the distinction of being the only nocturnal anthropoid. They are found in one-male, one-female pair-bonded family groups. They weigh .78–1.1 kg and eat primarily fruit, leaves, and insects.

The subfamily Callicebinae includes the titi monkeys of the genus *Callicebus.* There are thirteen species, most found in Brazil, Peru, and Bolivia. They weigh .8–11.4 kg and eat a diet made up of fruit, leaves, and animal prey. Males and females form one-male, one-female pair-bonds. Including their offspring, group sizes range from two to six members. The females reach sexual maturity between 2 to 3 years of age and give birth to single offspring yearly. The adult male and female often sit close together on a branch with their tails entwined.

The subfamily Cebinae includes the capuchins (*Cebus*) and the squirrel monkeys (*Saimiri*). Capuchin monkeys range from Ecuador to Honduras in Central America and throughout northern and central South America. They are divided into four species. Their multimale, multifemale groups range from eight to thirty individuals. Capuchins are very active foragers and eat a very broad diet, which includes fruit, seeds, leaves, and a variety of small animal prey. They range in weight from 1.35 kg to 4.8 kg.

Squirrel monkeys are relatively small monkeys (.6–1.25 kg) who live in multimale, multifemale social groups that contain up to fifty members. They are found in Costa Rica and Honduras, Panama, and throughout northern South America. Their diet contains a large percentage of animal prey, along with fruit and seeds. Mating and births are highly seasonal for this genus.

The saki and uakari are classified in the subfamily Pitheciinae. These monkeys have specialized stout incisors, which they use to process hard fruits and nuts. The five species of saki monkeys (*Pithecia*) are located throughout northern South America. They form one-male, one-female family groups. They range in size from .8 kg to 3 kg in size and live on a diet of fruit, seeds, and leaves.

The two species of bearded sakis (*Chiropotes*) are found in northeastern South America. These monkeys are named for the long patches of hair found around their necks, which resemble a human beard. They form multimale, multifemale groups that range in size from two to thirty members. Their diet is composed of fruit, leaves, and flowers.

The uakari is found in Brazil, Peru, and Venezuela. They live in one-male, multifemale groups or multimale, multifemale groups ranging in size from five individuals up to a hundred. The bald uakari (*Cacajao calvus*) is striking with its completely bald, bright red head and long red or white coat. They live on a diet of fruit, leaves, and small animal prey. They weigh between 2.9 kg and 4 kg.

The eight species of howler monkeys (*Alouatta*) that make up the subfamily Alouattinae are widely distributed from southern Mexico through Central America and throughout South America. They are found in either multimale, multifemale groups or one-male, multifemale groups of up to twenty-one individuals. They range in size from 3.8 kg to 10 kg, with marked sexual dimorphism. In some species the males are a different color from the females, which is called **sexual dichromotism.** The howler monkey diet includes a large proportion of leaves as well as fruit. A **prehensile** (grasping) **tail** allows these monkeys to hang off of branches and forage more extensively. These monkeys are named for their loud territorial vocalizations, which are enhanced by use of an enlarged hyoid bone that resonates the sound.

The spider, woolly spider, and woolly monkeys who make up the subgenus *Atelinae* are the largest of the New World primates, weighing up to 12 kg. Like the howler monkeys, they all have prehensile tails. This group has a slow development rate compared to other primates of its size.

The spider monkey (*Ateles*) is found from the southern tip of Mexico through Central America and throughout northern South America. They feed primarily on ripe fruit, which is rich in carbohydrates but patchily distributed. Perhaps to reduce competition for this food resource, they live in fission-fusion social communities of up to thirty-five individuals who split into small subgroups to forage. Their hands are adapted for suspensory locomotion, with long, hook-like fingers and a reduced or absent thumb.

The two species of woolly monkey (*Lagothrix*) are found in Peru and in the Amazon Basin of South America. They live in multimale, multifemale groups of up to seventy individuals. Their diet is made up of fruit, leaves, and animal prey (including some mammals). They are highly sought after by hunters for meat and as pets.

The woolly spider monkey or muriqui (*Brachyteles*) is found only in two limited areas of eastern Brazil. They have a variable social structure, being found in both fission-fusion and multimale, multifemale groups averaging twenty-six individuals. They eat more leaves than the spider monkeys do, but also eat fruit, nectar, and seeds. They range in size between 9.4 kg and 1.2 kg, with some sexual dimorphism. They are reported to be one of the least aggressive primate species.

11

The Atelines

Karen B. Strier

The Atelines are members of a subfamily of New World monkeys divided into two tribes, the Alouattini, represented by a single genus, *Alouatta,* or the howler monkeys, and the Atelini, represented by three genera: *Ateles,* or spider monkeys; *Lagothrix,* or woolly monkeys; and *Brachyteles,* or muriquis. Morphological, molecular, and behavioral data are consistent in recognizing the division between *Alouatta* and the atelines, but the precise relationships among the three ateline genera are still controversial (Schneider and Rosenberger 1996).

Howler monkeys, which earn their English common name from their loud vocalizations, have one of the most widespread distributions of all New World monkeys, with various species occurring from southern Mexico through northern Argentina. Spider monkeys, with their long, spindly arms and legs, may occur sympatrically with howler monkeys from southern Mexico through Central America and into the vast Amazonian rain forest. Woolly monkeys, aptly named for their thick furry appearance, are restricted to pockets of the Amazon where they are sometimes found sympatrically with their spider and howler monkey kin. Muriquis, named by the Tupi Indians who once shared the forests with them, have one of the most limited distributions of all, being restricted to what remains of the Atlantic forest of southeastern Brazil. Only one other ateline, the brown howler monkey (*Alouatta fusca*), occurs in the Atlantic forest alongside muriquis.

SYSTEMATICS AND CONSERVATION STATUS

Recent taxonomic classifications of the ateline primates recognize nine species of howler monkeys, six species of spider monkeys, two species of woolly monkeys, and two species of muriquis (Rylands, Mittermeier, and Luna 1995, 1997). Many of these species are poorly known, however, and the more numerous subspecies designations (forty-seven ateline subspecies) may more accurately reflect their present diversity than species per se (Rylands et al. 1995; Strier 1997a; Strier and Fonseca, in press). The contraction of forests into isolated refuges created by the Pleistocene glaciations (e.g., Kinzey 1982) along with more recent habitat destruction, which has severely disrupted the historical distributions of many atelines (and other platyrrhines), further confounds efforts to distinguish species from subspecies and populations.

Habitat destruction has also left the future of many atelines in a precarious state. Of the forty-seven recognizable subspecies of atelines, 15% are now considered to be critically endangered, 11% endangered, and 15% vulnerable to extinction. Some of these are known only from a single population (Rylands et al. 1997). Howler monkeys and muriquis, which possess morphological adaptations that permit them to rely heavily on leaves, have managed to adapt to the altered conditions that habitat disturbances like selected logging have

109

caused. Spider monkeys, in contrast, are more specialized to the fruity diets that only large tracts of undisturbed forests can provide.

ATELINE PATTERNS

Their large body size and high **biomass** (Peres 1996) make atelines prized prey for hunters in unprotected areas where they still occur. Female muriquis, at 9.45 kg, are the largest of all female New World primates, followed by female spider monkeys at 7.45–8.8 kg. Weights of female woolly monkeys, at 5.75 kg, and howler monkeys, at 4.55–6.43 kg (*Alouatta fusca* and *A. pigra,* respectively), overlap depending on species (Ford 1994).

Ateline male body weights are more variable, largely as a result of differences in the degree of sexual dimorphism resulting from variation in the level of **male-male competition** across taxa (Ford 1994). Male woolly monkeys and howler monkeys may weigh up to 12 kg (Peres 1996) and 11.35 kg (Ford 1994), respectively, although most woolly monkey weights (8.34 kg) fall within the species variation of howler monkeys (6.18–11.35 kg; Ford 1994). Male spider monkeys and muriquis are more similar to their female counterparts in body size, whereas the larger sizes of woolly and howler monkey males make these genera highly sexually dimorphic (Ford 1994).

The effects of female and male body sizes on behavior are profound. Differences in ateline female body sizes correspond to aspects of their life history strategies that affect reproductive rates (Ross 1991; Fedigan and Rose 1995; Strier, in prep.). Their relatively slow reproductive rates, compared to many other monkeys, make it more difficult for populations that have been reduced in size to recover in numbers.

Differences in the degree of sexual dimorphism correspond to striking differences in the relationships between males and females as well as to relationships among males (Strier 1994a). Comparisons across New World primates suggest that female reproductive rates and male competitive regimes may be linked through the degree to which female reproduction can be influenced by male

behavioral strategies (Strier 1996a). Thus, understanding the interacting effects of body size and life histories, which are often treated as **phylogenetic constraints,** is critical to understanding the behavioral variation among the atelines.

Despite these differences in body size and sexual dimorphism, ateline societies resemble one another in a variety of ways. Some of these similarities, such as the absence of female kin bonding so prevalent among the Old World cercopithecines and the prevalence of female dispersal accompanied by either male dispersal (as in howler monkeys) or male philopatry (as in the three atelines), can be attributed to their phylogenetic ancestry (Rosenberger and Strier 1989; Strier, in press). Others, such as their ability to shift from cohesive to fluid patterns of association, can be attributed to the proportion and distributions of different food types in their diets, which vary both among different genera and among populations within each genus in response to local ecological conditions (Strier 1992a). Indeed, both female dispersal (Strier 1990) and flexible patterns of association (Kinzey and Cunningham 1994) have been identified as probable primitive conditions in ancestral platyrrhines. Exploring the behavioral consequences of these ateline adaptations may provide broad, comparative insights into the behavioral evolution of other New World primates as well as contributing to the development of informed conservation programs on their behalf.

BODY SIZE AND
LIFE HISTORY VARIABLES

Body size is generally a good predictor of female primate life history variables that affect reproductive rates, including gestation length, age at first reproduction, interbirth intervals, and longevity. The large-bodied atelines, however, have even slower reproductive rates than expected for their body size, making them more like forest-dwelling apes than woodland- or savanna-dwelling Old World monkeys (Ross 1991).

Their slow reproductive rates also make the atelines more vulnerable than other monkeys to the

TABLE 1 Female Life History Variables from Wild Ateline Populations

| | Body Weight | Age (in years) at | | Interbirth Interval (in months) |
		Emigration	First Reproduction	
Alouatta				
A. palliata[1]	5.35 kg	2.7	3.5	20–22.5
A. seniculus[2]	5.60 kg	2–4	5.2	17–20
Lagothrix lagothricha[3]	5.75 kg	4–5	6–10	34.5
Ateles geoffroyi[4]	7.46 kg	5–7	7	34.7
Brachyteles[5]	9.45 kg	5–7	8–14	36.0

NOTES: [1]Glander 1980; Fedigan and Rose 1995; [2]Crockett and Pope 1993; [3]Nishimura 1992, 1994; [4]Fedigan and Rose 1995; [5]Strier 1996b.

deleterious consequences of small population size. Female spider monkeys (Fedigan and Rose 1995) and muriquis (Strier 1996b) are typically 5–7 years of age when they emigrate from their natal groups and 7–14 years of age when they give birth to their first infants in the wild. Although female woolly and howler monkeys are similar to one another in body size, woolly females are older than howler females when they emigrate and give birth to their first infants (Table 1). The delayed maturation of female woolly monkeys appears to resemble that of their ateline relatives more closely than that of howler monkeys of similar body size.

Interbirth intervals among the atelines also vary more closely with taxonomic affinity than with body size (see Table 1). Howler monkey interbirth intervals range from 19.9 to 22.5 months, whereas those of all three atelines, including the smaller-bodied woolly monkeys, range from 34.5 to 36 months.

Gestation accounts for a greater proportion of interbirth intervals for howler monkeys (31%) than for spider monkeys (22%; Fedigan and Rose 1995) or muriquis (19%; Strier and Ziegler, 1997). The comparatively low postnatal investment by howler mothers in their offspring might also contribute to higher infant mortality, but such comparisons across genera are difficult to make because other factors that affect infant mortality, including risks of predation and both intra- and interspecific competitor pressures, vary widely across study sites.

SOCIAL CONSEQUENCES OF SEXUAL DIMORPHISM

The degree of sexual dimorphism in primates correlates with the level and intensity of male-male competition for access to mates (Ford 1994; Mitani, Gors-Lewis, and Richards 1996). Variation in levels of sexual dimorphism among the atelines also corresponds to differences in the relationships between males and females (Rosenberger and Strier 1989; Plavcan and van Schaik 1992; reviewed in Strier 1994a). Among the atelines, for example, both howler and woolly monkeys exhibit high levels of sexual dimorphism in body size and canine size, and males in these genera are individually dominant over females. Spider monkeys are sexually monomorphic in body size but dimorphic in canine size, and male subgroups in this genus can dominate individual females. Muriquis have relatively sexually monomorphic body sizes and canine sizes, and relationships between the sexes are egalitarian (reviewed in Strier 1994a). Not surprisingly, as the ability of males to harass females through aggression declines, opportunities for female mate choice increase and the risks that aggressive males pose to females and their offspring decrease (Strier 1992b).

It may be that differences in the degree of within- and between-group competition among males are responsible for the variable patterns of sexual dimorphism observed among atelines (Kelley and

Strier 1994, in prep.). From this perspective, the benefits of cooperating with male kin to monitor and monopolize fluid groups of females in spider monkeys and muriquis may override the benefits of aggressive competition among male group members for access to mates. Stronger within-group competition for access to mates among woolly and howler monkeys might give males that can not only dominate other males but that also can coerce females into choosing them as mates reproductive advantages (Strier 1994a).

It is also possible that levels of competition among male atelines are a direct result of the degree to which males can influence female reproductive rates (Strier 1996a). The faster reproductive rates of female howlers might raise the stakes for aggression among male howler monkeys compared to the atelines, particularly if coupled with fewer seasonal constraints on howler female reproduction. The woolly monkey's pattern of howler-like sexual dimorphism and ateline-like reproductive rates is more difficult to explain, unless the more cohesive grouping associations that female woolly monkeys form alter the relative tradeoffs between inter- and intragroup competition among males for access to mates.

CONSEQUENCES OF
FEMALE DISPERSAL

Nearly all ateline females disperse from their natal groups before they begin to reproduce, but their options upon emigration are different. Male philopatry in the three atelines means that young females must join existing groups composed of males who are related to one another and other females who have previously joined the group. Dispersing females may sometimes end up in groups with maternal or paternal sisters who previously transferred from the same natal groups, particularly in small populations where only two to three groups occur (Strier 1997a), but determining whether females preferentially join groups containing female kin will require data from large populations where such options exist.

Female howler monkeys have more options when they disperse than female atelines because, unlike male atelines, male howler monkeys also tend to leave their natal troops. Theoretically, both male and female howler monkeys can fight their way into existing troops or they can join a similarly disenfranchised mate in establishing a new troop.

In one long-term study of red howler monkeys (*A. seniculus*) in Venezuela, over 20% of natal females remained to breed in their natal troops (Crockett and Pope 1993). Once the number of adult females reached a maximum of four, however, additional natal females were expelled through aggression by the other adult females (Crockett 1996). Because recruitment of females into troops in this species appears to be largely through natal females, those expelled from their natal troops were also unable to join established troops composed of unrelated females.

In Costa Rican mantled howlers (*A. palliata*), females may insinuate themselves into established troops by fighting their way to the top of the female dominance hierarchy. Their success comes with a price, however, as indicated by the 100% infant mortality that these first-time dominant mothers experience (Glander 1980).

Both red and mantled howler monkeys appear to respond to expanding populations by increasing the number and density of troops instead of their troop sizes (Clarke and Zucker 1994; Crockett 1996). As a result, the alternatives of forming a new troop as opposed to joining an established troop may simply reflect local population densities (Crockett 1996). Red howler monkey males are tolerated as nonbreeders in their natal troops much longer than mantled howler monkey males (4–6 versus 1–2 years), but again, it is difficult to evaluate whether this difference is a result of variation in population densities or species specific patterns (Glander 1992; Crockett 1996). For example, secondary dispersal has been reported for red but not for mantled howler males (Glander 1992; Crockett and Pope 1993), and red howler males may emigrate as kin cohorts (Crockett and Pope 1993) in growing populations where there are greater opportunities to establish new troops (Crockett 1996).

The correspondingly lower levels of competition among males may lead to greater tolerance toward natal males in this red howler monkey population.

Despite male philopatry in the atelines, the strength of cooperative and affiliative relationships among male kin in these genera is variable. Unlike woolly monkeys, male spider monkeys and muriquis both maintain strong spatial associations with one another and cooperate in intergroup encounters against other groups of male kin. Yet, unlike muriquis, both spider and woolly monkey males maintain dominance hierarchies based on the outcomes of agonistic interactions, and dominant males in both of these genera accounted for a disproportionate number of copulations (reviewed in Strier 1994a).

Agonistic-based dominance relationships among male muriquis have not been detected, in part because rates of intragroup aggression are unusually low (Mendes 1990; Strier 1992b). Individual males may be more popular than others as a result of their own efforts to associate with other males, as in the case among young males (Strier 1993), or through their tolerance toward males attempting to associate with them, as appears to be the case with some older males (Strier 1997b). Likewise, some males achieve disproportionately high mating success (Strier 1997c), but it is not yet known whether their success is a result of their greater initiative or female preference (Costa, in prep.), or whether their higher mating success also translates into higher reproductive success.

GROUPING PATTERNS AND DIET

Whether primates remain together year-round in cohesive groups or split up, either occasionally or routinely, into smaller feeding parties has typically been associated with the spatial and temporal distribution of preferred food resources and the size of food patches (Chapman, Wrangham, and Chapman 1995). Among the atelines, however, variation in both diet and grouping patterns among populations of the same genus can be as great as the variation apparent among genera. For example, muriquis at

three study sites devoted over 50% of their annual feeding time to leaves, yet they differed from one another in their degree of group cohesion (Fazenda Barreiro Rico: Milton 1984; Fazenda Esmeralda: Lemos de Sá 1991; Estação Biologica de Caratinga [formerly Fazenda Montes Claros]: Strier 1991). Furthermore, although muriquis adjust the number of individuals feeding in fruit patches in response to patch size (Strier 1989; Moraes, Carralho, and Strier 1998), between-site comparisons indicate that higher densities of large fruit patches did not necessarily lead to larger feeding parties (Moraes et al. 1998).

Comparable variability has been reported for woolly monkeys. Those at La Macarena, Colombia, maintain cohesive groups year-round (Stevenson, Quiñoes, and Ahumada 1994), whereas those in the Brazil Amazon maintain much looser aggregations (Peres 1996). Stevenson et al. (1994) attribute these differences to the greater proportion of arthropods (24%) in the diet of Colombian woolly monkeys, which provide a more constant and evenly distributed food source. By contrast, 90% of the diet of Brazilian woolly monkeys consisted of clumped fruits and seeds (Peres 1994). Although Brazilian woolly monkey groups do not split up entirely, Peres (1996) notes that they do adjust their intragroup spacing patterns in response to the size of their fruit patches.

Like Brazilian woolly monkeys and muriquis, both mantled howler monkeys in Panama (Leighton and Leighton 1982) and spider monkeys in Peru (Symington 1990) and Costa Rica (Chapman 1990) adjust their party size in response to the size of fruit patches. Small howler monkey troops tend to be more cohesive, and large troops of mantled howler monkeys in Costa Rica have been reported to fragment for more than a month at a time (Chapman 1990).

Flexible patterns of association are clearly a characteristic of the atelines, which often, but not always, corresponds to the proportion of fruits in their diets. The most consistently fluid patterns of association occur among spider monkeys, which are also the atelines that rely most heavily on fruit (over 70%; reviewed in Strier 1992a). Recent reports of loose or fluid grouping patterns in populations of Brazilian woolly monkeys (Peres 1996) and muriquis (Carvalho 1996) with comparable or greater levels of frugivory emphasize the importance of population variation as well as general adaptive patterns to understanding the behavioral ecology of the ateline primates.

CONCLUSIONS AND CAUTIONS

Some of the ateline adaptations reviewed in this essay diverge from those of other primates. For example, in contrast to many other primates, body size is a poor predictor of ateline diets (Ford and Davis 1992). The degree of insectivory practiced by Colombian woolly monkeys is greater than expected from their body size when compared to other much smaller primates with comparable degrees of insectivory (Stevenson et al. 1994). Similarly, the higher proportion of fruit in the diet of muriquis compared to sympatric howler monkeys deviates from predictions based on body size, suggesting that muriquis occupying seasonal Atlantic forest habitats with howler monkeys fill the more frugivorous niche that their spider monkey sisters occupy in more equatorial regions (Strier 1992a).

Other ateline adaptations provide broader insights into the relationships between behavioral and ecological variables that may operate in other primates as well. For example, the occurrence of male philopatry with slow, ape-like reproductive rates in the atelines may be indicative of a more general, causal relationship between female reproductive rates and male reproductive strategies (Strier 1996a). The fact that the African hominoids, with their slow reproductive rates, also exhibit male kin bonding and female dispersal supports the suggestion that primate dispersal patterns are linked to life history variables, which affect reproductive rates, and that both are strongly influenced by phylogeny.

It is important to note that robust generalizations about atelines, or any other group of primates, require extensive comparative data that encompass both the full range of interpopulation variation and the long-term effects of demographic fluctuations in particular populations (Strier 1997a, 1997b). It is rare to encounter such broad coverage for any taxon, and particularly so for primates like many atelines whose habitats have been altered and whose populations have been fragmented. Recent studies on neglected populations, such as those on Colombian and Amazonian woolly monkeys and on muriquis occupying the few remaining large, pristine forests available to them, have begun to provide some of the comparative perspectives on atelines that have previously been lacking. Expanding our comparative framework on atelines will improve our understanding of this fascinating subfamily and will provide valuable insights into the behavioral diversity that characterizes the Primate Order.

ACKNOWLEDGMENTS

I am grateful to the Brazilian government and CNPq for permission to conduct research on muriquis, and to Dr. G. Fonseca for serving as my Brazilian sponsor. I thank Drs. Fuentes and Dolhinow for inviting me to contribute this essay to their book, and for their helpful comments.

12

Capuchin Object Manipulation

Melissa Panger

During most of the twentieth century, humans distinguished themselves from other animals largely on the basis of their tool-using abilities. For example (overlooking the archaic use of the word "man" for "humans"), Leakey (1960) defined humans as "Man the Tool Maker," and Oakley (1964) argued that "[m]an is a social animal, distinguished by 'culture': by the ability to make tools and communicate ideas" (p. 1). Although tool use is still considered one of the hallmarks of human evolution, it is no longer seen as a distinguishing "human" characteristic because tool use has been seen in a wide variety of animal species (see Beck 1980).

*Because tool use is considered by many to be an important aspect of human evolution (e.g., Kortlandt 1986; Klein 1992), much of the animal tool-use research conducted to date has concentrated on primates due to their phylogenetic proximity to humans. This focus on nonhuman primate **object manipulation** has been conducted in attempts to gain an understanding of the evolution of tool use in early hominids.*

Many people (including nonprimatologists) have become familiar with chimpanzee (Pan spp.) tool-using abilities, especially the use of probing tools while "termite fishing." In addition to probing tools, free-ranging and captive chimpanzees also regularly use stone tools (hammer and anvil), make and use sponges, and use sticks as clubs (see McGrew 1992). However, there is another nonhuman primate that "stands out" in regard to its tool-using abilities both in terms of the variety and the rates of its tool use. These primates, capuchins (Cebus spp.), are monkeys, not apes, and thus are phylogenetically distant from both

humans and chimpanzees (the two other habitual tool-using primates). In spite of their phylogenetic distance—capuchins shared a last common ancestor with apes and humans over 30 mya—capuchins possess a remarkable aptitude for using tools.

Capuchins, named for the Capuchin Monks because of the "capped" pattern of fur on the top of their heads, are medium-sized (2.5–4 kg) New World monkeys and are members of the Ceboidea superfamily and Cebidae family. They have arguably the largest geographic distribution of any New World primate genus (rivaled only by howler monkeys, Alouatta spp.) and can be found throughout Central America and into South America from Colombia to Argentina. Capuchins are found and are able to survive in a wide variety of habitat types from tropical dry forest to gallery forest, palm forest, mangrove, premontane forest, liana forest, and swamp areas and from sea level to elevations of over 2500 m (Wolfheim 1983). There are currently four recognized capuchin species: Cebus albifrons, C. apella, C. capucinus, and C. olivacious. These species can be distinguished easily by coat and geographic distribution, but they seem to vary little in regard to general social behavior. For example, they live primarily in multifemale, multimale groups of three to thirty-five individuals and exhibit relatively low rates of intragroup aggression.

In regard to diet, capuchins are generalist omnivores, eating a wide variety of food types including fruits, young leaves, some flower parts, insects, bird eggs and, occasionally, vertebrate prey. While foraging in the wild, these monkeys rely heavily on extractive foraging techniques and often probe into tree holes with their hands, break small branches, unroll dried leaves, and dig through leaf litter in search of food (Fragaszy, Visalberghi, and Robinson 1990). They also process a variety of foods using various objects as tools. Their extractive foraging techniques and generalist diet may account for the overall success of the genus as measured by its wide geographic distribution.

Although capuchins demonstrate a wide range of complex manipulative behavior, I will be focusing on their object manipulation and tool use in this essay because it is these behaviors that seem unique to capuchins when compared to all other monkeys and, in fact, when compared to most other primates (e.g., Torigoe 1985). Care must be taken, however, when proclaiming such uniqueness. Several assumptions can easily, but not necessarily correctly, be associated with such a statement, most notably assumptions relating to intelligence.

CAPUCHIN INTELLIGENCE

A full discussion of intelligence is beyond the scope of this essay. However, there does seem to be a rough correlation between increased brain size and increased intelligence in the animal kingdom (Jerison 1973), but this relationship is far from clear. Capuchins do have relatively large brains when compared with other monkeys, both in terms of whole brain size to body size and, more specifically, in regard to the size of the **cerebellum, neocortex,** and the dorsal nucleus of the thalamus relative to body size (Bauchot 1982; Stephan, Baron, and Frahm 1988). However, although capuchins do rate higher than other monkeys on some types of intelligence tests (e.g., sensorimotor tests), they are even with them in others (e.g., tests involving object discrimination learning sets, cross-modal recognition tests, and maximum auditory retention interval tests) (Parker and Gibson 1977; Adams-Curtis 1990; Anderson 1996). And in relation to apes, capuchins seem to lack the mental representation abilities of chimpanzees, relying almost wholly on trial and error attempts to solve problems relating to tool use (e.g., Visalberghi and Fragaszy 1990; Fragaszy and Adams-Curtis 1991; but see Anderson and Henneman 1994). This seems to indicate

that if capuchins are more "intelligent" than other monkeys it is in a narrow and specific sense.

WHAT IS TOOL OR OBJECT USE?

The criteria for tool use vary slightly among fields of research. For animal behaviorists, the most widely accepted operational definition is Beck's (1980), which states that tool use is "the external employment of an unattached environmental object to alter more efficiently the form, position, or condition of another object, another organism, or the user itself when the user holds or carries the tool during or just prior to use" (p. 10). One important aspect of tool use is that both the "object of change" and the "agent of change" (i.e., the tool) are manipulated by the user (Parker and Gibson 1977).

This differs from the definition of object use, which is any time an individual manipulates (to alter) a detached object relative to a fixed substrate or medium (adapted from Parker and Gibson's [1977] definition of "proto tool use"). One important difference between object use and tool use is that with object use only the "object of change" is detached and manipulated. Both tool use and object use require an interpretation of motivation or intention; that is, the activity is performed by the individual to alter an object or another individual.

The distinction between tool use and object use may seem trivial; however, it is a useful and perhaps necessary distinction to make. At the level of technology demonstrated by nonhuman primates, any increase in complexity is a considerable advance (e.g., manipulating and detaching both the agents and the objects of change instead of just the objects of change). This can be illustrated by considering the evolution of tool use in another primate group, the early hominids.

EARLY HOMINID STONE TOOL TECHNOLOGY

An interesting pattern emerges when we look at the evolution of modified stone tools (the most complete tool record we have). The first modified stone tools belonged to the **Oldowan Industrial Complex,** which began at least 2.3 mya (Isaac 1984; Susman 1991). Oldowan stone tools were most likely initially made and used by the first members of our genus, *Homo habilis,* who lived in Africa from about 2.4 to 1.5 mya. These early hominids were similar to modern chimpanzees in stature but had brain sizes that fell outside of modern ape range (an average size of 630 cc). *H. habilis* was in fact the first hominid within our lineage that had, on average, a larger than ape-sized brain. Based largely on brain size estimates and a lack of stone tool remains, earlier known hominids (members of the genera *Ardipithecus* and *Australopithecus*) were most likely using the types of tools associated with chimpanzees and capuchins (i.e., nonstone tools and unmodified stone tools).

Although a "jump" in brain size is correlated with a "jump" in technology (the modification of stone tools), the types of stone tools associated with *H. habilis* are relatively simple. Oldowan tools are typified by tools called **choppers.** Choppers are smooth stones about the size of tennis balls in which a few **flakes** were struck off to produce sharp edges (Klein 1989). Despite their relative crudeness, however, both the chopper (i.e., the **core**) and the flakes broken off the stone could have been very useful in processing foods. This was illustrated several years ago by Louis Leakey when he effectively butchered an elephant using only Oldowan tools.

What is interesting for our purposes here is that Oldowan tools remained relatively unchanged for almost 1 million years, barring minor variations due to differences in available raw materials (Susman 1991). Therefore, the technological advance associated with modifying stones was followed by a long period of technological stasis (at least in regard to the manufacture of stone tools).

Another change in stone tool technology did not occur until approximately 1.3 million years ago with the origin of the **Achuelian Industry.** This tool tradition is associated with some *Homo erectus* populations, most notably in Africa (other populations continued to make and use Oldowan tools). Members of the species *H. erectus* lived from about 1.8 mya to 200,000 ya. They were the first hominids to expand their geographic range beyond Africa, and they were found throughout the temperate regions of the Old World. In regard to morphology, *H. erectus* had approximately modern human stature and exhibited an expanded brain size over earlier hominids (average size of 1000 cc).

The Acheulian Industry is characterized by large **bifaced tools** known as **handaxes** and **cleavers.** These tools were generally larger and flatter than the earlier choppers and involved more sophisticated **stoneknapping,** which produced sharper, straighter edges. Although Acheulian tools were slightly more advanced from a technical perspective (and potentially more effective) when compared to earlier forms, they are seen as a logical progression from preceding Oldowan choppers (Klein 1989). Therefore, Acheulian tools represent a technological advance, but not a dramatic one. And again, as with the Oldowan Industry, Acheulian tool technology remained relatively unchanged for approximately one million years (Klein 1989).

This pattern of a jump in technology followed by a long period of technological stasis seems to indicate that changes at this level of technology do not occur easily. Thus, what appear to be relatively minor increases in technology, measured by today's technological standards, are actually considerable advances. Therefore, making a distinction between object manipulation and tool use is warranted.

Also, because of the apparently "slow" innovative process associated with early hominid technology, it is logical to assume that object use predated and led to tool use in our ancestors (i.e., tool use probably did not spontaneously occur prior to less complex object manipulation; see Gruber 1969). Therefore, a complete understanding of the evolution of tool use in early hominids requires both an understanding of the tool-using aptitude of early hominids and an examination of what led to the evolution of object use. Because we do not have the luxury of studying the behavior of early hominids directly, one way we can understand their behavior is by studying our closest living relatives, the nonhuman primates. Capuchins, because of their complex manipulative behavior, provide a potential model for gaining insight into the evolution of tool use in early hominids.

CAPUCHIN TOOL USE AND OBJECT USE IN CAPTIVITY

The study of tool use in capuchins has a long and interesting history (see Visalberghi 1990 and Mc-Grew and Marchant 1997 for reviews). In captivity capuchin tool use has been extensively studied (primarily in *C. apella*), and capuchins are known to exhibit an incredible array of complex manipulative behavior when provided with adequate materials and problems (e.g., objects that can be used as tools and food resources that require tools to process). The types of tool use reported for captive capuchins include hitting conspecifics with sticks (Cooper and Harlow, as reported in Visalberghi 1990), using sticks as probing tools (Anderson and Henneman 1994), using sponging tools (Westergaard and Fragaszy 1987), using rocks and wood to pound open hard-shelled nuts (Antinucci and Visalberghi 1986), using sticks as levers and as chisel-and-hammers (Jalles-Filho 1995), using stones and sticks as pestles (Westergaard et al. 1995), modifying bones with rock to make appropriate probing tools (Westergaard and Suomi 1994b), modifying bamboo to make probing and cutting tools (Westergaard and Suomi 1995), and modifying stones to make cutting tools (Westergaard 1995). Essentially, captive capuchins are capable of performing just about every type of tool use exhibited by free-ranging and captive chimpanzees (McGrew and Marchant 1997).

With the exception of the tools described by Westergaard and Suomi (1994b, 1995) and Westergaard (1995), the objects used as tools by captive capuchins were "co-opted" (using Ingold's 1995 term loosely), meaning that the tools were not modified or constructed by the monkeys. Most of the tool use was also "enabled" (i.e., researchers provided a problem and a means of solution but no direct interaction with the monkeys) or "induced" (i.e., researchers interacted with the monkeys and shaped their behavior using principles of learning theory; McGrew and Marchant 1997). These differ from "spontaneous" behaviors in which animals exhibit a task without any human intervention.

Perhaps at least partly because of the enabled and induced nature of the tasks, the reported rates of tool use among captive capuchins are often very high. Studies that provide explicit rate information include 1.7 bouts/hr (Chevalier-Skolnikoff 1989) and 1.6 bouts/hr (Westergaard and Fragaszy 1987). However, there are often significant differences among individuals in the amount of tool use exhibited. Some individuals never use tools, and others use tools in almost every trial within the same study group (Anderson and Henneman 1994). This is most likely due to the potential ability of some individuals to monopolize tools or at least to socially inhibit others from using them (Visalberghi 1988).

Unfortunately, there is little data regarding capuchin object use because nearly all of the captive literature has examined tool use only. One study has discussed object-use behavior quantitatively, although many captive studies do mention that rubbing and pounding behaviors are common among capuchins (e.g., Visalberghi and Vitale 1990). This is probably because tool use has been considered more interesting than object use. (Why study object use if your monkeys are using tools?) The one captive study that considered object use reports it at a rate of 16 bouts/hr, although their definition of object use was very inclusive and included such things as licking or picking food off the wall (Fragaszy and Adams-Curtis 1991).

CAPUCHIN TOOL USE AND OBJECT MANIPULATION UNDER FREE-RANGING CONDITIONS

Much less is known about what capuchins are doing under free-ranging conditions. Capuchins do demonstrate tool use under free-ranging conditions, however, such behavior appears to be rare. Most of the information regarding this comes from anecdotal reports, which include accounts of capuchins hitting a potential snake predator with sticks (in *C. capucinus*: Chapman 1986; Boinski 1988), pounding oysters open with pieces of an oyster bed (in *C. apella*: Fernandes 1991), and wrapping caterpillars in leaves and rubbing them against tree branches to remove stinging hairs (in *C. capucinus*: Susan Perry, pers. comm.). Two quantitative studies (both with *C. capucinus*) have examined the complex object manipulation of capuchins: a five-month study that focused strictly on tool use (Chevalier-Skolnikoff 1990) and an eleven-month study in which I examined both tool and object use (Panger 1998).

The monkeys in Chevalier-Skolnikoff's (1990) study exhibited tool use at a rate of .02 bouts/hr (excluding most of the dropping of sticks and all of the defecation on conspecifics because of the possible difficulty in determining the intended goals of the behavior; see Panger 1998). The five tool-use bouts Chevalier-Skolnikoff observed included these behaviors: poking a conspecific with a stick, probing a hole with a stick, breaking and dropping branches directly on an individual, and flailing sticks at another. During my study, however, I did not see a single tool-use behavior in more than 300 hours of observation. These studies taken together indicate that even though free-ranging capuchins are capable of tool use, it is not a common behavior pattern. Although capuchins habitually use a wide array of tools under captive conditions, this does not seem to be the case for their free-ranging counterparts. There are many potential reasons for the differences in tool-use behavior of free-ranging capuchins when compared to captive ones, including differential motivational responses to objects, arboreal lifestyle, absence of adequate tool material, and absence of food resources that require extraction involving tool use (see Panger 1998). Instead, what appears to be habitual in free-ranging capuchins is object use.

Several qualitative studies of object use in free-ranging capuchins have described pounding hard-shelled fruits and nuts against tree branches (e.g., in *C. apella*: Izawa and Mizuno 1977; in *C. apella* and *C. albifrons*: Terborgh 1983), however only one long-term field study has examined object use quantitatively, the study I conducted at Palo Verde, Costa Rica (Panger 1998).

The monkeys in my study exhibited three different types of object use: pound, rub, and fulcrum use. Pound use involved an individual hitting an object against a tree branch or rock with either one or two hands. This was by far the most common type of object use exhibited by the monkeys. Rub use was the next most common, and it involved an

TABLE 1 Assumed Functions of Object Use

Function	Object Use		
	Pound	Rub	Fulcrum
To break into fruits or animal products with a hard outer layer	X	X	X
To soften unripe fruit for easier ingestion	X	X	
To damage the rind of certain fruits prior to fur rubbing (see Baker 1996 for a full description of fur rubbing)	X	X	
To remove wind-dispersed seeds from certain fruits	X	X	
To remove noxious substances from the outer layer of certain plants and animals	X	X	
To detach fruits from fruit bunches	X		

individual sliding an object against a tree branch or rock with either one or two hands. Fulcrum use was less common than either rub or pound use and involved applying force on an object working against a substrate (which was used as a fulcrum). These behaviors together occurred at a rate of .19/hr and made up less than 1% of the total waking time of the monkeys (there were no differences among age or sex classes). Most object-use behavior was associated with processing foods (Table 1).

CONCLUSIONS

Using the expansive captive capuchin literature together with the information emerging from recent quantitative field studies, a more complete picture of capuchin object manipulation is becoming apparent. Although capuchins appear to be unique among monkeys in regard to their incredible aptitude for tool use, their habitual use of tools (at this point) seems to be limited to captivity where such behaviors can be induced. These captive data can lend insight into the potential range of tool types used by early hominids prior to and during the periods in which stones were being modified, tools that tend not to be readily apparent in the fossil record. Although capuchins do use tools under free-ranging conditions, object use rather than tool use appears to be the habitual behavior pattern.

The importance of examining capuchin object use becomes clear when the pattern of innovation involving early hominid stone tool technologies is considered. The first technological advance in stone tools that can be detected in the fossil record (the modification of stone) is associated with simple Oldowan choppers. This stone tool innovation was followed by a period of technological stasis that lasted nearly a million years. The stasis was broken with the advent of the Acheulian tradition, which was characterized by large, bifaced handaxes. The advance of Acheulian tools over Oldowan tools was largely related to more sophisticated stoneknapping, which produced sharper cutting edges.

This technological advance also was followed by a period of "stone tool" stasis that lasted over a million years, demonstrating that technological advances did not come easily to early hominids and that "minor" increases in their technology were actually "major." Therefore, we can logically assume that tool use probably did not spontaneously occur prior to less complex object manipulation. Object manipulation probably predated and led to tool use in our ancestors. Consequently, a complete understanding of the evolution of tool use in early hominids requires an understanding of what led to the evolution of object use in their ancestors. Capuchins, because of their habitual and unique (when compared to other monkeys) object-using abilities under free-ranging conditions, are potential models for the evolution of object use in primates. An examination of how and why capuchins use objects under natural ecological constraints may provide clues as to how and why these behaviors evolved in our hominid ancestors.

What is apparent from free-ranging studies is that capuchins use objects primarily to access difficult to process food resources. Object use allows these monkeys access to food resources not readily available to other, even sympatric, primates (Terborgh 1983). Therefore, the adaptive value of object use is not difficult to argue. These data, taken together with the information from chimpanzee studies, seem to indicate that the evolution of object use, which most likely led to tool use in some primates (including humans), grew out of the requirements of a highly omnivorous diet that relied heavily on extractive foraging techniques (see also Parker and Gibson 1977).

The Prosimians

The members of the suborder Prosimii are an interesting group of primates that have retained a number of more **primitive features**, such as a moist rhinarium nose (similar to that of your dog) and unfused mandible and frontal bones. They also have eye sockets that are not completely enclosed in bone and elongated, specialized incisor teeth called a **dental comb.** Most also have a claw on the second or third digit called a **grooming claw.** They are all nocturnal, with the exception of the lemurs, and many have specialized scent glands, which they use to communicate with each other and to mark their territory.

Five of the eight prosimian families live on the island of Madagascar and are grouped in the superfamily Lemuroidea, which includes thirteen genera and twenty to twenty-three species of lemurs. Two of the families contain only one genus each. There is little sexual dimorphism in body size or weight among lemuroids. Because there are no anthropoid primates on the island to compete for resources, the lemurs have differentiated in body size and in temporal use of the environment more than prosimians found elsewhere. They have retained the **tapetum lucidem** (reflective layer in the retina that increases the effectiveness of night vision), although many lemurs are diurnal. Lemurs range in size from the pygmy mouse lemur (.03 kg) to the indri (6.5 kg). Lemurs live on a diet that consists mainly of fruit, flowers, nectar, insects, small fauna (frogs, bird eggs, lizards, and so forth), gums, saps, and leaves. Some lemurs are specialized feeders, such as the fork-marked lemur that specializes on gums, whereas others primarily eat leaves. The diet of the bamboo lemur (family Lemuridae) is made up almost entirely of bamboo. In contrast, the aye-aye (family Daubentonidae) has a long, thin middle finger adapted for reaching insect larvae that are burrowed in trees. All members of the family Megaladapidae and Indriidae eat plant matter only. All but a few lemur species are highly arboreal, some moving about by means of vertical clinging and leaping from one tree trunk to another, and others walking on all fours along tree branches, a mode of locomotion called arboreal quadrupedalism. Home range size varies from .5 to 23 hectares. All Malagasy primates are threatened by habitat destruction.

The nocturnal lemuriformes may be solitary (foraging independently but communicating vocally and having brief social encounters with others on a regular basis) or found in mated pairs or in variable social systems. The diurnal lemurs tend to have more variable social systems. Some are pair-bonded, and others can be found in multimale, multifemale and community social groups with up to thirty members.

All species of lemuriformes are seasonal breeders. Gestation length varies from 60 days for the smallest lemurs to 160 days for the larger species. Age at first birth ranges from approximately 1 year up to 6 years, with interbirth intervals lasting from one year to three years, on average. Several species of lemurs keep their infants in nests or holes in tree trunks.

The members of the superfamily Lorisoidea are all small (less than 2.2 kg), and they are nocturnal. They are divided into two families, the Lorisidae, which include the lorises and pottos, and the Galagonidae, which include the bush babies. The lorises are found in southern Asia, and the pottos are found in Africa. They are arboreal quadrupeds and move in a very slow manner, using their powerful hands to grip the branches. Some specialize on insects and small animal prey, whereas others include a great deal of fruit and gums in their diet. They are mostly solitary foragers and will sometimes forage in pairs. The range of females varies from 6 to 16 hectares. The range of a male may overlap that of several females, and varies from 9 to 60 hectares. Females have their first infant anywhere from 9 to 18 months of age. Gestation ranges from 4.5 to 6.5 months, with an interbirth interval of 9 to 18 months.

There are four genera of galagos and eleven species found in equatorial Africa. They eat a diet composed of gums, fruit, insects, and small animal prey and move around by means of leaping, quadrupedal running, and climbing. They are mostly solitary foragers, but two to five females may sleep in the same hollow. A female and her offspring often forage as a group, forming a matriarchy. Galagos have their first infants between 8 and 24 months of age, and gestation varies from 3.5 to 5.5 months, with an interbirth interval of 6 to 12 months. The range of a female galago is between .5 and 16 hectares, whereas the male range may be as large as 40 hectares, overlapping several female ranges.

The tarsier shares some characteristics with the lorises and lemurs and some with anthropoids. Unlike the lemurs and lorises, tarsiers have a dry nose and complete postorbital closure. They do have a grooming claw and an unfused mandible and frontal bones and are nocturnal. They weigh only .11–.12 kg and are all nocturnal. There is one genus and five species encompassed by the Tarsiidae. The tarsiers are named for their elongated tarsal bones, which are an adaptation for their vertical clinging and leaping form of locomotion. They eat a diet composed entirely of insects and animal prey and are found in the Philippines and in Indonesia. Their range varies from .5 to 11 hectares, and they are found in a variety of social systems, including solitary foragers, pairs, and multimale, multifemale groups of two to six individuals. Tarsiers have their first infants at around 24 months, with a gestation of 178–194 days.

13

An Introduction to the Ecology of Daylight-Active Lemurs

Benjamin Z. Freed

Lemurs are a group of approximately forty-five species and subspecies of prosimian primates found only in Madagascar and on the nearby Comoro Islands. There are six extant groups of these endangered primates:[1]

1. Lemurids: seven species of medium-sized (1–4 kg), daylight-active, often quadrupedal, "true" lemurs (an **intermembral index** or IM = 68–72)

2. Indriids: five species of variable-sized (1–8 kg; see Powzyk 1997), vertically oriented or orthograde lemurs (IM = 58–65)

3. Bamboo lemurs: three species of variable-sized (1–3 kg), short-faced lemurs that may prefer large bamboo stands (IM = 64–65)

4. Lepilemurids: one to six species of small (< 1 kg) nocturnal lemurs (IM = 59)

5. Cheirogaleids: nine to ten species of tiny (< 0.5 kg) nocturnal lemurs (IM = 68–72)

6. Aye-aye (*Daubentonia madagascariensis*): a medium-sized (2–3 kg), anatomically strange, nocturnal lemur (IM = 70)

For many years, lemurs were among the most understudied groups of primates. Before 1990, only four daylight-active[2] species of Malagasy (Madagascan) lemurids and indriids were the focus of year-round ecological field studies (e.g., Sussman 1973; Pollock 1975, 1977; Richard 1977, 1978). Knowledge about lemurs was largely the result of descriptive surveys, preliminary studies, or short-term work (e.g., Petter 1962; Tattersall 1976a, 1977a, 1977b; Petter, Albignac, and Rumpier 1977; Wilson et al. 1989), with long-term work limited to a few sites. Although ecologists provided vital socioecological data on lemurs, long-term data on resource availability and plant phenology throughout Madagascar was largely uncollected until recently (see, e.g., Hemingway 1995). Little was known about the year-round use of resources and group composition of the strictly nocturnal Malagasy lemurs (cf. Martin 1973; Charles-Dominique 1977; Pages 1978; Petter 1978). Lemurs were living fossils, and the specifics of their geographical distribution, resource use, and social behavior were essentially unknown. Since 1990, lemurs have become the focus of intensive data collection, with fifteen species or more the subjects of year-round ecological studies throughout Madagascar (Figure 1).

In this essay I will focus on the habitat use and group composition of one set of lemurs, the lemurids: *Lemur catta, L. coronatus, L. fulvus,*

---

[1]This taxonomy is from Tattersall (1982) and Tattersall and Coopman (1989). Simons and Rumpler (1988) place "true" lemurs in three genera: *Lemur catta* is genus *Lemur,* other *Lemur* species are genus *Eulemur,* and ruffed lemurs are genus *Varecia.*

[2]The term *daylight-active* refers to those species reported as either diurnal or cathemeral (active both during daylight and nighttime). Those species active only at night are strictly nocturnal.

FIGURE 1   Map of Madagascar showing locations of year-round field studies of daylight-active Malagasy lemurs.

L. macaco, L. mongoz, L. rubriventer, and *Varecia variegata.* I will summarize each species' diet (species diversity and food item), use of space (horizontal and vertical), activity patterns, and social structure (group composition and density) as well as reporting overall trends in the habits of these primates.

RINGTAILED LEMURS (LEMUR CATTA)

Ringtailed lemurs have perhaps been the most studied of all lemurs (see Essay 14). Jolly (1966) produced the first detailed descriptions of ringtailed lemur behavior in Berenty Reserve in southern Madagascar. Budnitz and Dainis (1975), O'Connor (1987), and Rasamaminana and Rafidinarivo (1993) also studied ringtailed lemur behavior and

ecology at Berenty. Sussman (1973, 1974, 1977) collected quantitative data about ringtailed lemur habitat preferences, resource use, and behavior at Berenty and Antserananomby. Sussman studied allopatric and sympatric populations of ringtailed lemurs and rufous lemurs (*Lemur fulvus rufus*). In Beza-Mahafaly Reserve, Sauther (1992) collected year-round phenological and behavioral data on ringtailed lemur diet, ranging behavior, activity patterns, and social behavior. The purpose of this study was to examine interindividual differences in diet and habitat use within ringtailed lemur groups. Since 1984, the ringtailed lemurs in southwestern Madagascar have been followed as part of a long-term study of social organization and ecology.

Ringtailed lemurs inhabit the dry scrub and brush forests of southern Madagascar (Figure 2). Ringtailed lemurs are generally opportunistic feeders, eating many plant species from different heights in the forest. When resources are least abundant, ringtailed lemurs are less active and eat fewer species and preferred plants (Sauther 1992). Sussman (1974) showed that populations in different forests essentially select diets of similar species diversity. Ringtailed lemurs also eat a variety of items: pods, fruit, leaves, flowers, herbs, and insects. Food item choice differs between populations, with lemurs in the Berenty Reserve selecting fruit more than twice as often as leaves, whereas the population in the Antserananomby Reserve eats leaves more than fruit. Even between groups within a site, ringtailed lemurs may select food species and items differently throughout the year (Rasamaminana and Rafidinarivo 1993).

Ringtailed lemurs have home ranges of 6 to 35 ha; those groups that live in drier or more disturbed habitats have larger home ranges (Sauther and Sussman 1993). Although conspecific groups do not tolerate one another, home ranges overlap greatly, and territories are not readily observed. Jolly et al. (1993), however, argued that ringtailed lemurs at Berenty actively defend territories, at least during the birth season.

Ringtailed lemurs are more terrestrial than any other lemur species. Both Sussman (1973, 1974) and Sauther (1992) report that lemurs use re-

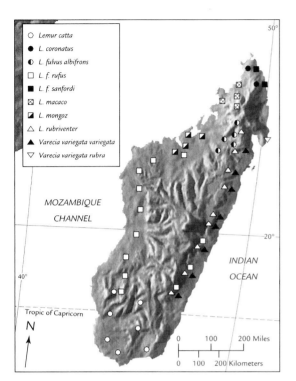

Figure legend (in map):

O *Lemur catta*
● *L. coronatus*
◑ *L. fulvus albifrons*
□ *L. f. rufus*
■ *L. f. sanfordi*
⊠ *L. macaco*
◪ *L. mongoz*
△ *L. rubriventer*
▲ *Varecia variegata variegata*
▽ *Varecia variegata rubra*

MOZAMBIQUE
CHANNEL

INDIAN
OCEAN

Tropic of Capricorn

N

0   100   200 Miles

0   100   200 Kilometers

50°

—20°

40°

FIGURE 2   Map of Madagascar showing geographical ranges of daylight-active lemurs that have been the focus of year-round ecological research (based on Tattersall, 1982).

sources in different heights of the forest, but they spend significant time on the ground. At these three sites, ringtailed lemurs spend 20–30% or more of their time on the ground.

The activity pattern of ringtailed lemurs varies greatly both between sites and within groups. Perhaps due to differences in ambient temperature, lemurs in Berenty begin their activities and their main resting period earlier in the day than do lemurs in Antserananomby (Sussman 1974). Sauther (1992) showed that resting rates differ significantly with reproductive state and the time of year.

Groups include several adult males, several adult females, and nonadults and average between thirteen and fifteen individuals. Adult sex ratios are near 1:1, and population densities vary from 17.4 to 350 individuals per km[2] (Sauther and Sussman 1993).

CROWNED LEMURS (*LEMUR CORONATUS*)

Crowned lemurs inhabit forests on the northern tip of Madagascar that vary in elevation, climate, and structure (see Figure 2). From preliminary studies and surveys, crowned lemurs were thought to prefer scrub forests, but few specifics were known about their diet, habitat use, and social structure (Petter et al. 1977; Arbelot-Tracqui 1983; Wilson et al. 1989). Freed (1996) conducted surveys, monitored plant phenology, and collected year-round data on crowned lemur and Sanford's lemur resource use and social behavior. Freed showed that crowned lemurs use a variety of resources and have a social structure that may ease food acquisition in different habitats. Crowned lemurs and Sanford's lemurs use the same resources differently both year-round and within seasons.

Freed's study occurred in a mixed primary and secondary forest in humid western Mt. d'Ambre (see Figure 1). Ten food species accounted for two-thirds of the annual diet, but food species diversity varied seasonally. Dietary diversity doubled during greatest resource scarcity, the wet season. Otherwise, two plant species accounted for nearly half the diet. Crowned lemurs are highly frugivorous; fruit makes up more than 70% of their diet. Flowers make up nearly one-fourth of the diet in the dry season, but at no other time did a nonfruit account for 10% of their diet. Crowned lemurs generally forage and feed in the bushes, treelets, and mid-sized trees below the canopy. As these resources contain only small amounts of fruit, crowned lemurs forage more throughout the day.

Crowned lemur home ranges are small (6.5–15.5 ha) and highly overlapping. Six or more groups share parts of each study group's home range. Lemurs are usually found below the canopy, and 60% of observations occurred in the small trees and bushes of the understory. Crowned lemurs use mid-sized trees and the middle story nearly one-third of the time, and they rarely use the ground or the canopy. Crowned lemurs are least active in the early morning but are more active as the day progresses. They are less active and range least daily during the dry season. Crowned lemurs are active both day and night year-round.

Most groups have a multimale, multifemale social structure. Groups consist of two or more adult males, two or more adult females, and nonadults and average between six and eight individuals. Adult sex ratios are 0.75–0.98 adult males for every adult female. Population density at the study site was 105 individuals per km^2. Although spatially cohesive for most of the year, crowned lemur groups divide into subgroups each day during the dry season. Subgroups function independently of one another but join later each day to re-form the original group.

BROWN LEMURS
(*LEMUR FULVUS*)

Seven brown lemur subspecies inhabit continuous canopy forest throughout Madagascar: the northern Mt. d'Ambre, the eastern rain forest, northwest, western forests, and the Comoro Islands (see Figure 2). Brown lemurs co-occur with other true lemurs in their range. Year-round quantitative ecological data have been reported on three subspecies: rufous lemurs (*L. fulvus rufus*), Sanford's lemurs (*L. f. sanfordi*), and white-fronted lemurs (*L. f. albifrons*) (Sussman 1973; Overdorff 1991; Freed 1996; Vasey 1997). Brown lemur ecology varies in communities throughout Madagascar.

Results on western rufous lemurs differ greatly from those on other brown lemurs. Sussman (1973, 1974) observed that allopatric and sympatric populations in southwestern Madagascar have a monotonous diet. Three plant species account for more than 80% of the rufous lemur diet. Leaves make up 50–90% of the diet; fruit never made up more than 40% of the diet. Rufous lemurs also rarely venture beneath the forest canopy; 80% or more of their time is spent in either the canopy or emergent level of the forest. They live in small (1.0 ha), highly overlapping home ranges and generally rest from mid-morning through mid-afternoon. Groups include three or more males, four or more females, and nonadults (average group size = 9.5 individuals). The sex ratio (M:F) is 1:1.24. Densities of

rufous lemurs are much greater here than elsewhere (1061 individuals per km^2).

Brown lemurs studied elsewhere have more diverse diets, are highly frugivorous, range differently, and live in lower densities. Overdorff (1991, 1993) observed eastern rufous lemurs in the rain forest of Ranomafana National Park (Vatoharanana). These lemurs co-occurred with red-bellied lemurs (*L. rubriventer*) and ruffed lemurs (*Varecia variegata*). Rufous lemurs consume one hundred or more plant species throughout the year, and food species diversity varies monthly. In several months, one species accounts for most of the diet; in other months five species compose most of the diet. These lemurs rely on ripe fruit, with fruit making up more than 65% of the diet and leaves no more than 20%. They also eat flowers. Rufous lemurs range over large home ranges (70–75 ha) that overlap extensively. During fruit scarcity, study groups may migrate nearly 4 km away to an area in which guava fruit (*Psidium cattleyanum*) is widely abundant. Although rufous lemurs spend half their time near the forest canopy, they are often observed in the understory. They are most active in the mid-morning and early evening; social activities occur most often in the mid-morning and mid-afternoon. Rufous lemurs also were active at night throughout the study. Social groups consist of three or more adult males, two or more adult females, and nonadults (average group size = 8). Groups have more males than females (M:F sex ratio = 1.9:1). The density of rufous lemurs is 25–70 individuals per km^2.

Sanford's lemurs behave much as eastern rufous lemurs, but do not migrate from their core areas. Freed (1996) studied Sanford's lemurs in Mt. d'Ambre (see the section on crowned lemurs). Sanford's lemurs eat nearly ninety plant species throughout the year, with dietary diversity doubling during greatest resource scarcity, the wet season. These lemurs otherwise rely on five species to compose half the diet. They eat ripe fruit; more than 85% of their diet is fruit. No other item makes up more than 12% of the diet. Brown lemurs feed in mid-sized trees, large trees, and treelets and use those resources that offer large amounts of fruit for several weeks. Compared with the sympatric crowned

urs, Sanford's lemurs spend less time foraging
d range over less daily distance. Home ranges are
nall (5.0–8.9 ha) and highly overlapping. These
ΛON· lurs spend their time beneath the forest canopy,
ostly in the middle story and exhibit no peaks in
ΔAY ylight activity. Sanford's lemurs are somewhat ac-
ve at night. Group composition was not unlike
ner brown lemurs: two or more adult males, two
more adult females, and one or more nonadults
(average group size = 7–11; M:F sex ratio 1:1.3;
density = 86 lemurs per km²).

White-fronted lemurs behave very much as Sanford's lemurs. Vasey (1997) studied white-fronted
lemurs and red-ruffed lemurs (*Varecia variegata
rubra*) in rain forest on the Masoala Peninsula.
White-fronted lemurs rely on ripe fruit for two-
thirds or more of their diet. They eat flowers, nectar, and leaves infrequently. They feed and remain
most active in the tops of small and mid-sized
trees; nearly 80% of all activities take place below
15 meters, which is beneath their potential competitors, the ruffed lemurs. Home ranges of white-
fronted lemurs are small (13.1 ha), overlapping,
and nonterritorial. Although most activities occur
during the day, these lemurs are also active at night.
Groups include two or more adult males, two or
more adult females, and nonadults (average group
size = 7–11; density = less than 50 individuals per
km²).

BLACK LEMURS
(*LEMUR MACACO*)

Black lemurs inhabit primary and secondary forests
in the Sambirano region of northwestern Madagascar (see Figure 2). Colquhoun (1997) conducted a
year-round quantitative study of black lemur socioecology in a secondary forest on the Ambato
Massif where black lemurs share the habitat with
no other lemurid.

Colquhoun observed that black lemurs adapt
well to a variety of habitats. Black lemurs eat many
plant species throughout the year, but three or four
species compose most of the diet in any month.
Each study group ate many species in similar proportions. Nearly two-thirds of the diet of any group

is fruit, and 20 to 25% are l
lemurs are highly frugivorou. Although black
sonally on nectar and flowers also rely sea-
available. On average, feeding ar ruit is less
meters above the ground.

Each black lemur group ranged occur 5
ranges are small (3.5–7.0 ha), with
overlap between the ranges of study me
lemurs are not territorial. Home ra %
used exclusively, and aggressive, conspi
group encounters occur infrequently. Bl
are found in similar heights off the gro
forest canopy is discontinuous, and nev
than 15 meters tall. Groups spend time in th
dle and upper parts of trees, and black l
rarely use the ground. Activity patterns vary
between groups. Black lemurs are most active .
the morning and in the late afternoon, resting in
the middle of the day. In the dry season, black
lemurs are much less active, but they are active at
night throughout the year.

Most black lemurs live in multimale, multifemale groups. Groups consist of three adult males,
three adult females, and three nonadults. The sex
ratio of black lemurs is nearly 1:1. Population density is 200 individuals per km². Black lemur groups
are spatially cohesive much of the year. During the
dry season, however, black lemur groups subdivide
and rejoin daily, much as described earlier for
crowned lemurs.

MONGOOSE LEMURS
(*LEMUR MONGOZ*)

Mongoose lemurs inhabit forests in Madagascar
and the Comoro Islands (see Figure 2). Tattersall
and Sussman (1975) observed groups during the
dry season in a deciduous forest of northwestern
Madagascar. Mongoose lemurs are nocturnal, have
a monotonous diet made up mostly of flowers and
nectar, and live in monogamous groups (one adult
male, one adult female, and nonadults).

Curtis (1997) studied the year-round ecology,
activity rhythms, and social organization of mongoose lemurs in Anjamena (see Figure 1), where
these lemurs co-occur with brown lemurs (*Lemur*

The Prosi...

...ts from this study confirm that
fulvus fulvus ...ized compared with that of other
mongo... black lemurs or crowned lemurs).
be ... up most of the diet, but seasonal dif-
l... ...cur in food item choice. During the wet
...ongoose lemurs consume more seeds and
... but in the dry season they eat more unripe
... young leaves, and mature flowers.

Mongoose lemurs have small home ranges (2.8–
.9 ha) with moderate overlap (less than 35%) between groups. These lemurs are territorial, and individuals monitor the borders of ranges. Chases
and vocalizations often occur when conspecific
groups meet in these regions. Mongoose lemurs are
usually observed between 5 and 10 meters above
the ground, and rarely do they move below 2 meters. Throughout the study they rested nearly 70%
of the time. Nighttime activity levels increase during the dry season. The estimated population density is 100 individuals per km^2.

RED-BELLIED LEMURS
(LEMUR RUBRIVENTER)

Red-bellied lemurs inhabit the eastern rain forest
from the northern Tsaratanana Massif to just south
of Ranomafana National Park (see Figure 2). These
lemurs have been the subject of intensive ecological
study and have been monitored each year in Ranomafana National Park at the Vatoharanana site
since 1988 (Overdorff 1991, 1996). Red-bellied
lemurs co-occur with other daytime-active lemurids, including rufous lemurs (*L. fulvus rufus*) and
black-and-white ruffed lemurs (*Varecia variegata
variegata*). Overdorff found significant year-round
differences and monthly variations in how rufous
lemurs and red-bellied lemurs use resources and
organize themselves socially.

Red-bellied lemurs eat ninety species or more,
but in any month five species account for most of
the diet. Fruit makes up 80% or more of their diet,
and leaves make up most of the remainder. When
fruit and leaf production is not at its peak, red-
bellied lemurs include flowers in their diet. They

are territorial and have small home ranges (11–19
ha) that overlap less than 10%. Red-bellied lemurs
live in small monogamous groups, and population
density is 15 to 30 individuals per km^2. They are
usually seen in the canopy above 20 meters; rarely
are they near the ground. These lemurs are most
active in the mid-morning and in the early evening.
Social behaviors occur in the mid-morning and in
the late afternoon. Red-bellied lemurs are also active at night throughout the year.

RUFFED LEMURS
(VARECIA VARIEGATA)

Ruffed lemurs inhabit the eastern rain forest from
the Masoala Peninsula to just south of Ranomafana
(see Figure 2). One subspecies, the red-ruffed
lemur (*Varecia variegata rubra*), is limited to the
Masoala Peninsula; the other subspecies, the black-
and-white ruffed lemur (*V. v. variegata*), occurs elsewhere. Rigamonti (1993) studied the ecology of
red-ruffed lemurs during an eleven-month period.
Vasey (1997) collected year-round quantitative
data on the habitat use and social structure of a
red-ruffed lemur community. Morland (1991)
studied black-and-white ruffed lemurs in the rain
forest of Nosy Mangabe. Balko (1998) studied how
black-and-white ruffed lemur resource use varied
between forests of different structure near Ranomafana. Red-ruffed lemurs co-occur with white-
fronted lemurs (*Lemur fulvus albifrons*) in Masoala;
ruffed lemurs are sympatric with red-bellied lemurs (*L. rubriventer*) and rufous lemurs (*L. f. rufus*)
in Ranomafana.

Ruffed lemurs have similar food species diversity, eat the same items, and feed in similar locations. Ruffed lemurs feed on sixty-five or more
species annually, but they rely on only a few food
species at any time. Wherever food species diversity was reported, the top five food species in each
month accounted for most feeding records. Food
species diversity fluctuated with black-and-white
ruffed lemurs. Morland found that food species diversity increased in the warm, nonmating season.
Balko saw that groups in resource scarce areas had

ore diverse diets than did those in resource rich reas. Ruffed lemurs are highly frugivorous. No atter the site, ripe fruit accounts for two-thirds or more of their diet. Red-ruffed lemurs supplement their diet with mature flowers; black-and-white ruffed lemurs consume either nectar (Nosy Mangabe) or young leaves (Ranomafana). Ruffed lemurs generally live either just below or within the forest canopy, spending 70% or more of their time at least 10 meters above the ground. Rigamonti found that red-ruffed lemurs prefer those resources that bear enough fruit to sustain groups for several weeks.

Morland reported seasonal shifts in activity rhythms. During the cool season, these lemurs are most active near dawn and dusk and remain largely inactive throughout the day. They rest close to food, and travel less daily distance. In the warm season, the lemurs are more active in the morning and late afternoon. They travel more distance and include more species in their diet. Inactivity occurs most during midday. Morland observed infrequent nocturnal activity among study groups.

Home range size varied greatly between sites (Rigamonti: 23–26 ha; Vasey: 58 ha; Morland: 8.5 ha; Balko: 100–150 ha). This variation may reflect methodology, group size, food distribution, or forest structure. Yet in each site, ruffed lemur home ranges overlapped less than 10%. Ruffed lemurs are highly intolerant of conspecific groups, and groups meet infrequently at home range boundaries. Chases, vocal displays, intensive **scent-marking** bouts, and aggressive interactions typify these interactions. Vasey and Balko noted that ruffed lemurs in their sites were territorial; communal members consistently monitored boundaries and excluded potential intruders. In Nosy Mangabe, however, Morland did not observe whether communal members consistently monitored boundaries.

Ruffed lemurs live in multimale, multifemale communities of 5 to 31 individuals. Densities range from 5 to 54 lemurs per km². Each community has two or more adult males, two or more adult females, and nonadults. Groups are not spatially cohesive, and an individual's range within a com-

munity could overlap extensively with those of other community members. The highly stereotypical behaviors that occur between members of different communities do not occur between members of the same community. Ruffed lemurs are most often seen alone or in subgroups. Rigamonti found seasonal variation in the time that members remain in subgroups. In the dry season subgroups form, but all members reunite as a group daily. In the cold, wet season subgroups form that last for several weeks. Balko noted that this flexible social system may enhance the ability of ruffed lemurs to adapt to forests that vary in structure and resource distribution.

TRENDS IN LEMUR ECOLOGY AND SOCIAL STRUCTURE

Overall, lemurids tend to rely on a core of four or five food species during any month or season (Table 1). In most studies, the percentage of diet devoted to top food species varies monthly or seasonally. Lemurids also are highly frugivorous. In almost all studies, fruit makes up two-thirds or more of the diet at most times. Other items, such as flowers, leaves, and nectar, are important supplements to diets, especially during fruit scarcity. Home ranges are generally small (less than 20 ha), and most lemurids are strictly arboreal. Nearly all are active during the day and night. Forest structure, resource availability, population density, and the presence of other primates may influence lemurid diet, ranging patterns, and activity rhythms.

Although lemurids behave similarly in many habitats, many significant between species differences occur (Tables 1 and 2). Ringtailed lemurs are unlike lemurids in that they are semiterrestrial. Their varied diet perhaps reflects resource diversity and availability near the ground. In most locations, brown lemurs use the middle story or canopy. Deviations from the typical lemurid diet, home range size, social structure, and group size may be due to factors such as high population density and fruit scarcity. Crowned lemurs and black lemurs inhabit the lower forest levels and use resources similar to

TABLE 1 Cross-Species Comparison of Diet, Ranging Patterns, Density, and Habitat Type
Based on Information from Year-Round, Ecological, Studies of Lemurids

Species (with common name)	Monthly or Seasonal Food Species Diversity	Food Item (P = primary, S = supplement)	Home Range (in hectares)	Forest Level	Density (lemurs/ km²)	Forest Type
Lemur catta Ringtailed	Varied	Varied	6–35 Nonterritorial?	Semi-terrestrial	17–350	Dry
Lemur fulvus Brown	Monotonous or seasonally varied	Fruit or leaves (P) Varied (S)	1–75 Nonterritorial	Middle story or canopy	25–1061	Continuous canopy (wet & dry)
Lemur coronatus Crowned	2 spp. = 50%, seasonally varied	Fruit (P) Flowers (S)	6–16 Nonterritorial	Lower forest levels	105	Wet & dry
Lemur macaco Black	4 spp. > 50%, varied	Fruit (P) Leaves & nectar (S)	3–7 Nonterritorial	Lower forest levels	200	Wet & dry
Lemur mongoz Mongoose	Not reported	Fruit (P) Varied (S)	3 Territorial	Lower forest levels	100	Deciduous
Lemur rubriventer Red-bellied	5 spp. > 50%, varied	Fruit (P) Leaves & flowers (S)	11–19 Territorial	Canopy	15–30	Wet
Varecia variegata Ruffed	5 spp. > 50%, varied	Fruit (P) Varied (S)	8–150 Variably territorial	Canopy	5–54	Wet

SOURCE: Morland 1991; Overdorff 1991; Rasamaminana and Rafidinarivo 1993; Rigamonti 1993;
Sauther and Sussman 1993; Freed 1996; Colquhoun 1997; Curtis 1997; Vasey 1997; Balko 1998.

other lemurids. Groups of both species form subgroups daily during the same season, perhaps to exploit those resources that would otherwise not support many individuals. This flexible social system may be quite necessary for those species that live in a variety of habitats. Mongoose lemurs also live in lower forest levels, yet they live in smaller monogamous groups that actively defend their ranges. They are also at least seasonally more nocturnal. Their social system, range defense, and nocturnality may reflect adaptations for life in deciduous forests where resource availability can fluctuate greatly. Red-bellied lemurs and ruffed lemurs are canopy or near-canopy dwellers in wet forests, but the density or number of individuals that use this forest level is quite low. Red-bellied lemurs live

in small monogamous groups, whereas ruffed lemurs live in small communities that are not spatially cohesive.

Within those species in which studies were conducted in two or more sites, habitat use and social structure vary widely (see Table 1). Among ringtailed lemurs, food species diversity, food item choice, home range, territoriality, and density vary between groups, months, seasons, and sites. For some categories, brown lemur ecology varies greatly between sites. Western rufous lemurs have a monotonous diet, feed on leaves, and live in large densities. Other brown lemurs have more diverse diets, eat fruit, and live in much lower densities (25–86 individuals per km²). Home ranges also differ between forests. Whereas eastern rufous

TABLE 2 Cross-Species Comparison of Social Structure and Habitat Type
Based on Information from Year-Round, Ecological Studies of Lemurids

Species (with common name)	Social Structure	Average Group Size	Spatial Cohesion	Forest Type
Lemur catta Ringtailed	Multimale, multifemale	13–15	Cohesive	Dry
Lemur fulvus Brown	Multimale, multifemale	7–11	Cohesive	Continuous canopy (wet and dry)
Lemur coronatus Crowned	Multimale, multifemale	6–8	Seasonal subgroups	Wet and dry
Lemur macaco Black	Multimale, multifemale	9	Seasonal subgroups	Wet and dry
Lemur mongoz Mongoose	Monogamy	3	Cohesive	Deciduous
Lemur rubriventer Red-bellied	Monogamy	3	Cohesive	Wet
Varecia variegata Ruffed	Community	5–31	Not cohesive	Wet

SOURCE: Morland 1991; Overdorff 1991; Rasamaminana and Rafidinarivo 1993; Rigamonti 1993; Sauther and Sussman 1993; Freed 1996; Colquhoun 1997; Curtis 1997; Vasey 1997; Balko 1998.

lemurs have large home ranges (75 ha) and perhaps migrate, other brown lemurs live in small home ranges (less than 13 ha). Ruffed lemurs have diets of similar species diversity, are highly frugivorous, and mostly live in the canopy. Yet their home range size, territorial defense, and population density differs between sites.

LEMUR COMMUNITIES

Much of the work on lemurids is focused on how closely related morphologically similar species share the same habitat. Many Malagasy forests contain brown lemurs and at least one other lemurid species. Brown lemurs and their sympatric species partition resources within each study site. Sussman (1973) found significant year-round differences between how ringtailed lemurs and rufous lemurs feed, range, and conduct activities. Whereas the former are frugivorous, terrestrial, and live in large groups, the latter eat more leaves, are more arbo-

real, and live in smaller groups. The two species essentially ignored one another throughout the study. Ward and Sussman (1978) observed that many "metric and morphological differences in the hindlimb anatomy of Lemur catta are consistent with differences in habitat and substrate utilization." Overdorff (1991, 1993) showed that red-bellied lemurs and rufous lemurs avoid potential competition during resource scarcity as rufous lemurs migrate and use areas of nonoverlap. The lemurs otherwise minimize or avoid competing with one another by selecting food items somewhat differently. Freed (1996) also reported significant year-round and seasonal differences in how crowned lemurs and Sanford's lemurs choose food species, select food items, range, conduct activities, and organize themselves socially. Freed hypothesized that body size might account for differences in lemur habitat preferences and resource use. Gross year-round differences occur whenever ruffed lemurs co-occur with brown lemurs (Morland 1991; Vasey 1997; Balko 1998). In each study, ruffed lemurs accessed fruit higher in the trees than did brown lemurs.

Within most large Malagasy forests, not only do one to three lemurids co-occur, but so do one or two diurnal indriids, one to three bamboo lemur species, several nocturnal cheirogaleids and Lepilemurids, and aye-aye. Within these larger communities, lemurs use the same resources differently in highly overlapping ranges. Whereas lemurids are mostly frugivorous, indriids incorporate more seeds and foliage in their diets (Pollock 1975; Richard 1977; Meyers 1993; Hemingway 1995). Where two diurnal indriids co-occur, each species has a different feeding strategy and relies on different plant parts (Powzyk 1997). Indriids, not unlike African guerezas, may rely on foliage when fruit and flowers are otherwise unavailable (Oates 1977a). Bamboo lemurs may rely greatly on several species of bamboo, but year-round dietary data are not yet readily available (e.g., Meier et al. 1987). Compared with lemurids, nocturnal lemurs have more specialized diets and often eat more insects than do lemurids (e.g., Hladik, Charles-Dominique, and Petter 1980). Finally, Sterling found that aye-ayes consume several food items (insect larvae, seeds, fungi, and nectar) but focus on few species of any one item (Sterling 1993).

In most communities that contain multiple lemur species, rarely do two species interact extensively with one another. One species tolerates, ignores, or perhaps displaces another from shared resources. In northern Madagascar, however, crowned lemurs and Sanford's lemurs not only readily tolerate each other, they seek out one another and associate. Freed (1996) observed that when resources become scarce in the understory, crowned lemurs seek Sanford's lemurs feeding in the middle story. Likewise, Sanford's lemurs seek crowned lemurs when resources become scarce in the middle story. Mixed species associations, or groups that contain both species, usually form for three hours or more each day during the wet season. Other populations of crowned lemurs and Sanford's lemurs may also form these associations (Petter et al. 1977; Wilson et al. 1989). Freed sug-

gested that by forming associations both species expand their resource base without having to monitor both forest levels. Mixed species associations may help these lemurids in habitats where there are sudden fluctuations in resource availability.

CONCLUSION

Lemurs use resources and organize themselves in ways not unlike those of other primates. Lemurids consume similarly diverse numbers of species, rely on fruit, are quite arboreal, range over areas less than 35 hectares, and are mostly active during the day but are somewhat active at night. These same primates, however, may vary considerably in their diet, arboreality, ranging patterns, activity patterns, social structure, and interactions with other primates. Lemurids also share the same habitat with each other and with other lemurs. The mechanisms that influence lemur distribution are now being investigated in primate communities throughout Madagascar. The effects of year-round or seasonal variation in habitat use may reflect subtle, yet significant, differences in the morphology and adaptations of these primates. By studying these creatures, we may gain valuable insight as to the forces that influence primate adaptation and evolution.

ACKNOWLEDGMENTS

I thank four groups of people who have inspired and assisted me: the Malagasy officials, assistants, and local people who let me into their world, especially Madame Berthe Rakotosamimanana, Benjamin Andriamihaja, Dr. Andrianasolo Ranaivoson, Celestine Ravaoarinoromanga, and Patrice Antilahimena; the senior researchers, especially Kenneth Glander, Robert W. Sussman, and Ian Tattersall; fellow researchers who provide lively debate, including Liz Balko, Ian Colquhoun, Claire Hemingway, Deborah Overdorff, and Natalia Vasey; and my number one field assistant, Rose Anne Freed. Financial assistance was provided by National Science Foundation grant BNS-8722340, a Fulbright Collaborative Research Grant, Boise Fund, Sigma Xi, and Harriet and Joshua Freed. Finally, I thank Michael Hayes, Abbie, Ivan, Yevgeny, Tatyana, and the rest of the lemurs of Ampamelonabe.

Color Plate 1 Tarsier *(Tarsius spectrum)*. Photo by Sharon Gursky.

Color Plate 2 Tarsier *(Tarsius spectrum)*. Photo by Sharon Gursky.

Color Plate 3 Adult male sanfords lemur *(Lemur fulvus sanfordi)*. Photo by Benjamin Freed.

Color Plate 4 Crowned lemur *(Lemur coronatus)* feeding. Photo by Benjamin Freed.

Color Plate 5 Slender loris (*Loris tardigradus*) with young. Photo by Benjamin Freed.

Color Plate 6 Crowned lemur (*Lemur coronatus*) in terminal branches. Photo by Benjamin Freed.

Color Plate 7 Adult ringtailed lemur (*Lemur catta*) and two immatures. Photo by Benjamin Freed.

Color Plate 8 Adult male crowned lemur (*Lemur coronatus*) feeding on fruit. Photo by Benjamin Freed.

Color Plate 9 Adult female chimpanzee *(Pan troglodytes)* begs for a piece of cardboard from an adolescent female. Photo by Phyllis Dolhinow.

Color Plate 10 Chimpanzee *(Pan troglodytes)* extended family and others relax. Photo by Phyllis Dolhinow.

Color Plate 11 A gibbon group *(Hylobates lar)*. Photo by Thad Bartlett.

Color Plate 12 A gibbon *(Hylobates lar)* demonstrating its anatomical specialization. Photo by Thad Bartlett.

Color Plate 13 Red leaf monkey *(Presbytis rubicunda)* in a fig tree. Photo by Tim Laman.

Color Plate 14 Adult female orangutan *(Pomgo pygmaeus)* with infant. Photo by Tim Laman.

Color Plate 15 Adult male orangutan (*Pomgo pygmaeus*). Photo by Tim Laman.

Color Plate 16 Pregnant adult female orangutan (*Pomgo pygmaeus*). Photo by Tim Laman.

Color Plate 17 Adult male gorilla. Photo by Tim Laman.

Color Plate 18 Capuchin monkey (*Cebus capucinus*). Photo by Phyllis Dolhinow.

Color Plate 19 Capuchin monkey *(Cebus capucinus)*. Note the prehensile tail. Photo by Phyllis Dolhinow.

Color Plate 20 Black and white colobus monkeys *(Colobus guereza)*. Photo by Phyllis Dolhinow.

Color Plate 21 Baboon troop (*Papio anubis*) in Nairobi Park. Photo by Phyllis Dolhinow.

Color Plate 22 A group of rhesus macaques (*Macaca mulatta*) on a rocky hillside. Photo by Phyllis Dolhinow.

Color Plate 23 Adult female Balinese longtailed macaque (*Macaca fasicularis*) and two immatures. Photo by Katherine MacKinnon.

Color Plate 24 Toque macaque (*Macaca sinica*) filling its cheek pouches. Photo by Phyllis Dolhinow.

Color Plate 25 Captive hanuman langur group *(Semnopithecus entellus)*. Photo by Phyllis Dolhinow.

Color Plate 26 Balinese longtailed macaques *(Macaca fasicularis)* grooming. Photo by Phyllis Dolhinow.

Color Plate 27 Adult Barbary macaque *(Macaca sylvanus)* and young in Gibraltar. Photo by Agustín Fuentes.

Color Plate 28 Adult male patas monkey *(Erythrocebus patas)*. Photo by Phyllis Dolhinow.

Color Plate 29 Pileated langur group (*Trachypithecus pileatus*). Photo by Craig Stanford.

Color Plate 30 Vervet group (*Chlorocebus aethiops*) with a young infant in the center. Photo by Phyllis Dolhinow.

Color Plate 31 Vervets *(Chlorocebus aethiops)* grooming. Photo by Phyllis Dolhinow.

Color Plate 32 Vervets *(Chlorocebus aethiops)* grooming. Photo by Phyllis Dolhinow.

14

How Female Dominance and Reproductive Seasonality Affect the Social Lives of Adult Male Ringtailed Lemurs

Lisa Gould

Female dominance occurs in only a small number of mammalian species and is rare among primates (Ralls 1976; Hrdy 1981; Richard 1987). The extent of and adaptive reasons for such a pattern differ from one species to another. For example, female reproductive condition influences the outcome of male-female agonistic interactions in golden hamsters, and in Maxwell's duikers females have priority of access to preferred food whereas males have priority over preferred resting areas (Ralls 1976). In some anthropoid primates, coalitions of females can be dominant to a male or males, or the alpha female can displace or exhibit aggression toward a single male or a few males. However, a single female would not be dominant to all males (see review in Smuts 1987). Among lemurs, several species are considered female dominant, and characteristics of such dominance differ interspecifically (Richard 1987; Pereira et al. 1990). Richard (1987) suggests that because of such interspecific variability a single definition of female dominance is inappropriate, and the state of female dominance is not likely homologous among mammals, nor has it evolved to serve a similar function across taxa.

In this essay I will examine patterns of sociality among adult males in a markedly female dominant primate species, the ringtailed lemur (Lemur catta), and discuss the effects of strict reproductive seasonality on male social relationships, as well as the benefits to males of living in social groups in which the females have priority of access to all resources. But first, I will *outline the social organization and reproductive pattern of the ringtailed lemur and discuss hypotheses that suggest why such strict female dominance exists in this species.*

SOCIAL ORGANIZATION

The ringtailed lemur (*Lemur catta*), is found in riverine and **xerophytic forests** in southern and southwestern Madagascar (Jolly 1966; Sussman 1977). This species lives in multimale, multifemale social groups and exhibits female residence and male dispersal (Jolly 1966; Budnitz and Dainis 1975; Sussman 1977, 1991, 1992). Social groups average thirteen to fifteen animals and range in size from five to twenty-seven individuals, with a sex ratio of approximately 1:1 (Jolly 1966; Budnitz and Dainis 1975; Sussman 1992; Sauther and Sussman 1993). There is little to no sexual dimorphism between males and females. All females residing in a social group are related, and a female remains in the group into which she is born all of her life. Females, their infants, and subadult offspring are generally found in close proximity to one another and spatially form the central core of the group (Jolly 1966; Budnitz and Dainis 1975; Sussman 1991; Sauther 1992). Young natal males who have not yet migrated are often found in close proximity to their mothers and other female kin (Sauther and

Sussman 1993). The highest ranking nonnatal male in a *Lemur catta* social group has been described as the "central male" (Sauther 1991; Sauther and Sussman 1993). Such males have been observed to spend more time than do the lower ranking males in close proximity to, and in social interaction with, the central core of females in a group throughout the year (Jolly 1966; Sussman 1977; Sauther 1992; Gould 1994). Lower ranking or **peripheral males** have been described as generally peripheral to the female core of the group, except during the brief mating period (Jolly 1966; Budnitz and Dainis 1975; Jones 1983). However, lower ranking males are by no means exclusively peripheral, and they do engage in affiliative interactions with adult females and immatures (Taylor 1986; Sauther 1992; Gould 1994, 1996, 1997).

The ringtailed lemur exhibits strict **reproductive seasonality** (Table 1). There are distinct mating, gestation, birth/lactation, male migration, and postmigration seasons (Jolly 1966; Sussman 1977, 1991, 1992; Jones 1983; Sauther 1991). Adult males transfer to new social groups approximately every three to five years, and young males make their first migration at about 3 to 4 years of age (Sussman 1991; Sauther and Sussman 1993). There is also marked resource seasonality (distinct wet and dry seasons) in the geographic range of this species; thus, periods of both food abundance and food scarcity occur each year.

WHY DOES THE RINGTAILED LEMUR EXHIBIT FEMALE DOMINANCE?

Ringtailed lemur society has been described as "the extreme example of female dominance among primates" (Jolly et al. 1993: 106). Adult females are dominant to males in all feeding and social contexts and across annual cycles (Budnitz and Dainis 1975; Jolly 1984; Kappeler 1990; Sauther 1992). One explanation for female dominance that applies to seasonally breeding mammals with strong **reproductive synchrony** is that because females in such

TABLE 1 Reproductive Seasons at Beza-Mahafaly

Reproductive season	Time of year
Postmigration period	March to May
Mating season	mid-May to mid-June
Gestation season	mid-June to October
Lactation/migration season (concurrent)	October to February

species experience marked seasonal stress with respect to food resources during gestation and lactation it would be advantageous for a male to defer to a female because she may be carrying or nursing his offspring (Hrdy 1981). The dry season in southern Madagascar is often extreme, in some years actual drought conditions occur. The highly synchronized birth season in ringtailed lemurs occurs near the end of the dry season, and most females in a population give birth within one three-to-four-week interval of time. Thus, all females begin lactating during a period when many important food resources are markedly scarce (Jolly 1984; Sauther 1991, 1993). Infants begin to ingest solid foods at approximately 6 to 8 weeks of age, a time that coincides with the onset of the rainy season; however, females continue to nurse infants until the infants are 4 to 6 months of age (Jolly 1966; Gould 1990). In addition, ringtailed lemur infants exhibit a relatively rapid growth rate relative to body size, which results in a high energy demand being placed on the mother (Richard 1987; Sauther 1991; Rasamaminana and Rafidinarivo 1993). Thus, to ensure infant survival, males need to allow lactating females priority of access to resources during this critical period (Jolly 1984; Richard 1987). One of the consequences for adult males of female priority of access to resources is that males experience strong agonism from females in all feeding contexts (Jolly 1966; Sauther 1992, 1993).

Ringtailed lemur females are dominant to males, have priority of access to all resources, and commonly exhibit agonism toward males. What do the males living in such groups get out of it? A number of advantages have, in fact, been documented. A male's membership in a group can offset his nutritional stress and vulnerability to predation (Sauther 1989, 1991; Sussman 1991). Predators of ringtailed lemurs include large raptors, the endemic fossa (a cat-like carnivore of the mongoose family), and feral dogs and cats (Sauther 1989; Goodman, O'Connor, and Langrand 1993). Potential mating success is another advantage to group living, as females tend to mate with group males before non-group males (Koyama 1988; Sauther 1991, 1992; Gould 1996). However, to live in a social group with these advantages, an adult male must be accepted by both females and other resident adult males. How is this accomplished? One particular research interest of mine has been to determine how males organize themselves socially and become accepted members of the group in a primate society that exhibits marked female dominance.

In 1992 and 1993 I spent twelve months at the Beza-Mahafaly Reserve in southwestern Madagascar collecting data on affiliative behavior between adult male ringtailed lemurs and other group members, including 1102 hours of **focal animal sampling** on nine focal males residing in three social groups within the reserve boundaries. Six of the nine adult males in the three study groups had been previously tagged and collared for identification purposes as they are part of a long-term demographic project at Beza-Mahafaly begun in 1987 (Sussman 1991). The remaining three males were captured and collared and tagged during the study. Thus, age class and migration status were known for all nine study animals.

The following behaviors were considered affiliative: **allogrooming**, sitting, or resting in contact with another group member; sitting and resting in close proximity (less than one meter) to another animal; and huddling with one or more animals during rest periods. Rates per hour of affiliative behavior between focal males, focal males and females, and focal males and immature group members were calculated.

One of the notable results of this research was that reproductive seasonality in particular appeared to have a strong effect on patterns of affiliative behavior between males and all other group members in this sample. Let's take a closer look at these data.

INTERMALE AFFILIATIVE RELATIONSHIPS AND REPRODUCTIVE SEASONALITY

The frequency of affiliative behavior between males differed significantly according to reproductive seasons (Figure 1). Rates per hour of affiliative behavior during the lactation season are higher for most of the focal males than those found in other seasons. This may be an effect of male migration, which occurs during part of the lactation season. Because successful immigration into a new social group can take several months, migrating males tend to form dyads or triads while in the process of migration (Sussman 1992). Males RG3 and RG4 emigrated from one social group (Red group) to another (Green group), and their rates of interaction with each other were comparatively very high throughout the migration and immediate postmigration season. However, five of the seven resident males also exhibited higher rates of affiliation with other males in their groups during the lactation/migration season. Resident males in a group collectively exhibit agonistic and defensive behavior toward outside males attempting to immigrate; therefore, the need to cooperate with each other, and hence the motivation to affiliate with familiar males, may be heightened at this time.

The lowest rates of intermale affiliative behavior occurred during the brief (four-week) mating season. During this short period of time, strong intermale competition for access to estrous females and high rates of male-male agonism occur. Predictably, rates of intermale affiliative behavior during mating season are lower compared with other periods.

Intermale affiliative behavior can result in a number of benefits. Ringtailed lemurs are highly social animals, and activities such as allogrooming and sitting or resting in contact are important. Affiliative behavior between males can also lead to health benefits such as keeping warm during the cold season by huddling and resting in contact with another animal. Temperatures during the austral winter in southwestern Madagascar can fall as low as 3 degrees centigrade, and close physical contact at this time can be crucial to survival. Males

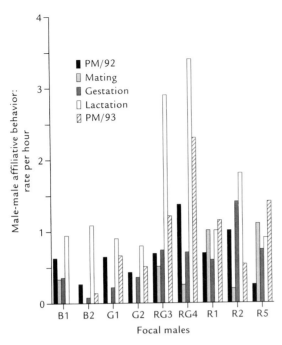

FIGURE 1   Rates per hour of affiliative behavior between each focal male and other males in his group. A significant difference was found over reproductive seasons (Friedman's two-way analysis of variance, $r^2 = 19.29$, $p < .001$). Males RG3 and RG4 are the two males that migrated from Red to Green group. Pm/92 and pm/93 represent the postmigration seasons of 1992 and 1993. Migration season occurs at the same time as lactation season.

also benefit healthwise from ectoparasite control through allogrooming. Males in the process of migration can benefit from affiliation with other migrating males in relation to enhanced predator detection and protection, enhanced detection of attack by resident males when attempting to immigrate into a new group, and social contact during the lengthy migration process.

MALE-FEMALE AFFILIATION

In contrast to intermale social behavior, rates of affiliative behavior between males and females did not differ significantly when examined across reproductive seasons (Figure 2); however, interindividual and intergroup differences are apparent. Of particular note is that the two males in Blue group (B1 and B2) displayed higher rates of affiliative behavior with the females in their group than most of the other focal males over all reproductive seasons but one (postmigration, 1992). Green group gained two males during the migration period, totalling four adult males after migration season. Rates of affiliation between the original two resident males (G1 and G2) and the females in Green group were higher in some seasons than those of Red group males. Overall, the males in Red group affiliated less frequently with the females in their group than the males in either of the other study groups. Red group contained six males during the first seven months of the study, then four after migration season. Thus, the number of males in a group may negatively affect rates of affiliation between males and females.

I was curious to discover if female involvement with infants had an effect on male-female affiliation. I divided the four-month lactation season into four segments of one month each and examined the rate per hour of affiliative behavior with females for each focal male. By doing so, it was possible to determine if maternal care at different stages of infant development and dependency affected the amount of affiliation between adult males and females. Again, no significant difference was found across these four periods (Figure 3). The three males that exhibited the lowest rates of social interaction with females were the two males that migrated out of Red group during the lactation period, as well as R5, who began the migration process coinciding with the first two months of the lactation period; however, he returned to Red group and remained there for the duration of the study. His rates of affiliative behavior with females increased in the final two months of the lactation period.

Females have priority of access to all resources and are socially dominant to males, so what kinds of benefits could males accrue by affiliating with adult females? I suggest that friendly relationships with females allow a male to spend time in closer proximity to the central female core of the group. This, in turn, can lead to better predator protec-

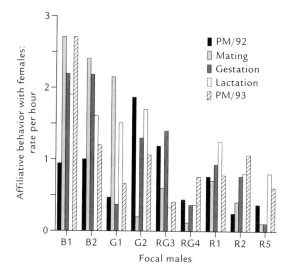

FIGURE 2   Rates per hour of affiliative behavior between each focal male and the adult females in his group over reproductive seasons. No seasonal difference was found (Friedman's two-way analysis of variance, p > .05). Males RG3 and RG4 are the two males that migrated from Red to Green group.

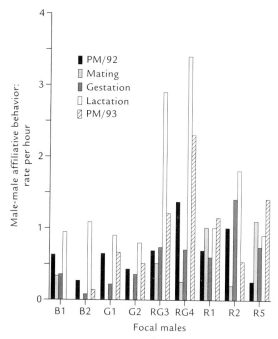

FIGURE 3   Affiliative behavior between adult males and females over each month of the lactation period.

tion, greater opportunities for social contact with all group members, and potentially greater access to estrous females in the mating season. With respect to mating, both Sauther (1991, 1992) and Gould (1996) noted that higher ranking, more central males were consistently chosen by females as first mating partners. Furthermore, affiliative relations with females expose a male to a greater number of social partners, which can lead to the health benefits previously discussed.

Friendly relationships with females do not, however, result in any type of feeding advantage for a male. Jolly (1966) first noted that females consistently displace males in feeding contexts. Sauther (1993) found that 63% of all feeding displacements by females toward males at Beza-Mahafaly involved severe and aggressive behavior such as chasing, pushing, and biting. Sauther also noted that such aggressive displacement was not restricted to any particular season: it occurred throughout the yearly cycle. I found that all males experience feeding agonism by females, regardless of whether or not

they have formed an affiliative relationship with a female.

The fact that affiliative relationships with females do not enhance access to food resources contrasts with the behavior of some male dominant primate species. Smuts (1983, 1985) suggested that one way in which adult female baboons benefit from their relationships with males is that they experience reduced interference with maintenance activities (such as feeding) by higher ranking females and other adult males. Hill (1990) commented that rhesus macaque females who have affiliative relationships with males may gain increased access to food resources.

MALES AND IMMATURES

The category "immatures" refers to pre-reproductive group members of the following age classes: infants (0–6 months), juveniles (6–18 months), and adolescents (18–30 months). The frequency of affiliative interactions between adult males and immatures did not differ significantly according to reproductive season. In two of the study groups (Blue and Red), however, an empirical trend existed. In these groups, adult males affiliated more often with older immatures (juveniles and adolescents) during the lactation and subsequent postmigration season (Figure 4). Maternal care did not affect rates of male-female affiliative behavior, but it may have had an effect on rates of social interaction between males and older immatures as these young group members would not have the same access to their mothers when mothers are engaged in nursing and other infant care activities. A similar trend has been noted in Japanese and rhesus macaques. Adult males in these two species exhibit a high degree of affiliation and care toward yearling and 2-year-olds during the lactation period when mothers have less time to spend with their older offspring (Itani 1959; Alexander 1970; Hasegawa and Hiraiwa 1980; Gouzoules 1984; Hill, 1986).

Both adult males and immatures can benefit from social relationships with one another. Adult males, by affiliating with immatures, are afforded closer proximity to the central core of the group because immatures tend to stay in fairly close proximity to their mothers until they become sexually mature. Frequent close proximity to the center of the group can lead to greater tolerance by females of a male's presence, which could potentially lead to the development of affiliative relationships with females. As well, all other social and health-related benefits discussed previously can be gained.

Furthermore, male ringtailed lemurs do exhibit an interest in infants and may derive contact comfort from interaction with them as Strum (1984) has suggested is the case in olive baboon male-infant interactions. Six of the nine focal males were observed engaging in alloparental and affiliative behavior with the infants in their groups. Such behavior consisted of grooming and holding the infant and occasional play.

Immature ringtailed lemurs can also benefit from social interaction with males with respect to greater protection from predators, development of social skills, and alloparental care.

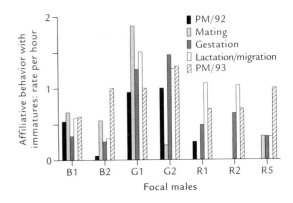

FIGURE 4   Rates per hour of affiliative behavior between focal males and the juveniles and adolescents in the group over reproductive seasons. No significant difference was found (Friedman's two-way analysis of variance, p > .05). The two migrating males RG3 and RG4 are not included in this figure as they did not interact with immatures over the long migration process.

CONCLUSIONS

Reproductive seasonality in ringtailed lemurs affects patterns of affiliative behavior between males and all group members. Social interaction between males appears most strongly affected during mating and male migration seasons. During the mating period, adult males are in competition for access to estrous females. Such competition can lead to a high degree of both indirect (scent-marking and ritual stink-fighting) and direct (physical fighting) reproductive competition; thus, little intermale affiliative behavior occurs at this time. Conversely, during the migration season, migrating males tend to band together in groups of two or three and affiliate almost exclusively with each other during the migration process, which can last from one to six months. Resident males also exhibit high degrees of affiliative behavior with each other at this time, which may be a result of much time spent together attempting to repel migrating males from entering their social group.

Although reproductive seasonality per se did not directly affect rates of male-female affiliative behavior in the study animals, group size did. Males residing in groups with few males and several females engaged in more frequent affiliative behavior with adult females than did males living in groups with several males. Male migration can affect this trend because males living in groups with several males stand to benefit if some of the males in their group emigrate. This situation occurred in one study group, Red group, when two of the five males emigrated. Rates of affiliative behavior between the three remaining males and the females in the group increased in the months subsequent to migration season. Surprisingly, female involvement with infants did not affect rates of affiliative behavior between males and females during the lactation/infant care period.

Some of the adult males in the sample affiliated more often with older immatures during the lactation season. Mothers have less time to spend with older immatures once birth season occurs, and yearlings and 2-year-olds in two of the study groups consequently spent more time in social interactions with adult males.

Adult males benefit from affiliative behavior with all group members. Affiliation with females as well as with immatures appears to provide the greatest benefit, as males in such situations experience greater opportunities to spend more time in the spatially central core of the group. This, in turn, leads to benefits such as greater protection against predators, greater opportunities for social interaction in a highly social species, ectoparasite control through allogrooming, and protection from cold temperatures during the austral winter in southern Madagascar. Being more spatially central can also result in greater tolerance by females, which could potentially lead to both affiliative relationships with

females and greater mating opportunities during the brief mating period. Affiliative relations with other males in the group may be considered less beneficial, as such relationships would not lead to greater spatial centrality or potential social and mating opportunities with females. However, inter-male affiliation does allow for social and health benefits. During the migration process, dispersing males can greatly benefit from affiliative behavior with other migrating males through increased predator detection and protection, increased detection of attack by resident males, and having a social partner or partners with which to interact.

Furuichi (1985) and Hill (1994) suggested that among Japanese macaques adult females were the preferred social partners of adult males, however, when females were not available, males affiliated with other males. I suggest that for adult male ringtailed lemurs, this may also be the case as it seems most beneficial for males to affiliate and form social relationships with adult females.

ACKNOWLEDGMENTS

This research was funded by NSF Grant BNS-9119122, Wenner-Gren Pre-doctoral Research Grant 5401, National Geographic Research Grant 4734–92, a grant from the Boise Fund of Oxford, and a fellowship from the Alberta Heritage Foundation. I am grateful to Mme. Berthe Rakotosamimanana, M. Benjamin Andriamihaja, M. Pothin Rakotomanga, Dr. Adrianasolo Ranaivoson, Joseph Andrianmampianina, Mme. Celestine Ravaoarinoromanga, the School of Agronomy at the University of Antananarivo, and Direction des Eaux et Fôret, Madagascar, for granting me permission to conduct research at the Beza-Mahafaly Reserve.

15

The Tarsiidae: Taxonomy, Behavior, and Conservation Status

Sharon Gursky

TAXONOMY

Tarsiers first became known to Western scientists based on a description written by Petiver in 1705. Petiver (1705) named the animal *Cercopithecus luzonis minimus* due to its primate-like features. In 1765, Buffon also described a tarsier, which he gave the name *Didelphis macrotarsus; Didelphis* because he believed tarsiers were related to opossums, and *macrotarsus* because of the extremely long tarsal bones exhibited by this animal. Erxleben (1777) was the first scientist to recognize the similarities between tarsiers and other prosimian primates, and consequently he named them *Lemur tarsier*. Storr, in 1780, recognized the numerous differences between lemurs and tarsiers and argued for the generic separation of these two taxa. Storr coined the genus name *Tarsius* for these unusual primates who possessed exceptionally long tarsal bones.

Since the time that tarsiers were finally recognized as primates, and distinct from the lemurs, they have been the focus of numerous controversies. Specifically, there has been considerable debate over the classification of the tarsiers within the order Primates. There are two major schools of thought.

The first school of thought is based on the work of Pocock (1918), who believed tarsiers are more similar to the higher primates (monkeys, apes, and humans) than to the lemurs and lorises. To express this relationship, Pocock established two infra-orders within the order Primates: the Haplorrhini, which included the suborder Tarsoidea as well as the suborders Ceboidea, Cercopithecoidea, and Hominoidea (monkeys, apes, and humans), and Strepsirhini, which included the lemurs and lorises. Pocock believed tarsiers were more similar to the anthropoid primates because of numerous shared derived characteristics (**synapomorphies**) such as the lack of a moist rhinarium. Among the characteristics shared by tarsiers and anthropoid primates are haemochorial placentation, absence of a tapetum lucidum, presence of a fovea centralis, reduced olfactory bulbs, lack of a wet rhinarium, well-developed promontory artery, and lack of an attached upper lip (Pocock 1918; Wolin and Massoupust 1970; Cave 1973; Luckett 1976; Cartmill and Kay 1978; Rosenberger and Szalay 1980; Aiello 1986; MacPhee and Cartmill 1986; Schwartz and Tatersall 1987; Fleagle 1988).

The second school of classification is based on the idea that the lemurs, lorises, and tarsiers are more closely related to one another and should be grouped together in the suborder Prosimii, with the higher primates all grouped together in the Anthropoidea (Simpson 1945b; Cartmill and Kay 1978; Rosenberger and Szalay 1980; Schwartz and Tatersall 1987; Fleagle 1988; Boyd and Silk 1997). This classification scheme is based on numerous ancestral characters such as the nocturnal habits of the tarsier, small body size, and the tarsiers' parenting strategy (infant parking and oral transport). This classification scheme represents a gradistic

140

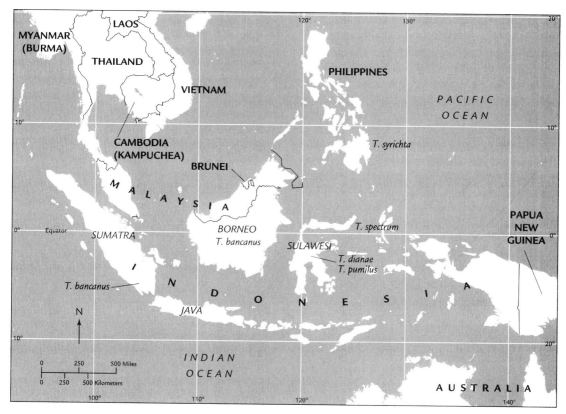

FIGURE 1   Distribution of the five formally recognized tarsier species.

classification scheme compared to the cladistic classification scheme proposed by Pocock (1918). Anatomical characteristics that are shared by tarsiers and other prosimian primates include an un-fused **mandibular symphysis,** a grooming claw, multiple pairs of mammae, and a **bicornuate uterus** (Pocock 1918; Hill 1955; Cartmill and Kay 1978; Rosenberger and Szalay 1980; Aiello 1986; Fleagle 1988). It is interesting that introductory textbooks in physical anthropology persist in using a gradistic approach in grouping tarsiers with the other prosimians but employ a cladistic approach when studying the relationship of the great apes (Boyd and Silk 1997).

Not only has there been substantial disagreement concerning the taxonomic classification of the tarsiers, but there has also been considerable disagreement regarding the number of tarsier species

(Hill 1955; Niemitz 1984; Musser and Dagosto 1987). At present, five species of tarsier are formally recognized (Figure 1): *Tarsius syrichta* (Linnaeus 1758); *Tarsius bancanus* (Horsfield 1821); *Tarsius pumilus* (Miller and Hollister 1921; Musser and Dagosto 1987); *Tarsius spectrum* (Pallas 1778); and *Tarsius dianae* (Niemitz et al. 1991). Two additional Sulawesian tarsier species, *Tarsius sangirensis* and *Tarsius togianensis,* have been tentatively proposed and are awaiting additional studies (Groves 1993; Nietsch 1996; Shekelle et al. 1997).

T. syrichta is distributed in the southern Philippines on the islands of Samar, Leyte, Dinagat, Siargao, Bohol, and Mindanao. *T. bancanus* is distributed within Borneo, Bangka, Belitung, Karimata, South Natuna, and the southern tip of Sumatra. Three tarsier species are presently recognized within Sulawesi: *T. pumilus,* from the montane mossy forest in the central part of the island; *T. dianae* (Niemitz et al. 1991), from the lowland forest in central Sulawesi; and *T. spectrum* (Pallas 1778), found throughout Sulawesi (Sody 1949; Laurie and Hill 1954). *T. spectrum* is reported to occur within the altitudinal range of *T. dianae*, although it is unclear whether the two populations live sympatrically (Niemitz et al. 1991). *T. pumilus*, the pygmy tarsier, is the smallest tarsier known, but it has not yet been observed in the wild (Shekelle et al. 1997; Gursky, pers. obser.).

These tarsier species differ morphologically from one another in a variety of ways. They differ in their absolute orbit size, their absolute tooth size, the proportion of tail that is covered by hair, and in their limb proportions. Musser and Dagosto (1987) observed that the distribution of these characteristics in tarsiers represents a **cline.** In terms of absolute orbit size and absolute tooth size, the Bornean tarsier possesses the largest orbits and the largest teeth of any of the species, followed by the Philippine tarsier, the spectral tarsier, and then the pygmy tarsier. No data are available for Dian's tarsier. There is also a cline in proportion of the tail that is covered by hair. *Tarsius spectrum* and the other Sulawesian tarsier species possess the most tail hair, followed by the Bornean tarsier, and the Philippine tarsier, whose tail is often described as naked due to the sparse fine hairs that cover it. Niemitz (1977) also recorded numerous differences in limb proportions between the three major tarsier species (*T. spectrum, T. bancanus,* and *T. syrichta*). The Bornean tarsier has the longest hindlimb and hand, followed by the Philippine tarsier, whose hindlimbs and hands are intermediate in length, followed by the spectral tarsier, whose hindlimbs and hands are the shortest in length.

Interestingly, although there are only minor differences in morphology, there are substantial chromosomal differences between some tarsier species. The Bornean and Philippine tarsier are each reported to have a karotype of 80 chromosomes (Klinger 1963; Chiarelli and Egozcue 1968; Poorman et al. 1985), whereas *Tarsius dianae* is reported to have only 46 chromosomes (Niemitz et al. 1991). The karotypes for both *T. spectrum* and *T. pumilus* are still unknown.

BEHAVIORAL STUDIES

Tarsius bancanus

The first field study of wild tarsiers was conducted by Fogden (1974) in Semongok Forest Reserve in Sarawak on *T. bancanus,* the Bornean tarsier. Fogden observed that Bornean tarsiers have home ranges of 2.5–3.0 hectares and that the male's range overlaps that of the female. In several cases the male's range overlapped the ranges of several females. He noted that this species primarily consumes insects, and they do not exhibit much social behavior. During 11% of his observations, Fogden observed more than one individual traveling or foraging together. In each instance, a male-female pair was observed.

Fogden's study (1974) was the inspiration for much of the later work on tarsiers. Niemitz's (1974, 1979, 1984) long-term studies of *T. bancanus* were based on his observations of semiwild individuals in a cage enclosure in the Semongok Forest Reserve in Sarawak. Niemitz (1979, 1984) reported that the home range of this species is approximately 1.5 hectares. In Niemitz's work, the male's range never overlapped the range of more than one female. He reported that individuals probably live in pairs (1984). Niemitz also observed that Bornean tarsiers not only consume insects but also birds, snakes, and other small mammals. According to Niemitz's observations (1984), the Bornean tarsier's primary mode of locomotion is vertical clinging and leaping (VCL), although individuals do spend time climbing, hopping on the ground, and in quadrupedal locomotion.

Crompton and Andau (1986, 1987) conducted a study of four *T. bancanus* using radio telemetry equipment in Sepilok Forest Reserve, Sabah. This was the first time that radio telemetry was used to study free-ranging tarsiers. Their results indicated that adult males range over 8.75–11.25 hectares and adult females range over 4.5–9.5 hectares. Crompton and Andau also noted the presence of two adult males in the home range of a single female and four adult males in the home range of another female. They observed that males and females did not sleep together during the day but were observed sleeping at an average of 50 meters from one another.

Although others have recorded that *T. bancanus* is ordinarily silent (Fogden 1974; Niemitz 1984), Crompton and Andau heard numerous clear calls while following the tarsiers at Sepilok. They believe that vocal communication is very important in Bornean tarsiers. Three calls were repeatedly heard: (1) a whistle of unknown association; (2) a "chick chick chick" that might indicate disturbance; and (3) a "tsit tsit tsit." A remarkable feature of Crompton and Andau's observations of vocalizations concerned the "calling concerts"; three to five tarsiers were heard calling "tsit tsit tsit" within a radius of 50 meters of the observer. In one instance, the "calling concert" lasted for four hours. It should be noted that most vocal calls were single. Of ninety-one calling records, 68% were single calls, 18.7% involved simultaneous calling or duets, and the rest were cases of three and four or more tarsiers calling simultaneously. Nonetheless, the authors claim that the calls are quite distinct from the "family choruses" that have been reported for spectral tarsiers.

Wright, Izard, and Simons (1986), Wright, Toyama, and Simons (1988), Haring and Wright (1989), and Roberts (1994) each studied the life history of captive Bornean tarsiers. Their results indicate that infants have a 6-month gestation where upon they weigh nearly one-quarter to one-third of adult weight. This is followed by a 2-month period of lactation and rapid postnatal growth. Males are not involved in caring for infants and are known to be aggressive toward young.

Tarsius spectrum

The first field study of wild spectral tarsiers was undertaken by MacKinnon and MacKinnon (1980a). This study revealed that spectral tarsiers are primarily monogamous and exhibit a large amount of territoriality in the form of vocal battles, early morning family choruses, and scent-marking behavior. Group members were observed to sleep together in hollow strangling *Ficus* (fig) trees. MacKinnon and MacKinnon were able to recognize fifteen distinct vocalizations.

The observed diet of their study animals was 100% insectivorous. No feeding on mammals, birds, reptiles, or amphibians was observed as was

reported by Niemitz (1984) for *T. bancanus*. According to MacKinnon and MacKinnon's observations (1980a), the spectral tarsier's primary mode of locomotion is vertical clinging and leaping, followed by climbing up supports, climbing down supports, hopping on the ground, and quadrupedal locomotion.

MacKinnon and MacKinnon (1980a) also observed that males seem to range widest and are more active territorially in terms of both calling and urine marking. Juveniles often remain in a small area close to the sleeping sites while their parents hunt over a larger area. Individuals followed the same routes night after night. Niemitz (1984) estimated the home range of *T. spectrum,* based on a figure drawn by MacKinnon and MacKinnon (1980a), to be between .9–1.1 hectares. This is considerably smaller than the home range observed by Gursky (1997) when utilizing radio telemetry. During this study, Gursky found that female spectral tarsiers utilized a home range of approximately 2.32 hectares, whereas male spectral tarsiers utilized a range of approximately 3.07 hectares (Gursky, in press b).

Nietsch and Niemitz (1992) and Gursky (1995) each found that group composition in the spectral tarsiers is not always representative of monogamous pairs and that some males are polygynous. At least one of the groups Nietsch and Niemitz trapped contained three adult females, and others contained one or two adult females (Nietsch and Niemitz 1992; Gursky 1995). The size of male spectral tarsiers' testes are in agreement with the interpretation that spectral tarsiers are not always monogamous; testes size was large relative to body size (Gursky 1997). Spectral tarsier males and females are sexually dimorphic, with males weighing approximately 15% more than females.

The life history strategy of the spectral tarsier is very unusual. Spectral tarsiers were found to have a 6- to 7-month gestation period followed by a 2- to 3-month period of lactation. Infants are one-quarter to one-third of adult weight at birth and grow rapidly thereafter. Infants are not continually transported by the mother or other group member following birth. Spectral tarsiers exhibit a "cache and carry" infant caretaking strategy (Gursky

1997). Infants are transported in the mother's mouth, similar to domestic cats. In contrast, Le-Gros Clark (1924) and Niemitz (1984) each report that Bornean tarsiers were never observed transporting their infants in their mouths. However, all observations of *Tarsius bancanus* in captivity indicate that the Bornean tarsiers transport their infants orally (Roberts et al. 1984; Haring and Wright 1989). Subadult females were observed to provide some allocare to their infant siblings in the form of food sharing, guarding, and retrieving infants following a fall. There was no substantial care of infants by adult males.

Tarsius dianae

T. dianae was formally recognized in 1991 (Niemitz et al. 1991), and the behavioral observations distinguishing *T. dianae* from the spectral tarsier involved the observation that *T. dianae* groups did not always return to the same sleeping site each night and that this species produced unusual family choruses each morning.

A study of the home range of *T. dianae* was conducted by Tremble, Muskita, and Supriatna (1993) in Lore Lindu National Park, central Sulawesi. Home range for individuals of this species varied from .5 to .8 hectares, considerably smaller than the home range obtained for either *T. bancanus* or *T. spectrum* when radio telemetry was utilized (Crompton and Andau 1987; Gursk, in press a).

Nietsch (1994) conducted playback experiments wherein the vocal family chorus of the Tangkoko *T. spectrum* population was played for a group she identified as *T. dianae*. The group did not recognize the vocal calls and did not respond to the recorded calls. In contrast, when she played the vocal calls of one *T. dianae* group for another *T. dianae* group, the group responded by traveling toward the intruder (the recorded vocal call) as well as by vocalizing themselves.

Gursky (1997) compared the morphometrics of two freshly killed individuals of Dian's tarsiers and was unable to identify any morphological differences between *T. dianae* and *T. spectrum*. However, when comparing cranial measurements of Dian's tarsier with the spectral tarsier, four major differences were identified. Dian's tarsiers had greater length of skull, zygomatic breadth, breadth of the palate at M^3, and length of the tooth row from the canine to M^3 than did the spectral tarsier (Gursky and Alvard, in prep.).

Tarsius syrichta

There has only been one short-term study of the behavior of wild *Tarsius syrichta,* the Philippine tarsier (Gebo and Dagosto, in press). Dagosto and Gebo radio-collared two adult males and found they had a home range of approximately .6 and 1.7 hectares, respectively. Minimum nightly travel distance was 260 and 342 meters for each individual, respectively. This is substantially shorter than the nightly path length reported for other tarsier species. The locomotor behavior of the Philippine tarsier is similar to that of other tarsier species, with vertical clinging and leaping utilized in 62% of all locomotor bouts, climbing in 23%, and quadrupedalism in 13%. Sleeping sites were located in dense tangles of ferns and saplings or at the base of bamboo clumps.

Tarsius pumilus

There have been no wild studies of the behavior and ecology of *Tarsius pumilus,* the pygmy tarsier, from the highlands of central Sulawesi. In fact, pygmy tarsiers have not been observed since the 1930s. Shekelle et al. (1997) surveyed the area where they were previously reported but were unsuccessful in locating them.

CONSERVATION STATUS

The population density for three of the five tarsier species is presented in Table 1. The density of tarsier individuals ranges from as few as 12 individuals per km^2 to as many as 156 individuals per km^2 (Fogden 1974; Niemitz 1984; Gursky 1997; Gursky, in press a, in press b). This variation in population density is quite deceptive because density values change substantially with altitude and habitat type. For example, the density of both the spectral tarsier and Dian's tarsier were lower at higher altitudes and increased at lower altitudes.

TABLE 1 Conservation Status of the Five Recognized Tarsier Species

Species	Population Density/km^2	Conservation Status	Reference
T. bancanus	12	Low Risk	Fogden 1974
T. bancanus	17	Low Risk	Niemitz 1984
T. spectrum	300–800	Data Deficient	MacKinnon and MacKinnon 1980a
T. spectrum	156	Data Deficient	Gursky, in press a
T. dianae	129	Data Deficient	Gursky, in press b
T. syrichta	N/A	Low Risk	N/A
T. pumilus	N/A	Data Deficient	N/A

Population density for both Sulawesian tarsier species was also higher in secondary disturbed habitat and lower in the primary less disturbed habitat (Gursky, in press a). No studies of the population density of T. syrichta or T. pumilus have been conducted.

The conservation status for each of these species varies from low risk (T. syrichta and T. bancanus) to data deficient due to a lack of information (T. dianae, T. spectrum, and T. pumilus) (Wolfheim 1986; Eudey 1996; IUCN 1996; Rowe 1996).

As a result of their uncertain conservation status, numerous attempts have been made to maintain both the Bornean and the Philippine tarsier species in captivity (Ulmer 1963; Wright et al. 1986, 1988; Roberts and Kohn 1993; Roberts 1994). Although many copulations and conceptions have occurred, infant survivorship has been quite poor. At present, only eight captive-born infants are reported to have been reared to weaning: one T. syrichta at the Frankfurt zoo; two T. syrichta at the Cincinnati zoo; one T. syrichta that was hand-reared at the Duke University Primate Center (Haring and Wright 1989), and four T. bancanus infants born at the National Zoological Park (Roberts 1994). Consequently, there are no active captive breeding populations for any tarsier species.

Primate Conservation

Biodiversity and conservation-related themes have become a critical part of primate studies. It is no longer possible to study a group or population of free-ranging nonhuman primates without coming into contact with human disturbance, manipulation, or destruction of the habitat. Ninety percent of the world's primates are found in tropical forests, and it is precisely these forests that are being converted to human use faster and more dramatically than any other habitat on earth. Fifty percent of all primate species are a conservation concern to the Species Survival Commission (SSC) and the World Conservation Union (IUCN), and 20% are considered endangered or critically endangered. Today these numbers continue to rise in the face of ongoing threats. For this reason we have included a few essays on conservation in this text.

Nonhuman primates play an important, sometimes critical, role in the structure and maintenance of tropical forests. Nonhuman primates frequently make up a large portion of the overall biomass of tropical rain forests and fill a primary role as consumers. They exist in many mutualistic associations with the flora, and much recent attention has been given to the role of nonhuman primates as seed dispersers and pollinators. Given that many forest primates consume large amounts of ripe (and unripe) fruit without digesting the seeds and that these primates also range widely throughout forest areas, it is probable that these animals play an integral role in the reproduction and distribution of forest plants and contribute to the overall forest structure. If, in fact, nonhuman primates are as crucial to the survival of the forest as the survival of the forest is crucial to them, then conservation and primate studies become linked by necessity.

The primary threats to nonhuman primates are the conversion of tropical forest land to agriculture and grassland and to destruction of forests by logging. Varying estimates for the rate of conversion are constantly bandied about; however, a conservative estimate of between 50,000 to 100,000 km^2 per year demonstrates the severity and urgency of the situation. In addition to the conversion and destruction of forests, hunting and the illegal bushmeat and pet trade are also taking an enormous toll on nonhuman primates. The tropical areas that are home to most nonhuman primates are in some of the most economically devastated and politically unstable nations on the planet. Dramatic food shortages, lack of solid educational foundations and environmental awareness, and severe poverty lead to dramatic overuse and destruction of natural habitat by the populations of these countries. This destruction takes a heavy toll on the nonhuman primates, many of whom are traditional foods, readily accessible large meat sources, and cost-effective prey items. Also, despite international condemnation, nonhuman primates are still sought as exotic pets and as vital components of costly traditional medicines. The combination of threats facing nonhuman primates is daunting indeed, and although we have not lost a primate species to extinction this century, the next one may make up for it in spades (Table 1).

What can be done to slow the assault on the nonhuman primates (and all nonhuman animals and habitat)? A few things. Legal protection in the form of parks and reserves has some positive effects. However, even the most strictly enforced park boundaries will crumble in the wake of a civil war, famine, or just plain old severe poverty and hunger. It has become readily apparent that no form of conservation action is possible without taking into account the human role in local utilization of protected areas. Education, sustainable development programs, and a focus on solving human problems are probably the only permanent answers to the conservation dilemma. We are both the cause and the solution to our cousins' predicament.

Not all is bleak however. In the last twenty years nine new species of primates have been discovered, some populations we thought terminally endangered have stabilized, and the international community has begun to make primate conservation a top priority. Public education campaigns, captive breeding and reintroduction programs, and a dramatic increase in a focus on conservation studies have appeared throughout the world. Importantly, data continue to roll in. Continued and growing interest in the nonhuman primates is resulting in vast amounts of new information on these species, information that is a vital first step in establishing any sort of conservation program.

In this section the essay by Ardith Eudey describes the state of primate conservation in Asia, and a specific case study in Vietnam is presented by Lois Lippold. Carey Yeager and Scott Silver describe the success and failure of reintroduction and translocation programs in primate conservation, and Bruce Wheatley presents the results of a specific conservation census of a small Pacific island on which macaques are severely threatened. These four articles scratch the surface enough to reveal the diverse nature of primate conservation problems and some of the methods being used to tackle them. Every individual who wishes to study the nonhuman primates must wear two hats, scientist and conservationist.

TABLE 1 Endangered Species in Order Primates

Family	Genus	Species	Conservation Status
Cheirogaleidae	Allocebus	trichotis	critically endangered
	Cheirogaleus	major	endangered
		medius	endangered
	Microcebus	murinus	endangered
		rufus	endangered
	Phaner	furcifer	endangered
Lemuridae	Lepilemur	dorsalis	endangered
		microdon	endangered
		mustelinus	endangered
		ruficaudatus	endangered
		sepentrionalis	endangered
	Lemur	catta	endangered
	Eulemur	coronatus	endangered
		fulvus	endangered
		mongoz	endangered
		rubriventer	endangered
	Varecia	variegata	endangered
	Hapalemur	aureus	endangered
		griseus	endangered
		simus	endangered
Indriidae	Avahi	laniger	endangered
	Propithecus	diadema	endangered
		tattersalli	endangered
		verreauxi	endangered
	Indri	indri	endangered
Daubentoniidae	Daubentonia	madagascariensis	endangered
Tarsiidae	Tarsius	syrichta	endangered
Callitrichidae	Callimico	goeldii	endangered
	Callithrix	aurita	endangered
		flaviceps	endangered
	Saguinus	geoffroyi	endangered
		leucopus	endangered
		oedipus	endangered
	Leontopithecus	caissara	critically endangered
		chrysomelas	endangered
		chrysopygus	critically endangered
		rosalia	critically endangered
Cebidae	Callicebus	donacophilus	endangered
		personatus	endangered
	Saimiri	oerstedii	endangered
	Chiropotes	albinasus	endangered
		satanas	endangered
	Cacajao	calvus	endangered
		melanocephalus	endangered
	Alouatta	fusca	endangered

Family	Genus	Species	Conservation Status
	Ateles	belzebuth	endangered
		fusciceps	endangered
	Lagothrix	flavicauda	endangered
	Brachyteles	arachnoides	endangered
Cercopithecidae	Macacca	fuscata	endangered
		nigra	endangered
		pagensis	endangered
		silenus	endangered
	Mandrillus	leucophaeus	endangered
		sphinx	endangered
	Cercocebus	agilis	endangered
		galeritus	endangered
		torquatus	endangered
	Cercopithecus	diana	endangered
		erythrogaster	endangered
		erythrotis	endangered
		lhoesti	endangered
		sclateri	endangered
		solatus	endangered
	Colobus	satanas	endangered
		vellerosus	endangered
	Procolobus	pennanti	endangered
		preussi	endangered
		rufomitratis	endangered
	Presbytis	comata	endangered
		potenziani	endangered
	Presbytis (Semnopithecus)	entellus	endangered
	Presbytis (Trachypithecus)	delacouri	critically endangered
		francoisi	endangered
		geei	endangered
		johnii	endangered
		pileatus	endangered
	Pygathrix	nemaeus	endangered
		nigripes	endangered
	Rhinopithecus	avunculus	critically endangered
		bieti	endangered
		brelichi	endangered
		roxellana	endangered
	Nasalis	larvatus	endangered
	Simias	concolor	endangered
Hylobatidae	Hylobates	hoolock	endangered
		agilis	endangered
		klossii	endangered
		lar	endangered

(continued)

TABLE 1 Endangered Species in Order Primates *continued*

Family	Genus	Species	Conservation Status
Hylobatidae	Hylobates	moloch	endangered
		muelleri	endangered
		pileatus	endangered
		concolor	endangered
		gabriellae	endangered
		leucogenys	endangered
		syndactylus	endangered
Pongidae	Pongo	pygmaeus	endangered (both subspecies)
	Gorilla	gorilla	endangered (all three subspecies)
	Pan	paniscus	endangered
		troglodytes	endangered

SOURCE: IUCN, USESA, and CITES lists and the African, Asian, and Madagascar IUCN Action Plan Reports.

16

Asian Primate Conservation—My Perspective

Ardith A. Eudey

PERSONAL ODYSSEY

As a graduate student in anthropology at the University of California at Davis in 1973, I initiated a field study in west-central Thailand to learn how the five species of macaque monkeys (*Macaca* spp.) previously recorded in the area were able to partition the resources of their environment while retaining their specific identity. My theoretical interest is the process of speciation, and I envisioned the results of my study contributing to a better understanding of the operation of premating isolating mechanisms in a higher vertebrate (Eudey 1979). The fieldwork was to be a perfunctory exercise, to satisfy the requirements for a doctoral degree. Instead, my field experience ignited within me a passion for, and a dedication to, the complex ecosystem in which I found myself and the human residents and caretakers of Huai Kha Khaeng Wildlife Sanctuary.

For more than twenty years I have been studying the distribution and habitat preference of the sympatric macaque species within the sanctuary (see, for example, Eudey 1981, 1991b). At the same time, I have been attempting to reconcile conservation objectives with the socioeconomic needs of the hill tribe minorities within the region (Eudey 1986, 1988, 1989, 1991a). These experiences, along with a stint as a "primate private eye," investigating irregular and illegal shipments of gibbons (*Hylobates lar*) from Thailand to a laboratory at my own university (Anon. 1980), surely inclined me to become a conservationist. Presently I am vice chair of the Primate

Specialist Group, Species Survival Commission, IUCN–The World Conservation Union, in which capacity I serve as editor of the newsletter *Asian Primates* and compiler of the Action Plan for Asian Primate Conservation. Because of the unfamiliarity of students and many professionals in the United States with the structure and activities of IUCN, let me provide a brief overview of the union and the Primate Specialist Group.

THE IUCN SPECIES SURVIVAL COMMISSION AND PRIMATE SPECIALIST GROUP

IUCN–The World Conservation Union, founded in 1948 with its Secretariat in Switzerland, is a unique global union composed of more than 880 state government agencies and nongovernmental organizations (NGOs) in 133 countries. Individuals also participate as members of the union's six expert commissions as well as being volunteers in networks that currently comprise some 8500 people. IUCN members are united in their acceptance of the *World Conservation Strategy*, a document prepared in 1980 by IUCN in collaboration with the United Nations Environment Programme (UNEP) and the World Wide Fund for Nature (WWF). The strategy stresses three basic principles: (1) conservation of biological diversity, (2) preservation of life-support systems, and (3) sustainable use of living natural resources. Much of the information contained in this section is condensed from a

1996–97 pocket guide to the union (IUCN 1996). One of the most important services that IUCN provides member organizations is technical expertise and theoretical guidance on a wide range of conservation-oriented issues. Much of this is carried out through the voluntary networks that presently constitute these commissions: Species Survival Commission (SSC), Commission on National Parks and Protected Areas (CNPPA), Commission on Ecosystem Management (CEM), Commission on Education and Communication (CEC), Commission on Environmental Law (CEL), and Commission on Environmental Strategy and Planning (CESP). The Species Survival Commission began in 1949 and is the largest and most active commission, with some 6800 volunteer members from 179 countries. The SSC membership, which is composed of scientists, field researchers, government officials, and conservation leaders, provides scientific and technical guidance for (biodiversity) conservation projects worldwide and serves as a resource to governments, international conventions such as CITES (Convention on International Trade in Endangered Species of Wild Fauna and Flora), and conservation organizations. Actvities are carried out primarily through about 110 specialist groups, most of which represent specific plant or animal groups threatened or potentially threatened with extinction, including the order Primates. A few groups deal with conservation issues, including veterinary medicine, conservation (captive) breeding, reintroduction of species into former ranges, invasive species, and sustainable use of wildlife or trade.

The major initiatives of the SSC include: (1) assessing the status of and threats to species, which are summarized in global Red Lists of threatened plants and animals; (2) promoting priorities for conservation identified in conservation action plans; (3) gathering, managing, and disseminating information about species and their conservation throughout the SSC network, which is linked to other disciplines through the Biodiversity Conservation Information System; (4) promoting sound conservation policy in the form of scientific guidelines to assist governments, NGOs, and others; (5) providing technical advice and guidance to intergov-

ernmental mechanisms such as the CITES, Convention on Migratory Species, International Whaling Commission, and Convention on Biological Diversity; and (6) understanding the ecological impacts of uses of wild species. The production of conservation action plans—launched with the publication of the *Action Plan for African Primate Conservation: 1986–90* (Oates 1986) and the *Action Plan for Asian Primate Conservation: 1987–91* (Eudey 1987)—is one of the most important activities carried out by the population-based specialist groups.

Since 1977, the IUCN/SSC Primate Specialist Group (PSG) has attempted to coordinate primate conservation activities on a global scale under the chairmanship of Dr. Russell A. Mittermeier, president of Conservation International, Washington, D.C. By 1981, the PSG had been divided into five sections: Africa, Asia, Madagascar, South and Central America, and a Special Section for experts working with captive populations. I began compilation of the *Action Plan for Asian Primate Conservation* in 1983 with the assistance of some fifty primatologists and conservationists working on Asian primates. At the meeting of the PSG held during the XIV Congress of the International Primatological Society in 1992 in Strasbourg, France, the decision was made to formalize the four regional sections with coordinators (now vice chairs). This action mirrored the process of decentralization occurring within IUCN itself. In 1990, at the 18th IUCN General Assembly held in Perth, Australia, I volunteered to publish a (quarterly) newsletter to facilitate communication among members of the Asian section of the PSG. The inaugural issue of *Asian Primates*, the first of the PSG newsletters, was published in June 1991 under my editorship. Each of the regional sections now publishes a newsletter, which is widely distributed free of charge, not only to PSG members but to other people, agencies, and organizations involved in research on, and conservation of, primates.

As part of the policy encouraging regional autonomy, I have been forming PSG regional committees in Asia. To date, committees have been established for Japan, Indonesia, South India, North-East India, Nepal, and China. Lack of funding has limited the effectiveness of some of the committees or, at least, my ability to work with them. The Primate Society of Great Britain (PSGB) recently made a small contribution to the operation of the two Indian committees and to help establish a committee in Bangladesh, which has not yet been accomplished. Likewise, lack of systematic implementation may have reduced the effectiveness of the Asian action plan in contributing to the conservation of Asian primates. Although no funding mechanism for projects is included in the 1987 plan, as has occurred in some subsequent SSC action plans, individuals have used its species and project ratings to secure funding, and these same ratings have been used in the evaluation of research proposals.

THE PLAYERS

According to figures compiled in November 1997 by Anthony Rylands (pers. comm.) on behalf of the IUCN/SSC Primate Specialist Group, worldwide there are 62 genera of primates composed of 266 to 270 species and 577 to 627 taxa or distinct populations such as subspecies. The regional breakdown includes:

Africa: 20 genera; 64–68 species; 150–200 taxa (25% of all species)

Asia: 12 genera; 72 species; 175 taxa (27% of all species)

Madagascar: 14 genera; 32 species; 50 taxa (12% of all species)

Neotropics: 16 genera; 98 species; 202 taxa (36% of all species)

In a widely read volume reviewing primate species and theoretical issues, Mittermeir and Cheney (1987) recognize ten to fifteen genera and about fifty-five species in Africa; nine to sixteen genera and fifty to fifty-six species in Asia; thirteen genera and twenty-eight species in Madagascar; and sixteen genera and sixty-four species in the Neotropics. No attempt is made to enumerate all taxa or subspecies. The overall increase in species may be attributed, in Asia and elsewhere, to taxonomic reassessment of known specimens and to new discoveries in the wild.

Recently, as part of the process of reviewing and revising the 1987 Asian action plan, I evaluated the status of all Asian species (but not all subspecies) using a new set of categories and criteria formally adopted in November 1994 by the IUCN Council, the body that guides the IUCN Secretariat in the implementation of policies and programs. The aim of these criteria is to provide a more objective framework for classification of species according to their extinction risk. This evaluation made possible the recent comparison of primate numbers by region. The results were incorporated into the *1996 Red List of Threatened Animals* (IUCN 1996; see also Eudey, in press).

The seventy-two Asian species provisionally were assigned to seven categories; the numbers in each category are indicated in parenthesis. Three categories—Critically Endangered (4), Endangered (11), and Vulnerable (18)—contain 33% to 46% of Asian species and constitute the highest degree of threat. The Critically Endangered (CR) species are: *Macaca pagensis* (Mentanwais, Indonesia), *Trachypithecus delacouri* (northern Vietnam), *Rhinopithecus avunculus* (northern Vietnam), and *Hylobates moloch* (Java, Indonesia). All four are rapidly declining populations and exhibit extremely small population size, as defined by the new IUCN criteria (IUCN 1996). At lower risk are the categories Conservation Dependent (3), Near Threatened (13) and Least Concern (9). Fourteen Data Deficient species should not be considered to be nonthreatened until they actually have been evaluated; this category includes, among others, taxa of problematic taxonomic assignment. The taxonomy as well as the evaluations should be considered provisional. Current data suggest, for example, that both the proboscis monkey (*Nasalis larvarus:* Yeager 1996) and the orangutan (*Pongo pygmaeus*) should be upgraded from Vulnerable (VU) to Endangered.

In the 1987 Asian action plan, thirty-seven (59%) of the then sixty-three species recognized were judged to need some kind of conservation action to survive into the twenty-first century, and forty-seven subspecies are identified as requiring special conservation attention. Some of the major threats to Asian primate populations are discussed next.

WORLDWIDE THREATS

To write about primate conservation in Asia in 1998 is not the same as writing about the topic in the year 2001, or even in 1996. A comparable statement probably could be made about conservation in the three other regions of the world where nonhuman primates occur: Africa, Madagascar, and the Neotropics. Several factors contribute to this phenomenon. Some are universal and shared among regions, such as environmental catastrophe or the commercialization of hunting for "bushmeat" trade (Kemf and Wilson 1997), but others are specific to a given area. A report released in December 1997 by the World Wide Fund for Nature (Dudley 1997) identifies 1997 as the year in which more tropical forest burned than at any other time in recorded history and characterizes the fires as "a planetary disaster." Up to 12.4 million acres of forest and other land burned in Indonesia and Brazil, where the Amazon alone had more than 45,000 fires. Large-scale fires also were reported in Africa, Colombia, and Papua New Guinea.

More specifically for Asia, the Indonesian fires reportedly destroyed more than 4.9 million acres of forest. Smog caused by fires in Kalimantan (Borneo), Irian Jaya, and Sumatra, as well as in Sulawesi and Java, enveloped an area in Southeast Asia from Thailand and the Philippines to Malaysia and Irian Jaya for several months in the summer and autumn of 1997. Regions as far away as Sri Lanka and northern Australia were subsequently affected by the haze. Preliminary estimates place the cost of the fires in terms of tourism, health effects, legal costs, and lost productivity at $20 billion (Dudley 1997).

At least nineteen protected areas appear to have been threatened by fire in Indonesia, including Tanjung Puting National Park in Central Kalimantan, which is known for both orangutans and proboscis monkeys (Dudley 1997). El Niño (the El Niño Southern Oscillation [ENSO]), the cyclical phenomenon of warming Pacific Ocean temperatures that disrupts climate patterns, delayed monsoon rains that usually extinguish many naturally occurring forest fires. The drought was the most severe in 150 years (Dudley 1997). Subsequent rainfall is reported to have been "unnaturally" acid as a result of air pollution, causing further damage to vegetation (Dudley 1997).

Of the primate fauna in Indonesia, the orangutan may have suffered the most adverse effects from the fires, although reports are difficult to verify (Dudley 1997). According to Willie Smits, advisor on orangutans to the Indonesian Ministry of Forestry, animal traders were capturing young orangutans for the pet trade as their mothers fled the fires (Dudley 1997). By November 1997 Smits was reporting that at least 120 orangutans had been killed as a result of the fires and estimating that up to a thousand animals had been affected by them (Dudley 1997). The onset of rain at the end of the year brought little relief to some areas in Indonesia. By May 1998 forest fires were reported to have burned more than 400,000 hectares in East Kalimantan, and more than 170 young orangutans had been taken in at the Wanariset Orangutan Rehabilitation Center (V. Watkins, posted on Primate-Talk, 18 May 1998).

The Indonesian government has blamed plantation owners, industrial estates, and transmigration land-clearing projects for about 80% of the fires (Dudley 1997). Fire is a quick and cheap way to clear away secondary growth to establish plantations and may be used to deliberately blur concession boundaries, to acquire more land, or to cover up the evidence of timber poaching. Fires even may have increased as a deliberate act of defiance against government efforts to crack down on illegal activity (Dudley 1997). Deliberate fire-raising appears to be the largest cause of forest fires in many countries and has been attributed to a breakdown in the "rule of law" as applied to the environment (Dudley 1997).

ASIAN ECONOMIC GROWTH AND POPULATION NUMBERS

Until July 1997 it was possible to speak of apparent booming economic growth throughout much of Asia. More than half of the world's population, 3.3 billion people, is found in Asia, including three of the world's four most populous nations (China, India, and Indonesia). In 1996 at the XVIth Congress of the International Primatological Society in Madison, Wisconsin, I (Eudey, in press) felt confident to report predictions that by the year 2020 Asian economies would have raised some 2 billion people out of poverty and that Asia would account for half the world's economic growth in the four years remaining in this century. The 1995 *Forbes* list of the world's wealthiest individuals already contained 123 Asians, of whom 82 were from countries other than Japan (see Anon. 1996). On 2 July 1997, however, Thailand effectively devalued its currency after months of attack by speculators amid a massive banking and real estate crisis. The government had spent 15% of its foreign currency reserves over the previous eight months trying to bolster the basic monetary unit (the baht) from attack. Like many other Southeast Asian countries, Thailand had "managed" its currency, keeping it stable versus the U.S. dollar.

An economic crisis subsequently swept Asia, affecting most seriously South Korea, Malaysia, and Indonesia as well as Thailand (Kapstein 1998). Further analysis reveals that these four countries combined only approximate France in economic size and that their exports have been less than 8% of the world's total. During the decade 1985 to 1995, their rapid growth did little for the world's economy; rather, while the world's per capita income increased by less than 1%, that in East Asia rose, on average, by more than 7% annually, representing tremendous economic gains (Kapstein 1998). The political problems raised by the financial collapse, at both national and international levels of governance, appear to be a far more serious problem and have led to parliamentary change in Thailand and the end of the thirty-two years of rule by the president of Indonesia following massive protests and deadly riots.

Increased human populations and economic growth have combined in Asia to threaten the environment and all wildlife. Although among the most species-rich nations in the world, the three most populous Asian countries also have a high proportion of mammals (and birds) that are threatened with extinction: Indonesia 29%, India 24%, and China 19% (IUCN 1996). The National Audubon Society's Habitat and Population Campaign (Rousseau 1998) reports that the United Nations anticipates that there will be at least 8 billion people in the year 2050. This represents an increase of 35%, or 2.1 billion people, over the present population of 5.9 billion. Industrialized northern countries, many of which have populations at replacement level, and developing southern countries have had success lowering their birth rates, but high population growth rates in the past have resulted in a high concentration of women in childbearing ages in lesser developed countries.

Recently, Costanza et al. (1997) estimate the current economic value of the entire biosphere and the global ecosystem services it provides at a minimum of US$16–54 trillion per year, with an average of US$33 trillion per year. According to their definition, ecosystem functions refer variously to the habitat, biological system properties, and processes of ecosystems, whereas ecosystem goods such as food and services, of which they differentiate seventeen, including waste assimilation, climate regulation, and recreation, collectively may be referred to as ecosystem services and represent the benefits human populations derive, directly or indirectly, from ecosystem functions. Against this backdrop it is instructive to consider that the recent fires in Asia, which may be associated with economic growth as previously discussed, constitute a debit estimated at US$20 billion (Dudley 1997). Similarly, China's booming economy is being confronted by a US$34.5 billion debit to clean up an environmental disaster caused by lax enforcement of pollution laws, outdated technology, and major underfunding, according to a new report, "The China Environmental Market: A Technology Transfer Approach" (Anon. 1997; see also Hertsgaard 1997).

TRADE AND TRAFFICKING IN PRIMATES

Commercial trade and trafficking both appear to have contributed to the decline of widespread species such as macaques (*Macaca* spp.) and rarer species such as the orangutan (Eudey 1995a, 1995b). Although rarely the major factor in the decline of a species, demand for live, wild-caught primates may add to other pressures such as habitat loss and result in serious depletion of populations. This appears to be true especially of Asian primates.

The United States has been the world's major importer and user of primates, and U.S. demand has driven international trade in primates, including that in Asia (Kavanagh 1984; Mack and Eudey 1984). Most importations into the United States have been for biomedical research, especially those subsequent to 1975 when the U.S. Public Health Service eliminated primates from the pet trade (Mack and Eudey 1984; Kavanagh, Eudey, and Mack 1987). During the period 1964–1980, almost 42% of the more than 1,178,300 primates imported into the United States originated in Asia (Mack and Eudey 1984). In 1973, Asia replaced the Neotropics as the major supplier of primates to the United States, largely as a consequence of the demand for rhesus macaques (*Macaca mulatta*) for use in the development and testing of polio vaccine and other medical research. India supplied more than 90% of the species annually until the country banned the export of all primates in 1978 (Mack and Eudey 1984).

Significant numbers of Southeast Asian long-tailed or crab-eating macaques (*Macaca fascicularis*), primarily, and pigtailed macaques (*M. nemestrina*), secondarily, entered the trade as a consequence of the curtailment of rhesus macaque exports from South Asia. The subsequent imposition of quotas and bans on primates by the major exporting countries in Southeast Asia (Indonesia, Malaysia, Philippines, and Thailand) mirrors the earlier situation in South Asia, however. Exports are still available from Indonesia and the Philippines, although legally they are restricted to captive-born monkeys.

TRADE ROUTES FOR ILLEGAL WILDLIFE TRADE

Destruction of forest habitat through legal and illegal timbering, conversion to agriculture, and hydroelectric projects has resulted in both the direct loss of primate populations and their increased vulnerability to hunting and capture for illegal trade.

The percentage of (primary) forest cover remaining in a country almost may be used as a measure of its economic development (or exploitation by neighboring countries). Development of investment pacts and trading alliances within Asia, such as the expanding ASEAN (Association of South East Asian Nations), have propelled the region's economic growth while establishing routes for illegal wildlife trade. In March 1998, for example, Thailand's prime minister ordered completion of the US$1 billion joint venture natural gas pipeline between Myanmar (formerly Burma) and Thailand. The project had been delayed by human rights and environmental groups protesting that it would involve slave labor and destroy areas of Thailand's remaining primary forest and that it would endanger primates and other wildlife. There is a strong suspicion that many of the primates that continue to appear in the illegal trade in Thailand are from Myanmar. Trade routes between Taiwan and Indonesia, southern China and Vietnam, and China and Vietnam already have been documented. All available evidence indicates that hunting continues to be a major threat to primates and other wildlife in Vietnam (and the neighboring countries of Cambodia and Laos). The demand of an increasingly affluent population within China for wildlife as food and for traditional medicine has resulted in considerable cross-border trade with Vietnam.

TRAFFICKING IN ORANGUTANS

Recent illegal trade in orangutans takes on special significance because of the devastating effects that the 1997–98 fires in Indonesia, especially Kalimantan, appear to have had on the species. During approximately two to three years bracketed by the period 1988–89 to 1990, as many as 1000 to 3000 young orangutans may have been smuggled by boat from Indonesia, especially Kalimantan, to Taiwan, where they were sold as pets and for publicity purposes to affluent buyers for the equivalent of between US$6,000 and US$15,000. A popular television program featuring an orangutan was a major impetus to the trade. Taiwan, Republic of China

(ROC), has one of Asia's strongest economies and is a major investor in East Asian countries, including the People's Republic of China, Indonesia, and Vietnam. At the present time, Taiwan is politically constrained from becoming a party to CITES because the China seat in the United Nations is occupied by the People's Republic of China. Taiwan wildlife laws are in conformity with CITES, however, and provide a mechanism to end illegal traffic in exotic wildlife.

Publicity attendant on the return of the orangutans known as the "Taiwan Ten" to Indonesia in 1990 and a general antismuggling campaign appeared to result in a dramatic decline in trade in the species and in other primates in Taiwan throughout 1991 (Phipps 1992). According to the 10 January 1992 *China Post,* 283 orangutans had been registered with Taiwan authorities, and the number of orangutans in Taiwan unofficially was estimated to be between 400 and 800 by the Orangutan Foundation Taiwan (Phipps 1992).

The 1986 decision by the Indonesian government to open up Kalimantan (Indonesian Borneo) to timber concessions and other economic ventures made the orangutan vulnerable to capture. Within Kalimantan, infant orangutans are reported to be purchased as "prestigious pets" by wealthy Indonesians, and the skulls of adult orangutans are sold to foreign tourists (Anon. 1990; Kemf and Wilson 1997) even though the orangutan was given legal protection in Indonesia as early as 1925. Within a brief span of time, the number of Bornean orangutans may have declined to no more than 12,300–20,571 as a consequence of habitat loss and capture (Anon. 1992).

The possibility of resumption of large-scale smuggling of orangutans into Taiwan may be minimal, although the possibility of animals being smuggled out of Taiwan to other countries is very real (Phipps 1992). However, an increase in the market for small primates may be occurring. According to Phipps (1992), there is little information on gibbons, but the demand for them seemed to continue after the demand for orangutans waned. As of 1991, gibbons, some of which probably were obtained from southern China, were in high demand as pets in Taiwan during 1990.

PROGNOSIS

In 1996 the proportion of Asia's land area reported to fall within protected area systems was 5.3%. This compares with 5.2% in Africa, 5.6% in Central America, and 7.4% in South America (World Resources Institute 1998). This is not a commentary on the adequacy of protection, however. Thailand, with 13.1% of its land area assigned some kind of protection, appears to have brought nearly all significant remaining forest (primate) habitat within its protected area system (W. Brockelman, pers. comm., 1994). Vietnam, in contrast, with only 3.1% of its land area designated as protected, may have many threatened primate populations living outside protected areas. Protection for the Critically Endangered Tonkin snub-nosed monkey, for example, was only obtained in the last decade and then in the form of a nature reserve. The taxonomy, distribution, and habitat preference of many other primate taxa in Vietnam are only now in the process of being worked out. The *Action Plan for Asian Primate Conservation* (Eudey 1987), which currently is under review and revision, identifies the kind of conservation action necessary to maintain primate biodiversity and establishes priorities for action. An outgrowth of the action plan has been a regional workshop in Beijing in 1997, which is leading to an action plan specific to the endangered genus *Rhinopithecus* in China and Vietnam and the planning of a national workshop in Hanoi in 1998 to draft an action plan for Vietnam's primates.

In many respects conservation may be entering a phase in which ethical considerations, or "quality control," should be given special consideration. Myanmar (formerly Burma) offers one example. The human rights violations of the ruling military junta, the State Law and Order Restoration Council (SLORC), and its failure to relinquish political power to the democratically elected government headed by Aung San Suu Kyi, the 1991 Nobel Peace Prize recipient, have resulted in economic sanctions being imposed by the United States and other northern countries, although not by neighboring countries such as Thailand for which Myanmar is a source of natural resources. Although only

.3% of Myanmar's land area falls within a protected area system (World Resources Institute 1998), private or bilateral aid for conservation in Myanmar could well be interpreted as endorsement of the present regime.

Ultimately, the fate of primates in Asia may hinge on the recruitment of young field primatologists or biologists and conservationists within the habitat countries. Obtaining support for their academic and field experience is critical. Any tendency to relegate nationals to a secondary role in achieving conservation objectives must be overcome. Empowering nationals to be effective conservationists, frequently through collaborative efforts, is a goal that I have set throughout Asia for the Primate Specialist Group.

17

The Effects of Hunting on the Longtailed Macaques of Ngeaur Island, Palau

Bruce P. Wheatley, Rebecca Stephenson, and Hiro Kurashina

Human hunting is a major threat to primates that leads to local extinction in some areas (Mittermeir 1987), yet there is a reluctance to consider humans as "natural" predators when the effects of predation are investigated (van Schaik and van Noordwijk 1983). Are the effects of human hunting different or similar to the effects of other "natural" predators?

For thousands of years the longtailed macaque (Macacca fascicularis) and other macaques have prospered, raiding human crops in riverine habitats and other areas of Asia (Wheatley 1980; Richard, Goldstein, and Dewar 1989). There is little information on the effects of human predation on primates, but it is not uncommon for these primates to be captured, shot at, or killed. If our models on sociality, sex roles, and other evolutionary responses to predation are to have validity, we need to include human influences on primate social organization and behavior.

We studied longtailed macaques on Ngeaur, a small, 830 ha coral atoll in the Republic of Palau, and the easternmost location for Macacca fascicularis in the Pacific. These animals are significantly smaller in body weight and other morphological dimensions than populations of longtailed macaques found elsewhere (Matsubayashi et al. 1989). These monkeys were introduced to the island during the German occupation, probably between 1909 and 1914 when phosphate mining began (Poirier and Smith 1974; Wheatley et al. 1997). Between 1914 and 1945, the Japanese killed some of these monkeys. The macaques of Ngeaur are considered a major agricultural pest by

the local people because they raid gardens, eating oranges, bananas, coconuts and, especially, taro. In response, the local people may hunt the monkeys.

CONDUCTING THE SURVEY

We, along with nine trained assistants, spent ten days on Ngeaur in July 1994, and approximately 700 hours of survey work were conducted. Long-tailed macaques are known for their cryptic behavior, especially where they are hunted, so we used a variety of methods to estimate their population density. We divided up into two-person groups every day and repeatedly and slowly walked along the many roads and trails on the island. During these surveys, at the first minute of detection we recorded a range of information: time, location, detection distance of the first animal sighted, animal's vertical height, whether the animal was exposed (an unobstructed view for a clear shot), the animal's sex and age, whether the animal was vigilant (head up and looking around rather than inspecting vegetation or partners at close range), the animal's activity (moving, resting, feeding; social or agonistic), nearest neighbor within 5 meters, method of detection (visual of animal or branch movement; hear animal calls or branch noises), the number of calls and calling individuals in each minute, and whether the observer was detected by the animal. A total of sixty-one samples was collected for statistical analyses.

To increase the reliability of our population estimate, we also counted the number of troops on the island and estimated the average troop size. Samples were also obtained during each of the next ten minutes of contact in regard to the number of calls per minute and age and sex information on vigilance, flight, approach, or threat toward the observer. A final troop count was obtained by recording the number of adult males and females, the total number of individuals seen and otherwise detected through noises, and the dispersion distances. The data were analyzed using StatPac, a computerized data manager and analysis program.

We also conducted a playback experiment using an audiotape of a barking dog, as dogs are often used in hunting. If hunting is a threat to these animals, we predicted that the animals would change their behavior upon hearing the barking dog.

POPULATION ESTIMATES

We surveyed approximately 62,362 meters of roads and trails. The mean detection distance was 41.8 meters. The number of individuals sighted and detected through other means such as crossing gaps in the forest was 286 over the ten-day period.

We estimate the number of troops on the island at twenty-seven. This figure does not include the three lone individuals detected. To estimate the number of individuals per troop, we determined the total number of individuals seen or unseen in the first minute of observation when we were *undetected* by the troop. There was a significant difference between the total number of individuals seen or unseen when individuals of the troop detected the observer as opposed to when the observer was undetected. Estimation of the 99% confidence interval around the mean yields a maximum troop size of 12.5 individuals and an estimated population size of 338 individuals. If the three lone individuals are included, the estimated population size is 341 individuals. This does not count the number of pets and caged animals on the island.

HUNTING PRACTICES

The police from Koror shot three monkeys during the four days they were present on Ngeaur. We examined an old juvenile male that was shot by a shotgun near our guesthouse in the village. The police also used M15 military assault weapons. Although the Constitution of Palau forbids the use of firearms, local hunters can be commissioned for their use, and hunters indicated that they shot at monkeys whenever they could. Another hunting method was to spread out and chase the monkeys with dogs, isolate them in trees with no escape routes, and shoot them, although the monkeys' sleeping trees had too many branches for hunters to be effective. Another hunter said he was more effective without using dogs. Hunters said that they preferred to hunt larger groups of monkeys because it was easier and they could shoot more animals either with shotguns or with semi-automatic 22s. The animals are not eaten. The hunters prefer to shoot mothers of infants so they can sell the infants. The standard price is $100 for an infant. This is a handy sum considering that most of the middle-aged people have left the island seeking employment elsewhere. It is illegal to transport a monkey to another island unless it is a male and a permit has been obtained, but some animals are probably smuggled.

Trapping also occurred, and we saw several baited traps. The traps have funnel-like entrances that prevent escape once the animal is inside. Up to twenty animals at a time have been said to be trapped.

BEHAVIORAL DIFFERENCES
DUE TO HUNTING

To determine some of the effects of hunting, we conducted detailed investigations on two troops in two different areas of the island. One troop is known as the lighthouse troop because of its proximity to a destroyed Japanese lighthouse north of the village. Several hunters told us that they did not hunt in this area because there are no gardens and it is too rocky, so this troop is not often hunted. The other troop is called the church troop because of its location behind a Catholic church. This troop ranges in the major taro growing and flat area of the village and just behind many of the houses of the village where several successful hunters live. This troop is often hunted and was very wary. We had to be quite stealthy to contact this troop. Both troops are multimale, and both have young infants in them. The total troop count for the lighthouse troop was sixteen. There were two adult males, one subadult male, at least three adult females, three old juveniles (one male and two females), two young juveniles (one of which was male), and two infants (a yearling and a black one only a few months old). The church troop had a total troop count of fifteen. Its age and sex composition is less certain, but there were at least two adult males, three adult females, one old and one young juvenile, and one old and one young infant.

Testing for behavioral differences between these two troops revealed the following statistically significant results:

1. The most obvious differences related to vocal behavior. There were significantly more alarm calls during the first minute of contact and a higher total numbers of calls and a greater number of minutes of alarm calls were heard from the lighthouse troop than from the church troop. There was no significant difference in maximum dispersion distances between the two troops, so the difference in calling behavior between the two troops is not related to a difference in intratroop dispersion distances. The church troop was silent during the entire sample more frequently than the lighthouse troop when the observer was detected. The number of calling individuals during the first minute of contact was significantly greater from the lighthouse troop than from the church troop.

2. There were also significant differences in visibility between the two troops. The number of individuals seen during the sample was significantly more at the lighthouse troop than at the church troop. There was no significant difference in the total numbers of individuals between the two troops

when individuals that were not seen but that were detected from moving branches or calling were included. There was no significant difference between the two troops in detection distance. Animals from the lighthouse troop were also exposed to the observer during the first minute of contact significantly more often than animals from the church troop. Animals from the church troop were never exposed to the observer, in contrast to the animals from the lighthouse troop. There were no significant differences in horizontal and vertical detection distances between the two troops. There was no significant sex difference in exposure; however, males were twice as likely to be exposed as females. Animals from the lighthouse troop approached or threatened the observer significantly more than animals from the church troop.

We also tested the data for sex differences and found significant sex differences in exposure and approaching and threatening the observer. There was a significant difference in the number of minutes adult males as opposed to adult females were exposed to the observer, regardless of whether the animal had detected the observer. The tested samples are when both adult males and adult females were detected during the record; that is, adult females were seen in the group but were not exposed to the observer as frequently as adult males were. Adult males approached or threatened the observer significantly more often than adult females. There was also a significant difference between the number of minutes a lighthouse troop adult male was exposed as opposed to the number of minutes a church troop adult male was exposed.

We found no significant differences between the sexes in some behaviors, however. For example, no significant difference was found in the number of minutes an adult male was vigilant at the lighthouse and the number of minutes an adult male was vigilant at the church. There was no significant difference in the number of minutes an adult male was vigilant, regardless of whether or not the animal detected the observer, and the number of minutes an adult female was vigilant. There was also no significant difference between the number of minutes adult females were vigilant at the light-house and the number of minutes adult females were vigilant at the church. There also was no significant relationship in which sex was detected in the first minute of observation at the lighthouse or at the church.

The playback experiment was conducted with the tape recorder placed approximately equidistant between the lighthouse troop's sleeping tree and the lighthouse. The tape of the barking dog was played sixteen minutes after the troop arrived. Upon our detection and prior to the experiment there was an average of eleven alarm calls per minute with an average of 1.9 calling individuals per minute, including an adult female and an old juvenile female. After the tape was played, however, only one subadult male called at a rate of .5 calls per minute. The two calling females fled and became silent and vigilant. A mother and black infant and two young juveniles fled into the trees and remained hiding. An adult male named Scarnose became vigilant, and two minutes into the sample he and the subadult male became exposed to the observers. One juvenile did not flee but remained vigilant.

There were also a number of significant relationships between the observers and behaviors exhibited by troops upon detection. For example, the method of first contact is significantly related to whether the animal detected the observer. Almost half of all animals were detected by hearing the animals' alarm calls. Another third of all detections were made visually. Each of these two methods of detection were significantly more successful than the other two methods of seeing or hearing branch movements.

Given the increasing rate of disappearance of nonhuman primates throughout the world, it is strange that there is so little information on the effects of human hunting, especially as it has been stated that the major threat to nonhuman primates is habitat destruction followed by hunting (Cheney and Wrangham 1987; Mittermeir 1987; Jorgenson and Redford 1993). This reluctance may be due to the tendency to view the intermixing of humans with other primates as disturbed and unnatural. Sponsel (1997) has also noted this neglect to con-

sider human predation on primates despite their coevolution in Amazonia. Data on indigenous peoples in Amazonia show monkeys to be an important source of protein (Bodmer, Fang et al. 1994; Sponsel 1997). Modern weaponry allows humans to take two to four times more prey than do other predators such as jaguars and pumas.

Our data on Ngeaur qualify previously proposed hypotheses on nonhuman primate predation. When Poirier and Smith (1974) conducted their studies in 1973, "the animals were not constantly vigilant" and would even "approach within 4.5 m," showing "no signs of disturbance." Human hunting and trapping of longtailed macaques on Ngeaur Island is probably responsible for the population decline from an estimated 825–900 individuals in 1981 (Farslow 1987) to an estimated 400 individuals today. In contrast to nonhuman predators such as the gavial (Galdikas and Yeager 1984), the Philippine eagle (*Pithecophagia jefferi*: Rabor 1968), and the python (van Schaik et al. 1983), human predators can seriously deplete the macaque population. On Ngeaur, for example, 10% of the population (ninety-four monkeys) was shot in 1980 (Farslow, 1987). Given this high mortality, it would be surprising if there were no effects on the behavior of these animals. Primates respond differently to different predators including humans (Struhsaker 1967; Tilson and Tenaza 1976; Tilson 1977, 1980; Tenaza 1987; Tenaza and Fuentes 1995). Legislation was passed in 1975 calling for the eradication of monkeys, and rewards were offered for their tails. Trapping was not observed by Farslow (pers. comm.), but sixty-six animals were trapped in 1986, mostly in the north, including monkeys around the lighthouse and in the south by the taro gardens (Kawamoto et al. 1988).

Our data on Ngeaur also modify previously proposed hypotheses accounting for primate defense against predation. It is sometimes stated that the risk of predation is the only selective force favoring group living; that is, larger groups can avoid predators better either through defensive action or through better detection (van Schaik 1983; van Schaik et al. 1983; Dunbar 1988). On Ngeaur, however, troop size is significantly smaller now than it was fifteen to twenty years ago when Poirier and Smith (1974) and Farslow (1987) studied them. All thirteen troops residing in areas we surveyed, and whose sizes were reported by Farslow, are about one-fourth the size today. The mean for troop size in 1980 was fifty-two individuals as opposed to eleven today. Matsubayashi et al. (1989) also suggested that troop sizes appeared to be in the range of ten to twenty individuals in 1987. There also appear to be twice as many troops today as there were when Farslow (1987) studied the animals in 1980. Farslow estimated thirteen troops on the island, whereas our data show twenty-seven troops. If hunters are more successful when they hunt larger troops (as they maintain), then selection would not seem to favor large troops. Barking hunting dogs are easy to detect, and the best anti-hunting tactic might be quiet evasion. On Ngeaur we found no significant correlation between the total number of animals in the group and detection distance. All animals on Ngeaur seem to be extremely vigilant.

The response of the Ngeaur animals to hunting pressure can best be seen in a comparison between the often hunted church troop and the less hunted lighthouse troop. Our results show that the church troop, which was exposed to more hunting, was significantly quieter and more evasive than the lighthouse troop. The church troop had significantly fewer alarm calls, fewer calling individuals, fewer animals visually detected by the observer, fewer exposed individuals, and fewer animals that threatened or approached the observer. Some of their alarms were barely audible. The only copulation call we heard on the island was from this troop, and it was only a second long, a marked contrast with Balinese *M. fascicularis* where calls can exceed five seconds in length (Wheatley, in press). Most of our first contacts were from their alarm calls, and those animals that call may be tracked and shot. Our attempt to simulate a hunt at the lighthouse with a playback of a barking dog corroborated some of these findings. In this experiment the animals fled and became silent. The

Ngeaur macaques do not quickly communicate the presence of human predators as they do for non-human predators (van Schaik and van Noordwijk 1983). We did find a significant sex difference in males approaching and threatening the observer and being exposed to the observer more than females. These findings are similar to those of van Schaik and van Noordwijk (1983), but we did not see a significant difference in vigilance between the sexes as these researchers had found. Even Poirier and Smith (1974) "were most impressed by the role of the adult female in threatening us." Vigilance by females would appear to be more important in human hunting than in nonhuman hunting, especially with the small group sizes on Ngeaur. There is also no confirmation for the hypothesis that Asian macaques outside the Philippines live in one-male groups because of the absence of large raptors (van Schaik and van Noordwijk 1983). The two troops that we intensively investigated were both multimale.

We doubt that the population can be totally exterminated because of the protection offered by the very rocky limestone terrain of the northern part of the island. Our experiences on Ngeaur also underline the importance of community support for conservation to be successful, such as that of the Monkey Forest at Ubud in Bali, Indonesia (Wheatley and Harya Putra 1994; Wheatley, in press). Despite laws preventing the use of firearms on Ngeaur, the monkey population continues to decline.

ACKNOWLEDGMENTS

We thank the Republic of Palau, especially David K. Idip, Ben Gulibert, and Riosang Salvador, for their help and permission to conduct research on Ngeaur. The University of Guam kindly offered financial and other support as did Continental Airlines. We also express our gratitude to the people of Ngeaur for their support. We thank the following students at the University of Guam who participated in the research: M. Akapito, R. Barrett, J. Drake, W. Johnson, K. Kautz, J. Matter, Y. Singeo, D. Tibbetts, and C. Ogo.

18

Translocation and Rehabilitation as Primate Conservation Tools: Are They Worth the Cost?

Carey P. Yeager and Scott C. Silver

Picture haze so thick you can't see more than a few meters ahead of you—haze caused by the smoke from fires burning enormous tracts of land. Imagine a new dam being constructed that will flood a lowland forest, resulting in an area larger than the city of New York under 75 meters of water. Or imagine hundreds of thousands of hectares of forest being converted for plantations or cleared by logging. What are the consequences of these scenarios? Millions of animals, including threatened and endangered primate species, are displaced, injured, and killed. This can't be real, but it is: forest fires raged in Indonesia and Brazil in 1997; a new dam was built on the Yang Tze River in China, and logging and land conversion projects abound. All of this is happening now. What can you do?

One immediate natural response is to want to rush in and rescue as many individuals as possible. News organizations such as CNN and nature-oriented television channels like the Discovery Channel have been very effective in showing us pictures of animals in need of assistance, from monkeys left homeless by flooding to injured baby orangutans. Rescuing injured babies makes for good news, but does it make for good conservation?

CONSERVATION STRATEGIES

Just think about some of what's involved in rescuing these animals. To begin with, you must be able to reach the areas where these animals are found,

often in some of the most remote and difficult places in the world. You will need to locate, capture, and at least temporarily house the animals you are trying to help. You need appropriate trapping equipment and temporary caging, a good veterinarian to anaesthetize the animals, and a way to transport the animals out of the area to a new location. In short, you have a logistical nightmare. Of course, it is only possible to accomplish all of this with a very substantial bank account.

Finally, and perhaps most important, you need a place to release the animals where they will be safe without causing damage to the plants and animals that already live there. Not just any patch of forest will do. The forest has to have the right type and sufficient amounts of food and shelter. If there is already a healthy population of the species that can survive in the area, you could upset the social interactions already in place. You also run a risk of introducing disease that may prove harmful to the resident animals. Animals should only be released into areas where they were known to have occurred at some time in the past to guard against upsetting the ecological balance in the area. You don't want other indigenous species to go locally extinct because of your releases. So the trick to finding a feasible release site is to find an area where the species was present previously, but not currently. You must also be reasonably certain that whatever caused the previous local extinction is no longer a threat to new animals. If it is, all the efforts at moving the animals will be for naught, and all the resources of time and money, not to mention the animals you are trying to rescue, will be lost.

From a conservation perspective, saving animals in situ (in their natural habitat) is almost always the preferred conservation strategy. We use other methods, such as captive breeding in zoos, to augment or complement conservation in the natural habitat. The hope, of course, is that some of those animals living in captivity will serve as a potential population for "restocking" as well as increasing the genetic diversity of dwindling wild populations. Captive animals also serve an educational or research purpose that has conservation benefits. Education may cause people to stop engaging in environmentally destructive behaviors, help influence government policy, and generate financial resources for conservation and research. Research may help us find newer and more effective ways to conserve threatened species.

TRANSLOCATION EFFORTS

Let us first turn our attention to **translocation.** Most conservationists define translocation as the movement of a wild, free-roaming individual animal or group of animals from one location to another. As a conservation tool, translocation can help alleviate the problems of **local extinctions** and the potential problem of inbreeding in isolated populations (Soule and Simberloff 1986). Translocation has been used to rescue animals whose habitat is being destroyed, to increase the number of separate populations of a species, to recolonize newly protected suitable habitat, or to expand the geographic range of a species. It often involves moving species into a habitat in which they had formerly been found, but had become locally extinct, a process referred to as "reintroduction."

There have been numerous instances of individual translocations that were not planned. Historically, humans have intentionally or unintentionally contributed to the movement of many species into new areas (e.g., domestic animals escape to become feral, such as goats, pigs, cats, dogs, and horses; nondomesticated species such as the brown snake and, of course, rats are transported). These introductions usually have overwhelmingly negative consequences for the local flora and fauna. Among primates, populations of escaped squirrel monkeys and rhesus macaques have been established in Florida, and Japanese macaques now reside in Texas. There are also intentional introductions of primate populations (for research and breeding purposes), such as those of the rhesus macaque on Cayo Santiago, Puerto Rico, and longtailed macaques on Tinjil Island, Indonesia.

The intentional translocation of primates as a means of reestablishing populations within their historical range is much less common. Most previous primate translocations have occurred to save specific groups or individuals from habitat destruction or human threats. For example, in the early 1980s Strum translocated three baboon troops to prevent them from being shot by local farmers for crop raiding (Strum and Southwick 1986). The animals were captured and moved to another area of similar habitat. Details on the long-term success are not known, but the procedure appears to have worked well in the short term, with the baboons establishing themselves in home ranges within six months. In this instance, entire groups were captured and moved as a unit for release. In addition, groups were provisioned after translocation to encourage them to stay in the release area.

Howler monkeys have been translocated on a number of occasions. In French Guiana howler monkeys were translocated along with many other animals (including two other primate species) as part of a widespread rescue of wildlife from 310 km[2] of flooded forest following the damming of the Sinnamary River (Vie 1996; Richard-Hansen, Vie, and de Thoisy in review). In Venezuela and Surinam (Konstant and Mittermeier 1982) howlers were also translocated primarily as an emergency response to the loss of their habitat through flooding due to construction of a dam. There was no follow-up on the translocations in Venezuela and Surinam, but most of the howler monkeys in French Guiana survived their release into a nearby forest. Howler monkeys were also translocated in Costa Rica (de Vries 1991), Mexico (Rodriguez-Luna et al. 1993), and Belize (Horwich et al. 1993; Koontz et al. 1994, in prep) with mixed success.

Individuals or groups were caught and immediately released in new areas that sometimes contained resident populations of howler monkeys. The results of these translocations varied. In some cases the social groups broke up subsequent to release (de Vries 1991); in other cases the groups were known to remain intact, establishing home ranges within the release areas and becoming reproductively active (Horwich et al. 1993; Rodriguez-Luna et al. 1993; Koontz et al. 1994, in prep).

Even major translocation efforts may not be enough to save large numbers of animals that are at risk, however. Construction of the Chiew Larn Dam in Thailand flooded a 165 km² area of lowland forest. Only 1364 animals of 116 species were rescued, including 152 primates of 6 species (Nakhasathien 1989). If we assume a density of approximately one group per species per square kilometer, there should have been at least 11,000 primates in the area. This means that only about 1% of the primates were rescued, perhaps less. Of course, some animals may have moved outside the affected area without becoming stranded on isolated islands as the water rose. Almost all of the animals were released into the immediate surrounding area, potentially increasing pressure on the populations already present. Nakhasathien (1989) led the translocation project and goes into great detail concerning the problems encountered.

Orangutans have been translocated in Sabah as an emergency response to habitat loss (Andau, Hiong, and Sale 1994). The orangutan habitat was being lost primarily through burning for conversion to palm oil plantations. The Sabah Wildlife Department captured 84 orangutans and released 74 in a nearby conservation area that had a low orangutan density and appropriate food trees present. According to Andau et. al. (1994), a follow-up study was planned.

Recent translocations of howler monkeys in Belize (Koontz et al. 1994, in prep; Silver 1998) have met with more success. These translocations were planned carefully in advance, building on past translocations, and were not made under the same time constraints as those that often accompany emergency rescue operations. The purpose of the translocation was to reestablish a population of black howler monkeys (*Alouatta nigra*) in a recently established park. Groups were translocated to an area in which howlers had been present previously but had gone locally extinct due to a combination of natural disasters and human hunting prior to the area being designated as a wildlife sanctuary. After both a feasibility study and a pilot release of three groups, a decision was made to attempt a more extensive translocation. Groups were carefully chosen for the translocation based on demographics and group size. Groups that contained youngsters too small to be tranquilized but no longer consistently carried by their mothers were not considered for translocation. Groups also had to be small enough to ensure that all group members could be captured. Most groups were given a "soft release"; they were temporarily housed in a large enclosure in the forest, which was especially constructed for this purpose. During their time in the enclosures, animals were offered a diet of familiar foods and new foods from the release area and allowed to recover from the stress of capture and transportation. After one or two days in these enclosures, the doors were opened, and the animals were allowed to leave on their own.

Unlike the majority of translocation studies, data on some of these groups were collected prior to capture, and for a year to three years (depending on the group) after their release. The data indicate that the groups adjusted rapidly to their new habitat. They were able to successfully forage, reproduce, and, although some groups broke up, maintain cohesive social groups (Koontz et al. 1994, in prep; Silver 1998; Ostro et al., in prep). In a number of cases, individuals who left their original groups established new groups with other lone individuals.

SOME CONSTRAINTS ON TRANSLOCATION

It appears that translocation, albeit expensive, can be quite effective. Successful new populations can be established, given healthy wild animals who experience a minimum of stress and are released into appropriate habitat. However, appropriate habitat is a definite constraint. We define appropriate habitat as habitat with sufficient food resources, sufficient shelter, no viable wild population of the same species, and no known threats that preclude the likelihood of survival of the species in question. Threats may include ongoing hunting or a disease to which the translocated animals have no resistance. Appropriate habitat is also an area in which the release of translocated primate species will not have negative effects on other resident species. As we often know little about interactions between species, it is safest to release animals into areas in which they have recently become locally extinct from some known danger that has since been eliminated, or is not likely to recur. Another possibility is to release animals into degraded habitat (preferably with enrichment planting to increase the food base) with no known threatened species present. However, most areas that have sufficient food resources already have a viable population of the species under consideration for translocation or rehabilitation. If a viable population of the species is already present, introducing additional animals to the area could cause food shortages, increased social stress, or possibly introduce disease. New individuals may be attacked and wounded or killed. This is particularly true for primates that defend their territory.

Disease transmission is one of the risks associated with translocation. A released individual may be a carrier of a disease to which the local population has had no prior exposure. Primates are vulnerable to infection by human diseases, and during even short interactions they may pick up easily transmitted respiratory illnesses, which mutate rapidly (e.g., colds and flu). During subsequent interactions with the local wild population, the disease can be spread. Disease epidemics have been suggested as a major constraint on primate population growth by Young (1994). For example, it is believed that a yellow fever epidemic wiped out a large portion of the howler population on Barro Colorado Island (Collias and Southwick 1952) and decimated many other Central American primate populations (including the Belize howlers described here).

REHABILITATION PROGRAMS

Unlike translocation, **rehabilitation** is the process by which individual animals that have been in captivity for some time, or have recuperated from injury or disease, are released back into the wild. These animals may need to be taught the necessary skills to survive, how to interact appropriately with other individuals of the same species, and perhaps even how to rear their young. Successfully rehabilitated animals are then released into appropriate habitat. In reality, the term is also used to describe the release of captive animals into any habitat deemed suitable, with or without any training. Rehabilitation may involve reintroduction as well. Rehabilitation has worked quite well for numerous species, notably peregrine falcons (Barclay and Cade 1983), Arabian oryx (Stanley Price 1989), and Mauritius kestrels (Cade and Jones 1993), but does it work for primates?

A review by Hannah and McGrew (1991) asserts that rehabilitation is an important tool for conservation, and they provide an excellent review of the literature. Animals have been released on numerous occasions, everywhere from Africa to Asia. Hannah and McGrew deem rehabilitation worthwhile if the primates are released and survive, and they define primate releases where provisioning is still carried out as successful. For example, they cite a release of chimpanzees that were provisioned in Liberia with a 55% success rate five years later.

Although many of these primate rehabilitation programs serve a humane function, it is unfortunate that these release sites probably do not serve a major conservation purpose. This is not an isolated view; numerous scientific articles have reached the same conclusion, including Harcourt (1976), Caldecott and Kavenaugh (1983), Bennett (1992), and Yeager (1997). These programs may more accurately be viewed as free-ranging breeding programs; for example, provisioned orangutans breed at a faster rate at the rehabilitation center in Tanjung Puting than they do in the wild (Yeager 1997). These animals can possibly serve as a "genetic reservoir" (i.e., as a source of genetic variability for the wild population), but the majority of rehabilitated animals are not able to function normally and survive, reproduce, and rear young on their own without some provisioning (Bennett 1992; Yeager 1997). Therefore, many rehabilitants do not contribute significantly to in situ conservation of wild populations. The exceptions here may be more recent releases of golden lion tamarins (Kleiman et al. 1991) and the chimpanzees of Rubondo (Borner 1985). The earlier releases of golden lion tamarins had high mortality rates, but more recent releases have met with much greater success (Kleiman et al. 1991). After an assessment of the training techniques, modifications were made that resulted in greater survival of released tamarins. These modifications included pairing captive-born animals with wild mates. On Rubondo, seventeen wild-caught chimpanzees were released after being in captivity in zoos. No records were kept, so it is not known what the exact outcome was for individuals. However, a nonprovisioned chimpanzee population has been established on the island and is reproducing. This, however, is an isolated population that cannot disperse, which means there may be inbreeding problems in the future if additional translocations or other methods of increasing genetic variability are not carried out.

Primates have a long development period in which they learn from their mother or other group members how to interact with others of the same species and how to find food, avoid predators, and rear young. If this learning process is interrupted, the young animal often never behaves completely normally, even when given opportunities to acquire the information at a later point in time (Mason 1986; Suomi 1986). Thus, a female raised in captivity may never be able to successfully rear offspring that can become completely independent because she herself does not have the necessary survival information to pass on. A good example of this phenomenon is seen among orangutan females released in Tanjung Puting National Park in Indonesia. The orangutan females reproduce, but they and their offspring appear to remain dependent on feedings provided by humans (Yeager 1997).

Gibbon release programs have met with limited success according to Bennett (1992). Survival rates following release at Semengok in Sarawak, Malaysia, are only about 10%. In a release program in

Thailand, only eight out of twenty-one gibbons were able to survive and establish territories on an island despite provisioning. The remainder (62%) either died or were removed. If the purpose of the rehabilitation program is to increase primate welfare and psychological well-being, those programs that continue to provision and provide long-term medical care may meet that objective for some individuals. Those programs that do not may be sentencing animals to psychological and physical stress. For example, many of the gibbons released at Semengok are believed to have starved to death or died from disease or aggression (Bennett 1992). Successful rehabilitation can be accomplished given healthy individuals with sufficient skills (or capacity to acquire those skills quickly) and appropriate habitat. Few animals reared in captivity for long periods of time meet these criteria, and there is very little appropriate habitat available.

SUCCESS OF CONSERVATION EFFORTS

Both translocation and rehabilitation are often extremely expensive if implemented properly. Implementing these techniques successfully takes tremendous amounts of preplanning, time, and money—all things most conservationists find in short supply. Nonetheless, both translocation and rehabilitation can work if a number of important factors are considered, not the least of which is employing the appropriate methods for specific situations. In practice, there are few situations in nature where translocation projects stand a reasonable chance of long-term success. Places with suitable habitat, where a particular species is absent despite previously being found there, where the original cause of that species disappearance has been removed, and that will not have a negative impact on resident flora and fauna are understandably few and far between. However, if appropriate habitat is made available (for example, by protecting areas denuded of their natural species composition by hunting or other human activities), well-planned translocation and rehabilitation projects may be used to restore appropriate species within that area.

Although both translocation and rehabilitation offer a chance to return animals into wild areas and thereby make a positive contribution to conservation, the time, cost, and difficulty of appropriate implementation clearly point to conservation in situ as the best possible approach for providing benefits to threatened nonhuman primate species, the ecosystem, and humans. Preserving habitats and the wildlife within them costs the least and gives us clean air and water, flood regulation, and climate control, to name just a few of the benefits. From the view of a cost-benefit analysis, no modern conservation technique can match the conservation of wildlife and their natural habitats. In conservation, as in so much else, an ounce of prevention is worth a pound of cure.

ACKNOWLEDGMENTS

C. P. Yeager wishes to thank the WWF–Indonesia Program, the Margot Marsh Biodiversity Foundation, the Center for Field Research, and Conservation International for partial support during preparation of this manuscript. S. C. Silver wishes to thank the Wildlife Conservation Society, Dr. Fred Koontz, and Dr. Rob Horwich. We are grateful for inputs from colleagues, which helped us improve the quality of this essay; they include R. Lilley, B. Manullang, and L. Ostro.

19

Doing Fieldwork Among the Doucs in Vietnam

Lois K. Lippold

Doucs are brilliantly colored monkeys found living high in the forest canopy in the mountainous tropical forests of Vietnam and Laos. Endangered and previously thought to be close to extinction due to the effects of the war, new studies have revealed not only the diversity of their distribution but also their ecological and behavioral flexibility. Although doucs are restricted to wooded habitats, they are found in a variety of forest types ranging from rain forests to semi-evergreen and wet-dry forests. Much of the douc day is taken up moving from one food source to another and collecting and consuming favorite menu items such as tender young tree leaves, flowers, buds, fruits, and seeds. The remainder of the daylight hours are taken up in napping, grooming, and playing (by the youngsters primarily). Doucs choose sleeping places at dusk and don't arise until dawn. Groups range in size from less than half a dozen individuals to more than fifty and are composed of family members. The core of the group is composed of related females, usually with two times as many females as males. The number of juveniles and infants varies because infants are born year-round.

COLLECTING DATA IN THE FIELD

"It is our destiny to study the douc together," stated my Vietnamese colleague as we started our survey one morning this January. The first phase of our fieldwork involves locating the forests of Vietnam that still contain populations of doucs and estimating the size of the monkey populations. It is also our job to assess whether the forest conditions are adequate to support the douc. Sadly, it is an economic reality that Vietnam cannot conserve all of the remaining forests, and our findings will form the basis for decisions by the government concerning which forests will receive concentrated protection efforts.

After spending more than two years studying doucs at the San Diego Zoo, I went to Vietnam in 1974, during the war, to conduct fieldwork at a site near Danang, Vietnam, aptly named Monkey Mountain. My fieldwork journey to Vietnam met with limited success because of the difficulties of carrying out research in areas where there was military activity: low-flying helicopters and missile attacks of the nearby airfields had a tendency to scatter my study groups. When the North Vietnamese Army began a massive infiltration into the south, I was forced to abandon the site. It is perhaps ironic that my Vietnamese colleague was a member of that North Vietnamese Army force.

DOING FIELDWORK AMONG THE DOUCS OF VIETNAM

I returned to Vietnam in 1993 and have spent eleven seasons studying the doucs. Seasons last from one to four months depending on the funding and the time of year. The dry season is the best time to do fieldwork in Vietnam as many trails are under water or not passable during the wet season.

Successful fieldwork depends on a variety of talents. A mastery of field methods and techniques must be combined with a thorough understanding of the cultural, social, and political situation of the country and the people. A high tolerance for adventure, bugs, new food, and cultural misunderstandings—not to mention extreme climatic conditions (heat, rain, and so forth)—is imperative. Finally, it is absolutely essential to remain flexible concerning study objectives, location of field sites, the daily operation of fieldwork, and types of foods consumed. Every day brings a new challenge in any one or all of these areas.

THE PLACE

Vietnam is situated along the southeastern margin of the Indo-Chinese Peninsula and extends from latitudes 8° 30′ N to 23° 30′ N. Three-quarters of the country is hilly or mountainous, with the highest peaks rising to more than 3000 m (9000 feet) in the northwest but grading into rolling dissected plateaus in the south. The Annamite mountain chain forms the natural boundary between Vietnam, Laos, and Cambodia.

The climate varies from humid tropical conditions in the southern lowlands to temperate conditions in the northern highlands. Mean annual sea level temperatures correspondingly decline from 27°C in the south to 21°C in the extreme north. The approximate mean annual rainfall is 2000 mm, but this increases in the central mountainous region to 3000 mm. There are three monsoon seasons: the northeast winter monsoon and the southeast and western summer monsoons.

The tropical monsoons and the broken and heavily dissected countryside have produced abundant and diverse forests in Vietnam. Forests occur all over the country, covering more than 9 million hectares (in 1989). The plant cover is very rich and diverse with more than 12,000 different kinds of

plants. Vietnam also has many plants and animals that occur nowhere else in the world.

Vietnam is the most densely populated country in mainland Southeast Asia, with more than 70 million residents in 1990 and an annual growth rate of 2.4%. More than 80% of the population is rural, with the largest concentrations of population in the Mekong and Red River deltas (Collins, Sayer, and Whitmore 1991). This high human population has undoubtedly influenced the distribution of the doucs.

GETTING THERE
IS HALF THE FUN

It takes more than 18 hours to fly from the west coast of the United States to Vietnam. This January it took more than 24 hours due to high head winds and the need for several refueling stops. Flying from the west coast means crossing the International Dateline: if I start on Saturday, I don't arrive in Vietnam until Monday. On the return trip I start in Hanoi in the afternoon and arrive in Los Angeles 15 minutes after I leave Hanoi. This makes for a very long day. Turbulence on the flights is common, and since the flights are usually at night the cabin temperature is lowered and the lights are turned out. On the last flight I took (January) I had to wrap myself in four blankets to keep warm. The return trip is even more difficult in terms of temperature regulation because it occurs after becoming acclimated to humid tropical conditions.

But these difficulties are eclipsed by flights within Vietnam. Many developing countries utilize outdated and old aircraft. I recently flew from Hanoi to a small city in southern Vietnam on an aircraft with Russian signs and equipment. To my horror, smoke appeared to pour out of the ventilation system as we gained speed and the plane lifted off the runway. It turned out to be the humid conditions within the cabin mixing with the ancient air conditioning system to produce a harmless fog. The tray tables were also equipped with resident cockroaches that ran to the end of the trays as soon as they were opened for the food service.

A countrywide survey calls for a four-wheel-drive vehicle able to negotiate unpaved roads. In my first season, my colleague hired a four-wheel-drive Land Rover. In Costa Rica I had driven the vehicle myself, but I was informed that in Vietnam vehicle and driver go together as a unit. When we got to the first obvious need for the four-wheel-drive, I wondered why the driver did not engage it. Instead we slipped off the road. After being hoisted back onto the road, I asked him why he had not put the vehicle into four-wheel-drive. He informed me calmly that the vehicle's four-wheel-drive did not work. "But I asked for a vehicle with four-wheel-drive," I said. "Yes," he said, "this vehicle has four-wheel-drive, but you did not ask for it to work."

Most of the roads we travel aren't really roads at all and would be better called trails. We were astonished recently when we decided to take what appeared to be a main road across one part of the country. The country map showed it as a main thoroughfare, with a wide red line designating it exactly like the heavily traveled Highway 1. It looked as if it would cut our driving time by at least two days, a precious commodity since each day costs more than $100 of research funds. I asked the driver if he had ever driven the road. "Once," he said, "a very long time ago, and it was not very good." As we started off, the road was paved. We all sighed a sigh of relief. About ten miles down the road it became dirt, and after another fifty miles it became an almost impassable track. It took us more than three days to get to our destination. There was no turning back, and there were no other roads in the area.

DATA COLLECTION METHODS

Vietnam contains five national parks and more than seventy-five nature reserves. At last count we have surveyed more than forty of these for the presence of doucs. In each location systematic walks exclusively on trails are conducted in forest habitat. These are done with local field guides who know the terrain and the wildlife. In most cases we have been extremely lucky to obtain guides who really know something about the park terrain, but on some occasions we have hiked all day in leech-infested forests only to find out later that doucs have never been spotted in these areas.

Field observations are made from 6:00 A.M. to 6:00 P.M., concentrating on early morning and later afternoon hours. Field sites are selected based on the best chances of finding monkeys according to the opinions of local guides, experienced hunters, existing scientific reports, and previous experience in the area. Further methods for evaluating survey localities include discussions with local scientists and Ministry of Forestry officials. Additionally, recent vegetation maps, aerial photographs, and satellite imagery photos are reviewed.

The resulting surveys are concentrated in areas where live animals are known to be sold in markets, where stuffed doucs are for sale to tourists, and on the borders of ranges. During the present phase of distribution surveys, existing trails are utilized because of the possible danger of coming into contact with undetected live ammunition left over from the war. We often work in areas that were bombed during the war, and it is not uncommon to hike between or around old bomb craters in the nature reserves in the Central Highlands.

Every time a douc group is observed, the number of individuals is recorded and the time of observation and location are noted on a reserve map. The number of individuals, their sex, and an estimation of each individual's age are also recorded. This is followed by a detailed description of the face and coat coloration of adults and infants of both sexes. Photographs and recordings of vocalizations are made whenever possible. Ten days to two weeks are spent in each locality, and walks are repeated at different times of the day.

DOUC IDENTIFICATION METHODS

A successful survey depends on the ability to differentiate doucs from other primates that are also found in these forests. Doucs are relatively easy to distinguish from other arboreal primates because of their large size and brilliant coloring. We carried pictures of all the primates that might be encountered, and when we met anyone in the forest we would show these pictures and ask if they had seen any of these primates recently and in which locations.

There are two separate varieties of douc, and these are differentiated by coloration. The primary colors of the douc are black, white, and gray. In the red-shanked douc langur (*Pygathrix nemaeus*), the legs are maroon from the knees to the ankle, and the thighs, fingers, and toes are black. The body is gray with agouti (a single hair with three colors) hairs of black, white, and gray. The arms are white from the elbows to the wrists, and the upper arms are gray like the body. In the black-shanked douc (*Pygathrix nigripes*), the hind limbs are entirely black, and the forelimbs (except the fingers) and the body are gray (agouti hairs), with the chest being a lighter gray than the rest of the body.

A prominent white triangular rump patch surrounds the long white tail. While studying doucs in captivity, I noticed that even young males could be distinguished from females from the back by a circular white spot found on either side and above the corners of the rump patch.

This trait became very valuable to me when working in the field as I could use it to sex the animals even if they were moving away from me (which they usually were because they are heavily hunted). This characteristic, which differentiates males from females, is found in both the red- and black-shanked doucs.

The white hairs on the cheeks of the red-shanked douc are long (in comparison to the black-shanked douc) and red predominates over black in the two-colored frontal band over the eyes. The face around the eyes is reddish yellow. In the black-shanked douc the cheek hairs are short, and black predominates over red in the two-color frontal band. The region around the eyes is blue, conveying a blue coloring to the entire face.

While studying doucs in captive conditions, I found that their coat color changed as they developed into adults (Lippold 1977). Knowledge of these color changes allowed me to estimate the ages of the young doucs I observed in the field. A newborn douc is characterized by a black face with light stripes beneath each eye. The head is black, with chestnut color bands extending from forehead to ears. The body is light chestnut, with a wide black stripe running from the shoulders to the triangular rump patch. Arms, legs, and rump patch are a slightly darker chestnut, the hands and feet are black, and the tail is reddish gray. Between 8 and 18 months, the adult color is attained although the face remains black. Young males can be differentiated from females by the presence of the circular white spot which develops above and to either side of the triangular rump patch at about 8 months of age. The infant's face gradually changes to adult coloration between 18 and 24 months. The face change starts around the eyes and then proceeds to the cheeks; the last places to change color are around the mouth, chin, and between the eyes.

DOUC DISTRIBUTION

One of the major objectives of our surveys is to collect data to help design a strategy to conserve the doucs. Before effective conservation measures can be designed, viable douc populations must be located. Recent fieldwork has contributed new and important information concerning douc distribution in Vietnam. Recent field surveys have been successful in locating both red-shanked and black-shanked doucs in nature reserves and the national parks of Vietnam. Once thought to be rare with limited distributions, douc populations are actually quite widespread, and doucs are found in a variety of habitats.

Doucs have also been found to utilize a number of different habitat types and a wide array of vegetation. They live in old growth primary forest but also have been found in secondary forests. All of the forests were above the 1000-foot level, and some were much higher. Douc group size was found to be variable and dependent on habitat and human disturbance. The smallest groups, those numbering five individuals, were located near human occupations or in small reserves. The largest groups, numbering over fifty individuals, were found in locations remote from humans.

CONSERVATION

Vietnam has a number of environmental laws that prohibit hunting, capture, or sale of endangered animals, yet endangered animals, including doucs, are found regularly in the local markets. Primates are hunted for food or to sell for medicinal purposes in all the areas we surveyed. Adult primates are eaten or reduced to monkey balm, and infant doucs are either kept and fattened for eating or are sold at the market or offered to foreigners for rescue or as pets. Illegal hunting is big business in Vietnam. Our Vietnamese guides often carried guns to protect us (and themselves) from poachers who commonly threaten to kill park guards and conservationists.

We found that habitat destruction and hunting (even in national parks and nature reserves) are major threats to the survival of the doucs (and other endangered species) in all the areas we surveyed. Primates are on the menu for the Vietnamese, and these animals are frequently supplied by the ethnic minority peoples who traditionally live inside the forest. Primates are also sold to local Vietnamese populations for use in traditional medicine, and large numbers of endangered primates are transported to adjoining countries (China primarily) for use in traditional medicine and for sale to animal dealers. Despite efforts by local, provincial, and state authorities, no effective protection of the endangered douc langur populations exists at the present time (Lippold 1995).

ACKNOWLEDGMENTS

This research was supported by National Geographic Society (NGS 5167–94, 5792–96), Primate Conservation, Inc., Save the Earth Foundation, and the San Diego State Foundation. I owe a special debt of gratitude to Professor Charles Southwick, whose steadfast support over the years has sustained and inspired me. It is a very special honor to contribute to the present volume for it was Dr. Phyllis Dolhinow who encouraged me to study doucs many years ago. Thanks to both Dr. Phyllis Dolhinow and Dr. Agustín Fuentes for including me among such admired colleagues in this present volume. Thanks also to my family for putting up with the long absences required by fieldwork and for their unfailing love and support.

P A R T   2

The Realm of Primate Behavior

The realm of primate behavior is vast and ever changing. Our focus here is on understanding the integration of biological and behavioral aspects of life. To know what an animal does and to understand why it does what it does requires knowledge of different aspects of the **phenotype**: development, behavior, and form. Natural selection, a major force of evolution, acts on phenotypes. Phenotypes, in turn, are constructed by the interaction of the organism with its environment from conception to maturity. An evolutionary perspective provides the framework for our questions and is implicit in our selection of evidence to solve the problems we pose.

Some of the topics in Part 2 will demonstrate the importance of being able to investigate the biological base for behaviors by means of new techniques, invasive as well as noninvasive, that monitor physiological changes over time. We then correlate these changes with our documentation of changes in behavior. The goal is to identify and understand the interactions among the behavioral, psychological, and biological mechanisms underlying what we observe. Primatology has advanced a long way from the days of simply watching and describing what animals do by themselves and with each other.

Once again it has been necessary to be very selective in our choice of essay topics. Many themes of behavior that are well studied are not represented here. The field of primatology has grown rapidly, investigating an ever increasing number of species with a similarly increasing array of investigative techniques. Much of this research could not be included here. If you are intrigued by what you have read here, we encourage you to delve into the rich literature that is available.

The first essay, a general statement on behavior, sets the stage for those that follow. Causes for behavior are to be found in evolutionary time—the distant past, during development, and in the immediate past and present. Different strategies of investigation assist in revealing these varied causes, and the products of the patterns of behavior so revealed are evidenced in primate social relations, cognition, growth, and development.

20

The Study of Behavior

Irwin S. Bernstein

All of us have a fundamental interest in geology, for it is the study of the very earth on which we stand. As living creatures many of us are fascinated by biology, the study of life. Things that move and change right before our eyes attract our attention. Some of us are more interested in animals than plants, even if the technical difference between animals and plants is not based on movement. We are interested in animals because of their behavior, the things they do in relatively short time spans that influence the way they interact with their environment. Behavior encompasses all of the actions of an organism, from the simplest reflexes to the most extraordinarily complex cognitive feats of the most gifted among us. Our favorite animal subject will be dictated, at least in part, by the degree of behavioral complexity we choose to study.

Undoubtedly, the most complex behavior will be observed in our own species, *Homo sapiens,* but many of us prefer to study nonhuman primates. We hope to better understand our own species by studying those animals most like ourselves either because we believe these are indeed good models for our species or because we believe common patterns will reveal the biological origins (evolutionary and genetic contributions) of human behavior. Sometimes the very complexity of human behavior overwhelms us, and we hope to better understand the processes involved by beginning with a similar but less complex system. In this way we hope to understand how complex behavior gets organized and develops over the lifetime of an individual or during the evolution of a taxonomic group.

Of course some of us are just interested in the fundamental behavior of nonhuman primates without regard to whether it is a model of our own behavior. Still others are interested in a particular process, such as learning or socialization, and believe the fundamentals will be found in almost any animal species. Regardless of which perspective we take in the study of nonhuman primate behavior, we observe behavior and then ask how it comes about. If we study what an animal does, we are interested in activities that do not occur all the time, but only at particular times. Then we ask why it does occur at those particular times rather than all the time. Our first approach will be to examine the situations in which the behavior of interest occurs and to search for something in those situations that is different from situations where the behavior does not occur. We look at the time just prior to the behavior for some trigger or stimulus that might have elicited the behavior.

Tinbergen (1951) said that the environmental change that elicits a particular behavior in an organism is the **proximal cause** of that behavior. He also recognized, however, that the proximal stimulus for a behavior may not always elicit the same response over the lifetime of an individual. Maturation and various experiences from conception to the moment of interest may operate to alter the response of an individual to the same stimulus at different points in its lifetime. The events during an individual's lifetime that altered an individual's response to a stimulus are called the ontogenetic causes of behavior. Behavioral scientists usually focus on proximal and ontogenetic causes of behavior in trying to explain why an individual acts in a particular manner at a particular time.

Biological scientists, in contrast, note that individual differences in responses to stimuli cannot always be attributed to differences in events that occurred during the lifetimes of these individuals. Some individuals differ in their behavior because they began life with a different set of genetic material than that found in others. Those differences may exist only in a particular individual or they may be general in a specific **population** of individuals, perhaps a population that can be described as a species or other taxonomic unit.

The problem then becomes one of accounting for the genetic differences among populations. Evolutionary theory indicates that genetic changes come about largely due to random processes (mutations) but that natural selection may favor individuals showing the phenotypic effects of some genetic combinations over individuals lacking those phenotypic features. The task now is one of identifying a suite of selective pressures that would have favored individuals with the genetic material that the current population begins life with. Tinbergen called this the ultimate cause of behavior, but I prefer Kummer's (1971) term, the evolutionary cause. Whereas there is often little difficulty in demonstrating genetic differences between populations, the selective pressures that account for those differences are often hidden in a past that we cannot reconstruct with any confidence. Surely there are multiple possible causes for any observed outcome.

All three of the causes of behavior discussed so far focus on events that happened prior to the behavior being examined: the proximal cause in the time just before the event, the ontogenetic cause in the time between an individual's conception and the moment of interest, and the evolutionary cause stretching back to the time when selection was acting so as to favor ancestors with the same genetic material that is now found in the individual. The fourth "why" question for behavior, however, looks to the future and asks about the consequences of a behavior. It is the question that my aunt poses when she asked me why do I study monkeys. She wants to know what good this will do me, her, or

anyone else. This is usually considered to be the function of an activity, producing a specific consequence, like a paycheck, an increase in knowledge, or the satisfaction of having solved a problem. When biologists ask about function, however, they focus on the influence the behavior has on the genetic fitness of the individual; they ask about the adaptive significance of the behavior.

Examining the function of behavior can mean looking for the immediate and observable consequences that follow from an activity or it can mean trying to understand how this activity influences the survival and reproduction of the individual. It is relatively easy to objectively describe the immediate consequence of an action—for example, pressing the bar released a pellet of food. It is far more difficult to ascertain how that same bar press influenced the genetic fitness of the animal.

Not all behavior is ideally or even positively adaptive, and selection will operate against individuals showing maladaptive behavior. But selection is not (1) instantaneous nor (2) based on single events and a particular outcome but rather on the usual consequence of a response. We know all too well how behavior that normally produces perfectly satisfactory consequences can go awry. If I normally drive to work in the morning and arrive on time, that in no way precludes my driving to work one morning and having a flat tire and arriving embarrassingly late. The flat tire (a consequence of my driving to work that morning) does not mean I will always have a flat tire when I drive to work, nor does it mean I should cease driving to work. Selection operates on the usual outcomes of an activity, whether it is natural selection influencing differential replication of genes as a consequence of their influences on the phenotype or an individual selecting response options based on a memory of the various consequences that occurred in the past following each of these options. Extreme variants may strongly influence selection. For example, a fatal accident will permanently alter my driving habits, whereas a flat tire will not.

More important, the function of behavior need not be the same as the consequences that natural selection favored in the past. Not only will some patterns fail to serve the same functions they served in ancestral populations at a time long gone but these same patterns may now serve entirely different functions that were not available in ancestral populations. For example, individual digit control functions to allow me to use a computer keyboard, but I am confident that whatever benefits accrued to my ancestors as a function of this same ability to move each finger independently, it was not related to computer keyboards. In this case, individual digit control—selected for some unknown function in the past—is an **exaptation**; it now permits functioning as an entirely new behavior to meet current environmental demands. The world is not static, and environmental demands change constantly. If the world were not dynamic, we might expect that millions of years of natural selection would have eliminated all deleterious behavior patterns and that our behavior today would be optimal—near perfectly suited to the world in which we live. That would be wonderful if it were true, but in fact many presumably genetically programmed responses that served our ancestors well are downright maladaptive in the present day and age.

When I am frightened because a child runs in front of my moving automobile and I only just succeed in stopping on time, my body mobilizes in response to this fright in a manner well suited to sudden violent physical activity. Responding to a charging elephant may indeed favor individuals who rapidly mobilize for physical flight, but when I get out of my car to assure myself that the child was indeed not hurt, I only stand quietly or kneel, and the bodily mobilization only serves to make me a bit faint and queasy in the stomach, neither of which is a particularly adaptive response at that moment.

Function can also be confused with intent and motivation. One can erroneously conclude that because a behavior results in a particular consequence that consequence was the goal the actor was attempting to attain; the actor intended, or was motivated to achieve, that consequence. Of course I did not intend to have a flat tire driving to work this morning, but that was surely the consequence of my driving to work this morning. Would that the consequences of behavior were always our intentions achieved!

Motivation and intention precede the activity; consequences lie in the future. Since the future has not yet occurred, the consequence of a behavior can never be the proximal cause of the behavior. Likewise, the consequence cannot be used as a reliable indicator of the actor's intentions at the time of the activity. To believe the future is predetermined and thus causes the present to happen is a belief in teleology. Some people do believe this is true, but such beliefs lie outside of the realm of science. There is no known **scientific method** to test such propositions.

Scientific examination of proximal, ontogenetic, and evolutionary causes, as well as function, is possible and requires substantially different methodologies (Table 1). If proximal causes are viewed as the internal states of an individual—its motives and intentions—then each of us has access to only one mind, our own. We can ask each other what our intentions were, but we have not learned how to ask nonhumans about their intentions and motivations, nor have we learned to understand their answers, even if they do understand our questions. If we believe their motives and intentions are exactly the same as ours would be under similar circumstances, we are guilty of **anthropomorphism,** that is, ascribing our thoughts and intentions to another species. I am not even comfortable with "egomorphism," where I ascribe to you what I believe I would be feeling were I in your situation. Although some of us are remarkably good at it, most of us are notoriously poor at judging the motivations and intentions of others (else there would be no con artists, flimflam specialists, or sharp business practices). Why then do we think we understand what a monkey or ape is thinking? We act as if they were people without guile, whereas we do not even attempt to understand the cognitive world of clams and starfish. Anthropomorphism, then, is the erroneous belief that animals that look like us must think exactly the same things we think.

Being denied ready access to the internal states of another, we still have access to the world to which that individual is responding. Of course, the world as we know it depends on our sensory apparatus, and whereas I have no idea what a lobster's view of the world is like, the sensory apparatus of

TABLE 1 The Four "Why" Questions for a Structure

Distant Past	Past Since Conception	Immediate Past	Present	Future
Selective pressures influence gene frequencies	Maturation and experience influence the individual	Motivation (intention) Physiological (Biological/cause) Environmental stimuli	Behavior at the moment	Consequence or effect of the behavior on the environment and the individual
Evolutionary Cause	Ontogenetic Cause	Proximal Cause	Structure	Function

nonhuman primates and ourselves are sufficiently similar for me to believe I can identify the stimuli that a nonhuman primate perceives. If I can detect changes in those stimuli that reliably predict a particular behavior on the part of the subject, then I can hope to identify the proximal cause of its behavior. Of course I am dealing with a correlation between stimulus and response and can never know for sure about causation, but if I can predict with near 100% accuracy, I am satisfied indeed to call that a causal chain.

Likewise with immediate consequences: I can readily measure the physical outcomes of behavior and call these the usual functions of the activity. However, to measure adaptive significance, I will need to follow enough individuals through their lifetimes and the generations to follow to know whether individuals showing a particular response ended up with higher genetic fitness than individuals that failed to do so. Since I cannot keep all other activities in their lives exactly the same, the task is statistically daunting. At this point we tend to retreat into theory and speculation.

Ontogenetic causes are only a little less difficult. Scientists usually focus on particular rearing environments or behavioral treatments at specific points in an individual's life and then ask how these experiences alter behavior at a later specified time. Such developmental studies take patience and are particularly demanding with nonhuman primates where development is measured over many years.

Evolutionary causes can be examined if we can identify genetically different populations with different phenotypes and then ask about differential survival and reproduction. Nonhuman primates

would hardly be the experimental animal of choice given their long generation times. Nematodes or fruit flies are far better suited to multigenerational studies that must be conducted within the lifetime of the investigator. Barring such research, we are once again reduced to theory and speculation about what the evolutionary selective pressures must have been in the dim distant past such that the world ended up as we know it now. A plausible scenario accounts for the outcome, but the outcome is not proof of the scenario. There is more than one way to achieve most ends, and belief in the truth of a single explanation because the result did happen is called the "error of affirming the consequent." It is the basis of most folk mythology.

The study of behavior, then, may be far more difficult than we first imagined. We begin by watching things happen and describing the events, but this can be as accurate as a recording device and deadly dull if we never understand why things happen as they do. Having asked "Why?" we are then faced with Tinbergen's four answers, each of which may be answered at multiple levels. Behavioral scientists face the proximal cause question and answer with descriptions of physiology, neuroanatomy, biochemistry, and motor mechanics; or intentions, drives, and motivations; or environmental stimuli that the subject may be responding to. Behavioral scientists asking ontogenetic questions are faced with all of the possible interactions of genes, maturation, learning, and environmental influences. Behavior genetics asks about heritability, the amount of variance in a specified population accounted for by genetic and environmental variables. Case study approaches try to link early experiences with later outcomes. Learning theorists talk about the particular conditions that account for the somewhat less than permanent changes in behavior that follow from individual experiences. Biological scientists focus on evolutionary theory, trying to understand how natural selection has shaped the genetic heritage each individual begins life with and how selective pressures at the present time are acting on the phenotypic expressions of our genetic material.

All of these are good questions. All of these are difficult to answer. None of us has to address all of them, but a complete understanding will require answers to all of them. We may never achieve full knowledge, but it is a goal most of us enjoy pursuing.

How Things Came to Be

Primate behavior is remarkably variable both within and among species. The origin of this diversity lies in several time dimensions from ultimate or evolutionary to ontogenetic or developmental to proximate or very recent times. The variability we observe today exists in part as a product of the many different environments of life, and it also comes about as a result of the many normal stages and constant changes that take place during an individual animal's life cycle. We see highly significant dissimilarities even among individuals growing up together in the same social group. Although this untidy degree of variability is unwieldy, to say the least, we can discern some general patterns that represent adjustments or adaptations to an animal's environment. Other patterns of behavior are not yet understood; we do not know how they have come about or what purpose they serve. Understanding the evolution of behavior is an enormously complex task. As is the case with morphological features, behaviors that served one purpose in the past may change over time and serve another purpose today (Gould and Vrba 1982).

In discussing morphological change over time, we examine the history of the group of animals under consideration and look as deeply into the past as possible (see Hartwig, Essay 1). The variation in structure that appears in the fossil record is scrutinized in an attempt to distinguish structural trends and similarities. Once a trend or pattern is identified, we construct hypotheses invoking natural selection and/or other forces of selection and sorting to explain the changes we observed. We use many lines of evidence in addition to the fossils, such as paleontological data, associated flora and fauna, and reconstructions of climate, to construct our hypotheses about the causes of change and to fill out our understanding of the context in which the animals lived. Combining all these sources of information has allowed us to begin to understand some of the major trends of primate evolution and to identify periods of slow and gradual change, *gradualism,* and relatively rapid shifts in morphology, *punctuated equilibrium.*

When our focus is on the evolution of behavior, scenario building is rather more difficult. We have only analogy to use as a base for discussing the behavior of organisms no longer living. We know next to nothing about the genetics of behavior in any complex long-lived species of animal such as a primate. Finally, behavior change can be very rapid and occur in the span of one generation. Other patterns of behavior can remain stable for generations and under a wide range of living conditions. Our understanding of the causes and mechanisms of behavioral change is so limited as to be of little use when the time under consideration is the distant past. As a result, colorful and at times rather Kipling-esque scenarios of the evolution of behavior patterns are often constructed on assumptions and speculation rather than on data that allow hypothesis testing.

We attempt to understand all of the behavioral as well as morphological aspects of the phenotype by identifying the mechanisms of origin, perpetuation, and change for each item or unit. It is this comprehension of underlying mechanisms that eventually will enable us to characterize the evolutionary significance and function, if any, of a given behavior. It is a temptation, not always resisted, to rush to an evolutionary explanation for a behavior or a set of related behaviors without understanding or identifying the causes of or mechanisms producing them. Keep in mind that behavior and biology are inseparable, although the nature of the relation between them is not always clear. It is an easy matter and sometimes the source of great amusement to speculate as to the function of something, but this alone is not science. Fantasy seldom gives rise to testable hypotheses.

Another area in which caution is advisable is in the choice of words we use to label or to describe a behavior. It is important to resist the temptation to project ourselves onto other animals, to anthropomorphize, especially when we are dealing with the nonhuman primates. There are substantial morphological and behavioral similarities among many of the living primates. However, grave pitfalls are created by projecting us onto them. The common practice of popularizing by anthropomorphizing only muddies our perspective and subverts our understanding of what the nonhuman primates are actually doing in their lives and with each other.

The three essays in this section present different ways to examine and investigate the meaning and evolution of behavior. We begin by looking at the most complex of behavior systems, the social group structures of living primates. The second essay describes a case study that has been the basis for a rapidly developing view of the adaptive nature of behavior, a reproductive strategy. The final essay examines the use of the behavior of our closest living relatives, the apes, in reconstructing our own hominid behavioral evolution.

21

Variable Social Organization: What Can Looking at Primate Groups Tell Us About the Evolution of Plasticity in Primate Societies?

Agustín Fuentes

Primates live in societies that can be identified as sets of animals that interact regularly and more so with each other than with members of other such sets. Compared to other mammals, primate societies are characterized by tremendous interspecific diversity in size and age-sex composition.

—Kappeler 1997

Sociality is the cornerstone of primate existence. From the so-called solitary lorises to 100-plus gelada baboon herds, sociality is the tie that binds the primate order. It may very well be that living in social groups, or sociality per se, is the main adaptation and key to this order's success (Kummer 1971; Foley 1996). Whatever the case, it is obvious to both professional and casual observers that social interactions and their relationship to group composition are the primary elements in a primate's everyday life.

This set of interactions between individuals and groups in a species is labeled **social organization** and it can be defined as "multi-layered sets of coalitions based on relationships that differ in intensity, character and function" (Dunbar 1988) or as "a set of 34 traits encompassing several major dimensions of primate social life" (Di Fiore and Rendall 1994), as well as many other variants on this theme (see Wilson 1975; Wrangham 1987a; Kappeler 1997). For this discussion social organization will include the entire set of interactions between individuals within a group and between groups within a species.

Given this definition, the focal point for any examination of social organization has to be the group. We can look at group structure (or composition) both within and between species to establish patterns and generalities. We then look to specific individuals within groups to follow the day-to-day social interactions. We rely on descriptions of group patterns and behavior within a species to assist us in formulating a larger scale concept of species social organization. However, it is vital that any theoretical discussion begin with a few words of caution. Social organization is an emergent property of layered sets of individual relationships (Dunbar 1988; Ray, Essay 25). Although social organization is not a discrete, independent entity, we can observe it as constraints at lower levels (individual, group interactions) and as changing characteristics of relationships over time. In fact groups themselves are not static units but rather fluid ongoing processes shaped and constrained by interactions between their members, other groups, and the environment in which they exist.

With this in mind, let us proceed to a discussion of primate groups: what we think about them, what we know about them, and what this might tell us about the evolution of primate social organization.

WHY PRIMATES LIVE IN GROUPS

There are a number of hypotheses to explain why organisms live in groups, but the primate literature focuses on the ideas of differential parental investment (Trivers 1972; Wilson 1975) and Wrangham's (1980) concept of female bonding. Van Schaik (1996) summarizes these ideas, explaining that resources and risks determine the distribution of and relationship amongst females who in turn (via length and synchrony of estrus) affect the distribution of and relationship amongst males. Van Schaik goes on to point out that this model may be "elegant, but inevitably oversimplifies" (p. 11). The dramatic simplicity of this model tends to ignore social factors that may influence female distribution and grouping patterns. This model also assumes that overall male reproductive investment is invariably small compared to females, when it actually may not be (Rowell 1988b; Travis and Yeager 1991; see also Berkovitch 1997, Essay 30).

Aside from (or in addition to) this general primate model, four major hypotheses have been put forth to explain the selective pressures affecting group formation in primates.

The *food competition* or *foraging hypothesis* suggests that group size is adjusted to the distribution and abundance of resources in time and space. That is, species relying on small, evenly distributed resources will best be able to utilize these resources if in small groups so as to avoid high intragroup competition for food. Conversely, those specializing on large, scattered resources would benefit from larger groups both because of a relaxation of intragroup competition via a large food patch size and the advantage that increased group size gives them in intergroup competition for resources (however, see Rodman 1988 for a review of the variations within this hypothesis).

The *predation pressure hypothesis* suggests that when predation pressure is high primates live in larger groups for protection via greater numbers and increased detection abilities (however, see Tilson 1980 for an alternative predation hypothesis favoring very small groups that rely on predator avoidance via cryptic habits).

The *assistance rearing offspring hypothesis* relates to group composition and is usually invoked for species that exhibit a high degree of paternal care. This hypothesis suggests that some species require a minimum of two adults to successfully raise offspring and has frequently been proposed as an explanation for the high occurrence of one-male, one-female and one-female, multimale groups in the callitrichids.

The *infanticide hypothesis* (van Schaik and Dunbar 1990; van Schaik 1996) suggests that infanticide (infant killing by males who did not father the offspring) is very common in primates. Due to the potential threat of infant loss, females should seek out males who can protect the female's investments (the infants) from other infanticidal males. Barring other severe limitations on group size and composition, van Schaik and Dunbar (1990), van Schaik and Kappeler (1993), and van Schaik (1996) have proposed this as the driving selective force behind a majority of primate social systems. However, there is tremendous disagreement over whether infanticide of any form is common in primates and some strong evidence that males killing unrelated infants is extremely uncommon (or nonexistent) in most primate species (Bartlett, Sussman, and Cheverud 1993; Sussman, Cheverud, and Bartlett 1995).

Other hypotheses include the phylogenetic hypothesis and the neocortex hypothesis. The *phylogenetic hypothesis* suggests that the current grouping pattern or social organization in a species is due primarily to phylogenetic constraints and inertia (Rodman 1988). The *neocortex hypothesis* (Dunbar 1992) suggests that neocortex size constrains group size in primates due to the finite number of individuals any given primate can continuously interact with in a cohesive social manner. Although frequently presented as singular causal elements, these hypotheses are not mutually exclusive. Robin Dunbar (1988, 1996) has taken these single explanation hypotheses a step or two further with an attempt to model multiple lines of selection for group size and composition parameters. Dunbar's (1996) recent models include ecological variables, rainfall, predation, and neocortex size all interacting to establish minimum and maximum group sizes for specific species in specific habitats.

TRADITIONAL DESCRIPTIONS OF PRIMATE GROUPS

Although primate groups are fluid temporal processes, traditional descriptive classifications that reflect the average pattern of group age-sex composition at any given moment in time are still useful in any discussion of primate social organization. Five types of traditional group descriptions are used for primate species.

Multimale, multifemale groups range greatly in size and include two or more adult males, two or more adult females, and their offspring. This is the most varied of the traditional group types and probably the least useful for detailed description. Within this type are a number of subtypes (for example, communities, fission-fusion groups, and multilevel bands). The multimale, multifemale grouping pattern is represented in one form or another in most primate families.

One-male, multifemale groups have one adult male and two or more adult females and offspring. Although common in cercopithecoids, this grouping pattern is less widespread than previously assumed in other primate taxa. One-male, multifemale groups are frequently (and erroneously) referred to as "harem groups." This term, which conjures up images of subservient females and domineering males, does not belong in a serious discussion of primate sociality.

One-female, multimale groups contain one adult female and two or more adult males and offspring. Sometimes this label is used to refer to multimale, multifemale groups with only one breeding female. This group type is very rare and only consistently reported for some callitrichid species.

One-male, one-female groups have only one adult of each sex plus offspring. This grouping pattern was thought to be common in primates as compared with other mammals, but recently it has been shown to be rather rare (Fuentes, in press).

Solitary or semi-solitary primates are those in which a female and her dependent offspring utilize a home range that overlaps with those of other female-offspring units and with multiple males. Although not truly a traditional group, these primates can be fairly social and may form sleeping associations, temporary multifemale associations, or male-female associations. This pattern is common in many prosimians and in one hominoid.

Although these groupings are identified by the sex of the members, they do not necessarily reflect mating patterns. One or more mating patterns may be exhibited within these grouping types, depending on the species in question. Unfortunately, many people still use mating pattern terminology (polygynous, polyandrous, monogamous) as shorthand for group types. I discourage that practice due to the confusion it can cause.

As traditional descriptions, these five patterns are frequently used to describe what is typical of a species. In some cases primate species steadfastly adhere to our labels, but there are also many instances in which they do not (Table 1).

PRIMATE GROUPS: NOTES FROM THE FIELD

As noted by Kappeler in the quote opening this essay, extant primate species vary dramatically in group composition, structure, and size. Nearly all primatologists will agree with that statement on interspecific (between species) variation. However, intraspecific (within species) variation of the same kind is often underemphasized. Most discussions of primate social organization begin with the assumption that species-wide grouping patterns can be sufficiently characterized using the traditional descriptions. But when discussing the ultimate causality of systems, care must be taken to ensure that the assumptions you are starting with are valid. A brief examination of a few primate species will make it clear that there is more to species grouping patterns than the traditional descriptions indicate.

The hanuman langur (*Semnopithecus entellus*) ranges across the Indian subcontinent, from southern

TABLE 1 Traditional Labels and Intraspecific Variation

Traditional Group Type	Species Used as an Example	What the Field Data Tell Us
multimale, multifemale	*Presbytis entellus**	4 of 22 populations one-male, multifemale, large variation in group size
	*Saguinus fuscicolis** *Saguinus oedipus**	some groups reproductively monogamous; some groups one-female, multimale; some groups one-male, one-female
one-male, multifemale	*Semnopithecus entellus**	18 of 22 populations predominantly multimale, multifemale (avg. 2.2 males per group)
one-female, multimale	*Saguinus fuscicolis** *Saguinus oedipus**	most, but not all, groups multimale, multifemale
one-male, one-female	*Hylobate syndactylus** *Hylobates lar**	most populations have some groups with more than 2 adults; some populations exhibit significant extra-pair copulation; potentially variable group genetic structure
	*Saguinus fuscicolis** *Saguinus oedipus**	some groups reproductively monogamous; some groups one-female, multimale; most, but not all, groups multimale, multifemale
solitary	*Pongo pygmaeus***	18–54% of observations are of multiple (2–4) individuals (not including dependent offspring)

*See text for citations; **Galdikas 1985a; this table is a small sample only, see Chism, Essay 9; Kirkpatrick, Essay 10; and Strier, Essay 11 for a few other examples.

Nepal in the north to Sri Lanka in the south. This highly successful colobine flourishes in a wide variety of habitats. Hanuman langurs have been alternately labeled one-male, multifemale; multimale, multifemale; and a mix of the two at various sites where they have been studied. Additionally, many adult males in this species spend some portion of their lives in cohesive all-male groups, some of which have great stability over time.

Treves and Chapman (1996) compared twenty-two sites at which hanuman langurs have been studied and found that the mean number of males per group ranged from 1 (4 sites) to 6 (1 site) and averaged 2.2 adult males per group across all sites. Group size reaches 118 individuals, and mixing between all-male groups and bisexual groups can produce groups with more males than females, although these groups are usually unstable and short-lived.

Tamarins of the genus *Saguinus* range from southern Central America through much of South America. At least four of the species in this genus (*S. fuscicolis, S. mystax, S. nigricolis,* and *S. oedipus*) have been labeled as one-male, one-female; multimale, multifemale; and one-female, multifemale. These species occur in groups of one to nineteen individuals, frequently have more than one adult of each sex per group, and mate in monogamous, polygynous, and polyandrous patterns (Goldizen 1988; Caine 1993a; Garber 1994; Goldizen et. al. 1996; Savage et. al. 1996).

The gibbons (genus *Hylobates*) have long been classified strictly as one-male, one-female groups. However, nearly every long-term study of gibbons has reported some groups with more than two adults (see Fuentes 1998 for a review). Also, recent research on *H. syndactylus* and *H. lar* suggests that even though the two-adult group may be the demographic norm for these species the actual group structure may be quite distinct. Extra-pair copulations, very short dispersal distances, and a high degree of variability in individual tenure of adults within the group paint a highly varied picture of group genetic relationships (Palombit 1994a, 1994b, 1994c; Reichard 1995; Bartlett, Essay 4).

It is critical that we also recognize that not all species of primates vary dramatically across their distribution in group composition, size, or genetic or behavioral profiles. Some species are generally consistent in group composition (some macaques, see Berkovitch and Huffman, Essay 8) or size. However, the range of individual variation that occurs on behavioral and ecological lines within these species remains unclear.

Although the traditional descriptions of groups serve an important function in general classification, the variability within those classifications is also important. There are many dangers in consigning a species to a "typical" group type. For example, variation in grouping patterns may be obscured, which can be quite deleterious when trying to pinpoint the evolutionary path of a species' social organization. Primatologists do, however, agree that primates live in groups and that these groups can be variable in a variety of ways.

VARIABLE SOCIAL ORGANIZATION IN PRIMATES

Rather than seeing social organization as an adaptation itself, we can look at the individuals that make up a species or a population within a species. The behavior of these individuals is the result of both ultimate (overall fitness) and proximate (behavioral, molecular, or physiological) factors. Therefore, the social organization of any population can be seen as a reflection of the interaction patterns of the individuals within it.

Even a brief examination of primate species indicates that grouping patterns, group composition, and the subsequent set of interactions within and between groups can be highly variable (Rylands 1993; Treves and Chapman 1996; Vasey 1997; Fuentes, 1998; Chism, Essay 9; Freed, Essay 13; Kirkpatrick, Essay 10; Strier, Essay 11). Because these elements can be highly variable, it is likely that selection has favored individuals who are highly adaptable in their behavior potentials. Natural selection may set the constraints for individual behavior, but any number of proximate mechanisms may be in process at any given moment within the lifetime of individuals and groups. In proposing a variable social organization in primates, my intent is to encompass both the ultimate and proximate mechanisms involved in the process we call social organization.

The hypotheses put forward to explain why primates live in groups (or what kinds of groups they live in) are examples of natural selection acting on the individuals within a population with the result of regulating group formation and composition. However, all of these hypotheses focus on singular elements as explanatory tools.

The reality of within-species variation for many primates forces us to question the explanatory role of any one of these hypotheses to the exclusion of other factors. It is highly likely that one or more of the scenarios put forward in these hypotheses may affect a primate population at varying points in time.

The food competition, predation pressure, assistance rearing offspring, and infanticide hypotheses are all best seen as potential selection pressures that may contribute (singularly or in unison) to the constraints on individual behavior (and therefore social organization) in a population of primates. Although useful at the level of hypotheses, caution must be exerted when such specific scenarios are used, especially when the assumptions they are based on may lack strong, quantifiable support (such as in the infanticide hypothesis). These hypotheses provide us with enticing evolutionary scenarios for specific elements of a species' social system. However, the high levels of complexity in behavioral and life history elements related to social organization require that models put forward to explain these systems set broad parameters and involve as many variables as possible.

The phylogenetic hypothesis and the neocortex hypothesis are by-products of other complexes brought about by natural selection. Both of these hypotheses could work in conjunction with other processes in establishing constraints on group size and composition. The phylogenetic hypothesis reflects the continuation of a previously established set of adaptations in spite of (or due to the lack of) a change in environment or a speciation event. The neocortex hypothesis reflects the possibility that group size is limited by mode of social communication and that group size among some primate species may reflect the minimum and maximum possible given the neocortical development of those species.

In addition to these hypotheses, many historical and stochastic (by chance) processes are also active in influencing group size, composition, and social organization. Groups and populations within species can be affected by differential mortality and uneven birth ratios, which could potentially skew the demographic patterns (group size, composition, and intergroup transfer). Disease, epidemics, and short-term changes in local habitat or specific environmental niche also can have long-lasting effects on the sets of interactions within and between groups. Massive geological and climatological changes can affect many elements in primate populations by changing selection pressures, reducing (or increasing) gene flow, and potentially increasing the impact of genetic drift. Many of these causal agents may be invisible if observations are restricted to present population demography, ecology, and behavior.

The complexity in behavior and grouping patterns observed within primate species across a range of habitats suggests that individuals within these species are best characterized as generalized adaptive complexes. That is, individuals are the result of selective pressures that establish the parameters of physiological and behavioral expression (potential behavior). Habitat, social interactions, and other elements in an individual's life history elicit specific responses (exhibited behavior) within the individual's potential (see Bernstein, Essay 20). These adaptive complexes (individuals) are highly changeable and can potentially exhibit novel or varied behavior given differing ecological, social, and physiological circumstances. This is not to say that primates are capable of adapting to all chal-

lenges. Rather, their biological parameters allow them a wide range of potential expression. Therefore, the reason we see so much flexibility in primate social organization is because of the high degree of plasticity at the individual, and therefore the group, level.

WHERE TO NOW?

This brief overview illustrates the multitude of factors that influence the social organization of a primate species. Social organization is a complex interconnected web of ultimate, proximate, and stochastic processes that are neither easily identified nor untangled. By viewing primate social organization as a highly variable system, the emphasis on ultimate or proximate explanations disappears, and we can then search for the complex of factors that have contributed to the current set of within-group and between-group behaviors. This is a highly complex and rather cumbersome way to study organisms, however, I believe it has the potential to produce more accurate statements about the emergent property we call social organization.

The task of modeling the factors involved in social organization is already being undertaken by many researchers (see Dunbar 1996 for examples). By viewing primates as somewhat plastic rather than rigid in their potential behavioral expression, we can more easily understand the variation we see at the level of the group. Then, instead of focusing on single element explanatory hypotheses, we can include variability in our models rather than ignore it. It is becoming increasingly clear that any model for primate social organization must take into account phylogenetic history, paleohistories, physiology, historical demographics, environmental variation, and ranges of group size and composition in addition to the traditional hypotheses reviewed here. This is a daunting task, but it has the potential to produce truly holistic, meaningful results.

22

Understanding Behavior:
A Langur Monkey Case Study

Phyllis Dolhinow

If we look at all the living primates, it is difficult to avoid being awed by the amount of variability in behavior among them. Some species will survive in many different habitats and act so differently from one place to another that a person may wonder whether it is really the same kind of primate. Behavior variability among and within species has been an important theme of primate studies for decades (Jay 1965; Dolhinow 1972a; Fedigan and Strum, Essay 33), and this array of diversity has provoked a multitude of ideas as to its meaning and what has produced it. One well-known species that exhibits great variability in social organization and in the behavior of individuals is the common gray langur monkey, *Semnopithecus* (= *Presbytis*) *entellus,* found in Nepal and throughout India to Sri Lanka.

Langur monkeys live in one-male or multimale **bisexual groups** (groups containing both males and females) and in all-male groups. There is great variation among study locations as to which group pattern is most common (Jay 1965; Dolhinow 1972b; Hrdy 1977a; Boggess 1980; Newton 1988). Group size ranges from as few as 3 to more than 100 members. Local populations may differ in density of animals, group size and composition, rate of males moving from one social unit to another, and level of seasonal aggression. The last category includes events ranging from mild face threat to the violent killing of immatures and adults.

Langurs have been studied in areas so diverse— the Himalayas, semi-desert, thick forest, cultivated acres, villages, temples, and cities—that a monkey transported from one extreme to another would certainly perish. Two sites from this array of habitats, Rajaji in Uttar Pradesh in northern India and Abu in Rajasthan, illustrate important contrasts in langur behavior.

The Rajaji Wildlife Sanctuary in the Siwalik forests of northern India is a relatively undisturbed habitat for the bisexual and all-male langur groups living there. Bisexual groups, with from 1 to 8 adult male members, range in size from 25 to 80. Special attention was paid to social relations among adult males as the patterns characteristic of the Rajaji langurs were very different from those of males in some other Indian populations. At Rajaji the level of aggression between males in the bisexual and all-male groups was very low, and during the months when females were sexually receptive, they mated with both group and nongroup males. As reported by Laws and Vonder Haar Laws (1984),

> Relations between bisexual troops and all-male bands are characterized by relatively low levels of aggression, and members of all-male bands are able to associate with bisexual troops for prolonged periods during the mating season. As a result of these associations, nontroop males are about as successful as troop males in achieving reproductive access to troop females. These associations between bisexual troops and all-male bands occurred with a minimal amount of agonistic behavior and without mortality or injury to troop females or immatures. (p. 31)

Adult male aggressive behavior was not significantly higher in frequency during mating season than at other times of the year, but in nonmating months spats between troop males and those in all-male groups were more intense. As a result, males from the bisexual group managed to keep outside males from joining their group. Laws and Vonder Haar Laws argue that the nontroop males are sufficiently motivated to up the ante during mating season and increase the intensity of their threats, thereby managing to stay with the bisexual group for months at a time. All of these shifting association patterns are worked out with no significant injuries even to the adult males and absolutely none to immatures. Rajaji langurs have sufficient space, food, and freedom from human harassment to allow them to act as most if not all langurs undoubtedly acted a few millennia ago before humans changed the ecological face of the subcontinent.

Now let's turn our attention to the langurs of the dry deforested area of Mount Abu, a hill station that is the annual destination of thousands of tourists. Abu is an ancient religious center with little cultivation and a long history of human-monkey interaction. It is here that langur monkeys gained their dark-side reputation for murder and mayhem.

The typical Abu scenario drawn from the interactions of males from all-male groups with the bisexual group is very different from that at Rajaji and many other locations. At Abu males from all-male groups are described as invading the bisexual group to replace and to "take over" control of the group, usually violently, from males already living there. So-called stranger males propel their way into established groups, forcing out resident males by targeting them for attack. In addition, new resident males were reported to stalk females with unweaned infants to attack and kill the immatures. The purpose of these destructive and often fatal attacks on the young langurs was stated by the human observer to have been to destroy all young fathered by other males. As a direct result of these intentional "infanticides," the incoming male made efficient use of what was typically a short reign over the troop (Hrdy 1974). Mothers of dead infants were hastened into sexual receptivity and insemi-

nated by the invader male, who would then become the father of the next generation (Hrdy 1977a; Hausfater and Vogel 1982). A few of these fatal attacks by invading males were witnessed, but unfortunately most were not. Attacks were assumed to have taken place because infants disappeared or were injured by unobserved causes (Bartlett et al. 1993).

At some locations the extent of reported killings was extraordinarily high. For example, 35.5% of 110 male and female infants at Jodhpur—alive at the time troops were invaded—were presumed killed by the immigrating adult males. Approximately 50% of male infants up to the age of 8 months were killed during takeovers (Rajpurohit and Sommer 1993). Here, as well as at other locations, langur monkey population density is very high. The highest frequency of troop takeovers occur in high density locations (Hrdy 1974). At Abu there are more than 130 monkeys per square mile, and at the southern Indian site of Dharwar, where infanticides are reported, there are from 220 to as many as 349 langurs per square mile (Hrdy 1974).

Eventually the scenario of male takeovers accompanied by infanticide achieved the status of being an evolved male reproductive strategy of heritable behavior (Hausfater and Hrdy 1984; Hrdy and Hausfater 1984). This was the case even though the hypothesis was based on "pitifully incomplete data sets" (Hrdy, Janson, and van Schaik 1994–95: 154). Nonetheless, it achieved the explanatory stature of being a major reason for primate sociality (van Schaik and Dunbar 1990). DeWaal (1997) suggested that this was important in bonobo social organization as well but wrote, "I must confess to being uncomfortable with hanging an entire evolutionary scenario on the menace of infanticide, which has never been reported for bonobos, captive or wild" (p. 130).

ONTOGENY

Although there have been many studies of langurs living in different habitats, researchers have not focused their observations on the behavior of immatures. A study of langur monkey development spanning five generations offers some startling clues as to how we may fill a critical gap in our understanding of what is happening at places in India where immatures are attacked and sometimes fatally injured. Information from this long-term study of development in a captive colony, combined with observations of langur development and behavior in India, provides us with an appreciation of the roles regularly taken by young in many different social situations (Dolhinow, in press).

Newborn langurs are far from the helpless and needy stereotypes many people have of the very young. Infants can signal their comfort or displeasure with a wide range of movement and sound (Dolhinow 1991). Mothers are critical to survival, however, and to a large extent they determine the range and quality of early experiences (Dolhinow and Murphy 1982; Dolhinow and Krusko 1984). From day one, the normal infant watches what is going on around it. Within a few days it focuses sharply on events in the group and struggles to get a good view of all that is happening. Infants are a focus of attention to many group females, and for the first five to six weeks after birth youngsters are passed from one female to another. Almost as though by magic, in the fifth week of life the infant starts to climb. This might not seem a nodal point in development, but it is.

The increasingly active infant is now able to go much farther—and in three dimensions—and it does so with rapidly escalating speed and strength. This mobility provides new and pressing management problems for mom, as the infant can now get into all manner of predicaments. Anything that attracts the infant's attention is fair game, and it is attentive to all that surrounds it. With growing independence from a mother who becomes less intent on supervision and restriction, the large infant expands its physical and social world. Always curious and investigative, infants are attracted to commotion and action. Very importantly, langur infants are responsible for most of the interactions that occur between them and adult males. When there is contact, and there is a good deal with some adult males, it is initiated by the infant. Far from being passive, immatures are initiators and intruders. This is the way they learn.

Immatures 2 months to 2 years of age were observed during a twelve-week study of agonism in a stable two-adult-male captive langur group. Results were consistent with observations from the field (Dolhinow, pers. obser.). Of a total of 864 acts of **agonism**, immatures as actors were responsible for 35, or 4.4%, and were receivers of 100, or 11.57%. Young females were actors in 2.1% of all group agonism. Many factors were associated with these scores, including whether the mother of the immature was sexually receptive, a situation in which increased agonism is often the case. Clearly, young langurs are active in group agonism: when there is excitement, they are out there interacting and, at times, getting in the way.

There have been a number of special circumstances in the captive colony history that made it necessary to introduce a new adult male or males into an established group containing infants less than 2 years old. In the last six such introductions, involving eight adult males, there was no detectable injury sustained by any immature in the group. In our introductions, or male replacements, aggression by unfamiliar males against females and immatures arose from interactions largely defined by the females and immatures. For example, in one male replacement, interactions with two juveniles were the most important determinant of an adult male's aggression. Constant close monitoring by this pair of 2-year-olds stimulated the adult's approach. Regardless of which animal was the actor, increased proximity led to avoidance by the young and adult following. Interactions became chases, and females frequently became involved. In another introduction, 27 of 40 aggressive acts directed by females toward the new male were in protection of young, and 6 of 13 male aggressive acts were in response to these interventions. When two new males came into the group at once, the same scenarios took place although they were complicated by the interactions between the males as they established relations.

Immatures are potentially put at risk by aggression when unfamiliar males enter established groups. The processes underlying such aggression are complex, and there are times when the male is more a passive figure than the controller and initiator of interactions. Constant attention of and frequency of approach by immatures can create tension, and this tension can lead to aggression that usually also involves adult females. Under normal circumstances, adult males and females take care not to injure youngsters, but with tensions high the storyline can be very different. These observations show how young langurs can be endangered in situations that arise in part from their own and their mother's actions. The general pattern of immature involvement in adult affairs is much greater than commonly credited, and by 2 years of age the immature is often responsible for placing itself in peril or at risk.

INTERPRETING BEHAVIOR

Clearly, langur monkeys are capable of behaving differently depending in part at least on where they live. The fatal aggression by adult males toward the young at Abu has been explained as a case of evolved reproductive strategy to enable infanticidal males to take advantage over males who do not kill young. However, to be a reproductive strategy, the male must identify the immatures who are not his own and target them specifically. The infant's death produces an effect—the mother becomes sexually receptive, which enables the killer male to inseminate her on his route to fatherhood of the next generation. In this scenario, infanticide becomes a deliberate plan to increase reproductive success for the aggressive male. But think about what a langur male presumably must be able to understand and calculate to activate this reproductive strategy. He must count back the 6½-month gestation period and add the age of the infant to determine whether a given infant might be his own. For a yearling this means the adult male's calendar of reckoning must extend back a total of 18 months. In addition, of course, he must know that his copulations that many months ago produced the young langur.

In stark contrast to the male reproductive strategy interpretation, others have suggested that the

mayhem of male takeovers and the deaths that follow are nonadaptive and are not an evolved reproductive strategy at all (Curtin 1977; Curtin and Dolhinow 1978; Boggess 1984; Dolhinow, in press). It has even been referred to as unabashedly manipulating data to fit a model, "a myth of our contemporary academic culture rather than . . . a scientific fact" (Schubert 1982: 201).

What is it that we need to know to sort this out? Ideally we ought to understand both the proximate and the ultimate causes of this behavior (Bernstein, Essay 24). We seek the mechanisms for proximate, or recent, causes. First off, we need accurate descriptions of what happened. Who did what to whom? How were they related? It is asserted that infant death produces female sexual receptivity sooner than if her infant survived. However, we know that many of the presumed victims were too old to influence the mother's reproduction patterns for the next year. Both the paternity of assumed victims and the fathers of subsequent infants were unknown. These are essential elements in the equation and must be known if the killing is to be considered a reproductive strategy.

In addition to all this missing but critical information, keep in mind that the future is not nor can it ever be the cause of the past. Consequences cannot be the proximate causes for an individual's actions. We cannot look into the mind of the monkey; hence, we do not know the intention of the aggressive male at the time he committed his brutal attacks. But it has been assumed that he killed for the future—a long time into the future.

Once the immediate or proximate aspects of behavior are understood—these are the mechanisms by which specific behaviors are produced in individual animals—we can investigate long-term meanings. In the case of infanticide, however, researchers have skipped over the short term to concentrate on creating evolutionary or ultimate explanations. Do the few cases of infant killing represent an evolved male reproductive strategy? Selection favors behaviors that are acceptable, on average, over lifetimes; it does not focus on single events. If we had observations for generations of male langur monkeys—those that kill and those that do not—we might then be able to address the question of whether killers are at an advantage. We do not have these data even for a tiny portion of one lifetime, and the data we do have are inconclusive at best (Bartlett et al. 1993).

Does behavior evolve? Behavior is part of the phenotype and may be acted on by selection, but can these patterns of behavior be transmitted from one generation to the next by genetic means? Or, given the average environment of development, are these behaviors constructed during development? Is there a genetic basis for infant killing? Hrdy states, "no one takes seriously the idea of a gene for infanticide" (1984a: 49–50), but others note that "a mutation for infanticide should spread rapidly in such a population" (Jolly 1985: 260). Genetic transmission of the trait of killing immatures was assumed to have reproductive advantage and to have been the result of natural selection. But this assumption was not itself examined. This is a classic example of the "'Sower's Fallacy': the error committed in assuming that a correlation between phenotype and reproductive success necessarily implies the operation of natural selection on genetically transmitted differences" (Colwell and King 1983: 232). Genes do not code for function, and there is no direct route from genes to behavior no matter whose atlas you use.

Infanticide is asserted to be an adaptation, genetically based and heritable, and it was further described as adaptive for the males who kill. But is it either? The available evidence supports neither contention. What is mistakenly labeled an adaptation can be behavior observed in successive generations that is without a known genetic base. Adaptation is not interchangeable with adaptive. Adaptive signifies the current utility a trait has for its possessor (Jacob 1977; Gould and Lewontin 1979; Gould and Vrba 1982; Sober 1984). Only over generations, by natural selection, can traits become adaptations (Williams 1966). But traits with high adaptive value do not need to have been produced by natural selection. Selection will act to favor phenotypic behaviors that, on average, have acceptable consequences. Whether something is an adaptation is testable only by looking at the long run. The adaptive significance of a behavior can be measured only in the future; it is never part of the calculus of the origin of the behavior. Once again, the future obviously cannot be the cause of the past, and it is a tautology to offer an adaptive explanation by searching for and creating the problem for which the behavior is a solution (Estling 1983). In this case, a male reproductive strategy is offered as a reason for increasing fitness, getting one's genes to the head of the line by destroying infants that are not your own—infanticide. Explanations that are created because they sound plausible are suitable for novels, not science.

Reference is often made to fitness as though it were a trait, which it is not. Rather, it is a technical assessment of selection, either short or long term. One thing is certain: it changes. Behaviors may increase fitness and have adaptive value in some contexts, but they need not have been shaped by evolution (Jamieson 1986). Fitness definitions are mental aids, and the way fitness is defined may be changed to increase prediction and explanation. There are no universal definitions of fitness because the problems we consider or seek to answer vary. The problem defines what fitness is. To claim that we measure genetic fitness requires identification of a genetic basis for the trait. Not only that, it demands that we demonstrate that variability among the animals with that set of genes corresponds with differential reproductive success. This is a daunting task, never accomplished for any set of behaviors, including so-called infanticide.

MISSING PIECES

With all these caveats, what can we say that may help us understand why langurs kill infants in some areas of India and not in others?

A good place to start is with studies of normal development in the field and in captivity, permitting immatures to take center stage. Even very young infants are far from helpless; they are active, persistent, opportunistic manipulators of their social world. Their attention is drawn to the social milieu surrounding them, and they are tuned in to all activity. As soon as they can, infants investigate, up close, all that is happening—from play to serious aggression. Under most circumstances, an immature's actions do not place it in peril. Under some circumstances, however, the identical behavior could prove fatal.

Explaining infant death by aggression as the result of an evolved male reproductive strategy based solely on benefit for the adult male ignores critical facts that could have led to a different understanding of what transpired and why. By looking at the behavior of the victims we might have realized that it was the immatures themselves who, by their natural interest in all that transpires about them, may have placed themselves in danger. Young do not avoid adult males when there is fighting, even when being close to the action places them at risk. An approach with contact that normally has no penalty for the youngster can carry a high price if done at the wrong time. This well might be the case in some locations when males are fighting seriously in a takeover situation.

Unfortunately, even when our attention is focused on the infants and juveniles, we still may not be able to determine which animal—the mother or the offspring—was the target of an attack. Most presumed instances of infanticide are not witnessed. It is possible that males are not always the perpetrators of destruction. Females can wound and kill infants, intentionally during fighting as well as unintentionally or accidentally. Having an infant clinging to her belly does not stop an adult female from serious fighting with other adults or from making perilous jumps that might dislodge the infant. It is an act of faith to blame males for all infant damage. In addition to reevaluating the role of the immature, we must also make certain we know the perpetrator of the violence.

CONCLUSION

Infant death by aggression (infanticide) has been reported for several locations in India, but it has not been witnessed at many other study sites. Where infanticide has been reported, high levels of aggression have been noted, mainly during and after so-called takeovers of bisexual groups by adult males from all-male bands. Male transfer from one kind of group into another, especially during the months when females are sexually receptive, characterizes langurs all over India. But what is not typical is the high degree of mayhem and damage associated with these transfers in Abu. Rajaji langur males, in marked contrast, moved in and out of bisexual groups with minimal aggression and no fatalities, adult or immature. Evidently, the lack of human harassment, the natural habitat, and the ample space available at Rajaji, plus a host of other factors, produced a far less costly way of reproduction and development than at the temple city of Abu.

There is no doubt that some immatures died as a result of takeovers at Abu, but perhaps not as many as reported, and perhaps not all at the hands and teeth of males. This loss does not allow us to assume that all behaviors that resulted in damage to young were done to serve that end. The adaptive significance of the aggression can only be measured in the future; it cannot have been responsible for the origin of the behavior. We need to know the effects of infant death on mother and all relations among the actors: living, dead, and yet to be born. Only lifetime reproduction records for all males will demonstrate whether killers did better than nonkillers. Short of knowing all this, we can only guess.

Patterns of social behavior, part of the phenotype constructed by the processes of development, can change very rapidly, far faster than morphological features. One genotype can produce a wealth of different phenotypes, depending on the environment of development from the moment of conception. It is not surprising, then, that species such as langurs are able to survive in diverse habitats and to do so by behaving differently. What would our understanding of primate behavior be if so many species did not exist in habitats that differ substantially from those in which they evolved? Habitat degradation and the insults from human cultural invasion have affected most primates, and some to a grave extent. We cannot turn back the clock 5000 years or so to see the widespread forests that covered much of northern India, but we know the forests were there for the ancestors of the langurs we study today in vastly altered conditions.

We will only discover what behavior might mean by studying the animal's development in detail and paying close attention to all of the actors in every drama, not just the loudest, largest, or most obvious ones. Even then, we have no assurance that we will understand what an act or event signifies to the actor. This means it is very important for us not to jump to conclusions that might seem reasonable if we were that actor. Never lower standards of evidence, not even for a good story.

Causes of behavior lie in many dimensions, from proximate just before the event in question, to ontogenetic in the lifetime of the animal, to long-term ultimate or evolutionary. All can serve to produce variability in what animals will do in different situations but, on average, allow for normal development and survival. Behavior is labile and is adaptive under most circumstances, but in others it can place the animal in grave jeopardy. Actions taken in normal or average circumstances may prove fatal in atypical circumstances. Immature langurs may have gotten in the way when intruding males attacked the group, a common behavior turned fatal.

Young primates are intelligent, perceptive, opportunistic, and motivated to take an active part in their social world (Pereira and Fairbanks 1993). Each has a history, memories, options, and needs. What has been selected for is the ability to learn, to modify, to experiment, and to vary responses to challenges of all sorts on a day-to-day and minute-to-minute basis. Constant adjustments to behavior are required in an ever changing environment. This is a key to survival.

23

Great Apes and Early Hominids: Reconstructing Ancestral Behavior

Craig B. Stanford

We will never know more than the most basic details of the lives of our earliest ancestors. This is due in part to the fragmentary nature of the fossil record and in part to the difficulty in projecting the details of an extinct animal's social behavior from its fossilized morphology. It is also due to what might be called the "Rashomon Effect," after the Japanese film of the same name.

In *Rashomon* a murder is committed and a suspect confesses; there are several eyewitnesses. However, as the police interview each person who was present at the crime, the facts of the case, which had seemed clear, become confused. Each witness provides a different rendering of the facts, and each story is supported by fragments of evidence. In the end, the observers' perspectives have muddied the account rather than clarified it, and it becomes impossible to find the reality among the varying stories.

This is analogous to the task of reconstructing the behavior of hominid ancestors. The fossil evidence for human evolution is the only direct physical information we have about our ancestry, but this record is still extremely fragmentary. The small samples of fossil material available for each of the links in our phylogeny allow for much latitude in interpretation. However, early hominid anatomy is better understood with each decade of paleontological research. Their ecology and diet are being resolved to a degree never thought possible only twenty years ago. Advances in technologies allow

us to test predictions about the relationship between dental anatomy and feeding behavior, and between postcranial anatomy and positional behavior, using living primates as exemplars.

For hundreds of years, great apes have served humans as reflections of who we once were, and of what we might have become had evolution taken a different course. The chimpanzee, bonobo, gorilla, and orangutan are the four pongid species, and each represents a different example of social evolution and behavioral adaptation. Each of these has been used to reconstruct the likely behavior of our earliest hominid ancestors. We refer to these reconstructions as "models," a term that is loosely defined as a plausible scenario for how early humans behaved based on relevant pieces of evidence (Moore 1996). A good model should accord with the known world and make predictions that are testable against empirical evidence. Unfortunately, evolution is not like physics or chemistry, in which known, quantifiable forces produce predictable, replicable results. We can explain the evolutionary process in hindsight, but it is not amenable to prediction.

TYPES OF MODELS

Human evolutionary scholars have used two different types of models extensively. Comprehensive models are theories of human origins that amass a large number of intersecting lines of evidence from disparate sources in an attempt to create a complete portrait of what early hominids were like. They are stories of our origins, rich in detail and with a set of facts that are internally consistent. These models will stand the test of time and scientific scrutiny only if they are not just internally consistent but externally consistent as well. For instance, one scenario for human behavioral origins, the so-called Aquatic Ape theory (Morgan 1982), is widely believed by the reading public but has nearly no scientific acceptance. The idea that humans passed through an aquatic phase in prehistory has no support in the fossil record, but Morgan compiled many pieces of evidence that, taken as a whole, tell an engaging and internally consistent story of early humans. A model with greater scientific credibility, the Lovejoy model, attempts to account for human monogamy and concealed ovulation with a comprehensive model (Lovejoy 1981), the specific details of which have been called into question ever since its publication (Allen et al. 1983). Nevertheless, the model has been influential due to its all-encompassing nature.

The second type of models is component models, which try to reconstruct one element of early humans using available data from living and extinct forms. For example, Rodman and McHenry (1980) hypothesized that **bipedalism** arose in earliest hominids because it provided greater foraging efficiency than quadrupedal travel. They based this assertion on a study of the energetics of walking in humans and chimpanzees (Taylor and Rowntree 1973) and on the foraging patterns of modern apes. Other researchers have since questioned Rodman and McHenry's finding (e.g., Steudel 1994). Overall, this model of one crucial aspect of human origins has enjoyed far less attention than Lovejoy, primarily because it makes no attempt to erect a unitary model.

Models using the great apes are limited by the very small number of these species living in the world today. The chimpanzee, bonobo, gorilla, and orangutan have varying social systems, and choosing the features of their behavior that are most informative to our own social evolution is highly subjective. Using any one species as a referent for a human ancestor is problematic because each early hominid was a unique species. Chimpanzees may share nearly all of the human DNA sequence and live in habitats similar to those in which early humans evolved, but they may be very different from the earliest ape-like hominids in important ways. However, those scholars who have advocated using models that rely on disparate evidence rather than analogy with a single species (e.g., Tooby and DeVore 1987) have usually settled on a chimpanzee-like creature as the last common ancestor with the Hominidae.

One way to use information on great ape social systems to reconstruct hominid behavior is to use a cladistic approach. Wrangham (1987b) and Ghiglieri (1987) both compared the great apes to see which features all had in common and were, therefore, most likely to be ancestral and also present in extinct forms. Both found that male bonding and associated behaviors such as territorial defense were shared by chimpanzees and bonobos but not by gorillas and orangutans. Female transfer between social groups at or after puberty characterized all four species and thus seems likely to have characterized the ancestral species as well. This cladistic method is, of course, limited by the quantity and quality of information available on modern great apes.

USING THE COMPONENT APPROACH: MODEL OF THE ORIGINS OF HOMINID MEAT-EATING

Using primate field information, I have investigated one crucial feature of early human behavior, the advent of meat-eating. Meat-eating lends itself to the use of a primate model in the following way. First, we know that beginning about 2.5 million years ago stone tools were used by early genus *Homo* to obtain meat from carcasses. Before this time, there is no archaeological trace of meat-eating since the divergence of apes from hominids. Thus, we know nothing about the earliest roots of meat-eating in the Hominidae, and our window onto it is through the observation of primates. Second, whether the primary mode of obtaining meat was by hunting live animals or by scavenging carcasses can also be addressed by studying living primates. Third, hunting and eating other mammals occurs rarely in the Primate order, so we can compare those species that hunt to see if there are other similarities between them.

Chimpanzees live in a community fission-fusion social system in which there are no permanent stable subgroupings except mothers and their dependent offspring. Females typically emigrate to another community as they reach sexual maturity or thereafter, and neighboring communities recognize territorial boundaries that are defended by males, sometimes violently (Goodall 1986). Since males usually remain on their natal territory throughout life, a community's males usually consist of some near and some more distant kin (Morin et al. 1993).

Chimpanzees hunt wherever they have been studied on a long-term basis. Although both males and females kill prey animals, most kills (91% at Gombe since 1982: Stanford et al. 1994) are by adult and adolescent males hunting in groups. In addition, three longer term studies of well-habituated populations have recorded hunting on a frequent basis (Goodall 1986; Boesch and Boesch 1989). In some of the other field studies in which hunting was documented only rarely (Kibale Forest: Ghiglieri 1984), the failure to observe hunting may have been due to incomplete habituation of the chimpanzee community. When chimpanzees became habituated, hunting was seen frequently. The early debate about whether hunting by chimpanzees is a natural part of their behavioral ecology has thus been resolved; hunting is a natural feature of chimpanzee behavioral ecology.

Chimpanzees hunt at least thirty-five species of mammals, most of which weigh less than 15 kg (Uehara 1997). Hunts can be solitary or social and can involve apparent planning of execution or be spontaneous discoveries of hidden prey. They can involve the capture of one or many prey animals in one hunting episode. The size of the prey animals and the method of capture are important; Isaac and

Crader (1981), for example, considered hunting of smaller animals to be gathering, and distinguish both hunting and scavenging by Pliocene hominids as of large game only. **Scavenging** refers to a foraging mode in which the foragers feed on the carcasses of other mammalian species the foragers themselves have not killed. Scavenging can be passive, in which the meat is procured from a dead animal without challenge, or active, in which a freshly killed prey animal is taken from predators by active pirating (Bunn and Ezzo 1993). The vast majority of observed cases of scavenging in wild chimpanzees are of the pirating mode of carcass procurement. Red colobus are the major prey species of chimpanzees at all long-term chimpanzee study sites.

Hunting by chimpanzees is seasonal (Stanford et al. 1994). At Gombe, nearly 40% of the kills of colobus monkeys occur in the dry season months of August and September. Why would chimpanzees hunt more often in some months than in others? This is an important question. Studies of early hominid diets have shown that meat-eating occurred most often in the dry season, at the same time that meat-eating peaks among Gombe chimpanzees (Speth 1989). The amount of meat eaten, even though it composes a small percentage of the chimpanzee diet, is substantial. In some years, the forty-five chimpanzees of the Kasakela community at Gombe kill and consume more than 700 kg of prey animals of all species (Stanford 1996). This is far more than previous estimates of the weight of live animals eaten by chimpanzees. Even though meat is not consumed every day, the estimated meat consumption during the dry season is about .065 kg of meat per day for each adult chimpanzee. This approaches the meat intake by the members of some human foraging societies. Chimpanzee dietary strategies thus approximate those of human **hunter-gatherers** to a greater degree than we had previously thought.

Although most successful hunts result in a kill of a single colobus monkey, up to seven colobus may be killed at a time. The likelihood of such a multiple kill is related to the number of hunters in the hunting party. The number of adult and adolescent male chimpanzees in the study community rose from five to twelve over the 1980s as a large number of young males matured and began to take their places in hunting parties. The annual number of multiple kills and overall colobus eaten also rose during this period. The fate of the Gombe red colobus population is thus in the hands of the chimpanzee population.

Chimpanzee hunting resembles hunting by human foragers, and perhaps by earliest hominids, in a number of important ways. First, the diet of both is mainly plant matter, and meat is hunted as a supplement. Chimpanzees do not search for prey; instead, they forage for plant foods and hunt only when the opportunity arises. Meat is eaten seasonally, and the importance of meat in the diet of both species may vary radically between rainy and dry seasons. Most hunting is by males in both humans and chimpanzees (Stanford et al. 1994). This is probably because it is risky for females of either species to confront toothed prey while carrying vulnerable infants. After a kill, meat is shared. Researchers in the Mahale Mountains have shown that the **alpha male** uses sharing opportunities in shrewd political ways, both to cement alliances and to snub rivals. Sharing at Gombe is highly nepotistic, with captors sharing mainly with their family members. Sharing at Taï is more reciprocal, as participants in the hunt receive meat for their cooperative efforts (Boesch and Boesch 1989). In general, sharing may be liberal, but it may also be done strategically with an eye toward enhancing the status of the meat possessor. Kills are mainly of quite small animals (less than 10 kg). However, the occurrence of multiple kills means that the total biomass consumed per hunt may be quite large.

There are three striking distinctions between chimpanzee and human hunters. First, humans travel bipedally, a very efficient mode of locomotion that allows them to walk long distances in search of meat. Chimpanzees cannot afford to waste hours or days walking quadrupedally in search of relatively small quantities of meat. Second, human hunting is technologically assisted: we use weapons to capture prey and tools to butcher it prior to consumption. Third, weapons allow humans to target large animal prey that can be captured by coordinated hunting and butchered using tools.

WHAT DOES CHIMPANZEE HUNTING TELL US?

Hunting by chimpanzees informs us about the possible range of behavior performed by early hominids in the period before stone tools provide clear evidence of meat-eating in the fossil record. For instance, claims that earliest hominids could not have hunted for a living because they lacked the cognitive ability to cooperate fall apart in the face of chimpanzee cooperative predatory behavior. The observation that chimpanzee populations show cultural variation between study sites also informs us about the likely range of variation among early hominid populations. While anthropologists debate scavenging versus hunting as subsistence modes, a "chimpologist" would observe that both are likely. Perhaps *Homo habilis* scavenged for a living in the Olduvai Gorge of the Pliocene, while another *habilis* population 100 kilometers away hunted for a living (Stanford, in press).

One of the most important questions about chimpanzee hunting is why the other great apes do not hunt. In fact, few primate species prey on other mammals. Among the apes, only chimpanzees are avid meat-eaters in the wild. Bonobos, although very closely related to chimpanzees, have been observed to hunt only about a dozen times in more than two decades of observation (Kano 1992). This may be in part because neither long-term bonobo study site offers ideal conditions for documenting predation, but it seems clear that these apes are not the avid hunters that chimpanzees are. In fact, bonobos are even known to capture small monkeys and use them as playthings rather than consider eating them (Sabater Pi et al. 1993). Gorillas ignore small antelope that stray within their reach, and orangutans occasionally eat small animals found in tree cavities but do not actively hunt for them (Sugardjito and Nurhada 1981).

Of the nonhuman primates, chimpanzees, baboons (*Papio* spp.), and capuchin monkeys (*Cebus* spp.) are the most highly predatory. Baboons at one site, Gilgil, recorded the highest predation rate of any wild nonhuman primate population, with about one prey item per day captured by a group (Strum 1981). Both *Cebus apella* and *Cebus albifrons* are voracious predators of small mammals such as squirrels, immature coatis, and even other monkeys (Perry and Rose 1994; Rose 1997; Dietz, pers. comm.). Great apes, Old World monkeys, and New World monkeys can all be avid predators.

Are there other features that link these species? One notable common feature is their intelligence, as measured by their skills of social manipulation. All three rank highest among the nonhuman primates in the frequency of tactical deception, or the tendency to deceive others in their group about some state of knowledge (Byrne 1995). Chimpanzees and *Cebus* spp. also have among the highest brain to body size ratios among the nonhuman primates, further suggesting cognitive abilities. Capuchins and chimpanzees are also the most highly skilled tool users of the nonhuman primates. Thus, hunting for mammals, manipulative intelligence involved in tool using, and social intelligence involved in tactical deception are all traits linking two distantly related primates. This suggests that hunting is a feature related somehow to intelligence. Accounting for the roots of human intelligence and the beginning of the rapid expansion of the human neocortex is thus possible through the use of a nonhuman primate predation model.

IS RECONSTRUCTING THE BEHAVIOR OF EXTINCT SPECIES JUST A PARLOR GAME?

Reconstructing the behavior of any extinct creature is always fraught with error. We can be sure that the Darwinian principles that guide us in making sense of the present were also operating in the past. We cannot, however, be sure that the fit between behavior and ecology is close enough that we can accurately analogize the past from the present. Skeletal remains provide us with the only direct evidence of our ancestors, and the behavior of those remains in life can only be inferred from careful consideration of their form and function. Using modern species to inform us about aspects of extinct ones is the only approach that will ever apply behavioral flesh to the bones. Even though we cannot be sure that Pliocene hominids were like chimpanzees are today, we can be sure that the range of possible social and ecological adaptations seen in wild chimpanzees approximates those of early humans.

The Primate Group

Primates are extraordinarily social, and the arena in which sociality is most obviously expressed is the group. The topic of the primate group has appeared, in one form or another, in nearly every essay in this volume. Here we have chosen three specific contributions to highlight key structural factors and important filters through which to observe the primate group. The contributions in this section touch on two of the most important elements of group living: kinship (or familiarity) and the hierarchy of social interaction.

Familiarity plays an integral role in all primate social interactions. The most familiar individuals are those who share the same space for long periods of time (groups). Kinship plays a very important role for human primates; it is how we define many of our most important social groups. However, what (if anything) is kinship for nonhuman primates? How would we measure, recognize, and evaluate it? Perhaps more important, how could a nonhuman primate have this concept? Bernstein outlines these concepts and suggests a few interesting directions for inquiry.

Social dominance is far more broadly conceived today than it was in early studies when adult males were the primary focus of attention. Modern studies investigate every individual in the group as we try to unravel and understand the impact of their complex social relations. The rank of individuals can be affected or determined by the social relations that exist within the group. Importantly, females play a very significant role in the power structure that encompasses and is built on the actions of both sexes.

Hierarchy in primate relations is frequently mentioned yet rarely studied. Aside from attention to dominance relations via priority of access tests, the structure of primate interactions at the individual and group level has been underrepresented in the primatological literature. In the third essay in this section, Ray highlights the complexity and structure surrounding primate hierarchies of social interaction and puts forward a set of suggestions for watching primates interact within and above the level of the group.

24

Kinship and the Behavior of Nonhuman Primates

Irwin S. Bernstein

When told I am related to a person I have just met, I usually suggest that we trace our lineages to identify an ancestor in common. We know who our parents are, and they told us who their parents were and that these were our grandparents. For a species with language, tracing one's recent ancestry is usually straightforward (except in the cases of uncertain paternity). Moreover, since we can count, it is no problem to count the steps to a common ancestor, multiply by one-half, and thus decide on the degree of relatedness between two individuals. If we have to count back more than a few generations, we may conclude that if there is any kinship involved it is so distal that it doesn't matter. Language and counting skills make kinship determination relatively easy.

Of course, I could suggest a more "scientific" approach and ask to have our genetic material analyzed. In truth, I am not certain how many alleles I should expect to share with a random member of my own species. Two people do not have to be related to share the same blood type and any number of alleles, but I expect it will be more if two people are kin. I have been told, however, that humans and chimpanzees have as much as 98% of their DNA in common, so kinship is not based on shared DNA but rather shared genes derived by recent common descent. In outbred species the number of genes shared by two individuals due to common descent will be roughly proportional to the number of steps to a common ancestor. In inbred species, however, two individuals may have nearly identical genotypes without a recent common ancestor. Kinship and genetic similarity are not two terms for the same thing. I often wonder how animals are expected to be able to recognize genes shared due to recent common descent, even if they could detect genes in common.

Kinship is a concept that is culturally defined. It is not biologically defined nor necessarily related to biological descent. In Western societies, and many others, my father's sister and my father's brother's wife are both my aunts, although the latter is not biologically related to me. Kinship, nonetheless, is central to the organization of most human societies, and we often ask how kinship, as defined in that society, influences the social patterns observed.

Evolutionary theory indicates that individuals behaving preferentially toward their own biological kin improve both their classical genetic fitness and their inclusive fitness. Natural selection will favor individuals that positively influence the survival and reproduction of their descendants and other kin that they share genes with by common descent. Given infinite time, all possible mutations will occur. In a static universe, natural selection will operate on this variation to produce populations optimally adapted to their environments. Of course the universe is not constant, and no species has existed through infinite time. Environments are dynamic and ever changing, and not only are mutations essentially random but there are a number of random factors, in addition to natural selection, that influence the gene pool of a species. Rather than assuming that individuals will always act in ways that will maximize their fitness, we still must examine the behavior of individuals in a population to see what they actually do.

Observations of nonhuman primates do indicate that there is a strong correlation between biological relatedness (kinship) and preferential treatment. Inasmuch as this correlation is less than perfect, we cannot consider kinship to be the necessary and sufficient cause for the distribution of beneficial interactions. The correlation between altruistic acts (behavior that benefits another at some cost to oneself) and genetic relatedness cannot be blindly accepted. We ask, instead, how this consequence is achieved. Stressing the functional consequence and ignoring the mechanism—the proximal cause that brings this about—reflects a blind faith in natural selection to "find a way" that borders on mysticism. Even if it is to an animal's advantage to recognize its kin and treat them nepotistically, we must ask first if they can actually recognize their kin (the **independent variable**) and then if they do treat them preferentially (the **dependent variable**). A correlation between kinship and preferential treatment does not necessarily mean that the subjects recognize kinship. Such correlations may occur due to response to other variables that correlate with relatedness rather than being due to biological relatedness per se.

Now it is possible that an animal might have some innate mechanism that would allow it to discriminate the proportion of genes it shares in common with others. Such a "kin" detection system would not mean that the animals had a cognitive concept of kinship but only that their behavior was influenced by the sensory data they received based on shared genetic material. Mechanisms from phenotype matching to chemical discrimination have been proposed, but for nonhuman primates there is no evidence for a preprogrammed mechanism to recognize genetic relatedness. Whereas Wu et al. (1980) did find some evidence suggestive of paternal kin recognition in one of two experiments using

pigtailed monkeys (*Macaca nemestrina*), efforts to replicate and extend these findings by one of the co-authors and a colleague (Fredrickson and Sackett 1984; Sackett and Fredrickson 1987) failed to find any evidence for preferential association with kin not based on previous familiarity. They concluded that the single anomalous result was a type one statistical error and that preferential associations were accounted for by a history of previous association.

There is no question, given the mass of available data, that many species of nonhuman primates behave in ways that benefit their usual associates. Groups act jointly against external sources of disturbance, including other groups of conspecifics. Within groups, members of various cliques support one another against members of other cliques. These groups and cliques are often composed of biologically related individuals, and association partners are often biological kin. In species with a long period of biological dependence, successive offspring are simultaneously associated with and dependent on the same parent(s) for prolonged periods. Siblings reared together have a long history of close association, and the association between parent and offspring need not be severed when the young mature, unless the parent or young independently emigrate from the group.

This close familiarity correlates strongly with biological relatedness, but it does not mean that animals use familiarity to classify one another into cognitive classes involving the concept of kinship. The correlation between the independent variable, kinship, and the dependent variable, behavior that benefits another functionally, does not mean that the animals are aware of either. That is, it does not mean that they know about genes or kinship, nor that they understand the beneficial functional consequences of their behavior on the recipient. The proximal cause for a mother nursing her infant is not necessarily her desire to nourish her young, have it survive, and live to produce grandchildren for her. Certainly that is the function, but the proximal cause of her behavior is likely much more mundane, like breast distension and the stimuli provided by the infant. Similarly, the same female did not necessarily engage in copulation one gestation period ago because she was trying to conceive and replicate her genes. Copulation may function to produce conceptions and replicates of one's genes, but the proximal cause will more likely lie in courtship and hormonal influences on the subject preceding copulation. Ontogenetic causes may include reinforcement of past behavior along the same lines, but that reinforcement must occur reasonably close to the event rather than lying in the far future, a gestation period away, when an infant is born.

How can an animal lacking an innate kin recognition device learn that it is kin to another? Mothers are present at the birth of their offspring, and it might seem that they could recognize these infants as products of their own bodies. But many primiparous mothers nonetheless seem unsure of what to do with their neonates, and virtually all require some period of time to recognize and bond with their infants. They do not "just know." How much more difficult for the father! What extraordinary learning capacity it would take for an individual to relate a copulation a gestation period ago (a period of 5 to 9 months for monkeys and apes) to the infant produced today! What is there in the experience of any nonhuman primate (male or female) that would lead it to believe that infants have both a father and a mother? I have been told that some humans do not know where babies come from. Am I then to believe that monkeys and apes understand paternity? It would be a wise monkey indeed that would know its own father.

It is not helpful to argue that animals "act as if" they understood paternity and that "concealed ovulation" and "fooling a male into believing that he is the father" are only metaphors or similes. Even when this is indeed the case, we must still identify the independent variable that the animals can detect and respond to, given that they cannot know how many genes they share in common, tell each other who their grandparents are, or count the number of steps to a common ancestor. There must be some variable that they respond to that correlates with kinship (even if not perfectly), and this must be the proximal cause for the widespread observation of nepotistic behavior among at least some classes of related individuals.

The available literature indicates that a wide range of behavior, from aiding in agonistic encounters to grooming and toleration of close proximity during feeding, and even food sharing, correlate to some degree with kinship. Such correlations are usually limited to matrilineal kin in female bonded groups. In groups where a single male associates with his offspring for a prolonged period of time and where all such offspring live in a cohesive social group, patrilineal kin are also sometimes described as showing preferential treatment toward one another.

In all of these cases a period of long and intimate association seems to be the best predictor of preferential treatment. Group members are more familiar with one another than strangers, and they usually unite to oppose strangers. Where the long period of biological dependence produces sustained intimate contact between a mother and her child, preferential treatment within a matriline may result. Long-term familiarity and intimate association need not correlate perfectly with kinship. Kidnapping or adoption of infants occurs, and the infants so acquired do not seem to be treated differently as they mature.

Long-term familiarity may come about simply by living in the same social group for a long time. More intimate association may be expected for individuals that were both simultaneously dependent on the same mother, and greater association may be expected for individuals that both associate with the same common partner (a mother for example). Deborah Martin, in a recent dissertation (1997), demonstrated exactly this in a pigtailed monkey group (*Macaca nemestrina*). Old matriarchs showed a strong preference for each other. Sisters born several years apart associated less as adults than sisters born within two years of one another, and sisters whose mother had died associated less than sisters whose mother was still alive. The varying degrees of preferential association correlated almost perfectly with years of living together and the amount of intimate association. This did correlate with kinship, but this preferential association was much better predicted by familiarity.

Familiarity then seems to be the ontogenetic factor and proximal cause for nepotism in nonhuman primates. Natural selection would favor this association if preferential treatment of familiar individuals was correlated with preferential treatment of descendants and individuals with whom one shares genes by common descent. Natural selection will favor genes that have phenotypic expressions that function to promote better survival or higher genetic fitness under specified circumstances. Natural selection may occur in response to functional consequences, but genes are selected that influence the phenotypic expressions that produce these consequences. Natural selection cannot operate to produce the consequences per se. One cannot have genes for high genetic fitness or genes for survival or an instinct for self-preservation, or any other such functional outcome. Natural selection must operate through proximal mechanisms, which elicit genetically influenced phenotypic expressions. Natural selection cannot short circuit to the function, which follows after the structure is expressed, and therefore cannot be the "cause" of the structure (a teleological error).

Now there is no question that animals act in ways that improve their genetic fitness. This does not mean that animals know about genetic fitness. Animals that dislike copulation will certainly be selected against, but those that engage in copulation do not need to know that it leads to conception. Those individuals that act in ways that benefit their offspring and kin will have higher genetic fitness, but this does not mean they understand kinship or parentage.

Whatever the mechanism, the existence of a correlation between kinship and preferential treatment is not proof of the existence of the cognitive concept of kinship. Just because being able to identify kin would be beneficial does not mean that animals can identify their kin. Treating familiar associates preferentially seems to suggest that animals can discriminate based on familiarity. If familiarity also correlates with some classes of kinship, this does not mean the animals use familiarity to identify their kin.

Dasser (1988) has shown that longtailed macaques (*Macaca fascicularis*) recognize mother-infant pairs. Monkeys also seem to recognize the usual allies of their opponents. Reconciliations and decisions to engage in agonistic encounters seem to be influenced by such knowledge. These data clearly indicate that monkeys can learn and remember past association patterns and that they associate certain animals with one another. They may also know what group an extra-group individual is associated with, but in neither case does such recognition imply more than a knowledge of association. It is gratuitous to assume that pairing an infant with the female that it is usually with, and that usually responds to its distress cries, is proof that the monkeys know this is mother and child, or that two males that aid one another are kin. (In fact, males that aid one another are often not kin, and reciprocal altruism and mutualism has been invoked to "explain" such alliances.) Explanations at the level of function may be useful in understanding how evolution could have produced such a result, but in every instance we must demonstrate what it is that the animals actually do (the structure of their behavior) and the proximal cause that elicits that behavior under the specific conditions where it produces the functional consequences noted.

So too with kinship. Nonhuman primates do behave in ways that function to selectively benefit their kin. Natural selection would have favored such behavior. It is up to us to identify what it is that the monkeys and apes are actually doing, and what the proximal stimuli are that they are responding to such that the functional consequences noted are obtained. To understand behavior one must first identify the structure under study, and then address each of Tinbergen's "why" questions. What is the function (consequence) of the behavior? Why would natural selection favor such behavior? What in the lifetime of the individual influences the expression of that behavior? What are the environmental stimuli that elicit the behavior of interest at the observed times? These are all important questions, and answering one does not answer any of the others. It is up to us to seek out the answers to all.

25

Social Dominance
in Nonhuman Primates

Elsworth Ray

Few ethological concepts have garnered as much atten-tion or acceptance in the general public as the concept of dominance. In coming to the primatological litera-ture for the first time, people commonly hold estab-lished notions as to the supremacy of the alpha male within his social group. He is the leader of his troop, achieving his status through his strength and ability to win fights, gaining privilege to all he desires: mates, food, resting places, and so forth. He is the "king," master of his harem and domain, a leader. It is a sim-ple picture bordering on a mythological tale, replete with rites of passage and a quest for the attainment of goals. Like many fables, it contains elements of the observable, empirical world, but in its telling much is left out.

The common perception of dominance in nonhuman primates excludes much that is of importance to pri-matologists. Most people envision a society of a domi-nant male with his females and are unaware of the dominance system among females or the roles females play in determining who is dominant in some species. The ability of an individual to dominate is based not only on its ability to win fights but also on its ability to garner support from others when conflicts arise.

Dominance is a concept with dual meanings (Hinde 1978). Fundamentally, dominance is a statement about a type of relationship that exists

between two individuals (Bernstein 1981). More specifically, the term is an adjective describing an individual that consistently prevails over another. Second, dominance applies to the rank order as-signed to individuals in a social group, the pecking order. Hierarchies are often complex social struc-tures (see Ray, Essay 26). The common perception of an ordinal, or linear, pecking order among the members of a primate group may or may not hold true for any specific group. Often it does not. The rank of an individual can be affected, or deter-mined, by the social relationships within its group.

The issue of how dominance is identified by re-searchers requires attention, particularly as we seek to understand the role of this social phenomenon in nonhuman societies and in evolution. The be-haviors we choose to determine dominance rank-ings strongly affect much of what we can say about the role of dominance in primate societies. Aggres-sive behaviors are at the heart of most, but not all, definitions of dominance. But if dominance is just a synonym for aggressiveness, why use the term at all? It becomes misleading. More is meant than simple aggression. Some important concerns re-garding dominance that are not directly addressed in this brief review are sex differences in the ex-pression of dominance (Fedigan 1982), life history factors (Pereira 1995), mate choice and reproduc-tive success (Fedigan 1982, 1983), the physiology of dominance (Sapolsky 1993), social inheritance (Chapais 1988), and the role of group structure on dominance relationships (Mendoza 1984; Dolhinow and Taff 1993).

AN ABBREVIATED HISTORY OF THE DOMINANCE CONCEPT

Using the ratio of wins to losses as the basic method of establishing who is dominant in a relationship dates to the pioneering studies of Schjelderup-Ebbe (1922), who noted in his research on chickens that the distribution of aggressive acts was not random among his subjects. Those chickens that pecked others did not receive pecks in return. Schjelderup-Ebbe referred to the overall pattern of who was able to peck whom in a group as a pecking order.

Zuckermann was among the first to argue that aggressive dominance was a cornerstone of primate social systems. He saw male competitive dominance as a way of ordering the individuals in primate societies (Zuckermann 1932), and this method of using aggressive dominance has continued amid debate.

The concept of dominance has not been limited to statements on social relationships. In 1962 Stuart Altmann presented a formal linear-rank model tying male dominance to the evolutionary process via natural selection. This model, termed the priority of access model, proposed that the number of females with whom a male mates was proportionate to his rank. Male 1 would mate with the largest number of females, Male 2 in rank would have the second highest number of females, Male 3 the third most, and so on down the line. Because the number of matings achieved was a result of a male's competitive ranking, a correlation could be made with the number of offspring sired by a given male through his dominance status. Consequently, an evolutionary role was given to high rank, and, concordantly, it was argued that dominance was a selected trait as high-ranking males passed more of their genes into subsequent generations. This model, with adjustments such as selective mating by alpha males, remains prevalent in both the public view and the primatological literature (cf., Popp

and DeVore 1979; Cowlishaw and Dunbar 1991; de Ruiter and Inoue 1993).

A few years after the publication of the priority of access model, a number of researchers (e.g., Rowell 1966) began to question the role of dominance in primate societies. Rowell noted that she could discern a dominance hierarchy in a captive group of savanna baboons but not in the wild group she studied at the same time.

In addition, other researchers (e.g., Gartlan 1968) began to ask if dominance was largely an artifact of captivity with little relevance to wild populations. The enclosures used to hold nonhuman primate social groups are much smaller than the area used by a primate throughout a day, forcing more encounters, including aggressive interactions between group members. Not only was limited space seen as a factor in captive groups but so was the amount of time available for social interactions. In natural habitats, primates often spend a great deal of their time engaged in obtaining food. In captivity, animals are fed two or three times a day, leaving many more hours each day to engage in social activities.

Based on his own research and a review of the literature, Gartlan (1968) found little substance to the traditional view of the place of dominance in primate lives. His work, and that of others (e.g., Bernstein 1970; Fedigan 1983), showed little or no correlation between dominance and reproductive success as predicted by the priority of access model. A different perspective on the function of dominance in primate societies was presented by Hall (cited in Gartlan 1968). Hall argued that aggressive dominance functioned to establish norms of behavior in societies. As individuals engaged in inappropriate behaviors, other members of the group would act aggressively toward the originator of the unacceptable actions. Through punishment, subordinate individuals learned to act appropriately.

Rowell (1966, 1974) and Gartlan (1968) also questioned how dominance was achieved. Their observations led them to conclude that dominance, to the extent it existed in wild populations, was due more to the actions of subordinates than to the actions of higher ranked individuals. Their studies on savanna baboons (Rowell) and vervet monkeys (Gartlan) showed that dominant individuals committed little aggressive behavior. Instead, they maintained, dominance relations result from the approach-retreat patterns and grimaces of the subordinate.

Despite this debate on how dominance was maintained and its role in primate societies, most researchers continued to apply the concept in their studies of primates. For example, Hausfater (1975) tested the priority of access model on baboons, concluding that although dominance did not directly correlate to mating success it may correlate to reproductive success as dominant males could monopolize females when the females were most likely to conceive. He cautioned, however, that as dominance status changes throughout a male's life there may not be a serious reproductive advantage to individuals over the course of their life because of their status at any given point in time.

Among the papers that strongly supported the traditional priority of access model, with alteration, was that of Popp and DeVore (1979). They proposed a cost-benefit model of aggressive dominance in response to a problem they perceived in the idea that dominance served to establish social norms. The idea that dominance functioned to bring stability to the group struck them as suggestive of a group level function, and as such the stability model violated tenets of evolutionary theory based in self-interested reproductive success.

In 1978 and 1981 important papers were published that attempted to deal with the conflicting views of the role of dominance in primate societies. Hinde's paper (1978) delineated two distinct meanings used by researchers for the word "dominance." One usage is as a type of dyadic relationship, the other as a reference to rankings in a hierarchy. Bernstein's paper (1981) focused on the nature of dominance relationships. Both papers discussed difficulties inherent in dealing with dominance hierarchies. Central among their concerns were issues of meaningful correlations of other behaviors with the dominance hierarchies and issues regarding the linear structure of the hierarchies constructed by primatologists.

DOMINANCE RELATIONSHIPS

A misperception regarding dominance is that it is a characteristic, or trait, of an individual. It is not. Dominance is a type of relationship that consists of a pattern of interaction between two individuals (Hinde 1978; Chase 1980; Bernstein 1981). It is dyadic, and the pattern is most easily identified during competitive situations. Dominance relationships are dynamic, with the degree and the direction of the relationship changing throughout the lives of the individuals engaged in the relationship.

The outcomes of aggressive encounters are the most common means used to identify dominance relationships. When an individual consistently enforces its will or obtains a contested resource over another individual, we label the former individual as dominant in the relationship and the latter as subordinate. The traditional use of aggressive acts to denote dominance is common, but aggression occurs in many contexts in primate life and can serve many functions (Mason 1993). Further, the use of aggression varies considerably among different species, with some species rarely if ever engaging in aggressive behaviors (Strier 1992b, 1994a).

A number of factors or variables can influence the pattern of interaction in a dominance relationship, and often several factors are acting on any given relationship. These factors include size and sexual dimorphism, age, health, social skills, kinship, ecological conditions, and group demographics. Size is one variable that has received a great deal of attention. Larger individuals tend to dominate smaller individuals. The degree of sexual dimorphism in a species has long been considered a major factor in the dominance relationships between males and females (see Strier, Essay 11). Age is another variable, along with health. Adults in their prime are often able to maintain dominance over subadults or aged individuals as are healthy animals over those with disabilities.

With age comes experience, providing individuals with the skills to use the social system of which they are a part. Experience allows an animal to make decisions such as whom it should support, when and how to participate in conflicts, or when to ignore them. The ability to garner support from others, to form coalitions and networks, can be vital in gaining or maintaining high rank. This ability to use and manipulate the social milieu of a group is itself affected by other variables such as kinship, migration patterns, and tenure within a group.

Ecological and demographic factors are also important. Scarcity of food, water, or refuges can lead to conflict and competition between members of a group. Individuals may fight with greater determination when resources are scarce, either reinforcing the dominance pattern or causing reversals in relationships. Adult sex ratios, the number of males to females, and group size also influence dominance by focusing or diffusing competition. When several females are in estrus at the same time (for example, when mating is seasonal) and there are several males in the group, the degree of competition for access to preferred mating partners is less intense than when several males compete for only one or two estrous females.

DOMINANCE RANKS

Dominance rankings are created by first identifying dominance relationships between all individuals. Having determined the dominance relationships within a group, researchers then order the individuals according to the criterion of who dominates whom. These rank orders constitute a linear hierarchical structure. An important factor in establishing dominance rankings is the behaviors chosen by researchers to represent dominance.

As noted, the two most common measures are agonism scores of winners/losers and approach-avoidance scores. Behaviors such as who grooms whom or who receives the greatest amount of grooming have been used to establish dominance ranks, as have the presenting of hindquarters, mounting, and acts of sex. Dominance is assigned to the individual who does the mounting, and subordination is assigned to the presenter. High rank is assigned to individuals with the greatest number of partners or the most copulations.

Dominance relationships do not rely solely on overt gestures but are often expressed subtly. A simple look or shift in posture by a dominant individual can convey all that is needed to check a subordinate's actions. Sometimes it is a show of indifference through a lack of a response to gestures by others that communicates dominance. In the langur monkeys (*Semnopithecus entellus*) I study, the dominant individual often ignores threats directed at him or her, or squabbles among others in their group (Ray, in prep.)

The behaviors we use to establish dominance are important because they become signifiers of what we as observers of primate societies want the term dominance to mean. Not all species show the same behaviors, and different species may use similar behaviors in different ways. As a result, determining higher level functions for dominance, such as giving it evolutionary significance, can be problematic when scientists attempt to correlate the different measures of dominance from various studies. It is easy to fall into the trap of correlating distinctly different social phenomena than originally intended.

There is no reason to assume that dominance rankings based on aggressive encounters are equivalent to rankings based on avoidance or grooming patterns. All researchers want their rankings to depict the real world of the animals they observe, and most are sensitive to the fact that when they use a single behavioral measure to establish rankings they may simply be renaming a social phenomenon. If aggressive behaviors are used to determine ranks, how broadly or appropriately do those specific behaviors represent other aspects of the group? Is there correspondence with grooming patterns, mating patterns, and accessibility to food, or does the ranking simply show who is most likely to win a fight when aggressive interactions occur? What are the implications of dominance systems in the lives of the primates we study? These are questions we want to answer.

Given the issues surrounding which behaviors to use in establishing dominance rankings, researchers also need to consider the linearity of their ranks. Dominance relationships are not always transitive. That is, if individual A dominates individual B, and

B dominates C, it does not automatically follow that A can dominate C. If A do in fact dominate all individuals below it in rank, as do B and C, then the dominance rankings are transitive in nature. However, it is not uncommon for an individual to be able to dominate another regardless of where those two stand in the overall rankings. Dominance rankings that are not linear (that is, A dominates B, who dominates C, who then in turn dominates A) are said to be nontransitive. The rankings do not extend from one relationship to another. This is often observed in mid- to low-ranked individuals, although it can apply to those of high rank as well.

Another aspect of dominance rankings is rank dependence. When constructing dominance ranks, each individual is assigned a position. This ranking, based on the individual's ability to dominate others, is referred to as its **independent rank.** However, it is not uncommon for individuals to be able to dominate others not because of their own abilities but because of support received from members of their group in the form of coalitions or social networks. This is **dependent rank.** Dependent rank was first identified by Japanese researchers studying *Macaca fuscata* (Kawai 1958). They noted that strong support among members of matrilines provided higher ranks than the individuals would hold if not in association with members of their networks. DeVore (1965a) observed a similar phenomenon in savanna baboons and delineated central versus peripheral ranks. A more formal appraisal of dependent dominance ranks has been put forth by Thierry (1990, 1993).

Dependent rank does not always result from participation in a matrilineal network. Studies of rank and reproduction in savanna baboons, for example, demonstrate that males often form coalitions against those with higher rank. These studies show that factors such as tenure (Strum 1982), self-interest (Bercovitch 1988), or the abilities and ranks of others (Chapais and Schulman 1980; Noë 1990) are important variables used by individuals to increase their own rank, or to gain access to re-

wards otherwise unavailable to them if dominance rankings were the only structure or system operating in primate societies.

CONCLUSION

The study of dominance in nonhuman societies has a long history, and researchers continue to study its function in nonhuman societies. The conceptual issues regarding dominance—some of which date to the early work of Schjelderup-Ebbe (1922)—include the use of aggression to measure dominance, the problems of transitive and nontransitive rank orders, and the dyadic nature of dominance relations. These considerations remain important in understanding dominance. More recent considerations include explicit recognition of the concept's dual meanings as relationship and as a rank order. The importance of dependent ranks through coalition formation was raised in recognition of the role social support plays as a tactic to maintain, subvert, or undermine the effects of dominance systems.

Bernstein (1981) raised an important question when he asked, What do we want the concept of dominance to mean? Do we want the concept to designate, as it does in human societies, the ability to control the actions of others? Or should dominance reflect the ability to achieve that which one desires? Whichever definition gains consensus will determine how we measure dominance, and what we can say about its role or function in social groups. Dominance must mean more than simple aggression.

The problem of defining dominance seems to be most acute when dealing with hierarchies. Dominance relationships are grounded in the interaction patterns between individuals and, as such, are observable and measurable. Dominance rankings are less tangible. What does it mean to beta or gamma? How will we know? Only serious reflection and further research will enable us to answer.

26

Hierarchy in Primate Social Organization

Elsworth Ray

Primate social groups are not merely a number of individuals living in the same area, using the same resources, and avoiding the same predators. Primate groups consist of individuals of all ages and both sexes interacting with one another as each strives to satisfy its own needs. Primate societies are dynamic entities that are constantly changing with births and deaths, emigration and immigration.

Conceptually, the social systems of primates are hierarchically structured. To say that primate social systems are hierarchic does not denote what, if any, systems or structures of social power or social inequality exist in primate groups. Rather, it is a statement regarding the social organizations created by primates through their social behavior and by us as observers of primates. Systems of domi-

nance relations can be seen in many primate groups, and these relationships can be assigned rankings (Chase 1980; Bernstein 1981). But the focus here will be on a different hierarchy—the social system of primates. Primate social systems can be examined and compared using basic principles of hierarchy theory (Pattee 1973; Salthe 1985; Dyke 1988; Ahl and Allen 1996).

Primate social systems can be organized into distinct levels: individuals, relationships, networks, and in some species, communities (Table 1). These levels represent discrete strata of organization within a hierarchical structure. Not all primate groups manifest all four levels of this conceptualization, nor do these four levels represent the total extent of social groupings present in primate social

TABLE 1 Nonhuman Primate Social Structure Hierarchy

Structural Level	Components of Level	Information Content of Level	Examples
Individual	Single organism	Me	Adult female
			Juvenile male
Relationships	Dyadic	You–Me	Mother-infant
			Play partners
			Dominant-subordinate
Networks	Triadic (plus)	We	Macaque matrilines
			Chimpanzee male cohorts
Community	Sets of networks	Us–Them	Ateline or chimpanzee social groups (not seen in all species)

systems. Humans, for example, manifest many more levels of organization than these four strata. Gorillas and gibbons do not create formal communities, although at different times they may come together into congregations. Still these basic levels of social organization are common elements of most primate social systems.

THE HIERARCHY WITHIN PRIMATE SYSTEMS

Before discussing the basic structural components of primate social systems, a few terms require clarification. First it is necessary to delineate what it means to be social. Sociality stems from the sustained interactions between members of a group, but it denotes more than simple interaction. It denotes association between individuals due to the presence of one another. Unlike simple collectives, or aggregations, the attractant for primates is not solely some external aspect of the world about them. Primates do not come together in groups for the sole purpose of exploiting food or water resources; the attractant is each other.

The phrase **social system** refers to all the components and processes at work in maintaining the organization of primate groups. "Social organization" refers to the actual structural elements of primate groups. The term "group" signifies any set of individuals living in an area. It does not provide information about how the individuals interact or about the complexity of their social structures.

INDIVIDUALS IN INTERACTION

In a hierarchical formulation of primate social systems, the individuals of the group constitute the base level of social organization, the foundation of the society. Individuals establish the starting point of the structural hierarchy through their behavioral patterns. Through affiliation, toleration, and antagonism, the individuals of a society create and maintain their social world. It is through these social processes, the behaviors of individuals, that the components of a social system are structured and identified.

It is important to recognize that each individual of a social group has its own personal needs and desires, and individuals act to obtain these requirements. Dietary, social, sexual, personal security, and health needs are among these requirements (see Goldsmith, Essay 6; Bercovitch, Essay 30). Further, as individuals mature, their needs change. The requirements of an infant are not the same as those of a juvenile or an adult (Dolhinow, Essay 29). Not only do needs change throughout a lifetime but so do the means individuals use to obtain their requirements.

Individuals do not act for "the good of the group," and it is not unusual for two or more group members to try to obtain the same resource at the same time. Consequently, conflict is a common feature of primate social life, and primate societies are dynamic systems (Mason 1993).

To obtain their goals, primates interact with other members of their group. The types of activities engaged in by each individual strongly affect each group's social organization. Primate social actions can be placed into three basic categories: affiliation, toleration, and antagonism. Of these three categories, affiliative behaviors are those most important to the formation and maintenance of social organization. Without affiliative behaviors, no larger social units of any significance can emerge.

Simple toleration, the acceptance of others, creates exposure, but tolerance itself is not a mechanism through which sociality emerges. Tolerance allows for the formation of aggregate clusters, as seen in the colony nesting sites of birds or in sea lion rookeries. It can be hypothesized that toleration is a first step toward social living, but in itself acceptance of the presence of others does not promote prolonged association or mutual involvement, particularly as individuals find themselves in conflict over resources.

Antagonistic acts (fighting or displaying threats) generate discord, not unity. Although agonism is one means by which primates establish norms of behavior and as such promote social order

(Bernstein and Gordon 1974; Lyons 1993), it does not establish a condition through which sociality emerges. Some social linkages do result as individuals act in concert to avoid or deter their own chances of receiving an agonistic act. These linkages, however, tend to be opportunistic, short-lived, and context dependent. Often referred to as coalitions, or factions, these units fail to create recognizably higher levels of social organization (Nicholas 1965). Overall, one would have a hard time making a case for two individuals consistently associating for the purpose of engaging in agonism with each other. Still, agonism is a common occurrence in many social groups as primates come into conflict with one another. To counter agonism's disruptive force many primates engage in reconciliatory gestures to maintain stability within the group.

For sociality to occur, individuals need to act in a manner that promotes continued association with each other. The behaviors of the individuals must send a signal that promotes mutualism within the group. This information must be specific and consistent so the signal is not misinterpreted. Conventionalized affiliative behaviors act as messengers of associative intent from one individual to another. Initial gestures, such as presenting or allowing prolonged spatial proximity or contact, promote continued association between individuals. As these initial gestures are accepted and as they persist, stronger signaling behaviors such as touching, embracing, or grooming may develop. As these behaviors become established elements of normal discourse between two individuals, a new level of social structure emerges. Dyadic in nature, this new level is the affiliative relationship (Hinde 1976, 1987).

PREDICTABLE INTERACTIONS IN RELATIONSHIPS

Until relationships develop within groups, there are simply individuals in action. No social emergence has occurred. Individuals may be gregarious in their activities, but their actions cannot be considered to be social until they display the condition of being sustained through time with specific others. The emergence of relationships as a structural unit in social groups comes through the sustained pattern of interactive behavior between two individuals. All relationships are dyadic in their structure, and the behavior between the two individuals follows a consistent pattern (Hinde 1976, 1987).

Both continuity and context are important in determining the existence and nature of relationships. Primates often form short-lived association patterns that are affiliative or cooperative in nature. These short-lived interactions represent context specific social entities serving a singular function. They do not act as structural components of the social organization. Both sexes form these short-term units of association. Male coalitions that form to gain access to estrous females in savanna baboons are such a unit (Bercovitch 1988). Consortships, wherein a female and a male interact extensively and nearly exclusively when the female is in estrus, are another example. Consortships have been observed in chimpanzees (Tutin 1979), Japanese macaques (Baxter and Fedigan 1979), and savanna baboons (Seyfarth 1978).

Although sustained over time and therefore stable, relationships are also dynamic structures. The rates of interaction between two individuals change over time as individuals adjust to and accept each other. But as long as the interaction pattern is consistent, the relationship persists. The consistency of the pattern enables the individuals to predict each other's behavior when they interact, and this social information provides stability throughout the group. Not only can the individuals of a given relationship predict future behaviors but so can other group members.

There are many types of relationships in primate groups: mother-infant, play partners, male-female associates, rivals, dominant-subordinate, and so on. Although affiliative behaviors provide the basis of social emergence, they do not preclude the possibility of agonistic actions (Bernstein, Judge, and Ruehlmann 1993). Conflicts arise. However, agonistic behaviors expressed within affiliative relationships occur at rates lower than the rates of behaviors that establish and maintain the overall pattern of interaction. Should new interaction patterns emerge between two individuals, their relationship will change accordingly.

RELATIONSHIP SETS

Relationships are dyadically structured, and each individual in a group has many relationships within its group. An individual not only has many relationships but many types of relationships. As relationships are predictable patterns of behaviors between two individuals, relationships can be assigned to the same three basic categories as are behaviors. The totality of an individual's relationships of a specific behavioral category with the members of its group can be conceptualized as a relationship set.

Although relationship sets are important facets in social systems, by themselves they do not form a distinct level of structural organization. Since relationship sets are summations of all the relationships of a specific type held by a single individual, they are bounded social entities constrained by the actions of the focal individual. In themselves, relationship sets provide no qualitatively new social information nor represent distinctive social dynamics.

Affiliative relationship sets, however, do bring a number of individuals into association. As the members of several relationship sets come into association, affiliative relationships between the members of differing sets may develop. As this clustering of sets involves many individuals, the cluster represents novel social information. Again continuity is a key feature in the emergence of this new level of social organization. This new level is the social network.

SOCIAL NETWORKS: NEXUS TO PLEXUS

As the members of affiliative relationship sets interact with one another, **social networks** emerge. Constrained by the characteristics of the individuals and the relationships that establish them, net-works are distinctly social entities, separate but not divorced from the biological realm. No longer anchored by a single individual, the network consists of the sustained interaction patterns between a number of individuals (Mayer 1966; Blau 1975).

The minimum number of individuals required for the formation of a network is three, but logically there is no upper boundary to the number of participants. Practically, the number of individuals in a network is constrained by the number of individuals in the group, the cognitive abilities of the species, the amount of time available to individuals for engaging in social activities, and the degree to which a given society has created social roles.

Another feature identifying networks is the distinctively pluralistic signal they convey throughout the groups in which they occur. For individuals the message is "I"; for relationships the message is a "you–me" statement. For the first time the information content of the social unit is the plural "we." This transformation to a pluralistic statement has serious ramifications for primate social life. The individuals of a society must take this dynamic into account when interacting with other members in their group.

In vervet, rhesus, and Japanese macaque societies, networks emerge from relationships developed within matrilines. Aggressive acts toward one individual of a matriline seriously affect the probabilities that the original aggressor will receive an act of retribution (Cheney and Seyfarth 1990). If the original aggressor is a member of a strong, or higher ranking, matriline, then the odds of that individual receiving retribution are reduced. However, should the aggressor belong to a less influential network, then there exists a strong likelihood that a member of the victim's matriline will direct an aggressive act toward the original perpetrator or another member of the perpetrator's own social network.

Kinship is not the only criterion for the formation of networks. Age, sex, and dominance ranks are also factors in the interaction patterns of primates. Adult males of chimpanzee groups form networks at Mahale (Takahata 1990) and at Gombe (Goodall 1986). Within male chimpanzee networks, smaller social units centered on single males seeking high social rank exist. These smaller units correspond to the relationship sets noted previously. These factions are very dynamic entities, and support for specific males changes often. Despite the dynamic nature of the factions, the male cohorts engage in a number of cross-faction affiliative behaviors including grooming, play, and meat sharing (Takahata 1990), which maintain the male social network.

Squirrel monkeys in Costa Rica also have been observed to form male networks, although this pattern has not been reported at other locations where squirrel monkeys have been studied. Males of the same birth cohort maintain their association well into adulthood, displaying little aggression between network members, engaging in joint predator defense, and cooperating in reproductive behaviors (Boinski and Mitchell 1994).

COMMUNITIES: SETS OF NETWORKS

Communities consist of the sets of interacting networks and relationships maintained by a group of individuals living together within a specific area. The lower levels of social organization from which communities emerge vary in terms of their composition, duration, and function. This local population is extremely dynamic internally, with multiple linkages across the networks that compose the overall group.

The local population must be sufficiently large for networks to coalesce and emerge into this highest level of nonhuman primate social organization, the community. Also, networks need to interact with each other, signaling their unity to noncommunity members. One means by which this is accomplished is joint defense of resources. Internally, unity is accomplished through the maintenance of relationships by individuals with members of the community outside their primary social network, creating cross-linkages throughout the group. Not all individuals in an affiliative relationship set establish affiliative patterns of association with all other individuals of that set. Nor are the individuals participating in a social network restricted to having affiliative relationships only within the basic

network. Male chimpanzees are noted for their long matrilineal bonds as well as their participation in the male network (Goodall 1986). The community emerges through this cross-linkage of social units.

In designating the term "community" as a distinct social structure, it is worthwhile to note that community is used in the scientific literature to differing purposes. For example, the term is often used in the ecological sense of all the biota of a particular region: fungi, plants, and animals (Allen and Starr 1982). Conceptually, the term contains the same central concept as that applied for the social hierarchy, an overriding unit of existence emerging from integrated and interactive elements.

Communities are seen in both species of *Pan* (Kano 1992) and in the atelines (Strier, Essay 11) and should be considered for other species as well (e.g., *Papio* and *Macaca* species). Although no two communities are identical, all communities contain a similar message: us–them. This signal imposes constraints on members and on nongroup members alike. Nonmembers are less likely to attempt to utilize resources encompassed within a community's home range. Community members are less likely to associate with nongroup individuals.

The diversity of community types results from differences in the underlying structures of the communities. The expression of relationships and networks are not manifested by identical social processes. Female-female relationships are more important (or at least more common) in *Pan paniscus* groups than in *Pan troglodytes* groups (Kano 1992). Even among common chimpanzees there are differences in the underlying social structures of the communities of Mahale and Gombe. Mahale females spend more time in association with one another than do females at Gombe (Hasegawa 1990).

Another factor affecting the specific type of community that emerges is the group's demographic features. How many adults? How many females? How many males? What is the mortality rate? The birth rate? When the physiological differences both within and across species, variation in cognitive abilities, and ecological parameters are considered, it is easy to see why so much variation exists in the social systems of the primates (Fuentes, Essay 21).

THE PRINCIPLE OF HIERARCHY
IN SOCIAL ORGANIZATION

As noted previously, the organization of primate social groups is structured hierarchically. Primate groups are not simple collectives. For a system to be considered hierarchic, it must fulfill a number of requirements (Pattee 1973; Allen and Starr 1982; Dyke 1988; Ahl and Allen 1996). Among these basic requirements are three overriding conditions. First, the system's structure must be stratified with stable layers. Second, each higher level in the structure must emerge from the interactions of the components that occupy the level beneath it. And third, the levels must exert influence on each other; that is, they must impose constraints.

Stratification

Primate social groups are structurally stratified systems. Each strata is made up of units identifiable in their own right, by us, as researchers, and by the primates whose social behaviors make up these units. Our means of identifying and establishing the reality of these levels are those used by the animals themselves. The strata are recognizable through the types of behaviors engaged in and through the rates of interaction among the primates.

These social strata are stable through time. The stability of the social units provides an advantage that stems from the system of organization. Hierarchical organization allows change to occur within social levels without forcing a complete restructuring of the social system. As a single relationship changes or dissolves, networks and communities may be affected but need not re-form anew. The other relationships and the networks provide continuity within which individuals adjust to change.

Emergent Properties

Although each level is distinct from the others, all strata are composed from the interactions of the components of the level immediately beneath it in the hierarchical structure. Hierarchy theory terms any structure that comes into being from the interactions of lower level components an **emergent property.** Emergent properties have characteristics that are not reducible to the components that produced them (Allen and Starr 1982).

For example, the pluralistic information content of the social network signal "we" is not a summation of all the "I" signals of the individuals identified as members of a network. A concrete form of this can be seen in the deference, or rank, given to the young of influential matrilines in vervet groups. Very young vervets of strong matrilines outrank adult members of less influential matrilines in their group and can maintain or hold resources from adults due to the matriline's social standing rather than their own abilities (Cheney and Seyfarth 1990).

Constraints

The presence of constraints is another condition that must be satisfied for a system to be considered hierarchic (Dyke 1988). For primates the lowest level in the system, the individuals, establishes constraints on all higher levels by setting the initiating condition or starting point from which the hierarchy develops. The possible numbers of relationships and the types of relationships in a primate group are constrained by the individuals that constitute the group. The demeanor, motivation, and inclination of the individuals to engage in social activities establish the probabilities of relationship formation as well as the relationship types formed.

Gibbon groups, for example, contain few individuals, generally a single adult male and a single adult female along with the female's offspring. Consequently, each group member has only a limited number of possible relationships. The highest level of social organization equates to a single social network. The types of relationships available to each member in a gibbon group are also constrained by the initiating condition of a small number of individuals. Matrilineal networks cannot emerge in gibbon groups, nor can linear power structures of the type found among savanna baboons. There simply are not enough individuals for such structures to form.

Constraint can also be imposed on lower levels by higher level units in a hierarchy. Gelada males engage in few affiliative acts with each other, instead focusing their attention on the females with whom they develop relationships. Female gelada monkeys direct their affiliative gestures toward their female offspring and a specific adult male (Dunbar 1984). As a result, tight social networks emerge from the relationships of gelada monkeys. This tightness of gelada networks constrains the possibilities of forming relationships outside the immediate unit.

WHY ADOPT A HIERARCHIC APPROACH TO STUDYING SOCIAL SYSTEMS?

There are advantages to examining primate social systems within a hierarchical perspective. This approach brings fresh insight to primate social systems by focusing research questions and data collection on the social processes occurring at, and between, distinctly different levels of social existence. Primate social behaviors can be examined as process mechanisms of the social structures we observe. Hierarchy theory recognizes the complexity of primate life and provides a much needed means to examine and compare that complexity through identification of the components and the constraints at work in primate social systems. As a result, models of social evolution can become more focused.

Instead of modeling the evolution of social categories (one-male, multimale, and so forth), theorists can address the structural components of social systems (Mendoza 1984; Thierry 1990). Through understanding the components that make up each species' social system, the variation in primate societies can be more fruitfully examined. Are the social units of nonhuman primate and other animal societies unique social forms not seen in human societies? How are the social systems similar? What structures do they hold in common? What processes and constraints are at work producing and maintaining the system? As noted by Gould and Vrba (1982), structures and processes that are not identified or named seldom receive attention.

Finally, hierarchy theory explicitly recognizes that an important feature of being a primate is living in a social world. Consequently, greater consideration in our models of social evolution will be given to the pivotal role of affiliation. Primate life is not simply a world of competition and competitive cooperation. The primate group is a complex milieu wherein different social entities affect each individual even as the individuals create that complexity. Primates do compete with each other. They have conflicts. They also must maintain their social order, and that cannot be accomplished without affiliation between individuals.

Behavioral and Biological Dimensions of the Life Span

Acknowledging and attempting to understand the many components that create and facilitate behavior of an organism is one of the goals of the study of nonhuman primates. The essays in this section offer strong testimony to the complex interrelatedness of biology and behavior throughout the life course of all primates. Although it is entirely appropriate to study a single strand of the tapestry of life, such as play, aging, reproduction, dominance, or diet, to comprehend the dynamics of the whole organism we must try to target as much as possible in our study. Selection acts on the behavior of the entire animal, and to understand adaptation and evolution we must strive to appreciate the many sources of development and behavior. The essays in this section follow a few of these physiological and behavioral strands as they weave together the complicated tapestry we call an organism.

Much primate literature focuses on the behavior of adulthood, and much less focuses on the process of aging or the aged animal. Our human preconceptions of what it is to be old have colored our interpretation of the nonhuman primate data, and Pavelka's essay on primate gerontology takes a fresh look at this field. The relationship between physical aging and patterns of social behavior is greatly affected by many factors in the ecology and social context of life. Aging is not a simple process, but it can be understood by taking into consideration the complex context in which the individual primate achieves old age.

The smallest monkeys are the subject of the essay on energy expenditure, physiology, and behavior. It appears that energy limitations may play a very important role in the life of callitrichid monkeys. Information on many aspects of behavior and physiology are presented. Although most large-bodied primates are diurnal and the majority of nocturnal primates small, most of our information is derived from study of the former. A number of long-standing assumptions are questioned in light of recent studies. Power concludes that the evolution of food sharing and group co-sleeping may have had a great impact on callitrichid reproduction rates, increasing it at lower cost to the female.

Playful activity is an important, and common, behavior of the early period of life. It is considered part of the process of development with benefits for the young animal as well as for later years of life. But most important, an infant or juvenile's play behavior is an adaptation for survival and success at the time play occurs, the present, not for a time in the future.

The final essay in this section considers the ramifications of male reproductive behavior as a subset of life history strategies. It presents reproductive behavior in its biological hormonal context but not without considering the importance of social factors. Physiology is linked with behavior to illustrate the critical importance of proximate mechanisms to reproductive success.

27

Primate Gerontology

M. S. M. Pavelka

*Since the early 1980s primatologists have been study-
ing aging in nonhuman primates. Interest in old age
in nonhuman primates has paralleled the increased
interest in aging phenomena in humans, and a human-
centered perspective has influenced some of the expectations and assumptions about aging in other
primates. Early reports of the behavior of old nonhuman primates, often based on short-term observations of small numbers of animals whose exact ages
were not known, tended to depict aged monkeys in
much the same way that Western society often depicts
elderly people—slow and tired and socially isolated
(Waser 1978; Hauser and Tyrell 1984; Nakamichi
1984). Recent developments in primate social gerontology clarify the distinctions between human and nonhuman primates. Studies of Japanese monkeys and
chimpanzees illustrate the inter- and intraspecies variation in aging that is being revealed by continuing
research in this new field of study.*

HUMAN VERSUS NONHUMAN
PRIMATE AGING

It is surely not a coincidence that the earliest reports of old monkey behavior corresponded so
closely to a long-standing popular perception of the
elderly in modern industrialized society. Whether
this image of the elderly as lonely, marginalized,
and socially isolated accurately reflects the real situation for a significant portion of the human elderly
population is not clear. What is clear is that this
popular perception influenced the earliest reports

of old monkeys. But cross-cultural variation in the
experiences and social realities of the elderly members of society suggest that no simple human pattern of increased isolation exists at the species level.

What does seem to be universally true in human
society is that the elderly are recognized as a social
entity or subgroup. Despite variation both within
and between societies, in all human societies the elderly are an identifiable subgroup with certain
characteristic social and behavioral patterns. The
behavior and social roles of the elderly are different
in many ways from those of young and middle-
aged adults. From the start, studies of the behavior
of aged monkeys made the assumption that this
would be true of nonhuman primates as well. The
expectation that old animals would become socially disengaged was just one specific idea within
the larger expectation that old animals would exhibit behaviors different from those of younger
adults. However, prior to the emergence of "primate gerontology" old animals were not identified
or recognized by researchers as distinctive in their
behavior.

Primatologists have long noted behavioral distinctions between classes of animals, and it was recognized that juveniles, for example, are socially
and behaviorally distinguishable from adults, that
males are socially and behaviorally distinguishable
from females, and so on. In 1976 Fedigan demonstrated empirically that subgroups of animals, with
characteristic behavior patterns, do exist in Japanese monkeys, but aged animals were not one of
these groups. Yet from the first flicker of interest in

gerontology came the expectation that old monkeys could be regarded as a socially and behaviorally distinct group. Indeed, the earliest reports of the behavior of old females came from studies of the same population of Japanese monkeys analyzed by Fedigan. Later research challenged this view, presenting research results in which advancing age did not correlate with significant changes in sociability or mobility in Japanese (Pavelka 1990, 1991; Pavelka, Gillespie, and Griffin 1991) or rhesus macaques (Lippold and Lehman 1992; Parks, Musante, and Novak 1992).

Further investigation of aging phenomena in human and nonhuman primates made it clear that there are good reasons to expect the behavior and social position of elderly humans to be different from that of young and middle-aged adults, but these reasons do not necessarily apply to nonhumans (Pavelka 1991). For example, in human society the knowledge that one is approaching the end of the life span has profound implications for the way in which individuals and societies regard old age. It is unknown, and will likely remain unknown for some time, whether any of the nonhuman primates possess such an awareness of mortality. It is true of apes, and probably monkeys, that the death of group members is recognized and may even be mourned, but this is not the same as individual animals having a sense of personal mortality. Human and nonhuman primates experience similar biological changes associated with aging, but we have no evidence that monkeys or apes are able to interpret and give meaning, either as individuals or as a group, to the biological changes that are occurring. Our awareness of our own mortality—the knowledge that we are approaching the end of life—surely influences how we respond socially and behaviorally to old age and contributes to differential social patterns for us during this stage of life. Likewise, we might expect a lack of such awareness to be associated with a more continuous life course from the attainment of adulthood to death.

Another distinctive feature of human aging pertains to the loss of independence that is possible in a species that has a division of labor. A division of labor involving production and exchange creates interdependence among the individuals in human societies, and this interdependence is generally considered to be one of the primary diagnostic features of human social life. Individual humans are not independent subsistence units but rely on production (the acquisition of greater amounts of goods than the individual is able to make use of) and exchange (sharing these goods with one another) for survival. Humans depend on one another in a direct and fundamental way. The fact of interindividual dependence is exemplified in the case of individuals who are unable to care for themselves, or to reciprocate in the exchange of goods and services. Nonproductive members, such as children and the ill or infirm, can survive because other members of the society will continue to exchange with them, even if they cannot fully reciprocate. The concept and reality of dependence, or loss of independence, is central to social gerontology. Because of the tendency for the elderly to have a higher likelihood of infirmity, and because of social norms (in industrial societies at least) regarding continued labor in the years when the end of the life span is approaching, the elderly often play a different role in the system of production and exchange.

Nonhuman primates do not possess a division of labor involving production and exchange. Each individual animal, once weaned, is a complete subsistence unit, not directly dependent for survival on any other individual. Nothing like the care and feeding of incapacitated adult humans has been reported for any nonhuman primate species. Frailty to the point of dependence is not a characteristic of old monkeys because animals in this position simply die. Dependent individuals do not continue as members of the social group. The division of labor and subsequent interindividual dependence characteristic of humans are absent in the other primates, and this has important ramifications for aging in human compared to nonhuman primate groups.

Finally, the complete cessation of reproduction in all women halfway through the species specific life span (human female menopause) is qualitatively different from the continued reproduction until death that characterizes the vast majority of monkey and ape females, regardless of their age at death. The lengthy, population-wide, postreproductive life span of the human female is unique among the primates. Although there is some variation within and between nonhuman primate species in the likelihood of finding old females who appear to have ceased reproducing (Caro et al. 1995), postreproductive females tend to be few in number, and the length of postreproductive life is relatively short. There is no predictable or sizable cohort of postreproductive old females in any nonhuman primate society. Most of the old females are still producing babies.

In contrast to women, many human males are able to reproduce into extreme old age. The decline of reproductive ability in men is highly variable and gradual and thus quite distinct from the abrupt cessation of reproductive function in middle-aged women. The continued reproductive potential of men does not necessarily become expressed, however, because male reproduction depends on access to reproductive females. Reproductive opportunities may be largely denied to aged men due to the nonreproductive nature of their partners, limited access to younger women, and increased difficulty achieving ejaculation (Barber 1988).

A regular, predictable cohort of old females who are no longer producing babies is a universal element of human societies, regardless of local life expectancy values. Even a society with a life expectancy at birth value of less than 50 years will regularly and consistently include many individuals who live well beyond 50. For example, based on data from 94 completed lives, Howell (1979) reported that life expectancy at birth of a !Kung population was only 34.57 years, however 38 of these 94 individuals, 40% of the population, lived to be 50 years of age and older. Twenty-three individuals (24% of the population) lived to be 65 and older, and two lived beyond 85 years. The human maximum life span of 95 to 100 years is known to be both species-wide and species specific, as is the cessation of reproduction at 50 years (see Pavelka and Fedigan 1991 for discussion). Menopause, an event that characterizes the lives of middle-aged women, has obvious implications for the distinctive social and behavioral characteristics of the elderly.

Awareness of mortality, division of labor with the subsequent potential for loss of independence for individual members, and menopause are three

characteristics of humans—absent in nonhuman primates—that have a direct impact on the latter portion of the life course, contributing directly to the distinctive experiences of the elderly as compared with young or middle-aged adults. The subject matter of human social gerontology would be radically different if women continued to have babies into their 60s and 70s, if everyone were economically independent, and if there were no knowledge that one's life would soon, or even eventually, end. Conversely, why would we expect there to be a social category for elderly monkeys who are economically independent and continue to reproduce right up to an end that they do not know is coming? Aging in nonhuman primates is distinctive from aging in human primates. In nonhuman primates, old age is a less obvious social and behavioral category, and less distinct from middle age, with adulthood being more socially continuous from the attainment of adulthood until death.

VARIATION IN AGING IN NONHUMAN PRIMATE SPECIES

Nonhuman primate aging may be more gradual and less differentiated from the earlier life course than it is in humans, but nonhuman primates are far from a homogenous group in this or any other regard. With upwards of 200 different species exhibiting a diversity of phylogenetic histories, ecological conditions, and social organizations, it should be expected that the behavior and social position of older animals will vary greatly from group to group and species to species. Although all human societies have a recognizable subgroup of elderly individuals, cross-cultural gerontology has revealed that the specific manifestations of aging vary greatly depending on a host of social and cultural factors (for example, see Amoss and Harrell 1981). Likewise, the cross-species perspective established that the changes experienced by individual animals as they move through the adult life course will depend heavily on the social structure of the species to which they belong and the type of social group in which they live (Pavelka 1994).

Aging is the gradual physical decline of the organism as it approaches the end of the life span, but whether this physical aging translates into observable behavioral or social changes (as well as the form such changes might take) will depend on a host of sociological (and ecological) factors. Aging takes place within a social context, and variation in the structure of the society will have a direct impact on the way in which individuals move through the life course, from beginning to end.

Japanese monkey females, for example, have a smooth life course with a pattern of continuity in adult social life, and this is tied to the continuous nature of the kinship bonds that organize Japanese macaque social life. Macaque societies are characterized by male dispersal and female philopatry; females live out their lives in the group to which they were born. The kinship bonds between related females, particularly the intergenerational bonds, explain many of the intragroup social dynamics (see Gouzoules and Gouzoules 1987). Thus, female lives are structured from birth to death within the framework of the matriline. Matriline membership largely determines the primary social partners of each female, and these partners provide affiliation as well as support in situations of conflict. Relatively few changes in female social networks or behavior occur as they approach the end of their life span. The important organizing principles of adult female Japanese monkey society are not age-related, and nothing occurs in the later portion of the life course to change this. The gradual biological changes are not sufficient to set in motion changes in social behavior, social relationships, or social organization.

The mother-offspring bond has long been heralded as the basic unit of primate society, and its importance in youth and endurance into adulthood has received much attention. The continuity in this fundamental unit of society is responsible for the essential continuity in the life course of female Japanese monkeys. One change, easily understood in demographic terms, is the switch from the mother as primary social partner in youth to a daughter as primary social partner in old age (Pavelka 1994). The social support of a female is solidified and strengthened with advanced age. There is no change in social dominance as a direct result of aging for female Japanese macaques because female dominance is tightly tied to kinship.

It too becomes solidified in old age for most females. Exceptions to the norm occur in Japanese macaques in the case of females who do not have any daughters who survive to adulthood. Such females may well find themselves without a substantial social network or without a primary social partner in adulthood (including old age).

A comparison of aging female chimpanzees with aging female Japanese macaques illustrates that the social manifestations of aging depend on the social structure and the social bonds throughout life. Since an old female Japanese monkey lives out her life within a tight kinship network of strong intergenerational bonds, there is no reason to expect much change in old age. But old chimpanzee females lose their daughters to dispersal and thus do not have such intergenerational bonds with daughters to structure their old age. Getting older may or may not introduce changes in the structure of social bonds that characterize adulthood.

Huffman (1990) reported on the sociobehavioral manifestations of old age in chimpanzees. Chimpanzees are characterized by female dispersal. Females normally disperse from the natal group at puberty and settle for life in the group in which they begin reproducing. As a female chimpanzee ages, she does not normally have any close female kin in the group, but she will likely have strong social bonds with her sons, who remain in the group with their mother from birth to death. Huffman described a narrowing of the social network of old females as they begin to spend more time interacting with prime adult males than do younger adult females.

Intraspecies variation in the behavioral and social manifestations of aging are also to be expected. For example, the sexes may age differently in the same society, just as they live their earlier lives differently. The description of a continuous life course, in which the social bonds are not altered but are solidified in old age, is specific to female Japanese monkeys. Male Japanese monkeys may transfer to new groups repeatedly over the course of their lives, and their lives are not organized around kinship lines as are those of females. Consequently, aging for male Japanese monkeys (not yet studied) may prove to be quite different. Likewise, different habitats may yield differential patterns of locomotor behavior in individuals who are past their physical prime. A terrestrial habitat is less likely to pose the kind of challenges to an aging individual than is an arboreal one. Indeed, old female Japanese macaques living in forested environments in Japan have been described as having increased difficulty climbing to get food.

Where social life is organized around dominance, and to the extent that dominance is dependent on physical prowess, one might expect the physical decline of the body that occurs in old age to be consistently associated with an alteration in the social position of the aging animal. Dominance is an important organizing principle in the lives of adult male chimpanzees, and according to Huffman (1990), old male chimps experience declining rank in old age and a tendency to become more solitary as a result. Further, old male chimps can threaten younger adult males without retaliation, presumably because of the expected decline in the ability of old males to influence coalitions. Younger individuals exercise restraint toward old adults, who are less likely to destabilize established social relationships (Huffman 1990).

CONCLUSION

The field of primate social gerontology is relatively new, and our understanding of the social manifes-tations of aging in nonhuman primates is based on relatively few studies of animals of known age. Early studies made the assumption that the aged members of nonhuman primate societies would be socially distinct, or at least recognizable, as they are in human societies, and sought to describe the behavior of the aged as compared to that of younger adults. The first descriptions tended to depict old monkeys as being much like the popular perception of the elderly in Western societies: slow, tired, and socially isolated. Later it became clear that the human life course, particularly the human female life course, involves important changes in later life, but these conditions associated with a distinctive period of old age may not be present in other primates. These include an awareness of mortality, a division of labor, and menopause. In the absence of these features, the life course of other primates might be much more continuous from the attainment of adulthood to death. Field studies present conflicting evidence about the impact of physiological aging on behavior (DeRousseau 1994); however, inter- and intraspecies variation is to be expected in the way individual members of the social group age. The extent to which the physical realities of aging translate into distinctive social and behavioral patterns will depend heavily on the habitat and social structure and on the role of variables such as kinship and rank in organizing social life at all ages.

28

Aspects of Energy Expenditure of Callitrichid Primates: Physiology and Behavior

Michael L. Power

The smallest monkeys belong to the neotropical primate family Callitrichidae. Members of this monophyletic taxon range in size from the diminutive pygmy marmoset (approximately .1 kg) to the lion tamarins (approximately .7 kg). Although all primates probably face circumstances where they are energy limited, at least on a seasonal basis, a number of theoretical considerations imply that energy limitations might be especially critical in the lives of callitrichid monkeys.

Small body size affects the ability of animals to meet energy needs in at least two ways. Although small animals will generally have absolutely lower energy requirements than large animals, the **allometry** of energy expenditure is less than one (approximately .75: Kleiber 1975). This means that an animal that has twice the mass of another has less than twice the energy requirement. This phenomenon would be of little consequence if the allometries of the aspects of morphology and physiology that affect energy (food) acquisition and storage were similar. However, this does not appear to be the case.

The total volume of the gut appears to increase linearly with body mass (Demment and Van Soest 1985). Thus, the animal that is twice the size of the other has twice the capacity to process food, but not twice the need. Small animals must refill their guts more times than large animals to satisfy energy requirements. Small animals are also unlikely to be

able to store as high a proportion of energy needs as body fat as large animals do because their energy requirement to mass ratio is higher. Small animals would have to carry a higher percentage of body fat to match the equivalent proportion of energy needs. But if any generalization can be made, it would be that small animals generally have a lower percentage of body fat. If true, this implies a double disadvantage of small body size; both a higher energy requirement to gut capacity ratio and a higher energy requirement to energy storage ratio than a larger animal.

Callitrichids are also unusual among anthropoids in routinely bearing twin offspring. Callitrichids have the capacity to produce two litters per year, and many species routinely do so, both in captivity and in the wild (Soini 1982; Hearn 1983). This has led many authors to assert that the energy demands on females due to reproduction are likely significantly higher in callitrichids compared to other anthropoids. Thus, energy limitations are thought to have significantly influenced the evolution of the Callitrichidae (Garber, Maoya, and Malaga 1984; Sussman and Kinzey 1984; Goldizen 1987a; Sussman and Garber 1987).

I do not argue against these last assertions, although I will point out that there are few data in the literature relevant to the cost of reproduction for callitrichids, or other nonhuman primates for that matter. I will present data here on some aspects of metabolism and behavior relevant to energy expenditure in callitrichid monkeys and examine how the patterns compare with other primate species. I will then hypothesize how these patterns could be considered adaptations to the callitrichid "lifestyle."

DEFINITIONS

Resting metabolic rate (RMR) is the energy expenditure of a resting, postabsorptive (i.e., not digesting) adult animal that is neither pregnant nor lactating. At temperatures within thermal neutrality for the species, RMR will be minimal. This parameter is a measure of the minimal cost of existence at any particular ambient temperature. Minimal RMR (i.e., within thermal neutrality) is sometimes referred to as **basal metabolic rate (BMR)**.

The gross energy of milk (GE) is the total energy per gram of milk. It does not account for any of the metabolic costs and inefficiencies inherent in digesting and metabolizing milk, and thus it is an overestimate of the energetic gain by the infant. It also does not account for any of the metabolic costs of producing milk, and thus it is an underestimate of the cost of milk production to the mother.

THE CALLITRICHIDAE

Callitrichids form a monophyletic taxa consisting of either four or five genera, depending on the taxonomist, and well over twenty species. All authorities include the genera *Leontopithecus* (the lion tamarins), *Saguinus* (the tamarins), and *Callithrix* and *Cebuella* (the marmosets). Most also include Goeldi's monkey (*Callimico goeldii*) within the taxa (Schneider and Rosenberger 1996). All these monkeys share small body size and many aspects of reproductive social behavior thought to be related to energy limitations. It should be noted, however, that Goeldi's monkey does not twin. Also, despite being a monophyletic taxa, all callitrichids cannot necessarily be considered to be closely related, as the estimated divergence times for the various genera are 10 to 15 million years (except for the divergence of *Callithrix* and *Cebuella,* which is much

less). Although I will often refer to "callitrichid traits," only a handful of these species have been well studied. There are undoubtedly many significant differences among these species that are hidden from us by our ignorance.

THE CALLITRICHID LIFESTYLE

Callitrichids are diurnal omnivores. Many, but not all callitrichids, travel large distances during each day, feeding from widely dispersed fruit sources and actively foraging for arthropod prey. This would be the pattern for the genera *Leontopithecus, Saguinus,* and *Callimico.* The marmosets are known to spend more time feeding on gums and other plant exudates than the other callitrichids, although many Amazonian *Callithrix* species have a foraging ecology similar to the nonmarmoset callitrichids. Gum-feeding generally is associated with reduced travel time and distance. Indeed, the pygmy marmoset may be considered a gum specialist. Family groups typically live on a few exudate-producing trees spread over less than .5 ha (Soini 1982).

All callitrichids have a relatively short active period of the day. They typically retire to a sleeping site before sunset and do not reemerge until after dawn (Dawson 1976; Coimbra-Filho 1977). Thus, the callitrichid lifestyle can be (perhaps oversimply) summarized as 10 to 11 hours of high activity predominantly related to food acquisition (especially if you stretch the definition to include territorial defense as, in part, an attempt to ensure priority of access to food resources over extra-group conspecifics) followed by 13 to 14 hours of complete inactivity.

CALLITRICHID REPRODUCTIVE STRATEGY

In general, there is only one breeding female within a callitrichid social group, which typically consists of four to twelve animals equally split between the sexes. The number of breeding males within a group is more controversial (Goldizen 1987b; Sussman and Garber 1987). Callitrichids have a communal infant care system (Garber et al. 1984). Infants are predominantly carried by group members other than their mother, and group members both passively and actively provision infants with food beginning at one month of age. There are species differences in the timing of these behaviors. In the marmoset species for which there are data, infants are carried by nonmaternal group members within a few days of birth, whereas it is typically several weeks before this occurs in Goeldi's monkey. Marmoset infants also appear to achieve (or are forced to achieve) independent locomotor and foraging status at an earlier age than the nonmarmoset callitrichids (Tardif et al. 1993).

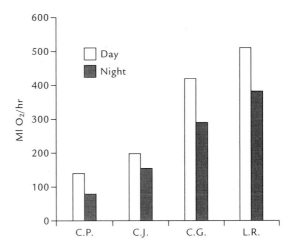

FIGURE 1   Callitrichid RMR day and night.

RMR OF CALLITRICHIDS

There is a profound difference between the RMR within thermal neutrality of a callitrichid during the active period and the inactive period (based on data from four species; Figure 1). During daylight hours, callitrichid RMR within thermal neutrality is, as would be expected for a primate of their body size, perhaps 10% to 20% higher than the mammalian expected as predicted by Kleiber's equation (1975). During the night, however, RMR is significantly reduced by 30 to 45% (Petry, Riehl, and Zucker 1986; Power 1991; Thompson et al. 1994; Power, Tardif, Power, and Layne, unpublished data). This reduction in metabolic rate is accompanied by a reduction in core body temperature (Hetherington 1978; Thompson et al. 1994). Homeothermy is not abandoned (i.e., they do not enter torpor), but body temperature is less tightly regulated (Figure 2).

Thus, during the day, callitrichids metabolize energy at a rate consistent with their active foraging ecology. During the night, energy metabolism is reduced to a low level. At night, callitrichids are difficult to awaken and generally unresponsive, both in captivity (Power, pers. obser.) and in the wild (Dawson 1976). Their nighttime survival strategy appears to be to remain as inconspicuous as possible, expend minimal energy, and wait for dawn to arrive. This could be interpreted as an energy saving adaptation. Certainly it results in far less energy expenditure during sleep than if RMR was maintained at active phase levels.

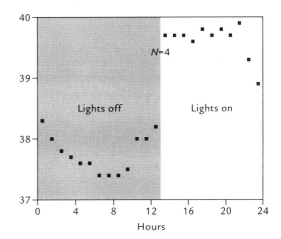

FIGURE 2   Circadian rhythm of T_B in *Leontopitheus rosalia*.

This pattern is not unique to callitrichids. Rodents under 1 kg in mass also exhibit a substantial decline in RMR during their inactive phase (average of 25%: Kenagy and Vleck 1982). In Figure 3 active and inactive phase RMR data for thirty-two species of primates are graphed in relation to Kleiber's relationship of RMR with body mass. Most active phase RMR are at or slightly above Kleiber's line, whereas most inactive phase RMR are below Kleiber's line, some of them substantially lower. Notice also that the majority of inactive phase data points are for smaller primates. This reflects the

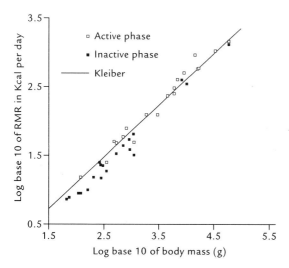

FIGURE 3   Primate RMR.

fact that the majority of primate RMR in the literature were measured during the day, and most large-bodied primates are diurnal, whereas nocturnal primates are mostly small. There are data on both phases for relatively few primates, a fact that casts doubt on many of the statements concerning metabolic rates in primates. For example, prosimians have been asserted to have lower RMR than anthropoids. However, the comparison of the two groups largely was made using active phase data for anthropoids and inactive phase data for prosimians. When nocturnal bushbabies are compared with similar-sized diurnal callitrichids, their inactive phase RMR are virtually identical. Unfortunately, there are no active phase RMR data for bushbabies in the literature, but a reasonable hypothesis would be that they would show a similar shift between active and inactive phase RMR as do callitrichids. Thus, the hypothesized difference between anthropoid and prosimian RMR may be an artifact of comparing large-bodied diurnal anthropoids with small-bodied nocturnal prosimians, all measured during the day!

A large shift in RMR between the active and inactive phases may be normal for small-bodied primates or, indeed, for any small-bodied mammal that has an extended inactive phase. Large-bodied species likely do exhibit some reduction in RMR

between phases, but not to the same extent. For example, human RMR during sleep is only about 10% lower than when awake. In the pygmy marmoset the difference between active and inactive RMR is almost 45%. This apparent effect of body size is consistent with the hypothesized differences in energy requirement to energy storage ratios between large and small mammals discussed earlier in this essay. Of course this does not mean that the reduction of RMR in callitrichids during sleep is merely due to allometry and does not serve an energy conserving function. That is likely its primary function. However, it does not appear to be a special callitrichid adaptation but rather reflects a fundamental difference between large and small animals, which require different energetic strategies.

One last point relevant to callitrichid energy expenditure during sleep. Callitrichids are unusual among anthropoid primates in that the social group sleeps huddled together, often within a vine tangle or tree hole. Although this behavior has been suggested to serve to reduce predation by nocturnal predators (Coimbra-Filho 1977; Caine 1993b), huddling also may decrease energy expenditure at night by reducing thermoregulatory costs. This has been demonstrated to be the case in golden lion tamarins (Figure 4) and will be discussed in the next section.

COSTS OF REPRODUCTION

The callitrichid infant care system, characterized by nonbreeding helpers, is hypothesized to have evolved to reduce the energetic burden of reproduction on reproductive females. The proposed costs to the breeding female that are reduced by helpers include both direct costs associated with the effort required to carry the infants and various indirect costs, such as reduced foraging time and efficiency and increased vulnerability to predators when carrying infants. The proposed benefits to the helpers include increased inclusive fitness (if they are related to the breeding animals), experience in parental care, and recruitment of emigration partners (Baker 1991).

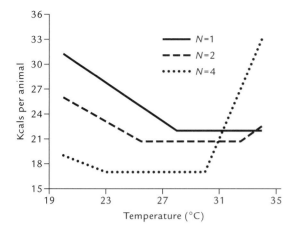

FIGURE 4   Effect of group size in golden lion tamarins.

My colleagues and I (Power et al., submitted) have proposed that there is at least one additional benefit to having helpers of a group, a benefit that affects every individual in the group to some extent but that could have a substantial effect on the survivorship of infants and juveniles. Put simply, that benefit is body heat. Open circuit respirometry measurements of six singletons, three pairs, and groups of four, five, and eight golden lion tamarins were conducted at ambient temperatures ranging from 10 to 35°C. Over a wide range of temperatures, the average per animal energy expenditure during rest in *L. rosalia* was lower for animals in groups than for pairs, and lower in pairs than for individual animals. Per animal energy expenditure relative to solitary individuals ranged from a few percent lower among pairs within thermal neutrality to almost 40% lower for larger groups at lower temperatures (see Figure 4). This energy savings was accounted for in part by an increased tolerance of cool temperatures by huddled animals. But even at ambient temperatures within thermal neutrality for all group sizes, average energy expenditure per animal was lower in groups than for pairs or individuals. Thus, the practice of sleeping together in groups provides golden lion tamarins with an energy-saving device that could permit breeding females in groups to allocate more energy to reproduction than could females in pairs.

LACTATION

Lactation generally is the most energetically expensive part of mammalian reproduction. For one thing, the nursing infant is larger than the gestating fetus, so maintenance energy costs are larger. A nursing infant also has thermoregulatory costs and may have costs associated with independent locomotion. For all these reasons, a nursing infant is more "expensive" than is a fetus.

Callitrichid females are thought to expend proportionally more energy for reproduction than most anthropoids because of the large combined mass of the twin offspring relative to maternal mass, and because many species routinely become pregnant during lactation. However, gestation is long in callitrichids (4 to 6 months), with relatively little fetal mass accumulated in the first trimester (Jaquish et al. 1995), and lactation is short, with infants being weaned by 2 to 3 months (at which time they receive a large quantity of food through food sharing behavior by other group members). Thus, the costs of lactation and gestation appear to be temporally separated.

COMPOSITION OF CALLITRICHID MILK

Primates have been thought to produce dilute milks with low levels of fat, protein, and gross energy. However, this characterization is based on data primarily from large-bodied anthropoids, such as baboons and humans, and may not correctly represent the entire order Primates (Oftedal 1984). In general, small body size in mammals is associated with relatively concentrated milk, as might be predicted from the high ratio of energy requirement to gastrointestinal capacity found in most small mammals (Blaxter 1961; Payne and Wheller 1968). Recent data from prosimian primates demonstrate that primate milks are variable, with small-bodied lorisoids producing more concentrated milks than larger lemuroids (Tilden and Oftedal 1997).

Both allometric considerations and the brevity of lactation suggest that a rapid rate of nutrient transfer from mother to young may be necessary for callitrichids. This could imply that callitrichid milk would be higher in dry matter, fat, protein, and gross energy (GE) than the milks of larger primates such as humans and baboons. However, the results from studies on the composition of milk of callitrichids are mixed. Mid-lactation milks of pygmy and common marmosets appear not to differ from that of most anthropoids and large prosimians in mean GE, although they are intermediate between large primates and lorisoids in protein content (Power, Oftedal, and Tardif 1998). In contrast, the GE of mid-lactation milk of golden lion tamarins is higher than other anthropoids and quite similar to the lorisoid milks (Oftedal and Iverson 1995).

It is not clear why small primates such as the pygmy marmoset produce relatively dilute milk. There may be physiological advantages to dilute milks, especially for tropical animals that must contend with high heat loads (Oftedal and Iverson 1995; Tilden and Oftedal 1997). Evaporative cooling requires a large flux of water through the body, which in young infants must be obtained from milk. High water content in milk may be important for thermal regulation by many primate infants (Tilden and Oftedal 1997).

In some mammals, milk composition is related to nursing patterns. Species that tend to nurse frequently tend to have more dilute milks than do species that nurse infrequently (Oftedal and Iverson 1995). This can be explained by volume limitations on both the mother's mammary glands and the gastrointestinal tract of the infant. Among primates, infants are generally presumed to have "on demand" access to the nipple. However, some primate species park their infants in nests while they forage. In these species the mother will have more, and the infant less, control over nursing frequency. Tilden and Oftedal (1997) found that prosimian species that "parked" their infants had more concentrated milks than species that carried their infants. *Varecia variegata* is an example of a large-bodied "parker" that has more concentrated milk than similar-sized

primates who carry their offspring (Tilden and Oftedal 1997).

It is unclear how callitrichids fit into this dichotomy. Infants certainly are carried, but usually not by the mother. Mothers control infant access to the nipple during early infancy by retrieving infants from other carriers and by harassing infants they are carrying until another caregiver retrieves them (Tardif 1994). Callitrichid infants might be less able to nurse on demand than other anthropoids, at least during daylight hours. Wild golden lion tamarins travel an average of 33.5% of their active period (Dietz, Peres, and Pinder 1997) as compared to a mean of 14% of time spent traveling in common marmosets (Digby and Barreto 1996). Even in captivity, 8-week-old infants of the genera *Saguinus* and *Leontopithecus* are carried more frequently than are 8-week-old common marmoset infants (Tardif, Harrison, and Simel 1993). It is possible that the observed differences in milk composition between golden lion tamarins and the marmoset species relate to different nursing patterns. However, many more milk samples from golden lion tamarins and other callitrichid species need to be analyzed to test this hypothesis.

In summary, *Cebuella pygmaea* and *Callithrix jacchus* produce milks that are similar, on average, to those of most anthropoids in GE, and intermediate in protein concentration between the dilute milks of most large primates and the more concentrated milks of the lorisoids. The milk of *Leontopithecus rosalia* appears to be among the most energy-rich among studied primates, although only a small number of samples have been assayed. From these data it is not clear that callitrichids expend more energy in reproduction than would be expected of a primate of their body size. The evolution of food sharing may have enabled callitrichids to increase their reproductive rate at a lower cost to the female by reducing the length of lactation and keeping the costs of gestation and lactation temporally separated.

29

Play: A Critical Process in the Developmental System

Phyllis Dolhinow

If each of us could follow a monkey or an ape from birth through its entire life span, we would be struck by the remarkable continuity of development and flow of events over the years. If we did this for a number of individuals, the amount of variability among them would test our powers of generalization and leave us with a deep appreciation of the complexity of development—even among individuals that live and grow at the same time in the same social group. Select a single word to describe what you have witnessed and it would probably be "change." The animal never stops changing, physically and socially, throughout its life, and this includes the adult years when we have often mistakenly considered animals to have concluded the process of growth.

Each segment of the life span that for our convenience we label a stage—infant, juvenile, subadult, and adult—has its distinguishing characteristics, but there are no sudden events or whistles that signal passage from one to the next. The primate must survive every day, one at a time, and as it grows to maturity and then gradually to old age its needs and wants change. Steadily, and at every step, it is confronted with distinctive challenges to staying alive and healthy. Consider that primates in general are notably social, intelligent, and opportunistic. Their sociability provides a powerful context for rearing young as well as a situation in which the pleasures and benefits of relationships are felt and maintained. Complex developmental processes are in place to help ensure that each animal will become a normally functioning member of its society.

Play and playful activities are an essential part of the environment of early development for most primates and continue throughout adulthood for many (Dolhinow and Bishop 1970; Fagen 1981, 1993; Bekoff 1984; Dolhinow 1984; Nash 1993; Watts and Pusey 1993). At the risk of underemphasizing other especially important aspects of life, I will focus on some of the many functions play serves, from social to physical.

Play is a very effective way of motivating the individual to become active, involved, and integrated into its world. It is an essential developmental process that ensures the acquisition of experiences to build the skills needed to survive. It may well also provide the youngster with a base on which future abilities are built, but selection can act only on traits in the present, not the future.

There are many routes to maturity, each starting in infancy, but we are a long way from understanding just how early experiences become part of the calculus of subadult then adult behavior patterns (Bateson 1981, 1982; Oyama 1985, 1989; Dolhinow 1991). Many studies of nonhuman primates focus on adults and adult activities. Of course, these are pivotal to understanding the nature of a species' behavior and adaptations to the environment in which it survives. Immatures are all too often given short shrift. When we focus on the immatures, we realize very quickly that there is an array of tactics available to young primates that enable survival every day from day one of life. Included in these tactics are the many ways by which infants, and later juveniles, gain advantage by responding to and deliberately manipulating their social environments. Infants are very sensitive to most of what surrounds them, especially other animals, and act to gain advantage in whatever they seek to get or to do. They make choices and communicate their feelings to all who will listen or look. It doesn't take long for youngsters to learn how to manipulate others to maximize the likelihood of getting what they want, whether this is access to the mother's ventrum or to a bit of desirable food.

YEARS OF IMMATURITY AND BEYOND

There is considerable variability in schedules of development among prosimians, monkeys, and apes. The Asian langur monkey (*Semnopithecus (= Presbytis) entellus*), though, is well studied in both the field and in captivity and serves as a excellent example for this discussion of development and the role of play and playful behaviors (Dolhinow and Bishop 1970). For the langur, as for other primates, immaturity is a period of rapid and profound change in all aspects of life. The dependent **neonate** becomes the intensely active infant whose physical and social world expands at an astonishing rate.

Infants are far from a uniform group. They vary in size, strength, sensory acuity, emotionality, reactivity to physical and social stimuli, perseverance, alertness, and maternal support, to name but a few distinguishing features. Relations with others in the group rapidly supplement the close bonds an infant has with immediate caregivers. Rates of maturation vary among different primates from exceedingly rapid to appositely slow, but infants of all kinds are provided with nourishment, transport, and protection by members of the group. It is recognizable to all who observe that reasonable psychological and physical growth in all primates produces adequate juveniles, subadults, and adults as time passes. There are many developmental pathways through

the life span, and each generates an array of attributes, skills, and degrees of success among adults. Although we can't point with any certainty to specific paths or qualities of immaturity that precede or predict specific aspects of adult behavior, we can identify areas of early experience of great consequence to adult capabilities.

There is a caveat for all who observe animals other than ourselves. We see through human eyes, and we translate what we see into words that, without our always being aware of it, by their standard definitions unbiddenly structure our interpretations of what we have seen. What we think are the options or choices of action available at a specific event for a langur monkey, or any other nonhuman primate, may not be those perceived by the monkey. We are aware of only a portion of their reality, and it might be a very small portion at that. Even so, we do see some of what happens, and having seen the actions and events repeatedly over long periods of time we can speculate as to what seem to be motivations, alternatives, and choices.

From years of viewing we can construct a list of qualities that constitute the structure of the tactical repertoires of young primates and, specifically, young langurs. High on the list are perseverance, inquisitiveness, alertness, opportunism, stubbornness, accommodation, cooperativeness, a good sense of timing, perceptiveness of the moods of others, and finally, but not least, ability to perceive and manipulate social responses with increasing accuracy (Dolhinow and DeMay 1982; Dolhinow 1991). Obviously, there is a prodigious range of ability among immatures in being able to use these traits, and by no means are all used at one time. However, they form an arsenal from which the youngster selects as it deems appropriate and in its best interest. Conflict and competition are often emphasized as the major events of life, including immaturity, but this is not an accurate reflection of the most important aspects of growing up. It would be far more accurate to emphasize patterns of cooperation and mutual adjustment as critical dimensions of social life (Bateson 1981; Dolhinow and Murphy 1982; Fedigan 1982).

Immatures are granted a much wider margin for error and hubris than are adults, and this latitude provides a context of relative safety for the elephantine amount of learning by trial and error that characterizes youthful activity. Young langur monkeys are provided protection by the group (Dolhinow, in press, pers. obser. in the field and colony). Early poor coordination of the newborn, combined with steady maternal oversight, prevent it from getting into much trouble. This changes very rapidly, and by the fifth week of life—almost as though someone threw a switch—the infant starts to climb (Dolhinow and Murphy 1982). At that point the infant is able to move toward anything it can see, and this quantum leap in mobility creates a real management challenge for the caregiver. Now the theme of the day is getting there and doing that. Rules change dramatically for the older animals, even for large juveniles and subadults. Little if any slack is cut for a mistake when subadults or adults err in judgment. Many lessons learned early carry throughout the life span, and most of the tactics for getting along and obtaining what is desired have been practiced and learned during formative years.

Increasing independence characterizes the large infant and then the juvenile. Weaning occurs before the next sibling is born and is marked more by the weanlings often boisterous and ear-splitting protests at being refused contact than by any objection at losing a source of nutrition. Social relations with members of the group are forged and amended during the time before reaching sexual and social adulthood. Maturity is not announced by obvious physical markers that suddenly appear to celebrate passing a life stage boundary. Instead, complex patterns of behavior change gradually and can be tracked over months to identify transitions from the time of immaturity through adolescence and into the early part of maturity.

DEVELOPMENTAL SYSTEMS

Insofar as it is thought to have a function, play has been postulated by many investigators to exist largely or in part to prepare young primates to practice skills that will be important to them when they become adults (Fagen 1993; Fairbanks 1993).

There is a problem in conceptualizing playful activity in this way, however. Selection does not act on future outcomes; it acts on aspects of the phenotype that, on average, have acceptable consequences at the time of selection (Sober 1984). The future can never be an effective cause of the past, and although significant consequences of behavior can be felt in the future, these future effects are not proximate causes for the action that happened long before. It is circular thinking to explain what a behavior does by asserting that it was selected to do just that (Estling 1983).

With this in mind, play and playful activity are understood to be very important parts of the immature's developmental system, which produces the animal's phenotype or nature. The primate inherits developmental processes, not traits, and through development constructs the phenotype that describes its existence. A developmental system consists of a set of interacting elements: the genome, intra- and extra-cellular elements, stimulation arising from itself, the surrounding physical environment, climate, and the multitude of influences from conspecifics (Oyama 1985, 1989). This speaks to the inseparability of behavior and biology, although the character of these bonds may not always be clear.

The characteristics defining an animal constitute its nature. Nature is not the result of a set of genetic plans or instructions; rather, nature is constructed during development—it is the phenotype (Oyama 1982, 1989). To live is to change; hence, natures are constantly mutable. Nurture, in contrast, consists in developmental interactions, the processes that produce the nature of the beast. Nature and nurture are distinct phenomena and are not simply different sources of form: "nature is the *product* of the *process* of the developmental interactions we call nurture. An organism's nature is simply its form and function. Because nature is phenotypic, it depends on developmental context as profoundly and intimately as it does on the genome" (Oyama 1989: 5). That which is inherited becomes evident during development; it is not fixed at conception. For these many reasons, playful activity is conceived as part of a process of development rather than part of a linear causal chain of events.

FORMS OF PLAYFUL BEHAVIOR

"It's hard to define, but I know it when I see it." This is a refrain often heard in discussions of play, and it hints at the difficulty of identification that all too often confronts the observer. Most of what we see and call play is fairly unambiguous, in part because we are using a behavior repertoire with units such as chase, chase with contact, wrestle, and solitary (Dolhinow 1978). When it isn't clear what the animals are doing but it looks a bit like play, we resort to calling it playful, or we add a modifier or two: play fighting, play mothering.

These problems of identification exist regardless of the age of the player. Young infants leaving the mother for the first times are unsteady and uncoordinated. Although their halting, stumbling, and tumbling progress amuses the observer, it is not play. Soon, however, the infant's enormous curiosity and drive to go and to explore—to investigate, taste, smell, and poke—are accompanied by bouts of what seems clearly to be playful activity often done in concert with other young. The forms of playful behavior change with age as young animals mature physically and socially. Content changes with development and the social context, undoubtedly reflecting changes in meaning of the activity to the actor. There are marked differences in play patterns among different primate genera, and additional variables related to demographics and habitat add more variability to our list of forms (Fagen 1993). Each animal, regardless of species, has its own rather unique context of development in which it expresses itself in all activities. Mothers, siblings, peers, and physical and social abilities all vary to produce different environments of maturation and, as a result, different phenotypes or natures.

So let us look at examples of play by a few Old World monkeys. Play can occur at any time of the day, when the group is quiet or in motion, but daily routines are such that feeding or quiet periods are prime time for youngsters to gather and play or to play separately. Depending on the habitat, play will be in trees, on open ground, in tall grass, or any combination thereof. When possible, all three dimensions of space are used. Play, with its rapid starts and stops and including one to many participants, is probably the most difficult of all behavior to describe accurately. Often play alternates with nonplay. Animals may join or drop out of a play group over and over again. When all this often frenetic activity among many individuals is embedded in a dense complex habitat, this creates a gigantic challenge to observers first of all to see and then to record.

Location and rapidity of action are only one set of problems for the observer. The players themselves are exchanging much more information than we can even guess at. Degree, strength or firmness of grasp, pinch, hair pull, nip, bite, squeeze, or poke are very important factors to the participants and quite unavailable to us. The players are feeling, tasting, smelling, and experiencing far more than can be measured by our looking or even filming. Without this array of information, how are we to evaluate fully what the experience means to them? We must take recourse in watching the entire scene unfold, all behavior, over time—a lifetime.

Some motor patterns appear regularly in the play of many species. Two or three macaques or langur monkeys, in the course of five minutes play, may chase, tag, hit, spin, push, pull, drag, rub, slap, scratch, run, jump, chase, charge, fall down, mouth, wrestle, and swing by the feet. Some patterns are situation specific, as when six young macaques chase each other, dashing and clambering 15 feet up into a tree from which they race with alarming speed to an outer small limb and drop, smack belly-flop, into a pool of water below. The observer wonders why are they doing this when it seems so risky, not to mention painful.

A fairly small infant and a rather large juvenile langur tussle near a group of grooming adults. The juvenile's mouth is wide open in a "play face" as he hugs and leans on the infant. After a few minutes, the infant tries in vain to break free, but the juvenile grabs the younger's tail in both hands and runs off pulling the infant behind him. The infant ups the ante and starts to squeal, then screech, as it bumps along and finally comes to a stop, again under the juvenile. As the juvenile picks the infant up to spin over his head, the infant's cries of distress reach siren level, and an adult female comes rushing to smack the juvenile and carry the infant away from its source of distress. Perhaps you are wondering whether this last example was much fun for the infant. It certainly started out well for both participants, but from the point of view of the smaller, it didn't end up that way. In any event, the start of the interaction was recorded as play for both.

Wrestling often turns into aggression when one player bites too hard or does something that changes the tenor of action. It is not clear what constitutes biting too hard because one time a juvenile bites the area on the back of an infant's head and literally lifts it off the ground without any protest from the one so bitten. A few minutes later much the same bite elicits a scream, seemingly of pain, and is followed by a rapid escape.

Although we have many examples of playful activity turning into something else, there are countless hours of play when each participant continues to be active until it appears exhausted. These tens of thousands of bouts have many qualities in common. This raises the question of what we mean when we use the term "play" to record interactions that are obviously composite in nature. The words we use do more than communicate a standard or common meaning; they also effectively, and often unbeknownst to us, structure what we see and how we record it. If we have a category listed as "play" in our behavior repertoire, and it has, say, six variant forms, then we do our best to record what we see in those six boxes.

Early studies considered play to be mainly practice of behaviors that would become part of adult life. The function of immaturity was viewed as preparation for the future. With this in mind it is not surprising that play was considered to be repetitive, awkward, incomplete, non-goal directed, uneconomical, and other qualities that signified it was of no real function to the animal at the time it played. With more studies focusing on development, this view has been amended dramatically. Play serves vital motivational purposes, getting the young primate moving and interacting, establishing physical competency as well as social relations. The list of play qualities now emphasizes mastering physical skills, exploring the environment, developing social skills of timing, learning tolerances,

and in all arenas, testing tolerances and pushing the limits.

And then we have the "gray" areas of behavior, when the solitary young animal is "messing around," tossing, pushing, investigating, dismantling, going over and over the same jump-climb-fall sequence, perhaps for many minutes at a time. Perhaps an obvious wrestle play bout turns into a furious brief fight, making it difficult if not impossible to determine the boundaries between the two very different kinds of behavior. Recall also the example of one animal wrestling with a smaller one that doesn't appear to consider the experience playful or enjoyable. The juvenile or large infant that takes a leap to grab and swing on the long tail of an adult sitting quietly on a branch is not a welcome intruder.

WHY PLAY?

Young primates devote countless hours to activities that serve to stretch their abilities and hone motor and social skills. It seems they find repetition and investigation to their liking, and familiarization with new objects, movements, and situations lends new knowledge (Dolhinow and Bishop 1970; Fairbanks 1993). The minutest increment of increase in ability that accrues from hours of play is an investment in the present with significant implications for the future. Playful activity serves to calibrate bodily and environmental experiences, including social experiences, the sum of the immature's world. Although various forms of play have been heralded as practice for adult behaviors, remember that the future can never be an effective cause of the past. Infants and juveniles are not practicing to be adults; they are acting as youngsters and surviving as a result.

The usefulness of patterns of play behavior are seldom apparent if only play is observed. The young macaques leaping from a tree into water far below, and running at breakneck speed to do it all over again, may seem to be taking unnecessary risks. If at a later time we see any of those individuals fleeing a predator or an attacker, we realize that the ability to move fast and accurately often is the difference between survival and death.

A great deal of attention has been given to adult dominance relations (Bernstein 1981), but very little heed has been paid to the genesis of tactics of competition itself. Curtin (1981) emphasized the highly opportunistic nature of adult langur monkey competition and the fact that success depended on the exploitation of temporary advantages. We see young langurs concentrating on the same tactics of opportunism, and as they grow they become more and more skillful in using them. Individual variability in most behaviors precludes our ability to predict adult patterns of behavior by studying the young. What we can assert is that the odds of survival change dramatically in favor of the monkey or ape that has learned its skills early and well.

CONCLUSION

Playful behavior is a complex, seemingly indispensable activity of primate immaturity, with boundaries that resist easy definition or understanding. Many areas of activity do not lend themselves readily to classification as play. It has been assumed that the long-term effects of immature play have an impact on adult behaviors ranging among, for example, caregiving, agonistic, affiliative, and reproductive behaviors. But selection that affects the behavior of any animal does not act on future outcomes but on aspects of the phenotype that, on average, have acceptable consequences at the time of selection. It is my contention that play (or playful activity when identification of the action is problematic) is a critical part of the environment of development and is most accurately viewed as a process rather than as only a series of repeated behavior items. It is a process in place to benefit the animal at whatever age it plays. The motivation for

playful behavior may change, however, with advancing age.

Consider that primates, in general, have evolved to be relatively intelligent creatures, explorative, curious, and to an extent, experimental. Young primates are motivated to play, and play is a powerful vehicle for learning, competing, practicing, and strategizing among peers with whom much time and energy is spent. Seen in this fashion, play is an exceedingly complex process of development, stimulated from within the animal but inseparable from the physical and social context of the actor. Playful actions encompass such a range of behaviors that vary with age and experience as well as with the social and ecological setting of the individual that in a very real sense it is a critical way of calibrating the young primate's reality.

Responsiveness to the environment is at the heart of development. Behavior and development are codependent, interacting elements of life history. Ontogeny is contingent on the full context of development rather than on preprogramming in the genome; hence, we must study systems as processes rather than as linear causal chains. In the more traditional view, play is preparation for adulthood. In our search for proximate mechanisms we must not confuse function and evolution. Consequences of behavior may be felt in the future, but the future consequences are not the proximate causes for the action. It is circular thinking to explain what a behavior does by asserting that it was selected to do just that.

Play serves real and urgent needs of young primates, including learning to move, interacting with companions, and discovering the physical environment in which all this takes place. By investigating activities we consider play, we can appreciate both the processes that shape the behaviors and the significance to the individual of what is gained and learned in every stage of life.

30

The Physiology of Male Reproductive Strategies

Fred B. Bercovitch

Penile rigidity is required for sexual intercourse. A limp penis secures an erection when venous blood is blocked from exiting the organ at the same time that smooth muscles relax to allow an increased inflow of arterial blood to accumulate (Sapolsky 1994). Only calm males can achieve an erection, because the physiological processes are stimulated by the parasympathetic nervous system, which is activated only in a relaxed state. A "raging bull" male primate who viciously defeats a competitor over access to a female must rapidly calm down to copulate. The physiology of male reproductive strategies can involve dynamic shifts in internal states. The goal of this essay is to explore the diversity of physiological mechanisms associated with male reproductive strategies across multiple primate species.

Reproductive strategies are a subset of life history strategies that include the timing of reproductive events, the energy expenditure related to reproduction, and behaviors associated with mate acquisition and retention, offspring production, and progeny rearing. Reproductive strategies consist of both mating and parental effort, although the two are often difficult to disentangle. Among mammals, males tend to emphasize mating effort, whereas females concentrate on parental effort, because of differences in reproductive physiology (Trivers 1972). Reproductive rates among female primates are constrained as a consequence of pregnancy and lacta-

tion; reproductive rates among males are limited by access to sexually receptive females (Trivers 1972).

As a result, research on nonhuman primate male reproductive strategies often focuses on aggressive competition. However, understanding the physiology of male reproductive strategies requires expanding our horizons beyond this perspective. Linking physiology with reproductive behavior is important in demonstrating how proximate mechanisms regulate relative reproductive success.

TESTOSTERONE, AGGRESSION, AND SEX

Testosterone is manufactured in the testicles and belongs to a class of hormones, called sex steroids, that are derived from cholesterol. **Hormones** are chemical messengers constructed in specific organs and transported through the circulatory system to particular target tissues. Upon reaching their destination, hormones trigger responses related to growth, development, metabolism, and behavior. The primary functions of androgenic hormones, such as testosterone, are to stimulate development of secondary sexual traits, foster growth of accessory sex organs, prime spermatogenesis (male gamete formation), and raise the prospects for aggressive and sexual behavior. Synthetic androgens, known as anabolic steroids, will promote the accumulation of muscle mass, but these short-term

Hercules-producing effects are accompanied by long-term effects such as testicular atrophy and impotence.

Testosterone begins to exert an effect on male behavior in utero when the fetal testes churn out massive amounts of testosterone, which alter brain formation and development (Goy and McEwen 1980). Testosterone injections administered to pregnant rhesus macaques carrying female fetuses result in offspring who have enlarged clitoral development, masculine behavioral attributes (Goy, Bercovitch, and McBrair 1988), and faulty ovarian cyclicity as adults (Dumesic et al. 1997).

Elevated testosterone increases the chances of aggressive and sexual behavior in males, but social factors constrain and guide the expression of these activities (Eaton and Resko 1974; Bernstein, Gordon, and Rose 1983; Bercovitch and Goy 1990; Zumpe and Michael 1996). For example, subordinate male talapoin monkeys (*Cercopithecus talapoin*) mate less than dominant males not due to lower testosterone levels but due to behavioral suppression by higher ranking males (Eberhardt, Keverne, and Meller 1980). Similarly, older male rhesus macaques (*Macaca mulatta*) copulate less than younger males, but the difference is not due to differences in testosterone concentrations (Robinson et al. 1975). Hormones prime the organism to respond in an appropriate fashion under certain conditions after a threshold level is surpassed and activate behavior by adjusting the probability of expression of an activity. Men with high testosterone concentrations achieve maximum penile erection size more rapidly than men with low testosterone levels in response to erotic stimuli (Lange et al. 1980), but inject a male monkey with anabolic steroids and he won't necessarily rise in rank, start fighting, or try to copulate.

Aggression and testosterone are commonly examined with respect to dominance status, but the relationship between the three variables is convoluted. When the dominance hierarchy is unstable, high ranking savanna baboon (*Papio cynocephalus*) males are characterized by elevated rates of aggression and increased concentrations of testosterone, but when the dominance structure is stable, young adolescent males frequently initiate fights and display high levels of testosterone (Sapolsky 1986). In

vervet monkeys (*Cercopithecus aethiops*) differences in testosterone levels do not distinguish high- and low-ranking males, but testosterone levels were associated with the amount of aggression initiated by dominant, but not subordinate, males (Steklis et al. 1985). Among male lesser mouse lemurs (*Microcebus murinus*), aggression and testosterone were unrelated, but dominant males had the highest testosterone concentrations (Perret 1992). In wild mountain gorillas (*Gorilla gorilla*) testosterone concentrations tended to be higher among dominant males compared to subordinate males (Robbins and Czekala 1997). In squirrel monkeys (*Saimiri sciurius*) testosterone levels corresponded to status differentials after group formation but were not indicative of future status prior to group formation (Mendoza et al. 1979). In Japanese macaques (*Macaca fuscata*) dominant males are not the most aggressive, and rank does not correlate with increased testosterone levels (Eaton and Resko 1974). The most parsimonious explanation for these discrepant results is that testosterone is a labile hormone that is influenced by, and influences, social behavior.

The arrow linking testosterone with aggression and sex does not point only in one direction. It is bidirectional: hormones and behavior influence each other. The ability of behavior to alter endocrine state is probably more consistent than the ability of hormones to alter behavioral activities. The most striking case of behavior influencing hormone concentration is that of induced ovulation in response to copulation. Another prominent example is the cascade of hormonal changes referred to as the endocrine stress response, where exposure to external threats stimulates an immediate outpouring of a variety of chemicals to cope with the challenge (Sapolsky 1994). The simple exposure of male rhesus macaques to sexually receptive females during the nonmating season yields increased testosterone concentrations (Vandenbergh 1969), and a similar pattern characterizes pigtailed macaques (*M. nemestrina*: Bernstein et al. 1978). In both rhesus macaques (Bernstein et al. 1983) and talapoin monkeys (Eberhardt et al. 1980), males who rise in dominance rank subsequently display elevated testosterone levels, whereas those who stumble in rank exhibit lowered testosterone levels.

In captive orangutans (*Pongo pygmaeus*) dominant males inhibit development of secondary sexual traits in subordinate males, but the precise endocrine pathway interfering with development is unclear (Graham and Nadler 1990).

Testosterone levels also fluctuate with environmental conditions. Food restriction suppresses sex steroid levels (Bronson 1989), and male savanna baboons have lower testosterone levels during a drought than during normal conditions (Sapolsky 1986). Dry, harsh conditions among baboons are associated with reduced levels of male-male competition (Popp 1983). Hence, decreased food availability seems to correspond to less energy for aggressive competition and reduced testosterone concentrations.

In summary, access to females sometimes depends on aggressive competition, and elevated testosterone increases the prospects for aggressive and sexual interactions. Surpassing a minimum testosterone level is probably a prerequisite for engaging in sex or aggression by males. Social and environmental factors strongly influence the ebb and flow of testosterone and constrain and guide male reproductive strategies. Social factors probably propel hormones more than hormones trigger specific behaviors.

SEASONAL REPRODUCTION AND MALE PHYSIOLOGY

Reproductive seasonality is common among primates, with the annual cycle linked to proximate factors such as daylight, altitude, rainfall, climate, food availability, and social cues (Lindburg 1987; Bronson 1989). These variables affect reproductive patterns by altering the hormonal milieu to either facilitate births at specific times of the year or to encourage mating at particular times of the year.

The annual reproductive cycle in males is marked by achieving peak body size, testes size, and testosterone levels during the mating season. Confining males to indoor environments does not eliminate the annual fluctuations in endocrine profiles (Bercovitch and Goy 1990), suggesting that proximate environmental variables operate to fine-tune a deeply set neurobiological rhythm.

Among patas monkeys (*Erythrocebus patas*), testosterone concentrations during the mating season are three to four times higher than during the birth season, and testes volume doubles from birth to mating season (Bercovitch 1996; Figure 1). Among squirrel monkeys, testosterone levels are twice as high during the mating season as during the birth season, and body weight increases by 10 to 20% (DuMond and Hutchinson 1967; Mendoza et al. 1978). Rhesus macaque males lose about 10% of body weight during the mating season (Bercovitch 1992a).

The seasonal increase in body mass among rhesus macaques has been linked to increased food intake (Lindburg 1977; Bercovitch 1997), whereas that of squirrel monkeys has been posited to accrue from altered metabolic patterns (Boinski 1987). Weight gain in rhesus monkeys manifests itself primarily as an increase in body fat levels. During the mating season, fat reserves are utilized as energy sources that enable males to guard mates and to reduce their level of food intake (Bercovitch 1992a, 1997). In squirrel monkeys seasonal amplification of male size might mediate male-male competition, as well as female choice (Boinski 1987).

The annual pattern of mating season enlargement of male body size has been called the "fatted male phenomenon" (DuMond and Hutchinson 1967). Adipose tissue, or fat, is a key site for aromatization (McCamant et al. 1987), which is the process of converting testosterone to estrogen. In both squirrel monkeys (McCamant et al. 1987) and rhesus monkeys (Bercovitch 1992a), male estrogen concentrations reach their peak at the onset of the mating season (Figure 2). Bercovitch (1992a) has suggested that fat deposition by males is a reproductive strategy that provides males with a substrate for adipose tissue aromatization that results in elevated estrogen concentrations and enables males to forgo feeding in favor of mate acquisition and retention. Rhodes et al. (1997) added an additional twist to this hypothesis by revealing that the redness of the sexual skin in male rhesus macaques is correlated with their estrogen levels.

In summary, male physiology changes during the year concurrent with reproductive cyclicity. Males achieve maximum body size at the commencement of the mating season and suffer weight

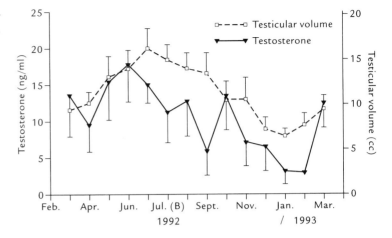

FIGURE 1 Annual variation in testes volume and testosterone levels. SOURCE: Bercovitch, 1996.

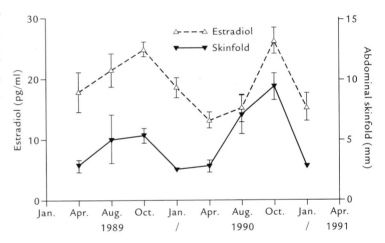

FIGURE 2 Circannual patterns of systemic estradiol and abdominal skinfold thickness in adult male rhesus macaques across a two-year period. Values graphed are the mean ± SEM (N = 4). SOURCE: Bercovitch, 1992a.

loss during the mating season. Annual fluctuations in body mass are primarily a consequence of fat deposition and usage.

SPERM COMPETITION AND REPRODUCTIVE SUCCESS

From puberty to death, testicles ceaselessly fabricate spermatozoa. Although only a single sperm successful penetrates the egg, men who ejaculate "only" 50 or 60 million sperm are considered subfertile because a normal ejaculate contains about 250 million sperm (Pollard, 1994). The number of sperm that are produced depends on the number of Sertoli cells in the testes, and the number of Ser-

toli cells is the key determinant of testicle size (Sharpe 1994). The Sertoli cells are packed tightly into the seminiferous tubules, which stretch to 100 meters in length in human beings (Pollard 1994).

Spermatogenesis in primates is under the primary control of follicle stimulating hormone, or FSH, which is the same hormone influencing ovulation, with testosterone acting as an assistant in the process (Rommerts 1988; Pollard 1994; Sharpe 1994). Sperm count is not correlated with testicular androgen concentrations (Weinbauer and Nieschlag 1991). Following testicular production, spermatozoa journey through the epididymis, where they undergo chemical changes enabling them to fertilize eggs (Pollard 1994). Transit time from production to maturation is about one to two months in primates (Sharpe 1994; Pollard 1994). Variation in relative testes size across species differs according to the type of mating system and frequency of copulatory behavior (Harcourt et al. 1981; Dixson 1987; Bercovitch 1992b).

Among primate species where females mate with multiple males, copulation frequency is about once per hour. In species characterized by females tending to mate with a single male, copulation frequency is approximately once per ten hours (Dixson 1995). For example, savanna baboons ejaculate about once per hour (Bercovitch 1989), whereas Galdikas (1981) recorded only thirty copulations over a four-year period in orangutans. Orangutans weigh about three times as much as baboons but have testicles less than half the size those of baboons (compare Bercovitch 1992b with Dahl, Gould, and Nadler 1993). Although testes size influences sperm production rates, and relatively large testes occur in species residing in multimale mating systems, male reproductive success within a population is not a function of testes size (Bercovitch 1989; Bercovitch and Nürnberg 1996; Figure 3). The timing of mating has a greater impact on male reproductive success than testicle size (Bercovitch 1989).

Dunbar (1988) has suggested that males can suppress the reproductive success of competitors by disrupting spermatogenesis, but Bercovitch and Goy (1990) reasoned that such a tactic would be nonproductive. Spermatogenesis proceeds even if testicular testosterone concentrations fall to 15% of baseline (Rommerts 1988), and males are still fertile if sperm count is at least 20% of normal. Males are more likely to increase their relative reproductive success by mating with a female at the appropriate time, and by saturating her reproductive tract with sperm, than by trying to hinder spermatogenesis in other males.

Sperm competition refers to a nonagonistic form of male rivalry that occurs when multiple males inseminate a female. Sperm competition is more pronounced in multimale than in unimale or monogamous mating systems and yields relatively large testicles and high rates of sexual activity. Very little is actually known about the mechanics of sperm competition within the female reproductive

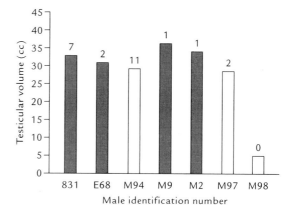

FIGURE 3 The relationship between testes size and paternity among the seven high-ranking males listed in descending dominance order ($r = 0.254$, $p > 0.50$). The number above the histogram bar is the number of offspring sired during the 1991 birth season in Group M. Gray bars are males ≥ 6 years of age; white bars are males 4–6 years of age. SOURCE: Bercovitch and Nürnberg, 1997.

tract (see Bercovitch 1992b), and some investigators have suggested that female control of fertilization mediates male reproductive success (Eberhard 1997).

In summary, the amount of sperm produced by males is strongly dependent on testes size, but the amount of sperm deposited by males in the female reproductive tract will depend on patterns of mate acquisition, retention, and choice. Across primate species, relative testicular size reflects mating system structure, but, within a population, paternity depends more on the timing of mating than on the size of the testicles.

STRESS AND MALE REPRODUCTION

Exercise is a stressor. As a fitness fanatic, my self-imposed workout routine subjects my body to the same physiological processes experienced by a red colobus (*Colobus badius*) monkey when crashing through the canopy attempting to avoid becoming a chimpanzee meal (see Goodall 1986). The stress response is a biological mechanism that functions by dampening digestive, immune, and reproductive functions, while energizing cardiovascular and musculoskeletal activity (Sapolsky 1990, 1994). Breathing rate increases, blood pressure rises, blood flow to the muscles expands, and glucose delivery to the muscles soars. Although the endocrine stress response suppresses reproductive processes, a well-tuned stress response can augment reproductive success (Pollard 1994).

Stress activates the adrenal glands, which are small organs resting atop the kidneys. Unlike other endocrine glands, the adrenals develop in utero from two distinct tissue regions: the neural crest and the mesoderm (Norman and Litwack 1987). Hence, the adrenal medulla, or center, is nervous tissue acting as an extension of the brain, whereas the adrenal cortex, or outer layer, is not. The essence of the endocrine stress response consists of an outpouring of **glucocorticoids** and **catecholamines,** accompanied by discharges of prolactin, β-endorphin, and other chemicals. In primates, the main glucocorticoid is cortisol, and the key catecholamine is epinephrine, also called adrenaline (Sapolsky 1994). Both prolactin and β-endorphin suppress testosterone levels during stress by altering brain regions regulating the production and discharge of GnRH (gonadotropin releasing hormone), which inhibits LH (luteinizing hormone) from stimulating testosterone output (Norman and Litwack 1987; Sapolsky 1990, 1994; Pollard 1994). Elevated prolactin is also associated with impotence and inhibited copulatory activity, whereas β-endorphin is a morphine-like substance contributing to a "runner's high" and accounting for the similarity between superathletes and drug addicts in their lower testosterone concentrations, smaller testes, and reduced sperm counts (Sapolsky 1994).

Because acute stress elevates glucocorticoid concentrations and dampens testosterone concentrations, one might expect that low-ranking animals would be characterized by high cortisol levels and low testosterone concentrations. However, the connection between low rank and low testosterone was questioned earlier, and social subordination and high cortisol levels do not necessarily coincide either. Male exposure to a female not only elevates testosterone values but increases cortisol concentrations in both longtailed macaques (*M. fascicu-*

laris: Glick 1984) and talapoin monkeys (Martensz et al. 1987).

In groups of squirrel monkeys, dominant males have higher concentrations of both testosterone and cortisol than subordinate males (Coe, Mendoza, and Levine 1979). Among lesser mouse lemurs, dominant males have significantly higher testosterone concentrations than subordinate males, but cortisol levels do not differ by rank (Perret 1992). A two-year study of rhesus macaques revealed that cortisol concentrations were not a function of dominance status and were independent of testosterone levels (Bercovitch and Clarke 1995). Cortisol levels corresponded with the amount of aggression received among talapoin monkeys but was not related to dominance rank (Martensz et al. 1987). Dominant male savanna baboons have lower cortisol levels than subordinate males when the rank relationships are stable, but low-ranking males who have extensive social affiliations and are able to displace aggression after losing fights also exhibit low cortisol concentrations (Sapolsky 1994). Sapolsky (1990, 1994) has reasoned that personality, behavioral strategies of coping with adversity, social control of interactions, and structure of social relationships (e.g., relative stability of the dominance hierarchy, the extent of reconciliation and frequency of attack) have a more pronounced impact on cortisol levels among primates than does dominance rank. Among primates, behavioral mechanisms regulating social relationships provide a strong basis for coping with unfavorable circumstances (Judge and de Waal 1997). Social skills contribute to mitigating the expression of the endocrine stress response (Sapolsky 1994).

The capacity to cope with stress could be an outcome of pre- and neonatal stress levels modifying the development of the neuroendocrine feedback system (Clarke et al. 1994). Pubescent rhesus macaques who experienced high levels of prenatal stress play less, cling to others more, and show lower levels of sociability than do control subjects (Clarke et al. 1996). In addition, the neuroendocrine profiles of prenatally stressed monkeys is altered compared to that of the control subjects (Clarke et al. 1994). Among baboons in Kenya, dominant males with low cortisol levels display a more rapid rise in cortisol when confronted with a stressor than do subordinate males (Sapolsky 1990, 1994). An appropriate stress response can augment reproductive success by buffering the animal against external challenges (Pollard 1994), whereas an inappropriate stress response can result in excess glucocorticoid production that nibbles away at bodily functions and brain performance (Sapolsky 1994).

Hormones released in response to stress interact with each other, and it is unlikely that elevated glucocorticoids are a major element reducing the reproductive success of subordinate males (Bercovitch and Clarke 1995). Stress has a greater impact on male reproductive function by interfering with erectile capacity than by suppressing testosterone concentrations or reducing sperm count (Sapolsky 1994).

In summary, acute stress launches a series of endocrine replies that include elevated cortisol and diminished testosterone. But the two hormones do not necessarily circulate in a mirror image of each other, and both rise on exposure to strange females. Stress is likely to affect male reproductive success not by obstructing spermatogenesis but by hindering male access to females and by stymieing erectile capacity. Coping with stress is a major behavioral strategy required for male reproduction, and high cortisol levels are an appropriate short-term stress response. Probably one of the most stressful events encountered by male primates is dispersal from their natal troop.

DISPERSAL IN MALE PRIMATES

Among cercopithecines, females tend to spend their entire lives in their natal troop, whereas males disperse during adolescence to other troops. As adults, males periodically shift troops, so an individual male resides in multiple troops during his lifetime.

The process of dispersal has physiological consequences, rendering males more susceptible to disease (Raleigh and McGuire 1990). Stress has a pronounced impact on immune response by lowering the ability to defend the body against infection and disease (Sapolsky 1994). Male rhesus macaques reintroduced to a social group after a one-year absence had significant decreases in T-lymphocyte counts (Gust, Gordon, and Hambright 1993), a pattern similar to that reported for a new immigrant male savanna baboon in Kenya (Alberts, Sapolsky, and Altmann 1992).

In rhesus macaques natal dispersal occurs between 3 and 6 years of age (Colvin 1986), bracketing the time period of adolescence (Bercovitch and Goy 1990). Dominant males remain in their natal troops longer than subordinate males (Colvin 1986), and a relatively young age at natal dispersal corresponds to low levels of CSF 5-HIAA,[1] which is a metabolite of the chemical serotonin (Mehlmann et al. 1995). Suppressed concentrations of CSF 5-HIAA are also linked to reduced social competence, impulsive behavior, excessive aggression, and increased mortality (Mehlmann et al. 1995; Higley et al. 1996). In a free-ranging population of rhesus macaques, Higley et al. (1996) were able to demonstrate that young males who died in fights had the lowest CSF 5-HIAA levels.

In summary, troop dispersal is a key event in male cercopithecine life history trajectories. Males who smoothly merge into a new troop probably have different neuroendocrine profiles than those having difficulty making the transition. Dispersal by male primates poses potential costs in terms of increased likelihood of succumbing to predators, diseases, or wounds inflicted by new troop residents, and these costs ought to be balanced by benefits associated with increased prospects for mating in the new troop. In many noncercopithecine species, either both sexes or females disperse from their natal troop, but the physiological correlates of dispersal in these species have not yet been subjected to systematic investigation.

PATERNAL CARE OF INFANTS

Male primates are generally not exalted for their level of parental care, but one fairly unique attribute of many primate societies is year-round heterosexual associations accompanied by strong male-infant bonds (van Schaik and Paul 1996).

---

[1] cerebrospinal fluid concentrations of 5-hydroxyindoleactic acid

Male care of infants includes carrying, grooming, playing, sharing food, protecting, "babysitting," and even adoption (Hrdy 1976; Whitten 1987). Whether tight male-infant affiliations reflect paternal relationships or not is a subject of heated debate, with close ties observed in a variety of mating systems (see Whitten 1987; Snowdon 1990b; Smuts and Gubernick 1992; van Schaik and Paul 1996). Notwithstanding the widespread evidence of close male-infant bonds, the only extensive work on the physiological correlates of male care has involved callitrichids.

Callitrichid infants spend most of the day atop males, and return to their mothers primarily for suckling (Dixson and Fleming 1981; Wright 1990). Among common marmosets (*Callithrix jacchus*), males who carry infants have prolactin levels five times as high as males without infants (Dixson and George 1982). In cotton-top tamarins (*Saguinus oedipus*) fathers have prolactin levels triple that of nonfathers and comparable to that of nursing mothers (Ziegler, Wegner, and Snowdon 1996). Male rhesus macaques do not display intense male care of infants, but prolactin levels during the birth season are significantly greater than during the mating season (Bercovitch, unpublished data). Elevated prolactin levels in nonbreeding helpers characterize many bird and avian species as well as cotton-top tamarins (Ziegler 1997), but whether prolactin concentrations are a cause or a consequence of infant care remains to be established (Snowdon 1990b).

In summary, a relatively uncharted area of the physiology of male reproductive strategies concerns male parental effort. Across a range of vertebrates, including primates, increased prolactin concentrations coincide with increased care of infants. Among callitrichids and some other primate species, infants spend more time with males than with their mothers. Determining whether male-infant affiliates are father-offspring dyads and uncovering the hormonal correlates of male tolerance and care in primates are two of the biggest tasks confronting future primate research.

CONCLUSION

Male reproductive strategies arise from the confluence of physiology and behavior. The social environment, as well as the physical environment, affect patterns of male reproduction. Under situations where female cooperation influences male sexual activity (see Huffman 1991b), one might expect that male mating frequency will depend more on female behavior, and female endocrine status, than on male testosterone concentrations. Partner preferences, familiarity, and dominance rank are three important social factors that modulate the interactions between hormones and behavior (Zumpe and Michael 1996). Social behavior is both a catalyst for, and a consequence of, changes in hormone concentrations.

Maximizing reproductive output involves more than fighting for females, producing prodigious quantities of sperm, and impregnating as many females as possible. Social skills have a tremendous impact on male reproductive success (Bercovitch 1991; Strum 1994). Physiological mechanisms regulating male reproduction involve a complex interplay of a variety of hormones and neurotransmitters. Understanding the evolution of male reproductive strategies entails unraveling the proximate mechanisms responsible for forming affiliations between individuals that germinate their reproductive success and for fomenting aggression between individuals that can augment or suppress their reproductive success.

ACKNOWLEDGMENTS

Constructive criticisms have been contributed by Phyllis Dolhinow, Agustín Fuentes, and Robert Sapolsky. The Caribbean Primate Research Center is supported by NIH Grant RR03640.

The Mind

Long considered to be the hallmark of humanness, the human mind is often held aloft as unique in the animal kingdom. However, it is critical to realize that humans are primates and that we lie along a broad, multidimensional spectrum of cognitive ability. Our nonhuman primate cousins join us, along with other mammals, on this spectrum. Similar in some respects and different in others, the nonhuman primates reflect a wide array of morphological adaptations and behavioral variants related to cognitive function as well as to environmental factors.

The first essay in this section describes a scheme of cognitive development in the primates from a phylogenetic perspective. The second essay illustrates some of the intriguing results of studies in communication between humans and our close cousins, the chimpanzees. Neither of these essays seeks to answer or provide a definitive statement on the cognitive abilities of nonhuman primates. Rather, they serve as suggestive illustrations of our current understanding of and viewpoint on nonhuman primate cognition.

31

The Comparative Method in Studies of Cognitive Evolution

Sue Taylor Parker

In a wonderful article entitled "The Snark was a Boojum," Frank Beach (1965) chides researchers for focusing their "comparative psychology" on one species, the white rat. He notes that this tendency began when someone at Clark University in 1899 began studying *Rattus norvegicus* and it rapidly caught on as a convenient experimental animal. This highly limited formulation led to bizarre equations between the behavior of rats and humans.

Similar accidents of history and matters of convenience have inspired experimental researchers to use so-called model organisms that are reliable and easy to care for (Raff 1996): *E. coli* bacteria, the fruit fly (*Drosophila melanogaster*), and bread mold (*Neurospora*) in molecular genetics; the nematode (*Caenorhabditis elegans*), the house mouse (*Mus musculus*), the frog (*Xenpus laevis*), and now the Zebrafish (*Brachydanio rerio*) in embryology; and the rhesus monkey (*Macaca rhesus*) in behavioral biology. Unfortunately, the characteristics that make these species reproduce and develop reliably in the laboratory may be uncharacteristic of their taxonomic group.

Harry Harlow noted that he had begun his Primate Research Laboratory in Madison, Wisconsin, studying many primate species but had settled on the rhesus monkey because he had serious problems keeping other monkeys healthy (Suomi and Leroy 1982). Robert Hinde's (1983) laboratory in Cambridge, England, also focused on this species, as did many other laboratories. Because of this, and the rhesus research colony established in Puerto Rico, more is known about this monkey than any other primate. This research led to widespread comparisons of mother-infant bonding between rhesus monkeys and humans. Whereas rhesus monkeys are certainly closer to humans than rats are, they are not as relevant for comparative studies as our closest living relatives, the chimpanzees and bonobos.

But who can argue with the success of studies of model organisms? The model organism approach has led to many important discoveries: universal laws of learning have been discovered through studies of the white rat; the regulation of gene action through the study of *E. coli;* the stages of embryo development through the study of sea urchins and nematodes; much about mother-infant attachment from the study of rhesus monkeys; and much more. This approach works well if the goal is to understand universal phenomena.

EVOLUTIONARY RECONSTRUCTION

Limitations of the model organism strategy only become apparent when the goal is to understand the evolution of form and function, be it physiology, morphology, development, behavior, or cognitive abilities. Evolutionary reconstruction depends on comparison of a characteristic in closely related species. Using comparative data, it is possible to determine which species share the same patterns and to infer the common ancestor from whom they inherited it. This comparative method was applied to the study of anatomy of the apes by Darwin's associate Thomas Henry Huxley (1863/1959). Later, it became the staple of ethology (Lorenz 1950), as seen, for example, in Leyhausen's study of the ontogeny of prey-catching in several species of wild cats and their hybrids (1973).

A recent, highly codified version of the comparative method can be found in a branch of phylogenetic taxonomy known as cladistics. Cladistics has two primary applications. First, it offers a systematic methodology for determining phylogenetic relationships. Second, it offers a methodology for identifying the common ancestry of characters. Both of these applications rely on the concept of shared derived character states (Hennig 1979; Wiley 1981; Ridley 1986).

The primary application of cladistics involves constructing **cladograms** by mapping character states of hypothetically related species on alternative branching diagrams (cladograms) until the most likely tree is found. (The most parsimonious tree is the one that requires the fewest evolutionary transformations.) Based on the most likely evolutionary tree, evolutionary taxonomists identify sister species on adjacent branches and classify them into higher taxonomic groups such as genera and families based on common ancestry (Hennig 1979; Wiley 1981; Ridley 1986).[1]

Hennig, who codified this methodology, argued that evolutionary trees must be based on the distinction between kinds of homologous characters: (1) those that are uniquely shared by a given group of sister species (shared derived character states) owing to their origin in a recent common ancestor,

and (2) primitive homologous characters that are broadly shared by a larger group of species (shared character states) owing to their ancient origin in a distant common ancestor.

Biologists distinguish between shared and shared derived characters by comparing character states of closely related species with those of more distantly related species. So, for example, the form of locomotion known as brachiation, which occurs in all the living apes but in none of the Old World monkeys, is a shared derived character state among the apes (the ingroup) relative to the Old World monkeys (the outgroup).

Homologous characters contrast with analogous characters, which have arisen in only one species (uniquely derived character states). They also contrast with characters that have evolved through convergent evolution in distantly related species who did not inherit them from their common ancestor (homoplasies: Wiley 1981). Bipedal locomotion in birds and hominids, for example, is a homoplastic character because it was not present in the common ancestor of birds and mammals (and is only present in one derived group of mammals).

Determining whether character states shared by various species are homoplastic, shared, or shared derived is the key to constructing evolutionary trees. Shared derived character states indicate closeness of phyletic relationship, whereas shared or homoplastic character states do not. Evolutionary trees are constructed on the basis of shared derived character states because only these character states indicate common ancestry. These cladograms may then be transformed into phylogenies in which putative common ancestors of the various branches are identified (Skelton, McHenry, and Drawhorn 1986).

The second application of cladistic methodology—the one that concerns us here—begins once tree construction is complete. At this point, the cladistic method can be reversed to do character mapping, that is, to discover the ancestry and sequence of evolution of character states. This can be done by mapping character states onto a previously constructed tree to see which common ancestor gave rise to shared derived characters. To

---

[1]The procedures described here are those developed by the school of evolutionary taxonomists known as cladists. The branching diagrams they construct, cladograms, differ from conventional family trees in that all species are represented at the ends of branches. None are represented at the nodes, as they sometimes are on phylogenies. Phylogenies, in contrast, represent purported common ancestors at the nodes or branch points.

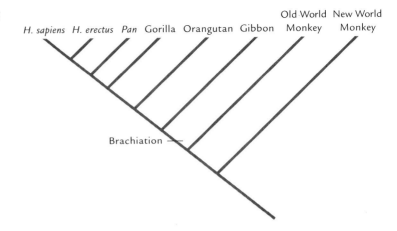

FIGURE 1 Phyletic origins of brachiation.

avoid circularity, only characteristics other than those used to construct the tree can be mapped on it to reconstruct common ancestry (Brooks and McLennan 1991). Character mapping is a vital part of evolutionary modeling because it alone can identify the common ancestor in whom a given character originated.

If we wanted to reconstruct the phylogeny of some characteristic, we would begin to compare that phenomenon in all the closely related species in the genus or family (the ingroup), and then compare those with related behaviors in a distantly related group (the outgroup). If, for example, we wanted to reconstruct the evolution of mother-infant behavior in Old World monkeys, we would compare that phenomenon in all the macaque species (or as many as possible), and then compare it with that in other cercopithecine monkeys (baboons, guenons, and other cheek-pouch monkeys). Then we would compare it with that in colobine monkeys (langurs, colobus, proboscis, and other leaf-eaters), and finally with that of New World monkeys (cebus, squirrel, marmosets, spider, woolly, and others).

If, however, we wanted to reconstruct the evolution of mother-infant behavior in humans, we would compare that system in ourselves and our closest relatives, the African apes (the ingroup), then all the great apes, then the lesser apes, and finally with the Old World monkeys (the outgroup). We would look to see which species share the same

derived characters, map these characters onto an existing primate phylogeny, and then infer the common ancestor from which the characters arose. In this case we see that brachiation is seen in all the apes, and none of the Old World monkeys. We can infer, therefore, that it must have evolved in the common ancestor of all the apes. The same principle would apply in reconstructing the evolution of any other characteristic. Figure 1 illustrates character mapping of one locomotor system in primates.

An important question in phylogenetic reconstruction is what characteristics to study and how to study them. Ideally, the same methodology is used to study all the species. This question is more difficult to answer than you might think because there are an infinite number of possible features to describe or measure. The general rule is to look for functional systems, that is, structures and/or behaviors that operate together under natural circumstances. In studies of primate morphology these have been described as the "total morphological pattern" of functional complexes (Clark 1959, 1964). The brachiation complex, for example, includes the configuration of the bones and muscles of the broad trunk, the rotational shoulder, the flexible elongated arms, and the hook-like hands that make arm-over-arm suspensory locomotion under branches possible. It is a shared derived character in apes inherited from their common ancestor.

THE EVOLUTION OF COGNITION

Because I am interested in the evolution of human mentality, problem solving or intelligence has been my focus. I began by studying intellectual development in an infant stumptailed macaque (Parker 1977). Later, I studied intellectual development in an infant gorilla (Parker, in press), an infant chimpanzee, and an infant human.

Intelligence is a vast subject that has been approached in many ways. Because I thought it would reveal important similarities and differences among primate species, I chose to use Jean Piaget's model of sensorimotor intellectual development in human children (Piaget 1952, 1954, 1962, 1966; Parker, in press). Many primatologists have used Piagetian models and other models of cognitive development in children to study intelligence in monkeys and apes (Jolly 1972a; Dore and Dumas 1987; Parker

1990; Tomasello and Call 1997; Parker and Mc-Kinney, in press).

One advantage of the Piagetian and neo-Piagetian models is that they cover a wide range of intelligent behaviors in several domains: imitation and pretend play and theory of mind in the social domain, causality and space in the physical domain, and classification and number in the logical-mathematical domain. This allows investigators to compare several kinds of intelligence. Even better, these models describe spontaneous behaviors that can be observed as primates go about their normal activities in colonies or even in the wild, as well as being elicited and tested in the laboratory. (Table 1 provides a summary of Piagetian developmental periods and subperiods.)

Another advantage of this approach is that developmental stages represent increasingly more sophisticated levels of intellectual ability, providing a

TABLE 1 Piaget's Periods of Cognitive Development

	Cognitive Domains		
Periods and Subperiods	Physical Knowledge	Logical-Mathematical Knowledge	Social and Interpersonal Knowledge
Sensorimotor period Early subperiod, birth to 1 year Late subperiod, 1 to 2 years	Discovery of practical properties, of objects, space, time, and causality	Practical construction of logical relationships among objects	Discovery of interpersonal efficacy through circular reactions, and novel schemes through imitation
Preoperations period Symbolic subperiod, 2 to 4 years Intuitive subperiod, 4 to 6 years	Discovery of immediate causes of actions and reactions	Construction of nonreversible classes	Construction of new routines and social roles through imitation and pretend play
Concrete operations period Early subperiod, 6 to 9 years Late subperiod, 9 to 12 years	Discovery of simple mediated causes of actions and reaction	Construction of reversible hierarchical classes	Construction of more complex routines and roles based on rules
Formal operations period Early subperiod, 12 to 15 years Late subperiod, 16 to 18 years	Discovery of simple laws of physics through measurement and control of variables	Discovery of logical necessity through hypothetical deductive reasoning	Construction of universal rules and principles

FIGURE 2 Phyletic origins of cognitive characters.

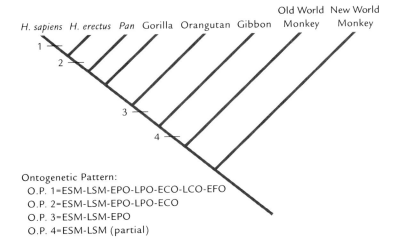

Ontogenetic Pattern:
O.P. 1=ESM-LSM-EPO-LPO-ECO-LCO-EFO
O.P. 2=ESM-LSM-EPO-LPO-ECO
O.P. 3=ESM-LSM-EPO
O.P. 4=ESM-LSM (partial)

natural scale or criteria for judging the relative levels of intelligence of nonhuman primate species. This scaling feature arises naturally from the fact that each new stage is constructed out of the raw materials of the preceding stage. This suggests that in the evolutionary history of primates the ability to develop to higher stages depended on prior evolution of the preceding level in an ancestor. This idea need not be taken on faith; it can be tested by comparing these abilities in monkeys and apes and mapping them onto phylogenies.

If we map the highest level of cognitive development in various domains onto the family tree of monkeys and apes, we see that the great apes show higher levels of intelligence than Old World monkeys. The highest level they achieve is equivalent to that of a 2- to 4-year-old human child, depending on which domain we consider. The highest level macaques achieve is similar to that of a 1-year-old child. (Figure 2 depicts these patterns.)

Some primatologists worry that using frameworks from human development for comparative studies is anthropomorphic. This would certainly be a concern if anthropomorphism were not the null hypothesis, that is, the hypothesis that human and nonhuman primates are identical. Any species differences we discover disprove this null hypothesis. The question then becomes how well a given framework is at identifying species similarities and differences. The richer and more diverse the frame-

work, the better it should be at this task (Parker 1997).

The other point to remember is that the more closely related species are, and the more recent their divergence from their common ancestor, the greater the number of similarities we should expect. Since humans and chimpanzees (and bonobos) had a common ancestor approximately 5 million years ago, similarities are not surprising. In terms of cognitive evolution, perhaps the most surprising finding is that so many of our human cognitive abilities—all those that develop after 2 to 4 years of age—evolved after hominids arose.

Describing the cognitive abilities of various closely related ingroup species and comparing them with those of an outgroup is the first step in evolutionary construction. The second step is to map these abilities onto a family tree. The third step is to propose a story, a scenario, to explain the evolution of those abilities. Several scenarios have been proposed to explain the evolution of intelligence in monkeys and apes. These may be classified as social, ecological, socialization, and locomotor hypotheses (Parker and McKinney, in press).

If we want to go on in our evolutionary analysis to understand the factors that favored particular intellectual abilities, we can turn to the third application of cladistic methodology. This application defines *adaptation* as shared derived character states. According to this approach, our adaptive scenario should specify the phylogeny of the character as well as the selection pressures. If we can specify all of these features in one taxonomic group, we have an adaptive hypothesis. If we can specify these features in two distantly related taxonomic groups that show *convergent* functions, we have a stronger hypothesis.[2]

Because primatologists are just beginning to think in terms of evolutionary reconstruction, few of our models for primate intelligence have been couched in these terms. The extractive foraging scenario for the evolution of intelligent tool use is one example of an evolutionary hypothesis that fits this definition. According to this scenario (Parker and Gibson 1977, 1979; Parker, 1996; Parker and McKinney, in press), intelligent tool use is defined in terms of Piaget's fifth sensorimotor stage, understanding of causality (i.e., that a stick or other tool may be used as an intermediary to influence the position or state of another object). Comparative studies have shown that great apes but not Old World monkeys display this understanding. Hence, it fits the definition of a shared derived character state among great apes. It evolved out of the simpler object manipulation abilities of ancestral primates.

The extractive foraging scenario proposes that intelligent tool use arose in the common ancestor of the great apes as an adaptation for extracting a variety of valuable embedded food sources from their casings or matrices with the aid of tools: termites and ants from their nests, honey from bees nests with sticks and probes, nuts and fruits from hard shells with hammers, juices from cavities with sponges, and so forth. Although intelligent tool use seems to be absent among Old World monkeys and most New World monkeys, it does occur in one New World genus, *Cebus,* the organ grinder monkeys. Interestingly, cebus monkeys, like great apes, engage in tool use—or more often proto-tool use (for example, banging or dropping objects to open them)—for the purpose of opening encased and embedded foods. Given that none of their close relatives (nor by implication their common ancestor with great apes) show this pattern, we can conclude that it evolved through convergent evolution. From the cladistics perspective, this is evidence in favor of the extractive foraging scenario for the evolution of intelligent tool use.

[2]Adaptation has been defined many ways. The most common approach is to define it in terms of design features that indicate selection for specific functions (Williams 1966, 1992).

32

Chimpanzee Sign Language Research

Roger S. Fouts and Deborah H. Fouts

Project Washoe is the first successful attempt to teach a human language to a nonhuman being. Previous attempts had failed because inappropriate expectations were placed on the apes involved, such as attempting to teach them spoken English (Wilmer 1909; Furness 1916, Hayes and Hayes 1951). Hayes and Hayes (1951) attempted to teach spoken English to the chimpanzee Viki, and after seven years of training, Viki had a vocabulary of four, largely voiceless words (Hayes and Hayes 1951; Hayes and Nissen 1971). Unlike their vocal ability, chimpanzees can freely move their hands, which means that a gestural language is better suited to the chimpanzee's abilities. The Gardners confirmed this as Washoe acquired a vocabulary of 132 signs in the first 51 months of the project (Gardner and Gardner 1974). The Gardners' research efforts, along with several later projects, have resulted in challenges to the evolutionarily naive anthropocentric claims of human uniqueness with regard to the ability to learn and use language. Following the Gardners' research, other investigators have looked at language acquisition in other great ape species such as gorillas (Patterson and Cohn 1990), orangutans (Miles 1980, 1990), and bonobos (Savage-Rumbaugh and Lewin 1994). The Gardners used a cross-fostering approach, but other investigators taught specific language-like abilities in different modes, using plastic tokens or lexigram boards (Premack 1971; Savage-Rumbaugh 1986).

CROSS-FOSTERING RESEARCH

The first ape sign language project was begun in 1966 with the infant chimpanzee Washoe, who was raised by Allen and Beatrix Gardner at the University of Nevada, Reno. Washoe was cross-fostered by the Gardners and their students, who used only American Sign Language (ASL) in her presence (Gardner and Gardner 1969, 1971, 1974, 1989). The cross-fostering method is simply one species raising another. In Washoe's case this involved her being raised in an environment similar to that of a deaf human child, in others words, in the context of a home and family rather than an operant conditioning laboratory. As a result, she learned her ASL signs during the first years of the project in a natural social environment comparable to that of a human deaf child. The Gardners state:

> She asked for goods and services, and she also asked questions about the world of objects and events around her. When Washoe had about eight signs in her expressive vocabulary, she began to combine them into meaningful phrases. YOU ME HIDE, and YOU ME GO OUT HURRY were common. She called her doll, BABY MINE; the sound of a barking dog, LISTEN DOG; the refrigerator, OPEN EAT DRINK; and her potty-chair, DIRTY GOOD. Along with her skill with cups and spoons, and pencils and crayons, her signing developed stage for stage much like

the speaking and signing of human children. (Gardner and Gardner 1989: 6)

Soon after Project Washoe ended, the Gardners continued their work with other cross-fostered chimpanzees. Moja, Pili, Tatu, and Dar were each raised in the same type of environment as Washoe except that these chimpanzees had each other to sign with as well as more deaf human signers than Project Washoe (Gardner and Gardner 1989). This replication confirmed and expanded on the Gardners' previous findings with Washoe. Taking the two projects together, the Gardners found that the five chimpanzees evinced the stage-by-stage replication of basic aspects of the acquisition of language by hearing and deaf children (B. T. Gardner and Gardner 1994; R. A. Gardner and Gardner 1994). The Gardners also used double-blind testing conditions to demonstrate that the chimpanzees communicated information using the signs of ASL to humans, that interobserver reliability between independent human observers in identifying the signs made by the chimpanzees could be obtained under these testing conditions, and that the five chimpanzees used their signs in reference to natural language categories (e.g., the sign TREE for any tree, BABY for any baby or doll: Gardner and Gardner 1985).

POST-RENO RESEARCH

In 1970 Washoe moved to the Institute for Primate Studies (IPS) at the University of Oklahoma, and the research was expanded to other captive chimpanzees. It was found that Washoe was not unique and that other chimpanzees could acquire the signs of ASL. With the help of human caregivers, the young chimpanzees Booee, Bruno, Cindy, and Thelma acquired signs (Fouts 1973). Other chimpanzees associated with the IPS who were being home-reared by humans, such as Lucy and Ally (aka Ali), were also taught the signs of ASL. Ally was able to comprehend and produce novel prepositional phrases, demonstrating his ability to use sign order (Fouts, Shapiro, and O'Neil 1978). In a

study with Lucy it was found that she was able to categorize and conceptualize fruits as different from vegetables and that she would describe novel objects by combining signs already existing in her vocabulary. For example, Lucy referred to a watermelon as a CANDY DRINK and a DRINK FRUIT, and she called an old bitter radish a CRY HURT FOOD after she took a bite of it and spit it out (Fouts 1975). Like Lucy, Washoe also combined signs to produce novel phrases to describe objects for which she did not have signs in her vocabulary, such as WATER BIRD for a swan on a lake and ROCK BERRY for Brazil nuts (Fouts and Rigby 1977). Ally also demonstrated that he could be taught ASL signs using vocal English words as exemplars and then in a blind condition transfer these signs to their physical referents (Fouts, Chown, and Goodin 1976). Later, Shaw (1989) reconfirmed the ability of chimpanzees to comprehend spoken English when she tested Tatu's ability to translate vocal English words into their ASL signs under a blind testing condition.

One of the advantages of the cross-fostering approach and the use of a natural language was that the use of sign language became a normal part of the chimpanzees' lives, not just a means for requesting food (Gardner and Gardner 1989). Today, Washoe, Moja, Tatu, and Dar, and one new addition, Loulis, continue to use sign language in a variety of contexts and situations here at the Chimpanzee and Human Communication Institute. Within this natural social context we have been able to demonstrate the cultural transmission of signs between chimpanzees. Ten-month-old Loulis was adopted by Washoe and acquired signing and other skills from her and the other signing chimpanzees in his community. To ensure that Loulis would acquire his signs only from the chimpanzees, the humans in his presence restricted their signing to seven specific signs or used vocal English to communicate with him. Washoe was observed to teach Loulis through modeling, molding and signing on his body. Most of his signs appeared to be delayed imitations of signs he had seen Washoe and the other chimpanzees use in similar contexts. We were able to examine the development of social behavior, communication, and other skills in Loulis without disrupting them. In this way, we obtained a comprehensive record of the cultural transmission of signing (Fouts, Hirsch, and Fouts 1982; Fouts and Fouts 1989; Fouts, Fouts, and Van Cantfort 1989).

To verify the use of the signs of ASL by Loulis, a remote videorecording technique was developed. Cameras were placed in the chimpanzee areas, and the chimpanzees' signing was recorded with no human presence whatsoever. Research using this technique demonstrated that Loulis, as well as the other four chimpanzees, would sign to communicate when no humans were present. In this study it was found that the chimpanzees mainly sign about social issues such as play, reassurance, and grooming (Fouts, Fouts, and Schoenfeld 1984; Fouts and Fouts 1989).

The remote videorecording technique was also used to study how the chimpanzees sign to themselves, which is called private signing. This method was used to record 368 instances of the chimpanzees using their signs in a nonsocial fashion to sign to themselves. These instances were classified into nine different functional categories, as has been done with private speech in humans. Similar to the human research, it was found that a few of the categories accounted for the majority of the chimpanzees' private signing. The Referential category accounted for 59% of the instances and is an utterance that refers to an object or event that is present. An example of this category was when Tatu signed THAT FLOWER to a picture of a flower in a magazine. The second highest category was the Informative category, which accounted for 12% of the instances and is an utterance that refers to an object or event that is *not* present. An example of this category was when Washoe signed DEBBI to herself when Debbi was not present (Bodamer, Fouts, Fouts, and Jensvold 1994).

The remote videorecording technique was also used to study imaginary play in the five chimpanzees. It was found that in fifteen hours of remote videorecording six instances of imaginary play were observed. These were classified into two different types of imaginary play: animation, in which an inanimate object is treated as if it is ani-

mate, and substitution, in which an object is given a new identity (Jensvold and Fouts 1993).

The remote videorecording technique was also used to examine the five chimpanzees' nighttime behavior. It was found that the chimpanzees were more active than previously assumed. With regard to signing, a few instances of behavior that meet the formal definition of a sign were recorded (Williams 1995).

Another study used both remote videotapes with humans absent and nonremote videotapes that were made with humans present who recorded the chimpanzees' behavior. Cianelli and Fouts (in press) examined high arousal interactions of the chimpanzees and found that they often emphatically signed ASL signs during high arousal interactions such as fights and active play. For example, after separating Dar and Loulis during a fight, and with all the chimpanzees still screaming, Washoe signed "COME HUG" to Loulis, who responded with the sign "NO." Results such as these indicate that the chimpanzees' signing is very robust indeed.

Other studies have involved more traditional methods of research, with the exception that they are subject paced. In other words, the chimpanzees are not required or forced to participate but do so in a voluntary fashion. Davis (1995) found that when a human distorted a sign while signing to a chimpanzee, if the distortion was low, the chimpanzee would restore the sign to its nondistorted form. A low distortion was defined as moving the place where the sign is made from 2.54 cm to 10.16 cm from the standard place where it is made. If the sign was a high distortion, the typical reaction of the chimpanzees was not to respond. A high distortion sign was defined as moving the place where the sign is made from 22.86 cm to 30.48 cm from the standard place where it is made. The chimpanzees demonstrated a flexibility similar to humans in their ability to comprehend and adjust to distorted verbal material.

Beaucher (1995) examined the semantic range of how a signing chimpanzee would categorize novel food stimuli that were manipulated on three dimensions. First, the chimpanzees were presented with Oreo® cookies and Saltine® crackers to verify that the chimpanzees would refer to these two food items with the signs for COOKIE and CRACKER, which they reliably did. She then devised recipes for novel food items that were varied on the dimensions of sweetened to nonsweetened, salty to not salty, and circle to square. She found that Washoe significantly used the sweet and nonsalty dimensions when comparing novel food items. These results indicated that Washoe was using a prototype model, which requires the subject to abstract attributes or dimensions of a category when applying them to novel objects.

Krause and Fouts (1997) examined referential pointing, eye gaze, and pointing accuracy in a study with Moja and Tatu in two experiments. The first experiment examined how Moja and Tatu attracted the attention of a human and then directed the human to an out-of-reach object. It was found that the chimpanzees would first acquire the visual attention of the human (e.g., make a noise to get the human to turn toward them and look at them) before they would point to the out-of-reach object. Once the human was looking at the chimpanzee, then Moja or Tatu would alternate their eye gaze direction between the human and the out-of-reach object. The chimpanzees used attention-getting devices, mutual gaze, and concomitant gaze alternation between the out-of-reach object and the human. This is evidence that the chimpanzees' pointing was indeed referential and communicative. The second experiment tested the chimpanzees' accuracy of pointing toward objects when the objects were placed in close proximity to each other and whether the humans could reliably determine where the chimpanzees were pointing. It was found that the humans were able to accurately respond to the chimpanzees' points under this condition. It was interesting to note that in the second experiment, which required a greater degree of precise pointing on the chimpanzees' part, both chimpanzees showed a left-hand bias, which was not found in the previous experiment.

Fouts, Haislip, Iwaszuk, Sanz, and Fouts (1997) have begun a long-term research project examining the use of gestural dialects and idiolects in wild and captive chimpanzees. The Fouts et al. (1997) study examined Washoe, Moja, Tatu, Dar, and Loulis's interactions for non-ASL sign gestures (nonverbal gestures) that were used during communicative interactions. They found eight gestures, both dialectical gestures and idiolect gestures, among these five chimpanzees. For example a subtle "chin tip" (a quick raising of the head with a directional component) was observed in chase games, where the direction of the tip (left or right) would indicate direction of the chase, and the active "chin tipper" would indicate the chaser.

Evidence already exists in the literature that chimpanzees in the wild use different gestural dialects in different communities. For example, this was first noted in 1978 when two researchers, William McGrew and Carolyn Tutin, from the Gombe Stream Research Centre traveled 80 kilometers south to study the Kasoje community of chimpanzees that Nishida studies in the Mahale Mountains in Tanzania. McGrew and Tutin (1978) reported observing a "grooming-hand-clasp" that was different from the grooming gesture they had observed used by the Kasakela chimpanzees at Gombe. Whereas the Kasakela chimpanzees will raise one arm straight into the air above their head to solicit grooming, the Kasoje chimpanzees approach each other at the beginning of a grooming session and each of the participants simultaneously raises an arm over its head and then grasps wrists with the other. Though similar to the Gombe pattern, this is an apparent dialectical variant of that pattern. McGrew and Tutin observed the "grooming-hand-clasp" to occur on the average of once every 2.4 hours, which exceeds the frequency for sexual behavior, agnostic behavior, or food-sharing, demonstrating that it plays a very important role in the Kasoje chimpanzees' social behavior. It is remarkable that this behavior has never been observed in the thousands of hours of observation in the past thirty-five years at Gombe. This finding, along with the discoveries of variation in food preferences, "tool kits," and other differences between communities, has led scientists such as McGrew (1992) to argue that this evidence meets the definition of culture.

The discovery of the dialectical difference between the Gombe's Kasakela and the Mahale Mountain's Kasoje communities of chimpanzees has begun to bring some attention to this area. Nishida (1987) observed a behavior he refers to as "leaf-clipping," which occurs in courtship. Apparently, for a male to successfully leave a group of chimpanzees with a female for consort, he must rely on female cooperation to slip away unnoticed. The "leaf-clipping" seems to serve this function. A male will make eye-contact with a female in estrus while placing a leaf in his mouth and then tearing the leaf and letting it drop. The male then quietly leaves, and shortly thereafter the estrous female will follow him. McGrew (1992) states that the male uses the "leaf-clipping" gesture as a subtle tool for capturing the attention of females. What Nishida noted was that this gesture is another cultural dialect difference between the two communities. The sexual behavior of the chimpanzees at Gombe has been extensively studied (McGinnes 1979; Tutin 1979; Goodall 1986), and there have been no reported observations of this behavior.

We are presently beginning a study of different communities of wild chimpanzees in hopes of examining other gestures that might be dialectical. The importance of the finding among the wild chimpanzees is that it demonstrates that gestural communication and acquisition of different forms of gestural communication is a behavior that is natural to chimpanzees, wild or captive.

CONCLUSION

The ape language research has demonstrated that apes can acquire and communicate with the signs of American Sign Language as well as other artificial communication systems. It has been found that chimpanzees can pass their signing skills on to the next generation, demonstrating the ability to culturally transmit their acquired language. In addition, they use their signs to spontaneously converse with each other when no humans are present. They will sign to themselves, they use their signs during imaginary play, and much more. The ape language behavior was found rich enough to provide texts that could be analyzed for a number of linguistic traits that are shared with human language.

Why has this research held such a controversial place in science when Darwinism maintains that the cognitive differences between apes and humans is one of degree? It is because many scientists still adhere to the Cartesian dark ages notion that "humans are outside of nature," in other words, different in kind from our fellow animals. Although this arrogant position may be popular and handy to justify exploitation and abuse, it is out of touch with biological reality and serves little else than to puff up human pretensions. A second problem is that the questions regarding ape language should not have been framed in the Aristotelian/Cartesian dichotomy of "is it language or is it not?" A better question would be: "To what degree do we share common communicative characteristics with our fellow animals and what are the adaptive functions that the similarities and differences serve in helping the individual and species survive?" The scientific evidence presented here clearly demonstrates that the difference between chimpanzees and humans is one of degree, just as it is with all our fellow animals. This evidence is consistent with the Darwinian notion of continuity—that we are all relatives. The chimpanzee and our other fellow apes just happen to be the next of kin in our phylogenetic family.

Primates in the Broader Context

Throughout this volume our focus has been on the nonhuman primates, their biology, behavior, and evolution. Although humans are mentioned in the context of cross-primate comparisons, no explicit discussions of humans are presented. In this brief section we turn our gaze inward and examine two important aspects of primate studies that are rarely mentioned: the history of the field of primatology and the way human cultures view and interact with our nonhuman primate relatives.

The field of primatology is an exciting hybrid of many disciplines with a dynamic and important history. It is always wise to get to know the individuals and history behind the data, hypotheses, and theories with which you are presented. The astute reader will have noticed the wide array of theoretical orientations, perspectives, and personalities amongst the more than thirty contributors in this volume. Here we have the embodiment of modern primatology, a diversity of opinion revolving around key concepts, traditions, and foci. Fedigan and Strum move quickly through a brief history of primatology, which will allow you to add a little context to the essays you have read.

Carter and Carter diverge from the "scientific" data-based analysis of nonhuman primate behavior to introduce a bit of human behavior: varied cultures' concepts, roles, and uses of the nonhuman primates. This essay provides a taste of the importance of the "other" primates in our human primate cultural world. Whether your goal is asking evolutionary questions, drawing physiological comparisons, or constructing mythical tales, there is no escaping the monkeys, apes, and prosimians climbing about in your family tree.

33

A Brief History of Primate Studies:
National Traditions, Disciplinary Origins,
and Stages in North American Field Research

Linda Marie Fedigan and Shirley C. Strum

The relationship of humans to our nonhuman primate relatives goes back almost as far as we can trace the human record in history and prehistory. Throughout this time and around the world, we have expressed strikingly diverse attitudes toward our primate relatives: we have eaten them as food, venerated them as deities and ancestral spirits, kept them for entertainment, portrayed them as symbols of evil and sin, seen them as comic imitations of ourselves, and used them as substitutes for humans in scientific study. Out of 3 million years of living alongside our primate relatives, it is only in the last 100 years, particularly in the 50 years since World War II, that humans have considered primates to be worthy of study in their own right. This science is sometimes called "primatology"—the study of the biology, behavior, ecology, and evolution of the prosimians, monkeys, and apes.

Even though the study of primates is relatively recent, the amount of research on primates is diverse. In this essay we will focus primarily on field studies of primate social behavior since 1950 in North America. Our objective is to trace some of the ideas about the nature of primate societies through different stages in the development of the discipline. To do this, we will outline the major stages and themes of each stage, as well as the key questions that have endured throughout the history of primate studies. And, to place this focused history into a larger context, we will begin by briefly describing how the study of primates arose in different places and how the major parental disciplines affected its development.

DIFFERENT NATIONAL TRADITIONS OF PRIMATE STUDIES

One of the unusual aspects of primatology is that it was independently and simultaneously invented at least twice in the 1950s, once by the Japanese and once by the Europeans and North Americans. Although they were aware of each other, Eastern and Western primatologists worked in relative isolation until the 1960s when translation of publications and visits to each other's field sites facilitated communication. There were also somewhat independent origins of British, Continental European, East Indian, Chinese, North American, and South American primate studies, but these groups of scientists communicated with each other a good bit more from the beginning. The national traditions of primatology that began relatively late (East Indian, Chinese, South American) developed in the climate of global conferences and international journals that prevailed after the early 1970s and so were not as isolated as the early ones. And some of the earlier national traditions (British and European) developed in parallel out of the field of ethology and so shared similar origins. Still, it is possible to characterize all of these national traditions as having had different histories and objectives, different influential figures and ideas, and different methodological preferences. At the risk of oversimplification, we will briefly introduce some of the distinctive features of several national traditions of primate studies.

Japanese primatology differs from Western primatology most clearly in its overriding emphasis on richly detailed descriptions of primate social behavior, its willingness to use anthropomorphic interpretation, its emphasis on proximate mechanisms (immediate causes of behavior), and its training of young scientists by sending them into the field with few preconceived theories about how the animals should behave and how scientists should collect data. As Pamela Asquith (1986) has described, the fundamental assumptions about primates are different in Japan and in the West. In North America and Europe, our Judeo-Christian heritage, Cartesian-based science, and more recent history of behaviorism and sociobiological theory make us reluctant to infer mental states in animals—that is, to grant them an inner life that might be contiguous with our own. The Japanese, however, do not see humans as set apart in nature from animals and find it appropriate to attribute motivation, feelings, and personality to monkeys. Even the possession of a soul is not believed to be unique to humans. Thus, anthropomorphism, the attribution of human-like mental states to animals, is not taboo in Japanese primatology as it is in the West.

Another distinguishing feature of our intellectual heritage is that Western scientists have been more profoundly influenced by Darwinian evolutionary theory than have the Japanese. Thus, we tend to be more concerned with ultimate, evolutionary adaptive explanations than with proximate mechanisms of behavior. The founding fathers of Japanese primatology, Kinji Imanishi and Junichiro Itani, established several practices that were later adopted by some Western scientists, for example: provisioning the animals to habituate them to human observation; taking the time to recognize and name individual animals and to track their kinship relations; attributing personality to individuals and culture to groups of primates; and conducting cooperative long-term studies over many years to understand individual life histories, group traditions, and population trends.

Today, the channels of communication between Japanese and Western scientists are more open, and the two sciences are converging. Some Japanese primatologists use theories and methods borrowed from the West and, when they do, their papers are sometimes indistinguishable from those of Western scientists. In spite of the many differences between the origins of Japanese and North American primatology, one interesting parallel did exist—scientists from both traditions began their study of primates with the primary objective of better understanding human origins.

Research on primates began somewhat differently in Britain and Continental Europe. Rather than a search for the origins of human sociality, the European study of primates grew out of the fields of ethology (the naturalistic and evolutionary study of animal behavior) and ecology. Primates were seen as simply another set of species (albeit complex, long-lived species) in which to investigate the evolution, ecology, and mechanisms of behavior. Hans Kummer, who supervised a large number of the current generation of Swiss and German primatologists, was influenced by Heini Hediger, among other ethologists. Trained specifically as an experimental psychologist, Kummer taught his own students that hypotheses about primate behavior need to be tested through experiments as well as by collecting observational data. Kummer (1995) established a long-term field site to study hamadryas baboons in Ethiopia and set up colonies of hamadryas baboons and longtailed macaques in Switzerland for captive research. Another influential European, who founded the "Dutch School" of primatology, is Jan van Hooff, who like Kummer was influenced by classical ethologists. Van Hooff studied under Desmond Morris in Britain (the latter a student of Niko Tinbergen) before returning to the University of Utrecht and establishing the colony of chimpanzees at Arnhem that have been the subject of much influential research. French primatologists, such as Annie and Jean-Pierre Gautier, were trained as ecologists and have been prominent in research on the guenons of Central and West

Africa, as well as establishing the captive colonies of *Cercopithecus* species maintained at the Paimpont Biological Station. The study of prosimians was also pioneered by French ecologists-zoologists, such as Arlette and Jean-Jacques Petter and Pierre Charles-Dominique.

In Britain, Robert Hinde, John Crook, and K. R. L. Hall are generally credited with having founded the study of primates. Both Hinde and Crook were originally influenced by founding ethologists such as Niko Tinbergen and ornithologists such as David Lack. Hinde and Crook both began their careers studying birds before moving to primates and, eventually, to humans. Hall was a psychologist who carried out extensive and pioneering fieldwork on the terrestrial monkey species of Africa, such as patas, vervets, and baboons, but he died tragically early in his career. Hinde (1983) supervised a large number of the current generation of primatologists who are prominent in both British and American primate studies, and he established the "Madingley" colony of rhesus macaques for the study of mother-infant relationships. Hinde's interest in infant development, and his distinction between three levels of social behavior (momentary interactions, long-term relationships, and the larger context of social structure), spawned a substantial body of diverse research on primate societies. His insistence on maintaining a balanced research program based on Tinbergen's classic "Four Whys" (i.e., four types of questions about behavior: causation, ontogeny, function, and evolution) means that his students have addressed research questions at many levels.

Thus far, with the exception of Japan, we have outlined the origins of primatology in countries where nonhuman primates themselves are not indigenous. What about places in which prosimians, monkeys, and apes are native, so-called host countries? The growth of primate studies in Argentina, Brazil, Mexico, Kenya, Madagascar, India, China, and Thailand, for example, has been slower and more recent than elsewhere, primarily because these economically underdeveloped nations have different concerns to address, such as poverty, population, and development. However, there are fledgling sciences of primatology in these nations,

and as one example we will very briefly outline the history of primate studies in Brazil.

The emergence of Brazilian primatology in the early 1980s can be traced to two major sources: laboratory studies of callitrichids (marmosets and tamarins) that focused on medically related topics as well as social behavior and field studies of monkeys that were motivated by conservation concerns. Although scientific interest in the monkeys of Brazil was originally stimulated by visiting European and North American researchers, a critical mass of Brazilian primatologists had formed by the mid-1980s and continues to grow. Emilia Yamamoto, a past president of the Brazilian Primatological Society, argues that Brazilian primatology is distinctive in drawing most of its students from the larger area of conservation research (rather than anthropology, psychology, or zoology) and in its strong focus on female relations, resulting from the prominent position of female monkeys in callitrichid social systems (Strum and Fedigan, in press a; Yamamoto and Alencar, in press).

DIFFERENT DISCIPLINARY ORIGINS (1920–1950)

If you attend one of the biennial meetings of the International Primatological Society, not only will you meet scientists from different nations around the world but you will also rub shoulders with researchers who come from many different disciplinary backgrounds. Primate studies are carried out by scientists affiliated with departments of anatomy, anthropology, biology, conservation, ecology, medicine, psychology, and zoology, to name a few. But it is fair to say that the study of primates in North America has had three major disciplinary sources—the fields of physical anthropology, psychology, and zoology.

In North America, systematic empirical research on the behavior of free-ranging primates was begun by the psychologist Robert M. Yerkes, who became interested in the study of great apes in the 1920s. In 1929 he and his wife, Ada, published a landmark volume, *The Great Apes,* summarizing all that was then known about these animals and calling for more and better research on them. Yerkes established the first major American primate breeding and research laboratory at Orange Park, Florida, which was later moved to Atlanta, Georgia, and renamed the Yerkes Regional Primate Research Center. Yerkes also encouraged young students to go out into the field to study primates in their natural habitat. The most successful of Yerkes's students was Clarence R. Carpenter, who is considered an early pioneer of primate field studies. Although he had been trained originally to study pigeons, Carpenter developed many successful techniques for observing primates in the wild that are still widely used today.

Carpenter conducted several influential studies of primates in the 1930s, studying howler monkeys and spider monkeys in Panama and gibbons in Thailand. He described the howlers of Barro Colorado Island as living in relaxed, communal harmony, with groups held together by affiliation and mutualistic relations (Carpenter 1934). After trapping and shipping 500 rhesus monkeys to Cayo Santiago Island off Puerto Rico in 1938, Carpenter subsequently studied the sexual behavior of these macaques for two years prior to the outbreak of World War II. His main concern was to integrate social behavior with physiology through the study of social patterns such as sexual behavior, but he was also very interested in the dynamics and maintenance of social groups. He recognized the two-way interaction between field and captive studies —that it would be impossible to understand the data from captive studies without knowledge of the species in the wild, and that experiments under controlled conditions in captivity would help us to understand the patterns of behavior in the field.

The integration of field and laboratory research continues to be an important issue in primate studies today. There is a tendency for psychologists to be associated with laboratory studies of the "mind" in areas such as learning and cognition, but many primatologists trained in psychology also carry out fieldwork. Probably the most famous body of research in psychologically based primatology is deprivation studies, originally carried out by Harry Harlow, who trained many of today's leading researchers in laboratory studies of primate behavior,

and whose infant deprivation research began as an accident. Trying to raise healthier monkeys for lab research, Harlow took infants away from their mothers at an early age. The results were surprising: these infants were psychologically, socially, and sexually disturbed. Thus began a series of experiments aimed at understanding the necessary elements for normal development in social primates (Harlow 1974).

Although Hugh Gilmore's (1981) historical analysis of primatology argues that zoologists had the easiest entry into primate field research because zoology already had a strong tradition in the naturalistic study of animal behavior, the fields of zoology and ecology were not as influential during the formative years of primate fieldwork in North America as were psychology and anthropology. Ecologists and zoologists did not have a special interest in primates per se and often found that shorter-lived species were more useful in exploring and testing evolutionary hypotheses. The relative contribution of these different parental disciplines has changed in recent years as scientists have begun to explore new ecological and evolutionary theories and models in the context of primate behavior (Southwick and Smith 1986).

Physical anthropology and anatomy were major sources of early interest in primate studies. Darwin himself devoted one appendix in his 1871 book, *Sexual Selection and the Descent of Man*, to a discussion of the anatomy or, more specifically, the "Faces and Hinder-ends" of primates. Two anatomists working in the 1920s who turned their research interests to primates were Adolph Schultz in the United States and Solly Zuckerman in Britain. Schultz established the measurement techniques that are still used in primate anatomy today, and Zuckerman is most remembered for his 1932 book, *The Social Life of Monkeys and Apes*. In it he proposed that female primates are continually receptive, that sexual bonds are the basis for primate society, and that dominance interactions between males over sexual access to females are a major force in primate social life. When Zuckerman conducted a study of the hamadryas baboons at the London Zoo in the late 1920s and early 1930s, the natural behavior patterns and social system of this species were unknown. Today we know that hamadryas in the wild live in polygynous (one male, multifemale) social groups. This was not the case at the London Zoo at that time, where 100 adult males, strangers to each other, were put on an island with only 30 females. In the resulting chaotic fighting, many monkeys (and almost all the females) died. Zuckerman thought he was watching normal behavior, and he extrapolated from this human-induced catastrophe to a general theory that sexual competition must be the basis of primate social life. Although the first wave of field studies after World War II would disprove most of Zuckerman's conclusions, his book was very influential in generating primate research.

It was a later anatomist who had the greatest influence on the origins of primate field studies. In the early 1950s, Sherwood Washburn published a rationale for the naturalistic study of primates as part of anthropology, and he began to train a long line of anthropological primatologists who went on to train their own students and to form a school of thought that became a major force in North American primate research. Washburn's "New Physical Anthropology" (1951) moved beyond a merely static measurement of bones or dissection of cadavers to an adaptive view of anatomical features. To understand these anatomical adaptations, Washburn argued that physical anthropology must become the dynamic, holistic study of human evolution and behavior. An important part of the "New Physical Anthropology," in his view, was the study of our nonhuman primate relatives in their natural environments, and thus Washburn established the value of watching how primates actually behave in the wild.

STAGES AND ISSUES IN NORTH AMERICAN PRIMATE FIELD STUDIES

Having outlined how field studies of primates originated and varied from nation to nation, we now turn to a selected history of how primate field research has developed in North America since the early 1950s. To make this still immense topic more manageable, we will concentrate on one aspect: how and why our ideas about primate society have changed over time. When we examined the history of ideas about primate society (see Strum and Fedigan, in press b), we found that there were regularities in the way data were collected and interpreted. These regularities suggest that the study of primate society since World War II can be divided into four stages:

Stage One (1950–1965): The Natural History Phase

Stage Two (1965–1975): The Discovery and Dilemma of Variability Phase

Stage Three (1975–1985): The Era of Sociobiology

Stage Four (1985–present): The Advent of Behavioral Ecology

Even though these stages are somewhat arbitrary, they help us to illustrate changing themes, theoretical issues, and methodological practices.

We also found that throughout this history scientists have been interested in a fundamental set of questions about primate societies. These enduring issues may be differently phrased and variably answered in the various stages, but they remain the foundational, driving questions of the study of primate society.

1. Why do primates live in social groups?

2. What is the social structure of the group, and what holds society together?

3. What is the relationship of the group to its environment?

4. What are the roles of aggression, dominance, sex, and affiliation in primate societies?

5. What is the basic nature of males, females, and the relationship between the sexes?

6. What is the pattern of ontogeny, development, and socialization?

7. What are the roles of instinct, learning, and cognition in behavior?

8. What are the patterns of intra- and interspecies variability?

9. What is the evolutionary relationship between different social grouping patterns?

10. What is unique about humans, and what is shared with our primate relatives?

By showing how the answers to these questions change and shift, we can begin to gain a concrete sense of how the naturalistic study of primate behavior in North America has developed in response to new methods and theories, the accumulation of data, and the larger social and cultural context.

The Natural History Phase (1950–1965)

Prior to 1950, Zuckerman and Carpenter had both conducted research on the social behavior of primates. Among their concerns was why primates live in social groups. They had each resolved this issue quite differently. Zuckerman asserted that sex was the social glue and that male competition, expressed through competition and dominance, was the organizing principle. Carpenter's communal howlers, in contrast, stayed together through cooperation, affiliation, and mutual interest. These two foundational ideas were to lay dormant for nearly twenty years until the disruptive effects of World War II finally abated and a number of other factors converged to produce the first big wave of primate field studies in the early 1950s. Some of the factors that played a role in the dramatic surge of primate field studies at that time were Washburn's "New Physical Anthropology"; the Darwin Centennial Celebrations; restored funding for field research; renewed interest in primates as biomedical and evolutionary models; and improved technology (i.e., easier air travel to remote areas and better antimalarial drugs).

The rush was on to get out into the field and study free-ranging primates. Scientists from the United States, Britain, France, Switzerland, and Japan traveled to the tropical countries where prosimians, monkeys, and apes are found. Many primate species, such as baboons, patas, vervets, macaques, langurs, and lemurs, had never before been the objects of sustained and systematic research in their native habitats, and everything observed about them in the wild was new to science.

The chimpanzees and gorillas that had eluded early attempts at naturalistic study were successfully observed during this stage by Jane Goodall and George Schaller, respectively. These first studies were very descriptive in nature and, much like early ethnographies in anthropology, covered a smorgasbord of topics: sexual behavior, maternal care, infant development, play, dominance hierarchies, ranging and feeding patterns, and territoriality. This can be termed the "natural history" phase of primatology because the major mandate was to collect descriptions of as many primate societies as possible using natural history methods.

Many of this first wave of primate researchers were trained as anthropologists and thus looked to the social sciences, especially to structural-functional models of human societies, for their interpretations. In structural-functional models, social behavior is seen as part of an ordered, integrated system in which individuals play patterned roles that function to fulfill the needs of the group. Washburn and his students were particularly interested in what came to be called the "primate pattern," basic adaptive features common across the order, and this framework helped us to understand human behavior and origins in an evolutionary context. In addition to anthropologists motivated by this agenda, biologists were also initiating important field projects in the 1950s. Some of these zoologists and ecologists returned to species and sites previously examined by Carpenter. For example, N. Collias and Charles Southwick returned to Barro Colorado Island to study howlers, Southwick went to India to study rhesus monkeys, and Stuart Altmann carried out a two-year study of the macaques that Carpenter had earlier transferred to Cayo Santiago.

Studies by two of Washburn's students can be used to exemplify this stage: Irven DeVore studied baboons in Rhodesia and Kenya, and Phyllis Dolhinow (formerly Phyllis Jay) studied langurs in North India. Although DeVore's reports described many different aspects of baboon behavior, his work is mainly remembered for its model of baboon society that emphasized male dominance, competition, and aggression (see DeVore 1965a). DeVore also collaborated with Hall to review baboon behavior in several locations and several species and concluded that baboon society was remarkably similar across locations and environments. In contrast, Dolhinow described langur groups from North India as peaceful and relaxed, with the presence of infants as the major cohesive factor. Infants were readily passed between females who acted as "aunts" or babysitters, and although males helped to coordinate group movement, they were otherwise rather peripheral (Jay 1965, 1968). These two models of what maintains cohesion in primate society show a striking parallel to the earlier, pre-World War II models that had been proposed: Zuckerman's baboon model (sex and dominance) and Carpenter's howler monkey model (communality and mutualism). Thus, in stage one, the answer to the nature of primate society was still unresolved. However, Zuckerman's theory that continual sex is the basis of primate society was seriously weakened when it was shown in this first wave of field studies that many primates have breeding and nonbreeding seasons.

In spite of the fact that many monkey and ape species were first successfully studied in the 1950s and 1960s, the predominant image of primates during this period was drawn from the idea that baboon society was structured around a male dominance hierarchy and relied heavily on male aggressive abilities. The subsequent baboon model of primate social life so captured the scientific and popular imagination, that baboons were often taken as representative of all monkey society, and monkey society was thought to represent all primate society, including that of humans. Popular interest in primates was intense after World War II as people looked to animals for answers about basic human nature. For example, researchers tried to determine the fundamental causes of aggressive behavior in animals in order to fathom what could give rise to aggressive levels so extreme in humans as to lead to global warfare.

The Discovery and Dilemma of Variability Phase (1965–1975)

Stage two is best characterized as the period that exposed the variability of primate behavior and so-

ciety. The number of species that were first studied during this decade is too large to enumerate here, but these studies served to emphasize the differences among species and to challenge the notion that there was a unified "primate pattern." It was, however, the reexamination of the *same* species in *new* locations that gave the most convincing evidence for the extent of variability in primate social and ecological patterns. During stage two, studies of baboons, vervets, chimpanzees, and langurs took place in different environments from the earlier research. The resulting descriptions of species behavior were diverse and often contradictory. This posed a major challenge to previous models and resulted in some skepticism about the usefulness of primate behavioral studies, particularly for anthropologists.

Studies of baboons and langurs during this period provide a useful illustration of the key themes and issues. In the late 1960s and early 1970s, studies of baboons in new locations by Thelma Rowell, Tim Ransom, Glen Hausfater, and Shirley Strum expanded and reevaluated parts of the stage one "male dominance" baboon model. For example, it was realized that females, not just males, had a dominance hierarchy and that females and their kin formed the core of the group since males transferred between groups. Even the importance of the male dominance hierarchy was questioned by Rowell (1974) and Strum (1982), and portrayal of the roles of males and females subsequently shifted.

During stage one, hanuman langurs had been studied by Phyllis Dolhinow (Jay) in North India, where they lived in multimale, multifemale groups characterized by peaceful, affiliative relations. A new study of these langurs in South India by Yukimara Sugiyama (1965) reported that they lived in groups containing only one male. Extra males lived in roving all-male groups that sometimes aggressively attacked the reproductive groups, defeating the alpha male and killing some of the infants in the group. Mothers who had lost their infants seemed to become sexually receptive soon thereafter and to mate with whichever of the new males had taken over leadership of the group. Following on the heels of the peace-loving langurs from the 1960s, this shocking finding did not seem to make sense. Existing theory, with its emphasis on a fundamental primate pattern and on a structural-functional model of society, suggested an interpretation of infant-killing as simply abnormal. But were the differences between the reports on langurs due to differences in the animals themselves, or to outside factors, such as observer bias?

Further evidence for other variations in social organization and behavior also raised the same question. Were the differences natural or artifacts? To reliably address this dilemma, better methods were championed. One way to reduce observer bias was to standardize the sampling of behavior and quantify the techniques used to collect data. Jean Altmann's influential review (1974) and evaluation of sampling methods in animal behavior was published at this time. But even with better methods variability persisted.

If the differences were due to variation in the primates themselves (i.e., "real" differences), the question then became: What causes behavioral variation? There were two main types of interpretations available: phylogenetic and ecological. Differences found *among* species were attributed to distinctive evolutionary heritages, that is, to phylogeny. Differences *within* species were ascribed to ecological pressures that varied between locations or habitats. Perhaps DeVore's baboons behaved differently from Rowell's because he studied them on the open savannah and she studied them in the forests of East Africa. Perhaps Sugiyama's langurs in South India were polygynous and aggressive because of the stresses of living near urban areas, whereas Dolhinow's langurs in North India lived in more rural areas with a lower population density of both humans and langurs.

Thus, attention turned to the relationship of the group to its environment and to the ecological and evolutionary significance of different social grouping patterns. At first, encompassing ecological models were proposed to account for social patterns. For example, John Crook and Steve Gartlan (1966) designed a model of "adaptive grades" of social organization where the species were sorted into one of five grades in relation to major environmental factors. This model failed, however, because there was as much variability within these "grades" as among them. However, this was the beginning of

an improved ecological context for primate behavioral studies.

The Era of Sociobiology (1975–1985)

Thomas Kuhn (1970), an influential philosopher of science, argued that a science matures and changes not through the gradual accretion of knowledge and slow development of more accurate theories but by the quantum replacement of one overarching explanatory model ("paradigm") with another. This he called a "scientific revolution." These revolutions, or major shifts in thinking, occur when the existing paradigm seems increasingly unable to explain certain observations. Often, an outsider or outside theory then succeeds in invading this fertile terrain as scientists become convinced that they need another model to explain their observations. Although not everyone agrees with Kuhn's thesis, it can be argued that something like a scientific revolution occurred in primate studies between 1975 and 1985. The Washburnian rationale for North American primate studies that had served the discipline so well since the 1950s began to falter. Two of its inherent assumptions were severely challenged: (1) that we can use the study of prosimians, monkeys, and apes to discern fundamental primate patterns that are also applicable to humans; and (2) that social science theories (e.g., structural-functionalism) can be applied to animal societies.

The major contender as a new explanatory model, or paradigm, for primate behavior was sociobiology. But sociobiology was not the only important contributor to organizing and interpreting ideas about primate behavior during stage three. At least four other factors played major roles: long-term studies began to bear fruit; new studies of previously unexamined species continued to provide exceptions and challenges to every rule; studies of female primates by women scientists challenged prior emphasis on males; and interest in cognitive theories emerged as Western scientists began to widely and seriously consider the possibility that animals, too, have minds.

The impact of sociobiology on primate research was revolutionary not in its insistence on an evolutionary framework but in its shift of the unit of selection from the group to the individual and, ultimately, to the gene. The theoretical framework of sociobiology explains social behavior entirely in terms of self-maximizing, biological processes, the most important of which are self-replication and reproductive success. Thus, this model focused questions of adaptive behavior on the individual rather than the group or the species. Fitness now had two components—that which belonged strictly to the individual and that which reflected back on the individual through the success or performance of closely related individuals (kin). Altruism and cooperation were both transformed into selfish strategies that could be used to improve reproductive success under certain conditions, and behaviors that had seemed strange and abnormal before now acquired evolutionary interpretations. For example, infanticide was viewed by sociobiologists as an evolutionary tactic instead of an abnormality (e.g., Hrdy 1977a). This extreme act of aggression was seen as one way that an individual could improve its reproductive success at the expense of others. Aggression in general was also reinterpreted as an individual rather than a group tactic, and whether it was advantageous to be aggressive or cooperative was seen to depend on a range of factors in the social and ecological environment. In the sociobiological framework, variability among and within species was expected and believed to result from strong selection on individuals to employ a variety of strategically adaptive behaviors in specific local circumstances.

Space does not permit a thorough discussion of the impact of sociobiological thinking on ideas about primate societies, but in general sociobiology addressed and reinterpreted almost every dimension of primate behavior, including the nature of competition and cooperation, the importance of family and kinship, and the relationship between individuals (particularly parents and offspring), between males, between females, and between males and females. Sociobiology also changed the language of explanation. By combining economic language with game theory, many new metaphors were generated about "trade-offs" of "costs and benefits" and "the battle" of "tactics" and "strategies." Three powerful subtheories of sociobiology—kin selection, reciprocal altru-

ism, and parental investment—have all been applied to primate behavior. These theories, and their fundamental premise of self-maximization, and the linguistic metaphors of sociobiology have all been hotly contested within primatology. Nonetheless, primate studies flourished in this new intellectual environment (Gray 1985).

A second factor that revolutionized this stage was the rich information that began to come in from long-term studies of primates in the wild. Even though these studies had been under way for some time, it was only when they had lasted at least as long as the life span of the species under study, that is twenty years or more, that their full effect was felt (e.g., Goodall 1986; Strum 1987). The best known examples of such longitudinal projects are the studies of chimpanzees at the Gombe Stream and Mahale Mountains Reserves in Tanzania; gorillas at Karisoke in Uganda; orangutans at Tanjung Puting in Borneo; ringtailed lemurs at Berenty in Madagascar; Japanese macaques at Arashiyama and Takasakiyama in Japan; rhesus macaques on Cayo Santiago; baboons at Amboseli, Gilgil/Chololo, Gombe, and Mikumi; howlers at Barro Colorado Island; and muriquis at Caratinga in Brazil. All of these long-term projects share some crucial characteristics. Foremost is the identification of individuals and the tracking of genealogical lines. Individuals become much more than members of age and sex classes, and following them through their lives and the lives of their offspring produces rich detail and essential information on many topics. Longitudinal studies demonstrated the value of life history, demographic, and ecological data and provided evidence that behavior varies over time as well as across groups and species, suggesting that local history may provide as much an explanation for current behavior as ultimate selective factors.

During this stage, researchers also made a more sustained effort to study the truly hard to observe species—those living in the tops of the canopy, or active by night, or showing a preference for mangrove swamps, or relying on cryptic concealment. Despite the difficulties of obtaining information on the social behavior of these animals, the new studies on prosimians and New World monkeys did yield some provocative results that challenged our generalizations based on the behavior of Old World primates. For example, the study of a substantial number of different lemur species raised the possibility that females may be dominant over males in most of this primate family (Jolly 1984). Research on the dispersal patterns of neotropical monkeys suggested that most species in the family Cebidae are female-dispersed, and that in some species, such as the muriquis and the spider monkeys, it is the males of a community that are related and closely bonded rather than the females, as in most Old World cercopithecines (Strier 1990).

Changing views of the cognitive abilities of animals also contributed to shifts in the images of primate society. Much earlier, Alison Jolly had argued for the central importance of social behavior in the evolution of primate intelligence, and Nicholas Humphrey had proposed that the large brain of primates was the result of adaptation to the complexities of social life. But it was really Donald Griffin (1976, 1984) who spearheaded a new movement to make animal "mind" part of the study of animal behavior, arguing that behaviorism had robbed animals of the cognitive abilities that were clearly essential to their survival.

Another prevalent theme of this stage was the study of female primates by women scientists. Although there had always been a number of women primatologists and many descriptions of female primates, the disproportionate influence of the baboon model, with its emphasis on male dominance and aggression, had sometimes made it seem as if females were unimportant. By the early 1980s women scientists began to change this view, some of them stating overtly that they were influenced by societal concerns over the Women's Movement (Fedigan 1982; Hrdy 1984b; Small 1984). Female primates were documented to be important social forces in their groups, and this argument was synergistic with other stage three trends: sociobiological theory included an emphasis on female competitive strategies, long-term studies showed that female kin groups formed the core structure of many primate societies, and the changing view of animal "mind" implied that both males and females made strategic decisions.

By the end of stage three the idea that there might be one basic nature of primate society had been abandoned. Variability, documented over the past twenty years, had become enshrined in theory. Now, to answer the question "what is the social structure of the group, and what holds society together?" we have to first consider what species, what group, what habitat, and at what point in the group's history.

The Advent of Behavioral Ecology (1985–present)

Stage four is the hardest to characterize for several reasons. The most obvious is that it is our current history, and thus, still unfinished. But the difficulty of depicting the present stage is also the result of growing fragmentation and specialization within the discipline and increasingly complex interactions among theories, methods, and other intrinsic aspects of science, as well as between science and its larger social context.

The sociobiological decade ended with a number of new answers to old questions. Yet despite its unifying "self-maximization" premise, there were anomalous observations that presaged the trends of the present period. For example, social complexity in primates implied higher cognitive abilities that were not just "gene strategies." And social strategies obviously involved cooperation and affiliation, as well as competition and exploitation. Stage four is perhaps best characterized as an era that has moved away from a strongly reductionist application of sociobiological theory. As it was used in the earlier decade, sociobiology emphasized genetic determinism. By contrast, the behavioral-ecological models favored in the present period espouse a more multicausal view of adaptation that emphasizes the interaction of ecological and social processes.

Behavioral ecology is primarily concerned with survival and reproductive strategies: how primates find enough food, avoid predators, and balance the conflicting demands their environment places on them. Both proximate and ultimate questions are asked about the ways in which animals interact with their living and nonliving environment. This broader perspective has placed greater emphasis on the idea that primates are part of larger communities, which contrasts with previous approaches that treated each species separately.

As one example, behavioral ecology has taken a fresh look at why primates live in social groups. During stage four, primatologists have pursued a lively debate about the relative importance of enhanced predator protection (van Schaik 1989) as compared to the cooperative defense of resources (Wrangham 1987a) as the ultimate and primary benefits of group living. Obviously, the answer to why primates live in groups is multifaceted and involves a trade-off between increased predator protection and decreased foraging opportunities.

How groups function has also become important. Research has shown that, far from living a simple life, many primates are immersed in systems of social complexity based on diverse strategies of competition and defense. These depend on social skills, knowledge, and the creation and careful management of social relationships. What makes an individual successful goes far beyond its age, size, or strength. Social complexity implies cognitive as well as social skills. To use social strategies, animal actors have to perceive the multiple dimensions of relationships, to predict the combined effects of sequential or simultaneous polyadic interactions, and to plan and manipulate such interactions for their own ends. Thus, the study of dominance and other aspects of competition has advanced from a rather mechanistic model of "brute" force to an approach that parallels the study of human politics, with all its intricacies of motivations, objectives, manipulations, and deceptions (de Waal 1982, 1989). Research now focuses on phenomena such as alliances and coalitions, reconciliation, and how aggressive and nonaggressive strategies are integrated during an individual's lifetime (e.g., Strum 1994).

The cognitive revolution stimulated by the discovery of social complexity ignited an interesting controversy about the evolutionary origins of primate intelligence. The case for the social function of primate intelligence had been made much earlier, but this idea lay dormant for many years. Katie Milton revived the discussion by constructing an ecological hypothesis that focused on the need for primates to have cognitive maps for tracking seasonally available food resources essential to survival. Subsequently, the origins and evolution of cognitive abilities in primates has been explored by a variety of investigators (Byrne and Whiten 1988). In general, the social origins hypothesis for primate intelligence has had more advocates than the ecological origins model. As just one example, Dorothy Cheney and Robert Seyfarth (1990) used experimental playbacks of vocalizations to demonstrate that vervets not only recognize other individuals from their calls but can also recognize relationships between other members of the group, such as that between a mother and her infant.

During this stage, as previously, shifting geopolitics have affected research patterns. For example, studies of New World monkeys and Malagasy lemurs have flourished, in part because these areas are now open to foreign researchers and are increasingly stable, whereas many parts of Africa and Asia are closed to primate research because of political unrest. Two other ways in which the worlds inside and outside primate studies have converged are in the areas of animal welfare (animal rights) and conservation. The recognition of animal "mind" by Western scientists had unintended consequences for social action. The link between mind, awareness, and suffering provided the animal welfare movement with its primate agenda and made captive primates the most obvious candidates for "liberation." Animal welfare advocates alienated many scientists when they targeted all laboratory research involving primates, but, by raising their concerns, they also convinced many scientists to design their research to take into account the welfare and emotional well-being of the captive primates (Blum 1994). Animal rights have also been championed. In its most ardent statement, known as the Great Ape Project, a variety of scientists and others have argued that we should extend basic human rights to the great apes (Cavalieri and Singer 1993). Their argument is based on scientific evidence about ape minds, as well as the social complexity and language abilities of great apes. For animal rights activists, admitting apes into the human family is the first step in reconsidering the rights of many other species. At present, this remains a very controversial and emotionally charged proposal.

Just as the line between science and advocacy is increasingly blurred in the arena of animal welfare and animal rights, so the line between basic and applied science has dissolved in the area of conservation. Although primatologists have always been concerned about the status of primates in the wild, now no one is able to ignore the vulnerability of their subjects. Habitat destruction, medical research that relies on certain primate species, conflicts between farmers and primate "pests" throughout the developing world, the increased killing of monkeys and apes for "bushmeat" as logging penetrates deeper and deeper into tropical forest, and the attraction of primates as pets and for exhibition have all spelled disaster for already dwindling populations. It has become very clear that more and better techniques are needed to assess the status of vulnerable populations and to safeguard them. New techniques, such as the rapid assessment of population viability, and management tools such as reintroduction and translocation are the beginning of this new wave (Arambulo et al. 1993; Benirschke 1986; Western, Wright, and Strum 1994).

CONCLUSION

We have used changing ideas of primate society to illustrate how the discipline has changed over the last fifty years, a small window into the history of primate field studies. It is obvious that our under-standing of primates is increasingly based on more information on more species in more environments. These data are both longitudinal and comparative among groups and species. Today, they include more ecology and biology than ever before. There have been important refinements in theory. Behavioral ecology, sociobiology, and cognitive ethology all present heuristic and intelligible frameworks for explaining the complexity that has been unearthed. Better methods of data collection, analysis, and modeling help us to agree on what constitutes data, even if we do not always agree on what the data mean. And, although many questions remain, no one could doubt that at the end of the twentieth century we have a better understanding of the diversity of primate societies and the reasons for this diversity than in the era of Zuckerman and Carpenter when field studies of primates first began.

ACKNOWLEDGMENTS

We would like to thank the participants of the 1996 Wenner-Gren conference in Brazil on "Changing Images of Primate Societies." These primatologists and science studies scholars from around the world expanded our horizons and increased our understanding of the multiple origins and different national traditions of primate studies. We also thank Sydel Silverman of the Wenner-Gren Foundation for Anthropological Research for supporting our inquiries into the history and nature of primate field studies. We gratefully acknowledge Rebecca Feasby for editorial assistance, and NSERCC (Natural Sciences and Engineering Research Council of Canada) for funding LMF's research.

34

Cultural Representations of Nonhuman Primates

Allisa Carter and Chris Carter

Humans and nonhuman primates have been interacting for a long time, perhaps as long as humanity has even existed. Almost everywhere that we find fossil hominid remains millions of years old we also find fossil monkeys. It is not surprising then that we have a long history of different representations of nonhuman primates in human culture. In some cultures, nonhuman primates are sacred figures, and monkeys may be seen as the embodiment of a god. In others, monkeys and apes are seen as evil and ugly and symbolize the worst in humanity. Sometimes nonhuman primates are seen as mischievous sidekicks that are always good for a laugh. Starting with the ancient Egyptian religion, we will see all of these representations of nonhuman primates in many cultures. From Chinese mythology to Zulu folktales, and from Medieval Europe to modern Hollywood, nonhuman primates have long been a focal point of human culture.

MONKEYS AS RELIGIOUS SYMBOLS

Some of the oldest cultural images of nonhuman primates are those of the sacred baboons of ancient Egypt, where hamadryas baboons were religious symbols over three thousand years ago. The monkey god was known as Thoth and is thought to have been a symbol of male virility (Morris and Morris 1966). Timekeeping, especially the lunar

and solar calendars, was also integral to Egyptian religion. Thoth was considered a lunar divinity, and images of hamadryas baboons have been recovered on ancient timepieces. Many of these sacred baboons were embalmed and mummified, some even in the same manner as important figures in Egyptian society. Apparently, many baboons were also kept in Thebes, where a large monkey cemetery was excavated (Morris and Morris 1966). Another Egyptian god, known as Hapi, was a human figure with a baboon head. This god was thought to watch over the spirits of the dead when they appeared before Osiris for judgment. Clearly Egyptians held their baboon neighbors in high esteem.

In Hindu society, the hanuman langur is second in importance amongst sacred animals only to the cow and snake. Hanuman is the Hindu god who rescued the wife of King Rama when she was stolen by Ravana, King of Lanka (Hrdy 1977b). The tales of Hanuman go back to the *Ramayana*, dated to around 500 B.C. Because of this noble association, the monkeys known as *Semnopithecus entellus* have enjoyed a privileged place in Indian society for thousands of years. "Originally, the hanuman monkey was the guardian god of each settlement, and, by tradition, the first duty of the founder of a new village was to erect a statue of the monkey-god and arrange for it to be kept decorated with daubs of vermilion" (Morris and Morris 1966: 21).

Indian langurs have a very distinct morphology, with a sleek gray coat and jet black hands and faces. A Hindu myth explains that this color pattern is due to the noble monkey's theft of a delicious mango, which he wanted to give to the people of Bengal, from the garden of a giant in Ceylon. Unfortunately, the monkey was caught, and the giant set him on fire. By the time the monkey could douse the flames, his hands and face were scorched. In modern Indian society, langurs typically are not harmed by the local human population, and this has contributed to their prolific spread across the continent, particularly in urban areas. In contrast to the Egyptians and Indians, some religious views of nonhuman primates were not so favorable.

It was during the Middle Ages in Europe that nonhuman primates first took on a more sinister image as Christian icons of evil. The repugnance shown at the idea of shared evolutionary ancestry with apes by such nineteenth-century figures as Disraeli, Bishop Wilberforce, and Owen has a long history in Christianity. The original impetus for symbolizing monkeys and apes as kin to the devil may have been a reaction against the Egyptian worship of Thoth and Hapi. In the early period of Christianity, Egypt was seen as a "land of darkness" and also as a prime example of the evils of idolatry. Their sacred baboon idol, then, was a symbol of everything Christianity was not. Over time, the image of the ape came to be associated with images of Satan because both were thought to be imitators of good beings. The devil imitated God, whereas apes were thought to be ugly imitations of humans. In an excellent volume that details the development of the ape as a Christian symbol, H. W. Janson (1952) shows that in ninth-century A.D. illustrations of Psalm 77, the people of Israel are menaced by "a goat-footed, horned satyr and hairy and sinister ape who bears the identifying notation *simia*" (p. 18). Over time, most Christian representations of apes metamorphosed the animals either into direct depictions of the devil or one of the devil's minions. Even pre-Christian stories about apes were adapted to take on a more wicked tone.

One of Aesop's fables has it that a mother ape gives birth to twins, one of whom she loves and the other she hates. She forces the hated infant to ride on her back and hugs the loved one to her bo-

som, but embraces it so tightly that it dies. In the thirteenth century, Christian preachers adapted this story so that the mother ape symbolized a sinner, and the hated child became the weight of her sins on her back. In the end, after killing the infant at her breast, the sins weigh her down so heavily that she is captured and killed by hunters. Thus, the story was transformed from having a moral of "sometimes too much affection is bad" to "if you sin, you will eventually be punished" (Janson 1952). In stark contrast to the Egyptian and Hindu images of monkeys and apes, Medieval Christianity demonized the animals, creating an archetype that persists to this day.

Monkeys also play an important role in the mythology of Buddhism. The story of how Buddhism came to be introduced to China is told in the *Hsi-yu-Chi,* or the *Record of a Journey to the Western Paradise,* written by Wu Cheng'en. In this story, the hero begins as a normal "stone monkey," but he soon leads his fellow monkeys to the magical Mountain of Many Flowers and is rewarded with a promotion to Monkey King. The story of the Monkey King is divided into two parts. In the first, the Monkey King stirs up trouble in heaven for the gods until finally Buddha himself must intervene, trapping the monkey under his cosmic thumb. In the second part of the story, the monkey is released by Buddha to serve the monk Xuan-zang as a pilgrim on a journey to the West (Lai 1994). Unlike the story of Hanuman, the *Hsi-yu-Chi* is not a pithy tale of heroic exploits. Instead, it is an epic story in which the monkey hero has many human qualities, both good and bad. In addition, the story of the Monkey King is a bit different from that of Hanuman or Thoth, as this monkey is not a religious icon in Buddhism. Taken together, these four examples show the ancient relationship of sacred (and not so sacred) monkeys and humans in four very different cultures. This relationship is further exemplified in folktales.

MONKEYS IN FOLKTALES

Nonhuman primates have been widely represented in folktales and stories in many different cultures.

In folktales, specific animals are commonly presented as stereotypes, having similar attributes in many different stories. In traditional Zulu folktales, the native baboons appear as vicious, cruel, and deceitful animals (unlike the sacred Egyptian baboon). This is similar to the depiction of the wolf in Western tales, such as the stories of the Three Little Pigs and Little Red Riding Hood.

In the Zulu tale "The Marriage Feast," a young woman marries a tall, handsome stranger. Just before they go to his homeland for a marriage feast, the young woman's little brother, Khokhoba, secretly witnesses the young man "slip out of his soft, chocolate-colored skin, to show beneath the rough hairy body of a big, black baboon!" (Savory 1964: 57). Here we see the transformation of the handsome stranger to the "evil and ugly" primate archetype. The woman does believe that her beautiful husband could be a "wicked baboon," so Khokhoba goes along to protect her. Deep in the wilderness, the baboon-in-disguise husband imprisons the brother and sister in a hut by blocking the exit with some large rocks, then sheds his skin and runs off as a baboon. The humans cut a hole in the roof with Khokhoba's knife, then make a raft to cross the river to escape the "large troupe of angry baboons" (p. 58) chasing them. When the "wicked leader" (p. 58) orders them to come back, Khokhoba outsmarts the baboons once again by getting the baboons to braid a rope of vines to pull the raft back to shore. The baboons throw them the rope and all pull on it, but Khokhoba pushes the raft into the current and all of the baboons are pulled into the river and drowned because "as you know, when a simian's hand closes on a thing, he *cannot* let go" (p. 60). The theme is thus established that although the baboon is stronger the human is smarter and is able to outwit the baboon.

Another theme found widely and with many variations in the folktales of the Zulu and other Bantu language groups is the intense desire of baboons to capture and raise a human child (Malcolm 1964). An example of this type of story is the tale of Fenisana (Savory 1964). This story is about a typically fierce troop of baboons, led by a cruel leader named Nymphere. In this case, however, a young baboon named Fenisana breaks the stereotype by being gentle and kind. She loves all living things and rescues small creatures being "roughly tortured by her fellow troopmates and nurse[s] them at her breast" (p. 38) and rocks the babies of the baboon mothers while they romped and played in their "senseless and foolish way" (p. 39).

The human protagonist of this story is Kumelele, who lays her 2-month-old son in the shade while she works in the fields. She looks up from her work and sees Fenisana cradling the baby and grunting to him. She yells at Fenisana, but the baboon begs "Please let me nurse your child, I love the little thing" (p. 39). Kumelele says to herself, "how strange, she speaks as one of us. Surely she would make a perfect nurse" (p. 39). By speaking the mother's language and expressing affection for the infant, Fenisana moves out of the evil and ugly stereotype and is viewed as a human. At first Fenisana does make a perfect nurse, but later she disappears with the infant. The mother finds them with the group, but Nymphere, the cruel baboon leader, wants to keep the baby. He declares, "The brains of man and the strength of us baboons will make us lords of *all* the beasts!" (p. 40). He plans to eat the mother the next day and threatens death to any of his troop members who release her. Fenisana appears to feel true remorse, crying tears like a human, and eventually defies Nymphere, risking her life to let Kumelele go.

In contrast to the typically evil and cruel baboons, some monkeys are portrayed in Zulu tales as being foolish and careless. In the tale "Nkalimeva" (Savory 1964), there is a benevolent and revered elephant king. The Nkau (monkeys) were "chatterboxes who could not mind their own business" (p. 34) and would chide the other animals of the adjoining kingdoms for their lack of law and order. They hung in the trees, laughing and chattering and throwing fruit at all who crossed the border, and sang the praises of their king. The carefree behavior of the monkeys led the animals from the nearby land to try to lure the great elephant to be their king instead, which they nearly succeed in doing. This depiction of the monkeys is another side to the Zulu representation of nonhuman primates in their folktales. The baboons are primarily very nasty and brutish (though they can behave nobly), but other types of monkeys can be much less sinister and play the role of the fool.

Japanese folktales are rich with monkey characters as well, most likely inspired by the macaques that inhabit their island country. The story of "The Monkey and the Crab" (Kani 1985) is one of the most popular traditional Japanese folktales and is told to nearly all Japanese children (Seki 1985). In this fairy tale, Mrs. Crab finds a rice ball while walking with Mr. Monkey. He convinces her to trade him the rice ball for a persimmon seed by explaining that she may plant it and harvest many juicy persimmons, compared to the one measly rice ball. Mrs. Crab trades for the seed and plants it. The persimmon tree grows up and produces lots of juicy persimmons, but Mrs. Crab is unable to get them out of the tree. Mr. Monkey offers to harvest the persimmons for her in exchange for a few, and Mrs. Crab invites him to take as many as he would like. He climbs in the tree and eats all the ripe persimmons. When Mrs. Crab complains, he says, "these are my persimmons because they grew from the seed that I found. Why should I give you any of them?" (Kani 1985: 9). Mr. Monkey then throws some hard, green persimmons at her, which hit her and break her shell. Once again, the primate emerges as a deceptive, heartless trickster. Just when it appears that he is going to be compassionate and help harvest the persimmons for Mrs. Crab, his basic monkey nature surfaces and he betrays her.

A different view of nonhuman primates is seen in "The Monkey's Haircut" (Bierhorst 1986), a Mayan folktale told by the Yucatec people who populated the Yucatan Peninsula. The monkey in this story lives in the house of a rich gentleman. He watches everything the gentleman does and tries to do those things too. After seeing the gentleman get a haircut, he finds some money and pays the barber for a haircut. The monkey then steals the razor and gives it to the butcher to cut meat with, then steals the butcher's guitar. He runs away, then ends up sitting on a wall singing a nonsensical song and playing the guitar. The butcher tells the monkey that

the devil is going to get him. The monkey replies, "What's it to you?" The monkey is then buried by the wall as it collapses on him. In this story the monkey is trying to be human but is unable to overcome his natural monkey ways. He can act human enough to live with the rich gentleman and learn about human culture—get the barber to give him a haircut and speak to the butcher—but he is aggressive and unpredictable. In the end, the monkey is punished for his actions.

MONKEYS IN LITERATURE

In all of these stories the monkeys were portrayed in a very negative light, as devious and conniving animals. In young children's books, monkeys are often portrayed in a more positive light. They may be curious or mischievous, but they are still basically good at heart. An excellent example of this genre is the Curious George series. This series is about a monkey taken from the jungle and brought to live in the city by the Man with the Yellow Hat, where he has many adventures that carry him through several books. Throughout these books several interesting themes recur.

George is portrayed as being very human in his behavior. For example, despite having recently been taken from his native jungle setting, he sits at the table, eats off of dishes while using a fork and knife, and sleeps in a four-poster bed in pajamas (Rey 1941). Yet, however human he appears, George makes the most of his natural nonhuman primate abilities: he easily climbs over a tall garden wall and scales a tree to retrieve a kite (Rey 1958) and a baby bear (Rey 1952). When George gets put in jail, he breaks out by walking along the top of the electric wires, thinking to himself how lucky he is to be a monkey (Rey 1941).

In some ways George acts and is treated like an adult. He smokes a pipe, is put in jail (Rey 1941), and is often left alone by the Man with the Yellow Hat (who for some reason continues to trust him to be by himself, even after all the trouble he perpetually gets himself into). In other ways, George acts like and is treated as a child. He plays with the telephone and accidentally makes a call (Rey 1941), makes paper boats out of the newspapers he's supposed to be delivering, and cries when he wrecks his bike (Rey 1952). Perhaps the greatest indication of George's childishness is that he always gets himself into so much trouble that he must be rescued by the Man with the Yellow Hat, who functions as a father figure (Rey 1941, 1952, 1958).

Perhaps what makes Curious George so appealing to children is his ability to straddle all kinds of categories that they are not allowed to cross. They identify with him as a character who has the freedom of an adult but the curious mind of a child. He behaves like a human—so much so that he can interact with humans on their level—yet has the strength and agility of a monkey. Possibly the most interesting irony of the Curious George stories is that he is often confronted with caged animals yet does not seem to see any parallels between those animals and himself. For instance, when the baby bear escapes from its cage at the exotic animal show, George sounds the alarm and brings it back to its captors (Rey 1952). Another example is when he encounters a cage full of baby bunnies with their mother, one of whom he releases for a time, but then he returns it to the cage "where it belongs" (Rey 1958). At the end of the story, he is given a bunny of his own as a pet! In light of these contrasting characteristics, Curious George is in an ambiguous position between animal and human.

In the first half of the twentieth century, Western knowledge of the natural behavior of nonhuman primates was just starting to increase. Several works around this time exemplify how facts about primates around the world were woven into semifictional (if not completely fictional) stories designed to recount tales of interactions with these animals. An 1896 book entitled *Four-handed Folk*, by Olive Thorne Miller, is a collection of anecdotes about primates of all kinds that were captured and taken to New York City. Miller describes, among other things, that her pet lemur particularly enjoyed playing a game of chase that involved the daily newspaper and that a marmoset in her care was fond of dipping his hand into bottles of cologne. Other books of this era relayed fantastic stories of meeting monkeys and apes on overseas trips, and they are written from the point of view of the monkeys! One such book, *Monkeyfolk of South Africa*, is a naturalist's tale of his encounters with African primates whom he "allows" to tell their own stories. This volume is full of wonderful photographs. The caption under a picture of a vervet monkey with an infant reads:

> I am a vervet, or Blaauw-aapje. I was caught in
> a trap by the humanfolk and kept in a cage.
> I reared my baby in captivity. We monkeyfolk
> love our children dearly. (Fitzsimons 1911: 122)

In another book, an epic tale of a kingdom of hanuman langurs springs from the imagination of Frieda Hauswirth Das (1932) after her stay in India from 1920–1929. In *Leap-home and Gentlebrawn*, Das includes many excellent and accurate details of langur life in her story about two heroic langurs, the title characters. The animal characters in these accounts are all given some degree of humanity, and it usually reflects very positively on them. In the same era, though, there were other fiction writers who presented a much dimmer view of our animal relatives.

One of the most popular American authors of the early twentieth century was Edgar Rice Burroughs (1914/1990), whose Tarzan novels (and the films based on them) have become a staple of American culture. Tarzan, of course, was the infant son of Lord Greystoke, a British nobleman. While visiting the jungles of Africa, a band of killer gorillas invades the Greystoke camp, killing all the adult humans and stealing the infant boy. The child is raised as a member of the gorilla group, and goes on to become "Lord of the Jungle." *Tarzan of the Apes*, the first in a series of twenty-four Tarzan books, was published in 1914. A key passage from the original novel shows Burroughs's impressions of gorillas. After describing the despotic king of the apes, Kerchak, killing numerous members of his group with malicious intent, Burroughs moves the scene to the Greystoke camp:

> He had seen many of his kind go to their
> deaths before the loud noise made by the little
> black stick in the hands of the strange white
> ape who lived in that wonderful lair, and Ker-

chak had made up his brute mind to own that death-dealing contrivance, and to explore the interior of the mysterious den.

He wanted very, very much, to feel his teeth sink into the neck of the queer animal that he had learned to hate and fear, and because of this, he came often with his tribe to reconnoiter, waiting for a time when the white ape should be off his guard. (1990: 32)

The distinction between ape and human is not particularly clear here. The ape is capable of reasoning that humans are simply "white apes" and that the source of their power is only their firearms; humans are just another animal in Burroughs's description. Both species are malevolent and capable of bloody violence. In fact, shortly after this passage, Kerchak and his cohorts slaughter Lord Greystoke and his companions while the young Tarzan is saved by a female gorilla whose infant has just died at the hand of Kerchak's earlier rampage. Thus, we see two opposing instincts simultaneously: bloodthirsty violence and motherly compassion. Reminiscent of the baboons in the Zulu stories, these primates embody some human traits but are clearly still wild animals.

MONKEYS IN THE MOVIES

The first Tarzan film followed shortly after the publication of the first Burroughs book, in 1918. Interestingly, the main ape character is not at all the malevolent killer described in the book but is instead the lovable Cheetah, Tarzan's chimpanzee sidekick. Cheetah is an excellent example of nonhuman primates in movies as comic relief. They are there to mimic humans, to do outrageous things and generally to play the role of the buffoon. We see this animal character again and again in such films as *Every Which Way but Loose* (which is still Clint Eastwood's top grossing film) and *Dunston Checks In,* a recent film starring Jason Alexander of *Seinfeld* fame. Both of these films star an orangutan in a very similar role. In the 1978 Eastwood movie, Clyde the orang is a drinking buddy for Eastwood's character. Clyde tags along as Eastwood drives an eighteen-wheeler around the country, stopping reg-

ularly for beer and bar fights. *Dunston Checks In* (1996) puts an orang in the environment of a five-star hotel, but the hijinks that result are much the same. As Alexander and Faye Dunaway try to keep everything running perfectly in their fancy hotel, you can bet that the sight of Dunston with panties on his head throws a big monkey wrench into their plans. From Cheetah to Dunston, then, the court jester role for nonhuman primates has become a staple of American film.

Another common role for nonhuman primates in movies is that of a menacing and evil villain, similar to Kerchak of the Tarzan novel. The beginnings of this go back to the classic film *King Kong* (1933), which is itself a reflection of nineteenth-century Christian views of nonhuman primates. Kong, a 40-foot-tall ape, steals the heroine, played by Faye Wray, and is hunted down by her shipmates. Kong kills most of the would-be rescuers, and along the way they get to watch the ape do battle with dinosaurs and other monsters on Skull Island. Finally Kong is subdued by sleeping gas and brought back to New York. For Kong, the city is just another jungle with different challenges, and the film hits its peak on top of the Empire State Building in a scene that has become an icon of American culture. Although there is certainly evidence that Kong himself is more misunderstood than a monster, this film set the stage for later nonhuman primate monster movies.

In *Monkey Shines: An Experiment in Fear,* filmed in 1988, we have the story of a quadriplegic human and a capuchin monkey who helps him out around the house. Ella, the monkey, gets injected with experimental brain cell drugs, and her mental abilities start to grow exponentially. By the end of the film she is able to read her master's mind. Uninhibited by his humanity, Ella acts out his darkest thoughts, which results in the unpleasant demise of some of his acquaintances. In *Congo* (1995) a group of specially bred and trained "gray gorillas" guard a lost city deep in the African jungle. These gorillas are lethal and kill most of a heavily armed expedition of treasure seekers. Though modern gadgets and concepts dress up these films, the basic concept of the nonhuman primate as an evil creature is not new.

Many films attempt to create a tone of authenticity by weaving scientific information into the plot. Some films of the last decade or so have done this with primatology. The clearest example of this is *Gorillas in the Mist,* loosely based on the work of the late primatologist Dian Fossey. We see Fossey first approach Louis Leakey about studying gorillas, then follow her career all the way to her tragic death. The film goes to extremes to portray the gorillas as completely peaceful and compassionate creatures, whereas the Africans with whom they share their territory are frequently seen to be violent and wasteful. This reversal of desirable and undesirable characteristics between humans and apes is the opposite of the typical pattern we have seen in other cultures.

Some film plots involving primates have been inspired by relatively recent developments in science and therefore have no historical precedent. Filmmakers are thus creating new cultural representations of nonhuman primates. An example of this is the movie *Outbreak,* a fictionalized account of the recent spread of the *ebola* virus. The plot of the movie is based on the hypothesis that the virus may have been transmitted initially from a monkey to a human. In the film, a capuchin actor plays the role of an African monkey, moving in and out of the plot as a lethal (yet unaware) figure. The chilling realization that such a deadly disease can pass between human and nonhuman may cause a return to a collective view of monkeys and apes as being dirty harbingers of disease as first articulated in medieval Europe.

Film representations of scientific advances in human-ape communication serve to change public perception of nonhuman primates in the opposite direction. Two recent movies depict apes that have been taught sign language and communicate with humans. In both *Project X* (1987) and *Congo* (1995) an ape character blurs the boundary between animal and human by communicating ideas and emotions through a language created by human culture. Although limited in what they can express, as are the real-life sign language apes, this ability to communicate creates a new level of empathy between ape and human that is unique in human history.

CONCLUSION

This survey merely scratches the surface of the rich history of nonhuman primates in human culture. Nonhuman primates have played a wide variety of roles in our collective conscience. Perhaps due to their physical similarity to humans, monkeys and apes often appear in many genres of cultural expression. This is true even in countries where no native nonhuman primates reside. Whether they are presented as creatures to be revered or despised, their significance is no less diminished. Nonhuman primates have symbolized important aspects of our humanity for eons, and through them we can gain a broader perspective on our own existence and our place in nature.

Suggested Readings

PART 1: The Nonhuman Primates: Who Are They, Where Are They, and How Are They Doing?

TAXONOMY AND PHYLOGENY OF THE PRIMATES

BEGUN, D., WARD, C. F., AND ROSE, K. D., eds. 1997. *Function, Phylogeny and Fossils: Miocene Hominid Origins and Adaptations.* New York, Plenum.

CONROY, G. C. 1990. *Primate Evolution.* New York, W. W. Norton.

FLEAGLE, J. 1999. *Primate Evolution and Adaptation,* 2nd ed. London, Academic Press.

HARTWIG, W. C. 1994. Patterns, puzzles and perspectives on platyrrhine origins. In *Integrative Paths to the Past: Paleoanthropological Essays in Honor of F. Clark Howell,* edited by R. S. Corrucini and R. L. Ciochon, pp. 69–94. Englewood Cliffs, NJ, Prentice-Hall.

STEWART, C. B., AND DISOTELL, T. R. 1998. Primate Evolution—In and Out of Africa. *Current Biology* 8(16): 582–588.

THE NONHUMAN PRIMATES

RICHARDS, A. 1985. *Primates in Nature.* New York, W. H. Freeman.

ROWE, N. 1996. *A Pictorial Guide to the Living Primates.* New York, Pogonias Press.

SMUTS, B. B., CHENEY, D. L., SEYFARTH, R. M., WRANGHAM, R. W., AND STRUHSAKER, T. T., eds. 1987. *Primate Societies.* Chicago, University of Chicago Press.

The Apes

KANO, T. 1992. *The Last Ape: Pygmy Chimpanzee Behavior and Ecology.* Stanford, Stanford University Press.

McGREW, W. C., MARCHANT, L. F., AND NISHIDA, T., eds. 1996. *Great Ape Societies.* Cambridge, Cambridge University Press.

WRANGHAM, R. W., McGREW, W. C., DE WAAL, F. B. M., AND HELTNE, P., eds. 1994. *Chimpanzee Cultures.* Cambridge, MA, Harvard University Press.

The Old World Monkeys

DAVIES, A. G., AND OATES, J. F., eds. 1994. *Colobine Monkeys: Their Ecology, Behaviour and Evolution.* Cambridge, Cambridge University Press.

FA, J. A., AND LINDBURG, D. G., eds. 1996. *Evolution and Ecology of Macaque Societies.* Cambridge, Cambridge University Press.

GAUTIER-HION, A., BOURLIERE, F., GAUTIER, J., AND KINGDON, J., eds. 1988. *A Primate Radiation: Evolutionary Biology of the African Guenons.* Cambridge, Cambridge University Press.

JABLONSKI, N. G., ed. 1998. *The Natural History of the Doucs and Snub-Nosed Monkeys.* Singapore, World Scientific Press.

WHITEHEAD, P. A., AND JOLLY, C. J., eds. In press. *Old World Monkeys.* Cambridge, Cambridge University Press.

The New World Monkeys

KINZEY, W. G., ed. 1997. *New World Primates: Ecology, Evolution and Behavior.* New York, Aldine de Gruyter.

NORCONK, M. A., ROSENBERGER, A. L., AND GARBER, P. A., eds. 1996. *Adaptive Radiations of Neotropical Primates.* New York, Plenum.

RYLANDS, A. B., ed. 1993. *Marmosets and Tamarins: Systematics, Behaviour, and Ecology.* Oxford, Oxford Science Press.

TERBORGH, J. 1985. *Five New World Primates: A Study in Comparative Ecology.* Princeton, NJ, Princeton University Press.

The Prosimians

BEARDER, S. K. 1987. Lorises, Bushbabies, and Tarsiers: Diverse Societies and Solitary Foragers. In *Primate Societies,* edited by B. B. Smuts, D. L. Cheney, R. M. Seyfarth, R. W. Wrangham and T. T. Struhsaker. Chicago, University of Chicago Press.

KAPPELER, P. M., AND GANZHORN, J. U., eds. 1993. *Lemur Social Systems and Their Ecological Basis.* New York, Plenum.

NIEMITZ, C. 1984. *The Biology of Tarsiers.* Stuttgart, Gustav Fischer.

TATTERSALL, I. 1982. *The Primates of Madagascar.* New York, Columbia University Press.

PRIMATE CONSERVATION

ELSE, J. G., AND LEE, P. C. 1986. *Primate Ecology and Conservation.* Cambridge, Cambridge University Press.

MARSH, C. W., AND MITTERMEIER, R. A., eds. 1987. *Primate Conservation in the Tropical Rainforest.* New York, Alan R. Liss.

Primate Conservation: A Retrospective and a Look into the 21st Century. 1996–97. Proceedings of the XVth Congress of the International Primatological Society. *Primate Conservation* 17.

PART 2: The Realm of Primate Behavior

BERNSTEIN, I. S. 1991. The Correlation Between Kinship and Behaviour in Non-human Primates. In *Kin Recognition,* edited by P. G. Hepper. Cambridge, Cambridge University Press.

DUNBAR, R. I. M. 1988. *Primate Social Systems.* Ithaca, NY, Cornell University Press.

FEDIGAN, L. M. 1992. *Primate Paradigms: Sex Roles and Social Bonds.* Chicago, University of Chicago Press.

HOW THINGS CAME TO BE

BARTLETT, T. Q., SUSSMAN, R. W., AND CHEVERUD, J. M. 1993. Infant Killing in Primates: A Review of Observed Cases with Specific Reference to the Sexual Selection Hypothesis. *American Anthropologist* 95(4): 958–990.

JAMIESON, I. G. 1986. The Functional Approach to Behavior: Is It Useful? *American Naturalist* 127:195–208.

MARTIN, R. D. 1990. *Primate Origins and Evolution: A Phylogenetic Reconstruction.* Princeton, NJ, Princeton University Press.

MORBECK, M. E., GALLOWAY, A., AND ZIHLMAN, A. 1997. *The Evolving Female: A Life-History Perspective.* Princeton, NJ, Princeton University Press.

OYAMA, S. 1985. *The Ontogeny of Information.* Cambridge, Cambridge University Press.

THE PRIMATE GROUP

BERNSTEIN, I. S. 1981. Dominance: The Baby and the Bathwater. *The Behavioral and Brain Sciences* 4:419–457.

HINDE, R., ed. 1983. *Primate Social Relationships: An Integrated Approach.* Oxford, Blackwell.

MASON, W. A., AND MENDOZA, S. P., eds. 1993. *Primate Social Conflict.* Albany, State University of New York Press.

SMUTS, B. B. 1985. *Sex and Friendship in Baboons.* New York, Aldine de Gruyter.

BEHAVIORAL AND BIOLOGICAL DIMENSIONS OF THE LIFE SPAN

CREWS, D. E., AND GARRUTO, R. M., eds. 1994. *Biological Anthropology and Aging.* Oxford, Oxford University Press.

SAPOLSKY, R. M. 1994. *Why Zebras Don't Get Ulcers.* New York, W. H. Freeman.

ZIEGLER, T. E., AND BERCOVITCH, F. B., eds. 1990. *Socioendocrinology of Primate Reproduction.* New York, Wiley-Liss.

THE MIND

BYRNE, R. W. 1995. *The Thinking Ape.* Oxford, Oxford University Press.

GARDNER, R. A., GARDNER, B. T., AND VAN CANTFORT, T., eds. 1989. *Teaching Sign Language to Chimpanzees.* Albany, State University of New York Press.

PARKER, S. T., AND GIBSON, K. R., eds. 1990. *"Language" and Intelligence in Monkeys and Apes: Comparative Developmental Perspectives.* Cambridge, Cambridge University Press.

PRIMATES IN THE BROADER CONTEXT

CH'ENG-EN, WU. 1961. *The Monkey King.* Translated by George Theiner. London, Westbook House.

JANSON, H. W. 1952. *Apes and Ape Lore in the Middle Ages and the Renaissance.* London, University of London Press.

OHNUKI-TIERNEY, E. 1987. *The Monkey as Mirror: Symbolic Transformations in Japanese History and Ritual.* Princeton, NJ, Princeton University Press.

The Ramayana of Valmiki: An Epic of Ancient India. 1984. Introduction and translation by Robert P. Goldman; annotation by Robert P. Goldman and Sally J. Sutherland. Princeton, NJ, Princeton University Press.

Glossary

Acheulian Industry stone tool technology associated with Pleistocene hominids, consisting largely of tools whose cutting edge is created by flaking on both sides of the edge.

adaptation (noun) any feature or characteristic of an organism whose current function arose via natural selection.

adaptation (verb) the process by which populations successfully interact with their environment.

adaptive radiation evolutionary event occurring when a species, or group of species, takes advantage of open environments or new resources and adapts to those circumstances, diversifying into several new species.

affiliative relationship a persistent pattern of socially reinforcing interactions between two individuals.

agonism actions that are self-assertive or defensive in nature and occur during conflict or competition.

agonistic buffering behavioral interaction where one individual uses a third party to lessen the likelihood of receiving aggression from another individual.

allele variants in the specific DNA sequence at a given locus within a species (alternate forms of a gene).

allogrooming the act of grooming another individual.

allometry the study of proportional changes in the morphology of different parts of the body due to growth and development.

allomother a female that engages in parenting behavior with an infant that is not her offspring.

allopatric when two or more species live in distinct, nonoverlapping environments or geographic areas.

alpha male a male in a social group that is capable of dominating all others.

analogy when taxa independently evolve similar traits but do not share these traits as a result of common ancestry.

Anthropoidea one of two suborders in the order Primates; also referred to as anthropoids and includes all monkeys, apes, and humans.

anthropomorphism assignment of human characteristics to nonhuman entities.

arboreal living primarily in the trees.

basal metabolic rate (BMR) rate of energy use required to maintain life in an organism at rest.

bicornuate uterus a uterus with two cavities, each descending from one of the two oviducts, which is found in all prosimians and differs from the simplex uterus of the Anthropoidea wherein the uterine cavity consists of a single chamber descending from both oviducts.

bifaced tools stone tools formed by flaking along both sides (faces) of the cutting edge.

bilophodont molars molars consisting of four cusps arranged in two pairs with a ridge bucco-lingually joining each pair; characteristic of the Cercopithecoidea.

binomial nomenclature formal scientific method for naming species by using two Latinized terms, one for the genus and one for the species name (e.g., *Homo sapiens*).

biomass the total amount of organic material in an ecosystem.

bipedalism locomotion achieved through striding on the hind limbs.

bisexual group a social group whose membership includes adults of both sexes.

brachiation locomotion wherein animals use their forelimbs to propel themselves by arm-over-arm swinging.

catecholamines a group of hormones produced by the adrenal glands (adrenaline, for example).

cerebellum portion of the brain whose main functions deal with motor coordination and voluntary movements.

chopper a simple stone tool made from a core whose cutting edge may be either unifacially or bifacially constructed.

cleaver stone tool made from the core with a long, bifacial cutting edge and a blunt end.

clade a taxonomic group that has evolved from a common ancestor; includes the ancestor and all descendent species.

cladistics   school of thought that classifies organisms according to the evolutionary relationships between them as determined by shared derived characteristics.

cladogram   depiction of the evolutionary relationships among different taxa.

cline   the distribution of a trait that varies gradually across a geographical area.

cluster technique   mathematical technique that examines multiple variables to reveal which of those variables intercorrelate, forming a group.

comparative method   scientific technique wherein differing taxa or populations are compared to reveal similarities and differences between them.

conspecific   members of the same species.

convergent evolution   independent evolution of similar characteristics by different taxa.

core   the primary stone from which tools are manufactured.

dental comb   a set of procumbent lower incisors and canines used for grooming or for gouging trees to get gums and sap.

dependent variable   the factor of interest in regression analysis; researchers seek to know what changes, if any, occur to it in response to another factor.

dependent rank   in a linear dominance system the ranking held by an individual due to support from others.

derived trait   a uniquely evolved characteristic of a species not seen in its ancestor; used in cladistic analyses to determine branching sequences in a taxon's evolutionary history.

displacement   interaction between two individuals where one individual approaches another and takes its place (physically or socially).

diurnal   carrying out basic activities during daylight.

divergent evolution   evolution of unique characteristics so that taxa become less alike.

dominance hierarchy   a set of power relationships between the individuals in a social group.

emergent property   any structure or entity that comes into being due to the interactions of lower level components in a hierarchically composed system; these characteristics are unique and cannot be explained by the actions of the lower level components that bring the property into being.

Eocene   geological epoch within the Cenozoic era lasting from 53 to 35 mya.

evolution   biological change over time resulting in the transformation of populations and species.

exaptation   any feature of an organism whose primary function is currently different from the function that originally arose via natural selection.

fission-fusion society   a social group that breaks into smaller subgroups that vary in composition and duration (fission); some or all of these subgroups may occasionally merge together (fussion).

flakes   pieces of stone that are removed from the core during stone tool manufacture; flakes are often modified to become stone tools.

focal animal sampling   technique of behavioral data collection wherein all actions performed by, or directed toward, a specific (focal) individual over a predetermined period of time are recorded.

folivore   animal that eats primarily leaves to obtain its dietary requirements.

fossil   any remains of an organism that have been converted into stone by geological processes; these remains often consist of recrystalized skeletal elements but also include casts or molds of organisms or traces of their behavior (e.g., footprints).

fossil record   the evolutionary history of a taxon based on fossils.

frugivore   animal that eats primarily fruit to obtain its dietary requirements.

gene   a segment of genetic material (either DNA or, for some viruses, RNA) that contains the coding sequence for an RNA product. In protein-coding genes this RNA product is translated into a polypeptide or protein.

gene expression   the process whereby the information contained in a gene is used to make an RNA or protein product. Expression requires transcription of a gene's DNA sequence into RNA and, for protein-coding genes, translation of the RNA sequence into a protein.

genotype   genetic makeup of a species or organism.

genus (plural **genera**)   a taxonomic level of classification consisting of closely related species.

glucocorticoids   a group of steroid hormones produced by the adrenal glands (cortisol, for example).

grooming   behavioral interaction wherein one individual examines and removes detritus and parasites from another; also considered to be important as a general affiliative social behavior.

grooming claw   the second digit of the hind limbs of prosimians.

hallux   the first digit at the end of the hind limbs (e.g., the big toe of humans).

handaxe   a bifaced stone tool made from the core that comes to a point and has a long cutting edge.

harem   metaphoric description for a social group consisting of one male, multiple females, and the offspring of the females.

herbivore   animal who uses plant matter as its primary dietary resource.

Hominidae   family of the Hominoidea distinguished by habitual bipedal locomotion; hominid is the general term for this taxonomic group.

Hominoidea   superfamily within the primate order consisting of the apes and humans, which is largely distinguished by morphological changes associated with brachiation; hominoid is the general term for this taxonomic group.

homology   characteristic of two or more species that is shared due to inheritance of the trait from a common ancestor.

homoplasy   trait seen in two or more species that has independently evolved in those taxa through convergent or parallel evolution.

hormone   chemical substance produced by structures in the body that affect other structures or organs in the body; hormones are transported primarily via the circulatory system.

hunter-gatherer   ecological lifestyle where foods are obtained through both hunting animals and collecting plants, with collecting generally contributing the majority of calories to the diet.

independent rank   in a linear dominance system the rank held by an individual without support from others.

independent variable   the factor used in regression analysis to test how changes in it affect some other factor(s).

inductive inquiry   nineteenth-century methodology of gathering and analyzing as many observable facts relating to a question as possible and deriving principles or laws from them to explain observed phenomena.

intermembral index (IM)   a measure of the relative lengths of the upper and lower limbs.

ischial callosities   thick pads formed on the hindquarters of an animal, seen in the Cercopithecoidea.

karyotype   the number and shape of chromosomes or photographs of the chromosomes of a species showing their number and shapes.

local extinction   extinction of a population within a specific geographic region but not throughout the entirety of a species' range.

lumpers   general term referring to taxonomists who tend to emphasize greater degrees of variation within taxonomic groups and consequently designate fewer taxa (c.f., splitters).

lyse   to break open or disintegrate.

male-male competition   form of sexual selection where males vie with each other for reproductive access to females.

mandibular symphysis   joint where the two halves of the mandible meet; fused in the anthropoids and tarsiers and unfused in the lemurs and lorises.

matriline   group of females related to one another through direct maternal descent.

Miocene   geological epoch of the Cenozoic era lasting from 25 to 5 mya.

monophyly   a clade consisting of a common ancestor and all of its descendent species.

morphology   shape of an organism or its parts.

mtDNA   the DNA located in the mitochondria of the cell, which is inherited through the maternal line.

natal group   social group into which an individual is born.

natural selection   the evolutionary process whereby changes are incorporated into a species, or by which species evolve into new species, through differential survival and reproduction.

neocortex   region covering the cerebral cortex, which is highly developed in primates as compared with other organisms.

neonate   newborn infant.

nuclear family   social group consisting of a male, a female, and the offspring of that male and female.

nucleotide sequencing   analysis of the order of chemical bases within a segment of DNA.

neutral mutation   change in the DNA that has no effect on the phenotype.

object manipulation   using an altered or unaltered object.

Oldowan Industrial Complex   the earliest (Pliocene) and simplest stone tool technology, with cutting edges unifacially formed by removing flakes from a core.

order   taxonomic subdivision of classes within the Linnean taxonomy; Primates is an order of the class Mammalia.

pairmates   social unit consisting of an adult male and female but not connoting exclusive reproduction within the unit.

perineum   the ano-genital region of a body.

peripheral male   any male in association with a social group but generally found at the edges of the group; these males may or may not be integrated members of the social unit.

phenotype   observable, measurable characteristics of an organism.

philopatry   dispersal pattern where females emigrate and males remain in their natal group upon reaching sexual maturity.

Pleistocene   geological epoch of the Cenozoic era lasting from 1.8 mya to 12 kya.

phylogenetic constraints   limitations on possible evolutionary innovations in a taxa due to characteristics of its ancestors.

phylogeny   the evolutionary history of a taxon, usually including ancestral and closely related species as well as the times of divergence; typically depicted as a branching tree diagram.

Pliocene   geological epoch of the Cenozoic era lasting from 5 to 1.8 mya.

polymerase chain reaction (PCR)   technique used to replicate segments of DNA for analysis.

polyphyly   a clade consisting of descendent species but not including the last common ancestor.

population   the individuals of a species living within the same geographic area.

prehensile tail   tail found in some neotropical primates that is capable of grasping objects; it has a tactile surface on its underside.

primitive features   characteristics of an organism retained from ancestral species; also referred to as primitive traits.

proximate causation   the immediate, localized agent of change.

quadrumanual clambering   arboreal locomotion in which individuals use their hands and feet to grab supports, boles, vines, and branches as they move through the trees.

quadruped   an animal that uses all four limbs to locomote.

ranging pattern   areas used and the paths taken by animals as they move about their home range.

rehabilitation   conservation technique that attempts to return animals to native habitats after teaching them survival techniques, such as food recognition.

reproductive seasonality   all females of a group give birth during a specific time of the year.

reproductive synchrony   the females of a group have similar timing in their ovulatory cycles.

resting metabolic rate (RMR)   see basal metabolic rate.

restriction site mapping   delineating the nucleotide sequence of a particular segment of DNA that has been specifically cut from the DNA molecule by a restriction enzyme.

sacculated stomach   a compartmentalized stomach allowing special digestion in the different compartments.

scavenging   ecological lifestyle where individuals obtain their dietary requirements by locating and using carrion for their primary food resource.

scent-marking   laying down olfactory cues from glands on elements in the environment.

scientific method   systematic investigation of natural phenomena through the testing of alternative hypotheses formulated to explain the phenomenon of interest.

sexual dichromatism   the two sexes of a species have differing coloration.

sexual dimorphism   sexes have different body sizes or shapes, exclusive of the reproductive organs.

sexual maturity   stage in an animal's life when it can successfully reproduce.

sexual monomorphism   sexes have identical body size and shape, exclusive of the reproductive organs.

shared derived trait   a feature held in common by two or more taxa due to the inheritance from a common ancestor; also known as synapomorphy.

sister-group   in cladistics one of two descendent groups from a common ancestor, not including the ancestor.

sister-taxa   two closely related species or taxa.

social network   sustained interaction patterns between a number of individuals in a social group.

social organization   the structural elements of social groups.

social system   components and processes at work in maintaining the organization of social groups.

socioecology   field that studies the interrelationship of social behavior and ecological conditions.

species   lowest formal level of the Linnean taxonomic system composed of individuals potentially capable of naturally reproducing with one another.

splitters   taxonomists that tend to limit the degree of variation within taxonomic groups and subsequently recognize a greater number of taxa (c.f., lumpers).

stoneknapping   the act of manufacturing stone tools.

symbolic communication   use of symbols to relate information from one individual to another.

sympatry   when two or more species live in the same environment or geographic area.

synapomorphy   derived features shared in two or more taxa that indicate that those taxa are descended from a common ancestor.

tapetum lucidum   layer within the retina that reflects light, enhances night vision.

taxon (plural **taxa**)   broad term for any grouping within the Linnean taxonomic system.

taxonomy   the science of systematically naming and classifying life forms.

terrestrial   use of the ground layer as primary habitat.

territorial   active defense of a home range.

translocation   to move a local population of a species to a new locality.

ultimate causation   force(s) responsible for long-term or overall change.

xerophytic forest   a highly seasonal dry forest in which much of the trees and shrubs store water and are protected by thorny outer layers.

References

ACHOKA, I. 1994. *Home range, group size, and group composition of mountain gorillas in the Bwindi-Impenetrable National Park, Southwest Uganda.* Master's thesis, Makerere University.

ADAMS-CURTIS, L. E. 1990. Conceptual learning in capuchin monkeys. *Folia Primatologica* 54:129–137.

ADKINS, R. M., AND HONEYCUTT, R. L. 1994. Evolution of the primate cytochrome oxidase subunit II gene. *Journal of Molecular Evolution* 38:215–231.

AGESTUMA, N. 1995a. Dietary selection by Yakushima macaques (*Macaca fuscata yakui*): The influence of food availability and temperature. *International Journal of Primatology* 16:611–627.

AGESTUMA, N. 1995b. Foraging synchrony in a group of Yakushima macaques (*Macaca fuscata yakui*). *Folia Primatologica* 64:167–179.

AHL, V., AND ALLEN, T. F. H. 1996. *Hierarchy theory: A vision, vocabulary, and epistemology.* New York, Columbia University Press.

AIELLO, L. 1986. The relationships of the Tarsiiformes: A review of the case for the Haplorrhini. In *Major topics in primate and human evolution,* edited by B. Wood, L. Martin, and P. Andrews, pp. 47–65. Cambridge, Cambridge University Press.

ALBERTS, S. C., SAPOLSKY, R. M., AND ALTMANN, J. 1992. Behavioral, endocrine, and immunological correlates of immigration by an aggressive male into a natural primate group. *Hormones and Behavior* 26:167–178.

ALEXANDER, B. K. 1970. Parental behaviour of adult male Japanese monkeys. *Behaviour* 36:270–285.

ALLEN, L. L., BRIDGES, P. S., EVON, D. L., ROSENBERG, K. R., RUSSELL, M. D., SCHEPARTZ, L. A., VITZTHUM, V. J., AND WOLPOFF, M. H. 1983. Demography and human origins. *American Anthropologist* 84:888–896.

ALLEN, T. F. H., AND STARR, T. B. 1982. *Hierarchy: Perspectives for ecological complexity.* Chicago, University of Chicago Press.

ALTMANN, J. 1974. Observational study of behavior: Sampling methods. *Behaviour* 49:227–267.

ALTMANN, S. A. 1962. A field study on the sociobiology of rhesus monkeys (*Macaca mulatta*). *Annals of the New York Academy of Sciences* 102:338–435.

AMOSS, P. T., AND HARRELL, S. 1981. An anthropological perspective on aging. In *Other ways of growing old: Anthropological perspectives,* edited by P. T. Amoss and S. Harrell, pp. 1–24. Stanford, Stanford University Press.

ANDAU, P. M., HIONG, L. K., AND SALE, J. B. 1994. Translocation of pocketed orang-utans in Sabah. *Oryx* 28:263–268.

ANDERSON, J. R. 1996. Chimpanzees and capuchin monkeys: Comparative cognition. In *Reaching into thought: The minds of the great apes,* edited by A. E. Russon, K. A. Bard, and S. T. Parker, pp. 23–56. Cambridge, Cambridge University Press.

ANDERSON, J. R., AND HENNEMAN, M. C. 1994. Solutions to a tool-use problem in a pair of *Cebus apella. Mammalia* 58(3):351–361.

ANDREWS, T. D., JERMIIN, L. S., AND EASTEAL, S. 1998. Accelerated evolution of cytochrome b in simian primates: Adaptive evolution in concert with other mitochondrial proteins. *Journal of Molecular Evolution* (in press).

ANON. 1980. Origin of comparative oncology laboratory gibbons. *IPPL Newsletter* 7(1).

ANON. 1990. Primate watch: In Indonesian Borneo, orangutans are for sale. *Wildlife Conservation* 93(6):26.

ANON. 1992–1993. Orang-utan population and habitat viability analysis workshop. *Asian Primates* 2(3&4): 3–4.

ANON. 1997 (24 November). China faces costly pollution cleanup. *Los Angeles Times,* p. D2.

ANTINUCCI, F., AND VISALBERGHI, E. 1986. Tool use in *Cebus apella*: A case study. *International Journal of Primatology* 7(4):351–363.

APPANAH, S. 1986. General flowering in the climax rain forests of South-east Asia. *Journal of Tropical Ecology* 1:225–250.

ARAMBULO, P., ENCARNACION, F., ESTUPINAN, J., SAMAME, H., WATSON, C. R., AND WELLER, R. E., eds. 1993. *Primates of the Americas: Strategies for conservation and sustained use in biomedical research.* Columbus, OH, Batelle Press.

ARBELOT-TRACQUI, V. 1983. *Etude ethoecologique de deux primates prosimiens:* Lemur coronatus *(Gray) et* Lemur fulvus sanfordi *(Archbold): Contribution a l'etude des mecanismes d'isolement reproductif intervenant dans la speciation.* Thesis, Universite Rennes.

ASANO, M. 1967. A note on the birth and rearing of an orang-utan *Pongo pygmaeus* at Tama Zoo, Tokyo. *International Zoo Yearbook* 7:95–96.

ASHTON, P. S., GIVINISH, T. J., AND APPANAH, S. 1988. Staggered flowering in the Dipterocarpaceae: New insights into floral induction and the evolution of mast fruiting. *American Naturalist* 132:44–66.

ASQUITH, P. 1986. Anthropomorphism and the Japanese and Western traditions in primatology. East and West. In *Primate ontogeny, cognition and behavior: Developments in field and laboratory research,* edited by J. Else and P. Lee, pp. 61–71. New York, Academic Press.

ASSINK, P., AND VAN DIJK, I. F. 1990. *Social organization, ranging, and density of* Presbytis thomasi *at Ketambe (Sumatra) and a comparison with other* Presbytis *species at several South East Asian locations.* M.Sc. thesis, University of Utrecht.

BABA, M. L., DARGA, L. L., AND GOODMAN, M. 1979. Immunodiffusion systematics of the primates. *Folia Primatologica* 32:207–238.

BAILEY W. J., FITCH D. H. A., TAGLE, D. A., CZELUSNIAK, J., SLIGHTOM, J. L., AND GOODMAN M. 1991. Molecular evolution of the yh-globin gene locus: Gibbon phylogeny and the hominoid slowdown. *Molecular Biology and Evolution* 8:155–184.

BAILEY, W. J., HAYASAKA, K., SKINNER, C. G., KEHOE, S., SIEU, L. C., SLIGHTOM, J. L., AND GOODMAN, M. 1992. Reexamination of the African hominoid trichotomy with additional sequences from the primate beta-globin gene cluster. *Molecular Phylogenetics and Evolution* 1:97–135.

BAKER, A. 1991. *Evolution of the social system of the golden lion tamarin* (Leontopithecus rosalia*): Mating system, group dynamics, and cooperative breeding.* Ph.D. thesis, University of Maryland, College Park.

BAKER, M. 1996. Fur rubbing: Use of medicinal plants by capuchin monkeys (*Cebus capucinus*). *American Journal of Primatology* 38:263–270.

BALDWIN, P. J., MCGREW, W. C., AND TUTIN, C. E. G. 1982. Wild-ranging chimpanzees at Mt. Assirik, Senegal. *International Journal of Primatology* 3(4):367–385.

BALKO, E. A. 1998. *A behaviorally plastic response to forest composition and logging disturbance by* Varecia variegata variegata *in Ranomafana National Park, Madagascar.* Ph.D. thesis, State University of New York, College of Environmental Science and Forestry, Syracuse.

BALL, H. L. 1996. Daddy's girl? Anomalous social rank of a female rhesus macaque (*Macaca mulatta*). *Folia Primatologica* 68:44–49.

BARBER, H. R. K. 1988. *Perimenopausal and geriatric gynecology.* New York, Macmillan.

BARCLAY, J. H., AND CADE, T. J. 1983. Restoration of the peregrine falcon in the eastern United States. *Bird Conservation* 1:3–40.

BARNARD, E. A. 1969. Biological function of pancreatic ribonuclease. *Nature* 221:340–344.

BARTLETT, T. Q., AND BROCKELMAN, W. Y. 1996. Gradual replacement of a male pairmate in white-handed gibbons (*Hylobates lar*) in Khao Yai National Park, Thailand. *American Journal of Physical Anthropology* Supplement 22:66.

BARTLETT, T. Q., SUSSMAN, R. W., AND CHEVERUD, J. M. 1993. Infant killing in primates: A review of observed cases with specific reference to the sexual selection hypothesis. *American Anthropologist* 95:958–990.

BATESON, P. 1981. Ontogeny of behavior patterns. *British Medical Bulletin* 37(2):159–164.

BATESON, P. 1982. Behavioural development and evolutionary processes. In *Current problems in sociobiology,* edited by Kings College Sociobiology Group, pp. 123–151. Cambridge, Cambridge University Press.

BAUCHOP, T. 1971. Stomach microbiology of primates. *Annual Review of Microbiology* 25:429–436.

BAUCHOP, T. 1977. Foregut fermentation. In *Microbial ecology of the gut,* edited by R. T. J. Clarke and T. Bauchop, pp. 223–250. New York, Academic Press.

BAUCHOP, T. 1978. Digestion of leaves in vertebrate arboreal folivores. In *The ecology of arboreal folivores,* edited by G. G. Montgomery, pp. 193–204. Washington, DC, Smithsonian Institution Press.

BAUCHOP, T., AND MARTUCCI, R. W. 1968. Ruminant-like digestion of the langur monkey. *Science* 161:698–700.

BAUCHOT, R. 1982. Brain organization and taxonomic relationships in Insectivora and Primates. In *Primate brain evolution,* edited by E. Armstrong, pp. 163–174. New York, Plenum.

BAUER, K., AND SCHREIBER, A. 1997. Double invasion of Tertiary Island South America by ancestral New World monkeys. *Biological Journal of the Linneanen Society* 60:1–20.

BAXTER, J. B., AND FEDIGAN, L. M. 1979. Grooming and consort partner selection in a troop of Japanese monkeys (*Macaca fuscata*). *Archives of Sexual Behavior* 8:445–458.

BEACH, F. 1965. The snark is a boojum. In *Readings in animal behavior,* edited by T. E. McGill, pp. 3–14. New York: Holt, Rinehart and Winston.

BEAUCHER, J. A. 1995. *Categorization models used by chimpanzees when forming basic-level categories.* Master's thesis, Central Washington University, Ellensburg.

BECK, B. 1980. *Animal tool behavior: The use and manufacture of tools by animals.* New York, Garland Press.

BEINTEMA, J. J. 1990. The primary structure of langur (*Presbytis entellus*) pancreatic ribonuclease: Adaptive features in digestive enzymes in mammals. *Molecular Biology and Evolution* 7:470–477.

BEINTEMA, J. J., AND LENSTRA, J. A. 1982. Evolution of mammalian pancreatic ribonucleases. In *Macromolecular sequences in systematic and evolutionary biology,* edited by M. Goodman, pp. 43–73. New York, Plenum.

BEINTEMA, J. J., SCHEFFER, A. J., VAN DIJK, H., WELLING, G. W., AND ZWIERS, H. 1973. Pancreatic ribonuclease: Distribution and comparisons in mammals. *Nature: New Biology* 241:76–78.

BEKOFF, M. 1984. Social play behavior. *BioScience* 34: 228–233.

BENIRSCHKE, K., ed. 1986. *Primates: The road to self-sustaining populations.* New York, Springer-Verlag.

BENNETT, E. L. 1983. *The banded langur: Ecology of a colobine in West Malaysian rain-forest.* Ph.D. thesis, Cambridge University.

BENNETT, E. L., AND SEBASTIAN, A. C. 1988. Social organization and ecology of proboscis monkeys (*Nasalis larvatus*) in mixed coastal forest in Sarawak. *International Journal of Primatology* 9:233–255.

BENNETT, J. 1992. A glut of gibbons in Sarawak—is rehabilitation the answer? *Oryx* 26:157–164.

BERARD, J. D., NÜRNBERG, P., EPPLEN, J. T., AND SCHMIDTKE, J. 1994. Alternative reproductive tactics and reproductive success in male rhesus macaques. *Behaviour* 129:177–201.

BERCOVITCH, F. 1988. Coalitions, cooperation, and reproductive tactics among adult savanna baboons. *Animal Behavior* 34:1198–1209.

BERCOVITCH, F. B. 1989. Body size, sperm competition, and determinants of reproductive success in male savanna baboons. *Evolution* 43:1507–1521.

BERCOVITCH, F. B. 1991. Social stratification, social strategies, and reproductive success in primates. *Ethology and Sociobiology* 12:315–333.

BERCOVITCH, F. B. 1992a. Estradiol concentrations, fat deposits, and reproductive strategies in male rhesus macaques. *Hormones and Behavior* 26:272–282.

BERCOVITCH, F. B. 1992b. Sperm competition, reproductive tactics and paternity in savanna baboons and rhesus macaques. In *Paternity in primates: Genetic tests and theories,* edited by R. D. Martin, A. F. Dixson, and E. J. Wickings, pp. 225–237. Basel, Karger.

BERCOVITCH, F. B. 1995. Female cooperation, consortship maintenance, and male mating success in savanna baboons. *Animal Behavior* 50:137–149.

BERCOVITCH, F. B. 1996. Testicular function and scrotal coloration in patas monkeys. *Journal of Zoology, London* 239:93–100.

BERCOVITCH, F. B. 1997. Reproductive strategies of rhesus macaques. *Primates* 38:247–263.

BERCOVITCH, F. B. 1998. Behavioral ecology and socioendocrinology of reproductive maturation in cercopithecines. In *Old World monkeys,* edited by P. A. Whitehead and C. J. Jolly. Cambridge, Cambridge University Press.

BERCOVITCH, F. B., AND BERARD, J. D. 1993. Life history costs and consequences of rapid reproductive maturation in female rhesus macaques. *Behavioral Ecology and Sociobiology* 32:103–109.

BERCOVITCH, F. B., AND CLARKE, A. S. 1995. Dominance rank, cortisol concentrations, and reproductive maturation in male rhesus macaques. *Physiology and Behavior* 58:215–221.

BERCOVITCH, F. B., AND GOY, R. W. 1990. The socioendocrinology of reproductive development and reproductive success in macaques. In *Socioendocrinology of primate reproduction,* edited by T. E. Ziegler and F. B. Bercovitch, pp. 59–93. New York, Wiley-Liss.

BERCOVITCH, F. B., LEBRON, M. R., MARTINEZ, H. S., AND KESSLER, M. J. 1998. Primigravidity, body weight, and costs of rearing first offspring in rhesus macaques. *American Journal of Primatology* (in press).

BERCOVITCH, F. B., AND NÜRNBERG, P. 1996. Socioendocrine and morphological correlates of paternity in rhesus macaques. *Journal of Reproduction and Fertility* 107: 59–68.

BERCOVITCH, F. B., AND NÜRNBERG, P. 1997. Genetic determination of paternity and variation in male reproductive success in two populations of rhesus macaque. *Electrophoresis* 18:1701–1705.

BERMAN, C. M. 1986. Maternal lineages as tools for understanding infant social development and social structure. In *The Cayo Santiago macaques,* edited by R. G. Rawlins and M. J. Kessler, pp. 73–92. Albany, State University of New York Press.

BERNSTEIN, I. S. 1967. Intertaxa interaction in a Malayan primate community. *Folia Primatologica* 7:198–207.

BERNSTEIN, I. S. 1968. The lutong of Kuala Selangor. *Behaviour* 32:1–16.

BERNSTEIN, I. S. 1970. Primate status hierarchies. In *Primate behavior: Developments in field and laboratory research,* edited by L. Rosenblum, vol. 1, pp. 71–109. New York, Academic Press.

BERNSTEIN, I. S. 1981. Dominance: The baby and the bathwater. *Behavioral and Brain Sciences* 4:419–457.

BERNSTEIN, I. S., AND GORDON, T. P. 1974. The function of aggression in primate societies. *American Scientist* 62:304–311.

BERNSTEIN, I. S., GORDON, T. P., AND ROSE, R. M. 1983. The interaction of hormones, behavior, and social context in nonhuman primates. In *Hormones and aggressive behavior,* edited by B. B. Svare, pp. 535–561. New York, Plenum.

BERNSTEIN, I. S., GORDON, T. P., ROSE, R. M., AND PETERSON, M. S. 1978. Influence of sexual and social stimuli upon circulating levels of testosterone in male pigtail macaques. *Behavioral Biology* 24:400–404.

BERNSTEIN, I. S., JUDGE, P. G., AND RUEHLMANN, T. E. 1993. Kinship, association, and social relationships in rhesus monkeys (*Macaca mulatta*). *American Journal of Primatology* 31:41–53.

BIERHORST, J. 1986. *The monkey's haircut and other stories told by the Maya.* New York, Morrow.

BISHOP, N. H. 1975. *Social behavior of langur monkeys* (*Presbytis entellus) in a high altitude environment.* Ph.D. thesis, University of California, Berkeley.

BISHOP, N. H. 1979. Himalayan langurs: Temperate colobines. *Journal of Human Evolution* 8:251–281.

BLAU, P. 1975. Parameters of social structure. In *Approaches to the study of social structure,* edited by P. Blau, pp. 220–253. New York, Macmillan.

BLAXTER, K. L. 1961. Lactation and growth of the young. In *The mammary gland and its secretions,* edited by S. K. Kon and A. T. Cowie, pp. 305–361. New York, Academic Press.

BLEISH, W. V., CHENG, A. S., REN, X. D., AND XIE, J. H. 1993. Preliminary results from a field study of wild Guizhou snub-nosed monkeys (*Rhinopithecus brelichi*). *Folia Primatologica* 60:72–82.

BLEISH, W. V., AND XIE, J. H. In press. Ecology and behavior of the Guizhou snub-nosed monkey (*Rhinopithecus brelichi*). In *The natural history of the doucs and snub-nosed monkeys,* edited by N. G. Jablonski. Singapore, World Scientific Press.

BLUM, D. 1994. *The monkey wars.* New York, Oxford University Press.

BOCIAN, C. M. 1997. *Niche separation of black-and-white colobus monkeys* (Colobus angolensis *and* C. guereza) *in the Ituri Forest.* Ph.D. thesis, City University of New York.

BODAMER, M., FOUTS, R. S., FOUTS, D. H., AND JENSVOLD, M. L. A. 1994. Functional analysis of chimpanzee (*Pan troglodytes*) private signing. *Human Evolution* 9:281–296.

BODMER, R., FANG, T., MOYA, L., AND GILL, R. 1994. Managing wildlife to conserve Amazonian forests: Population biology and economic considerations of game hunting. *Biological Conservation* 67:29–35.

TE BOEKHORST, I. J. A., SCHÜRMANN, C. L., AND SUGARDJITO, J. 1990. Residential status and seasonal movements of wild orang-utans in the Gunung Leuser Reserve (Sumatra, Indonesia). *Animal Behaviour* 39:1098–1109.

BOESCH, C. 1991. The effects of leopard predation on grouping patterns in forest chimpanzees. *Behaviour* 117:220–242.

BOESCH, C. 1996. Social grouping in Taï chimpanzees. In *Great ape societies,* edited by W. C. McGrew, L. F. Marchant, and T. Nishida, pp. 101–113. Cambridge, Cambridge University Press.

BOESCH, C. 1997. Evidence for dominant wild female chimpanzees investing more in sons. *Animal Behaviour* 54:811–815.

BOESCH, C., AND BOESCH, H. 1984. Possible causes of sex differences in the use of natural hammers by wild chimpanzees. *Journal of Human Evolution* 13:415–440.

BOESCH, C., AND BOESCH, H. 1989. Hunting behavior of wild chimpanzees in the Taï National Park. *American Journal of Physical Anthropology* 78:547–573.

BOGGESS, J. E. 1976. *Social behavior of the Himalayan langur* (Presbytis entellus) *in eastern Nepal.* Ph.D. thesis, University of California, Berkeley.

BOGGESS, J. E. 1980. Intermale relations and troop male membership changes in langurs (*Presbytis entellus*) in Nepal. *International Journal of Primatology* 1(3):233–274.

BOGGESS, J. E. 1984. Infant killing and male reproductive strategies in langurs (*Presbytis entellus*). In *Infanticide: Comparative and evolutionary perspectives,* edited by G. Hausfater and S. B. Hrdy, pp. 283–310. New York, Aldine.

BOINSKI, S. 1987. Mating patterns in squirrel monkeys (*Saimiri oerstoedi*). *Behavioral Ecology and Sociobiology* 21:13–21.

BOINSKI, S. 1988. Use of a club by a wild white-faced capuchin (*Cebus capucinus*) to attack a venomous snake (*Bothrops asper*). *American Journal of Primatology* 14(2):177–179.

BOINSKI, S., AND MITCHELL, C. L. 1994. Male residence and association patterns in Costa Rican squirrel monkeys (*Saimiri oerstedi*). *American Journal of Primatology* 34:157–169.

BONNER, T. I., HEINEMANN, R., AND TODARO, G. J. 1980. Evolution of DNA sequences has been retarded in Malagasy primates. *Nature* 286:420–423.

BOONRATANA, R. 1994. *The ecology and behaviour of the proboscis monkey* (Nasalis larvatus) *in the lower Kinabatangan, Sabah.* Ph.D. thesis, Mahidol University.

BOONRATANA, R., AND LE, X. C. 1994. A report on the ecology, status and conservation of the Tonkin snub-nosed monkey (*Rhinopithecus avunculus*) in northern Vietnam. New York, Wildlife Conservation Society.

BORNER, M. 1985. The rehabilitated chimpanzees of Rubondo island. *Oryx* 19:151–154.

BOYD, R., AND SILK, J. 1997. *How humans evolved.* New York, W. W. Norton.

BROCKELMAN, W. Y., AND GITTINS, S. P. 1984. Natural hybridization in the *Hylobates lar* species group: Implications for speciation in gibbons. In *The lesser apes,* edited by H. Preuschoft, D. Chivers, W. Brockelman, and N. Creel, pp. 498–532. Edinburgh, Edinburgh University Press.

BROCKELMAN, W. Y., AND SRIKOSAMATARA, S. 1984. The maintenance and evolution of social structure in gibbons. In *The lesser apes,* edited by H. Preuschoft, D. Chivers, W. Brockelman, and N. Creel, pp. 298–323. Edinburgh, Edinburgh University Press.

BROCKELMAN, W. Y., TREESUCON, U., REICHARD, U., AND RAEMAEKERS, J. J. 1998. Dispersal, pair formation and social structure in gibbons (*Hylobates lar*). *Behavioral Ecology and Sociobiology* (in press).

BRONSON, F. H. 1989. *Mammalian reproductive biology.* Chicago, University of Chicago Press.

BROOKS, D., AND MCLENNAN, D. 1991. *Phylogeny, ecology, and behavior.* Chicago, University of Chicago Press.

BRUCE, E. J., AND AYALA, F. J. 1979. Phylogenetic relationships between man and apes: Electrophoretic evidence. *Evolution* 33:1040–1056.

BUDNITZ, N., AND DAINIS, K. 1975. *Lemur catta*: Ecology and behavior. In *Lemur biology,* edited by I. Tattersall and R. W. Sussman, pp. 219–235. New York, Plenum.

BUETTNER-JANUSCH, J., DAME, L., MASON, G. A., AND SADE, D. S. 1974a. Primate red cell enzymes: Glucose-6-phosphate dehydrogenase and 6-phosphogluconate dehydrogenase. *American Journal of Physical Anthropology* 41:7–14.

BUETTNER-JANUSCH, J., MASON, G. A., DAME, L., BUETTNER-JANUSCH, V., AND SADE, D. S. 1974b. Genetic studies of serum transferrins of free-ranging macaques of Cayo Santiago, *Macaca mulatta* (Zimmerman, 1780). *American Journal of Physical Anthropology* 41:217–232.

BUFFON, G. 1765. Histoire naturelle, generale et particuliere. *L'imprimeerie du Roi* 13:87–91.

BUNN, H.T., AND EZZO, J. A. 1993. Hunting and scavenging by Plio-Pleistocene hominids: Nutritional constraints, archaeological patterns, and behavioural implications. *Journal of Archaeological Science* 20:365–398.

BURROUGHS, E. 1990. *Tarzan of the apes.* New York, Penguin Books. (Originally published 1914.)

BUSSE, C. D. (1977). Chimpanzee predation as a possible factor in the evolution of red colobus monkey social organization. *Evolution* 31:907–911.

BUTYNSKI, T. M. 1984. Ecological survey of the Impenetrable (Bwindi) Forest, Uganda, and recommendations for its conservation and management. Report to the Government of Uganda.

BYRNE, R. 1995. *The thinking ape.* Oxford, Oxford University Press.

BYRNE, R., AND WHITEN, A., eds. 1988. *Machiavellian intelligence. Social expertise and the evolution of intelligence in monkeys, apes and humans.* Oxford, Clarendon Press.

CACCONE, A., AND POWELL, J. R. 1989. DNA divergence among hominoids. *Evolution* 43:925–942.

CADE, T. J., AND JONES, C. G. 1993. Progress in restoration of the Mauritius kestral. *Conservation Biology* 7:169–175.

CAINE, N. G. 1993a. Flexibility and cooperation as unifying themes in *Saguinus* social organization and behavior: The role of predation pressures. In *Marmosets and tamarins: Systematics, behavior and ecology,* edited by A. B. Rylands, pp. 200–219. Oxford, Oxford Scientific Publications.

CAINE, N. G. 1993b. Vigilance, vocalizations, and cryptic behavior at retirement in captive groups of red-bellied tamarins (*Saguinus labiatus*). *American Journal of Primatology* 12:241–250.

CALDECOTT, J. O., FEISTNER, A. T. C., AND GADSBY, E. L. 1996. A comparison of ecological strategies of pigtail macaques, mandrills and drills. In *Evolution and ecology of macaque societies,* edited by J. A. Fa and D. S. Lindburg, pp. 73–94. Cambridge, Cambridge University Press.

CALDECOTT, J. O., AND KAVANAGH, M. 1983. Can translocation help wild primates? *Oryx* 17:135–139.

CARO, T. M., SELLEN, D. W., PARISH, A., FRANK, R., BROWN, D. M., VOLAND, E., AND BORGERHOFF, M. M. 1995. Termination of reproduction in nonhuman and human female primates. *International Journal of Primatology* 16(2):205–220.

CARPENTER, C. R. 1934. A field study of the behavior and social relations of howling monkeys (*Aloutta palliata*). *Comparative Psychology Monographs* 10:1–168.

CARPENTER, C. R. 1940. Field study in Siam of the behavior and social relations of the gibbon (*Hylobates lar*). *Comparative Psychology Monographs* 16:1–212.

CARPENTER, C. R. 1942. Sexual behavior of free-ranging rhesus monkeys (*Macaca mulatta*). *Journal of Comparative Psychology* 33:113–162.

CARTMILL, M., AND KAY, R. 1978. Craniodental morphology, tarsier affinities and primate suborders. In *Recent advances in primatology,* vol. 3, *Evolution,* edited by D. Chivers and J. Joysey, pp. 205–214. New York, Academic Press.

CARVALHO, J. O. 1996. *Comportamento e ecologia de brachyteles no parque estadual de Carlos Botelho, SP.* Master's thesis, Universidade Federal de Bélem, Para.

CASIMIR, M. J., AND BUTENANDT, E. 1973. Migration and core area shifting in relation to some ecological factors in a mountain gorilla group (*Gorilla gorilla beringei*) in the Mt. Kahuzi Region (République du Zaïre). *Zeitschrift für Tierpsychologie* 33:514–522.

CAVALIERI, P., AND SINGER, P. 1993. *The great ape project.* London, Fourth Estate.

CAVE, A. 1973. The primate nasal fossa. *Biological Journal of the Linneanen Society* 5:377–387.

CHAPAIS, B. 1988. Experimental matrilineal inheritance of rank in female Japanese macaques. *Animal Behaviour* 36:1025–1037.

CHAPAIS, B., AND SCHULMAN, S. 1980. An evolutionary model of female dominance relations in primates. *Journal of Theoretical Biology* 82:47–89.

CHAPMAN, C. A. 1986. Boa constrictor predation and group response in white-faced cebus monkeys. *Biotropica* 18:171–172.

CHAPMAN, C. A. 1990. Ecological constraints on group size in three species of neotropical primates. *Folia Primatologica* 55:1–9.

CHAPMAN, C. A., WRANGHAM, R. W., AND CHAPMAN, L. J. 1995. Ecological constraints on group size: An analysis of spider monkey and chimpanzee subgroups. *Behavioral Ecology and Sociobiology* 36:59–70.

CHARLES-DOMINIQUE, P. 1977. *Ecology and behaviour of nocturnal primates.* New York, Columbia University Press.

CHASE, I. D. 1980. Social process and hierarchy formation in small groups: A comparative perspective. *American Sociological Review* 45:905–924.

CHENEY, D., AND SEYFARTH, R. 1990. *How monkeys see the world: Inside the mind of another species.* Chicago, University of Chicago Press.

CHENEY, D., AND WRANGHAM, W. 1987. Predation. In *Primate societies,* edited by B. B. Smuts, D. L. Cheney, R. M. Seyfarth, R. W. Wrangham, and T. T. Struhsaker. Chicago, University of Chicago Press.

CH'ENG-EN, WU. 1961. *The monkey king,* translated by George Theiner. London, Westbook House.

CHEVALIER-SKOLNIKOFF, S. 1974. Male-female, female-female, and male-male sexual behavior in the stump-tail monkey, with special attention to the female orgasm. *Archives of Sexual Behavior* 3:95–115.

CHEVALIER-SKOLNIKOFF, S. 1976. Homosexual behavior in a laboratory group of stumptail monkeys (*Macaca arctoides*): Forms, contexts, and possible social functions. *Archives of Sexual Behavior* 5:511–527.

CHEVALIER-SKOLNIKOFF, S. 1989. Tool use in cebus: Its relation to object manipulation, the brain, and ecological adaptations. *Behavioral and Brain Sciences* 12(3):610–627.

CHEVALIER-SKOLNIKOFF, S. 1990. Tool use by wild cebus monkeys at Santa Rosa National Park, Costa Rica. *Primates* 31(3):375–383.

CHIARELLI, A. B. 1980. The karyology of South American primates and their relationship to African and Asian species. In *Evolutionary biology of the New World monkeys and continental drift,* edited by R. Ciochon and A. B. Chiarelli. New York, Plenum.

CHIARELLI, A., AND EGOZCUE, J. 1968. The meiotic chromosome of some primates. *Mammal Chromosome Newsletter* 9:85–86.

CHISM, J. 1986. Development and mother-infant relations among captive patas monkeys. *International Journal of Primatology* 7:49–81.

CHISM, J. 1995. Allomaternal behavior and maternal time budgets in patas monkeys. *American Journal of Physical Anthropology* Supplement 20:75–76.

CHISM, J. In press. Allocare patterns among cercopithecines. *Folia Primatologica.*

CHISM, J., AND ROGERS, W. 1997. Male competition, mating success and female choice in a seasonally-breeding primate (*Erythrocebus patas*). *Ethology* 103:109–126.

CHISM, J., AND ROWELL, T. E. 1986. Mating and residence patterns of male patas monkeys. *Ethology* 72:31–39.

CHISM, J., AND ROWELL, T. E. 1988. The natural history of patas monkeys. In *A primate radiation: Evolutionary biology of the African guenons,* edited by A. Gautier-Hion, F. Bourliere, J.-P. Gautier, and J. Kingdon, pp. 412–438. Cambridge, Cambridge University Press.

CHISM, J., ROWELL, T. E., AND OLSON, D. K. 1984. Life history patterns of female patas monkeys. In *Female primates: Studies by women primatologists,* edited by M. Small, pp. 175–190. New York, Alan R. Liss.

CHISM, J., AND WOOD, C. 1994. Diet and feeding behavior of patas monkeys (*Erythrocebus patas*) in Kenya. *American Journal of Physical Anthropology* Supplement 18:67.

CHIVERS, D. J. 1974. *The siamang in Malaya.* Basel, Karger.

CHIVERS, D. J. 1977. The lesser apes. In *Primate conservation,* edited by Prince Rainier of Monaco and G. H. Bourne, pp. 539–598. New York, Academic Press.

CHIVERS, D. J. 1984. Feeding and ranging in gibbons: A summary. In *The lesser apes: Evolutionary and behav-*

ioral biology, edited by H. Preuschoft, D. Chivers, W. Brockelman, and N. Creel. Edinburgh, Edinburgh University Press.

CHIVERS, D. J. 1986. Current issues and new approaches in primate ecology and conservation. In *Primate ecology and conservation,* edited by J. G. Else and P. C. Lee. Cambridge, Cambridge University Press.

CHIVERS, D. J. 1994. Functional anatomy of the gastrointestinal tract. In *Colobine monkeys: Their ecology, behaviour and evolution,* edited by A. G. Davies and J. F. Oates, pp. 205–227. Cambridge, Cambridge University Press.

CHIVERS, D. J., AND HLADIK, C. M. 1980. Morphology of the gastrointestinal tract in primates: Comparisons with other mammals in relation to diet. *Journal of Morphology* 166:337–386.

CIANELLI, S. N., AND FOUTS, R. S. In press. Chimpanzee to chimpanzee American Sign Language communication during high arousal interactions. *Human Evolution.*

CLARK, W. L. G. 1959. *The antecedents of man.* New York, Harper and Row.

CLARK, W. L. G. 1964. *The fossil evidence for human evolution.* Chicago, University of Chicago Press.

CLARKE, A. S., SOTO, A., BERGHOLZ, T., AND SCHNEIDER, M. L. 1996. Maternal gestational stress alters adaptive and social behavior in adolescent rhesus monkey offspring. *Infant Behavior and Development* 19:451–461.

CLARKE, A. S., WITTWER, D. J., ABBOTT, D. H., AND SCHNEIDER, M. L. 1994. Long-term effects of prenatal stress on HPA axis activity in juvenile rhesus monkeys. *Developmental Psychobiology* 27:257–269.

CLARKE, M. R., AND ZUCKER, E. L. 1994. Survey of the howling monkey population at La Pacifica: A seven-year follow-up. *International Journal of Primatology* 15:61–73.

CLUTTON-BROCK, T. H. 1975. Feeding behavior of red colobus and black and white colobus in East Africa. *Folia Primatologica* 23:165–207.

CLUTTON-BROCK, T. H., ed. 1977. *Primate ecology: Studies of feeding and ranging behaviour in lemurs, monkeys and apes.* New York, Academic Press.

CLUTTON-BROCK, T. H., AND HARVEY, P. H. 1977a. Primate ecology and social organization. *Journal of Zoology, London* 183:1–39.

CLUTTON-BROCK, T. H., AND HARVEY, P. H. 1977b. Species differences in feeding and ranging behavior. In *Primate ecology,* edited by T. H. Clutton-Brock, pp. 557–584. New York, Academic Press.

COE, C. L., MENDOZA, S. P., AND LEVINE, S. 1979. Social status constrains the stress response in the squirrel monkey. *Physiology and Behavior* 23:633–638.

COIMBRA-FILHO, A. 1977. Natural shelters of *Leontopithecus rosalia* and some ecological implications. In *The biology of the Callitrichidae,* edited by D. G. Kleiman, pp. 79–89. Washington, DC, Smithsonian Institution Press.

COLLIAS, N., AND SOUTHWICK, C. 1952. A field study of population density and social organization in howling monkeys. *Proceedings of the American Philosophical Society* 96:143–156.

COLLINS, N. M., SAYER, J. A., AND WHITMORE, T. C. 1991. *The conservation atlas of tropical forests: Asia and the Pacific.* New York, Simon and Schuster.

COLLURA, R. V., AUERBACH, M. R., AND STEWART, C.-B. 1996. A quick, direct method that can differentiate expressed mitochondrial genes from their nuclear pseudogenes. *Current Biology* 6:1337–1339.

COLLURA, R. V., AND STEWART, C.-B. 1995. Insertions and duplications of mtDNA in the nuclear genomes of Old World monkeys and hominoids. *Nature* 378:485–489.

COLLURA, R.V., AND STEWART, C.-B. 1996. *Mitochondrial DNA phylogeny of the colobine Old World monkeys.* Abstracts. XVIth Congress of the International Primatological Society, August 11–16, Madison, Wisconsin.

COLQUHOUN, I. C. 1997. *A predictive socioecological study of the black lemur (Eulemur macaco macaco) in northwestern Madagascar.* Ph.D. thesis, Washington University, St. Louis.

COLVIN, J. D. 1986. Proximate causes of male emigration at puberty in rhesus monkeys. In *The Cayo Santiago macaques,* edited by R. G. Rawlins and M. J. Kessler, pp. 131–157. Albany, State University of New York Press.

COLWELL, R., AND KING, M. C. 1983. Disentangling genetic and cultural influences on human behavior: Problems and prospects. In *Comparing behavior: Studying man studying animals,* edited by D. W. Rajecki, pp. 227–249. Hillsdale, NJ, Lawrence Erlbaum.

COOLIDGE, H. J. 1933. *Pan paniscus.* Pygmy chimpanzee from south of the Congo River. *American Journal of Physical Anthropology* 18:1–57.

CORBET, G. B., AND HILL, J. E. 1992. *The mammals of the Indomalayan region.* Oxford, Oxford University Press.

CORDS, M. 1987. Forest guenons and patas monkeys: Male-male competition in one-male groups. In *Primate societies,* edited by B. Smuts, D. Cheney, R. Seyfarth, R. Wrangham, and T. Struhsaker, pp. 98–111. Chicago, University of Chicago Press.

COSTANZA, R., D'ARGE, R., DE GROOT, R., FARBER, S., GRASSO, M., HANNON, B., LIMBURG, K., NAEEM, S., O'NEILL, R. V., PARUELO, J., RASKIN, R. G., SUTTON, P., AND VAN DEN BELT, M. 1997. The value of the world's ecosystem services and natural capital. *Nature* 387: 253–259.

COWLISHAW, G. 1992. Song functions in gibbons. *Behaviour* 121(1&2):131–153.

COWLISHAW, G., AND DUNBAR, R. 1991. Dominance rank and mating success in male primates. *Animal Behaviour* 41:1045–1056.

CREEL, N., AND PREUSCHOFT, H. 1984. Pathways of speciation: An introduction. In *The lesser apes: Evolutionary and behavioral biology,* edited by H. Preuschoft, D. J. Chivers, W. Y. Brockelman, and N. Creel. Edinburgh, Edinburgh University Press.

CROCKETT, C. M. 1996. The relation between red howler monkey (*Alouatta seniculus*) troop size and population growth in two habitats. In *Adaptive radiations of neotropical primates,* edited by M. A. Norconk, A. L. Rosenberger, and P. A. Garber, pp. 489–510. New York, Plenum.

CROCKETT, C. M., AND POPE, T. R. 1993. Consequences of sex differences in dispersal for juvenile red howler monkeys. In *Juvenile primates: Life history, development, and behavior,* edited by M. E. Pereira and L. A. Fairbanks, pp. 104–118. New York, Oxford University Press.

CROMPTON, R., AND ANDAU, P. 1987. Ranging, activity rhythms, and sociality in free-ranging *Tarsius bancanus*: A preliminary report. *International Journal of Primatology* 8:43–71.

CRONIN, J. E., AND SARICH, V. M. 1975. Molecular systematics of the New World monkeys. *Journal of Human Evolution* 4:357–375.

CRONIN, J. E., AND SARICH, V. M. 1976. Molecular evidence for the dual origin of the mangabeys among Old World monkeys. *Nature* 260:700–702.

CRONIN, J. E., SARICH, V. M., AND RYDER, O. 1984. Molecular evolution and speciation in the lesser apes. In *The lesser apes: Evolutionary and behavioral biology,* edited by H. Preuschoft, D. J. Chivers, W. Y. Brockelman, and N. Creel. Edinburgh, Edinburgh University Press.

CROOK, J. H., AND GARTLAN, J. S. 1966. Evolution of primate societies. *Nature* 210:1200–1203.

CURTIN, R. A. 1975. *The socioecology of the common langur,* Presbytis entellus, *in the Nepal Himalayas*. Ph.D. thesis, University of California.

CURTIN R. A. 1977. Langur social behavior and infant mortality. *Kroeber Anthropological Society Papers* 50: 27–36.

CURTIN R. A. 1981. Strategy and tactics in male gray langur competition. *Journal of Human Evolution* 10:245–253.

CURTIN R. A., AND DOLHINOW, P. 1978. Primate social behavior in a changing world. *American Scientist* 66: 468–475.

CURTIN, S. H. 1976. Niche separation in sympatric Malaysian leaf-monkeys (*Presbytis obscura* and *Presbytis melalophos*). *Yearbook of Physical Anthropology* 20:421–439.

CURTIN, S. H. 1980. Dusky and banded leaf monkeys. In *Malayan forest primates,* edited by D. J. Chivers, pp. 107–145. New York, Plenum.

CURTIS, D. J. 1997. *The mongoose lemur (*Eulemur mongoz*): A study in behavior and ecology*. Ph.D. thesis, Universität Zurich, Zurich.

DAHL, J. F., GOULD, K. G., AND NADLER, R. D. 1993. Testicle size of orang-utans in relation to body size. *American Journal of Physical Anthropology* 90:229–236.

DARWIN, C. 1981. *The descent of man and selection in relation to sex*. Princeton, NJ, Princeton University Press. (Originally published 1871.)

DAS, F. 1932. *Leap-home and Gentlebrawn*. London, Dent and Sons.

DASILVA, G. L. 1994. Diet of *Colobus polykomos* on Tiwai Island: Selection of food in relation to its seasonal abundance and nutritional quality. *International Journal of Primatology* 15:655–680.

DASSER, V. 1988. A social concept in Java monkeys. *Animal Behaviour* 36:225–230.

DAVIES, A. G. 1984. *An ecological study of the red leaf monkey (*Presbytis rubicunda) *in the dipterocarp forest of northern Borneo*. Ph.D. thesis, Cambridge University.

DAVIES, A. G. 1991. Seed-eating by red leaf monkeys (*Presbytis rubicunda*) in dipterocarp forest of northern Borneo. *International Journal of Primatology* 12:119–144.

DAVIES, A. G., BENNETT, E. L., AND WATERMAN, P. G. 1988. Food selection by two south-east Asian colobine monkeys (*Presbytis rubicunda* and *Presbytis melalophos*) in relation to plant chemistry. *Biological Journal of the Linneanen Society* 34:33–56.

DAVIES, A. G., AND OATES, J. F., eds. 1994. *Colobine monkeys: Their ecology, behaviour and evolution*. Cambridge, Cambridge University Press.

DAVIS, J. Q. 1995. *The perception of distortions in the signs of American Sign Language by a group of cross-fostered chimpanzees (*Pan troglodytes*)*. Master's thesis, Central Washington University, Ellensburg.

DAWSON, G. A. 1976. *Behavioral ecology of the Panamanian tamarin,* Saguinus oedipus geoffroyi (*Callitrichidae, Primates*). Ph.D. thesis, Michigan State University.

DEAG, J. M., AND CROOK, J. H. 1971. Social behaviour and agonistic buffering in the wild Barbary macaque, *Macaca sylvana* L. *Folia Primatologica* 15:183–200.

DELSON, E. 1980. Fossil macaques, phyletic relationships and a scenario of development. In *The macaques,* edited by D. G. Lindburg, pp. 10–30. New York, Van Nostrand Reinhold.

DELSON, E. 1992. Evolution of Old World monkeys. In *Cambridge encyclopaedia of human evolution,* edited by S. Jones, R. D. Martin, and D. M. Pilbeam, pp. 217–222. Cambridge, Cambridge University Press.

DELSON, E. 1994. Evolutionary history of the colobine monkeys in paleoenvironmental perspective. In *Colobine monkeys: Their ecology, behavior and evolution,* edited by A. G. Davies and J. F. Oates, pp. 11–43. Cambridge, Cambridge University Press.

DEMMENT, M. W. 1983. Feeding ecology and the evolution of body size of baboons. *African Journal of Ecology* 21:219–233.

DEMMENT, M. W., AND VAN SOEST, P. J. 1985. A nutritional explanation for body-size patterns of ruminant and nonruminant herbivores. *American Naturalist* 125: 641–672.

DENE, H. T., GOODMAN, M., AND PRYCHODKO, W. 1976. Immunodiffusion evidence on the phylogeny of the primates. In *Molecular anthropology,* edited by M. Goodman and R. E. Tashian, pp. 171–195. New York, Plenum.

DENE, H. T., GOODMAN, M., AND PRYCHODKO, W. 1980. Immunodiffusion systematics of the primates. IV: Lemuriformes. *Mammalia* 44:211–223.

DENHAM, W. W. 1971. Energy relations and some basic properties of primate social organization. *American Anthropologist* 73:77–95.

DEROUSSEAU, C. J. 1994. Primate gerontology: An emerging discipline. In *Biological anthropology and aging,* edited by D. E. Crews and R. M. Garruto, pp. 127–153. Oxford, Oxford University Press.

DE RUITER, J., AND INOUE, M. 1993. Paternity, male social rank and sexual behaviour. *Primates* 34:553–555.

DE RUITER, J. R., SCHEFFRAHN, W., TROMMELEN, G. J. J. M., UITTERLINDEN, A. G., MARTIN, R. D., AND VAN HOOFF, J. A. R. A. M. 1992. Male social rank and reproductive success in wild longtailed macaques: Paternity exclusions by blood protein analysis and DNA fingerprinting. In *Paternity in primates: Genetic tests and theories,* edited by R. D. Martin, A. F. Dixson, and E. J. Wickings, pp. 175–191. Basel, Karger.

DEVORE, I. 1962. *Social behavior and organization of baboon troops.* Ph.D. thesis, Harvard University.

DEVORE, I. 1965a. Male dominance and mating behavior in baboons. In *Sex and behavior,* edited by F. Beach, pp. 266–289. New York, Wiley.

DEVORE, I., ed. 1965b. *Primate behavior: Field studies of monkeys and apes.* New York, Holt, Rinehart and Winston.

DE VRIES, A. 1991. *Translocation of mantled howling monkeys* (Alouatta palliata) *in Guanacaste, Costa Rica.* Master's thesis, University of Calgary, Alberta, Canada.

DE WAAL, F. B. M. 1982. *Chimpanzee politics: Power and sex among apes.* London, Unwin Paperbacks.

DE WAAL, F. B. M. 1989. *Peace-making among primates.* Cambridge, MA, Harvard University Press.

DE WAAL, F. B. M. 1993. Reconciliation among primates: A review of empirical evidence and unresolved issues. In *Primate social conflict,* edited by W. A. Mason and S. P. Mendoza, pp. 111–144. Albany, State University of New York Press.

DE WAAL, F. B. M. 1997. *Bonobo: The forgotten ape.* Berkeley, University of California Press.

DE WAAL, F. B. M., AND LANTING, F. 1998. *Bonobo: The forgotten ape.* Berkeley, University of California Press.

DE WAAL, F. B. M., AND LUTTRELL, L. M. 1989. Toward a comparative socioecology of the genus *Macaca*: Different dominance styles in rhesus and stumptail monkeys. *American Journal of Primatology* 19:83–109.

DE WAAL, F. B. M., VAN HOOFF, J., AND NETTO, W. J. 1976. An ethological analysis of types of agonistic interaction in a captive group of Java monkeys (*Macaca fascicularis*). *Primates* 17:257–290.

DIETZ, J. M., PERES, C. A., AND PINDER, L. 1997. Foraging ecology and use of space in wild golden lion tamarins (*Leontopithecus rosalia*). *American Journal of Primatology* 41:289–305.

DI FIORE, A., AND RENDALL, D. 1994. Evolution of social organization: A reappraisal for primates by using phylogenetic methods. *Proceedings of the National Academy of Sciences* 91:9941–9945.

DIGBY, L. J., AND BARRETO, C. E. 1996. Activity and ranging patterns in common marmosets (*Callithrix jacchus*). In *Adaptive radiations of neotropical primates.* edited by M. A. Norconk, A. L. Rosenberger, and P. A. Garber, pp. 173–185. New York, Plenum.

DISOTELL, T. R. 1994. Generic level relationships of the Papionini (Cercopithecoidea). *American Journal of Physical Anthropology* 94:47–57.

DISOTELL, T. R. 1996. The phylogeny of Old World monkeys. *Evolutionary Anthropology* 5:18–24.

DISOTELL, T. R. 1998. Molecular systematics of the Cercopithecinae. In *Old World monkeys,* edited by P. F. Whitehead and C. J. Jolly. Cambridge, Cambridge University Press.

DITTUS, W. P. J. 1980. The social regulation of primate populations: A synthesis. In *The macaques,* edited by D. G. Lindburg, pp. 263–286. New York, Van Nostrand Reinhold.

DITTUS, W. P. J. 1987. Group fusion among wild toque macaques: An extreme case of inter-group resource competition. *Behaviour* 100:247–291.

DITTUS, W. P. J. 1988. Group fission among wild toque macaques as a consequence of female resource competition and environmental stress. *Animal Behavior* 36:1626–1645.

DIXSON, A. F. 1983. Observations on the evolution and behavioral significance of sexual skin in female primates. *Advances in the Study of Behavior* 13:63–106.

DIXSON, A. F. 1987. Baculum length and copulatory behavior in primates. *American Journal of Primatology* 13:51–60.

DIXSON, A. F. 1995. Sexual selection and ejaculatory frequency in primates. *Folia Primatologica* 64:146–152.

DIXSON, A. F., AND FLEMING, D. 1981. Parental behaviour and infant development in owl monkeys (*Aotus trivirgatus grivemembra*). *Journal of Zoology, London* 194:25–39.

DIXSON, A. F., AND GEORGE, L. 1982. Prolactin and parental behaviour in a male New World primate. *Nature* 299:551–553.

DJOJOSUDHARMO, S., AND VAN SCHAIK, C. P. 1992. Why are orangutans so rare in the highlands?: Altitudinal changes in a Sumatran forest. *Tropical Biodiversity* 1(1):11–22.

DOBSON, D. E. 1981. *Evolution of ruminant lysozymes.* Berkeley, University of California Press.

DOBSON, D. E., PRAGER, E. M., AND WILSON, A. C. 1984. Stomach lysozymes of ruminants: I. Distribution and catalytic properties. *Journal of Biological Chemistry* 259:11607–11616.

DOLHINOW, P. 1972a. The north Indian langur. In *Primate patterns,* edited by P. Dolhinow, pp. 181–238. New York, Holt, Rinehart and Winston.

DOLHINOW, P., ed. 1972b. *Primate patterns.* New York, Holt, Rinehart and Winston.

DOLHINOW, P. 1978. A behavior repertoire for the Indian langur monkey (*Presbytis entellus*). *Primates* 19:449–472.

DOLHINOW, P. 1984. The primates: Age, behavior, and evolution. In *Age and anthropological theory.* edited by D. I. Kertzer and J. Keith, pp. 65–81. Ithaca, NY, Cornell University Press.

DOLHINOW, P. 1991. Tactics of primate immaturity. In *Man and beast revisited,* edited by M. H. Robinson and L. Tiger, pp. 139–240. Washington, DC, Smithsonian Institution Press.

DOLHINOW, P. In press. A mystery, explaining behavior. In *The new physical anthropology: Science, humanism and critical reflection.* edited by S. Strum, D. Lindburg, and D. Hamburg. New York, Prentice Hall.

DOLHINOW, P., AND BISHOP, N. 1970. The development of motor skills and social relations among primates through play. *Minnesota Symposium on Child Psychology* 4:141–198.

DOLHINOW, P., AND DEMAY, M. 1982. Adoption: The importance of infant choice. *Journal of Human Evolution* 11:391–420.

DOLHINOW, P., AND KRUSKO, N. 1984. Langur monkey females and infants: The female's point of view. In *Female primates,* edited by M. F. Small, pp. 37–57. New York, Alan R. Liss.

DOLHINOW, P., AND MURPHY, G. 1982. Langur monkey (*Presbytis entellus*) development. *Folia Primatologica* 39:305–331.

DOLHINOW, P., AND TAFF, M. 1993. Rivalry, resolution, and the individual: Cooperation among male langur monkeys. In *Milestones in human evolution,* edited by A. J. Almquist and A. Manyak, pp. 75–92. Prospect Heights, IL, Waveland Press.

DOOLITTLE, R. F. 1994. Convergent evolution: The need to be explicit. *Trends in Biochemical Sciences* 19:15–18.

DORAN, D. M. 1996. Comparative positional behavior of the African apes. In *Great ape societies,* edited by W. C. McGrew, L. F. Marchant, and T. Nishida, pp. 213–224. Cambridge, Cambridge University Press.

DORE, F., AND DUMAS, C. 1987. Psychology of animal cognition: Piagetian studies. *Psychological Bulletin* 102(2):242–248.

DRICKAMER, L. 1974. A ten-year summary of reproductive data for free-ranging *Macaca mulatta. Folia primatologica* 21:61–80.

DUDLEY, N. 1997. *The year the world caught fire.* Gland, Switzerland, World Wide Fund for Nature.

DUMESIC, D. A., ABBOTT, D. H., EISNER, J. R., AND GOY, R. W. 1997. Prenatal exposure of female rhesus monkeys to testosterone propionate increases serum luteinizing hormone levels in adulthood. *Fertility and Sterility* 67:155–163.

DUMOND, F. V., AND HUTCHINSON, T. C. 1967. Squirrel monkey reproduction: The fatted male phenomenon and seasonal spermatogenesis. *Science* 158:1067–1070.

DUNBAR, R. I. M. 1984. *Reproductive decisions: An economic analysis of gelada baboon social strategies.* Princeton, NJ, Princeton University Press.

DUNBAR, R. I. M. 1988. *Primate social systems.* Ithaca, NY, Comstock.

DUNBAR, R. I. M. 1992. Neocortex size as a constraint on group size in primates. *Journal of Human Evolution* 20:469–493.

DUNBAR, R. I. M. 1996. Determinants of group size in primates: A general model. In *Evolution of social behav-*

iour patterns in primates and man, edited by W. G. Runciman, J. M. Smith, and R. I. M. Dunbar, pp. 33–58. Oxford, Oxford University Press.

DUNBAR, R. I. M., AND DUNBAR, E. P. 1974. Ecology and population dynamics of *Colobus guereza* in Ethiopia. *Folia Primatologica* 21:188–208.

DUTRILLAUX, B. 1988. Chromosome evolution in primates. *Folia Primatologica* 50:134–135.

DUTRILLAUX, B., COUTURIER, J., MULERIS, M., LOMBARD, M., AND CHAUVIER, G. 1982. Chromosomal phylogeny of forty-two species or subspecies of cercopithecoids (Primates, Catarrhini). *Annales de genetique* 25:96–109.

DYKE, C. 1988. *The evolutionary dynamics of complex systems: A study in biosocial complexity.* New York, Oxford University Press.

EAMES, J. C., AND ROBSON, C. R. 1993. Threatened primates in southern Vietnam. *Oryx* 27(3):146–154.

EATON, G. G., AND RESKO, J. A. 1974. Plasma testosterone and male dominance in a Japanese macaque (*Macaca fuscata*) troop compared with repeated measures of testosterone in laboratory males. *Hormones and Behavior* 5:251–259.

EBERHARD, W. G. 1997. *Female control.* Princeton, NJ, Princeton University Press.

EBERHARDT, J. A., KEVERNE, E. B., AND MELLER, R. E. 1980. Social influences on plasma testosterone levels in male talapoin monkeys. *Hormones and Behavior* 14:247–266.

EHARDT, C. L., AND BERNSTEIN, I. S. 1992. Conflict intervention behaviour by adult male macaques: Structural and functional aspects. In *Coalitions and alliances in humans and other animals,* edited by A. H. Harcourt and F. B. M. de Waal, pp. 83–111. Oxford, Oxford University Press.

EISENBERG, J. F., MUCKENHIRN, N. A., AND RUDRAN, R. 1972. The relation between ecology and social structure in primates. *Science* 176:863–874.

ELLEFSON, J. O. 1968. Territorial behavior in the common white-handed gibbon, *Hylobates lar* linn. In *Primates: Studies in adaptation and variability,* edited by P. C. Jay, pp. 180–199. New York, Holt, Rinehart and Winston.

ELLEFSON, J. O. 1974. A natural history of white-handed gibbons in the Malayan peninsula. In *Gibbon and siamang,* edited by D. M. Rumbaugh, vol. 3. Basel, Karger.

ENDO, T., IKEO, K., AND GOJOBORI, T. 1996. Large-scale search for genes on which positive selection may operate. *Molecular Biology and Evolution* 13:685–690.

ERLANDSEN, S. L., PARSONS, J. A., AND TAYLOR, T. D. 1974. Ultrastructural immunocytochemical localization of lysozyme in the Paneth cells of man. *Journal of Histochemistry and Cytochemistry* 22:401–413.

ERXLEBEN, J. 1777. *Systema regni animalis.* Liepzig, Impensis Weygandianis.

ESTEP, D. Q., BRUCE, K. E. M., JOHNSTON, M. E., AND GORDON, T. P. 1984. Sexual behavior of group-housed stumptail macaques (*Macaca acrtoides*): Temporal, demographic and sociosexual relationships. *Folia Primatologica* 42:115–126.

ESTLING, R. 1983 (June). The trouble with thinking backwards. *New Scientist* 2:619–621.

ESTRADA, A. 1984. Male-infant interactions among free-ranging stumptail macaques. In *Primate paternalism,* edited by D. M. Taub, pp. 56–87. New York, Van Nostrand Reinhold.

EUDEY, A. A. 1979. *Differentiation and dispersal of macaques (Macaca spp.) in Asia.* Ph.D. thesis, University of California, Davis.

EUDEY, A. A. 1981. Morphological and ecological characters in sympatric populations of *Macaca* in the Dawna Range. In *Primate evolutionary biology,* edited by R. S. Corruccini and A. B. Chiarelli, pp. 44–50. Berlin, Springer-Verlag.

EUDEY, A. A. 1986. Hill tribe peoples and primate conservation in Thailand: A preliminary assessment of the problem of reconciling shifting cultivation with conservation objectives. In *Primate ecology and conservation,* edited by J. G. Else and P. C. Lee, pp. 237–248. Cambridge, Cambridge University Press.

EUDEY, A. A., compiler. 1987. *Action plan for Asian primate conservation: 1987–91.* Gland, Switzerland, IUCN.

EUDEY, A. A. 1988. Hmong relocated in northern Thailand. *Cultural Survival Quarterly* 12(1):79–82.

EUDEY, A. A. 1989 (14 April). Eviction orders to the Hmong of Huai Yew Yee village, Huai Kha Khaeng Wildlife Sanctuary, Thailand. In *Hill tribes today,* edited by J. McKinnon and B. Vienne, pp. 249–258. Bangkok, White Lotus and Orstom.

EUDEY, A. A. 1991a. Conservation's moral dilemma: A case study from Thailand. In *Primatology today,* edited by A. Ehara, T. Kimura, O. Takenaka, and M. Iwamoto, pp. 59–62. New York, Elsevier.

EUDEY, A. A. 1991b. Macaque habitat preference in west-central Thailand and Quaternary glacial events. In *Primatology today,* edited by A. Ehara, T. Kimura, O. Takenaka, and M. Iwamoto, pp. 21–24. New York, Elsevier.

EUDEY, A. A. 1995a. The impact of socioeconomic decisions on the status of the orangutan and other east Asian fauna. In *The neglected ape,* edited by R. D. Nadler, B. M. F. Galdikas, L. K. Sheeran, and N. Rosen, pp. 23–27. New York, Plenum.

EUDEY, A. A. 1995b. Southeast Asian primate trade routes. *Primate Report* 41:33–42.

EUDEY, A. A. 1996. *The conservation status of the Asian and African primates.* Paper presented at the International Primatological Society, Madison, Wisconsin.

EUDEY, A. A. 1996/1997. Asian primate conservation— the species and the network. *Primate Conservation,* 17:101–110.

EVANS, B. J., MORALES, J. C., AND MELNICK, D. J. In press. Mitochondrial phylogeography of macaques in southeast Asia, the Sunda shelf, and Sulawesi. *Biological Journal of the Linneanen Society.*

FA, J. A. 1989. The genus *Macaca:* A review of taxonomy and evolution. *Mammal Review* 19:45–81.

FAGEN, R. 1981. *Animal play behavior.* New York, Oxford University Press.

FAGEN, R. 1993. Primate juveniles and primate play. In *Juvenile primates: Life history, development, and behavior,* edited by M. E. Pereira and L. A. Fairbanks, pp. 182–196. New York, Oxford University Press.

FAIRBANKS, L. A. 1993. Juvenile vervet monkeys: Establishing relationships and practicing skills for the future. In *Juvenile primates: Life history, development, and behavior,* edited by M. E. Pereira and L. A. Fairbanks, pp. 211–227. New York, Oxford University Press.

FARSLOW, D. 1987. *The behavior and ecology of the long-tailed macaque,* Macaca fascicularis *on Angaur Island, Palau, Micronesia.* Ph.D. thesis, Ohio State University.

FEDIGAN, L. M. 1976. A study of roles in the Arashiyama West troop of Japanese monkeys (*Macaca fuscata*). *Contributions to Primatology,* vol. 9. New York, Karger.

FEDIGAN, L. M. 1982. *Primate paradigms: Sex roles and social bonds.* Montreal, Eden Press.

FEDIGAN, L. M. 1983. Dominance and reproductive success in primates. *Yearbook of Physical Anthropology* 26:91–129.

FEDIGAN, L. M. 1991. History of the Arashiyama West Japanese macaques in Texas. In *The monkeys of Arashiyama: Thirty-five years of research in Japan and the West,* edited by L. M. Fedigan and P. J. Asquith, pp. 54–73. Albany, State University of New York Press.

FEDIGAN, L., AND FEDIGAN, L. 1988. *Cercopithecus aethiops:* A review of field studies. In *A primate radiation: Evolutionary biology of the African guenons,* edited by A. Gautier-Hion, F. Bourliere, J.-P. Gautier, and J. Kingdon, pp. 389–411. Cambridge, Cambridge University Press.

FEDIGAN, L. M., FEDIGAN, L., GOUZOULES, S., GOUZOULES, H., AND KOYAMA, N. 1986. Lifetime reproductive success in female Japanese macaques. *Folia Primatologica* 47:143–157.

FEDIGAN, L. M., AND ROSE, L. M. 1995. Interbirth interval variation in three sympatric species of neotropical monkey. *American Journal of Primatology* 37:9–24.

FERNANDES, M. E. B. 1991. Tool use and predation of oysters (*Crassostrea rhizophorea*) by the tufted capuchin, *Cebus apella apella,* in brackish water mangrove swamp. *Primates* 32(4):529–531.

FITTINGHOFF, N. A., JR., AND LINDBURG, D. G. 1980. Riverine refuging in East Bornean *Macaca fascicularis.* In *The macaques,* edited by D. G. Lindburg, pp. 182–214. New York, Van Nostrand Reinhold.

FITZSIMONS, F. 1911. *The monkey-folk of South Africa.* London, Longmans, Green, and Co.

FLEAGLE, J. G. 1988. *Primate adaptation and evolution.* San Diego, CA, Academic Press.

FLEMING, T. H., BREITWISCH, R., AND WHITESIDES, G. H. 1987. Patterns of tropical vertebrate frugivore diversity. *Annual Review of Ecology and Systematics* 18:91–109.

FOGDEN, M. L. 1974. A preliminary field study of the western tarsier, *Tarsius bancanus* (Horsfield). In *Prosimian biology,* edited by R. D. Martin, G. A. Doyle, and A. C. Walker. London, Duckworth.

FOLEY, R. A. 1996. An evolutionary and chronological framework for human social behavior. In *Evolution of social behaviour patterns in primates and man,* edited by W. G. Runciman, J. M. Smith, and R. I. M. Dunbar, pp. 95–118. Oxford, Oxford University Press.

FOODEN, J. 1967. Complimentary specialization of male and female reproductive structures in the bear macaque, *Macaca arctoides. Nature* 214:939–941.

FOODEN, J. 1976. Provisional classification and key to the living species of macaques (Primates: *Macaca*). *Folia Primatologica* 25:225–236.

FOODEN, J. 1986. Taxonomy and evolution of the sinica group of macaques. 5. Overview of natural history. *Fieldiana, Zoology* 29:1–22.

FOODEN, J., AND LANYON, S. M. 1989. Blood-protein allele frequencies and phylogenetic relationships in *Macaca.* A review. *American Journal of Primatology* 17:209–241.

FORD, S. M. 1994. Evolution of sexual dimorphism in body weight in platyrrhines. *American Journal of Primatology* 34:221–244.

FORD, S. M., AND DAVIS, L. C. 1992. Systematics and body size: Implications for feeding adaptations in New World monkeys. *American Journal of Physical Anthropology* 88:415–468.

FOSSEY, D. 1983. *Gorillas in the mist.* Boston, Houghton Mifflin.

FOSSEY, D., AND HARCOURT, A. H. 1977. Feeding ecology of free-ranging mountain gorillas (*Gorilla gorilla beringei*). In *Primate ecology: Studies of feeding and ranging behaviour in lemurs, monkeys and apes,* edited by T. H. Clutton-Brock, pp. 415–447. London, Academic Press.

Fouts, R. S. 1973. Acquisition and testing of gestural signs in four young chimpanzees. *Science* 180:978–980.

Fouts, R. S. 1975. Communication with chimpanzees. In *Hominization and behavior,* edited by I. Eibl-Eibesfeldt and G. Kurth, pp. 137–158. Stuttgart, Gustav Fisher Verlag.

Fouts, R. S., Chown, B., and Goodin, L. 1976. Transfer of signed responses in American Sign Language from vocal English stimuli to physical object stimuli by a chimpanzee (*Pan*). *Learning and Motivation* 7:458–475.

Fouts, R. S., and Fouts, D. H. 1989. Loulis in conversation with the cross-fostered chimpanzees. In *Teaching sign language to chimpanzees,* edited by R. A. Gardner, B. T. Gardner, and T. Van Cantfort, pp. 293–307. Albany, State University of New York Press.

Fouts, R. S., Fouts, D. H., and Schoenfeld, D. 1984. Sign language conversational interactions between chimpanzees. *Sign Language Studies* 34:1–12.

Fouts, R. S., Fouts, D. H., and Van Cantfort, T. 1989. The infant Loulis learns signs from cross-fostered chimpanzees. In *Teaching sign language to chimpanzees,* edited by R. A. Gardner, B. T. Gardner, and T. Van Cantfort, pp. 280–292. Albany, State University of New York Press.

Fouts, R. S., Haislip, M., Iwaszuk, W., Sanz, C., and Fouts, D. H. 1997. *Chimpanzee communicative gestures: Idiolects and dialects.* Paper presented at the Rocky Mountain Psychological Association, Reno/Sparks, NV, April 18–20.

Fouts, R. S., Hirsch, A. D., and Fouts, D. H. 1982. Cultural transmission of a human language in a chimpanzee mother-infant relationship. In *Psychobiological perspectives: Child nurturance series,* edited by H. E. Fitzgerald, J. A. Mullins, and P. Page, vol. 3, pp. 159–193. New York, Plenum.

Fouts, R. S., and Rigby, R. 1977. Man-chimpanzee communication. In *How animals communicate,* edited by T. A. Sebeok, pp. 1034–1054. Bloomington, Indiana University Press.

Fouts, R. S., Shapiro, G., and O'Neil, C. 1978. Studies of linguistic behavior in apes and children. In *Understanding language through sign language research,* edited by P. Siple, pp. 163–185. New York, Academic Press.

Fox, E. 1998. The function of male sexual aggression and female resistance in wild Sumatran orangutans (*Pongo pygmaeus abelii*). *American Journal of Physical Anthropology* Supplement 26:84.

Fracasso, C., and Patarnello, T. 1998. Evolution of the dystrophin muscular promoter and 50 flanking regions in primates. *Journal of Molecular Evolution* 46: 168–179.

Fragaszy, D. M., and Adams-Curtis, L. E. 1991. Generative aspects of manipulation in tufted capuchin monkeys (*Cebus apella*). *Journal of Comparative Psychology* 105(4):387–397.

Fragaszy, D. M., Visalberghi, E., and Robinson, J. G. 1990. Variability and adaptability in the genus *Cebus. Folia Primatologica* 54:114–118.

Fredrickson, W. T., and Sackett, G. P. 1984. Kin preferences in primates (*Macaca nemestrina*): Relatedness or familiarity? *Journal of Comparative Psychology* 98: 29–34.

Freed, B. Z. 1996. *Co-occurrence among crowned lemurs (Lemur coronatus) and Sanford's lemurs (Lemur fulvus sanfordi) of Madagascar.* Ph.D. thesis, Washington University, St. Louis.

Fruth, B. 1995. *Nests and nest groups in wild bonobos (Pan paniscus): Ecological and behavioural correlates.* Aachen, Shaker.

Fruth, B. 1996. The terrestrial bonobo (*Pan paniscus*): New findings from a wild, habituated, non-provisioned community at Lomako (République du Zaïre). Paper presented at the XVIth Congress of the International Primatological Society, Madison, Wisconsin.

Fruth, B., and Hohmann, G. 1994. Comparative analyses of nest-building behavior in bonobos and chimpanzees. In *Chimpanzee cultures,* edited by R. W. Wrangham, W. C. McGrew, F. B. M. de Waal, and P. G. Heltne, pp. 109–128. Cambridge, MA, Harvard University Press.

Fruth, B., and Hohmann, G. 1996. Nest building behavior in the great apes: The great leap forward? In *Great ape societies,* edited by W. C. McGrew, L. F. Marchant, and T. Nishida, pp. 225–240. Cambridge, Cambridge University Press.

Fuentes, A. 1994. *The socioecology of the Mentawai Island langur (Presbytis potenziani).* Ph.D. thesis, University of California, Berkeley.

Fuentes, A. 1998. Re-evaluating primate monogamy. *American Anthropologist* (in press).

Furness, W. H. 1916. *Proceedings from the American Philosophical Society* 55:281.

Furuichi, T. 1983. Interindividual distance and influence of dominance on feeding in a natural Japanese macaque troop. *Primates* 24:445–455.

Furuichi, T. 1985. Inter-male associations in a wild Japanese macaque troop on Yakushima Island, Japan. *Primates* 26:219–237.

Furuichi, T. 1987. Sexual swelling, receptivity, and grouping of wild pygmy chimpanzee females at Wamba, Zaïre. *Primates* 28:309–318.

FURUICHI, T. 1997. Agonistic interactions and matrifocal dominance rank of wild bonobos (*Pan paniscus*) at Wamba. *International Journal of Primatology* 18:855–875.

FUTUYMA, D. J. 1986. *Evolutionary biology.* Sunderland, MA, Sinauer.

GAGNEUX, P., WOODRUFF, D. S., AND BOESCH, C. 1997. Furtive mating in female chimpanzees. *Nature* 387:348–350.

GALAT, G., AND GALAT-LUONG, A. 1985. La commuaute de primates diurnes de la foret de Tai, Cote-d'Ivoire. *Revue d'Ecologie (Terre et Vie)* 40:3–32.

GALDIKAS, B. M. F. 1981. Orangutan reproduction in the wild. In *Reproductive biology of the great apes,* edited by C. E. Graham, pp. 281–300. New York, Academic Press.

GALDIKAS, B. M. F. 1982. An unusual instance of tool-use among wild orang-utans in Tanjung Puting Reserve, Indonesian Borneo. *Primates* 23(1):138–139.

GALDIKAS, B. M. F. 1983. The orangutan long call and snag crashing at Tanjung Puting Reserve. *Primates* 24:371–384.

GALDIKAS, B. M. F. 1985a. Orangutan sociality at Tanjung Puting. *American Journal of Primatology* 9:101–119.

GALDIKAS, B. M. F. 1985b. Subadult male orangutan sociality and reproductive behavior at Tanjung Puting. *American Journal of Primatology* 8:87–99.

GALDIKAS, B. M. F. 1988. Orangutan diet, range, and activity at Tanjung Puting, Central Borneo. *International Journal of Primatology* 9(1):1–35.

GALDIKAS, B. M. F. 1995. Social and reproductive behavior of wild adolescent female orangutans. In *The neglected ape,* edited by R. D. Nadler, B. F. M. Galdikas, L. K. Sheeran, and N. Rosen, pp. 163–182. New York, Plenum.

GALDIKAS, B. M. F., AND WOOD, J. W. 1990. Birth spacing patterns in humans and apes. *American Journal of Physical Anthropology* 83:185–191.

GALDIKAS, B. M. F., AND YEAGER, C. 1984. Crocodile predation on a crab-eating macaque in Borneo. *American Journal of Primatology* 6:49–51.

GARBER, P. 1994. Phylogenetic approach to the study of tamarin and marmoset social systems. *American Journal of Primatology* 34:199–219.

GARBER, P. A., MAOYA, L., AND MALAGA, C. 1984. A preliminary field study of the moustached tamarin monkey (*Saguinus mystax*) in northeastern Peru: Questions concerned with the evolution of a communal breeding system. *Folia Primatologica* 42:17–32.

GARDNER, B. T., AND GARDNER, R. A. 1971. Two-way communication with an infant chimpanzee. In *Behavior of nonhuman primates,* edited by A. Schrier and F. Stollnitz, vol. 4, pp. 117–184. New York, Academic Press.

GARDNER, B. T., AND GARDNER, R. A. 1974. Comparing the early utterances of child and chimpanzee. In *Minnesota symposium on child psychology,* edited by A. Pick, vol. 8, pp. 3–23. Minneapolis, University of Minnesota Press.

GARDNER, B. T., AND GARDNER, R. A. 1985. Signs of intelligence in cross-fostered chimpanzees. *Philosophical Transactions of the Royal Society* B308:159–176.

GARDNER, B. T., AND GARDNER, R. A. 1994. Development of phrases in the utterances of children and cross-fostered chimpanzees. In *The ethological roots of culture,* edited by R. A. Gardner, B. T. Gardner, B. Chiarelli, and F. X. Plooij, pp. 223–255. Dordrechet/Boston/London, Kluwer Academic Publishers.

GARDNER, R. A., AND GARDNER, B. T. 1969. Teaching sign language to a chimpanzee. *Science* 165:664–672.

GARDNER, R. A., AND GARDNER, B. T. 1989. A cross-fostering laboratory. In *Teaching sign language to chimpanzees,* edited by R. A. Gardner, B. T. Gardner, and T. Van Cantfort, pp. 1–28. Albany, State University of New York Press.

GARDNER, R. A., AND GARDNER, B. T. 1994. Ethological roots of language. In *The ethological roots of culture,* edited by R. A. Gardner, B. T. Gardner, B. Chiarelli, and F. X. Plooij, pp. 199–222. Dordrechet/Boston/London, Kluwer Academic Publishers.

GARNER, K. J., AND RYDER, O. A. 1996. Mitochondrial DNA diversity in gorillas. *Molecular Phylogenetics and Evolution* 6:39–48.

GARTLAN, J. S. 1968. Structure and function in primate society. *Folia Primatologica* 8:89–120.

GARTLAN, J. S. 1975. Adaptive aspects of social structure in *Erythrocebus patas.* In *Proceedings of the Symposium of the 5th Congress of the International Primatological Society,* edited by S. Kondo, M. Kawai, A. Ehara, and S. Kawamura, pp. 161–171. Tokyo, Japan Science Press.

GARZA, J.C., AND WOODRUFF, D. S. 1992. A phylogenetic study of the gibbons (*Hylobates*) using DNA obtained non-invasively from hair. *Molecular Phylogenetics and Evolution* 1:202–210.

GATINOT, B. L. 1978. Characteristics of the diet of west African red colobus. In *Recent advances in primatology, vol. 1: Behaviour,* edited by D. J. Chivers and J. Herbert, pp. 253–255. New York, Academic Press.

GEBO, D., AND DAGOSTO, M. In press. A preliminary study of the Philippine tarsier in Leyte. *American Journal of Physical Anthropology* Supplement.

GEISSMANN, T. 1995a. Gibbon systematics and species identification. *International Zoo News* 42:467–501.

GEISSMANN, T. 1995b. The yellow-cheeked gibbon (*Hylobates gabriellae*) in Nam Bai Cat Tien (southern Viet Nam) revisited. *Primates* 36(3):447–455.

GERLOFF, U., SCHLÖTTERER, C., RASSMANN, K., RAMBOLD, I., HOHMANN, G., FRUTH, B., AND TAUTZ, D. 1995. Amplification of hypervariable simple sequence repeats (microsatellites) from excremental DNA of wild living bonobos (*Pan paniscus*). *Molecular Ecology* 4:515–518.

GHIGLIERI, M. P. 1984. *The chimpanzees of Kibale forest: A field study of ecology and social structure.* New York, Columbia University Press.

GHIGLIERI, M. P. 1987. Sociobiology of the great apes and the hominid ancestor. *Journal of Human Evolution* 16:319–357.

GILMORE, H. A. 1981. From Radcliffe-Brown to sociobiology: Some aspects of the rise of primatology within physical anthropology. *American Journal of Physical Anthropology* 56:387–392.

GITTINS, S. P. 1980. Territorial behavior in the agile gibbon. *International Journal of Primatology* 1:381–399.

GITTINS, S. P. 1982. Feeding and ranging in the agile gibbon. *Folia Primatologica* 38:39–71.

GITTINS, S. P. 1984. Territorial advertisement and defense in gibbons. In *The lesser apes: Evolutionary and behavioral ecology,* edited by H. Preuschoft, D. J. Chivers, W. Brockelman, and N. Creel, pp. 420–426. Edinburgh, Edinburgh University Press.

GITTINS, S. P., AND RAEMAEKERS, J. J. 1980. Siamang, lar, and agile gibbons. In *Malayan forest primates: Ten years' study in tropical rain forest,* edited by D. J. Chivers, pp. 63–105. New York, Plenum.

GIUSTO, J. P., AND MARGULIS, L. 1981. Karyotypic fission theory and the evolution of Old World monkeys and apes. *Biosystems* 13:267–302.

GLANDER, K. E. 1980. Reproduction and population growth in free-ranging mantled howling monkeys. *American Journal of Physical Anthropology* 53:25–36.

GLANDER, K. E. 1992. Dispersal patterns in Costa Rican mantled howling monkeys. *International Journal of Primatology* 13:415–436.

GLICK, B. B. 1984. Male endocrine responses to females: Effects of social cues in cynomologus macaques. *American Journal of Primatology* 6:229–239.

GOLDBERG, T. L., AND RUVOLO, M. 1997. The geographical apportionment of mitochondrial genetic diversity in east African chimpanzees, *Pan troglodytes schweinfurthii.* *Molecular Biology and Evolution* 14:976–984.

GOLDFOOT, D. A., SLOB, A. K., SCHEFFLER, G., ROBINSON, J. A., WIEGAND, S. J., AND CORDS, J. 1975. Multiple ejaculations during prolonged sexual tests and lack of resultant serum testosterone increases in male stump-tail macaques (*Macaca arctoides*). *Archives of Sexual Behavior* 4:547–560.

GOLDFOOT, D. A., WESTERBORG-VAN LOON, H., GROENEVELD, W., AND SLOB, A. K. 1980. Behavioral and physiological evidence of sexual climax in the female stump-tailed macaque (*Macaca arctoides*). *Science* 208: 1477–1479.

GOLDIZEN, A. W. 1987a. Facultative polyandry and the role of infant-carrying in wild saddle-back tamarins (*Saguinus fuscicollis*). *Behavioral Ecology and Sociobiology* 20:99–109.

GOLDIZEN, A. W. 1987b. Tamarins and marmosets: Communal care of offspring. In *Primate societies*, edited by B. B. Smuts, D. L. Cheney, R. M. Seyfarth, R. W. Wrangham, and T. T. Struhsaker, pp. 34–43. Chicago, University of Chicago Press.

GOLDIZEN, A. W. 1988. Tamarin and marmoset mating systems: Unusual flexibility. *Tree* 3(2):36–40.

GOLDIZEN, A. W., MENDELSON, M., VAN VLAARDINGEN, M., AND TERBORGH, J. 1996. Saddle-back tamarin (*Saguinus fuscicollis*) reproductive strategies: Evidence from a thirteen year study of a marked population. *American Journal of Primatology* 38:57–83.

GOLDSMITH, M. L. 1996. *Ecological influences on the ranging and grouping behavior of western lowland gorillas at Bai Hokōu in the Central African Republic.* Ph.D. thesis, State University of New York, Stony Brook.

GOLDSMITH, M. L. 1998. Ecological constraints on the foraging effort of western lowland gorillas at Bai Hokōu, Central African Republic. *International Journal of Primatology.*

GOLDSMITH, M. L., HANKE, A. E., NKURUNUNGI, J. B., AND STANFORD, C. B. 1998. Comparative behavioral ecology of sympatric Bwindi gorillas and chimpanzees, Uganda: Preliminary results. *American Journal of Physical Anthropology* Supplement 26:101

GONDER, M. K., OATES, J. F., DISOTELL, T. R., FORSTNER, M. R. J., MORALES, J. C., AND MELNICK, D. J. 1997. A new west African chimpanzee subspecies? *Nature* 388:337.

GOODALL, A. G. 1977. Feeding and ranging in Kahuzi gorillas. In *Primate ecology: Studies of feeding and ranging behaviour in lemurs, monkeys and apes,* edited by T. H. Clutton-Brock, pp. 450–479. London, Academic Press.

GOODALL, J. 1983. Population dynamics during a fifteen-year period in one community of free-living chimpanzees in the Gombe National Park, Tanzania. *Zeitschrift fur Tierpsychologie* 61:1–60.

GOODALL, J. 1986. *The chimpanzees of Gombe: Patterns of behavior.* Cambridge, MA, Harvard University Press.

GOODALL, J. 1996. Foreword: Conserving great apes. In *Great ape societies,* edited by W. C. McGrew, L. F. Marchant, and T. Nishida, pp. xv–xx. Cambridge, Cambridge University Press.

GOODMAN, M. 1963. Man's place in the phylogeny of the primates as reflected in serum proteins. In *Classification and human evolution,* edited by S. L. Washburn, pp. 204–234. Chicago, Aldine.

GOODMAN, M., BAILEY, W. J., HAYASAKA, K., STANHOPE, M. J., SLIGHTOM, J., AND CZELUSNIAK, J. 1994. Molecular evidence on primate phylogeny from DNA sequences. *American Journal of Physical Anthropology* 94:3–24.

GOODMAN, M., AND MOORE, G. W. 1971. Immunodiffusion systematics of the primates. I. The Catarrhines. *Systemic Zoology* 20:19–62.

GOODMAN, M., ROMERO-HERRERA, A. E., DENE, H., CZELUSNIAK, J., AND TASHIAN, R. E. 1982. Amino acid sequence evidence on the phylogeny of primates and other eutherians. In *Macromolecular sequences in systematic and evolutionary biology,* edited by M. Goodman, pp. 115–191. New York, Plenum.

GOODMAN, S. M., O'CONNOR, S., AND LANGRAND, O. 1993. A review of predation on lemurs: Implications for the evolution of social behavior in small nocturnal primates. In *Lemur social systems and their ecological basis,* edited by P. M. Kappeler and J. U. Ganzhorn, pp. 51–66. New York, Plenum.

GOULD, L. 1990. The social development of free-ranging infant *Lemur catta* at Berenty Reserve, Madagascar. *International Journal of Primatology* 11:297–318.

GOULD L. 1994. *Patterns of affiliative behavior in adult male ringtailed lemurs* (Lemur catta) *at the Beza-Mahafaly Reserve, Madagascar.* Ph.D. thesis, Washington University, St. Louis.

GOULD L. 1996. Male-female affiliative relationships in naturally occurring ringtailed lemurs (*Lemur catta*) at Beza-Mahafaly Reserve, Madagascar. *American Journal of Primatology* 39:63–78.

GOULD, L. 1997. Affiliative relationships between adult males and immature group members in naturally occurring ringtailed lemurs (*Lemur catta*). *American Journal of Physical Anthropology* 103:163–171.

GOULD, S. J., AND LEWONTIN, R. C. 1979. The spandrels of San Marco and the Panglossian paradigm: A critique of the adaptationist programme. *Proceedings of the Royal Society of London* B205:581–598.

GOULD, S. J., AND VRBA, E. S. 1982. Exaptation—a missing term in the science of form. *Paleobiology* 8:4–15.

GOUZOULES, H. 1984. Social relations of males and infants in a troop of Japanese monkeys: A consideration of causal mechanisms. In *Primate paternalism,* edited by D. M. Taub, pp. 127–145. New York, Van Nostrand Reinhold.

GOUZOULES, H., AND GOUZOULES, S. 1989a. Design features and developmental modification of pigtail macaque, *Macaca nemestrina,* agonistic screams. *Animal Behavior* 37:383–401.

GOUZOULES, H., AND GOUZOULES, S. 1989b. Sex differences in the acquisition of communicative competence by pigtail macaques (*Macaca nemestrina*). *American Journal of Primatology* 19:163–174.

GOUZOULES, H., AND GOUZOULES, S. 1990. Matrilineal signatures in the recruitment screams of pigtail macaques, *Macaca nemestrina. Behaviour* 115:327–347.

GOUZOULES, S., AND GOUZOULES, H. 1987. Kinship. In *Primate societies,* edited by B. Smuts, D. Cheney, R. Seyfarth, R. Wrangham, and T. Struhsaker, pp. 299–305. Chicago, University of Chicago Press.

GOY, R. W., BERCOVITCH, F. B., AND MCBRAIR, M. C. 1988. Behavioral masculinization is independent of genital masculinization in prenatally androgenized female rhesus macaques. *Hormones and Behavior* 22:552–571.

GOY, R. W., AND MCEWEN, B. S. 1980. *Sexual differentiation of the brain.* Cambridge, MA, MIT Press.

GRAHAM, C. E., AND NADLER, R. D. 1990. Socioendocrine interactions in great ape reproduction. In *Socioendocrinology of primate reproduction,* edited by T. E. Ziegler and F. B. Bercovitch, pp. 33–58. New York, Wiley-Liss.

GRAHAM-JONES, O., AND HILL, W. C. O. 1962. Pregnancy and parturition in a Bornean orangutan. *Proceedings of the Zoological Society of London* 139:503–510.

GRAND, T. I. 1972. A mechanical interpretation of terminal branch feeding. *Journal of Mammalogy* 53:198–201.

GRAY, J. P. 1985. *Primate sociobiology.* New Haven, CT, HRAF Press.

GRETHER, G. F., PALOMBIT, R. A., AND RODMAN, P. S. 1992. Gibbon foraging decisions and the marginal value model. *International Journal of Primatology* 13(1):1–17.

GRIFFIN, D. R. 1976. *The question of animal awareness: Evolutionary continuity of mental experience.* New York, Rockefeller University Press.

GRIFFIN, D. R. 1984. *Animal thinking.* Cambridge, MA, Harvard University Press.

GROVES, C. P. 1970. Population systematics of the gorilla. *Man* 6:44–51.

GROVES, C. P. 1972. Systematics and phylogeny of gibbons. In *Gibbon and siamang,* edited by D. Rumbaugh, vol. 1, pp. 1–89. Basel, Karger.

GROVES, C. P. 1989. *A theory of human and primate evolution.* Oxford, Clarendon Press.

GROVES, C. P. 1993. Order Primates. In *Mammalian species of the world: A taxonomic and geographic reference,* edited by D. Wilson and D. Reader, pp. 243–277. Washington, DC, Smithsonian Institution Press.

GRUBER, A. 1969. Functional definition of primate tool-making. *Man* 4:573–579.

GUNDERSON, V. 1977. Some observations on the ecology of *Colobus badius temmincki*, Abuko Nature Reserve, the Gambia, west Africa. *Primates* 18:305–314.

GURMAYA, K. J. 1986. Ecology and behavior of *Presbytis thomasi* in northern Sumatra. *Primates* 27:151–172.

GURSKY, S. 1995. Group size and composition in the spectral tarsier, *Tarsius spectrum,* Sulawesi, Indonesia: Implications for social organization. *Tropical Biodiversity* 3(1):57–62.

GURSKY, S. 1997. *Modeling maternal time budgets: The impact of lactation and gestation on the behavior of the spectral tarsier,* Tarsius spectrum. Ph.D. thesis, Doctoral Program in Anthropological Sciences, State University of New York, Stony Brook.

GURSKY, S. In press a. Conservation status of the spectral tarsier, *Tarsius spectrum:* Data on population density and home range. *Folia Primatologica.*

GURSKY, S. In press b. The effect of altitude and habitat type on the population density of the spectral tarsier (*Tarsius spectrum*) and Dian's tarsier (*Tarsius dianae*). *Primate Conservation.*

GUST, D. A., GORDON, T. P., AND HAMBRIGHT, M. K. 1993. Response to removal from and return to a social group in adult male rhesus monkeys. *Physiology and Behavior* 53:599–602.

HAIMOFF, E. H. 1984. Acoustic and organizational features of gibbons songs. In *The lesser apes,* edited by H. Preuschoft, D. Chivers, W. Brockelman, and N. Creel, pp. 333–353. Edinburgh, Edinburgh University Press.

HAIMOFF, E. H., GITTINS, S. P., WHITTEN, A. J., AND CHIVERS, D. J. 1984. A phylogeny and classification of gibbons based on morphology and ethology. In *The lesser apes: Evolutionary and behavioral biology,* edited by H. Preuschoft, D. J. Chivers, W. Y. Brockelman, and N. Creel, pp. 614–632. Edinburgh, Edinburgh University Press.

HAIMOFF, E. H., YANG, X-J., HE, S-J., AND CHEN, N. 1987. Preliminary observations of wild black-crested gibbons (*Hylobates concolor concolor*) in Yunnan Province, People's Republic of China. *Primates* 28(3):319–335.

HALL, J. S., SALTONSTALL, K., INOGWABINI, B. I., AND OMARI, I. 1998. Distribution, abundance, and conservation status of Grauer's gorilla. *Oryx* 32(2):122–130.

HALL, K. R. L. 1965. Behaviour and ecology of the wild patas monkey, *Erythrocebus patas,* in Uganda. *Journal of Zoology* 148:15–87.

HANKE, A. E., AND GOLDSMITH, M. L. 1998. Nesting behavior: Implications for determining group dynamics of mountain gorillas in Bwindi-Impenetrable National Park, Uganda. *American Journal of Physical Anthropology* Supplement 26:96–97.

HANNAH, A. C., AND MCGREW, W. C. 1991. Rehabilitation of captive chimpanzees. In *Primate responses to environmental change,* edited by H. O. Box, pp. 167–186. New York, Chapman and Hall.

HARADA, M. L., SCHNEIDER, H., SCHNEIDER, M. P. C., SAMPAIO, I., CZELUSNIAK, J., AND GOODMAN, M. 1995. DNA evidence of the phylogenetic systematics of New World monkeys: Support for the sister-grouping of *Cebus* and *Saimiri* from two unlinked nuclear genes. *Molecular Phylogenetics and Evolution* 4:331–349.

HARAWAY, D. 1978. Animal sociology and a natural economy of the body politic. *Signs* 4:21–60.

HARCOURT, A. H. 1976. Virunga gorillas—the case against translocations. *Oryx* 13:469–472.

HARCOURT, A. H., AND DE WAAL, F. B. M. 1992. *Coalitions and alliances in humans and other animals.* Oxford, Oxford University Press.

HARCOURT, A. H, FOSSEY, D., AND SABATER PI, J. 1981. Demography of *Gorilla gorilla. Journal of Zoology, London* 195:215–233.

HARCOURT, A. H., HARVEY, P. H., LARSON, S. G., AND SHORT, R. V. 1981. Testis weight, body weight and breeding system in primates. *Nature* 293:55–57.

HARDING, R. S. O., AND OLSON, D. K. 1986. Patterns of mating among male patas monkeys (*Erythrocebus patas*) in Kenya. *American Journal of Primatology* 11:343–358.

HARING, D., AND WRIGHT, P. 1989. Hand raising a Philippine tarsier, *Tarsius syrichta. Zoo Biology* 8:265–274.

HARLOW, H. F. 1974. *Learning to love.* New York, J. Aronson.

HARRIS, E. E., AND DISOTELL, T. R. 1998. Nuclear gene trees and the phylogenetic relationships of the mangabeys (Primates: *Papionini*). *Molecular Biology and Evolution* 15 (in press).

HARRISON, M. J. S. 1986. Feeding ecology of black colobus (*Colobus satanas*) in central Gabon. In *Primate ecology and conservation,* edited by J. G. Else and P. C. Lee, pp. 31–37. Cambridge, Cambridge University Press.

HASEGAWA, T. 1990. Sex differences in ranging patterns. In *The chimpanzees of the Mahale mountains: Sexual and life history strategies,* edited by T. Nishida, pp. 99–114. Tokyo, University of Tokyo Press.

HASEGAWA, T., AND HIRAIWA, M. 1980. Social interactions of orphans observed in a free-ranging troop of Japanese monkeys. *Folia Primatologica* 33:129–158.

HASEGAWA, T., AND HIRAIWA-HASEGAWA, M. 1983. Opportunistic and restrictive matings among wild chimpanzees in the Mahale mountains, Tanzania. *Journal of Ethology* 1:75–85.

HAUSER, M.D., AND TYRELL, G. 1984. Old age and its behavioral manifestations: A study on two species of macaque. *Folia Primatologica* 43:24–35.

HAUSFATER, G. 1975. *Dominance and reproduction in baboons* (Papio cynocephalus*): A quantitative study.* Basel, Karger.

HAUSFATER, G., AND HRDY, S. B., eds. 1984. *Infanticide: Comparative and evolutionary perspectives.* New York, Aldine.

HAUSFATER, G., AND VOGEL, C. 1982. Infanticide in langur monkeys (*Presbytis entellus*): Recent research and a review of hypotheses. In *Advanced view in primate biology,* edited by A. B. Chiarelli and R. S. Corruccini, pp. 160–176. Berlin, Springer-Verlag.

HAYASAKA, K., GOJOBORI, T., AND HORAI, S. 1988. Molecular phylogeny and evolution of primate mitochondrial DNA. *Molecular Biology and Evolution* 5:626–644.

HAYES, K. J., AND HAYES, C. 1951. The intellectual development of a home-raised chimpanzee. *Proceedings of the American Philosophical Society* 95(2):105–109.

HAYES, K. J., AND NISSEN, C. H. 1971. Higher mental functions of a home-raised chimpanzee. In *Behavior of nonhuman primates,* edited by A. Schrier and F. Stollnitz, pp. 59–115. New York, Academic Press.

HEARN, J. P. 1983. The common marmoset. In *Reproduction in New World primates,* edited by J. P. Hearn, pp. 181–216. Lancaster, UK, MTP Press.

HEMINGWAY, C. A. 1995. *Feeding and reproductive strategies of the Milne Edwards' sifaka,* Propithecus diadema edwardsi. Ph.D. thesis, Duke University, Durham, NC.

HENNIG, W. 1979. *Phylogenetic systematics.* Urbana, University of Illinois Press.

HERTSGAARD, M. 1997. Our real China problem. *Atlantic Monthly* 280(5):96–98, 100–102, 104–106, 108–109, 112, 114.

HETHERINGTON, C. M. 1978. Circadian oscillations of body temperature in the marmoset, *Callithrix jacchus. Laboratory Animals* 12:107–108.

HIGLEY, J. D., MEHLMAN, P. T., HIGLEY, S. B., FERNALD, B., VICKERS, J., LINDELL, S. G., TAUB, D. M., SUOMI, S. J., AND LINNOILA, M. 1996. Excessive mortality in young free-ranging male nonhuman primates with low cerebrospinal fluid 5-hydroxyindoleactic acid concentrations. *Archives of General Psychology* 53:537–543.

HILL, D. A. 1986. Social relationships between adult male and immature rhesus macaques. *Primates* 27:425–440.

HILL, D. A. 1990. Social relationships between adult male and female rhesus macaques: II Non-sexual affiliative behavior. *Primates* 31:33–50.

HILL, D. A. 1994. Affiliative behaviour between adult males of the genus *Macaca. Behaviour* 130:294–308.

HILL, W. 1955. *Primates. Haplorhini, Tarsoidea.* New York, Interscience.

HINDE, R. 1976. Interactions, relationships and social structure. *Man* 11:1–17.

HINDE, R. 1978. Dominance and role: Two concepts with dual meaning. *Journal of Social and Biological Structures* 1:27–38.

HINDE, R., ed. 1983. *Primate social relationships: An integrated approach.* Oxford, Blackwell.

HINDE, R. A. 1987. *Individuals, relationships and culture: Links between ethology and the social sciences.* Cambridge, Cambridge University Press.

HIRAWAI, M. 1981. Maternal and alloparental care in a troop of free-ranging Japanese monkeys. *Primates* 22:309–329.

HLADIK, C. M. 1977. A comparative study of the feeding strategies of two sympatric species of leaf monkeys: *Presbytis senex* and *Presbytis entellus.* In *Primate ecology: Studies of feeding and ranging behaviour in lemurs, monkeys and apes,* edited by T. H. Clutton-Brock, pp. 323–353. New York, Academic Press.

HLADIK, C. M., CHARLES-DOMINIQUE, P., AND PETTER, J.-J. 1980. Feeding strategies of five nocturnal prosimians in the dry forest of the west coast of Madagascar. In *Nocturnal Malagasy primates: Ecology, physiology, and behavior,* edited by P. Charles-Dominique, H. M. Cooper, A. Hladik, C. M. Hladik, E. Pages, G. F. Pariente, A. Petter-Rousseaux, and A. Schilling, pp. 41–73. New York, Academic Press.

HOELZER, G. A., AND MELNICK, D. J. 1996. Evolutionary relationships of the macaques. In *Evolution and ecology of macaque societies,* edited by J. E. Fa and D. G. Lindburg, pp. 3–19. Cambridge, Cambridge University Press.

HOHMANN, G. 1989. Group fission in Nilgiri langurs (*Presbytis johnii*). *International Journal of Primatology* 10:441–454.

HOHMANN, G., AND FRUTH, B. 1996. Food sharing and status in unprovisioned bonobos. In *Food and the status quest,* edited by P. Wiessner and W. Schiefenhövel, pp. 47–67. Providence, RI, Berghahn Books.

HOROVITZ, I., AND MEYER, A. 1995. Systematics of New World monkeys (Platyrrhini, Primates) based on 16S mitochondrial DNA sequences: A comparative analysis of different weighting methods in cladistic analysis. *Molecular Phylogenetics and Evolution* 4:448–456.

HOROVITZ, I., AND MEYER, A. 1997. Evolutionary trends in the ecology of New World monkeys inferred from combined phylogenetic analysis of nuclear, mitochondrial, and morphological data. In *Molecular evolution and adaptive radiation,* edited by T. J. Givnish and K. J. Sytsma. Cambridge, Cambridge University Press.

HOROVITZ, I., ZARDOYA, R., AND MEYER, A. 1998. Platyrrhine systematics: A simultaneous analysis of molecular and morphological data. *American Journal of Physical Anthropology* 106:261–281.

HORR, D. A. 1975. The Borneo orangutan: Population structure and dynamics in relationship to ecology and reproductive strategy. In *Primate behavior: Developments in field and laboratory research,* edited by L. A. Rosenblum, pp. 307–323. New York, Academic Press.

HORSFIELD, T. 1821. *Zoological researches in Java.* London, Black, Kingsbury, Parbury and Allen.

HORWICH, R. H., KOONTZ, F., SAQUI, E., SAQUI, H., AND GLANDER, K. E. 1993. A reintroduction program for the conservation of the black howler monkey in Belize. *Endangered Species Update* 10:1–6.

HOWELL, N. 1979. *Demography of the Dobe !Kung.* New York, Academic Press.

HRDY, S. B. 1974. Male-male competition and infanticide among the langurs (*Presbytis entellus*) of Abu, Rajasthan. *Folia Primatologica* 22:19–58.

HRDY, S. B. 1976. Care and exploitation of nonhuman primate infants by conspecifics other than the mother. *Advances in the Study of Behavior* 6:101–158.

HRDY, S. B. 1977a. Infanticide as a primate reproductive strategy. *American Scientist* 65:40–49.

HRDY, S. B. 1977b. *The langurs of Abu: Female and male strategies of reproduction.* Cambridge, MA, Harvard University Press.

HRDY, S. B. 1981. *The woman that never evolved.* Cambridge, MA, Harvard University Press.

HRDY, S. B. 1984a. When the bough breaks: There may be method in the madness of infanticide. *Sciences* 24(2):44–50.

HRDY, S. B. 1984b. *The woman that never evolved.* Cambridge, MA, Harvard University Press.

HRDY, S. B., AND HAUSFATER, G. 1984. In *Infanticide: Comparative and evolutionary perspectives,* edited by G. Hausfater and S. B. Hrdy, pp. xiii–xxxix. New York, Aldine.

HRDY, S. B., JANSON, C., AND VAN SCHAIK, C. 1994–95. Infanticide: Let's not throw out the baby with the bath water. *Evolutionary Anthropology* 3(5):151–154.

HUFFMAN, M. A. 1990. Some socio-behavioral manifestations of old age. In *The chimpanzees of the Mahale mountains: Sexual and life history strategies,* edited by

T. Nishida, pp. 237–255. Tokyo, University of Tokyo Press.

HUFFMAN, M. A. 1991a. History of the Arashiyama Japanese macaques in Kyoto, Japan. In *The monkeys of Arashiyama: Thirty-five years of research in Japan and the West,* edited by L. M. Fedigan and P. S. Asquith, pp. 21–53. Albany, State University of New York Press.

HUFFMAN, M. A. 1991b. Mate selection and partner preference in female Japanese macaques. In *The monkeys of Arashiyama: Thirty-five years of research in Japan and the West,* edited by L. M. Fedigan and P. S. Asquith, pp. 101–122. Albany, State University of New York Press.

HUFFMAN, M. A. 1992. Influences of female partner preference on potential reproductive outcome in Japanese macaques. *Folia Primatologica* 59:77–88.

HUFFMAN, M. A. 1996. Acquisition of innovative cultural behaviors in nonhuman primates: A case study of stone handling, a socially transmitted behavior in Japanese macaques. In *Social learning in animals: The roots of culture,* edited by B. Galef, Jr., and C. Heyes, pp. 267–289. Orlando, FL, Academic Press.

HUXLEY, T. H. 1959. *Man's place in nature.* Ann Arbor, University of Michigan Press. (Originally published 1863.)

IHOBE, H. 1992a. Male-male relationships among wild bonobos (*Pan paniscus*) at Wamba, Republic of Zaïre. *Primates* 33:163–179.

IHOBE, H. 1992b. Observations on the meat-eating behavior of wild bonobos (*Pan paniscus*) at Wamba, Republic of Zaïre. *Primates* 32:247–250.

INGMANSON, E. J. 1996. Tool-using behavior in wild *Pan paniscus*: Social and ecological considerations. In *Reaching into thought: The minds of the great apes,* edited by A. E. Russon, K. A. Bard, and S. T. Parker, pp. 190–210. Cambridge, Cambridge University Press.

INGOLD, T. 1995. Building, dwelling, living: How animals and people make themselves at home in the world. In *Shifting contexts: Transformations in anthropological knowledge,* edited by M. Strathern, pp. 57–80. New York, Routledge.

INTERNATIONAL UNION FOR THE CONSERVATION OF NATURE. 1994. *The criteria for classifying critically endangered and vulnerable primate species.* Gland, Switzerland, IUCN.

INTERNATIONAL UNION FOR THE CONSERVATION OF NATURE. 1996. *Red list of threatened animals.* Gland, Switzerland, IUCN.

IRWIN, D. M. 1996. Molecular evolution of ruminant lysozymes. In *Lysozymes: Model enzymes in biochem-*

istry and biology, edited by P. Jollès, pp. 347–361. Basel, Birkhäuser-Verlag.

ISAAC, G. L. 1984. The archeology of human origins: Studies of the lower Pleistocene in East Africa, 1971–1981. In *Advances in world archeology,* edited by F. Wendorf and A. Close, vol. 3, pp. 1–87. New York, Academic Press.

ISAAC, G. L., AND CRADER, D. C. 1981. To what extent were early hominids carnivorous? An archaeological perspective. In *Omnivorous primates,* edited by R. S. O. Harding and G. Teleki, pp. 37–103. New York, Columbia University Press.

ISBELL, L. A. 1991. Contest and scramble competition: Patterns of female aggression and ranging behavior among primates. *Behavioral Ecology* 2:143–155.

ISBELL, L. A. 1994. Predation on primates: Ecological patterns and evolutionary consequences. *Evolutionary Anthropology* 3:61–71.

ISLAM, M. A., AND FEEROZ, M. M. 1992. Ecology of hoolock gibbon of Bangladesh. *Primates* 33(4):451–464.

ISLAM, M. A., AND HUSAIN, K. Z. 1982. A preliminary study on the ecology of the capped langur. *Folia Primatologica* 39:145–159.

ITANI, J. 1954. *The monkeys of Takasakiyama.* (in Japanese) Tokyo, Iwanami Shinsho.

ITANI, J. 1958. On the acquisition and propagation of new food habit in the troop of Japanese monkeys at Takasakiyama. *Primates* 1:84–98.

ITANI, J. 1959. Paternal care in the wild Japanese monkey, *Macaca fuscata fuscata. Primates* 2:61–93.

IZAWA, K., AND MIZUNO, A. 1977. Palm-fruit cracking behavior of wild black-capped capuchin (*Cebus apella*). *Primates* 18(4):773–792.

JALLES-FILHO, E. 1995. Manipulative propensity and tool use in capuchin monkeys. *Current Anthropology* 36(4):664–667.

JAMIESON, I. G. 1986. The functional approach to behavior: Is it useful? *American Naturalist* 127:195–208.

JANSON, C. H., AND GOLDSMITH, M. L. 1995. Predicting group size in primates: Foraging costs and predation risks. *Behavioral Ecology* 6:326–336.

JANSON, H. W. 1952. *Apes and Ape Lore in the Middle Ages and the Renaissance.* London, University of London Press.

JANZEN, D. H. 1974. Tropical blackwater rivers, animals, and mast fruiting by the Dipterocarpaceae. *Biotropica* 6:69–103.

JAQUISH, C. E., TOAL, R. L., TARDIF, S. D., AND CARSON, R. L. 1995. Use of ultrasound to monitor prenatal growth and development in the common marmoset

(*Callithrix jacchus*). *American Journal of Primatology* 36:259–275.

JAWORSKI, C. J. 1995. A reassessment of mammalian aA-crystallin sequences using DNA sequencing: Implications for anthropoid affinities of tarsier. *Journal of Molecular Evolution* 41:901–908.

JAY, P. 1965. The common langur of north India. In *Primate behavior: Field studies of monkeys and apes,* edited by I. DeVore, pp. 114–123. New York, Holt, Rinehart and Winston.

JAY, P., ed. 1968. *Primates. Studies in adaptation and variability.* New York, Holt, Rinehart and Winston.

JENSVOLD, M. L. A., AND FOUTS, R. S. 1993. Imaginary play in chimpanzees (*Pan troglodytes*). *Human Evolution* 8(3):217–227.

JERISON, H. J. 1973. *The evolution of the brain and intelligence.* New York, Academic Press.

JOLLÈS, J., JOLLÈS, P., BOWMAN, B. H., PRAGER, E. M., STEWART, C.-B., AND WILSON, A. C. 1989. Episodic evolution in the stomach lysozymes of ruminants. *Journal of Molecular Evolution* 28:528–535.

JOLLÈS, J., PRAGER, E. M., ALNEMRI, E. S., JOLLÈS, P., IBRAHIMI, I. M., AND WILSON, A. C. 1990. Amino acid sequences of stomach and nonstomach lysozymes of ruminants. *Journal of Molecular Evolution* 30:370–382.

JOLLÈS, P., ed. 1996. *Lysozymes: Model enzymes in biochemistry and biology.* Basel, Birkhäuser-Verlag.

JOLLÈS, P., SCHOENTGEN, F., JOLLÈS, J., DOBSON, D. E., PRAGER, E. M., AND WILSON, A. C. 1984. Stomach lysozymes of ruminants: II. Amino acid sequence of cow lysozyme 2 and immunological comparisons with other lysozymes. *Journal of Biological Chemistry* 259:11617–11625.

JOLLY, A. 1966. *Lemur behavior.* Chicago, University of Chicago Press.

JOLLY, A. 1972a. *The evolution of primate behavior.* New York, McGraw-Hill.

JOLLY, A. 1972b. Troop continuity and troop spacing in *Propithecus verreauxi* and *Lemur catta* at Berenty, Madagascar. *Folia Primatologica* 17:335–362.

JOLLY, A. 1984. The puzzle of female feeding priority. In *Primates: Studies by women primatologists,* edited by M. F. Small. New York, Alan R. Liss.

JOLLY, A. 1985. *The evolution of primate behavior,* 2nd ed. New York, Macmillan.

JOLLY, A., RASAMIMANANA, H. R., KINNAIRD, M. F., O'BRIEN, T. G., CROWLEY, H. M., HARCOURT, C. S., GARDNER, S., AND DAVIDSON, J. M. 1993. Territoriality in *Lemur catta* groups during the birth season at Berenty, Madagascar. In *Lemur social systems and their ecological basis,* edited by P. M. Kappeler and J. U. Ganzhorn, pp. 85–110. New York, Plenum.

JOLLY, C. L., OATES, J. F., AND DISOTELL, T. R. 1995. Chimpanzee kinship. *Science* 268:185–188.

JONES, K. C. 1983. Inter-troop transfer of *Lemur catta* males at Berenty, Madagascar. *Folia Primatologica* 40: 145–160.

JORDAN, C. 1982. Object manipulation and tool-use in captive pygmy chimpanzees (*Pan paniscus*). *Journal of Human Evolution* 11:35–39.

JORGENSON, J., AND REDFORD, K. 1993. Humans and big cats as predators in the Neotropics. *Symposium of the Zoological Society of London* 65:367–390.

JUDGE, P. G., AND DE WAAL, F. B. M. 1997. Rhesus monkey behaviour under diverse population densities: Coping with long-term crowding. *Animal Behavior* 54: 643–662.

JUNGERS, W. L., AND SUSMAN, R. L. 1984. Body size and skeletal allometry in African apes. In *The pygmy chimpanzee,* edited by R. L. Susman, pp. 131–177. New York, Plenum.

KANI, S. 1985. *The monkey and the crab.* Union City, CA, Heian International.

KANO, T. 1971. The chimpanzees of Filabanga, western Tanzania. *Primates* 12:229–246.

KANO, T. 1980. Social behavior of wild pygmy chimpanzees (*Pan paniscus*) of Wamba: A preliminary report. *Journal of Human Evolution* 9:243–260.

KANO, T. 1982. The use of leafy twigs for rain cover by the pygmy chimpanzees of Wamba. *Primates* 23:453–457.

KANO, T. 1992. *The last ape: Pygmy chimpanzee behavior and ecology.* Stanford, CA, Stanford University Press.

KANO, T., AND MULAVWA, M. 1984. Feeding ecology of the pygmy chimpanzee (*Pan paniscus*) of Wamba. In *The pygmy chimpanzee,* edited by R. L. Susman, pp. 233–274. New York, Plenum.

KAPPELER, M. 1984. Diet and feeding behavior of the moloch gibbon. In *The lesser apes: Evolutionary and behavioral biology,* edited by H. Preuschoft, D. J. Chivers, W. Brockelman, and N. Creel, pp. 228–241. Edinburgh, Edinburgh University Press.

KAPPELER, P. M. 1990. Female dominance in *Lemur catta*: More than just female feeding priority? *Folia Primatologica* 55:92–95.

KAPPELER, P. M. 1997. Determinants of primate social organization: Comparative evidence and new insights from Malagasy lemurs. *Biological Reviews of the Cambridge Philosophical Society* 72:111–151.

KAPSTEIN, E. B. 1998 (18 January). I'm shocked, shocked, to find that cronyism is going on in east Asia. *Los Angeles Times,* pp. M1&6.

KAVANAGH, M. 1984. A review of the international primate trade. In *The international primate trade,* edited by D. Mack and R. A. Mittermeier, pp. 49–89. Washington, DC, WWF-US/TRAFFIC-USA.

KAVANAGH, M., EUDEY, A. A., AND MACK, D. 1987. The effects of live trapping and trade on primate populations. In *Primate conservation in the tropical rainforest,* edited by C. W. Marsh and R. A. Mittermeier, pp. 147–177. New York, Alan R. Liss.

KAWAI, M. 1958. On the system of social ranks in a natural troop of Japanese monkeys: (1) basic rank and dependent rank. *Primates* 1–2:111–130.

KAWAI, M. 1965. Newly acquired pre-cultural behavior of a natural troop of Japanese monkeys on Koshima Island. *Primates* 6:1–30.

KAWAMOTO, Y., NOZAWA, K., MATSUBAYASHI, K., AND GOTOH, S. 1988. A population-genetic study of crab-eating macaques (*Macaca fascicularis*) on the island of Angaur, Palau, Micronesia. *Folia Primatologica* 51: 169–181.

KAWAMURA, S. 1958. Matriarchal social ranks in the Minoo-B troop: A study of the rank system of Japanese monkeys. *Primates* 1:149–156.

KAY, R. N. B., AND DAVIES, A. G. 1994. Digestive physiology. In *Colobine monkeys: Their ecology, behaviour and evolution,* edited by A. G. Davies and J. F. Oates, pp. 229–250. Cambridge, Cambridge University Press.

KAY, R. N. B., HOPPE, P., AND MALOIY, G. M. O. 1976. Fermentative digestion of food in the colobus monkey, *Colobus polykomos. Experientia* 32:485–487.

KELLEY, J., AND STRIER, K. B. 1994. Male aggression and canine size in atelines and hominoids. *American Journal of Physical Anthropology* Supplement.

KEMF, E., AND WILSON, A. 1997. *Great apes in the wild. WWF species status report.* Gland, Switzerland, WWF.

KENAGY, G. J., AND VLECK, D. 1982. Daily temporal organization of metabolism in small mammals: Adaptations and adversity. In *Vertebrate circadian systems: Structure and physiology,* edited by J. Aschoff, S. Daan, and G. A. Groüss. Berlin, Springer.

KIMURA, M. 1983. *The neutral theory of molecular evolution.* Cambridge, Cambridge University Press.

KINGSLEY, S. 1982. Causes of non-breeding and the development of the secondary sexual characteristics in the male orangutan: A hormonal study. In *The orangutan: Its biology and conservation,* edited by L. E. M. de Boer, pp. 215–219. The Hague, Dr W. Junk.

KINGSLEY, S. R. 1988. Physiological development of male orang-utans and gorillas. In *Orang-utan biology,* edited by J. H. Schwartz, pp. 123–131. Oxford, Oxford University Press.

KINZEY, W. G. 1982. Distribution of primates and forest refuges. In *Biological diversification in the tropics,* edited by G. T. Prance, pp. 455–482. New York, Columbia University Press.

KINZEY, W. G., AND CUNNINGHAM, E. P. 1994. Variability in Platyrrhine social organization. *American Journal of Primatology* 34:185–198.

KIRKPATRICK, R. C. 1996. *Ecology and behavior of the Yunnan snub-nosed langur* (Rhinopithecus bieti, Colobinae). Ph.D. thesis, University of California, Davis.

KIRKPATRICK, R. C. In press. Ecology and behavior in snub-nosed and douc langurs. In *The natural history of the doucs and snub-nosed monkeys,* edited by N. G. Jablonski. Singapore, World Scientific Press.

KLEIBER, M. 1975. *The fire of life,* rev. ed. Huntington, NY, Robert E. Krieger.

KLEIMAN, D. G., BECK, B. B., DIETZ, J. M., AND DIETZ, L. A. 1991. Costs of a reintroduction and criteria for success: Accounting and accountability in the golden lion tamarin conservation program. In *Beyond captive breeding,* edited by J. H. W. Gibbs, pp. 125–144. Oxford, Clarendon Press.

KLEIN, R. G. 1989. *The human career: Human biological and cultural origins.* Chicago, University of Chicago Press.

KLEIN, R. G. 1992. The archeology of modern human origins. *Evolutionary Anthropology* 1:5–14.

KLINGER, H. 1963. The somatic chromosomes of some primates. *Cytogenetics* 2:140–151.

KLOCKARS, M., AND REITAMO, S. 1975. Tissue distribution of lysozyme in man. *Journal of Histochemistry and Cytochemistry* 23:932–940.

KNOTT, C. D. 1997a. The effects of changes in food availability on diet, activity, and hormonal patterns in wild Bornean orangutans (*Pongo pygmaeus*). *American Journal of Physical Anthropology* Supplement 24:145.

KNOTT, C. D. 1997b. Interactions between energy balance, hormonal patterns and mating behavior in wild Bornean orangutans (*Pongo pygmaeus*). *American Journal of Primatology* 42(2):124.

KNOTT, C. D. 1998a. Changes in orangutan diet, caloric intake and ketones in response to fluctuating fruit availability. *International Journal of Primatology* 19(6).

KNOTT, C. D. 1998b (August). Orangutans: In the wild. *National Geographic Magazine.*

KNOTT, C. D. 1999. *Reproductive, physiological and behavioral responses of orangutans in Borneo to fluctuations in food availability.* Ph.D. thesis, Harvard University.

KNOTT, C. D. 1998c. Social system dynamics, ranging patterns and male and female strategies in wild Bornean orangutans (*Pongo pygmaeus*). *American Journal of Physical Anthropology* Supplement 26:140.

KOCHER, T. D., THOMAS, W. K., MEYER, A., EDWARDS, S. V., PAABO, S., VILLABLANCA, F. X., AND WILSON, A. C. 1989.

Dynamics of mitochondrial DNA evolution in animals: Amplification and sequencing with conserved primers. *Proceedings of the National Academy of Sciences, USA* 86:6196–6200.

KOFORD, C. B. 1963. Rank of mothers and sons in bands of rhesus monkeys. *Science* 141:356–357.

KONSTANT, W. R., AND MITTERMEIER, R. A. 1982. Introduction, reintroduction and translocation of neotropical primates: Past experiences and future possibilities. *International Zoo Yearbook* 22:69–77.

KOOL, K. M. 1993. The diet and feeding behavior of the silver leaf monkey (*Trachypithecus auratus sondaicus*) in Indonesia. *International Journal of Primatology* 14: 667–699.

KOONTZ, F. W., HORWICH, R., SAQUI, E., SAQUI, H., GLANDER, K., KOONTZ, C., AND WESTROM, W. 1994. Reintroduction of black howler monkeys (*Alouatta pigra*) into the Cockscomb Basin Wildlife Sanctuary, Belize. In *American Zoo and Aquarium Association Annual Conference Proceedings,* pp. 104–111. Bethesda, MD, AZA.

KOOP, B. F., TAGLE, D. A., GOODMAN, M., AND SLIGHTOM, J. L. 1989. A molecular view of primate phylogeny and important systematic and evolutionary questions. *Molecular Biology and Evolution* 6:580–612.

KORTLANDT, A. 1986. The use of stone tools by wild-living chimpanzees and the earliest hominids. *Journal of Human Evolution* 15(2):77–132.

KOYAMA, N. 1967. On dominance rank and kinship of a wild Japanese monkey troop in Arashiyama. *Primates* 8:189–216.

KOYAMA, N. 1988. Mating behavior of ring-tailed lemurs (*Lemur catta*) at Berenty, Madagascar. *Primates* 29: 163–175.

KRAUSE, M. A., AND FOUTS, R. S. 1997. Chimpanzee (*Pan troglodytes*) pointing: Hand shapes, accuracy, and the role of eye gaze. *Journal of Comparative Psychology* 111(4):330–336.

KREITMAN, M. 1991. Detecting selection at the level of DNA. In *Evolution at the molecular level,* edited by A. G. Selander and T. S. Whittam, pp. 204–221. Sunderland, MA, Sinauer.

KREITMAN, M., AND AKASHI, J. 1995. Molecular evidence for natural selection. *Annual Review of Ecology and Systematics* 26:403–422.

KUESTER, J., AND PAUL, A. 1992. Influence of male competition and female mate choice on male mating success in Barbary macaques (*Macaca sylvanus*). *Behaviour* 120:192–217.

KUESTER, J., AND PAUL, A. 1998. Male migration in Barbary macaques (*Macaca sylvanus*) at Affenberg Salem. *International Journal of Primatology* (in press).

KUHN, T. S. 1970. *The nature of scientific revolution.* Chicago, University of Chicago Press.

KUMMER, H. 1971. *Primate societies: Group techniques of ecological adaptation.* Chicago, Aldine-Atherton Press.

KUMMER, H. 1995. *In quest of the sacred baboon: A scientist's journey.* Princeton, NJ, Princeton University Press.

KURODA, S. 1979. Grouping of the pygmy chimpanzees. *Primates* 20:161–183.

KURODA, S. 1980. Social behavior of the pygmy chimpanzees. *Primates* 21:181–197.

KURODA, S. 1984. Interactions over food among pygmy chimpanzees. In *The pygmy chimpanzee,* edited by R. L. Susman, pp. 301–324. New York, Plenum.

KURODA, S., NISHIHARA, T., SUZUKI, S., AND OKO, R. A. 1996. Sympatric chimpanzees and gorillas in the Ndoki Forest, Congo. In *Great ape societies,* edited by W. C. McGrew, L. T. Marchant, and T. Nishida, pp. 71–81. London, Cambridge University Press.

KURUP, G. U., AND KUMAR, A. 1993. Time budget and activity patterns of the liontailed macaque (*Macaca silenus*). *International Journal of Primatology* 14:27–39.

LAI, W. 1994. From protean ape to handsome saint: The monkey king. *Asian Folklore Studies* 53:29–65.

LAN DAOYING, HE SHUNJIN, AND SHU LIDE. 1990. Preliminary observations on the group composition of the wild concolor gibbons (*Hylobates concolor*) in Yunnan, China. *Primate Report* 26:89–96.

LANGE, J. D., BROWN, W. A., WINCZE, J. P., AND ZWICK, W. 1980. Serum testosterone concentrations and penile tumescence changes in men. *Hormones and Behavior* 14:267–270.

LASLEY, B., PRESLEY, S., AND CZEKALA, N. 1980. Monitoring ovulation in great apes; Urinary immunoreactive estrogen and bioactive lutenizing hormone. *Annual Proceedings of the American Society of Zoo Veterinarians,* 37–40.

LAURIE, E., AND HILL, J. 1954. *List of land mammals of New Guinea, Celebes and adjacent islands.* London, British Museum.

LAWRENCE, D. C., AND LEIGHTON, M. 1996. Ecological determinants of feeding bout length in long-tailed macaques (*Macaca fascicularis*). *Tropical Biodiversity* 3(3):227–241.

LAWS, J., AND VONDER HAAR LAWS, J. 1984. Social interactions among adult male langurs (*Presbytis entellus*) at Rajaji Wildlife Sanctuary. *International Journal of Primatology* 5:31–50.

LEAKEY, L. S. B. 1960. *Adam's ancestor: The evolution of man and his culture.* New York, Harper Torchbook.

LEDBETTER, D. H. 1981. *Chromosomal evolution and speciation in the genus Cercopithecus (Primates, Cercopithecinae).* Ph.D. thesis, University of Texas, Austin.

LEE, Y.-H., AND VACQUIER, V. D. 1992. The divergence of species-specific abalone sperm lysins is promoted by positive Darwinian selection. *Biological Bulletin* 182:97–104.

LEGROS CLARK, W. 1924. Notes on the living tarsier (*Tarsius spectrum*). *Proceedings of the Zoological Society of London* 14:216–223.

LEIGHTON, D. R. 1987. Gibbons: Territoriality and monogamy. In *Primate societies,* edited by B. Smuts, D. Cheney, R. Seyfarth, R. Wrangham, and T. Struhsaker, pp. 135–145. Chicago, University of Chicago Press.

LEIGHTON, M. 1993. Modeling diet selectivity by Bornean orangutans: Evidence for integration of multiple criteria for fruit selection. *International Journal of Primatology* 14(2):257–313.

LEIGHTON, M., AND LEIGHTON, D. R. 1982. The relationships of size of feeding aggregate to size of food patch: Howler monkeys (*Alouatta palliata*) feeding in Trichilia cipo fruit trees on Barro Colorado Island. *Biotropica* 14:81–90.

LEIGHTON, M., AND LEIGHTON, D. R. 1983. Vertebrate responses to fruiting seasonality within a Bornean rain forest. In *Tropical rain forest ecology and management,* edited by S. L. Sutton, T. C. Whitmore, and A. C. Chadwick, pp. 181–196. Oxford, Blackwell Scientific Publications.

LEMOS DE SÁ, R. M. 1991. População de *Brachyteles arachnoides* (Primates, Cebidae) da Fazenda Esmeralda, Rio Casca, Minas Gerais. In *A primatologia no Brasil-3,* edited by A. B. Rylands and A. T. Bernardes, pp. 235–238. Fundação Biodiversitas, Belo Horizonte.

LETHMATE, J. 1982. Tool-using skills of orangutans. *Journal of Human Evolution* 11:49–64.

LEYHAUSEN, P. 1973. On the function of the relative hierarchy of moods (as exemplified by the phylogenetic and ontogenetic development of prey-catching in carnivores). In *Motivation of human and animal behavior: An ethological view,* edited by K. Lorenz and P. Leyhausen, pp. 144–241. New York, Van Nostrand.

LI, W.-H., AND GRAUR, D. 1991. *Fundamentals of molecular evolution.* Sunderland, MA, Sinauer.

LINDBURG, D. G. 1977. Feeding behavior and diet of rhesus monkeys (*Macaca mulatta*) in a Siwalik Forest in North India. In *Primate ecology,* edited by T. H. Clutton-Brock, pp. 223–249. New York, Academic Press.

LINDBURG, D. G. 1987. Seasonality of reproduction in primates. In *Comparative primate biology: Behavior, cogni-*

tion, and motivation, edited by G. Mitchell, vol. 2B, pp. 167–218. New York, Alan R. Liss.

LINDBURG, D. G. 1991. Ecological requirements of macaques. *Laboratory Animal Science* 41:315–322.

LINNAEUS, C. 1758. *Systema naturae.* Vienna, J. T. Trrattner.

LIPPOLD, L. K. 1977. The douc langur: A time for conservation. In *Primate conservation,* edited by HSH Prince Rainier and G. H. Bourne, pp. 513–538. New York, Academic Press.

LIPPOLD, L. K. 1995. Distribution and conservation status of douc langurs in Vietnam. *Asian Primates* 4:4–6.

LIPPOLD, M. T., AND LEHMAN, S. M. 1992. An analysis of the social behaviors of aged rhesus macaques. Abstract. *American Journal of Primatology* 27(1):25.

LORENZ, K. 1950. The comparative method in studying innate behavior patterns. *Symposium of the Society for Experimental Biology* 42:166–181.

LOVEJOY, O. W. 1981. The origin of man. *Science* 211: 341–350.

LOY, J., ARGO, B., NESTELL, G., VALLETT, S., AND WANAMAKER, G. 1993. A reanalysis of patas monkeys' "grimace and gecker" display and a discussion of lack of formal dominance. *International Journal of Primatology* 14:879–893.

LU, Z., KARESH, W. B., JANCZEWSKI, D. N., FRAZIER-TAYLOR, H., SAJUTHI, D., ET AL. 1996. Genomic differentiation among natural populations of orangutan (*Pongo pygmaeus*). *Current Biology* 610:1326–1336.

LUCKETT, W. 1976. Cladistic relationships among primate higher categories: Evidence of the fetal membrane and placenta. *Folia Primatologica* 25:245–276.

LYONS, D. B. 1995. A vegetation analysis and study of mountain gorilla (*Gorilla g. beringei*) food plants in Bwindi-Impenetrable National Park, SW Uganda. *F.H.S. Project Report.* Oxford, Oxford University.

LYONS, D. M. 1993. Conflict as a constructive force in social life. In *Primate social conflict,* edited by W. A. Mason and S. P. Mendoza, pp. 387–408. Albany, State University of New York Press.

MACK, D., AND EUDEY, A. A. 1984. A review of the U.S. primate trade. In *The international primate trade,* edited by D. Mack and R. A. Mittermeier, pp. 91–136. Washington, DC, WWF-US/TRAFFIC-USA.

MACKINNON, J. R. 1971. The orangutan in Sabah today. *Oryx* 11:141–191.

MACKINNON, J. R. 1974. The behaviour and ecology of wild orang-utans (*Pongo pygmaeus*). *Animal Behaviour* 22:3–74.

MACKINNON, J. R. 1977. A comparative ecology of Asian apes. *Primates* 18(4):747–772.

MACKINNON, J. R., AND MACKINNON, K. S. 1978. Comparative feeding ecology of six sympatric primates in west Malaysia. In *Recent advances in primatology, vol. 1: Behaviour,* edited by D. J. Chivers and J. Herbert, pp. 305–321. New York, Academic Press.

MACKINNON, J. R., AND MACKINNON, K. S. 1980a. The behavior of wild spectral tarsiers. *International Journal of Primatology* 1:361–379.

MACKINNON, J. R., AND MACKINNON, K. S. 1980b. Niche differentiation in a primate community. In *Malayan forest primates: Ten years' study in tropical rain forest,* edited by D. J. Chivers, pp. 167–190. New York, Plenum.

MACKINNON, J. R., AND MACKINNON, K. S. 1984. Territoriality, monogamy and song in gibbons and tarsiers. In *The lesser apes: Evolutionary and behavioral biology,* edited by H. Preuschoft, D. J. Chivers, W. Brockelman, and N. Creel, pp. 291–297. Edinburgh, Edinburgh University Press.

MACLATCHY, L. M. 1996. Another look at the australopithecine hip. *Journal of Human Evolution* 31:455–476.

MACPHEE, R., AND CARTMILL, M. 1986. Basicranial structures and primate systematics. In *Comparative primate biology volume 1: Systematics, evolution and anatomy,* edited by R. MacPhee, pp. 219–275. New York, Alan R. Liss.

MAGGIONCALDA, A. N. 1995a. Testicular hormone and gonadotropin profiles of developmentally arrested adolescent male orangutans. *American Journal of Physical Anthropology* Supplement 20:140–141.

MAGGIONCALDA, A. N. 1995b. *The socioendocrinology of orangutan growth, development, and reproduction—an analysis of endocrine profiles of juvenile, developing adolescent, and developmentally arrested adolescent, adult, and aged captive male orangutans.* Ph.D. thesis, Duke University, Durham, NC.

MAISELS, F., GAUTIER-HION, A., AND GAUTIER, J. P. 1994. Diets of two sympatric colobines in Zaire: More evidence on seed-eating in forests on poor soils. *International Journal of Primatology* 15:681–701.

MALCOLM, D. 1964. Foreword. In *Zulu fireside tales,* by R. Savory. Cape Town, Howard Timmins.

MALENKY, R. K., AND WRANGHAM, R. W. 1994. A quantitative comparison of terrestrial herbaceous food consumption by *Pan paniscus* in the Lomako Forest, Zaïre, and *Pan troglodytes* in the Kibale Forest, Uganda. *American Journal of Primatology* 32:1–12.

MALLOW, E. B., HARRIS, A., SALZMAN, N., RUSSELL, J. P., DEBERARTDINIS, R. J., RUCHELLI, E., AND BEVINS, C. L. 1996. Human enteric defensins: Gene structure and developmental expression. *Journal of Biological Chemistry* 271:4038–4045.

MANSON, J. H. 1995. Do female rhesus macaques choose novel males? *American Journal of Primatology* 37: 285–296.

MANSON, J. H., AND WRANGHAM, R. W. 1991. Intergroup aggression in chimpanzees and humans. *Current Anthropology* 32:369–390.

MARKHAM, R. J. 1990. Breeding orangutans at Perth zoo: Twenty years of appropriate husbandry. *Zoo Biology* 9:171–182.

MARKHAM, R., AND GROVES, C. P. 1990. Brief communication: Weights of wild orangutans. *American Journal of Physical Anthropology* 81:1–3.

MARKS, J. 1991. What's old and new in molecular phylogenetics. *American Journal of Physical Anthropology* 85:207–219.

MARLER, P. 1969. *Colobus guereza:* Territoriality and group composition. *Science* 163:93–95.

MARSH, C. W. 1979. Comparative aspects of social organization in the Tana River red colobus, *Colobus badius rufomitratus. Zeitschrift für Tierpsychologie* 51:337–362.

MARSH, C. W. 1981. Diet choice among red colobus (*Colobus badius rufomitratus*) on the Tana River, Kenya. *Folia Primatologica* 35:147–178.

MARSHALL, J., AND SUGARDJITO, J. 1986. Gibbon systematics. In *Comparative primate biology,* vol. 1, *Systematics, evolution, and anatomy,* edited by R. MacPhee, pp. 137–185. New York, Alan R. Liss.

MARSHALL, J. T., AND MARSHAL, E. R. 1976. Gibbons and their territorial songs. *Science* 193:235–237.

MARSHALL, J. T., SUGARDJITO, J., AND MARKAYA, M. 1984. Gibbons of the *lar* group: Relationships based on voice. In *The lesser apes: Evolutionary and behavioral biology,* edited by H. Preuschoft, D. J. Chivers, W. Y. Brockelman, and N. Creel, pp. 533–541. Edinburgh, Edinburgh University Press.

MARTENSZ, N. D., YELLUCCI, S. V., FULLER, L. M., EVERITT, B. J., KEVERNE, E. B., AND HERBERT, J. 1987. Relation between aggressive behaviour and circadian rhythms in cortisol and testosterone in social groups of talapoin monkeys. *Journal of Endocrinology* 115:107–120.

MARTIN, D. A. 1997. *Kinship bias: A function of familiarity in pigtailed macaques* (Macaca nemestrina), pp. vi, 79. Ph.D. thesis, University of Georgia, Athens.

MARTIN, R. D. 1973. A review of the behavior and ecology of the lesser mouse lemur (*Microcebus murinus;* J. F. Miller, 1777). In *Comparative ecology and behavior of primates,* edited by R. P. Michael and J. H. Crook, pp. 1–68. London, Academic Press.

MARTIN, R. D. 1990. *Primate origins and evolution: A phylogenetic reconstruction.* Princeton, NJ, Princeton University Press.

MASON, W. A. 1986. Early socialization. In *Primates: The road to self-sustaining populations,* edited by K. Benirschke, pp. 321–330. New York, Springer-Verlag.

MASON, W. A. 1993. The nature of social conflict: A psycho-ethological perspective, In *Primate social conflict,* edited by W. A. Mason and S. P. Mendoza, pp. 13–47. Albany, State University of New York Press.

MASTERS, A., AND MARKHAM, R. 1991. Assessing reproductive status in orangutans by using urinary estrone. *Zoo Biology* 10(3):197–208.

MATSUBAYASHI, K., GOTOH, S., KAWAMOTO, Y., NOZAWA, K., AND SUZUKI, J. 1989. Biological characteristics of crab-eating monkeys on Angaur Island. *Primate Research* 5:46–57.

MATSUMURA, S. 1997. Relaxed dominance relations among female moor macaques (*Macaca maurus*) in their natural habitat, South Sulawesi, Indonesia. *Folia Primatologica.*

MATSUMURA, S., AND OKAMOTO, K. 1997. Factors affecting proximity among members of a wild group of moor macaques during feeding, moving, and resting. *International Journal of Primatology* 18:929–940.

MAYER, A. C. 1966. Quasi-groups in the study of complex societies. In *The social anthropology of complex societies,* edited by M. Banton, pp. 97–123. A.S.A. 4. London, Tavistok Publications.

McCAMENT, S. K., KLOSTERMAN, L. L., GOLDMAN, E. S., MURAI, J. T., AND SITTERI, P. K. 1987. Conversion of androgens to estrogens in the male squirrel monkey (*Saimiri sciurus*). *Steroids* 50:547–549.

McGINNES, P. R. 1979. Sexual behavior of free-living chimpanzees: Consort relationships. In *The great apes,* edited by D. A. Hamburg and E. R. McCown, pp. 429–439. Menlo Park, CA, Benjamin-Cummings.

McGREW, W. C. 1975. Patterns of plant food sharing by wild chimpanzees. In *Contemporary primatology,* edited by S. Kono, M. Dawai, and A. Ehara, pp. 304–309. Basel, S. Karger.

McGREW, W. C. 1979. Evolutionary implications of sex differences in chimpanzee predation and tool use. In *The great apes,* edited by D. A. Hamburg and E. R. McCown, pp. 440–463. Menlo Park, CA, Benjamin-Cummings.

McGREW, W. C. 1992. *Chimpanzee material culture.* Cambridge, Cambridge University Press.

McGREW, W. C. 1996. Dominance status, food sharing, and reproductive success in chimpanzees. In *Food and the status quest,* edited by P. Wiessner and W. Schiefenhövel, pp. 39–45. Providence, RI, Berghahn Books.

McGREW, W. C., BALDWIN, P. J., AND TUTIN, C. E. G. 1988. Diet of wild chimpanzees (*Pan troglodytes verus*) at Mt.

Assirik, Senegal. I. Composition. *American Journal of Primatology* 16:213–226.

McGrew, W. C., and Marchant, L. F. 1997. Using the tools at hand: Manual laterality and elementary technology in *Cebus* spp. and *Pan* spp. *International Journal of Primatology* 18:787–810.

McGrew, W. C., and Tutin, C. E. G. 1978. Evidence for a social custom in wild chimpanzees? *Man* 13:234–251.

McKeena, M. C., and Bell, S. K. 1997. *Classification of mammals above the species level.* New York, Columbia University Press.

McKey, D. B. 1978. Soils, vegetation and seed-eating by black colobus monkeys. In *The ecology of arboreal folivores,* edited by G. G. Montgomery, pp. 423–438. Washington, DC, Smithsonian Institution Press.

McKey, D. B., Gartlan, J. S., Waterman, P. G., and Choo, G. M. 1981. Food selection by black colobus monkeys (*Colobus satanas*) in relation to plant chemistry. *Biological Journal of the Linneanen Society* 16:115–146.

McKey, D. B., and Waterman, P. G. 1982. Ranging behavior of a group of black colobus (*Colobus satanas*) in the Douala-Edea Reserve, Cameroon. *Folia Primatologica* 39:264–304.

Medway, L. 1972. Phenology of a tropical rain forest in Malaya. *Biological Journal of the Linneanen Society* 4: 117–146.

Mehlmann, P. T., Higley, J. D., Faucher, I., Lilly, A. A., Taub, D. M., Vickers, J., Suomi, S. J., and Linnoila, M. 1995. Correlation of CSF 5-HIAA concentrations with sociality and the timing of emigration in free-ranging primates. *American Journal of Psychiatry* 152: 907–913.

Meier, B., Albignac, R., Peyrieras, A., Rumpler, Y., and Wright, P. 1987. A new species of *Hapalemur* (Primates) from southeast Madagascar. *Folia Primatologica* 48:211–215.

Mendes, F. D. C. 1990. *Afiliação e hierarquia no muriqui: O grupo Matão de Caratinga.* Master's thesis, Universidade de São Paulo, Brazil.

Mendoza, S. P. 1984. The psychobiology of relationships. In *Social cohesion: Essays toward a sociopsychological perspective,* edited by P. Brachas and S. Mendoza, pp. 3–29. Westport, CT, Greenwood Press.

Mendoza, S. P., Coe, C. L., Lowe, E. L., and Levine, S. 1979. The physiological response to group formation in adult male squirrel monkeys. *Psychoneuroendocrinology* 3:221–229.

Mendoza, S. P., Lowe, E. L., Davidson, J. M., and Levine, S. 1978. Annual cyclicity in the squirrel monkey (*Saimiri sciurius*): The relationship between testosterone, fatting, and sexual behavior. *Hormones and Behavior* 11:295–303.

Messier, W., and Stewart, C.-B. 1997. Episodic adaptive evolution of primate lysozymes. *Nature* 385:151–154.

Meyers, D. M. 1993. *The effects of resource seasonality on behavior and reproduction in the golden-crowned sifaka* (Propithecus tattersalli, Simons, 1988) *in three Malagasy forests.* Ph.D. thesis, Duke University, Durham, NC.

Miles, H. L. 1980. Acquisition of gestural signs by an infant orangutan (*Pongo pygmaeus*). *American Journal of Physical Anthropology* 52:256–257.

Miles, H. L. 1990. The cognitive foundations for reference in a signing orangutan. In *'Language' and intelligence in monkeys and apes: Comparative developmental perspectives,* edited by S. T. Parker and K. R. Gibson, pp. 511–539. Cambridge, Cambridge University Press.

Miller, G., and Hollister, F. 1921. A review of *Tarsius spectrum* from Celebes. *Proceedings of the Biological Society of Washington* 34:93–104.

Miller, O. 1896. *Four-handed folk.* Cambridge, MA, Riverside Press.

Milton, K. 1979. Factors influencing leaf choice by howler monkeys: A test of some hypotheses of food selection by generalist herbivores. *American Naturalist* 114:362–378.

Milton, K. 1984. Habitat, diet and activity patterns of free-ranging woolly spider monkeys (*Brachyteles arachnoides*; E. Geoffroy 1806). *International Journal of Primatology* 5:491–514.

Mitani, J. 1985a. Sexual selection and adult male orangutan long calls. *Animal Behaviour* 33:272–283.

Mitani, J. 1985b. Mating behaviour of male orangutans in the Kutai Game Reserve, Indonesia. *Animal Behaviour* 33:391–402.

Mitani, J. C. 1987. Territoriality and monogamy among agile gibbons (*Hylobates agilis*). *Behavioral Ecology and Sociobiology* 20:265–269.

Mitani, J. C. 1989. Orangutan activity budgets: Monthly variations and effect of body size, parturition, and sociality. *American Journal of Primatology* 18:87–100.

Mitani, J. C., Gors-Louis, J., and Richards, A. F. 1996. Sexual dimorphism, the operational sex ratio, and the intensity of male competition in polygynous primates. *American Naturalist* 147:966–980.

Mitani, J. C., and Rodman, P. S. 1979. Territoriality: The relation of ranging pattern and home range size to defendability, with an analysis of territoriality among primate species. *Behavioral Ecology and Sociobiology* 5:241–251.

Mitchell, A. H. 1994. *Ecology of Hose's langur,* Presbytis hosei, *in mixed logged and unlogged dipterocarp forest of northeast Borneo.* Ph.D. thesis, Yale University, New Haven, CT.

MITTERMEIR, R. 1987. Conservation of primates and their habitats. In *Primate societies,* edited by B. B. Smuts, D. L. Cheney, R. M. Seyfarth, R. W. Wrangham, and T. T. Struhsaker. Chicago, University of Chicago Press.

MOORE, J. 1996. Savanna chimpanzees, referential models and the last common ancestor. In *Great ape societies,* edited by W. C. McGrew, L. F. Marchant, and T. Nishida, pp. 275–292. Cambridge, Cambridge University Press.

MORAES, P. L. R., CARVALHO, O., JR., AND STRIER, K. B. 1998. Population variation in patch and party size in muriquis (*Brachyteles arachnoides*). *International Journal of Primatology,* 19:325–337.

MORALES, J. C., AND MELNICK, D. J. 1998. Phylogenetic relationships of the macaques (Cercopithecidae: *Macaca*), as revealed by high resolution restriction site mapping of mitochondrial ribosomal genes. *Journal of Human Evolution* 34:1–23.

MORELL, V. 1995. Chimpanzee outbreak heats up search for Ebola origin. *Science* 268:974–975.

MORENO-BLACK, G. S., AND BENT, E. F. 1982. Secondary compounds in the diet of *Colobus angolensis. African Journal of Ecology* 20:29–36.

MORENO-BLACK, G. S., AND MAPLES, W. R. 1977. Differential habitat utilization for four Cercopithecidae in a Kenyan forest. *Folia Primatologica* 27:85–107.

MORGAN, E. 1982. *The aquatic ape.* New York, Stein and Day.

MORIN, P. A., MOORE, J. J., CHAKRABORTY, R., JIN, L., GOODALL, J., AND WOODRUFF, D. S. 1994. Kin selection, social structure, gene flow, and the evolution of chimpanzees. *Science* 265:1193–1201.

MORIN, P. A., WALLIS, J., MOORE, J., CHAKRABORTY, R., AND WOODRUFF, D. S. 1993. Non-invasive sampling and DNA amplification for paternity exclusion, community structure, and phylogeography in wild chimpanzees. *Primates* 34:347–356.

MORIN, P. A., WALLIS, J., MOORE, J. J., AND WOODRUFF, S. 1994. Paternity exclusion in a community of wild chimpanzees using hypervariable simple sequence repeats. *Molecular Ecology* 3:469–478.

MORLAND, H. S. 1991. *Social organization and ecology of black and white ruffed lemurs (Varecia variegata variegata) in lowland rain forest, Nosy Mangabe, Madagascar.* Ph.D. thesis, Yale University, New Haven, CT.

MORRIS, R., AND MORRIS, D. 1966. *Men and apes.* London, Clowes and Sons.

MOURANT, A. E. 1954. *The distribution of human blood groups.* Oxford, Blackwell Scientific.

MOWRY, C. B., DECKER, B. S., AND SHURE, D. J. 1996. The role of phytochemistry in dietary choices of Tana River red colobus monkeys (*Procolobus badius rufomitratus*). *International Journal of Primatology* 17: 63–84.

MTURI, F. A. 1993. Ecology of the Zanzibar red colobus monkey, *Colobus badius kirkii* (Gray, 1968), in comparison with other red colobines. In *Biogeography and ecology of the rain forests of eastern Africa,* edited by J. C. Lovett and S. K. Wasser, pp. 243–266. Cambridge, Cambridge University Press.

MUCKENHIRN, N. A. 1972. *Leaf-eaters and their predators in Ceylon: Ecological roles of gray langurs, Presbytis entellus, and leopards.* Ph.D. thesis, University of Maryland, College Park.

MUIR, C., GALDIKAS, B. M. F., AND BECKENBACH, A. T. 1995. Genetic variability in orangutans. In *The neglected ape,* edited by R. D. Nadler, B. F. M. Galdikas, L. K. Sheeran, and N. Rosen, pp. 367–272. New York, Plenum.

MUKHERJEE, R. P. 1986. The ecology of the hoolock gibbon, *Hylobates hoolock,* in Tripura, India. In *Primate ecology and conservation,* edited by J. G. Else and P. C. Lee, pp. 115–123. Cambridge, Cambridge University Press.

MURNYAK, D. F. 1981. Censusing the gorillas in Kahuzi-Biega National Park. *Biological Conservation* 21:163–176.

MUSSER, G., AND DAGOSTO, M. 1987. The identity of *Tarsius pumilus,* a pygmy species endemic to montane mossy forests of central Sulawesi. *American Museum Novitiates* 2867:1–53.

NADLER, R. D. 1977. Sexual behavior of captive orangutans. *Archives of Sexual Behavior* 189:813–814.

NADLER, R. D. 1988. Sexual and reproductive behavior. In *Orang-utan biology,* edited by J. H. Schwartz, pp. 31–51. Oxford, Oxford University Press.

NAKAGAWA, N., IWAMOTO, T., YOKOTA, N., AND SOUMAH, A. G. 1996. Inter-regional and inter-seasonal variations of food quality in Japanese macaques: Constraints of digestive volume and feeding time. In *Evolution and ecology of macaque societies,* edited by J. E. Fa and D. G. Lindburg, pp. 207–234. Cambridge, Cambridge University Press.

NAKAMICHI, M. 1984. Behavioral characteristics of old female Japanese monkeys in a free-ranging group. *Primates* 25:192–203.

NAKHASATHIEN, S. 1989. Chiew Larn Dam wildlife rescue operation. *Oryx* 23:146–154.

NAPIER, J. R., AND NAPIER, P. H. 1985. *The natural history of the primates.* Cambridge, MA, MIT Press.

NASH, L. T. 1993. Juveniles in nongregarious primates. In *Juvenile primates: Life history, development, and behavior,* edited by M. E. Pereira and M. A. Fairbanks, pp. 119–137. New York, Oxford University Press.

NEI, M. 1987. *Molecular evolutionary genetics.* New York, Columbia University Press.

NEWTON, P. N. 1988. The variable social organization of hanuman langurs (*Presbytis entellus*), infanticide and the monopolization of females. *International Journal of Primatology* 9(1):59–77.

NEWTON, P. N. 1992. Feeding and ranging patterns of forest hanuman langurs (*Presbytis entellus*). *International Journal of Primatology* 13:245–285.

NEWTON, P. N. 1994. Social stability and change among forest hanuman langurs (*Presbytis entellus*). *Primates* 35:489–498.

NICHOLAS, R. W. 1965. Factions: A comparative analysis. In *Political systems and the distribution of power,* pp. 21–61. A.S.A. Monographs 2, London, Tavistock.

NIEMITZ, C. 1974. A contribution to the postnatal behavioral development of *Tarsius bancanus* studied in two cases. *Folia Primatologica* 21:250–276.

NIEMITZ, C. 1977. Can a primate be an owl? Convergence on the same ecological niche. *Fortechreift Zoologie* 30:667–670.

NIEMITZ, C. 1979. Results of a field study on the western tarsier in Sarawak. *Sarawak Museum Journal* 27:171–228.

NIEMITZ, C. 1984. *The biology of tarsiers.* Stuttgart, Gustav Fischer.

NIEMITZ, C., NIETSCH, A., WARTER, S., AND RUMPLER, Y. 1991. *Tarsius dianae:* A new primate species from central Sulawesi (Indonesia). *Folia Primatologica* 56:105–116.

NIETSCH, A. 1994. A comparative study of vocal communication in Sulawesi tarsiers. *IPS Abstracts,* Bali, p.427.

NIETSCH, A. 1996. A comparative study of vocal communication in Sulawesi tarsiers. *IPS Abstracts,* Wisconsin, p. 320.

NIETSCH, A., AND NIEMITZ, C. 1992. Indication for facultative polygamy in free-ranging *Tarsius spectrum,* supported by morphometric data. *IPS Abstracts,* Strasbourg, p. 318.

NIEUWENHUIJSEN, K., DE NEEF, K. J., AND SLOB, A. K. 1986. Sexual behaviour during ovarian cycles, pregnancy, and lactation in group-living stumptail macaques (*Macaca arctoides*). *Human Reproduction* 1:159–169.

NISHIDA, T. 1966. A sociological study of solitary male monkeys. *Primates* 7:141–204.

NISHIDA, T. 1968. The social group of wild chimpanzees in the Mahali mountains. *Primates* 9:167–224.

NISHIDA, T. 1979. The social structure of chimpanzees of the Mahale mountains. In *The great apes,* edited by

D. A. Hamburg and E. R. McCown, pp. 72–121. Menlo Park, CA, Benjamin-Cummings.

NISHIDA, T. 1987. Local traditions and cultural transmission. In *Primate societies,* edited by B. Smuts, D. Cheney, R. Seyfarth, R. Wrangham, and T. Struhsaker, pp. 462–474. Chicago, University of Chicago Press.

NISHIDA, T., HASEGAWA, T., HAYAKI, H., TAKAHATA, Y., AND UEHARA, S. 1992. Meat-sharing as a coalition strategy by an alpha male chimpanzee. In *Topics in primatology,* edited by T. Nishida, W. C. McGrew, P. Marler, and M. Pickford, vol. 1, pp. 159–174. Tokyo, University of Tokyo Press.

NISHIDA, T., AND KAWANAKA, K. 1985. Within-group cannibalism by adult male chimpanzees. *Primates* 26(3):247–284.

NISHIDA, T., TAKASAKI, H., AND TAKAHATA, Y. 1990. Demography and reproductive profiles. In *The chimpanzees of the Mahale mountains,* edited by T. Nishida, pp. 63–97. Tokyo, University of Tokyo Press.

NISHIDA, T., AND UEHARA, S. 1983. Natural diet of chimpanzees (*Pan troglodytes schweinfurthii*): A long-term record from the Mahale mountains, Tanzania. *African Study Monographs* 3:109–130.

NISHIHARA, T. 1995. Feeding ecology of western lowland gorillas in the Nouabalé-Ndoki National Park, Congo. *Primates* 36:151–168.

NISHIMURA, A. 1992. Mating behaviors of woolly monkeys, *Lagothrix lagotricha,* at La Macarena, Colombia (III): Reproductive parameters viewed from a long-term study. *Field Studies of New World Monkeys, La Macarena, Colombia* 7:1–7.

NISHIMURA, A. 1994. Social interaction patterns of woolly monkeys (*Lagothrix lagotricha*): A comparison among the atelines. *The Science and Engineering Review of Doshisha University* 35:235–254.

NISSEN, H. W. 1931. A field study of the chimpanzee. Observations of chimpanzee behavior and environment in western French Guinea. *Comparative Psychological Monographs* 8:1–122.

NOË, R. 1990. A veto game played by baboons: A challenge to the use of the prisoner's dilemma as a paradigm for reciprocity and cooperation. *Animal Behaviour* 39:78–90.

NORIKOSHI, K., AND KOYAMA, N. 1975. Group shifting and social organization among Japanese monkeys. In *Proceedings of the symposium of the 5th Congress of the International Primatological Society,* edited by S. Kondo, M. Kawai, A. Ehara, and S. Kawamura, pp. 43–61. Tokyo, Japan Science Press.

NORMAN, A., AND LITWACK, J. 1987. *Hormones.* New York, Academic Press.

NOZAKI, M., MITSUNAGA, F., AND SHIMIZU, K. 1995. Reproductive senescence in female Japanese monkeys (*Macaca fuscata*): Age- and season-related changes in hypothalamic-pituitary-ovarian functions and fecundity rates. *Biology of Reproduction* 52:1250–1257.

NUTTAL, G. H. F. 1904. *Blood immunity and blood relationship: A demonstration of certain blood-relationships amongst animals by means of the perception test for blood.* Cambridge, Cambridge University Press.

OAKLEY, K. 1964. *Man the tool-maker.* Chicago, University of Chicago Press.

OATES, J. F. 1977a. The guereza and its food. In *Primate ecology: Studies of feeding and ranging behaviour in lemurs, monkeys and apes,* edited by T. H. Clutton-Brock, pp. 275–321. New York, Academic Press.

OATES, J. F. 1977b. The social life of a black-and-white colobus monkey, *Colobus guereza. Zeitschrift für Tierpsychologie* 45:1–60.

OATES, J. F., compiler. 1986. *Action plan for African primate conservation: 1986–90.* Gland, Switzerland, IUCN.

OATES, J. F. 1988. The diet of the olive colobus monkey, *Procolobus verus,* in Sierra Leone. *International Journal of Primatology* 9:457–478.

OATES, J. F. 1994. The natural history of African colobines. In *Colobine monkeys: Their ecology, behaviour and evolution,* edited by A. G. Davies and J. F. Oates, pp. 75–128. Cambridge, Cambridge University Press.

OATES, J. F. 1996. *African primates.* Gland, Switzerland, IUCN.

OATES, J. F., AND DAVIES, G. 1994. What are the colobines? In *Colobine monkeys: Their ecology, behaviour and evolution,* edited by A. G. Davies and J. F. Oates. Cambridge, Cambridge University Press.

OATES, J. F., DAVIES, G., AND DELSON, E. 1994. The diversity of living colobines. In *Colobine monkeys: Their ecology, behaviour and evolution,* edited by A. G. Davies and J. F. Oates, pp. 45–73. Cambridge, Cambridge University Press.

OATES, J. F., SWAIN, T., AND ZANTOVSKA, J. 1977. Secondary compounds and food selection by colobus monkeys. *Biochemical Systematics and Ecology* 5:317–321.

OATES, J. F., WATERMAN, P. G., AND CHOO, G. M. 1980. Food selection by the South Indian leaf-monkey, *Presbytis johnii,* in relation to leaf chemistry. *Oecologia* 45:45–56.

O'CONNOR, S. M. 1987. *The effect of human impact on the vegetation and the consequences to primates in two riverine forests, southern Madagascar.* Ph.D. thesis, Dept. of Applied Biology, Cambridge University, Cambridge.

OFTEDAL, O. T. 1984. Milk composition, milk yield and energy output at peak lactation: A comparative review. *Symposium of the Zoological Society of London* 51:33–85.

OFTEDAL, O. T., AND IVERSON, S. J. 1995. Comparative analysis of nonhuman milks. A. Phylogenetic variation in gross composition of milks. In *Handbook of milk composition,* edited by R. G. Jensen, pp. 749–788. San Diego, Academic Press.

OGAWA, H. 1995a. Bridging behavior and other affiliative interactions among male Tibetan macaques (*Macaca thibetana*). *International Journal of Primatology* 16: 707–729.

OGAWA, H. 1995b. Recognition of social relationships in bridging behavior among Tibetan macaques (*Macaca thibetana*). *American Journal of Primatology* 35:305–310.

OHSAWA, H., INOUE, M., AND TAKENAKA, O. 1993. Mating strategy and reproductive success of male patas monkeys (*Erythrocebus patas*). *Primates* 34:533–544.

OHSAWA, H., AND SUGIYAMA, Y. 1996. Population dynamics of Japanese monkeys at Takasakiyama: Trends in 1985–1992. In *Variations in the Asian macaques,* edited by T. Shotake and K. Wada, pp. 163–179. Tokyo, Tokai University Press.

OLEJNICZAK, C. 1996. Update on the Mbeli Bai gorilla study in the Nouabale-Ndoki National Park, northern Congo. *Gorilla Conservation News* 10:5–8.

OUELLETTE, A. J., AND SELSTED, M. E. 1996. Paneth cell defensins: Endogenous peptide components of intestinal host defense. *FASEB Journal* 10:1280–1289.

OVERDORFF, D. J. 1991. *Ecological correlates to social structure in two prosimian primates:* Eulemur fulvus rufus *and* Eulemur rubriventer *in Madagascar.* Ph.D. thesis, Duke University, Durham, NC.

OVERDORFF, D. J. 1993. Similarities, differences, and seasonal patterns in the diets of *Eulemur rubriventer* and *Eulemur fulvus rufus* in the Ranomafana National Park, Madagascar. *International Journal of Primatology* 14:721–753.

OVERDORFF, D. J. 1996. Ecological correlates to activity and habitat use of two prosimian primates: *Eulemur rubriventer* and *Eulemur fulvus rufus* in Madagascar. *American Journal of Primatology* 40:327–342.

OYAMA, S. 1982. A reformulation of the idea of maturation. In *Perspectives in ethology 5,* edited by P. P. G. Bateson and P. H. Klopfer, pp. 101–131. New York, Plenum.

OYAMA, S. 1985. *The ontogeny of information.* Cambridge, Cambridge University Press.

OYAMA, S. 1989. Ontogeny and the central dogma: Do we need the concept of genetic programming in order to have an evolutionary perspective? In *Systems and development, the Minnesota symposia on child development,* edited by M. S. Gunnar and E. Thelen, vol. 22, pp. 1–34. Hillsdale, NJ, Lawrence Erlbaum.

PAGES, E. 1978. Home range, behaviour and tactile communication in a nocturnal Malagasy lemur *Microcebus coquereli.* In *Recent advances in primatology (3),* edited by D. Chivers and K. Joysey, pp. 171–177. London, Academic Press.

PAHUD, J. J., SCHELLENBERG, D., MONTI, J. C., AND SCHERZ, J. C. 1983. Lysozyme, an abomasal enzyme in the ruminants. *Annales de Recherches Veterinaires* 14: 493–501.

PALLAS, P. S. 1778. *Novae species quad e glirium ordinae cum illustrationibus variis complurium ex hoc ordinae animalium.* Erlangen, W. Walther.

PALOMBIT, R. A. 1993. Lethal territorial aggression in a white-handed gibbon. *American Journal of Primatology* 31:311–318.

PALOMBIT, R. A. 1994a. Dynamic pair bonds in hylobatids: Implications regarding monogamous social systems. *Behaviour* 128(1–2):65–101.

PALOMBIT, R. A. 1994b. Extra-pair copulations in a monogamous ape. *Animal Behaviour* 47:721–723.

PALOMBIT, R. A. 1994c. *Pair bonds and monogamy in wild siamang* (Hylobates syndactylus) *and white-handed gibbon* (Hylobates lar) *in northern Sumatra.* Ph.D. thesis, University of California, Davis.

PALOMBIT, R. A. 1995. Longitudinal patterns of reproduction in wild female siamangs (*Hylobates syndactylus*) and white-handed gibbons (*Hylobates lar*). *International Journal of Primatology* 16(5):739–760.

PALOMBIT R. A. 1996. Pair bonds in monogamous apes: A comparison of the siamang *Hylobates syndactylus* and the white-handed gibbon *Hylobates lar. Behaviour* 133:321–356.

PANGER, M. A. 1998. Object-use in free-ranging white-faced capuchins (*Cebus capucinus*) in Costa Rica. *American Journal of Physical Anthropology* 106(3): 311–321.

PARISH, A. R. 1994. Sex and food control in the "uncommon chimpanzee": How bonobo females overcome a phylogenetic legacy of male dominance. *Ethology and Sociobiology* 15:157–179.

PARISH, A. R. In review. Sexual dimorphism, maturation, and female dominance in bonobos (*Pan paniscus*). *American Journal of Physical Anthropology.*

PARISH, A. R., AND DE WAAL F. B. M. In review. Social relationships in the bonobo (*Pan paniscus*) redefined: Evidence for female-bonding in a "non-female bonded" primate. *Behaviour.*

PARKER, S. T. 1977. Paiget's sensorimotor series in an infant macaque: A model for comparing unstereotyped behavior and intelligence in human and nonhuman primates. In *Primate biosocial development,* edited by S. Chevalier-Skolnikoff and F. Poirier, pp. 43–112. New York, Garland.

PARKER, S. T. 1990. The origins of comparative developmental evolutionary studies of primate mental abilities. In *"Language" and intelligence in monkeys and apes,* edited by S. T. Parker and K. R. Gibson, pp. 3–64. New York, Cambridge University Press.

PARKER, S. T. 1996. Apprenticeship in tool-mediated extractive foraging: The origins of imitation, teaching, and self-awareness in great apes. In *Reaching into thought: The minds of great apes,* edited by A. Russon, K. Bard, and S. T. Parker, pp. 348–370. Cambridge, Cambridge University Press.

PARKER, S. T. 1997. Anthropomorphism is the null hypothesis and recapitulation is the bogey man in comparative developmental evolutionary studies. In *Anthropomorphism, anecdotes and animals,* edited by R. Mitchell, N. Thompson, and H. L. Miles, pp. 348–362. Albany, State University of New York Press.

PARKER, S. T. In press. Development of intelligence and social roles in the play of an infant gorilla. In *The mentalities of gorillas and orangutans,* edited by S. T. Parker, R. W. Mitchell, and H. L. Miles. Cambridge, Cambridge University Press.

PARKER, S. T., AND GIBSON, K. R. 1977. Object manipulation, tool use and sensorimotor intelligence as feeding adaptations in cebus monkeys and great apes. *Journal of Human Evolution* 6:623–641.

PARKER, S. T., AND GIBSON, K. R. 1979. A developmental model for the evolution of language and intelligence in early hominids. *Behavioral and Brain Sciences* 2:367–408.

PARKER, S. T., AND MCKINNEY, M. L. In press. *Origins of intelligence in apes and humans.* Baltimore, Johns Hopkins University Press.

PARKS, K., MUSANTE, A., AND NOVAK, M. 1992. Studies of aging in rhesus monkeys: A longitudinal perspective. *American Journal of Primatology* 27(1):49 (Abstract).

PASTORINI, J., FORTNER, M. R. J., MARTIN, R. D., AND MELNICK, D. J. 1998. A re-examination of the phylogenetic position of Callimico (Primates) incorporating new mitochondrial DNA sequence data. *Journal of Molecular Evolution* (in press).

PATTEE, H. H. 1973. The physical basis and origin of hierarchical control. In *Hierarchy theory: The challenge of complex systems,* edited by H. H. Pattee, pp. 73–108. New York, George Braziller.

PATTERSON, F. G., AND COHN, R. H. 1990. Language acquisition by a lowland gorilla: Koko's first ten years of vocabulary development. *Word* 41(2):97–143.

PAUL, A., AND KUESTER, J. 1996. Differential reproduction in male and female Barbary macaques. In *Evolution and ecology of macaque societies,* edited by J. E. Fa and D. G. Lindburg, pp. 293–317. Cambridge, Cambridge University Press.

PAUL, A., KUESTER, J., AND ARNEMANN, J. 1996. The sociobiology of male-infant interactions in Barbary macaques, *Macaca sylvanus. Animal Behaviour* 51: 155–170.

PAUL, A., KUESTER, J., AND PODZUWEIT, D. 1993. Reproductive senescence and terminal investment in female Barbary macaques (*Macaca sylvanus*) at Salem. *International Journal of Primatology* 14:105–124.

PAVELKA, M. S. M. 1990. Do old female monkeys have a specific social role? *Primates* 31(2):363–373.

PAVELKA, M. S. M. 1991. Sociability in old female Japanese monkeys: Human versus nonhuman primate aging. *American Anthropologist* 93(3):588–598.

PAVELKA, M. S. M. 1994. The nonhuman primate perspective: Old age, kinship and social partners in a monkey society. *Journal of Cross-Cultural Gerontology* 9:219–229.

PAVELKA, M. S. M., AND FEDIGAN, L. M. 1991. Menopause: A comparative life history perspective. *Yearbook of Physical Anthropology* 34:13–38.

PAVELKA, M. S. M., GILLESPIE, M. W., AND GRIFFIN, L. 1991. The interacting effect of age and rank on the sociability of adult female Japanese monkeys. In *The monkeys of Arashiyama,* edited by L. M. Fedigan and P. J. Asquith, pp. 194–207. Albany, State University of New York Press.

PAYNE, P. R., AND WHELLER, E. F. 1968. Comparative nutrition in pregnancy and lactation. *Proceedings of the Nutrition Society* 27:129–138.

PEREIRA, M. E. 1995. Development and social dominance among group-living primates. *American Journal of Primatology* 37:143–175.

PEREIRA, M. E., AND FAIRBANKS, L. A. 1993. *Juvenile primates: Life history, development, and behavior.* New York, Oxford University Press.

PEREIRA, M. E., KAUFMAN, R., KAPPELER, P. M., AND OVERDORFF, D. J. 1990. Female dominance does not characterize all of the Lemuridae. *Folia Primatologica* 55:96–103.

PERELYGIN, A. A., KAMMERER, C. M., STOWELL, N. C., AND ROGERS, J. 1996. Conservation of human chromosome 18 in baboons (*Papio hamadryas*): A linkage map of eight human microsatellites. *Cytogenetics and Cell Genetics* 75:207–209.

PERES, C. A. 1994. Diet and feeding ecology of gray woolly monkeys (*Lagothrix lagotricha cana*) in central Amazonia: Comparisons with other atelines. *International Journal of Primatology* 15:333–372.

PERES, C. A. 1996. Use of space, spatial group structure, and foraging group size of gray woolly monkeys (*Lagothrix lagotricha cana*) at Urucu, Brazil. In *Adaptive radiations of neotropical primates,* edited by M. A. Norconk, A. L. Rosenberger, and P. A. Garber, pp. 467–488. New York, Plenum.

PERNA, N. T., AND KOCHER, T. D. 1996. Mitochondrial DNA: Molecular fossils in the nucleus. *Current Biology* 6:128–129.

PERRET, M. 1992. Environmental and social determinants of sexual function in the male lesser mouse lemur (*Microcebus murinus*). *Folia Primatologica* 59:1–25.

PERRY, S., AND ROSE, L. M. 1994. Begging and transfer of coati meat by white-faced capuchin monkeys, *Cebus capucinus. Primates* 35:409–415.

PETIT, O., AND THIERRY, B. 1994. Aggressive and peaceful interventions in conflicts in Tonkean macaques. *Animal Behaviour* 48:1427–1436.

PETIVER, J. 1705. *Gazophylacii naturae et artis.* London.

PETRY, V. H., RIEHL, I., AND ZUCKER, H. 1986. Energieumsatzmessungen an Weissbüscheläffchen (*Callithrix jacchus*). *Journal of Animal Physiology and Animal Nutrition* 55:214–224.

PETTER, J.-J. 1962. Recherches sur l'écologie et l'éthologie des lémuriens malgaches. *Memoirs of the National Museum of Natural History (Paris)* 27:1–146.

PETTER, J.-J. 1978. Ecological and physiological adaptations of five sympatric nocturnal lemurs to seasonal variations in food production. In *Recent advances in primatology (1),* edited by D. Chivers and J. Herbert, pp. 211–223. London, Academic Press.

PETTER, J.-J., ALBIGNAC, R., AND RUMPLER, Y. 1977. *Faune de Madagascar 44: Mammifères Lémuriens (Primates Prosimiens).* Paris, ORSTOM/CNRS.

PHIPPS, M. 1992. Recent incidents involving illegal primate trade in Taiwan. *Asian Primates* 2(2):5–6.

PIAGET, J. 1952. *The origins of intelligence in children.* New York, International Universities Press.

PIAGET, J. 1954. *The construction of reality in the child.* New York, Basic Books.

PIAGET, J. 1962. *Play, dreams, and imitation.* New York, W. W. Norton.

PIAGET, J. 1966. *Psychology of intelligence.* New York, Littlefield Adams.

PILBEAM, D. R. 1996. Genetic and morphological records of the Hominoidea and hominid origins: A synthesis. *Molecular Phylogenetics and Evolution* 5:155–168.

PLAVCAN, J. M., AND VAN SCHAIK, C. P. 1992. Intrasexual competition and canine dimorphism in anthropoid primates. *American Journal of Physical Anthropology* 87:461–477.

POCOCK, R. 1918. On the external characteristics of lemurs and Tarsius. *Proceedings of the Zoological Society of London,* 19–53.

POIRIER, F. E. 1967. *The ecology and social behavior of the Nilgiri langur* (Presbytis johnii) *of south India.* Ph.D. thesis, University of Oregon, Eugene.

POIRIER, F. E. 1970. The Nilgiri langur (*Presbytis johnii*) of south India. In *Primate behavior: Developments in field and laboratory research,* edited by L. A. Rosenblum, vol. 1, pp. 251–383. New York, Academic Press.

POIRIER, F., AND SMITH, E. 1974. The crab-eating macaques (*Macaca fascicularis*) of Angaur Island, Palau, Micronesia. *Folia Primatologica* 22:258–306.

POLLARD, I. 1994. *A guide to reproduction.* Cambridge, Cambridge University Press.

POLLOCK, J. I. 1975. *The social behaviour and ecology of Indri indri.* Ph.D. thesis, University of London.

POORMAN, P., CARTMILL, M., MACPHEE, R., AND MOSES, M. 1985. The G-banded karotype of *Tarsius bancanus* and its implications for primate phylogeny. *American Journal of Physical Anthropology* 66:215.

POPP, J., AND DEVORE, I. 1979. Aggressive competition and social dominance theory: Synopsis. In *The great apes,* edited by D. A. Hamburg and E. R. McCown, pp. 317–338. Menlo Park, CA, Benjamin-Cummings.

POPP, J. L. 1983. Ecological determinism in the life histories of baboons. *Primates* 24:198–210.

PORTER, C. A., SAMPAIO, I., SCHNEIDER, H., SCHNEIDER, M. P. C., CZELUSNIAK, J., AND GOODMAN, M. 1995. Evidence of primate phylogeny from e-globin sequences and flanking regions. *Journal of Molecular Evolution* 40:30–55.

POWER, M. L. 1991. *Digestive function, energy intake and the response to dietary gum in captive callitrichids.* Ph.D. thesis, University of California, Berkeley.

POWER, M. L., OFTEDAL, O. T., AND TARDIF, S. D. 1998. Does the composition of milk of callitrichid monkeys reflect their small body size? *Symposia of the Comparative Nutrition Society,* vol. 2.

POWZYK, J. A. 1997. *The socio-ecology of two sympatric indriids:* Propithecus diadema diadema *and* Indri indri, *a comparison of feeding strategies and their possible repercussions on species-specific behaviors.* Ph.D. thesis, Duke University, Durham, NC.

PRAGER, E. M. 1996. Adaptive evolution of lysozyme: Changes in amino acid sequence, regulation of expression and gene number. In *Lysozymes: Model enzymes in biochemistry and biology,* edited by P. Jollès, pp. 323–345. Basel, Birkhauser-Verlag.

PREMACK, D. 1971. Language in chimpanzee? *Science* 172: 808–822.

PROUTY, L. A., BUCHANAN, P. D., POLLITZER, W. S., AND MOOTNICK, A. R. 1983a. A presumptive new hylobatid subgenus with 38 chromosomes. *Cytogenetics and Cell Genetics* 35:141–142.

PROUTY, L. A., BUCHANAN, P. D., POLLITZER, W. S., AND MOOTNICK, A. R. 1983b. Bunopoithecus: A genus-level taxon for the hoolock gibbon (*Hylobates hoolock*). *American Journal of Primatology* 5:83–87.

PYKE, G. H., PULLIAM, H. R., AND CHARNOV, E. L. 1977. Optimal foraging: A selective review of theory and tests. *Quarterly Review of Biology* 52:137–154.

RABOR, D. 1968. The present status of the monkey-eating eagle, *Pithecophagia jefferyi* Ogilvie-Grant, of the Philippines. *International Union Conservation Natural Resources Publication New Series* 10:312–314.

RAEMAEKERS, J. J. 1979. Ecology of sympatric gibbons. *Folia Primatologica* 31:227–245.

RAEMAEKERS, J. J. 1980. Causes of variation between months in the distance traveled daily by gibbons. *Folia Primatologica* 34:46–60.

RAEMAEKERS, J. J., AND RAEMAEKERS, P. M. 1984. Vocal interactions between two male gibbons, *Hylobates lar. Natural History Bulletin of the Siam Society* 32:95–106.

RAEMAEKERS, J. J., AND RAEMAEKERS, P. M. 1985a. Field playback of loud calls to gibbons (*Hylobates lar*): Territorial, sex-specific, and species-specific responses. *Animal Behaviour* 33:481–493.

RAEMAEKERS, J. J., AND RAEMAEKERS, P. M. 1985b. Long-range vocal interactions between groups of gibbons (*Hylobates lar*). *Behavior* 95:26–44.

RAEMAEKERS, J. J., RAEMAEKERS, P. M., AND HAIMOFF, E. H. 1984. Loud calls of the gibbon (*Hylobates lar*): Repetoire, organization and context. *Behaviour* 91: 146–189.

RAFF, R. A. 1996. *The shape of life.* Chicago, University of Chicago Press.

RAJANATHAN, R., AND BENNETT, E. L. 1990. Notes on the social behavior of wild proboscis monkeys (*Nasalis larvatus*). *Malaysian Nature Journal* 44:35–44.

RAJPUROHIT, L. S., AND SOMMER, V. 1993. Juvenile male emigration from natal one-male troops in hanuman langurs. In *Juvenile primates: Life history, development, and behavior,* edited by M. E. Pereira and L. A. Fairbanks, pp. 86–103. New York, Oxford University Press.

RALEIGH, M. J., AND MCGUIRE, M. T. 1990. Social influences on endocrine function in male vervet monkeys. In *Socioendocrinology of primate reproduction,* edited by

T. E. Ziegler and F. B. Bercovitch, pp. 95–111. New York, Wiley-Liss.

RALLS, K. 1976. Mammals in which females are larger than males. *Quarterly Review of Biology* 51:245–276.

RASAMAMINANA, H. R., AND RAFIDINARIVO, E. 1993. Feeding behavior of *Lemur catta* in relation to their physiological state. In *Lemur social systems and their ecological basis,* edited by P. M. Kappeler and J. U. Ganzhorn, pp. 123–134. New York, Plenum.

RAWLINS, R. G., AND KESSLER, M. J. 1986. The history of the Cayo Santiago colony. In *The Cayo Santiago macaques,* edited by R. G. Rawlins and M. J. Kessler, pp. 13–45. Albany, State University of New York Press.

REICHARD, U. 1995. Extra-pair copulations in a monogamous gibbon (*Hylobates lar*). *Ethology* 100:99–112.

REICHARD, U., AND SOMMER, V. 1994. Grooming site preferences in wild white-handed gibbons (*Hylobates lar*). *Primates* 35:369–374.

REICHARD, U., AND SOMMER, V. 1997. Group encounters in wild gibbons (*Hylobates lar*): Agonism, affiliation, and the concept of infanticide. *Behaviour* 134(15–16): 1135.

REMIS, M. J. 1994. *Feeding ecology and positional behavior of western lowland gorillas* (Gorilla gorilla gorilla) *in the Central African Republic.* Ph.D. thesis, Yale University, New Haven, CT.

REMIS, M. J. 1995. Effects of body size and social context on the arboreal activities of lowland gorillas in the Central African Republic. *American Journal of Primatology* 97:413–433.

REMIS, M. J. 1997a. Western lowland gorillas (*Gorilla gorilla gorilla*) as seasonal frugivores: Use of variable resources. *American Journal of Primatology* 43:87–109.

REMIS, M. J. 1997b. Ranging and grouping patterns of a western lowland gorilla group at Bai Hokōu, Central African Republic. *American Journal of Primatology* 43:111–133.

REN, R. M., SU, Y. J., YAN, K. H., LI, J. J., ZHOU, Y., ZHU, Z. Q., HU, Z. L., AND HU, Y. F. In press. Preliminary survey of the social organization of *Rhinopithecus roxellana* in Shennongjia National Natural Reserve, Hubei, China. In *The natural history of the doucs and snub-nosed monkeys,* edited by N. G. Jablonski. Singapore, World Scientific Press.

RENDALL, D., AND DiFIORE, A. 1995. The road less traveled: Phylogenetic perspectives in primatology. *Evolutionary Anthropology* 4:43–52.

REY, H. A. 1941. *Curious George.* Boston, Houghton Mifflin.

REY, H. A. 1952. *Curious George rides a bike.* Boston, Houghton Mifflin.

REY, H. A. 1958. *Curious George flies a kite.* Boston, Houghton Mifflin.

RHODES, L., ARGERSINGER, M. E., GANTERT, L. T., FRISCINO, B. H., HOM, G., PIKOUNIS, B., HESS, D. L., AND RHODES, W. L. 1997. Effects of administration of testosterone, dihydrotestosterone, oestrogen, and fadrozole, an aromatase inhibitor, on sex skin colour in intact male rhesus macaques. *Journal of Reproduction and Fertility* 111:51–57.

RICHARD, A. F. 1977. The feeding behaviour of *Propithecus verreauxi.* In *Primate ecology,* edited by T. H. Clutton-Brock, pp. 72–96. New York, Academic Press.

RICHARD, A. F. 1978. *Behavioral variation: A case study of a Malagasy lemur.* Lewisburg, PA, Bucknell University Press.

RICHARD, A. F. 1987. Malagasy prosimians: Female dominance. In *Primate societies,* edited by B. B. Smuts, D. L. Cheney, R. M. Seyfarth, R. W. Wrangham, and T. T. Struhsaker, pp. 25–33. Chicago, University of Chicago Press.

RICHARD, A., GOLDSTEIN, S., AND DEWAR, R. 1989. Weed macaques: The evolutionary implications of macaque feeding ecology. *International Journal of Primatology* 10(6):569–594.

RICHARD-HANSEN, C., VIE, J., AND de THOISY, B. In review. Translocation of red howler monkeys in French Guiana: Dispersal, settlement and sociality.

RIDLEY, M. 1986. *Evolution and classification.* New York, Longman.

RIGAMONTI, M. M. 1993. Home range and diet in red ruffed lemurs (*Varecia variegata rubra*) on the Masoala Peninsula, Madagascar. In *Lemur social systems and their ecological basis,* edited by P. M. Kappeler and J. U. Ganzhorn, pp. 25–40. New York, Plenum.

RIJKSEN, H. D. 1978. *A field study on Sumatran orang-utans* (Pongo pygmaeus abelii, *Lesson 1827*): Ecology, behavior, and conservation. Wageningen, The Netherlands, H. Veenman and Zonen.

RIPLEY, S. 1965. *The ecology and social behavior of the Ceylon gray langur,* Presbytis entellus thersites. Ph.D. thesis, University of California, Berkeley.

ROBBINS, D., CHAPMAN, C. A., AND WRANGHAM, R. W. 1991. Group size and stability: Why do gibbons and spider monkeys differ? *Primates* 32(3):301–305.

ROBBINS, M. M., AND CZEKALA, N. M. 1997. A preliminary investigation of urinary testosterone and cortisol levels in wild male mountain gorillas. *American Journal of Primatology* 43:51–64.

ROBERTS, M. 1994. Growth, development, and parental care patterns in the western tarsiers, *Tarsius bancanus,* in captivity: Evidence for a slow life history and nonmonogamous mating system. *International Journal of Primatology* 15(1):1–28.

ROBERTS, M., AND KOHN, F. 1993. Habitat use, foraging behavior and activity patterns in reproducing western tarsiers, *Tarsius bancanus,* in captivity: A management synthesis. *Zoo Biology* 12:217–232.

ROBERTS, M., KOHN, F., KEPPEL, A., MALINIAK, E., AND DEAL, M. 1984. Management and husbandry of the western tarsier, *Tarsius bancanus,* at the National Zoological Park. *AAZPA Regional Conference Proceedings,* 588–600.

ROBINSON, J. A., AND GOY, R. W. 1986. Steroid hormones and the ovarian cycle. In *Comparative primate biology,* edited by W. R. Dukelow and J. Erwin, vol. 3, pp. 63–91. New York, Alan R. Liss.

ROBINSON, J. A., SCHEFFLER, G., EISELE, S. G., AND GOY, R. W. 1975. Effects of age and season on sexual behavior and plasma testosterone and dihydrotestosterone concentrations of laboratory-housed male rhesus monkeys (*Macaca mulatta*). *Biology of Reproduction* 13:203–210.

RODMAN, P. S. 1973. Population composition and adaptive organisation among orangutans of the Kutai Reserve. In *Primate ecology: Studies of feeding and ranging behaviour in lemur, monkeys and apes,* edited by T. H. Clutton-Brock. London, Academic Press.

RODMAN, P. S. 1977. Feeding behavior of orangutans in the Kutai Reserve, East Kalimantan. In *Primate ecology,* edited by T. H. Clutton-Brock, pp. 383–413. London, Academic Press.

RODMAN, P. S. 1978. Diets, densities and distributions of Bornean primates. In *The ecology of arboreal folivores,* edited by G. G. Montgomery, pp. 465–678. Washington, DC, Smithsonian Institution Press.

RODMAN, P. S. 1979a. Individual activity profiles and the solitary nature of orangutans. In *The great apes,* edited by D. L. Hamburg and E. R. McCown, pp. 235–255. London, W. A. Benjamin.

RODMAN, P. S. 1979b. Skeletal differentiation of *Macaca fascicularis* and *Macaca nemestrina* in relation to arboreal and terrestrial quadrupedalism. *American Journal of Physical Anthropology* 51:51–62.

RODMAN, P. S. 1988. Resources and group size in primates. In *The ecology of social behavior,* edited by C. N. Slobodchikoff, pp. 83–108. New York, Academic Press.

RODMAN, P. S., AND MCHENRY, H. M. 1980. Bioenergetics and the origin of hominid bipedalism. *American Journal of Physical Anthropology* 52:103–106.

RODMAN, P. S., AND MITANI, J. C. 1987. Orangutans: Sexual dimorphism in a solitary species. In *Primate societies,* edited by B. B. Smuts, D. L. Cheney, R. M. Seyfarth, R. W. Wrangham, and T. T. Struhsaker, pp. 146–152. Chicago, University of Chicago Press.

RODRIGUEZ-LUNA, E., GARCIA-ORDUNA, F., ESPINOSA, D. C., AND SILVA, J. C. 1993. Translocation of the howler monkey; a four year record. *American Journal of Primatology* 30:345 (Abstract).

ROGERS, J. 1994. Levels of genealogical hierarchy and the problem of hominoid phylogeny. *American Journal of Physical Anthropology* 94:81–88.

ROGERS, M. E., MAISELS, F., WILLIAMSON, E. A., FERNANDEZ, M., AND TUTIN, C. E. G. 1990. Gorilla diet in the Lopé Reserve, Gabon: A nutritional analysis. *Oecologia* 84:326–339.

ROGERS, T. A. 1958. The metabolism of ruminants. *Scientific American* 198:34–38.

ROMMERTS, F. F. G. 1988. How much androgen is required for maintenance of spermatogenesis? *Journal of Endocrinology* 116:7–9.

ROSE, L. M. 1997. Vertebrate predation and food-sharing in *Cebus* and *Pan*. *International Journal of Primatology* 18:727–765.

ROSENBERG, H. F., DYER, K. D., TIFFANY, H. L., AND GONZALEZ, M. 1995. Rapid evolution of a unique family of primate ribonuclease genes. *Nature Genetics* 10: 219–223.

ROSENBERGER, A. L. 1992. Evolution of feeding niches in New World monkeys. *American Journal of Physical Anthropology* 88:525–562.

ROSENBERGER, A. L., AND STRIER, K. B. 1989. Adaptive radiation of the ateline primates. *Journal of Human Evolution* 18:717–750.

ROSENBERGER, A., AND SZALAY, F. 1980. On the tarsiiform origins of the Anthropoidea. In *Evolutionary biology of the New World monkeys and continental drift,* edited by R. Ciochon and A. Chiarelli, pp. 139–157. New York, Plenum.

ROSS, C. 1991. Life history patterns of New World primates. *International Journal of Primatology* 12:481–502.

ROUSSEAU, L. 1998. Negative population growth? *Population & Habitat Update* 10(2):1–2.

ROWE, N. 1996. *A pictorial guide to the living primates.* New York, Pogonias Press.

ROWELL, T. E. 1966. Hierarchy in the organization of a captive baboon group. *Animal Behavior* 14:430–433.

ROWELL, T. E. 1974. The concept of social dominance. *Behavioral Biology,* 131–154.

ROWELL, T. E. 1977. Variation in age at puberty in monkeys. *Folia Primatologica* 27:284–296.

ROWELL, T. E. 1984. What do male monkeys do besides competing? In *Behavioral evolution and integrative levels,* edited by G. Greenburg and E. Tobach, pp. 205–212. Hillsdale, NJ, Erlbaum.

ROWELL, T. E. 1988. Beyond the one-male group. *Behaviour* 104:189–201.

ROWELL, T. E., AND CHISM, J. 1986. The ontogeny of sex differences in the behavior of patas monkeys. *International Journal of Primatology* 7:83–106.

ROWELL, T. E., AND OLSON, D. K. 1983. Alternative mechanisms of social organization in monkeys. *Behaviour* 86:31–54.

RUDRAN, R. 1973. The reproductive cycles of two subspecies of purple-faced langurs (*Presbytis senex*) with relation to environmental factors. *Folia Primatologica* 19:41–60.

RUHIYAT, Y. 1983. Socio-ecological study of *Presbytis aygula* in West Java. *Primates* 24:344–359.

RUSSON, A. E., AND GALDIKAS, B. M. F. 1995. Imitation and tool use in rehabilitant orangutans. In *The neglected ape,* edited by R. D. Nadler, B. F. M. Galdikas, L. K. Sheeran, and N. Rosen, pp. 191–197. New York, Plenum.

RUVOLO, M. 1988. Genetic evolution in the African guenons. In *A primate radiation: Evolutionary biology of the African guenons,* edited by A. Gautier-Hion, F. Bourliere, J.-P. Gautier, and J. Kingdon, pp. 127–139. Cambridge, Cambridge University Press.

RUVOLO, M. 1997. Molecular phylogeny of the hominoids: Inferences from multiple independent DNA sequence data sets. *Molecular Biology and Evolution* 14:248–265.

RUVOLO, M., DISOTELL, T. R., ALLARD, M. W., BROWN, W. M., AND HONEYCUTT, R. L. 1994. Resolution of the African hominoid trichotomy by use of a mitochondrial gene sequence. *Proceedings of the National Academy of Sciences* 88:1570–1574.

RUVOLO, M., PAN, D., ZEHR, S., GOLDBERG, T., DISOTELL, T. R., AND VON DORNUM, M. 1994. Gene trees and hominoid phylogeny. *Proceedings of the National Academy of Sciences* 91:8900–8904.

RYDER, O. A., AND CHEMNICK, L. G. 1993. Chromosomal and mitochondrial DNA variation in orangutan. *Journal of Heredity* 84:405–409.

RYLANDS, A. B., ed. 1993. *Marmosets and tamarins: Systematics, behavior and ecology.* Oxford, Oxford Scientific Publications.

RYLANDS, A. B., MITTERMEIER, R. A., AND LUNA, E. R. 1995. A species list for the New World primates (Platyrrhini): Distribution by country, endemism, and conservation status according to the Mace-Land system. *Neotropical Primates* Supplement 3:113–160.

RYLANDS, A. B., MITTERMEIER, R. A., AND LUNA, E. R. 1997. Conservation of neotropical primates: Threatened species and an analysis of primate diversity by country and region. *Folia Primatologica* 68:134–169.

SABATER PI, J., BERMEJO, M., ILERA, G., AND VEA, J. J. 1993. Behavior of bonobos (*Pan paniscus*) following their capture of monkeys in Zaïre. *International Journal of Primatology* 14:797–804.

SACKETT, G. P., AND FREDRICKSON, W. T. 1987. Social preferences by pigtailed macaques: Familiarity versus degree and type of kinship. *Animal Behaviour* 35:603–606.

SADE, D. S. 1965. Some aspects of parent-offspring and sibling relations in a group of rhesus monkeys, with a discussion of grooming. *American Journal of Physical Anthropology* 23:1–18.

SADE, D. S. 1968. Inhibition of son-mother mating among free-ranging rhesus monkeys. *Science and Psychoanalysis* 12:18–38.

SAITO, C. 1996. Dominance and feeding success in female Japanese macaques, *Macaca fuscata*: Effects of food patch size and inter-patch distance. *Animal Behaviour* 51:967–980.

SALTHE, S. 1985. *Evolving hierarchical structures: Their structure and representation.* New York, Columbia University Press.

SANDERSON, M. J., AND HUFFORD, L., eds. 1996. *Homoplasy: The recurrence of similarity in evolution.* New York, Academic Press.

SAPOLSKY, R. M. 1986. Endocrine and behavioral correlates of drought in wild olive baboons (*Papio anubis*). *American Journal of Primatology* 11:217–227.

SAPOLSKY, R. M. 1990 (January). Stress in the wild. *Scientific American*, 116–123.

SAPOLSKY, R. M. 1993. The physiology of dominance in stable versus unstable hierarchies. In *Primate social conflict,* edited by W. A. Mason and S. P. Mendoza, pp. 171–204. Albany, State University of New York Press.

SAPOLSKY, R. M. 1994. *Why zebras don't get ulcers.* New York, W. H. Freeman.

SARICH, V. M. 1970. Primate systematics with special reference to Old World monkeys: A protein perspective. In *Old World monkeys. Evolution, systematics and behavior,* edited by J. R. Napier and P. H. Napier, pp. 175–226. New York, Academic Press.

SARICH, V. M., AND CRONIN, J. E. 1976. Molecular systematics of the primates. In *Molecular anthropology,* edited by M. Goodman and R. E. Tashian, pp. 141–170. New York, Plenum.

SARMIENTO, E. E., BUTYNSKI, T. M., AND KALINA, J. 1996. Gorillas of Bwindi-Impenetrable Forest and the Virunga Volcanoes: Taxonomic implications of morphological and ecological differences. *American Journal of Primatology* 40:1–21.

SAUTHER, M. L. 1989. Antipredator behavior in troops of free-ranging *Lemur catta* at Beza Mahafaly Special Reserve, Madagascar. *International Journal of Primatology* 10:595–606.

SAUTHER, M. L. 1991. Reproductive behavior of free-ranging *Lemur catta* at Beza Mahafaly Special Reserve, Madagascar. *American Journal of Physical Anthropology* 84:463–477.

SAUTHER, M. L. 1992. *The effect of reproductive state, social rank, and group size on resource use among free-ranging ringtailed lemurs* (Lemur catta) *of Madagascar.* Ph.D. thesis, Washington University, St. Louis.

SAUTHER, M. L. 1993. Resource competition in wild populations of ringtailed lemurs (*Lemur catta*): Implications for female dominance. In *Lemur social systems and their ecological basis,* edited by P. M. Kappeler and J. U. Ganzhorn, pp. 135–152. New York, Plenum.

SAUTHER, M. L., AND SUSSMAN, R. W. 1993. A new interpretation of the social organization and mating system of the ringtailed lemur (*Lemur catta*). In *Lemur social systems and their ecological basis,* edited by P. M. Kappeler and J. U. Ganzhorn, pp. 111–121. New York, Plenum.

SAVAGE, A., GIRALDO, L. H., SOTO, L. H., SNOWDON, C. T., AND INDERENA, R. I. 1996. Demography, group composition and dispersal in wild cotton-top tamarins (*Saguinus oedipus*). *American Journal of Primatology* 38:85–100.

SAVAGE-RUMBAUGH, E. S. 1986. *Ape language: From conditioned response to symbol.* New York, Columbia University Press.

SAVAGE-RUMBAUGH, E. S., AND LEWIN, R. 1994. *Kanzi: The ape at the brink of the human mind.* New York, Wiley.

SAVORY, P. 1964. *Zulu fireside tales.* Cape Town, Howard Timmins.

SCHALLER, G. B. 1963. *The mountain gorilla: Ecology and behavior.* Chicago, University of Chicago Press.

SCHJELDERUP-EBBE, T. 1922. Bieträge zur Sozialpsychologie des Haushuhns, Zeitschrift für. *Psychologie* 88: 225–252.

SCHNEIDER, H., AND ROSENBERGER, A. L. 1996. Molecules, morphology, and Platyrrhine systematics. In *Adaptive radiations of neotropical primates,* edited by M. A. Norconk, A. L. Rosenberger, and P. A. Garber, pp. 3–19. New York, Plenum.

SCHNEIDER, H., SAMPAIO, I., HARADA, M. L., BARROSO, C. M. L., SCHNEIDER, M. P. C., CZELUSNIAK, J., AND GOODMAN, M. 1996. Molecular phylogeny of the New World monkeys (Platyrrhini, Primates) based on two unlinked nuclear genes: IRBP intron 1 and epsilon-globin sequences. *American Journal of Physical Anthropology* 100:153–179.

SCHNEIDER, H., SCHNEIDER. M. P. C., SAMPAIO, I., HARADA, M. L., STANHOPE, M., AND GOODMAN, M. 1993. Molec-

ular phylogeny of the New World monkeys (Platyrrhini, Primates). *Molecular Phylogenetics and Evolution* 2:225–242.

SCHUBERT, G. 1982. Infanticide by usurper hanuman langur males: A sociobiological myth. *Biology and Social Life, Social Science Information (SAGE)* 21(2):199–244.

SCHULTZ, A. H. 1938. Genital swelling in the female orang-utan. *Journal of Mammalogy* 19:363–366.

SCHÜRMANN, C. 1982. Mating behaviour of wild orangutans. In *The orangutan: Its biology and conservation,* edited by L. de Boer, pp. 269–284. The Hague, W. Junk.

SCHÜRMANN, C. L., AND VAN HOOFF, J. 1986. Reproductive strategies of the orang-utan: New data and a reconsideration of existing sociosexual models. *International Journal of Primatology* 7:265–287.

SCHWARTZ, J., AND TATTERSALL, I. 1987. Tarsiers, adapids and the integrity of Strepsirhini. In *Primate phylogeny,* edited by F. Grine, J. Fleagle, and L. Martin, pp. 23–40. New York, Academic Press.

SEKI, K. 1985. Afterword. In *The monkey and the crab.* Union City, CA, Heian International.

SETIAWAN, E., KNOTT, C. D., AND BUDHI, S. 1996. Preliminary assessment of vigilance and predator avoidance behavior of orangutans in Gunung Palung National Park, Indonesia. *Tropical Biodiversity* 3(3):269–279.

SEYFARTH, R. 1978. Social relationships among adult male and female baboons. II. Behaviour throughout the female reproductive cycle. *Behaviour* 64:227–247.

SEYFARTH, R. M., AND CHENEY, D. L. 1994. The evolution of social cognition in primates. In *Behavioral mechanisms in evolutionary ecology,* edited by L. A. Real, pp. 371–389. Chicago, University of Chicago Press.

SHAFER, D. A., MYERS, R. H., AND SALTZMAN, D. 1984. Biogenetics of the siabon (gibbon-siamang hybrids). In *The lesser apes: Evolutionary and behavioral biology,* edited by H. Preuschoft, D. J. Chivers, W. Y. Brockelman, and N. Creel, pp. 486–497. Edinburgh, Edinburgh University Press.

SHAPIRO, G., AND GALDIKAS, B. M. F. 1995. Attentiveness in orangutans within the sign learning context. In *The neglected ape,* edited by R. D. Nadler, B. F. M. Galdikas, L. K. Sheeran, and N. Rosen, pp. 199–212. New York, Plenum.

SHARP, P. M. 1997. In search of molecular Darwinism. *Nature* 385:111–112.

SHARPE, R. M. 1994. Regulation of spermatogenesis. In *The physiology of reproduction,* edited by E. Knobil and J. D. Neill, vol. 1, pp. 1363–1434. New York, Raven Press.

SHAW, H. L. 1989. *Comprehension of the spoken word and ASL translation by chimpanzees.* Master's thesis, Central Washington University, Ellensburg.

SHEKELLE, M., MUKTI, S., ICHWAN, L., AND MASALA, Y. 1997. The natural history of the spectral tarsier. *Sulawesi Primate Project Newsletter.*

SHOLLEY, C. R. 1991. Conserving gorillas in the midst of guerrillas. *AAZPA Annual Conference Proceedings,* 30–37.

SILK, J. B. 1987. Social behavior in an evolutionary perspective. In *Primate societies,* edited by B. B. Smuts, D. L. Cheney, R. M. Seyfarth, R. W. Wrangham, and T. T. Struhsaker, pp. 318–329. Chicago, University of Chicago Press.

SILK, J. B. 1992. Patterns of intervention in agonistic contests among male bonnet macaques. In *Coalitions and alliances in humans and other animals,* edited by A. H. Harcourt and F. B. M. de Waal, pp. 215–232. Oxford, Oxford University Press.

SILK, J. B. 1997. The function of peaceful post-conflict contacts among primates. *Primates* 38:265–279.

SILVER, S. C. 1998. *The feeding ecology of translocated howler monkeys* (Alouatta pigra) *in Belize.* Ph.D. thesis, Fordham University, New York.

SIMONDS, P. E. 1965. The bonnet macaque in south India. In *Primate behavior,* edited by I. DeVore, pp. 175–196. New York, Holt, Rinehart and Winston.

SIMONS, E. L., AND RUMPLER, Y. 1988. *Eulemur:* New generic name for species of lemur other than *Lemur catta. Comptes rendus de L'Academie des Sciences* (Paris) Ser. 3 307:547–551.

SIMPSON, G. G. 1945a. The principles of classification and a classification of the mammals. *Bulletin of the American Museum of Natural History* 85:1–350.

SIMPSON, G. 1945b. Studies on the earliest primates. *Bulletin of the American Museum of Natural History* 77:185–212.

SKELTON, R. R., MCHENRY, H. M., AND DRAWHORN, G. 1986. Phylogenetic analysis of early hominids. *Current Anthropology* 27(1):21–43.

SMALL, M. E. 1984. *Female primates: Studies by women primatologists.* New York, Alan R. Liss.

SMITH, D. G. 1994. Male dominance and reproductive success in a captive group of rhesus macaques (*Macaca mulatta*). *Behaviour* 129:225–242.

SMUTS, B. B. 1983. Special relationships between adult male and female olive baboons: Selective advantages. In *Primate social relationships: An integrated approach,* edited by R. A. Hinde, pp. 262–266. Blackwell, Oxford Press.

SMUTS, B. B. 1985. *Sex and friendship in baboons.* New York, Aldine.

SMUTS, B. B. 1987. Gender, aggression, and influence. In *Primate societies,* edited by B. B. Smuts, D. L. Cheney, R. M. Seyfarth, R. W. Wrangham, and T. T. Struhsaker, pp. 400–412. Chicago, University of Chicago Press.

SMUTS, B. B., AND GUBERNICK, D. J. 1992. Male-infant relationships in nonhuman primates: Paternal investment or mating effort? In *Father-child relations in a cultural and biosocial context,* edited by B. S. Hewlett, pp. 1–30. New York, Aldine de Gruyter.

SMUTS, B. B., AND SMUTS, R. W. 1993. Male aggression and sexual coercion of females in nonhuman primates and other mammals: Evidence and theoretical implications. *Advances in the Study of Behavior* 22:1–63.

SNEATH, P. H. A., AND SOKAL, R. R. 1973. *Numerical taxonomy: The principles and practice of numerical classification.* San Francisco, W. H. Freeman.

SNOWDON, C. T. 1990a. Language capacities of nonhuman animals. *Yearbook of Physical Anthropology* 33:215–243.

SNOWDON, C. T. 1990b. Mechanisms maintaining monogamy in monkeys. In *Contemporary issues in comparative psychology,* edited by D. A. Doewsbury, pp. 225–252. Sunderland, MA, Sinauer Associates.

SOBER, E. 1984. *The nature of selection.* Cambridge, MA, MIT Press.

SODY, H. 1949. Notes on some primates, carnivora and the babirusa from the Indo-Malayan and Indo-Australian regions. *Treubia* 20:121–190.

SOINI, P. 1982. Ecology and population dynamics of the pygmy marmoset, *Cebuella pygmaea. Folia Primatologica* 49:11–32.

SOLTIS, J., MITSUNAGA, F., SHIMIZU, K., NOZAKI, M., YANAGIHARA, Y., DOMINGO-GOURA, X., AND TAKENAKA, O. 1997a. Sexual selection in Japanese macaques II: Female mate choice and male-male competition. *Animal Behaviour* 54:737–746.

SOLTIS, J., MITSUNAGA, F., SHIMUZU, K., YANAGIHARA, Y., AND NOZAKI, M. 1997b. Sexual selection in Japanese macaques I: Female mate choice or male sexual coercion. *Animal Behaviour* 54:725–736.

SOMMER, V., AND RAJPUROHIT, L. S. 1989. Male reproductive success in harem troops of hanuman langurs (*Presbytis entellus*). *International Journal of Primatology* 10:293–317.

SOULE, M. E., AND SIMBERLOFF, D. 1986. What do genetics and ecology tell us about the design of nature reserves? *Biological Conservation* 35:19–40.

SOUTHWICK, C. H., AND SMITH, R. B. 1986. The growth of primate field studies. In *Comparative primate biology,* vol. 2A: *Behavior, conservation and ecology,* edited by G. Mitchell and J. Erwin, pp. 73–91. New York, Alan R. Liss.

SPETH, J. D. 1989. Early hominid hunting and scavenging: The role of meat as an energy source. *Journal of Human Evolution* 18:329–343.

SPONSEL, L. 1997. The human niche in Amazonia: Explorations in ethnoprimatology. In *New World primates,* edited by W. G. Kinzey, pp. 143–165. New York, Aldine de Gruyter.

SPRAGUE, D. 1991a. Mating by nontroop males among the Japanese macaques of Yakushima Island. *Folia Primatologica* 57:156–158.

SPRAGUE, D. 1991b. Influences of mating on the troop choice of non-troop males among the Japanese macaques of Yakushima Island. In *Primatology today,* edited by A. Ehara et al., pp. 207–210. Amsterdam, Elsevier.

SRIKOSAMATARA, S. 1984. Ecology of pileated gibbons in south-east Thailand. In *The lesser apes: Evolutionary and behavioral ecology,* edited by H. Preuschoft, D. J. Chivers, W. Brockelman, and N. Creel, pp. 242–247. Edinburgh, Edinburgh University Press.

STANFORD, C. B. 1991a. The diet of the capped langur (*Presbytis pileata*) in a moist deciduous forest in Bangladesh. *International Journal of Primatology* 12:199–216.

STANFORD, C. B. 1991b. Social dynamics of intergroup encounters in the capped langur (*Presbytis pileata*). *American Journal of Primatology* 25:35–47.

STANFORD, C. B. 1996. The hunting ecology of wild chimpanzees: Implications for the behavioral ecology of Pliocene hominids. *American Anthropologist* 98:96–113.

STANFORD, C. B. 1998. The social behavior of chimpanzees and bonobos. Empirical evidence and shifting assumptions. *Current Anthropology* (in press).

STANFORD, C. B. In press. *The hunting apes.* Princeton, NJ, Princeton University Press.

STANFORD, C. B., WALLIS, J., MATAMA, H., AND GOODALL, J. 1994. Patterns of predation by chimpanzees on red colobus monkeys in Gombe National Park, Tanzania, 1982–1991. *American Journal of Physical Anthropology* 94:213–228.

STANHOPE, M. J., CZELUSNIAK, J., SI, J. S., NICKERSON, J., AND GOODMAN, M. 1992. A molecular perspective on mammalian evolution from the gene encoding interphotoreceptor retinoid binding protein, with convincing evidence for bat monophyly. *Molecular Phylogenetics and Evolution* 1:148–160.

STANLEY PRICE, M. R. 1989. *Animal re-introductions: The Arabian oryx in Oman.* Cambridge, Cambridge University Press.

STANYON, R. C, FANTINI, C., CAMPERIO-CIANI, A., CHIARELLI, B., AND ARDITO, G. 1988. Banded karyotypes of 20 Papionini species reveal no necessary correlation with speciation. *American Journal of Primatology* 16:3–17.

STARIN, E. D. 1991. *Socioecology of the red colobus monkey in the Gambia with particular reference to female-male differences and transfer patterns.* Ph.D. thesis, City University of New York.

STEKLIS, H. D., BRAMMER, G. L., RALEIGH, M. J., AND McGUIRE, M. T. 1985. Serum testosterone, male dominance and aggression in captive groups of male vervet monkeys (*Cercopithecus aethiops sabaeus*). *Hormones and Behavior* 19:154–163.

STEPHAN, H., BARON, G., AND FRAHM, H. D. 1988. Comparative size of brains and brain components. In *Comparative primate biology,* edited by H. D. Steklis and J. Erwin, pp. 1–39. New York, Alan R. Liss.

STERCK, E. H. M., AND STEENBEEK, R. 1997. Female dominance relationships and food competition in the sympatric Thomas langur and long-tailed macaque. *Behaviour* 134:749–774.

STERLING, E. J. 1993. *Behavioral ecology of the aye-aye* (Daubentonia madagascariensis) *on Nosy Mangabe, Madagascar.* Ph.D. thesis, Yale University, New Haven, CT.

STERN, B. R., AND SMITH, D. G. 1984. Sexual behavior and paternity in three captive groups of rhesus monkeys. *Animal Behaviour* 32:23–32.

STEUDEL, K. L. 1994. Locomotor energetics and hominid evolution. *Evolutionary Anthropology* 3:42–48.

STEVENS, C. E. 1988. *Comparative physiology of the vertebrate digestive system.* Cambridge, Cambridge University Press.

STEVENSON, P. R., QUIÑOES, M. J., AND AHUMADA, J. A. 1994. Ecological strategies of woolly monkeys (*Lagothrix lagotricha*) at Tinigua National Park, Colombia. *American Journal of Primatology* 32:123–140.

STEWART, C.-B. 1986. *Lysozyme evolution in Old World monkeys.* Berkeley, University of California Press.

STEWART, C.-B., AND DISOTELL, T. R. 1998. Primate evolution: In and out of Africa. *Current Biology* (in press).

STEWART, C.-B., SCHILLING, J. W., AND WILSON, A. C. 1987. Adaptive evolution in the stomach lysozymes of foregut fermenters. *Nature* 330:401–404.

STEWART, C.-B., AND WILSON, A. C. 1987. Sequence convergence and functional adaptation of stomach lysozyme from foregut fermenters. *Cold Spring Harbor Symposia on Quantitative Biology* 52:891–899.

STRASSER, E., AND DELSON, E. 1987. Cladistic analysis of cercopithecid relationships. *Journal of Human Evolution* 16:81–99.

STRIER, K. B. 1989. Effects of patch size on feeding associations in muriquis (*Brachyteles arachnoides*). *Folia Primatologica* 52:790–797.

STRIER, K. B. 1990. New World primates, new frontiers: Insights from the woolly spider monkey, or muriqui (*Brachyteles arachnoides*). *International Journal of Primatology* 11:7–19.

STRIER, K. B. 1991. Diet in one group of woolly spider monkeys, or muriquis (*Brachyteles arachnoides*). *American Journal of Primatology* 23:113–126.

STRIER, K. B. 1992a. Atelinae adaptations: Behavioral strategies and ecological constraints. *American Journal of Physical Anthropology* 88:515–524.

STRIER, K. B. 1992b. Causes and consequences of nonaggression in woolly spider monkeys. In *Aggression and peacefulness in humans and other primates*, edited by J. Silverberg and J. Grey, pp. 100–116. New York, Oxford University Press.

STRIER, K. B. 1993. Growing up in a patrifocal society: Sex differences in the spatial relations of immature muriquis (*Brachyteles arachnoides*). In *Juveniles: Life history, development, and behavior*, edited by M. E. Pereira and L. A. Fairbanks, pp. 138–147. New York, Oxford University Press.

STRIER, K. B. 1994a. Brotherhoods among atelines: Kinship, affiliation, and competition. *Behaviour* 130: 151–167.

STRIER, K. B. 1994b. Myth of the typical primate. *Yearbook of Physical Anthropology* 37:233–271.

STRIER, K. B. 1996a. Male reproductive strategies in New World primates. *Human Nature* 7:105–123.

STRIER, K. B. 1996b. Reproductive ecology of female muriquis. In *Adaptive radiations of neotropical primates*, edited by M. A. Norconk, A. L. Rosenberger, and P. A. Garber, pp. 511–532. New York, Plenum.

STRIER, K. B. 1997a. Behavioral ecology and conservation biology of primates and other animals. *Advances in the Study of Behavior* 26:101–158.

STRIER, K. B. 1997b. Subtle cues of social relations in male muriqui monkeys (*Brachyteles arachnoides*). In *New World primates: Evolution, ecology and behavior*, edited by W. G. Kinzey, pp. 109–118. New York, Aldine de Gruyter.

STRIER, K. B. 1997c. Mate preferences of wild muriqui monkeys (*Brachyteles arachnoides*): Reproductive and social correlates. *Folia Primatologica* 68:120–133.

STRIER, K. B. In press. Why is female kin bonding so rare: Comparative sociality of New World primates. In *Primate socioecology*, edited by P. C. Lee. Cambridge, Cambridge University Press.

STRIER, K. B., AND FONSECA, G. A. B. In press. The endangered muriquis of Brazil's Atlantic forest. *Primate Conservation*.

STRIER, K. B., AND ZIEGLER, T. E. 1997. Behavioral and endocrine characteristics of the reproductive cycle in wild muriqui monkeys, *Brachyteles arachnoides*. *American Journal of Primatology* 42:299–310.

STRUHSAKER, T. T. 1967. Auditory communication among vervet monkeys (*Cercopithecus aethiops*). In *Social communication among primates*, edited by S. Altmann, pp. 281–324. Chicago, University of Chicago Press.

STRUHSAKER, T. T. 1975. *The red colobus monkey*. Chicago, University of Chicago Press.

STRUHSAKER, T. T., AND GARTLAN, J. S. 1970. Observations on the behaviour and ecology of the patas monkey in the Waza Reserve, Cameroon. *Journal of Zoology, London* 161:49–63.

STRUHSAKER, T. T., AND OATES, J. F. 1975. Comparison of the behavior and ecology of red colobus and black-and-white colobus monkeys in Uganda: A summary. In *Socioecology and psychology of primates*, edited by R. H. Tuttle, pp. 103–123. The Hague, Mouton.

STRUM, S. C. 1981. Processes and products of change: Baboon predatory behavior at Gilgil, Kenya. In *Omnivorous primates*, edited by R. S. O. Harding and G. Teleki, pp. 255–302. New York, Columbia University Press.

STRUM, S. C. 1982. Agonistic dominance in male baboons: An alternative view. *International Journal of Primatology* 3:175–202.

STRUM, S. C. 1984. Why males use infants. In *Primate paternalism*, edited by D. M. Taub, pp. 146–185. New York, Van Nostrand Reinhold.

STRUM, S. C. 1987. *Almost human: A journey into the world of baboons*. New York, Random House.

STRUM, S. C. 1994. Reconciling aggression and social manipulation as means of competition, part 1: Life history perspective. *International Journal of Primatology* 15:739–765.

STRUM, S. C., AND FEDIGAN, L. M. In press a. *Primate encounters: Animals, scientists and science*. Chicago, University of Chicago Press.

STRUM, S. C., AND FEDIGAN L. M. In press b. Theory, method and gender: What changed our views of primate society? In *The new physical anthropology*, edited by S. C. Strum and D. Lindburg. New York, Prentice Hall.

STRUM, S. C., AND SOUTHWICK, C. H. 1986. Translocation of primates. In *Primates: The road to self-sustaining populations*, edited by K. Benirschke, pp. 449–457. New York, Springer-Verlag.

SU, Y. J., REN, R. M., YAN, K. H., LI, J. J., ZHOU, Y., ZHU, Z. Q., HU, Z. L., AND HU, Y. F. In press. Preliminary survey of the home range and ranging behavior of golden monkeys (*Rhinopithecus roxellana*) in Shennongjia National Nature Reserve, Hubei, China. In *The natural history of the doucs and snub-nosed monkeys*, edited by N. G. Joblonski. Singapore, World Scientific Press.

SUGARDJITO, J. 1983. Selecting nest-sites of Sumatran orang-utans, *Pongo pygmaeus abelii* in the Gunung Leuser National Park, Indonesia. *Primates* 24(4): 467–474.

SUGARDJITO, J. 1986. *Ecological constraints on the behaviour of Sumatran orang-utans* (Pongo pygmaeus abelii) *in the Gunung Leuser National Park, Indonesia*. Ph.D. thesis, Utrecht University.

SUGARDJITO, J., TE BOEKHORST, I. J. A., AND VAN HOOFF, J. 1987. Ecological constraints on the grouping of wild orang-utans (*Pongo pygmaeus*) in the Gunung Leuser National Park, Sumatra, Indonesia. *International Journal of Primatology* 8:17–41.

SUGARDJITO, J., AND NURHADA, N. 1981. Meat-eating behavior in wild orangutans. *Primates* 22:414–416.

SUGIYAMA, Y. 1964. Group composition, population density and some sociological observations of hanuman langurs (*Presbytis entellus*). *Primates* 5(3&4):7–37.

SUGIYAMA, Y. 1965. On the social change of hanuman langurs (*Presbytis entellus*) in their natural condition. *Primates* 6:381–418.

SUGIYAMA, Y. 1984. Population dynamics of wild chimpanzees at Bossou, Guinea, between 1976 and 1983. *Primates* 25:391–400.

SUGIYAMA, Y., AND OHSAWA, H. 1982. Population dynamics of Japanese monkeys with special reference to the effect of artificial feeding. *Folia Primatologica* 39:238–263.

SUOMI, S. J. 1986. Behavioral aspects of successful reproduction in primates. In *Primates: The road to self-sustaining populations,* edited by K. Benirschke, pp. 331–340. New York, Springer-Verlag.

SUOMI, S. J., AND LEROY, H. 1982. In memoriam: Harry F. Harlow (1905–1981). *American Journal of Primatology* 2:319–342.

SUPRIATNA, J., MANULLANG, B. O., AND SOEKARA, E. 1986. Group composition, home range, and diet of the maroon leaf monkey (*Presbytis rubicunda*) at Tanjung Puting Reserve, Central Kalimantan, Indonesia. *Primates* 27:185–190.

SUSMAN, R. L. 1991. Who made the Oldowan tools? Fossil evidence for tool behavior in Plio-Pleistocene hominids. *Journal of Anthropological Research* 47(2): 129–151.

SUSSMAN, R. W. 1973. *An ecological study of two Madagascan primates:* Lemur fulvus rufus (Audebert) *and* Lemur catta (Linnaeus). Ph.D. thesis, Duke University, Durham, NC.

SUSSMAN, R. W. 1974. Ecological distinctions in sympatric species of Lemur. In *Prosimian biology,* edited by

R. D. Martin, G. A. Doyle, and A. C. Walker, pp. 75–108. London, Duckworth.

SUSSMAN, R. W. 1977. Socialization, social structure and ecology of two sympatric species of Lemur. In *Primate bio-social development,* edited by S. Chevalier-Skolnikoff and F. Poirier, pp. 515–529. New York, Garland Press.

SUSSMAN, R. W. 1991. Demography and social organization of free-ranging *Lemur catta* in the Beza Mahafaly Reserve, Madagascar. *American Journal of Physical Anthropology* 84:43–58.

SUSSMAN, R. W. 1992. Male life histories and inter-group mobility among ringtailed lemurs (*Lemur catta*). *International Journal of Primatology* 13:395–413.

SUSSMAN, R. W., CHEVERUD, J. M, AND BARTLETT, T. Q. 1995. Infant killing as an evolutionary strategy: Reality or myth? *Evolutionary Anthropology* 3(5):149–151.

SUSSMAN, R. W., AND GARBER, P. A. 1987. A new interpretation of the social organization and mating system of the Callitrichidae. *International Journal of Primatology* 8:73–92.

SUSSMAN, R. W., AND KINZEY, W. G. 1984. The ecological role of the Callitrichidae: A review. *American Journal of Physical Anthropology* 64:419–449.

SUZUKI, A. 1979. The variation and adaptation of social groups of chimpanzees and black and white colobus monkeys. In *Primate ecology and human origins,* edited by I. S. Bernstein and E. O. Smith, pp. 153–173. New York, Garland Press.

SWANSON, K. W., IRWIN, D. M., AND WILSON, A. C. 1991. Stomach lysozyme gene of the langur monkey: Test for convergence and positive selection. *Journal of Molecular Evolution* 33:418–425.

SWANSON, W. J., AND VACQUIER, V. D. 1995. Extraordinary divergence and positive Darwinian selection in a fusagenic protein coating the acrosomal process of abalone spermatozoa. *Proceedings of the National Academy of Sciences, USA* 92:4957–4961.

SWOFFORD, D. L., OLSEN, G. J., WADDELL, P. J., AND HILLIS, D. M. 1996. Phylogenetic inference. In *Molecular systematics,* 2nd ed., edited by D. M. Hillis, C. Moritz, and B. K. Mable. Sunderland, Sinauer.

SYMINGTON, M. M. 1990. Fission-fusion social organization in *Ateles* and *Pan. International Journal of Primatology* 11:47–61.

SZALAY, F. S., AND DELSON, E. 1979. *Evolutionary history of the primates.* New York, Academic Press.

TAKAHATA, Y. 1980. The reproductive biology of a free-ranging troop of Japanese macaques. *Primates* 21: 303–329.

TAKAHATA, Y. 1990. Social relationships among adult males. In *The chimpanzees of the Mahale mountains: Sexual and life history strategies,* edited by T. Nishida, pp. 149–170. Tokyo, University of Tokyo Press.

TAKAHATA, Y., IHOBE, H., AND IDANI, G. 1996. Comparing copulations of chimpanzees and bonobos: Do females exhibit proceptivity or receptivity? In *Great ape societies,* edited by W. C. McGrew, L. F. Marchant, and T. Nishida, pp. 146–155. Cambridge, Cambridge University Press.

TAKAHATA, Y., SUZUKI, S., OKAYASU, N., AND HILL, D. 1994. Troop extinction and fusion in wild Japanese macaques of Yakushima Island, Japan. *American Journal of Primatology* 33:317–322.

TAKANAKA, O., HOTTA, Y., KAWAMOTO, Y., SURYOBROTO, B., AND BROTOISWORO, E. 1987. Origin and evolution of the Sulawesi macaques II: Complete amino acid sequences of seven β chains of three molecular types. *Primates* 28:99–109.

TARDIF, S. D. 1994. Relative energetic cost of infant care in small-bodied neotropical primates and its relation to infant-care patterns. *American Journal of Primatology,* 34:133–143.

TARDIF, S. D., HARRISON, M. L., AND SIMEL, M. A. 1993. Communal infant care in marmosets and tamarins: Relation to energetics, ecology, and social organization. In *Marmosets and tamarins: Systematics, behaviour, and ecology.* edited by A. B. Rylands, pp. 220–234. Oxford, Oxford Science Press.

TATTERSALL, I. 1976a. Notes on the status of *Lemur macaco* and *Lemur fulvus* (Primates, Lemuriformes). *Anthropological Papers of the American Museum of Natural History* 53:255–261.

TATTERSALL, I. 1976b. Group structure and activity rhythm in *Lemur mongoz* (Primates, Lemuriformes) on Anjouan and Mohéli Islands, Comoro Archipelago. *Anthropological Papers of the American Museum of Natural History* 53:367–380.

TATTERSALL, I. 1977a. The lemurs of the Comoros Islands. *Oryx* 13:445–448.

TATTERSALL, I. 1977b. Distribution of the Malagasy lemurs. Part 1: The lemurs of northern Madagascar. *Annals of the New York Academy of Sciences* 293:160–169.

TATTERSALL, I. 1982. *The primates of Madagascar.* New York, Columbia University Press.

TATTERSALL, I., AND COOPMAN, K. 1989. A further note on nomenclature in Lemuridae. *Journal of Human Evolution* 18:499–500.

TATTERSALL, I., AND SUSSMAN, R. W. 1975. Observations on the ecology and behavior of the mongoose lemur *Lemur mongoz mongoz* Linnaeus (Primates, Lemuri-

formes) at Ampijoroa, Madagascar. *Anthropological Papers of the American Museum of Natural History* 52: 193–216.

TAUB, D. M. 1980. Female choice and mating strategies among wild Barbary macaques (*Macaca sylvanus* L.). In *The macaques,* edited by D. G. Lindburg, pp. 287–344. New York, Van Nostrand Reinhold.

TAUB, D. M. 1984. Male caretaking behavior among wild Barbary macaques (*Macaca sylvanus*). In *Primate paternalism,* edited by D. M. Taub, pp. 20–55. New York, Van Nostrand Reinhold.

TAYLOR, C. R., AND ROWNTREE, V. J. 1973. Running on two or four legs: Which consumes more energy? *Science* 179:186–187.

TAYLOR, L. L. 1986. *Kinship, dominance, and social organization in a semi-free-ranging group of ring-tailed lemurs* (Lemur catta). Ph.D. thesis, Washington University, St. Louis.

TAYLOR, M., AND FEYEREISEN, R. 1996. Molecular biology and evolution of resistance to toxicants. *Molecular Biology and Evolution* 13:719–734.

TELEKI, G. 1973. *The predatory behavior of wild chimpanzees.* Lewisburg, PA, Bucknell University Press.

TENAZA, R. R. 1975. Territory and monogamy among Kloss' gibbons (*Hylobates klossii*) in Siberut Island, Indonesia. *Folia Primatologica* 24:60–80.

TENAZA, R. R. 1985. Human predation and Kloss' gibbons (*Hylobates klossii*) sleeping trees in Siberut Island, Indonesia. *American Journal of Primatology* 8: 299–308.

TENAZA, R. R. 1987. Studies of primates and their habitats in the Pagai Islands, Indonesia. *Primate Conservation* 8: 104–110.

TENAZA, R. R., AND FUENTES, A. 1995. Monandrous social organization of pigtailed langurs (*Simias concolor*) in the Pagai Islands, Indonesia. *International Journal of Primatology* 16:295–310.

TERBORGH, J. 1983. *Five New World primates: A study in comparative ecology.* Princeton, NJ, Princeton University Press.

TERBORGH, J., AND JANSON, C. H. 1986. The socioecology of primate groups. *Annual Review of Ecology and Systematics* 17:111–135.

THIERRY, B. 1990. Feedback loop between kinship and dominance: The macaque model. *Journal of Theoretical Biology* 145:511–521.

THIERRY, B. 1993. Emergent constraints condition the action of ultimate causes. *Journal of Theoretical Biology* 160:403–405.

THIERRY, B., GAUTHIER, C., AND PEIGNOT, P. 1990. Social grooming in Tonkean macaques (*Macaca tonkeana*). *International Journal of Primatology* 11:357–375.

THIERRY, B., HEISTERMANN, M., AUJARD, F., AND HODGES, J. K. 1996. Long-term data on basic reproductive parameters and evaluation of endocrine, morphological, and behavioral measures for monitoring reproductive status in a group of semifree-ranging Tonkean macaques (*Macaca tonkeana*). *American Journal of Primatology* 39:47–62.

THOMPSON, S. D., POWER, M. L., RUTLEDGE, C. E., AND KLEIMAN, D. G. 1994. Energy metabolism and thermoregulation in the golden lion tamarin (*Leontopithecus rosalia*). *Folia Primatologica* 63:131–143.

TILDEN, C., AND OFTEDAL, O. T. 1997. Milk composition reflects patterns of maternal care in prosimian primates. *American Journal of Primatology* 41:195–211.

TILSON, R. L. 1977. Social organization of simakobu monkeys (*Nasalis concolor*) in Siberut Island, Indonesia. *Journal of Mammalogy* 58:202–212.

TILSON, R. L. 1980. *Monogamous mating systems of gibbons and langurs in the Mentawai Islands, Indonesia.* Ph.D. thesis, University of California, Davis.

TILSON, R. L., SEAL, U. S., SOEMARNA, K., RAMONO, W., SUMARDJA, E., PONIRAN, S., VAN SCHAIK, C., LEIGHTON, M., RIJKSEN, H., AND EUDEY, A. 1993. Orangutan population and habitat viability analysis workshop. Medan, North Sumatra, Indonesia.

TILSON, R. L., AND TENAZA, R. R. 1976. Monogamy and dueting in an Old World monkey. *Nature* 263:320–321.

TILSON, R. L. AND TENAZA, R. R. 1977. The evolution of long-distance alarm calls in Kloss' gibbons. *Nature* 268:233–235.

TINBERGEN, N. 1951. *The study of instinct.* Oxford, Clarendon Press.

TOMASELLO, M., AND CALL, J. 1997. *Primate cognition.* New York, Oxford University Press.

TOOBY, J., AND DEVORE, I. 1987. The reconstruction of hominid behavioral evolution through strategic modeling. In *The evolution of human behavior: Primate models,* edited by W. G. Kinzey, pp. 183–238. Albany, State University of New York Press.

TORIGOE, T. 1985. Comparison of object manipulation among 74 species of non-human primates. *Primates* 26(2):182–194.

TRAVIS, C. B., AND YEAGER, C. P. 1991. Sexual selection, parental investment, and sexism. *Journal of Social Issues* 47(3):117–129.

TREESUCON, U., AND RAEMAEKERS, S. 1984. Group formation in gibbons through displacement of an adult. *International Journal of Primatology* 5:387.

TREMBLE, M., MUSKITA, Y., AND SUPRIATNA, J. 1993. Field observations of *Tarsius dianae* at Lore Lindu National Park, Central Sulawesi, Indonesia. *Tropical Biodiversity* 1(2):67–76.

TREVES, A., AND CHAPMAN, C. A. 1996. Conspecific threat, predation avoidance, and resource defense: Implications for grouping in langurs. *Behavioral Ecology and Sociobiology* 39:43–53.

TRIVERS, R. L. 1972. Parental investment and sexual selection. In *Sexual selection and the descent of man, 1871–1971,* edited by B. G. Campbell, pp. 136–179. Chicago, Aldine.

TUTIN, C. E. G. 1979. Mating patterns and reproductive strategies in a community of wild chimpanzees (*Pan troglodytes schweinfurthii*). *Behavioral Ecology and Sociobiology* 6:29–38.

TUTIN, C. E. G. 1996. Ranging and social structure of lowland gorillas in the Lopé Reserve, Gabon. In *Great ape societies,* edited by W. C. McGrew, L. T. Marchant, and T. Nishida, pp. 58–70. London, Cambridge University Press.

TUTIN, C. E. G., AND FERNANDEZ, M. 1984. Nationwide census of gorilla (*Gorilla g. gorilla*) and chimpanzee (*Pan t. troglodytes*) populations in Gabon. *American Journal of Primatology* 6:313–336.

TUTIN, C. E. G., AND FERNANDEZ, M. 1985. Foods consumed by sympatric populations of *Gorilla g. gorilla* and *Pan t. troglodytes* in Gabon: Some preliminary data. *International Journal of Primatology* 6:27–43.

TUTIN, C. E. G., AND FERNANDEZ, M. 1993. Composition of the diet of chimpanzees and comparisons with that of sympatric lowland gorillas in the Lopé Reserve, Gabon. *American Journal of Primatology* 30:195–211.

TUTIN, C. E. G., FERNANDEZ, M., ROGERS, M. E., AND WILLIAMSON, E. A. 1992. A preliminary analysis of the social structure of lowland gorillas in the Lopé Reserve, Gabon. In *Topics in primatology,* vol. 2, *Ecology and conservation,* edited by N. Itoigawa, Y. Sugiyama, G. P. Sackett, and R. K. R. Thompson, pp. 245–253. Tokyo, University of Tokyo Press.

UCHIDA, A. 1996. What we don't know about great ape variation. *Tree* 11(4):163–168.

UEHARA, S. 1997. Predation on mammals by the chimpanzee (*Pan troglodytes*). *Primates* 38:193–214.

ULMER, F. A. 1963. Observations on the tarsier in captivity. *Zoologischer Garten* 27:106–121.

UNGAR, P. S. 1992. *Incisor microwear and feeding behavior of four Sumatran anthropoids.* Ph.D. thesis, University of New York, Stony Brook.

UNGAR, P. S. 1996. Feeding height and niche separation in sympatric Sumatran monkeys and apes. *Folia Primatologica* 67:163–168.

UTAMI, S. 1997. Meat-eating behavior of adult female orangutans (*Pongo pygmaeus abelii*). *American Journal of Primatology* 43(2):159–165.

UTAMI, S., AND MITRA SETIA, T. 1995. Behavioral changes in wild male and female Sumatran orangutans (*Pongo pygmaeus abelii*) during and following a resident male take-over. In *The neglected ape,* edited by R. D. Nadler, B. F. M. Galdikas, L. K. Sheeran, and N. Rosen, pp. 183–190. New York, Plenum.

UTAMI, S., WICH, S. A., STERCK, E. H. M., AND VAN HOOFF, J. 1997. Food competition between wild orangutans in large fig trees. *International Journal of Primatology* 18(6):909–927.

VANDENBERGH, J. G. 1969. Endocrine coordination in monkeys: Male sexual responses to the female. *Physiology and Behavior* 4:261–264.

VAN DER KUYL, A. C., KUIKEN, C. L., DEKKER, J. T., AND GOUDSMIT, J. 1995a. Phylogeny of African monkeys based upon mitochondrial 12S rRNA sequences. *Journal of Molecular Evolution* 40:173–180.

VAN DER KUYL, A. C., KUIKEN, C. L., DEKKER, J. T., PERIZONIUS, W. R. K., AND GOUDSMIT, J. 1995b. Nuclear counterparts of the cytoplasmic mitochondrial 12S rRNA gene: A problem of ancient DNA and molecular phylogenies. *Journal of Molecular Evolution* 40:652–657.

VAN SCHAIK, C. P. 1983. Why are diurnal primates living in groups? *Behaviour* 87:120–144.

VAN SCHAIK, C. P. 1986. Phenological changes in a Sumatran rainforest. *Journal of Tropical Ecology* 2:327–347.

VAN SCHAIK, C. P. 1989. The ecology of social relationships amongst female primates. In *Comparative socioecology: The behavioural ecology of humans and other mammals,* edited by V. Standen and R. Foley, pp. 195–218. Oxford, Blackwell.

VAN SCHAIK, C. P. 1996. Social evolution in primates: The role of ecological factors and male behaviour. In *Evolution of social behaviour patterns in primates and man,* edited by W. G. Runciman, J. M. Smith, and R. I. M. Dunbar, pp. 9–31. Oxford, Oxford University Press.

VAN SCHAIK, C. P., AND DUNBAR, R. I. M. 1990. The evolution of monogamy in large primates: A new hypothesis and some crucial tests. *Behaviour* 115(1–2):30–62.

VAN SCHAIK, C. P., AND FOX, E. A. 1996. Manufacture and use of tools in wild Sumatran orangutans. *Naturwissenschaften* 83:186–188.

VAN SCHAIK, C. P., AND KAPPELER, P. M. 1993. Life history, activity period, and lemur social systems. In *Lemur social systems and their ecological basis,* edited by P. M. Kappeler and J. P. Ganzhorn, pp. 241–260. New York, Plenum.

VAN SCHAIK, C., AND KNOTT, C. D. 1998. Orangutan cultures? *American Journal of Physical Anthropology* Supplement 26.

VAN SCHAIK, C. P., AND PAUL, A. 1996. Male care in primates: Does it ever reflect paternity? *Evolutionary Anthropology* 5:152–156.

VAN SCHAIK, C. P., AND VAN HOOFF, J. 1996. Toward an understanding of the orangutan's social system. In *Great ape societies,* edited by W. C. McGrew, L. F. Marchant, and T. Nishida, pp. 3–15. Cambridge, Cambridge University Press.

VAN SCHAIK, C. P., AND VAN NOORDWIJK, M. 1983. The special role of male cebus monkeys in predation avoidance and its effect on group composition. *Behavioral Ecology and Sociobiology* 4:265–276.

VAN SCHAIK, C., VAN NOORDWIJK, M., WARSONO, B., AND SUTRIONO, E. 1983. Party size and early detection of predators in Sumatran forest primates. *Primates* 2: 211–221.

VAN TUINEN, P., AND LEDBETTER, D. H. 1983. Cytogenetic comparison and phylogeny of three species of Hylobatidae. *American Journal of Physical Anthropology* 61:453–466.

VASEY, N. 1997. *Community ecology and behavior of* Varecia variegata rubra *and* Lemur fulvus albifrons *on the Masoala Peninsula, Madagascar.* Ph.D. thesis, Washington University, St. Louis.

VEDDER, A. L. 1984. Movement patterns of a group of free-ranging mountain gorillas (*Gorilla gorilla beringei*) and their relation to food availability. *American Journal of Primatology* 7:73–88.

VELLAYAN, S. 1981. The nutritive value of ficus in the diet of lar gibbon (*Hylobates lar*). *Malaysian Applied Biology* 10:177–182.

VIE, J. 1996. Wildlife rescue in French Guiana: Objectives, methodology and preliminary results. *Proceedings of the 1996 annual conference of the American Association of Zoo Veterinarians.* Puerto Vallarta, Mexico.

VISALBERGHI, E. 1988. Responsiveness to objects in two social groups of tufted capuchin monkeys (*Cebus apella*). *American Journal of Primatology* 15:349–360.

VISALBERGHI, E. 1990. Tool use in *Cebus. Folia Primatologica* 54:146–154.

VISALBERGHI, E., AND FRAGASZY, D. M. 1990. Do monkeys ape? In *"Language" and intelligence in monkeys and apes,* edited by S. Parker and K. R. Gibson, pp. 247–273. Cambridge, Cambridge University Press.

VISALBERGHI, E., AND VITALE, A. F. 1990. Coated nuts as an enrichment device to elicit tool use in tufted capuchins (*Cebus apella*). *Zoo Biology* 9:65–71.

VON DORNUM, M. J. 1997. *DNA sequence data from mitochondrial COII and nuclear G6PD loci and a molecular phylogeny of the New World primates (Primates, Platyrrhini).* Ph.D. thesis, Harvard University, Cambridge, MA.

WALKER, M. L. 1995. Menopause in female rhesus monkeys. *American Journal of Primatology* 35:59–71.

WALLACE, D. C., STUGARD, C., MURDOCK, D., SCHURR, T., AND BROWN, M. D. 1997. Ancient mtDNA sequences in the human nuclear genome: A potential source of errors in identifying pathogenic mutations. *Proceedings of the National Academy of Sciences, USA* 94:14900–14905.

WALLIS, J. 1992. Chimpanzee genital swelling and its role in the pattern of sociosexual behavior. *American Journal of Primatology* 28:101–113.

WANG, W., FORNSTER, M. R. J., ZHANG, Y., LIU, Z., WEI, Y., HUANG, H., HU, H., XIE, Y., WU, D., AND MELNICK, D. J. 1997. A phylogeny of Chinese leaf monkeys using mitochondrial ND3-ND4 gene sequences. *International Journal of Primatology* 18:305–320.

WARD, S. C., AND SUSSMAN, R. W. 1978. Correlates between locomotor anatomy and behavior in two sympatric species of lemurs. *American Journal of Physical Anthropology* 50:575–590.

WASER, P. M. 1978. Postreproductive survival and behavior in a free-ranging female mangabey. *Folia Primatologica* 29:142–160.

WASHBURN, S. L. 1951. The new physical anthropology. *Transactions of the New York Academy of Sciences, Series II* 13:298–304.

WATANABE, K. 1989. Fish: A new addition to the diet of Japanese macaques on Koshima Island. *Folia Primatologica* 52:124–131.

WATERMAN, P. G., AND KOOL, K. M. 1994. Colobine food selection and plant chemistry. In *Colobine monkeys: Their ecology, behaviour and evolution,* edited by A. G. Davies and J. F. Oates, pp. 251–284. Cambridge, Cambridge University Press.

WATERMAN, P. G., CHOO, G. M., VEDDER, A. L., AND WATTS, D. P. 1983. Digestibility, digestion-inhibitors and nutrients of herbaceous foliage and green stems from an African montane flora and comparison with other tropical flora. *Oecologia* 60:244–249.

WATTS, D. P. 1984. Composition and variability of mountain gorilla diets in the central Virungas. *American Journal of Primatology* 7:323–356.

WATTS, D. P. 1985. Relations between group size and composition and feeding competition in mountain gorilla groups. *Animal Behavior* 33:72–85.

WATTS, D. P. 1989. Infanticide in mountain gorillas: New cases and a reconstruction of the evidence. *Ethology* 81:1–18.

WATTS, D. P. 1991. Strategies of habitat use by mountain gorillas. *Folia Primatologica* 56:1–16.

WATTS, D. P., AND PUSEY, A. E. 1993. Behavior of juvenile and adolescent great apes. In *Juvenile primates: Life history, development, and behavior,* edited by M. E. Pereira and L. A. Fairbanks, pp. 148–167. New York, Oxford University Press.

WEINBAUR, G. F., AND NIESCHLAG, E. 1991. Peptide and steroid regulation of spermatogenesis in primates. *Annals of the New York Academy of Sciences* 637:107–121.

WEINBERG, J., STANYON, R., JAUCH, A., AND CREMER, T. 1992. Homologies in human *Macaca fuscata* chromosomes revealed by in situ suppression hybridization with human chromosome specific DNA libraries. *Chromosoma* 101:265–270.

WESTERGAARD, G. C. 1995. The stone-tool technology of capuchin monkeys: Possible implications for the evolution of symbolic communication in hominids. *World Archaeology* 27(1):1–9.

WESTERGAARD, G. C., AND FRAGASZY, D. M. 1987. The manufacture and use of tools by capuchin monkeys (*Cebus apella*). *Journal of Comparative Psychology* 101(2):159–168.

WESTERGAARD, G. C., GREENE, J. A., BABITZ, M. A., AND SUOMI, S. J. 1995. Pestle use and modification by tufted capuchins (*Cebus apella*). *International Journal of Primatology* 16(4):643–651.

WESTERGAARD, G. C., LUNDQUIST, A. L., KUHN, H. E., AND SUOMI, S. J. 1997. Ant-gathering with tools by captive tufted capuchins (*Cebus apella*). *International Journal of Primatology* 18(1):95–103.

WESTERGAARD, G. C., AND SUOMI, S. J. 1994a. The use and modification of bone tools by capuchin monkeys. *Current Anthropology* 35(1):75–77.

WESTERGAARD, G. C., AND SUOMI, S. J. 1994b. Asymmetrical manipulation in the use of tools by tufted capuchin monkeys (*Cebus apella*). *Folia Primatologica* 63:96–98.

WESTERGAARD, G. C., AND SUOMI, S. J. 1995. The manufacture and use of bamboo tools by monkeys: Possible implications for the development of material culture among East Asian hominids. *Journal of Archaeological Science* 22:677–681.

WESTERN, J. D., WRIGHT, M, AND STRUM, S. C. 1994. *Natural connections: Perspectives on community based conservation.* Washington, DC, Island Press.

WHEATLEY, B. 1980. Feeding and ranging of East Bornean *Macaca fascicularis.* In *The macaques: Studies in ecology, behavior and evolution,* edited by D. G. Lindburg, pp. 215–246. New York, Van Nostrand.

WHEATLEY, B. P. 1982. Energetics of foraging in *Macaca fascicularis* and *Pongo pygmaeus* and a selective advantage of large body size in the orang-utan. *Primates* 23:348–363.

WHEATLEY, B. P. 1987. The evolution of large body size in orangutans: A model for hominoid divergence. *American Journal of Primatology* 13:313.

WHEATLEY, B. In press. *The sacred monkeys of Bali.* Prospect Heights, IL, Waveland Press.

WHEATLEY, B., AND HARYA PUTRA, D. K. 1994. The effects of tourism on conservation at the monkey forest in Ubud, Bali. *Revue D Ecologie (Terre et Vie)* 49:245–257.

WHEATLEY, B., STEPHENSON, R., KURASHINA, H., AND KAUTZ, K. 1997. *Cultural primatology of* Macaca fascicularis *on Ngeaur Island, Republic of Palau.* Unpublished manuscript.

WHITE, F. J., AND WRANGHAM, R. W. 1988. Feeding competition and patch size in the chimpanzee species *Pan paniscus* and *Pan troglodytes. Behaviour* 105:148–163.

WHITINGTON, C. L. 1992. Interactions between lar gibbons and pig-tailed macaques at fruit sources. *American Journal of Primatology* 26:61–64.

WHITTEN, A. J. 1982a. Diet and feeding behavior of Kloss gibbons on Siberut Island, Indonesia. *Folia Primatologica* 37:177–208.

WHITTEN, A. J. 1982b. Home range use by Kloss gibbons (*Hylobates klossii*) on Siberut Island, Indonesia. *Animal Behaviour* 30:182–198.

WHITTEN, A. J. 1984. Ecological comparisons between Kloss gibbons and other small gibbons. In *The lesser apes: Evolutionary and behavioral ecology,* edited by H. Preuschoft, D. J. Chivers, W. Brockelman, and N. Creel, pp. 219–227. Edinburgh, Edinburgh University Press.

WHITTEN, P. L. 1987. Infants and adult males. In *Primate societies,* edited by B. B. Smuts, D. L. Cheney, R. M. Seyfarth, R. W. Wrangham, and T. T. Struhsaker, pp. 343–357. Chicago, University of Chicago Press.

WILEY, E. O. 1981. *Phylogenetics: The theory and practice of phylogenetic systematics.* New York, Wiley.

WILLIAMS, G. C. 1966. *Adaptation and natural selection.* Princeton, NJ, Princeton University Press.

WILLIAMS, G. C. 1992. *Natural selection: Domains, levels, and challenges.* New York, Oxford University Press.

WILLIAMS, K. 1995. *Comprehensive nighttime activity budgets of captive chimpanzees* (Pan troglodytes). Master's thesis, Central Washington University, Ellensburg.

WILLIAMSON, E. A., TUTIN, C. E. G., ROGERS, M. E., AND FERNANDEZ, M. 1990. Composition of the diet of lowland gorillas at Lopé in Gabon. *American Journal of Primatology* 21:265–277.

WILMER, L. 1909. *Psychological Clinic* 3:179–205.

WILSON, A. C. 1975. *Evolutionary importance of gene regulation.* Columbia, University of Missouri (Stadler Symposium).

WILSON, A. C. 1985. The molecular basis of evolution. *Scientific American* 253:164–173.

WILSON, A. C., CARLSON, S. S., AND WHITE, T. J. 1977. Biochemical evolution. *Annual Review of Biochemistry* 46:573–639.

WILSON, A. C., AND SARICH, V. M. 1969. A molecular time scale for human evolution. *Proceedings of the National Academy of Sciences, USA* 63:1088–1093.

WILSON, J. M., STEWART, P. D., RAMANGASON, G. S., DENNING, A. M., AND HUTCHINGS, M. S. 1989. Ecology and conservation of the crowned lemur, *Lemur coronatus,* at Ankarana, N. Madagascar, with notes on Sanford's lemur, other sympatric and subfossil lemurs. *Folia Primatologica* 52:1–26.

WILSON, M. E., GORDON, T. P., AND COLLINS, D. C. 1982. Age differences in copulatory behavior and serum 17β-estradiol in female rhesus monkeys. *Physiology and Behavior* 28:733–737.

WINKLER, L. 1989. Morphology and relationships of the orangutan fatty cheek pads. *American Journal of Primatology* 17:305–319.

WISE, C. A., SRAML, M., RUBINSZTEIN, D. C., AND EASTEAL, S. 1997. Comparative nuclear and mitochondrial genome diversity in humans and chimpanzees. *Molecular Biology and Evolution* 14:707–716.

WOLFHEIM, J. H. 1983. *Primates of the world: Distribution, abundance, and conservation.* Seattle, University of Washington Press.

WOLFHEIM, J. H. 1986. *The distribution, ecology and habitat of primates.* Cambridge, Cambridge University Press.

WOLIN, L., AND MASSOPUST, L. 1970. Morphology of the primate retina. In *Primate brain,* edited by C. Noback and W. Montagna, pp. 1–27. New York, Appleton-Century-Crofts.

WORLD RESOURCES INSTITUTE. 1998. *World Resources 1998–99.* New York, Oxford University Press.

WRANGHAM, R. W. 1977. Feeding behaviour of chimpanzees in Gombe National Park, Tanzania. In *Primate ecology*, edited by T. H. Clutton-Brock, pp. 504–538. London, Academic Press.

WRANGHAM, R. W. 1979. On the evolution of ape social systems. *Social Science Information* 18:335–368.

WRANGHAM, R. W. 1980. An ecological model of female-bonded primate groups. *Behaviour* 75:262–300.

WRANGHAM, R. W. 1986. Ecology and social relationships in two species of chimpanzee. In *Ecological aspects of social evolution*, edited by D. I. Rubenstein and R. W. Wrangham, pp. 352–378. Princeton, NJ, Princeton University Press.

WRANGHAM, R. W. 1987a. Evolution of social structure. In *Primate societies*, edited by B. B. Smuts, D. L. Cheney, R. M. Seyfarth, R. W. Wrangham, and T. T. Struhsaker, pp. 282–296. Chicago, University of Chicago Press.

WRANGHAM, R. W. 1987b. The significance of African apes for reconstructing human social evolution. In *The evolution of human behavior: Primate models*, edited by W. G. Kinzey, pp. 51–71. Albany, State University of New York Press.

WRANGHAM, R. W. 1993. The evolution of sexuality in chimpanzees and bonobos. *Human Nature* 4:47–79.

WRANGHAM, R. W., AND VAN ZINNICQ BERGMANN RISS, E. 1990. Rates of predation on mammals by Gombe chimpanzees, 1972–1975. *Primates* 31:157–170.

WRIGHT, P. C. 1990. Patterns of paternal care in primates. *International Journal of Primatology* 11:89–102.

WRIGHT, P. C., IZARD, M., AND SIMONS, E. 1986. Reproductive cycles in *Tarsius bancanus*. *American Journal of Primatology* 11:207–215.

WRIGHT, P. C., TOYAMA, L., AND SIMONS, E. 1988. Courtship and copulation in *Tarsius bancanus*. *Folia Primatologica* 46:142–148.

WU, C. I. 1991. Inferences of species phylogeny in relation to segregation of ancient polymorphisms. *Genetics* 127:429–435.

YAMAGIWA, J., MARUHASHI, T., AND YUMOTO, T. 1996. Dietary and ranging overlap in sympatric gorillas and chimpanzees in Kahuzi-Biega National Park, Zaire. In *Great ape societies*, edited by W. C. McGrew, L. T. Marchant, and T. Nishida, pp. 82–98. London, Cambridge University Press.

YAMAGIWA, J., MWANZA, N., SPANGENBERG, A., MARUHASHI, T., YUMOTO, T., FISCHER, A., AND STEINHAUER-BUKART, B. 1993. A census of the eastern lowland gorilla (*Gorilla gorilla graueri*) in the Kahuzi-Biega National Park with reference to mountain gorillas (*G. g. beringei*) in

the Virunga region, Zaire. *Biological Conservation* 64:83–89.

YAMAGIWA, J., MWANZA, N., YUMOTO, T., AND MARUHASHI, T. 1992. Travel distances and food habits of eastern lowland gorillas: A comparative analysis. In *Topics in primatology*, vol. 2, *Ecology and conservation*, edited by N. Itoigawa, Y. Sugiyama, G. P. Sackett, and R. K. R. Thompson, pp. 267–281. Tokyo, University of Tokyo Press.

YAMAMOTO, M. E., AND ALENCAR, A. I. In press. Some characteristics of the scientific literature in Brazilian primatology, In *Primate encounters: Animals, scientists and science*, edited by S. C. Strum and L. M. Fedigan. Chicago, University of Chicago Press.

YANG, Z. 1998. Likelihood ratio tests for detecting positive selection and application to primate lysozyme evolution. *Molecular Biology and Evolution* 15:568–573.

YANG, Z., KUMAR, S., AND NEI, M. 1995. A new method of inference of ancestral nucleotide and amino acid sequences. *Genetics* 141:1641–1650.

YEAGER, C. P. 1989. Feeding ecology of the proboscis monkey (*Nasalis larvatus*). *International Journal of Primatology* 10:497–530.

YEAGER, C. P. 1991. Proboscis monkey (*Nasalis larvatus*) social organization: Intergroup patterns of association. *American Journal of Primatology* 23:73–86.

YEAGER, C. P. 1996. Conservation status of proboscis monkey groups and the effects of habitat degradation. *Asian Primates* 5(3&4):3–5.

YEAGER, C. P. 1997. Orangutan rehabilitation at Tanjung Puting National Park, Kalimantan Tengah, Indonesia. *Conservation Biology* 11:802–805.

YODER, A. D. 1996. Strepsirrhine phylogeny: Congruence of results from a mitochondrial and a nuclear gene. *American Journal of Physical Anthropology* 22:250.

YODER, A. D. 1997. Back to the future: A synthesis of strepsirrhine systematics. *Evolutionary Anthropology* 6:11–22.

YODER, A. D., RUVOLO, M., AND VIGALYS, R. 1996. Molecular evolutionary dynamics of cytochrome b in strepsirrhine primates: The phylogenetic significance of third position transversions. *Molecular Biology and Evolution* 13:1339–1350.

YOKOYAMA, R., AND YOKOYAMA, S. 1990. Convergent evolution of the red- and green-like visual pigment genes in fish, *Astyanax fasciatus*, and human. *Proceedings of the National Academy of Sciences, USA* 87:9315–9318.

YOSHIBA, K. 1967. An ecological study of hanuman langurs, *Presbytis entellus*. *Primates* 8:127–154.

YOUNG, T. 1994. Natural die-offs of large mammals: Implications for conservation. *Conservation Biology* 8: 410–418.

ZEHR, S., RUVOLO, M. HEIDER, J., AND MOOTNICK, A. 1996. Gibbon phylogeny inferred from mitochondrial DNA sequences. *American Journal of Physical Anthropology* Supplement 22:251.

ZHANG, D.-X., AND HEWITT, G. M. 1996. Nuclear integrations: Challenges for mitochondrial DNA markers. *Trends in Ecology and Evolution* 11:247–251.

ZHANG, J., AND KUMAR, S. 1997. Detection of convergent and parallel evolution at the amino acid sequence level. *Molecular Biology and Evolution* 14:527–536.

ZHANG, J., KUMAR, S., AND NEI, M. 1997. Small-sample tests of episodic adaptive evolution: A case study of primate lysozymes. *Molecular Biology and Evolution* 14:1335–1338.

ZHANG, Y., AND RYDER, O. A. 1998. Mitochondrial cytochrome b gene sequences of Old World monkeys: With special reference on evolution of Asian colobines. *Primates* 39:39–49.

ZHANG, Y., AND SHI, L. 1993. Phylogenetic relationships of macaques as inferred from restriction endonuclease analysis of mitochondrial DNA. *Folia Primatologica* 60:7–17.

ZIEGLER, T. E. 1997. Hormones associated with non-maternal care: A review of mammalian and avian studies. *Folia Primatologica.*

ZIEGLER, T. E., WEGNER, F. H., AND SNOWDON, C. T. 1996. Hormonal responses to parental and nonparental conditions in male cotton-top tamarins, *Saguinus oedipus,* a New World primate. *Hormones and Behavior* 30:287–297.

ZUCKERMAN, S. 1932. *The social life of monkeys and apes.* London, Routledge.

ZUMPE, D., AND MICHAEL, R. P. 1996. Social factors modulate the effects of hormones on the sexual and aggressive behavior of macaques. *American Journal of Primatology* 38:233–261.

Index

Page numbers in *italics* refer
to figures.

Acheulian Industry, 117, 120
Adapidae, 12
adaptive evolution
    behavior and, 177–178, 179, 193
    of colobine foregut fermentation,
        29–30, 32–38
    comparative method and, 29–30,
        250–251
    genetic mechanisms in, 29, 34
    in origin of primates, 12
    regulatory theory of, 34
adaptive grades, 59, 265
adaptive radiation, of New World
        monkeys, 21
adolescents, definition of, 137
adrenaline, 242
affiliative behaviors, 212, 213, 217
affiliative relationship sets, 214, 215
aggression
    in behavioral ecology, 268
    dominance and, 206, 207, 208,
        209
    functions of, 208
    in sociobiology, 266
    testosterone and, 238–239
aging in nonhuman primates, 218
    vs. human primates, 220–222
    variations in, 222–224
agonism scores, 209
agonistic behavior, 212–213
agonistic buffering, 81, 82
Allenopithecus, 23
allometry of energy expenditure,
        225, 228
allomothering, in colobines, 75
Alouatta. See howler monkeys
Alouattinae, 108
Alouattini, 109
alpha male, 199, 206, 207

altruism, 203, 205, 266
analogous characters, 247
analogous molecules, 30
anatomical research, 261, 262
anatomy of primates, 10, 12
Angolan colobus, 96, 97, 99
animal welfare, 268–269
antagonism, 212–213
Anthropoidea
    evolution of, 12–16, *15, 16, 17*
    taxonomic status of, 19, 20, 140
anthropomorphism, 178, 182, 250
    in Japanese primatology, 259
Aotinae, 107
Aotus. See owl monkeys
apes, 41–43
    brachiation, 41, 247, 248, *248*
    cognitive evolution, 249–251
    early hominid behavior and,
        196–200
    fossil record, 15–16, *15, 16, 17*
    molecular phylogeny, 26–28, *27*
    sign language research, 56,
        252–256
    See also specific apes
approach-avoidance scores, 209
Aquatic Ape theory, 197
Archeolemur, 17
arctoides group, 24, *24*
Assamese macaque (*M. assamensis*),
        82
Ateles. See spider monkeys
Atelidae, 21, 22
atelines, 21, 22, 108, 109–114
    communities in, 215
    See also spider monkeys; woolly
        monkeys; woolly spider
        monkey
Atelini, 109
Avahi, 21
aye-aye, 121, 123
    in communities, 132

molecular phylogeny, 20–21

baboons, 73–74
    consortships, 213
    dominance and female behavior,
        137, 267
    dominance and male hormones,
        238, 242
    dominance hierarchy, 207, 208,
        210
    folktales about, 272–273
    history of research, 259, 261–262,
        263–264
    male coalitions, 213
    male-immature interactions, 138
    male reproductive physiology,
        238, 239, 241, 242
    molecular phylogeny, 23, 24
    predation by, 199–200
    sacred, in ancient Egypt, 270
    stress response, 242–243
    translocation project, 165
    See also hamadryas baboon;
        savanna baboon
bamboo lemurs, 121, 123, 132
banded leaf monkey, 95, 101
Barbary macaque (*M. sylvanus*), 24,
        80, 81
basal metabolic rate (BMR), 226
behavior, 175
    . adaptive significance of, 177–178,
        179, 193
    causes of, 176–177, 178–180, 195
    consequences of, 177, 178, 179
    definition of, 176
    evolution of, 175, 177, 178, 179,
        181–182, 196–200
    functions of, 177–178, 179, 182,
        203–204, 205
    hormones and, 238
    human, origins of, 176
    structure of, 179, 205

behavior (continued)
   Tinbergen's "why" questions, 176,
      177, 179, 205, 260
   variability of, 181, 188, 189,
      264–265, 266, 267
   See also social organization
behavioral ecology, 262, 267–269
   See also socioecology
behaviorism, 259, 267
β-endorphin, 242
bilophodont molars, 73
binomial nomenclature, 6
bipedalism, in early hominids, 197
black-and-white colobus, 25, 94
black-and-white ruffed lemur, 128
black colobus, 93, 96, 100
black lemur, 127, 129–130, 131
BMR (basal metabolic rate), 226
bonnet macaque (M. radiata), 79, 80
bonobo (Pan paniscus), 42–43
   arboreality, 65, 66
   distribution, 42, 64, 65
   dominance in, 67, 71
   female-female relationships,
      70–71, 215
   food sharing, 66–67
   food sources, 42, 62, 65
   history of research, 64
   hunting by, 199
   infanticide hypothesis, 190
   kinship in, 71
   language acquisition, 252
   mating behavior, 69
   molecular phylogeny, 28
   sexual behavior, 68–70, 69, 70
   sexual dimorphism, 64
   social organization, 42, 59, 64–65,
      66–67, 67, 70–72
   threats to, 65–66
   tool use, 68
brachiation, 41, 247, 248, 248
   by gibbons, 44
   by orangutans, 51
Brachyteles, 21, 22, 109
Brazilian primatology, 260
British primatology, 259, 260,
   261–262
brown lemurs, 126–127, 129, 130,
   131–132
Buddhism, primate images in, 271
Bunopithecus (H. hoolock), 26, 45

bush babies, 122, 228
bushmeat trade, 146, 147, 154, 156,
   269
   gorillas, 58

Cacajao. See uakaris
Callicebinae, 107
Callicebus, 21, 22, 107
Callimico goeldi, 21, 22, 106, 107,
   226
   infant care, 227
Callithrix, 21, 22, 106, 226
   male-infant bonds, 244
   milk, 230
callitrichids, 106–107
   Brazilian primatology and, 260
   energy expenditure, 218, 225–230
   lactation, 229–230
   lifestyle, 226
   male-infant bonds, 244
   reproductive costs, 228–229
   reproductive strategy, 226–227
   social organization, 184, 185,
     260
   taxonomy, 21, 22, 106–107, 226
   See also marmosets; tamarins
calls. See vocalizations
capped langur, 95, 96
captive primates
   breeding in, 165
   social organization of, 207
capuchins, 107, 115–116
   intelligence, 116
   molecular phylogeny, 21, 22
   object manipulation by, 115–116,
     118–120, 200, 251
   predation by, 199–200
Cartesianism, 259
catarrhines. See apes; Old World
   monkeys
catecholamines, 242
cathemeral species, 123
Catopithecus, 13, 13
Cebidae, 21, 22, 107–108
   female dispersal in, 267
   See also capuchins
Cebinae, 107
   See also capuchins
Cebuella, 22, 106, 226, 230
Cebupithecia, 14
Cebus. See capuchins

Cercocebus, 23, 74
Cercopithecidae. See Old World
   monkeys
Cercopithecinae, 73
   male dispersal, 243
   taxonomy, 22–25, 23
   See also baboons; macaques; patas
     monkey
cercopithecins, 22–23
Cercopithecus, 23, 74
character mapping, 247–248
cheirogaleids, 20, 21, 123, 132
chimpanzees, 42–43
   aging, 223, 224
   arboreality, 65, 66
   cognitive abilities, 67–68
   distribution, 42, 64, 65
   dominance in, 67
   female-female relationships, 215
   food sharing, 66–67
   food sources, 42, 65
   gorillas sympatric with, 62, 63
   history of research, 64, 259
   human ancestors and, 197
   kinship in, 71
   male social networks, 214–215
   mating behavior, 68, 69, 69, 213
   molecular phylogeny, 27–28, 27
   rehabilitation programs, 167, 168
   sexual dimorphism, 64
   sign language research, 252–256
   social organization, 42, 59, 64–65,
     66–67, 67, 69, 70–72
   threats to, 65–66
   tool use, 42, 67–68, 68, 200, 255
Chiropotes, 21, 22, 107–108
Chlorocebus. See vervet monkey
Christianity, primate images in, 271
cladistics, 18, 247–248
   adaptation and, 250–251
   haplorhine concept and, 20, 141
   hominid behavior and, 197
cladograms, 247
cline, of tarsier characteristics, 142
cluster technique, 18
coalitions, 213, 268
cognitive abilities, 245, 267, 268
   See also intelligence; tool use
cognitive development, 249–250
cognitive evolution, 249–251, 267,
   268

colobines, 73, 74–76
  diet and social organization,
    93–105, 97
  foregut evolution, 29–30, 32–38
  molecular phylogeny, 22, 25–26,
    26, 30–32, 31
  See also langurs
Colobus, 25, 75, 99–100
  See also specific colobus monkeys
communication
  sign language, 56, 252–256
  See also vocalizations
communities, 185, 211, 215
comparative studies, 40
  cladistics in, 246–248, 250–251
  of cognitive evolution, 249–251
  of foregut evolution, 29–30
competition, 268
  See also dominance
conservation, 146–150, 269
  of Asian primates, 151–158
  of doucs in Vietnam, 170–174
  of gibbons, 49
  hunting by humans and, 154,
    156, 159–163, 174
  of orangutans, 56–57, 154, 155,
    156–157, 166, 167–168
  rehabilitation for, 167–169
  of tarsiers, 144–145
  taxonomic status and, 7
  trade in primates and, 155–157
  translocation for, 164–166,
    168–169
  World Conservation Union, 146,
    151–153
  See also endangered species
consortships, 213
constraints of hierarchy, 216–217
convergent evolution
  adaptive, 29, 30
  of amino acid sequences, 30,
    34–35
  of foregut fermentation, 29–30,
    32–38
  vs. homologous characters, 247
  phylogenetic interpretation and,
    19
copulation frequency, 241
cortisol, 242–243
crowned lemur, 125–126, 129–130,
    131, 132

cultural representations of primates,
    257, 258, 270–276
culture
  in chimpanzees, 255–256
  in Japanese macaques, 78
cytochrome b gene, 30–32

Daubentonia. See aye-aye
death, awareness of, 221, 222
deception, tactical, 200, 268
defensins, 33
dental comb, 121
dependent rank, 210
derived traits, 7, 8
  See also shared derived traits
development
  cognitive, 249–250
  play and, 231–232, 233, 235–236
  prenatal, testosterone and, 238
  studies of, 179
dichromatism, sexual, 108
dispersal
  female, 267
  male, 243
DNA sequences. See molecular phy-
    logenetic studies
dominance, 201, 206–210
  aggression and, 206, 207, 208,
    209
  aging and, 224
  behavioral ecology and, 268
  in captive vs. wild primates, 207
  concept of, 206, 207–208, 210
  factors affecting, 206–207,
    208–209, 210
  hormones and, 238, 242, 244
  normative function of, 207, 208
  priority of access model, 207, 208
  relationships in, 208–209, 268
  subordinate behavior and,
    207–208
  See also hierarchy
dominance rankings, 209–210
  vs. hierarchies, 211
  social networks and, 214–215
douc langurs, 75, 104
  molecular phylogeny, 25, 26
  Vietnam field studies, 170–174
drill, 23, 74
Dryopithecus, 16
dusky leaf monkey, 32, 36, 95, 103

Dutch School of primatology, 259
dyadic relationships, 213–214

eastern lowland gorillas, 58, 62
ecology, 261, 263
  See also behavioral ecology;
    socioecology
ecophysiological methods, 50
Egypt, ancient, primates in, 270,
    271
emergent properties, 183, 188, 216
endangered species, 146–147
  atelines as, 109–110
  list of, 148–150
  orangutans as, 56–57
  Pan species as, 66
  See also conservation
energy expenditure
  allometry of, 225, 228
  in callitrichids, 218, 225–230
Eocene fossils, 12, 13
epinephrine, 242
erection, penile, 237, 238, 243
Erythrocebus patas. See patas monkey
estrogen, male seasonal variations,
    239, 240
ethology, 258, 259, 269
Eulemur, 123
European primatology, 259–260
evolution of primates
  behavioral, 175, 177, 178, 179,
    181–182, 196–200
  cognitive, 249–251, 267, 268
  comparative method, 29–30,
    246–248, 250–251
  origins, 10, 12
  sociobiology and, 265–266
  taxonomy and, 7–8
  timeline, 11
  See also adaptive evolution; fossil
    record; molecular phylogenetic
    studies; natural selection
exaptation, 178, 181
exports of primates, 155–157
extractive foraging scenario, 251

factions, 213
familiarity, 201, 203, 204–205
  See also kinship
fascicularis group, 24, 24
fatted male phenomenon, 239–240

Fayum fossils, 13, *13*, 15
female bonding, 184
    in *Pan* species, 70–71, 215
female dispersal, in Cebidae, 267
female dominance, in lemurs,
    133–139, 267
feminism, 92, 267
film representations of primates,
    275–276
fission-fusion social organization,
    185
    in macaques, 79
    in *Pan* species, 42, 59, 65, 198
    in snub-nosed monkeys, 97
    in spider monkeys, 108
fitness
    genetic, 177, 179, 193, 202, 205
    inclusive, 202
focal animal sampling, with ring-
    tailed lemurs, 135
folivores
    gorillas as, 59–63
    protein-fiber ratios and, 95, 98
    social structures of, 59
    See also colobines
folktales, monkeys in, 271–273
food competition hypothesis, 184,
    187
food sharing
    in chimpanzees, 66–67, 199,
        215
    kinship and, 204
foraging hypothesis, 184, 187
foregut fermentation, evolution of,
    29–30, 32–38
forest destruction. *See* habitat
    destruction
fossil record, 10, 11, 16
    anthropoid origins, 12–14
    early radiations, 12–13
    geological timeline, 11
    hominids, 196
    hominoids, 15–16, *15, 16, 17*
    interpretation of, 181
    lemur, *17*
    New World monkeys, 14, *14, 17*
    Old World monkeys, 14–15, *15*
    origin of primates and, 10
frugivores
    early primates as, 12
    gorillas as, 60, 61–62
    social structures of, 59

Galagonidae, 122
galagos, 122
    See also bush babies, 122
gelada baboon, 23, 24, 74
    social networks, 216–217
gene regulation, 29, 34
genetic drift, 34, 188
genetic fitness, 177, 179, 193
    kinship and, 202, 205
genetics of populations, 177, 179
gene tree, 19
genus (genera), 6
geological timeline, 11
gerontology, 218, 220–224
gibbons, 41, 44–49
    distinguishing features, 41, 44, 45
    distribution, 44–45
    feeding behavior, 45–46
    future research, 49
    illegal trade in, 151, 157
    mating behavior, 48–49
    predation by orangutan, 53
    release programs, 168
    social activity, 49
    social organization, 41, 48–49,
        186–187, 216
    taxonomy, 26–27, 44–45
    territoriality, 46–48
    vocalizations, 27, 46
glucocorticoids, 242–243
Goeldi's monkey, 21, 22, 106, 107,
    226
    infant care, 227
golden lion tamarin
    conservation, 168
    energy expenditure, 228, 229,
        230
    See also lion tamarins
Goodman-Wilson-Sarich genetic
    revolution, 18
gorillas, 42
    cultural images of, 58
    intellectual development, 249
    language acquisition, 252
    socioecology, 58–63
    taxonomy, 27, *27,* 58
    testosterone and dominance, 238
gradistic classification, 140–141
Grauer's gorilla, 58, 62
gray langur. *See* hanuman langur
grooming
    affiliation and, 213, 215

chimpanzee communication
    about, 255
    dominance and, 209
    kinship and, 204
    by macaques, 79, 80, 82
grooming claw, 121, 122, 141
groups, social, 183, 201, 212
    definition of, 212
    traditional classifications, 185
    ultimate benefits of, 268
group size
    diet and, 59, 184
    energy expenditure and, 229
guenons, 22–23, 74, 259–260
guereza
    diet and social organization, 94,
        95, 96, 97, 98, 100
    lysozyme expression in, 36
gum-feeding, 226

habitat, in primate studies, 39–40
habitat destruction, 146–147, 154,
    156, 164, 165, 166
    activism by primatologists, 269
    atelines and, 109–110
    behavior and, 194
    orangutans and, 56–57
    Pan species and, 66
hallux, in callitrichids, 22
hamadryas baboon, 73, 259,
    261–262, 270
hanuman langur (*Semnopithecus
    entellus*), 75
    aggression in, 189–192
    development, 232–233, 234–235,
        236
    dominance in, 209
    infanticide in, 190–195
    in literature, 274
    lysozyme evolution in, 32, 35, 36,
        37
    phylogeny, 25, 26, 32
    sacred, in India, 270–271
    social organization and diet, 94,
        95, 97, 98, 103–104
    social organization variability,
        185–186, 189–195, 264–265
haplorhine concept, 19–20, 140
harem groups. *See* one-male, multi-
    female groups
hierarchy, 211–217
    basic requirements for, 216–217

communities in, 211, 215
dominance and, 206, 208
vs. dominance ranking, 211
individual in, 211, 212–213,
    216
levels of, 211–212
networks in, 211, 214–215, 216,
    217
relationships in, 211, 213–214,
    216
See also dominance
hierarchy theory, 211, 216, 217
Hindu society, primates in, 270–271
hominids, early
    behavior, reconstruction of,
        196–200
    fossil record, 16
    tool use, 116–117, 120
Hominoidea, 41
hominoids. *See* apes; humans
Homo erectus, 117
Homo habilis, 117, 199
homologous characters, 247
homologous molecules, 30
homoplasy, 30, 247
homosexual behavior
    in bonobos, 68–70, 71
    in stumptailed macaques, 85
hormones, 237–239, *240*, 242–243,
    244
howler monkeys, 108
    distribution, 109
    early field research, 77, 261
    taxonomy, 21, 22, 109
    translocation projects, 165–166
    yellow fever epidemic, 167
Human Genome Project, 28
humans
    behavior, origins of, 176
    molecular phylogeny, 27–28, *27*
    representations of primates by,
        257, 258, 270–276
    See also hominids, early
hunter-gatherers, 198
hunting by primates
    by baboons, 199–200
    by capuchins, 199–200
    by chimpanzees, 42, 67, 198–200
    by orangutans, 53
    See also meat-eating; scavenging
hunting of primates, 154, 156
    of longtailed macaques, 159–163

by other monkeys, 200
    in Vietnam, 174
Hylobates. See gibbons; siamang

immatures, definition of, 137
immune response, stress and, 243
inbred species, 202
inclusive fitness, 202
independent rank, 210
individual, within hierarchy, 211,
    212–213, 216
indriids, 21, 121, 123, 132
infant deprivation research, 261
infanticide
    in chimpanzees, 69
    in gorillas, 60, 61
    in langurs, 190–195, 264–265
    in macaques, 81
    sociobiological interpretation, 266
infanticide hypothesis, 184, 187
infants, definition of, 137
information content, social, 211,
    214, 216
intelligence
    of capuchins, 116, 200
    of chimpanzees, 67–68, 200
    development of, 249–251
    ecological function of, 268
    hunting and, 200
    of orangutans, 56
    social function of, 267, 268
    See also tool use
intention, 178, 179
intermembral index, of lemurs, 123
ischial callosities
    of gibbons, 44
    of Old World monkeys, 73
IUCN (World Conservation Union),
    146, 151–153

Japanese macaque (*M. fuscata*),
    77–78, 79, 80, 81
    aging, 220–221, 223, 224
    consortships in, 213
    dependent rank in, 210
    folktales about, 273
    male-immature affiliation, 82, 138
    matriarchies in, 82–83, *84*, 214,
        223
    testosterone and dominance, 238
Japanese primatology, 77–78, 258,
    259

Java leaf monkey, 101
juveniles, definition of, 137

kin selection, 266
kinship, 201, 202–205
    definition of, 202
    recognition of, 203–204, 205
    social networks and, 214

lactation, in callitrichids, 229–230
Lagothrix, 21, 22, 108, 109
language acquisition, 56, 252–256
langurs, 75
    doucs, 25, 26, 75, 104, 170–174
    lysozyme evolution in, 29, 36
    molecular phylogeny, 25, 26, 30,
        32
    See also hanuman langur;
        Trachypithecus
La Venta fossils, 14, *14*
leaf-eating primates. *See* colobines;
    folivores
leaf monkeys, 75
    diet and social organization, 93,
        95, 96, 97, 101–104
    molecular phylogeny, 25, 26, 30,
        32
Lemuridae. *See* lemurs
lemurids (*Lemur*), 123–132,
    133–139
    communities of multiple species,
        131–132
    comparison of species, 129–131
    description of species, 123–129
    L. catta, 124–125, 129, 130, 131,
        133–139
    L. coronatus, 125–126, 129–130,
        131, 132
    L. fulvus, 126–127, 129, 130,
        131–132
    L. macaco, 127, 129–130, 131
    L. mongoz, 127–128, 130, 131
    L. rubriventer, 126, 128, 130, 131
lemurs, 121–122
    aye-aye, 20–21, 121, 123, 132
    bamboo lemurs, 121, 123, 132
    cheirogaleids, 20, 21, 123, 132
    female dominance in, 133–139,
        267
    field studies of, 123, *124, 125*
    fossil skull, *17*
    indriids, 21, 121, 123, 132

lemurs (continued)
  lepilemurids, 123, 132
  molecular phylogeny, 19, 20–21
  mouse lemurs, 238, 242
  reproductive seasonality in,
    133–139
  taxonomy, 123
Leontopithecus. See lion tamarins
lepilemurids, 123, 132
lesser apes. See gibbons; siamang
Linnean system, 6
liontailed macaque (M. silenus), 24,
    79
lion tamarins (Leontopithecus), 21,
    22, 106, 225, 226
  conservation, 168
  energy expenditure, 228, 229, 230
literature, monkeys in, 273–275
long-branch attraction, 19
longtailed macaque (M. fascicularis),
    24, 79, 81, 82
  exports, 156
  hunting of, 159–163
  kinship recognition in, 205
  male reproductive physiology, 242
  Swiss research, 259
Lophocebus, 23, 24, 74
lorises, 122
  milk, 229, 230
  molecular phylogeny, 19, 20–21
  predation by orangutan, 53
Lovejoy model, 197
lumpers, taxonomic, 6–7
lysozyme, adaptive evolution of,
    29–30, 32–38

Macaca. See macaques
macaques, 73, 77–85
  aging, 220–221, 223, 224
  distribution, 73, 78
  dominance hierarchies in, 80, 81,
    210
  evolution, 78
  feeding behavior, 78–79
  folktales about, 273
  food sources, 78
  history of research, 77–78, 259,
    261
  hunting of longtailed macaque,
    159–163
  intellectual development, 249

kinship recognition in, 203, 204,
    205
male disperal, 243
male-immature interactions,
    81–82, 138, 244
mother-infant bonding, 246, 261
play, 234
reproductive biology, 80, 238,
    242
sexual behavior, 80–81, 83–85,
    92, 213
social structure, 77–78, 79–80,
    82–83, 84, 137, 138
stress in, 242
sympatric Thai species, 151
taxonomy, 23, 24–25, 24, 78
trade and trafficking in, 155, 156
vocalizations, longtailed, 161,
    162, 163
vocalizations, pigtailed, 83
See also specific macaques
Magaladapidae, 121
male bonding, 267
  in ringtailed lemur, 135–136,
    138–139
male dispersal, 243
male dominance, 206, 207
male-immature affiliation, 184,
    243–244
  in macaques, 81–82, 138, 244
  in ringtailed lemur, 137–138, 138,
    139
male reproductive strategies, 219,
    237–244
  aggression in, 237–239
  dispersal in, 243
  female behavior and, 237, 244
  paternal care in, 243–244
  social skills in, 244
  sperm competition in, 240–241
  stress and, 241–243
  testosterone and, 237–239
mandibular symphysis, unfused, 141
mandrill, 23, 24, 74
mangabeys, 23, 24, 74
marmosets, 21, 22, 106
  energy expenditure, 228, 230
  lifestyle, 226
  male-infant bonds, 244
  reproductive strategy, 227
mast fruiting, 51, 53

masturbation, in stumptailed
    macaques, 85
maternal deprivation research, 261
mating pattern, vs. grouping type,
    185
mating season. See reproductive
    seasonality
maximum likelihood models, 18–19
meat-eating
  in chimpanzees, 65, 66, 67,
    197–200, 215
  in early hominids, 197–198
  in orangutans, 53
  See also hunting by primates;
    scavenging
menopause, human, 221–222
mental states, 259, 267, 268
metabolism, 226, 227–228
milk
  body size and, 229, 230
  callitrichid, 229–230
  energy of, 226
mind, 259, 267, 268
Miocene fossils, 14, 14, 15–16, 15,
    16, 17
Miopithecus, 23
mitochondrial DNA, 30–32
  See also molecular phylogenetic
    studies
model organisms, 246
molecular genetics of paternity, 81,
    92
molecular phylogenetic studies, 7–8,
    18–28
  of colobines, 22, 25–26, 26,
    30–32, 31
  of hominoids, 26–28, 27
  of lemurs, 19, 20–21, 21
  of lorises, 19, 20–21, 21
  methods in, 18–19, 30–32
  most parsimonious tree, 18, 247
  of New World monkeys, 21–22,
    22
  of Old World monkeys, 22–26,
    23, 24, 26, 30–32, 31
  of tarsiers, 19–20, 21
mongoose lemur, 127–128, 130,
    131
monkeys. See New World monkeys;
    Old World monkeys
moor macaque (M. maura), 79–80

Morris, Desmond, 259
mother-infant bonding, in rhesus
      macaque, 246, 261
motivation, 178, 179
mountain gorillas, 58, 59, 60–61
      testosterone and dominance, 238
mouse lemurs, 238, 242
movies, primates in, 275–276
mtDNA, 30–32
      See also molecular phylogenetic
         studies
multilevel bands, 185
multimale, multifemale groups, 185,
      186
multivorous species, 10
muriqui (woolly spider monkey), 21,
      22, 109, 267

Nasalis. See proboscis monkey
natural history, in primatology, 262,
      263–264
natural selection, 177, 178, 179, 180
      behavior and, 193
      kinship and, 202–203, 204–205
      male dominance and, 207
      vs. neutral theory of evolution, 34
      See also selective pressures
neocortex hypothesis, 184–185,
      187–188
neotropical monkeys. *See* New
      World monkeys
nepotistic behavior, 203, 204
nests, of apes, 41, 42, 53, 65
networks, social, 211, 214–215,
      216, 217
neutral mutations, 29, 34
neutral rate violation, 34, 35
New World monkeys, 106–108
      fossil record, 14, *14*
      phylogeny, 21–22, *22*
      See also atelines; callitrichids;
         capuchins
Ngeaur, hunting of macaques on,
      159–163
night monkeys. *See* owl monkeys
Nilgiri langur, 95, 104
Nomascus (Hylobates concolor)
      taxonomy, 26, 27, 44, 45
North American primatology,
      260–269
Notharctus, 13

nuclear pseudogenes, 30, 31
nucleotide sequencing, 18

object use
   by capuchins, 118, 119, 120
   definition of, 116
   See also tool use
Oldowan Industrial Complex, 117,
      120
Old World monkeys, 73–76
   fossil record, 14–15, *15*
   molecular phylogeny, 22–26, *23,
      24, 26,* 30–32, *31*
   See also baboons; colobines;
      langurs; macaques; patas
      monkey
olive baboon, 138
olive colobus, 25, 36, 75, 100
omnivorous species, 10
Omomyidae, 12
one-female, multimale groups, 185,
      186
one-male, multifemale groups, 185,
      186
   in colobines, 93, 94–95, 96, 97,
      100–105
   in gorillas, 59
   in patas monkeys, 86, 87, 92
one-male, one-female groups, 185,
      186
one-male unit (OMU). *See* one-male,
      multifemale groups
ontogenetic causes of behavior,
      176–177, 178, 179, 204
optimal foraging models, 98
orangutans, 41–42, 50–57
   activity patterns, 53
   cognitive abilities, 56
   conservation status, 56–57, 154,
      155, 156–157, 166, 167–168
   distribution, 50
   environment, 51
   fat storage, 53–54
   feeding ecology, 53
   fossil ancestor, *16*
   language acquisition, 252
   life span, 55
   locomotion, 41, 51
   male development, 51–52, 55,
      239
   meat-eating by, 199

morphology, 51, 52
ranging patterns, 54
reproduction, 55
sexual behavior, 56, 241
social organization, 41–42, 54–55
taxonomy, 27, 50–51
tool use, 42, 56
Ouranopithecus, 16, *17*
outbred species, 202
ovulation, induced by copulation,
      238
owl monkeys, 21, 22, 107

Palau, hunting of macaques in,
      159–163
Pan paniscus. See bonobo
Pan troglodytes. See chimpanzee
Papio. See baboons
papionins, 23–25
      See also baboons; macaques; man-
         drill; mangabeys
paradigm shift, 265
Parapithecidae, 13
parental investment, 184, 266
      See also male-immature affiliation;
         mother-infant bonding
parsimonious tree, 18, 247
patas monkey, 74, 86–92
      food sources, 90, 91
      predator defense, 90–91, *90, 91*
      reproduction, 88–89, 91–92
      social organization, 86–90, 91–92
      taxonomy, 22–23
      testosterone levels, 239, *240*
paternal care, 184, 243–244
      See also male-immature affiliation
paternity
      molecular genetics of, 81, 92
      recognition of, 204
pecking order, 206, 207
      See also dominance; hierarchy
phenotypes
      development of, 233
      natural selection and, 177, 180
phylogenetic hypothesis, 184,
      187–188
phylogeny
      cladistics and, 247–248
      vs. taxonomy, 6
      See also evolution of primates;
         molecular phylogenetic studies

physical anthropology, 260, 261, 262
Piagetian models, 249–250, 251
pigtailed langur (*Simias*), 25, 76, 105
pigtailed macaque (*M. nemestrina*), 24, 79, 80, 81, 83
    exports, 156
    preferential association in, 203, 204
    testosterone levels, 238
Piliocolobus. See red colobus
pirating of carcass, 198
Pithecia, 21, 22, 107
pithecins, 21, 22, 107–108
platyrrhines. *see* New World monkeys
play, 218, 231–236
    in chimpanzee male networks, 215
    chimpanzee sign language in, 254, 255
    developmental functions, 231–232, 233, 235–236
    forms of, 234–235
    in gibbons, 49
Pleistocene fossils, 14–15, 16, *17*
Pliocene fossils, 15
Pongidae. *See* apes
Pongo. See orangutans
populations, genetics of, 177, 179
pottos, 122
predation. *See* hunting by primates
predation pressure hypothesis, 184, 187, 268
prehensile tail, of howler monkey, 108
Presbytina, 25
Presbytis, 75
    diet and social organization, 93, 94, 95, 101–104
    taxonomy, 25, 26
    See also hanuman langur; leaf monkeys
primate pattern, 263, 264, 265
primates
    anatomical traits of, 10, 12
    cultural representations of, 270–276
    numbers of species worldwide, 153

    See also conservation; evolution of primates; taxonomy of primates
primate studies, 257, 258–269
    disciplinary origins of, 260–262
    fundamental questions of, 262–263
    geopolitical influences on, 268
    key elements in, 39–40
    long-term field studies, 77–78, 266–267
    national traditions in, 258–260
    stage one: natural history, 262, 263–264
    stage two: variability, 262, 264–265, 266, 267
    stage three: sociobiology, 77, 92, 259, 262, 265–267
    stage four: behavioral ecology, 262, 267–269
    women in, 92, 265, 267
primitive traits, 7, 8
priority of access model, 207, 208
proboscis monkey, 76
    diet and social organization, 96, 97, 101
    foregut evolution, 29
    taxonomy, 25, 26, 30, 32
Procolobus. See olive colobus; red colobus
Proconsul, 15, *15,* 16
prolactin
    male-infant bonds and, 244
    stress and, 242
Propithecus, 21
Propliopithecidae, 13
prosimians, 121–122
    energy expenditure, 228
    history of research, 260
    milk, 229, 230
    social organization, 185
    taxonomy, 19–21, *21,* 140–141
    See also lemurs; lorises; tarsiers
Protopithecus, 17
proximal cause of behavior, 176–177, 178, 179
    with nepotistic behavior, 204–205
pseudogenes, nuclear, 30, 31
psychologists in primatology, 260, 261
Purgatorius, 12

purple-faced langur
    diet and social organization, 94, 95, 97, 98, 104
    molecular phylogeny, 32
Pygathrix, 75, 104
    doucs in Vietnam, 170–174
    molecular phylogeny, 25, 26, 32
pygmy chimpanzee. *See* bonobo
pygmy marmoset, 225, 226, 228, 230

quadrumanual clambering, 51

ranks, dominance, 209–210
    social networks and, 214–215
    See also dominance; hierarchy
Rashomon Effect, 196
reciprocal altruism, 266
recruitment screams, 83
red-bellied lemur, 126, 128, 130, 131
red colobus, 75
    diet and social organization, 94, 95, 96, 97, 98, 99–100
    as prey of chimpanzees, 198–199
    taxonomy, 25
red leaf monkey, 96, 97, 102
red-ruffed lemur, 127, 128, 129
rehabilitation programs, 167–169
reintroduction of species, 165, 269
relationships
    complexity of, 268
    dominance in, 208–209
    in hierarchies, 211, 213–214, 216
relationship sets, 214, 215
religious images of primates, 270–271
reproductive seasonality, 239–240, *240*
    in ringtailed lemur, 133–139
reproductive strategies
    behavioral ecology and, 267
    male, 219, 237–244
reproductive success
    dominance and, 207, 208
    vs. mating frequency, 92
    natural selection and, 193
    in sociobiology, 266
resting metabolic rate (RMR)
    vs. body mass, 227–228

of callitrichids, 227–228
definition of, 226
restriction site mapping, 18
rhesus macaque (*M. mulatta*)
aging, 221
early field studies, 77, 261
exports, 156
male dispersal, 243
male-immature affiliation, 82,
138, 244
male reproductive physiology,
238, 239, *240*, 242
male reproductive success, 81, 92
as model organism, 246
mother-infant bonding, 246, 261
prenatal stress, 242
social organization, 80, 137, 214
Rhinopithecus. See snub-nosed
monkeys
ribonuclease, adaptive evolution of,
29–30, 33, 38
ringtailed lemur
ecology, 124–125, 129, 130,
131
female dominance and reproductive seasonality, 133–139
RMR. *See* resting metabolic rate
ruffed lemur (*Varecia*), 126, 127,
128–129, 130, 131–132
milk, 230
rufous lemur, 124, 126, 128, 130,
131
ruminants, foregut fermentation in,
29, 32, 33–34 35, 38

Saguinus. See tamarins
Saimiri. See squirrel monkeys
sakis, 21, 22, 107–108
Sanford's lemur, 125, 126–127, 132
savanna baboon
consortships in, 213
copulation frequency, 241
cortisol levels, 242
dominance in, 207, 208, 210, 238,
242
male coalitions in, 213
male dispersal, 243
testosterone levels, 238, 239
scavenging, 198, 199
See also meat-eating

scientific revolutions, 265
seasonality. *See* reproductive
seasonality
seed dispersal by primates, 146
seed predator monkeys, 22,
107–108
selective pressures, 177, 178, 179,
180
social organization and, 184–185,
187–188
See also natural selection
Semnopithecus. See hanuman langur
serotonin, male dispersal and, 243
sexual coercion, in orangutans, 51,
55, 56
sexual dichromatism, 108
sexual dimorphism
dominance relationships and, 208
male-male competition and, 111
shared character states, 247
shared derived character states, 247,
248, 250–251
shared derived traits, 7, 8, 18
siamang, 41, 44, 45
feeding behavior, 45–46, 47
mating behavior, 48, 49
range use, 46, 47
sign language, 56, 252–256
silenus-sylvanus group, 24, *24*
silvered leaf monkey, 95
Simias, 25, 76, 105
sinica group, 24, *24*
Sivapithecus, *16*
snub-nosed monkeys, 75–76
conservation, 157
diet and social organization, 96,
104–105
taxonomy, 25, 26
social actions, basic categories of,
212
sociality, 212
social networks, 211, 214–215
social norms, enforcement of, 207,
208, 212–213
social organization, 183–188
adaptive grades of, 59, 265
definitions of, 183, 212
as emergent property, 183, 188,
216

historical and stochastic determinants of, 188
intraspecific variations in,
185–188
levels of, 183
plasticity of individual and, 188
primacy of, 183
selective pressures leading to,
184–185, 187–188
vs. social system, 212
traditional classifications, 185
variability in, 185–186, 264–265,
266, 267
See also dominance; hierarchy;
kinship
social system, 212
sociobiology, 77, 92, 259, 262,
265–267
socioecology, 59
of colobines, 93–105
of gorillas, 59–63
See also behavioral ecology
solitary primates, 185, 186
Sower's Fallacy, 193
species, in Linnean system, 6
species tree, 19
spermatogenesis, 240–241
sperm competition, 241
spider monkeys, *17*, 21, 22, 108,
109
male-male affiliation, 267
splitters, taxonomic, 6–7
squirrel monkeys, 21, 22, 107
cortisol levels, 242
male networks in, 215
male seasonality in body mass,
239
testosterone levels, 238, 239, 242
stimuli, 176–177, 178–179
stone tools
of early hominids, 116–117, 120
meat-eating and, 197, 199
stratification, social, 216
strepsirrhines, 19, 20–21
stress, 238, 241–243
structural-functional social models,
263, 265
stumptailed macaque (*M. arctoides*),
24, 80, 82, 83–85
intellectual development, 249

subordinate behavior, 207–208
Sulawesi macaques, 78, 80
swamp monkey, 23
symbolic communication, in pig-
    tailed macaques, 83
Symphalangus, 26, 45
synapomorphies. *See* shared derived
    traits

talapoin monkeys, 23, 74
    male reproductive strategy, 238,
        242
tamarins (*Saguinus*), 21, 22, 106,
        226
    lactation, 230
    male-infant bonds, 244
    social organization, 186
    See also lion tamarins
tannins, 95
tapetum lucidem, 121, 140
tarsiers, 122, 140–145
    behavior, 142–144
    conservation status, 144–145
    distribution, 141–142, *141*
    taxonomy, 19–20, 140–142
taxa, naming of, 6
taxonomy of primates, *9*
    cladistics in, 18–19, 247–248
    controversies, major divisions, 19,
        140–141
    controversies, species-level, 6–7
    Linnean system, 6
    molecular methods, 7–8, 18–28,
        30–32
    morphology in, 6, 7, 8

numbers of species worldwide,
    153
See also molecular phylogenetic
    studies
teleology, 178, 205
terminal branch feeders, 78–79
testes size, 239, 240, 241, *241*
testosterone
    aggression and, 238–239
    reproductive seasonality and,
        239–240, *240*
    in spermatogenesis, 240, 241
    stress and, 242
Theropithecus, 23, 24, 74
Tibetan macaque (*M. thibetana*), 82
Tinbergen's "why" questions, 176,
    177, 179, 205, 260
titi monkeys, 21, 22, 107
toleration, 212
Tonkean macaque (*M. tonkean*), 79
tool use
    by capuchins, 115–116, 118–120,
        200, 251
    by chimpanzees, 42, 67–68, *68,*
        200, 255
    definition of, 116
    by early hominids, 116–117, 120
    evolutionary hypothesis, 251
    by orangutans, 42, 56
toque macaque (*M. sinica*), 24, 79
Trachypithecus, 75
    diet and social organization,
        102–103
    molecular phylogeny, 25, 26, 32
trade in primates, 155–157

transitive dominance rankings,
    209–210
translocation strategies, 164–166,
    168–169, 269
twins, callitrichid, 225, 229

uakaris, 21, 22, 107, 108
uniquely derived character states,
    247
ursine colobus, 95, 100
uterus, bicornuate, 141

Varecia. See ruffed lemur
vervet monkey, 22–23, 74, 91
    dominance in, 208, 238
    matrilines in, 214, 216
    vocalizations, 268
Victoriapithecus, 15
vocalizations
    gibbons, 27, 46
    howler monkeys, 108
    macaques, longtailed, 161, 162,
        163
    macaques, pigtailed, 83
    tarsiers, 143, 144
    vervets, 268

western lowland gorillas, 58, 61–62
white-fronted leaf monkey, 101
white-fronted lemur, 126, 127, 128
woolly monkeys, 21, 22, 108, 109
woolly spider monkey (muriqui), 21,
    22, 109, 267
World Conservation Union (IUCN),
    146, 151–153